The Country Music Reader

The Country Music Reader

TRAVIS D. STIMELING

OXFORD
UNIVERSITY PRESS

OXFORD
UNIVERSITY PRESS

Oxford University Press is a department of the University of Oxford.
It furthers the University's objective of excellence in research, scholarship,
and education by publishing worldwide.

Oxford   New York
Auckland   Cape Town   Dar es Salaam   Hong Kong   Karachi
Kuala Lumpur   Madrid   Melbourne   Mexico City   Nairobi
New Delhi   Shanghai   Taipei   Toronto

With offices in
Argentina   Austria   Brazil   Chile   Czech Republic   France   Greece
Guatemala   Hungary   Italy   Japan   Poland   Portugal   Singapore
South Korea   Switzerland   Thailand   Turkey   Ukraine   Vietnam

Oxford is a registered trademark of Oxford University Press
in the UK and certain other countries.

Published in the United States of America by
Oxford University Press
198 Madison Avenue, New York, NY 10016

© Oxford University Press 2014

Library of Congress Cataloging-in-Publication Data
Stimeling, Travis D.
The country music reader / Travis D. Stimeling.
pages cm
Includes bibliographical references and index.
ISBN 978-0-19-931491-1 (hardback : alk. paper)—ISBN 978-0-19-931492-8 (pbk. : alk. paper)—
ISBN 978-0-19-931493-5 (electronic text)   1. Country music—History and criticism.   I. Title.
ML3524.S753 2015
781.64209—dc23
2014007768

1 3 5 7 9 8 6 4 2
Printed in the United States of America
on acid-free paper

FOR LOLA,

MY STEADFAST WRITING COMPANION

Contents

Preface   ix

Acknowledgments   xi

Note on Sources   xiii

1.   Linton K. Starr, "Georgia's Unwritten Airs Played by Old 'Fiddlers' for Atlanta Prizes: Untutored Players from Hillsides and Marshes Perform Traditional Southern Melodies on Wire-Stringed Violins—Society Folk and Workers in Audiences 'Shuffle Feet' to Contagious Strains—'Bald Mountain Caruso' and Treble-singing Dog at Unique Convention" (1914)   1
2.   Cecil B. Sharp, *English Folk Songs from the Southern Appalachians* (1917) [excerpt]   8
3.   John A. Lomax, *Cowboy Songs and Other Frontier Ballads* (1910)   16
4.   "What the Popularity of Hill-Billy Songs Means in Retail Profit Sensibilities: The Widespread Vogue of the Funereal Type of Songs Is Attested by Publishers and Record Manufacturers—Is It of Significance as Indication of Public Taste?" (1925)   22
5.   "Mountain Songs Recorded Here by Victor Co.: Notable Performers of This Section at Work at Station in This City" (1927)   26
6.   Ralph Peer, "Discovery of the 1st Hillbilly Great" (1953)   30
7.   Bill Williams, "Interview with Mother Maybelle Carter" (1968/1971)   37
8.   Harold A. Safford, "Bradley Kincaid" (1928)   47
9.   Paul Hobson, "Radio's Hillbilly King, Carson Robison, who is, with his Pioneers, a regular attraction for Oxydol every Sunday from Luxembourg, Lyons and Normandy, tells us in this interview how he writes his world-famous songs" (1938)   51
10.   John Wright, "J. E. Mainer" (1993)   55
11.   Virginia Seeds, "Back Stage Ramble: Cowboys and Cow Belles Enjoy the Barn Dance" (1936)   64
12.   "No Hill Billies in Radio: Ballads Are Still Written, Says John Lair" (1935)   69
13.   Alva Johnston, "Tenor on Horseback" (1939)   74
14.   George D. Hay, *A Story of the Grand Old Opry* (1945)   86
15.   Janis Stout, "The Light Crust Doughboys Were on the Air: A Memoir" (1996)   89
16.   "Okies Reverse Order of Steinbeck's Tale" (1941)   96
17.   Maurice Zolotow, "Hillbilly Boom" (1944)   99
18.   Nicholas Dawidoff, "Earl Scruggs: Three Fast Fingers" (1997)   107
19.   Rufus Jarman, "Country Music Goes to Town" (1953)   117
20.   Johnny Cash on Recording at Sun with Sam Phillips, *Cash: The Autobiography* (1997)   125
21.   Charlie Louvin, "Elvis" (2012)   131
22.   Murray Nash, "Miss Country Music and Her Family" (1955)   137
23.   Linda Lamendola, "Steve Sholes—Star Maker" (1956)   141
24.   Ben A. Green, "Chet Makes Guitar Talk with Rhythm and Melody" (1957)   146
25.   "Coast Country Biz Booms" (1957)   152

26. Alan Lomax, "Bluegrass Background: Folk Music with Overdrive" (1959)   156
27. Tom T. Hall, *The Storyteller's Nashville,* on Song Writing and Song Plugging (1979)   160
28. "The Story of the Country Music Association" (1968)   164
29. "Ask Trina" (1968)   169
30. John Grissim Jr., "California White Man's Shit Kickin' Blues" (1969)   179
31. Lee Arnold, "A DJ Tells Why—There's Country Music in the City Air" (1975)   205
32. Michael Bane, *The Outlaws: Revolution in Country Music* (1978)   208
33. Rex Rutkoski, "The Pill: Should It Be Banned from Airplay?" (1975)   223
34. George F. Will, "Of Pride and Country Music" (1975)   226
35. Aaron Latham, "The Ballad of the Urban Cowboy: America's Search for True Grit" (1978)   229
36. Tom Anthony, "Kenny Rogers: Drawing Full Houses" (1981)   244
37. Alanna Nash, "Emmylou Harris" (1988)   251
38. Holly G. Miller, "Randy Travis: Nice Guy Finishes First" (1988)   275
39. Bruce Feiler, *Dreaming Out Loud: Garth Brooks, Wynonna Judd, Wade Hayes, and the Changing Face of Nashville* (1998)   280
40. Debbie Holley, "Country Dancing Sparks Club Growth: New Nightclubs, Remixes Target Trend" (1992)   290
41. Eric Boehlert, "Classic Country Stations Fill Niche: Claim Fans of Currents, Standards Mix" (1993)   295
42. Peter Cronin, "Nashville's Studio Boom Alters Musical Landscape" (1993)   298
43. Kyle Ryan, "Any Kind of Music But Country: A Decade of Indie Country, Punk Rock, and the Struggle for Country's Soul" (2005)   304
44. Rich Kienzle, Review of *BR5-49* (1996)   315
45. Deborah Evans Price, "Has There Been 'Murder on Music Row'? Key Players Speak Out" (2000) and "Is There 'Murder on Music Row'? Debate Continues" (2000)   318
46. Scott Galupo, "The Critical Rockist and Gretchen" (2005)   325
47. Craig Havighurst, "Scenes from a Rose Garden (2006)   330
48. Jill Sobule, "Searching for the Republican Artist" (2008)   340
49. Vanessa Grigoriadis, "The Very Pink, Very Perfect Life of Taylor Swift" (2009)   345
50. Chet Flippo, "Why the Term 'Country Music' May Disappear: Marketers of the Future May Dissolve Music Genre Labels" (2010)   353
51. Skip Hollandsworth, "The Girl Who Played with Firearms" (2011)   357

Index   369

Song Index   379

Preface

When we have the opportunity to engage with the voices from the past, our understanding of history is significantly improved. As students of music history, we often use scores and recordings as key primary documents, but a sole focus on musical works presents only one side of the story. By reading criticism, memoirs, and reportage in conjunction with our listening and score study, we can begin to grasp the complexity of the historian's task. Such sources force us to make sense of complex debates, interrogate historical rhetorics, and engage with the life experiences of history's very human actors. Moreover, such readings allow us to understand music history not simply as the result of musicians' work but also as a product of many figures, often with competing interests and goals.

This book has been designed with the primary goal of providing access to the voices of people who have created country music culture over the course of the genre's nine-decade history. In addition to musicians, this collection also includes the thoughts of folksong collectors, radio producers, recording engineers, music critics, and—perhaps most important—country music fans. It is my hope that you will read these sources alongside such narrative histories as Bill C. Malone's *Country Music, U.S.A.* (3rd ed. [with Jocelyn R. Neal], Austin: University of Texas Press, 2010) or Jocelyn Neal's *Country Music: A Cultural and Stylistic History* (New York: Oxford University Press, 2012), listen to recordings made by pioneering country musicians, view documentary films about the genre, and watch the rich array of country music videos that are now widely available on the Internet.

Although *The Country Music Reader* is organized chronologically, the sources also lend themselves to topical or thematic treatment. In particular, readers will note a focus on the production and dissemination of country recordings, debates about country music authenticity, and gender in country music. It is my hope that readers will make use of the sources anthologized here in ways that suit their pedagogical styles and the learning goals of their particular courses.

In compiling and editing this collection, I have been inspired by the work of many music historians, and *The Country Music Reader* bears the traces of these influences. Richard Taruskin and Pierro Weiss's *Music in the Western World: A History in Documents* (Belmont, CA: 2nd ed., Thomson/Schirmer, 2008); David Brackett's *The Rock, Pop, and Soul Reader: Histories and Debates* (3rd ed., New York: Oxford University Press, 2013); Judith Tick and Paul Beaudoin's *Music in the USA: A Documentary Companion* (New York: Oxford University Press, 2008); Thomas Goldsmith's *The Bluegrass Reader* (Urbana and Chicago: University of Illinois Press, 2006); and Robert Gottlieb's *Reading Jazz: A Gathering of Authiography, Reportage, and Criticism from 1919 to Now* (New York: Vintage, 1999) have served as useful models as I have worked to select relevant sources, compose insightful critical introductions, annotate readings, and organize the anthology. Moreover, my decision to include many of the sources found here was influenced by the outstanding work of three generations of country music historians, and it is my hope that their voices also speak through *The Country Music Reader*.

Acknowledgments

A project of this magnitude would be impossible if not for the support and assistance of a wonderful group of colleagues, assistants, mentors, friends, and family members.

This project began with the assistance of Millikin University's Summer Undergraduate Research Fellowship and Undergraduate Research Fellowship programs, which facilitated the hiring of two outstanding undergraduate research assistants, Will Frankenberger and Alyssa Callaghan. Together, they compiled an initial bibliography of periodical sources and supplied me with a seemingly endless array of outstanding primary source material drawn from a wide range of music and general interest periodicals. Moreover, their willingness to jump headlong into a project as large as this has inspired me to continue moving forward, even when my own confidence flagged. I am especially grateful for the lasting friendships we have developed over the years since their graduation, and I am extremely proud of their accomplishments in life. Millikin University also granted me a semester of academic leave in the Fall 2010 term, which granted me the opportunity to begin putting this project together in earnest. After joining the faculty of West Virginia University's School of Music in the fall of 2013, I was fortunate to have the opportunity to work with Anne Stickley, an exceptional undergraduate student who provided valuable assistance with fact-checking, copyediting, and indexing. I would like to thank Keith Jackson, director of the WVU School of Music, and Paul Kreider, dean of the WVU College of Creative Arts, for their financial and intellectual support of this project.

Along the way, numerous librarians and archivists have pointed me to useful sources, made collections available, and helped me track down arcane publications. At Millikin University, Ruth Nihiser processed endless interlibrary loan requests for primary and secondary literature. A visit to Middle Tennessee State University's Center for Popular Music in May 2010 provided the opportunity to meet Linda Cockrell and Grover Baker, both of whom offered access to their repository of country music publications and provided great restaurant recommendations. Finally, Steve Weiss and Aaron Smithers at the Southern Folklife Collection at the University of North Carolina at Chapel Hill were gracious hosts in March 2012 when I visited to explore their extensive vertical files.

I am also deeply grateful for the many people who have granted permission to reprint many of the readings below. Several authors and their heirs generously offered these sources at no cost, while others were more than willing to negotiate reasonable fees.

I have also been the beneficiary of the remarkable support of my colleagues and mentors. At Millikin University, Steve Widenhofer, Laura Ledford, and Barry Pearson were more than generous in both their financial support of and enthusiasm for my research on this book, and Dave Burdick and Andy Heise's constant reminders of the need to pick and sing while I write about this wonderful music served me well throughout the development of this project. At WVU, I have had the great pleasure of receiving the support of my colleagues Andrea Houde, Janet Robbins, Nick Perna, Mike Vercelli, and Chris Nichter. Several colleagues have sent along materials that I considered for publication here, including Stephanie Vander Wel, Paul Wells, Kevin Fontenot, Nate Gibson, and David Pruett, and I am grateful for their generosity. Chris Wells read a draft of this book and challenged me to consider the subtleties of language and its impact on the ways we might read the people and practices discussed in these sources. Doug Shadle has been a steadfast supporter of my work and a true friend over the many years that this project has been in development. Rich Kienzle has been a regular correspondent over the past several years and has thoroughly enriched my appreciation for and knowledge of good country music journalism. Jocelyn Neal, Mark Katz, Christopher Wilkinson, and Mary Ferer have served as valuable mentors throughout this project and beyond. I strive to "pay it forward."

I have been blessed with many friends who deserve recognition for the things they have done to provide support over the years that this book has been developing, including Chuck Kerwin, Nancy Freeman, Matt Meacham, Ian and Anne Helmick, Jj Kidder, Katie Sullivan, Rachel Weiss, SarahEmily Lekberg, Cate Edwards, the members of the Millikin University Big Bluegrass Band, and the fine folks at the Unitarian Universalist Fellowship of Decatur, Illinois.

Suzanne Ryan has been especially instrumental in seeing this project from its infancy to its completion. Her encouragement has challenged me to consider possibilities that I may have never thought available to me and to push through the nagging voices of self-doubt to create something of which I am truly proud.

Finally, I know that I could not do anything without the love and support of my partner in this life, Melanie, who models kindness, patience, generosity, and love in all she does.

Note on Sources

The sources that are collected here are taken from a wide array of published memoirs, newspaper and magazine articles, fan newsletters, and trade publications. It was my goal to select articles that represented diverse perspectives on country music and its significance to the broader landscape of American popular music. Consequently, the voices of skeptical journalists, avid fans, and passionate songwriters and recording artists are placed alongside one another in an effort to situate country music within the broader contexts of its production and reception.

All sources are reprinted with permission of the copyright holder in the event that it was possible to determine who the copyright holder is. In several instances, however, the anthologized source was determined to be orphaned after significant effort to track down the copyright holder. Permissions are noted with each source, as specified.

In order to create a book of manageable length, the sources anthologized here have been lightly annotated. Readers are encouraged to consult such standard reference works as *The Grove Dictionary of American Music*, 2ⁿᵈ ed. (New York: Oxford University Press, 2013) and *The Encyclopedia of Country Music*, 2ⁿᵈ ed. (New York: Oxford University Press, 2012) for more information about the biographies of many people named here. Discographcial information is also readily available in numerous sources, including Tony Russell's magnificent *Country Music Records: A Discography, 1921–1942* (New York: Oxford University Press, 2004); Guthrie T. Meade, Jr., Dick Spottswood, and Douglas S. Meade's *Country Music Sources: A Biblio-Discography of Commercially Recorded Traditional Music* (Chapel Hill: Southern Folklife Collection, The University of North Carolina at Chapel Hill Libraries in Association with the John Edwards Memorial Forum, 2002); and Joel L. Whitburn's *Hot Country Songs, 1944–2012*, 8th ed. (Menomonee Falls, WI: Record Research, 2012). Finally, each source is followed by a list of suggested readings that can provide still more historical and cultural context, and it is hoped that readers will seek out this outstanding work.

The Country Music Reader

Linton K. Starr

"Georgia's Unwritten Airs Played by
Old 'Fiddlers' for Atlanta Prizes: Untutored Players
from Hillsides and Marshes Perform Traditional
Southern Melodies on Wire-Stringed Violins—Society
Folk and Workers in Audiences 'Shuffle Feet' to
Contagious Strains—'Bald Mountain Caruso' and
Treble-singing Dog at Unique Convention" (1914)

Although the decade of the 1920s is often referred to as the "Jazz Age," it might just as easily be described as the "Hillbilly Age." Much as jazz was thought to embody the noise and racial boundary-crossing of the modern age, early hillbilly recording artists were believed to hail from idyllic rural landscapes, invoking images of noble Anglo-Saxons and notions of pure and unbroken folk traditions that were untainted by the influence of the modern life and the popular music industry along the way.[1] Yet, even a cursory survey of the careers of the early hillbilly recording

1. Archie Green, "Hillbilly Music: Source and Symbol," *Journal of American Folklore* 78 (July 1965): 51–68, repr. in *Torching the Fink Books & Other Essays on Vernacular Culture* (Chapel Hill: University of North Carolina Press, 2001), 8–46; Richard

artists suggests that they were far more cosmopolitan than marketing materials might have suggested. Even if they had been born in a rural community, they were often shaped by the modern urban environments of such southern cities as Atlanta, Charlotte, Nashville, and Dallas, where they worked in mills and factories, played music for rural émigrés, and had face-to-face exchanges with African American musical traditions. Moreover, the urban environments in which many of these musicians and their audiences worked were filled with modern entertainment options, including motion pictures, radio broadcasts, and phonograph records.[2]

Many of the most successful of the early hillbilly recording artists drew upon their urban experiences to create repertories that reflected the unique experiences of the South's new urban dwellers, skillfully blending traditional tunes and styles with modern music, deliberately adopting the hillbilly image and portraying stereotypical behaviors,[3] and promoting their music through a variety of media.

Perhaps the most successful of this first group of hillbilly recording artists was Fiddlin' John Carson (ca. 1868–1949). Born in rural Fannin County, Georgia, and raised in the Reconstruction-era South, Carson has often been described as a transitional figure in the history of north Georgia fiddling, whose repertoire embraced both the late-nineteenth-century dance tunes and styles of north Georgia and the influences of the modern popular music industry.[4] In the 1890s, he frequently moved between the rail yards and cotton mills of the Atlanta area and the rural farmlands of north Georgia; and in 1900, he moved permanently to Atlanta, where he went to work at Exposition Cotton Mills. In 1913, Carson began performing at the annual Georgia Old-Time Fiddlers' Convention, a contest that he won multiple times, catapulting him to regional fame. The same year, Carson wrote "Little Mary Phagan," the first of three ballads he composed about the murder and sexual assault of a thirteen-year-old mill worker and the sensational murder trial of

A. Peterson, *Creating Country Music: Fabricating Authenticity* (Chicago: University of Chicago Press, 1997), 67–69; Anthony Harkins, *Hillbilly: A Cultural History of an American Icon* (New York: Oxford University Press, 2004), 71–72.

2. Patrick Huber has explored the role of urban and semi-urban textile mill towns in shaping the image, repertoire, and accessibility of hillbilly music in his *Linthead Stomp: The Creation of Country Music in the Piedmont South* (Chapel Hill: University of North Carolina Press, 2008).

3. Gavin James Campbell, *Music and the Making of a New South* (Chapel Hill: University of North Carolina Press, 2004), 121–23, 131–35; Huber, *Linthead Stomp*, 67–68; Edward P. Comentale, *Sweet Air: Modernism, Regionalism, and American Popular Song* (Urbana: University of Illinois Press, 2013), 72–116. An alternative thesis, which should probably be tempered by cases such as those provided by Carson, argues that the use of the hillbilly image in early country music was largely a product of record executives and radio promoters who forced musicians to take on the image and attitudes of the hillbilly. See, for instance, Green, "Hillbilly Music: Source and Symbol," 213; Peterson, *Creating Country Music*, 67–80; and Harkins, *Hillbilly*, 71–87.

4. Gene Wiggins, *Fiddlin' Georgia Crazy: Fiddlin' John Carson, His Real World, and the World of His Songs* (Urbana and Chicago: University of Illinois Press, 1987), 19–45; Huber, *Linthead Stomp*, 49–50.

mill superintendent Leo M. Frank, and he played a central role in encouraging populist anger that led to the Frank's lynching in 1915.[5]

In 1922, Carson became the first hillbilly musician to perform on radio, broadcasting on Atlanta radio station WSB ("Welcome South, Brother"), opening the door for many of the region's fiddlers to perform in the new medium and generating widespread regional interest in his music.[6] When Okeh Records producer Ralph Peer (1892–1960) traveled to Atlanta in June 1923 to record local talent, furniture store owner Polk Brockman, who owned the Atlanta Okeh dealership, convinced Peer to record Carson and to press five hundred copies for distribution in the Atlanta area. The record—"Little Old Log Cabin in the Lane" b/w "The Old Hen Cackled and the Rooster's Going to Crow"—sold briskly, demonstrating both the demand for Carson's music and a potentially greater demand for hillbilly music, and encouraged Peer to continue traveling throughout the South in search of new musicians and new songs.[7] Recording at various times for Okeh's "Popular Music Series" and "Old Time Tunes" series, Carson recorded 123 sides, including traditional fiddle tunes, topical ballads, and sentimental and popular numbers.

The following article, published in the art music–focused periodical *Musical America* in 1914, offers a richly detailed description of Atlanta's annual Old Fiddlers' Contest. The Contest was one of three major events on the city's musical and social calendar, along with an annual visit from New York's Metropolitan Opera and the spiritual performances at the "Colored Music Festival." As Gavin James Campbell has demonstrated in his study of turn-of-the-twentieth-century musical life of Atlanta, these events—all of which were held at the city's Armory-Auditorium—helped the residents of this dynamic southern city make sense of rapid social change in the city and the broader American South.[8] The juxtaposition of powerful political, business, and cultural leaders in attendance and the "untutored" musicians performing onstage was common in the

5. Saundra Keyes, "'Little Mary Phagan': A Native American Ballad in Context," *Journal of Country Music* 3, no. 1 (Spring 1972): 1–16; D. K. Wilgus and Nathan Hurvitz, "'Little Mary Phagan': Further Notes on a Native American Ballad in Context," *Journal of Country Music* 4, no. 1 (Spring 1973): 17–30; Huber, *Linthead Stomp*, 58–59.

For more details pertaining to the Leo Frank case, consult Leonard Dinnerstein, *The Leo Frank Case* (New York: Columbia University Press, 1966); Albert S. Lindemann, *The Jew Accused: Three Anti-Semitic Affairs: Dreyfus, Beilis, Frank, 1894-1915* (Cambridge: Cambridge University Press, 1992); Jeffrey Melnick, *Black-Jewish Relations on Trial: Leo Frank and Jim Conley in the New South* (Jackson: University Press of Mississippi, 2000).

6. Huber, 72. There is some uncertainty as to the precise date that Carson made his WSB debut. Wayne W. Daniel (*Pickin' on Peachtree: A History of Country Music in Atlanta, Georgia* [Urbana and Chicago: University of Illinois Press, 1990], 50) cites local legend that he performed on 23 March 1922, just eight days after the station went on the air, and Norm Cohen suggests that the debut was 9 September 1922 ("Riley Puckett: 'King of the Hillbillies,'" *JEMF Quarterly* [Winter 1976], repr. in *Exploring Roots Music: Twenty Years of the* JEMF Quarterly, ed. Nolan Porterfield [Lanham, MD and Oxford: Scarecrow Press, 2004], 145).

7. Peterson, *Creating Country Music*, 17–20.

8. Campbell, *Music and the Making of a New South*, 11–13.

emerging industrial center. The simultaneous fascination with and disdain for the "unwritten airs" that Lindon K. Starr, a music critic for the *Atlanta Journal* and correspondent to *Music America*,[9] heard at the Old Fiddlers' Contest was likely a commonplace, as well. Note, for instance, the representation of Carson's speech in dialect, the description of the music heard there as "contagious," and the comparisons between Carson and classical superstars Enrico Caruso and Jan Kubelík.[10]

The Atlanta convention also provides a view of the lively community of fiddlers who worked in and around the Georgia capital. Carson, who had earned fourth place in the inaugural contest the prior year, was a purported crowd favorite, perhaps as a consequence of his brashness and willingness to bend the rules of the contest—which prohibited singing—to please the audience.[11] But he was far from the only popular fiddler at the event. Gid Tanner, later the leader of the popular musical and comedic group the Skillet Lickers, performed and was photographed for the *Musical America* piece that follows; it was likely there that Tanner heard a string band known as the Lickskillet Orchestra, which likely influenced the name of Tanner's later group.[12] Additional fiddlers hailed from other parts of the South, allowing audiences, themselves arriving in Atlanta from the surrounding area, to hear a wide variety of fiddling styles and a tunes taken from traditional Irish fiddle music, as well as sentimental and minstrel songs.[13]

━━━━━━━━━

ATLANTA, GA., MARCH 16—This is the story of the recent gathering of a hundred Georgia country musicians, who played on wire-stringed fiddles unwritten tunes that tradition only has kept alive for years. It lasted for a whole week in the city auditorium in Atlanta, on the stage where the Metropolitan Opera stars will sing next month. There were "fiddlers" from the Blue Ridge mountains [sic] and the South Georgia marshes—a more nondescript collection has never before been grouped together on a single stage in Atlanta.

9. "Starr, Linton K.," in Emma L. Trapper, comp., *The Musical Blue Book of America, 1916-1917: Recording in Concise Form the Activities of Leading Musicians and Those Actively and Prominently Identified with Music in Its Various Departments* (New York: Musical Blue Book Corporation, 1916), 54, http://ia700500.us.archive.org/7/items/musicalbluebook00trapuoft/musicalbluebook00trapuoft.pdf; accessed 23 November 2011.

10. The hillbilly image of ignorant, lazy rural whites contrasted with an equally prominent image of the southern mountaineer as the last bastion of pure white masculinity in an era during which urban white men were increasingly concerned about the state of white masculinity. Several historians have traced this history, including Campbell, *Music and the Making of a New South*, 100–42; Harkins, *Hillbilly*, 3–9; and Huber, *Linthead Stomp*, 65–67.

11. Wiggins, *Fiddlin' Georgia Crazy*, 48.

12. Wiggins, *Fiddlin' Georgia Crazy*, 50–53.

13. Wiggins, *Fiddlin' Georgia Crazy*, 48–49.

It may have been the desire to hear "native" music, or the fact that many of Georgia's most prominent men spent joyous moments of their boyhood at country dances, but, anyway, at the opening night the front row was occupied by Col. William Lawson Peel, president of the Atlanta Music Festival Association and one of the south's leading bankers; Judge Richard Russell, of the Georgia Court of Appeals; James G. Woodward, mayor of Atlanta; Edwin Arthur Craft, Atlanta's municipal organist, and many other notables.

AUDIENCE OF 5,000

From front row to back sat richly gowned society leaders, side by side with working folk in rough attire. The big auditorium was packed with 5,000 persons, and on the stage sat the most picturesque looking bunch of "fiddlers" imaginable.

The chairman signaled for silence. "The next, ladies and gentlemen," he said, "is 'Fiddlin' John Carson, of Blue Ridge, Georgia."

"Fiddlin'" John edged forward to the cane-bottomed chair in the center of the stage, sat down, crossed his legs and tucked his "fiddle" under his chin. He drew his bow across the catgut, and his heel beat a *staccato* refrain on the floor as he coaxed out a familiar tune. The audience leaned forward. Droned "Fiddlin'" John:

"When I was playin' wid my brudder,

"Happy was I.

"Oh, take me to my kind old mudder,

"There let me live and die."

The audience began beating time to the refrain, and the Old Fiddlers' convention was well under way!

Suddenly "Fiddlin'" John swung into the strains of "Hop, Light, Ladies." Col. William Lawson Peel, musical expert, nudged Justice "Dick" Russell, of the Georgia Appellate Court, who sat next to him, and the two leaned forward. There was a soft shuffling of patent leather shoes on the floor, a little louder, louder still, and then—

"Swing your corners! Ladies change!" shouted Col. Peel, craning forward the better to watch the fiddler's bow. "All hands 'round!"

After that, joy reigned. Atlanta society folk shuffled their feet to the lilting strains of "Wild Hog in the Cane Brake" and cheered wildly when some unusually inspiring measure set the fiddlers to dancing. There was straw-beatin' and jig-steppin', singing and banjo-picking, and there was merriment from the first notes of "Cacklin' Hen" to the final [strains] of the good old Georgia tune, "Mullinax."

OLD TUNES RELISHED

It was the same on the second night and the following evenings. "Red-Necked" Jim Lawson of Milton County "woke 'em up" with "Joe Clark," another "fiddler" played "Devil in the Wheat Patch" in an entrancing manner. Such tunes as "Old Zip Coon," "Billy in the Low Ground," "Katie Hill," "Soapsuds Over the Fence" and "Moonshiner Bob" fairly poured from the fiddles.

And there was singing by Zeke Wardell, billed as the "Bald Mountain Caruso," a young mountaineer who turned out to be the possessor of a tenor that amazed his hearers.

On the last night of all the prizes were to be awarded to the best of all "fiddlers."
"Fiddlin'" John Carson started for the Auditorium in the early afternoon of that day, with many
a pause to view the sights of the city. His beloved fiddle was tucked under his arm in a pillow
slip, and at the heels, tugging at a bit of plow-line, trotted "Trail," the sorriest looking hound
that ever bayed at the moon.

"No dogs allowed," said the janitor at the Auditorium, curtly.

"This ain't no common dawg," retorted "Fiddlin'" John, pulling "Trail" closer into
view. "That there houn' is the best tribble [treble] singer in Gawgy. Ain't you, 'Trail'? Speak up,
now."

"MOUNTAIN KUBELIK" AND HIS DOG

By this time the custodian of the building, who knew of "Fiddlin'" John's fame, had reached
the door. He admitted the "fiddler" and his dog, and that night the mountain Kubelik played
while old "Trail" sang. His song was the echo of a fox chase under a Georgia moon, then a
memory of the biggest coon ever treed. As he warned to his work his master's playing became
gradually a more *obbligato* to his solo.

When he paused "Fiddlin'" John laid down his violin as the audience cheered. The
judges withdrew and "Fiddlin'" John sang "Run, Nigger, Run, Patterroll'll Ketch You,"[14] while
they made up their decision.

"Fiddlin'" John then was declared the best of Georgia fiddlers, with "Shortly" Harper
as next best, and the convention adjourned.

Georgia's own peculiar music floated back to the hills and lowlands for another year's
tuning up preparatory to the next Old Fiddlers' convention, and the stage was swept for grand
opera.

Source: Linton K. Starr, "Georgia's Unwritten Airs Played by Old 'Fiddlers' for Atlanta
Prizes: Untutored Players from Hillsides and Marshes Perform Traditional Southern
Melodies on Wire-Stringed Violins—Society Folk and Workers in Audiences 'Shuffle
Feet' to Contagious Strains—'Bald Mountain Caruso' and Treble-singing Dog at Unique
Convention," *Musical America*, 21 March 1914.

14. A popular and frequently documented song from the mid-nineteenth century,
the song warned of "patrollers, or white guards; on duty at night during the days of
slavery; whose duty it was to see that slaves without permission to go, stayed at home"
(Thomas W. Talley, quoted in Charles K. Wolfe, ed., *Thomas W. Talley's* Negro Folk
Rhymes (Knoxville: University of Tennessee Press, 1991), 30. The song was recorded
by musicians in Atlanta and Nashville (Guthrie T. Meade with Dick Spottswood
and Douglas S. Meade, *Country Music Sources: A Biblio-Discography of Commercially
Recorded Traditional Music* [Chapel Hill: Southern Folklife Collection, 2002], 762).

FOR FURTHER READING

Daniel, Wayne W. *Pickin' on Peachtree: A History of Country Music in Atlanta, Georgia.* Urbana and Chicago: University of Illinois Press, 1990, 15–108.

Huber, Patrick. *Linthead Stomp: The Creation of Country Music in the Piedmont South.* Chapel Hill and London: University of North Carolina Press, 2008, 43–102.

Peterson, Richard A. *Creating Country Music: Fabricating Authenticity.* Chicago and London: University of Chicago Press, 1997, 13–32.

Wiggins, Gene. *Fiddlin' Georgia Crazy: Fiddlin' John Carson, His Real World, and the World of His Songs.* Urbana and Chicago: University of Illinois Press, 1986.

Cecil B. Sharp

English Folk Songs from the Southern Appalachians
(1917) [excerpt]

During the last decades of the nineteenth century and the first decades of the twentieth, amateur and professional folklorists scoured the Appalachian Mountains in search of ballads, or narrative songs, that had been carried to the region with the earliest British migrants and passed down through the oral tradition for hundreds of years. Informed by the work of Francis James Child, who had published five volumes of ballads from the British Isles between 1883 and 1898, folklorists and "songcatchers" such as Cecil Sharp and Olive Dame Campbell, among others, worked under the premise that the isolation of the central and southern Appalachians would have preserved linguistic and musical practices that dated to Shakespeare's England.[1] Scouring small towns and rural communities

1. For more background on Sharp, consult Maud Karpeles, *Cecil Sharp: His Life and Work* (London: Faber and Faber, 2012); Ronald D. Cohen, *Folk Music: The Basics* (New York: Routledge, 2006), 19-26. For more on Campbell, consult chapter 2 of David E. Whisnant, *All That Is Native & Fine: The Politics of Culture in an American Region* (Chapel Hill: University of North Carolina Press, 1983); Elizaeth McCutchen Williams, ed., *Appalachian Travels: The Diary of Olive Dame Campbell* (Lexington: University of

throughout the Appalachian South, these scholars practiced what is commonly known as "salvage folklore" in a last-ditch effort to document these seemingly unchanged musical and literary practices before modern life encroached into the region.[2] Although folklorists failed to consider Appalachia as a dynamic region that had engaged in commerce and cultural exchange with the rest of the American South for decades prior to their arrival, their efforts to document the region's ballad traditions resulted in several valuable collections of music and lyrics that continue to inform traditional music-making throughout the region. Furthermore, many of the songs that were documented by Child, Sharp, and Campbell found their way onto early hillbilly recordings, often with string band accompaniments that refinished the ballads for a contemporary audience.

The following excerpt, drawn from the preface of Campbell and Sharp's landmark 1917 study *English Folk Songs from the Southern Appalachians*, presents Appalachia as an inherently musical region that unpretentiously bears the rich traditions of English balladry that had been nearly eradicated by the Industrial Revolution of Victorian England. Revealing their anxieties about the rapid modernization of British life, Sharp's preface depicts Appalachia as an idyllic rural hinterland where song is tied to the rituals of everyday life. Although their portrait of the region was certainly grounded in some element of the truth, it is important to note that such romanticized portrayals of Appalachia later filtered into the marketing of early hillbilly music and helped to perpetuate stereotypes about the region for generations to follow.

———

THE effort that has been made to collect and preserve in permanent form the folk-songs of England during the last twenty of thirty years has resulted in the salvage of many thousands of beautiful songs. It was pardonable, therefore, if those who, like myself, had assisted in the task had come to believe that the major part of the work had been completed. So far as the collection in England itself was concerned, this belief was no doubt well founded. Nevertheless, in arriving at this very consolatory conclusion, one important, albeit not very obvious consideration had been overlooked, namely, the possibility that one or other of those English communities that lie scattered in various parts of the world might provide as good a field for the collector as England itself, and yield as bountiful and rich a harvest. The investigation which my colleague Mrs. Campbell began, and in which later on I came to bear a hand, has proved that at least one such community does in fact exist in the Southern Appalachian Mountains of North American. The region is an extensive one, covering some 110,000 square miles, and is considerably larger than England, Wales, and Scotland combined. It includes about one third

Kentucky Press, 2012). Scott B. Spencer has traced the work of Child and its influence in "Ballad Collecting: Impetus and Impact," in *The Ballad Collectors of North America: How Gathering Folksongs Transformed Academic Thought and American Identity*, ed. Scott B. Spencer (Lanham, MD: Scarecrow Press, 2012), 5-13.

2. The concept of "salvage folklore" is discussed at greater length in Bruce Jackson, *Fieldwork* (Urbana: University of Illinois Press, 1987), 37-39.

of the total area of the States of North and South Carolina, Tennessee, Virginia, West Virginia, Kentucky, Alabama, and Georgia. The total population exceeds five millions, or, excluding city dwellers, about three millions.

The Country and its Inhabitants. The reader will, I think, be in a better position to appreciate and assess the value of the songs and ballads which form the major part of this volume if, by way of preface, I give some account of the way in which they were collected and record the impression which the inhabitants of this unique country made upon me. But I must beg him remember that I claim to speak with authority only with respect to that part of the mountain district into which I penetrated and that the statements and opinions which are now to follow must be accepted subject to this qualification.

I spent nine weeks only in the mountains, accompanied throughout by Miss Maud Karpeles, who took down, usually in shorthand, the words of the songs we heard, while I noted the tunes. Mr. John C. Campbell, the agent for the Southern Highland Division of the Russell Sage Foundation, went with us on our first expedition and afterwards directed our journeyings and, in general, gave us the benefit of his very full knowledge of the country and its people. Our usual procedure was to stay at one or other of the Presbyterian Missionary Settlements[3] and to make it our centre for a week or ten days while we visited the singers who lived within a walking radius. In this way[,] we successively visited Whit Rock, Allanstand, Alleghany and Carmen, Big Laurel and Hot Springs, in North Carolina, and thus succeeded in exploring the major portion of what is know as the Laural Country. Afterwards we spent ten days at Rock Fork, Tenn., and a similar period at Charlottesville, Va. I should add that had it not been for the generous hospitality extended to us by the heads of the Missionary Settlements at which we sojourned, it would have been quite impossible to prosecute our work.

The present inhabitants of the Laurel country are the direct descendants of the original settlers who were emigrants from England and, I suspect, the lowlands of Scotland. I was able to ascertain with some degree of certainty that the settlement of this particular section began about three or four generations ago, *i.e.* in the latter part of the eighteenth century or early years of the nineteenth. How many years prior to this the original emigration from England had taken place, I am unable to say; but it is fairly safe, I think, to conclude that the present-day residents of this section of the mountains are the descendants of those who left the shores of Britain some time in the eighteenth century.

The region is from its inaccessibility a very secluded one. There are but few roads—most of them little better than mountain tracks—and practically no railroads. Indeed, so remote and shut off from outside influence were, until quite recently, these sequestered mountain valleys that the inhabitants have for a hundred years or more been completely isolated and cut off from all traffic with the rest of the world. Their speech is English, not American, and, from the number of expressions they use which have long been obsolete elsewhere, and the old-fashioned way in which they pronounce many of their words, it is clear that they are talking the language of a past day, though exactly of what period I am not competent to decide. One peculiarity is perhaps worth the noting, namely the pronunciation of the impersonal pronoun with an aspirate—"hit"—a practice that seems to be universal.

3. Missionary projects proliferated in Appalachia during the late nineteenth and early twentieth centuries. For more on progressive reform efforts in Appalachia, consult William A. Link, *The Paradox of Southern Progressivism, 1880-1930* (Chapel Hill: University of North Carolina Press, 1992).

Economically they are independent. As there are practically no available markets, little or no surplus produce is grown, each family extracting from its holding just what is needed to support life, and no more. They have very little money, barter in kind being the customary form of exchange.

Many set the standard of bodily and material comfort perilously low, in order, presumably, that they may have the more leisure and so extract the maximum enjoyment out of life. The majority live in log-cabins, more or less water-tight, usually, but not always, lighted with windows; but some have built larger and more comfortable homesteads.

They are a leisurely, cheery people in their quiet way, in whom the social instinct is very highly developed. They dispense hospitality with an openhanded generosity and are extremely interested in and friendly toward strangers, communicative and unsuspicious. "But surely you will tarry with us for the night?" was said to us on more than one occasion when, after paying an afternoon's visit, we rose to say good-bye.

They know their Bible intimately and subscribe to an austere creed, charged with Calvinism and the unrelenting doctrines of determinism or fatalism. The majority we met were Baptists, but we met Methodists also, a few Presbyterians, and some who are attached to what is known as the "Holiness" sect, with whom, however, we had but little truck, as their creed forbids the singing of secular songs.[4]

They have an easy unaffected bearing and the unselfconscious manners of the well-bred. I have received salutations upon introduction or on bidding farewell, dignified and restrained, such as a courtier might make to his Sovereign. Our work naturally led to the making of many acquaintances, and, in not a few cases, to the formation of friendships of a more intimate nature, but on no single occasion did we receive anything but courteous and friendly treatment. Strangers that we met in the course of our long walks would usually bow, doff the hat, and extend the hand, saying, "My name is ————; what is yours?" an introduction which often led to a pleasant talk and sometimes to singing and the noting of interesting ballads. In their general characteristics[,] they reminded me of the English peasant, with whom my work in England for the past fifteen years or more has brought me into close contact. There are differences, however. The mountaineers is freer in his manner, more alert, and less inarticulate than his British prototype, and bears no trace of the obsequiousness of manner which, since the Enclosure Acts robbed him of his economic independence and made of him a hired labourer, has unhappily characterized the English villager. The difference is seen in the way the mountaineer, as I have already said, upon meeting a stranger, removes his hat, offers his hand and enters into conversation, where the English labourer would touch his cap, or pull his forelock, and pass on.

A few of those we met were able to read and write, but the majority were illiterate. They are, however, good talkers, using an abundant vocabulary racily and often picturesquely. Although uneducated, in the sense in which that term is usually understood, they possess that elemental wisdom, abundant knowledge and intuitive understanding which those only who live in constant touch with Nature and face to face with reality seem to be able to acquire. It is

4. For more on religious practices in Appalachia, consult Deborah Vansau McCauley, *Appalachian Mountain Religion: A History* (Urbana: University of Illinois Press, 1995); Loyal Jones, *Faith and Meaning in the Southern Uplands* (Urbana: University of Illinois Press, 1999); and Bill J. Leonard, eds., *Christianity in Appalachia: Profiles in Regional Pluralism* (Knoxville: University of Tennessee Press, 1999).

to be hoped that the schools which are beginning to be established in some districts, chiefly in the vicinity of the Missionary Settlements, will succeed in giving them what they lack without infecting their ideals, or depriving them of the charm of manner and the many engaging qualities which so happily distinguish them.

Physically, they are strong and of good stature, though usually spare in figure. Their features are clean-cut and often handsome; while their complexions testify to wholesome, out-of-door habits. They carry themselves superbly, and it was a never-failing delight to not their swinging, easy gait and the sureness with which they would negotiate the foot-logs over the creeks, the crossing of which caused us many anxious moments. The children usually go about barefooted, and, on occasion their elders too, at any rate in the summer time. Like all primitive peoples, or those who live under primitive conditions, they attain to physical maturity at a very early age, especially the women, with whom marriage at thirteen, or even younger, is not unknown.

I have been told that in past days there were blood-feuds—a species of vendetta— which were pursued for generations between members of certain families or clans; but, whenever circumstances connected with these were related to me, I was always given to understand that this barbarous custom had long since been discontinued. I have heard, too, that there is a good deal of illicit distilling of corn spirit by "moonshiners", [sic] as they are called, in defiance of the State excise laws; but of this, again, I personally saw nothing and heard but little. Nor did I see any consumption of alcohol in the houses I visited. On the other hand, the chewing or snuffing of tobacco is a common habit amongst the young and old; but, curiously enough, no one smokes. Indeed, many looked askance at my pipe and I rarely succeeded in extracting more than a half-hearted assent to my request for permission to light it.

That the illiterate may nevertheless reach a high level of culture will surprise those only who imagine that education and cultivation are convertible terms. The reason, I take it, why these mountain people, albeit unlettered, have acquired so many of the essentials of culture is partly to be attributed to the large amount of leisure they enjoy, without which, of course, no cultural development is possible, but chiefly to the fact that they have one and all entered at birth into the full enjoyment of their racial heritage. Their language, wisdom, manners, and the many graces of life that are theirs, are merely racial attributes which have been gradually acquired and accumulated in past centuries and handed down generation by generation, each generation adding its quotum to that which it received. It must be remembered, also, that in their everyday lives they are immune from that continuous, grinding, mental pressure, due to the attempt to "make a living," from which nearly all of us in the modern world suffer. Here no one is "on the make"; commercial competition and social rivalries are unknown. In this respect, at any rate, they have the advantage over those who habitually spend the greater part of every day in preparing to live, in acquiring the technique of life, rather than in its enjoyment.

I have dwelt at considerable length upon this aspect of mountain life because it was the first which struck me and further, because, without a realization of this background, it will be difficult for the reader to follow intelligently what I have to say. But before I leave this part of my subject[,] I must, in self-justification, add that I am aware that the outsider does not always see the whole of the game, and that I am fully conscious that there is another and less lovely side of the picture which in my appreciation I have ignored. I have deliberately done so because that side has, I believe, already been emphasized, perhaps with unnecessary insistence, by other observers.

The Singers and their Songs. My sole purpose in visiting this country was to collect the traditional songs and ballads which I had heard from Mrs. Campbell, and knew from other sources, were still being sung there. I naturally expected to find conditions very similar to those which I had encountered in England when engaged on the same quest. But of this I was soon to be agreeably disillusioned. Instead, for instance, of having to confine my attention to the aged, as in England where no one under the age of seventy ordinarily possesses the folk-song tradition, I discovered that I could get what I wanted from pretty nearly every one I met, young and old. In fact, I found myself for the first time in my life in a community in which singing was as common and almost as universal a practice as speaking. With us, of course, singing is an entertainment, something done by others for our delectation, the cult and close preserve of a professional caste of specialists. The fact has been forgotten that singing is the one form of artistic expression that can be practiced without any preliminary study or special training; that every normal human being can sing just as every one can talk; and that it is, consequently, just as ridiculous to restrict thte practice of singing to a chosen few as it would be to limit the art of speaking to orators, professors of elocution and other specialists. In an ideal society[,] every child in his earliest years would as a matter of course develop this inborn capacity and learn to sing the songs of his forefathers in the same natural and unselfconscious way in which he now learns his mother tongue and the elementary literature of the nation to which he belongs.

And it was precisely this ideal state of things that I found existing in the mountain communities. So closely, indeed, is the practice of this particular art interwoven with the ordinary avocations of everyday life that singers, unable to recall a song I had asked for, would often make some such remark as, "Oh, if only I were driving the cows home I could sing it at once!". [sic] On one occasion, too, I remember that a small boy tried to edge himself into my cabin in which a man was singing to me and, when I asked him what he wanted, he said, "I always like to go where there is sweet music." Of course, I let him in and, later one, when my singer failed to remember a song I had asked for, my little visitor came to the rescue and straightway sang the ballad from beginning to end in the true traditional manner, and in a way which would have shamed many a professional vocalist[....] I have no doubt but that this delightful habit of making beautiful music at all times and in all places largely compensates for any deficiencies in the matter of reading and writing.

But, of course, the cultural value of singing must depend upon the kind of songs that are sung. Happily, in this matter the hillsman is not called upon to exercise any choice, for the only music, or, at any rate, the only secular music, that he hears and has, therefore, any opportunity of learning is that which his British forefathers brought with them from their native country and has since survived by oral tradition.

When, by chance, the text of a modern street-song succeeds in penetrating into the mountains[,] it is at once mated to a traditional tune [...] and sometimes still further purified by being moulded into the form of a traditional ballad [....] But this happens but rarely, for, strange as it may seem, these mountain valleys are in fact far less affected by modern musical influences than the most remote and secluded English village, where there is always a Parsonage or Manor house, or both, to link it to the outside world.

We found little or no difficulty in persuading those we visited to sing to us. To prove our interest in the subject and to arouse their memories, we would ourselves sometimes sing folk-songs that I had collected in England, choosing, for preference, those with which they were unacquainted. Very often they misunderstood our requirements and would give us hymns instead of the secular songs and ballads which we wanted; but that was before we had learned to ask for "love-songs," which is their name for these ditties. It was evident, too, that it was often assumed that strangers like ourselves could have but one object and that to "improve", [sic] and their relief was obvious when they found that we came not to give but to receive.

It is no exaggeration to say that some of the hours I passed sitting on the porch (i.e. verandah) of a log-cabin, talking and listening to songs were amongst the pleasantest I have every spent. Very often we would call upon some of our friends early in the morning and remain till dusk, sharing the mid-day meal with the family, and I would go away in the evening with the feeling that I had never before been in a more musical atmosphere, nor benefited more greatly by the exchange of musical confidences.

The singers displayed much interest in watching me take down their music in my note-book and when at the conclusion of a song I hummed over the tune to test the accuracy of my transcription they were as delighted as though I had successfully performed a conjuring trick.

The mountain singers sing in very much the same way as English folk-singers, in the same straightforward, direct manner, without any conscious effort at expression, and with the even tone and clarity of enunciation with which all folk-song collectors are familiar. Perhaps, however, they are less unselfconscious and sing rather more freely and with somewhat less restraint than the English peasant; I certainly never saw any one of them close the eyes when he sang nor assume that rigid, passive expression to which collectors in England have so often called attention.

They have one vocal peculiarity, however, which I have never noticed amongst English folk-singers, namely, the habit of dwelling arbitrarily upon certain notes of the melody, generally the weaker accents. This practice, which is almost universal, by disguising the rhythm and breaking up the monotonous regularity of the phrases, produces an effect of improvisation and freedom from rule which is very pleasing. The effect is most characteristic in 6/8 tunes, as, for example, No. 16G, in which in the course of the tune pauses are made on each of the three notes of the subsidiary triplets.

The wonderful charm, fascinating and well-nigh magical, which the folk-singer produces upon those who are fortunate enough to hear him is to be attributed very largely to his method of singing, and this, it should be understood, is quite as traditional as the song itself. The genuine folk-singer is never conscious of his audience—indeed, as often as not, he has none—and he never, therefore, strives after effect, nor endeavours in this or in any other way to attract the attention, much less the admiration of his hearers. So far as I have been able to comprehend his mental attitude, I gather that, when singing a ballad, for instance, he is merely relating a story in a peculiarly effective way which he has learned from his elders, his conscious attention begin wholly concentrated upon what he singing and not upon the effect which he himself is producing. This is more true, perhaps, of the English than of the American singers, some of whom I found were able mentally to separate the tune from the text—which English singers can rarely do—and even in some cases to discuss the musical points of the former with considerable intelligence.

Source: Sharp, Cecil J. "Introduction." In Olive Dame Campbell and Cecil B. Sharp. *English Folk Songs from the Southern Appalachians*. New York and London: G.P. Putnam's Sons, 1917. iii–x.

FOR FURTHER READING

Spencer, Scott B. "Ballad Collecting: Impetus and Impact." In *The Ballad Collectors of North America: How Gathering Folksongs Transformed Academic Thought and American Identity.* Lanham, MD: Scarecrow Press, 2012. 1–16.

Whisnant, David E. *All That Is Native & Fine: The Politics of Culture in an American Region.* Chapel Hill: University of North Carolina Press, 1983.

John A. Lomax

Cowboy Songs and Other Frontier Ballads (1910)

Another important source of country music mythology and imagery has been the music and lore of the American cowboy. Fascinating American audiences since the dime novels about cowboy life were widely circulated in the late nineteenth century, the cowboy's life has been symbolic of Manifest Destiny, as well as American liberty and masculinity.[1] Although many popular cowboy singers performing at the height of the singing cowboy craze of the 1930s and 1940s sang compositions written by contemporary songwriters using modern harmonies and rhythms, cowboy singers have also drawn heavily from songs that have long histories on the ranges of North America.[2] A key source for many of these songs is folklorist John A. Lomax's

1. For a cogent discussion of cowboy masculinity, consult Jacqueline M. Moore, *Cow Boys and Cattle Men: Class and Masculinities on the Texas Frontier, 1865–1900* (New York: New York University Press, 2010). For more on the representative power of the American West, consult David M. Wrobel, *Global West, American Frontier: Travel, Empire, and Exceptionalism from Manifest Destiny to the Great Depression* (Albuquerque: University of New Mexico Press, 2013).

2. Douglas B. Green, *Singing in the Saddle: The History of the Singing Cowboy* (Nashville, TN: Country Music Foundation Press and Vanderbilt University Press, 2002), 9–19.

Cowboys Songs and Other Frontier Ballads, first published in 1910. The collection, which also provided the source material for composer Aaron Copland's ballet *Rodeo,*[3] included such famous songs as "I Ride an Old Paint," "Jesse James," and "The Cowboy's Lament." Like Cecil Sharp (see chapter 2) and Francis Child, Lomax was interested in preserving what was thought to be a dying vernacular art form, endangered by the end of America's westward expansion, the rise of railroads, and the increasing urbanization of early-twentieth-century America. At the same time, he seemed to have little concern about efforts to commercialize cowboy singing, transcribing the songs in his collection to regularize rhythms and pitches so that others might sing them, and even aiding the career of a young singer and former student named Tex Ritter, who went on to an acclaimed career on stage and recordings.[4]

In the excerpt that follows, extracted from the "Collector's Note" that prefaced *Cowboys Songs and Other Frontier Ballads,* Lomax describes the role that singing played in the lives of mid-nineteenth-century cowboys, revealing that singing was a key entertainment on the long trail rides and cattle drives that they led, an essential tool used to move the cattle along, and a way of documenting their work and play. Lomax's occasional lapses into romanticized language and comparisons between cowboys and the Knights of the Round Table also speak to his efforts to shape a distinctly American folklore built around the unique experiences of a diverse, multicultural America and equal to the lore of Europe.

"COLLECTOR'S NOTE"

Out in the wild, far-away places of the big and still unpeopled west,—in the cañons[5] along the Rocky Mountains, among the mining camps of Nevada and Montana, and on the remote cattle ranches of Texas, New Mexico, and Arizona,—yet survives the Anglo-Saxon ballad spirit that was active in secluded districts in England and Scotland even after the coming of Tennyson and Browning.[6] This spirit is manifested both in the preservation of the English ballad and in the creation of local songs. Illiterate people, and people

3. Consult Howard Pollack, *Aaron Copland: The Life and Work of an Uncommon Man* (Urbana: University of Illinois Press, 2000), 363–74, for more information on Copland's ballet.

4. For more on John Lomax, consult Nolan Porterfield, *Last Cavalier: The Life and Times of John A. Lomax, 1867-1948* (Urbana: University of Illinois Press, 1996). For broader context on the collection of cowboy songs and cowboy folklore, consult Barry Shank, *Dissonant Identities: The Rock 'n' Roll Scene in Austin, Texas* (New Hanover, NH: Wesleyan University Press/University Press of New England, 1994), 20–37; Guy Logsdon, "Songcatchers in the West: Cowboy Songs," in *The Ballad Collectors of North America: How Gathering Folksongs Transformed Academic Thought and American Identity* (Lanham, MD: Scarecrow Press, 2012), 51–65;

5. Spanish spelling of *canyons.*

6. Victorian-era poets Alfred Lord Tennyson (1809–1892) and Robert Browning (1812–1889).

cut off from newspapers and books, isolated and lonely,—thrown back on primal resources for entertainment and for the expression of emotion,—utter themselves through somewhat the same character of songs as did their fore-fathers of perhaps a thousand years ago. In some such way have been made and preserved the cowboy songs and other frontier ballads contained in this volume. The songs represent the operation of instinct and tradition. They are chiefly interesting to the present generation, however, because of the light they throw on the conditions of pioneer life, and more particularly because of the information they contain concerning that unique and romantic figure in modern civilization, the American cowboy.

The profession of cow-punching, not yet a lost art in a group of big western states, reached its greatest prominence during the first two decades succeeding the Civil War. In Texas, for example, immense tracts of open range, covered with luxuriant grass, encouraged the raising of cattle. One person in many instances owned thousands. To care for the cattle during the winter season, to round them up in the spring and mark and brand the yearlings, and later to drive from Texas to Fort Dodge, Kansas, those ready for market, required large forces of men. The drive from Texas to Kansas came to be known as "going up the trail," for the cattle really made permanent, deep-cut trails across the otherwise trackless hills and plains of the long way. It also became the custom to take large herds of young steers from Texas as far north as Montana, where grass at certain seasons grew more luxuriant than in the south. Texas was the best breeding ground, while the climate and grass of Montana developed young cattle for the market.

A trip up the trail made a distinct break in the monotonous life of the big ranches, often situated hundreds of miles from where the conventions of society were observed. The ranch community consisted usually of the boss, the straw-boss, the cowboys proper, the horse wrangler, and the cook—often a negro [sic].[7] These men lived on terms of practical equality. Except in the case of the boss, there was little difference in the amounts paid each for his services. Society, then, was here reduced to its lowest terms. The work of the men, their daily experiences, their thoughts, their interests, were all in com-mon. Such a community had necessarily to turn to itself for entertainment. Songs sprang up naturally, some of them tender and familiar lays of child-hood, others original compositions, all genuine, however crude and unpol-ished. Whatever the most gifted man could produce must bear the criticism of the entire camp, and agree with the ideas of a group of men. In this sense, therefore, any song that came from such a group would be the joint product of a number of them, telling perhaps the story of some stampede they had all fought to turn, some crime in which they had all shared equally, some com-rade's tragic death which they had all witnessed. The song-making did not cease as the men went up the trail. Indeed the songs were here utilized for very

7. For more on African American cowboys, consult Sara R. Massey, ed., *Black Cowboys of Texas* (College Station: Texas A&M University Press, 2000).

practical ends. Not only were sharp, rhythmic yells—sometimes beaten into verse—employed to stir up lagging cattle, but also during the long watches the night-guards, as they rode round and round the herd, improvised cattle lullabies which quieted the animals and soothed them to sleep. Some of the best of the so-called "dogie songs" seem to have been created for the purpose of preventing cattle stampedes,—such songs coming straight from the heart of the cowboy, speaking familiarly to his herd in the stillness of the night.

The long drives up the trail occupied months, and called for sleepless vigilance and tireless activity both day and night. When at last a shipping point was reached, the cattle marketed or loaded on the cars, the cowboys were paid off. It is not surprising that the consequent relaxation led to reckless deeds. The music, the dancing, the click of the roulette ball in the saloons, invited; the lure of crimson lights was irresistible. Drunken orgies, reactions from months of toil, deprivation, and loneliness on the ranch and on the trail, brought to death many a temporarily crazed buckaroo. To match this dare-deviltry, a saloon man in one frontier town, as a sign for his business, with psychological ingenuity painted across the broad front of his building in big black letters this challenge to God, man, and the devil: *The Road to Ruin.* Down this road, with swift and eager footsteps, has trod many a pioneer viking [sic] of the West. Quick to resent an insult real or fancied, inflamed by unaccustomed drink, the ready pistol always at his side, the tricks of the professional gambler to provoke his sense of fair play, and finally his own wild recklessness to urge him on,—all these combined forces sometimes brought him into tragic conflict with another spirit equally heedless and daring. Not nearly so often, however, as one might suppose, did he die with his boots on. Many of the most wealthy and respected citizens now living in border states served as cowboys before settling down to quiet domesticity.

A cow-camp in the seventies generally contained several types of men. It was not unusual to find a negro [sic] who, because of his ability to handle wild horses or because of his skill with a lasso, had been promoted from the chuck-wagon to a place in the ranks of the cowboys. Another familiar figure was the adventurous younger son of some British family, through whom perhaps became current the English ballads found in the West. Furthermore, so considerable was the number of men who had fled from the States because of grave impudence or crime, it was bad form to inquire too closely about a person's real name or where he came from. Most cowboys, however, were bold young spirits who emigrated to the West for the same reason that their ancestors had come across the seas. They loved roving; the loved freedom; they were pioneers by instinct; an impulse set their faces from the East, put the tang for roaming in their veins, and sent them ever, ever westward.

That the cowboy was brave has come to be axiomatic. If his life of isolation made him taciturn, it at the same time created a spirit of hospitality, primitive and hearty as that found in the mead-halls of Beowulf. He faced the wind and the rain, the snow of winter, the fearful dust-storms of alkali desert wastes, with the same uncomplaining quiet. Not all his work was on the ranch and the trail. To the cowboy, more than to the goldseekers, more than to Uncle Sam's soldiers, is due the conquest of the West. Along his winding cattle trails the Forty-Niners found their way to California. The cowboy has fought back the Indians ever since ranching became a business and as long as Indians remained to be fought. He played his part in winning the great slice of territory that the United States took away from Mexico. He has always been on the skirmish line of civilization. Restless, fearless, chivalric, elemental, he lived hard, shot quick and true, and died with his face to his foe. Still much misunderstood, he is often slandered, nearly always caricatured, both by the press and by the stage. Perhaps these songs, coming direct from the cowboy's experiences, giving vent to his careless and his tender emotions, will afford future generations a truer conception of what he really was than is now possessed by those who know him only through highly colored romances.

The big ranches of the West are now being cut up into small farms.[8] The nester has come, and come to stay. Gone is the buffalo, the Indian warwhoop, the free grass of the open plain;—even the stinging lizard, the horned frog, the centipede, the prairie dog, the rattlesnake, are fast disappearing. Save in some of the secluded valleys of southern New Mexico, the old-time round-up is no more; the trails to Kansas and Montana have become grass-grown or lost in fields of waving grain; the maverick steer, the regal longhorn, has been supplanted by his unpoetic but more beefy and profitable Polled Angus, Durham, and Hereford cousins from across the seas. The changing and romantic West of the early days lives mainly in story and in song. The last figure to vanish is the cowboy, the animating spirit of the vanishing era. He sits his horse easily as he rides through a wide valley, enclosed by mountains, clad in the hazy purple of coming night,—with his face turned steadily down the long, long road, "the road that the sun goes down." Dauntless, reckless, without the unearthly purity of Sir Galahad though as gentle to a pure woman as King Arthur, he is truly a knight of the twentieth century. A vagrant puff of wind shakes a corner of the crimson handkerchief knotted loosely at his throat; the thud of his pony's feet mingling with the jungle of his spurs is borne back; and as the careless, gracious, lovable figure disappears over the divide, the breeze brings to the ears, faint and far yet cheery still, the refrain of a cowboy song:

> *Whoopee ti yi, get along, little dogies;*
>
> *It's my misfortune and none of your own.*
>
> *Whoopee ti yi, get along, little dogies;*
>
> *For you know Wyoming will be your new home.*

8. This history is discussed at some length in Timothy Egan, *The Worst Hard Time: The Untold Story of Those Who Survived the Great American Dust Bowl* (New York: Houghton Mifflin, 2006).

As for the songs of this collection, I have violated the ethics of ballad-gatherers, in a few instances, by selecting and putting together what seemed to be the best lines from different versions, all telling the same story. Frankly, the volume is meant to be popular. The songs have been arranged in some such haphazard way as they were collected,—jotted down on a table in the rear of saloons, scrawled on an envelope while squatting about a campfire, caught behind the scenes of a broncho-busting outfit. Later, it is hoped that enough interest will be aroused to justify printing all the variants of these songs, accompanied by the music and such explanatory notes as may be useful; the negro [sic] folk-songs, the songs of the lumber jacks, the songs of the mountaineers, and the songs of the sea, already partially collected, being included in the final publication. The songs of this collection, never before in print, as a rule have been taken down from oral recitation. In only a few instances have I been able to discover the authorship of any song. They seem to have sprung up as quietly and mysteriously as does the grass on the plains. All have been popular with the range riders, several being current all the way from Texas to Montana, and quite as long as the old Chisholm Trail stretching between these states. Some of the songs the cowboy certainly composed; all of them he sang. Obviously, a number of the most characteristic cannot be printed for general circulation. To paraphrase slightly what Sidney Lanier said of Walt Whitman's poetry, they are raw collops slashed from the rump of Nature, and never mind the gristle. Likewise some of the strong adjectives and nouns have been softened,—Jonahed, as George Meredith would have said. There is, however, a Homeric quality about the cowboy's profanity and vulgarity that pleases rather than repulses. The broad sky under which he slept, the limitless plains over which he rode, the big, open, free life he lived near to Nature's breast, taught him simplicity, calm, directness. He spoke out plainly the impulses of his heart. But[,] as yet[,] so-called polite society is not quite willing to hear.

Source: John A. Lomax, *Cowboy Songs and Other Frontier Ballads* (New York: Macmillan, 1910), xvii–xxv.

FOR FURTHER READING

Green, Douglas B. *Singing in the Saddle: The History of the Singing Cowboy*. Nashville, TN: Country Music Foundation Press and Vanderbilt University Press, 2002.

Porterfield, Nolan. *Last Cavalier: The Life and Times of John A. Lomax, 1867–1948*. Urbana: University of Illinois Press, 1996.

4

"What the Popularity of Hill-Billy Songs Means in Retail Profit Sensibilities:

The Widespread Vogue of the Funereal Type of Songs Is Attested by Publishers and Record Manufacturers— Is It of Significance as Indication of Public Taste?"
(1925)

*T*he *Talking Machine World* was the most important consumer and trade publication treating the products and practices of the recording industry in the first decades of the twentieth century, and its contributors frequently used their columns to editorialize about the state of contemporary musical tastes.[1] Emerging alongside jazz and blues recordings, hillbilly recordings proved particularly problematic for some writers who were puzzled by the widespread acceptance of

---

1. For more on *The Talking Machine World*, consult Tim Gracyk with R. J. Wakeman, "Introduction to Talking Machine World," http://www.gracyk.com/tmw. shtml; accessed 27 January 2014. The Library of Congress has archived many back issues, which are available at https://archive.org/details/libraryofcongresspackard campus; accessed 27 January 2014.

"low-brow" musical entertainments that were created by marginalized peoples: working-class blacks and whites.[2] Many contemporary commentators saw the popularity of these genres not as evidence of American music's richness but as a sign of the nation's aesthetic and moral decay.[3] Although the writer in the excerpt that follows is hopeful that the rise of hillbilly recordings in the mid-1920s might diminish the popularity of jazz (which, by virtue of its obvious associations with African American culture, was deemed to be a serious problem), he also does not appear to appreciate Sharp's and Lomax's assertions that these songs might represent the truest expressions of American, and even European, folk cultures. Rather, the simplicity of hillbilly music's "weird funereal offerings" is cast here as little more than a welcome respite from the complex jazz arrangements.

At the same time, this report also highlights the important role that sheet music sales played in the success of the early-twentieth-century music industry. The essayist's excitement about the "return to songs" suggests that people might purchase sheet music of these new compositions so that they could play them in their own homes, just as they had during the nineteenth-century heyday of the American popular song publishing.[4] Dance arrangements, it seems, were not as lucrative as the new hillbilly songs, no matter how déclassé they may have seemed.

━━━━━━━━━━

The advent or revival, or whatever you choose to call it, of what are described as the "hill-billy" songs signifies more than the mere vogue of such publications. The "Death of Floyd Collins," "Wreck of the Shenandoah," "At My Mother's Grave," and other such songs which have had fairly widespread popularity may mark the initial move in the passing of jazz. Whether or not the popularity of such works continues, it is questionable that music lovers will accept the situation as an improvement. This, however, and other indications show a grasping out on the part of music purchasers for something besides the generally over-arranged jazz offerings.

It must be remembered that these weird funereal musical offerings have been preceded by several months by other offerings, the outstanding

2. For a general discussion of cultural hierarchies in American culture, consult Lawrence Levine, *Highbrow/Lowbrow: The Emergence of Cultural Hierarchy in America* (Cambridge, MA: Harvard University Press, 1988).

3. Kathy J. Ogren has noted that, during the 1920s, "many critics of jazz attacked the music as 'noise,' and compared it to a plague or disease threatening to destroy the civilized world. Most criticisms clustered around moral, aesthetic, or professional values challenged by jazz. All objections by whites to the music were, of course, based on the premise that blacks were inferior to whites" (Kathy J. Ogren, *The Jazz Revolution: Twenties America and the Meaning of Jazz* [New York: Oxford University Press, 1992], 153).

4. For a general overview of the nineteenth-century music publishing industry, consult Russell Sanjek, *American Popular Music and Its Business, The First Hundred Years, Vol. 2: From 1790 to 1909* (New York: Oxford University Press, 1988), 47–145.

feature of which was that they were in most simplified song form. In fact, some of the outstanding record sellers to-day and for the past few months have been solo numbers with minor accompaniment.[5] All of this undoubtedly shows the earmarks of a new phase of the popular music and record business. It would seemingly demonstrate that the public is returning to songs. The first love, of course, is songs of the ballad order because they are the most impressive, have the widest appeal and sale. We may expect other types of songs to follow closely. Probably we have had an over-production of songs of the fox-trot order and in self-defense the public has revolted and turned to that which was a most radical change, the sob songs of several generations ago, brought up to date and made into a pathetic song on some current topical event or catastrophe.[6] Psychologically this can be answered, it being well know that when groups revolt[,] they go to extremes.

The fact that the public or a fair portion of it has decided on a funeral dirge type of offering should not be taken as an atavistic tendency. It is rather a desire for something different. This desire can be taken advantage of by both the popular publisher and record maker, and songs of good ballad order, love songs and other numbers particularly lending themselves to solo voices with a minimum of arrangement[,] should meet the situation and bring on a period of prosperity that would be far larger than the results obtained by merely catering to what may be a limited vogue for songs of pathos.

Probably one of the best points for the publisher and record maker to remember in the present trend of public taste is the fact that at least for some period the sales of dance music will not markedly depreciate. It will probably be many months before any real indentation will be made in the sales of such works. The demands for songs are to a great extent added sales.

As far as dance music is concerned[,] there is hardly a likelihood that any considerable change will be made in the demand for dance. The situation may indicate, however, that we need a new type of dance or a new type of dance music. Something in more simplified form and one holding continuously to the melody of the piece without diverting to super accompaniments.

The modern dance orchestra[,] despite its many weaknesses, none of which is eradicable, has performed a very big work in disseminating music to the great multitudes. Not only that, but it has been the means of acting as an incentive to hundreds of thousands of the younger generation who have taken up musical instruments of every class[,] from the lowly ukulele to our almost as popular saxophone. None would wish to see a trend in musical taste that would in any measure kill off this power that is influencing, musically, so many of the younger generation.

5. Sparse instrumental accompaniment.
6. For an in-depth discussion of the nineteenth-century songwriting trends referenced here, consult chaps. 8–12 of Charles Hamm, *Yesterdays: Popular Song in America* (New York: W.W. Norton, 1979) and Jon W. Finson, *The Voices that are Gone: Themes in 19th-Century American Popular Song* (New York: Oxford University Press, 1994).

We would probably gladly, however, look forward to greater development of a little more simplification in our popular renditions. We would like to know the melodies that are being played and what they are all about rather than be led up to an approaching melody and abruptly be diverted to a semi-solo effect in obbligato form.

At any rate, as far as popular publishers are concerned, the situation is quite pleasing because it does show that the great American public is returning to songs and after all[,] "the song is the thing."

Source: "What the Popularity of Hill-Billy Songs Means in Retail Profit Sensibilities: The Widespread Vogue of the Funereal Type of Songs Is Attested by Publishers and Record Manufacturers—Is It of Significance as Indication of Public Taste?" *The Talking Machine World*, 15 December 1925.

FOR FURTHER READING

Miller, Karl Hagstrom. *Segregating Sound: Inventing Folk and Pop Music in the Age of Jim Crow*. Durham, NC: Duke University Press, 2010.

"Mountain Songs Recorded Here by Victor Co.:

Notable Performers of This Section at Work at Station in This City" (1927)

Country music historian Nolan Porterfield has described the series of recording sessions held in at the former Taylor-Christian Hat Company building in Bristol, Tennessee, between 25 July and 5 August 1927 as "the big bang of country music."[1] The first hillbilly recordings were made more than five years earlier and many record labels were promoting their own lines of "Old Familiar Tunes" (Columbia) or "Old-Time Music" (OKeh),[2] but the "Bristol sessions" have taken on

1. Nolan Porterfield, "Hey, Hey, Tell 'Em 'Bout Us: Jimmie Rodgers Visits the Carter Family," in Paul Kingsbury, Alan Axelrod, and Susan Costello, eds., *Country: The Music and the Musicians*, 2nd ed. (New York: Abbeville Press, 1994), 17.

2. Archie Green, "Hillbilly Music: Source and Symbol," *Journal of American Folklore* vol. 78, no. 309 (July-September 1965), 216–217; Charles K. Wolfe, "Columbia Records and Old-Time Music," reprinted in *Exploring Roots Music: Twenty Years of the* JEMF *Quarterly*, ed. Nolan Porterfield (Lanham, MD: Scarecrow Press, 2004), 199–217; Charles K. Wolfe, "The Bristol Syndrome: Field Recordings of Early Country Music," in *Country Music Annual 2002*, ed. Charles K. Wolfe and James E. Akenson (Lexington: University Press of Kentucky, 2002), 203–207; Bill C. Malone and Jocelyn R. Neal, *Country Music, U.S.A.*, 3rd rev. ed. (Austin: University of Texas Press, 2010), 39. For a more detailed

special significance in the history of country music. The Bristol sessions document the musical life of a particularly rich southern Appalachian region that stretched across five states.[3] Nineteen groups recorded seventy-six songs for Ralph Peer during the Bristol sessions, including vocal pieces and string band tunes.[4] Although many of these musicians never went on to great regional or national fame following the Bristol sessions, two of the acts that cut sides in Bristol in the summer of 1927 enjoyed long careers in the entertainment industry: the Carter Family (A.P., Sara, and Maybelle) and Jimmie Rodgers. Representing polar opposites in terms of musical style and image, the Carter Family and Rodgers were two of the earliest stars of the hillbilly music industry, exerting a significant influence not only on their contemporaries but also on subsequent generations of musicians and fans (see chapters 8 and 9).[5]

Described in early promotional materials as "a Victor recording expedition into the mountains of Tennessee," Ralph Peer's trip to Bristol was part of a two-month trip to the major cities of the American South that yielded several important recordings of American vernacular musics from a variety of musical traditions. Although Peer sometimes claimed that he could not recall why he chose to record in Bristol, country music historian Charles K. Wolfe has suggested a number of potential reasons.[6] First, the city, the largest in southern Appalachia at the time, was centrally

discussion of the formation of "race" and "hillbilly" series in the 1920s, consult chaps. 6 and 7 of William Howland Kinney, *Recorded Music in American Life: The Phonograph and Popular Memory, 1890-1945* (New York and Oxford: Oxford University Press, 1999) and chap. 6 of Karl Hagstrom Miller, *Segregating Sound: Inventing Folk and Pop Music in the Age of Jim Crow* (Durham, NC: Duke University Press, 2010).

3. Of the nineteen acts who recorded during the Bristol sessions, five hailed from within twenty miles of Bristol, four from within fifty miles, five from within one hundred miles, and five from more than one hundred miles away (Wolfe, "The Bristol Syndrome," 210).

4. The number of vocal pieces can likely be attributed to the recent development of the electric microphone, which allowed musicians to be more expressive than the previous "acoustic process" had permitted (Charles K. Wolfe, "The Legend That Peer Built: Reappraising the Bristol Sessions," *Journal of Country Music* 13, no. 2 [1989], repr. in *The Bristol Sessions: Writings about the Big Bang of Country Music*, ed. Charles K. Wolfe and Ted Olsen, *Contributions to Southern Appalachian Studies* 12]Jefferson, NC, and London: MacFarland, 2005], 12).

For a more detailed discussion of the differences between acoustic and electric recording, consult Mark Katz, *Capturing Sound: How Technology Has Changed Music* (Berkeley: University of California Press, 2005), 37–41; Andre Millard, *America on Record: A History of Recorded Sound*, 2nd ed. (Cambridge: Cambridge University Press, 2005), 115–57; Eric Morritt, "Early Sound Recording Technology and the Bristol Sessions," in *The Bristol Sessions: Writings about the Big Bang of Country Music*, ed. Charles K. Wolfe and Ted Olsen (Jefferson, NC, and London: McFarland, 2005), 7–13.

5. Ted Olsen and Ajay Kalra, "The Birthplace of Country Music, 75 Years Later: The Cradle Still Rocks," in *The Bristol Sessions: Writings about the Big Bang of Country Music*, ed. Charles K. Wolfe and Ted Olsen (Jefferson, NC, and London: McFarland, 2005), 257–70.

6. Charles K. Wolfe, "Ralph Peer at Work: The Victor 1927 Bristol Session," *Old Time Music* 5 (Summer 1972): 10–15; Wolfe, "The Legend That Peer Built," 17–39. The essay was also reprinted in moderately revised edition in *The Country Reader: 25 Years*

located in an area that was already well-known as a musically rich region.[7] Moreover, many of the musicians who recorded for Peer in Bristol had already demonstrated an ability to perform strongly on recordings, either for Victor or for the label's competitors.[8] Peer also deployed a network of talent scouts, including Bristol's Victor dealer Cecil McLister, Princeton, West Virginia musician Blind Alfred Reed, and Galax, Virginia carpenter and musician Ernest Stoneman, to audition potential musicians, and Peer himself made an advance trip to the city in June 1927 to make final arrangements.[9]

The following newspaper article describes a recording session with Ernest Stoneman, a veteran recording artist and regionally renowned musician. Perhaps intended to drum up interest among local musicians, this piece, which appeared in the Bristol *News Bulletin* on the second day of the recording sessions, offers useful insights into the recording process, the possible financial benefits that recording offered local musicians, and the musical tastes of dancers and listeners around Bristol.

━━━━━━━━━

Intensely interesting is a visit to the Victor Talking Machine recording station in Bristol, located on the second floor of the building formerly occupied by the Taylor-Christian Hat company [*sic*] in Bristol. There each day can be witnessed notables of this mountain country doing their best stunts for the microphone, turned into records, and spread at home and abroad.

This morning Earnest [*sic*] Stoneman and company from near Gal[a]x, Va. were the performers and they played and sang into the microphone a favorite in Grayson County, Va., namely, "I Love My Lulu Bell[e]." Eck Dumford [*sic*] was the principal singer while a matron, 26 years of age, and the mother of five children, joined in for a couple of stanzas. Lulu Belle is nothing like the production witnessed on the New York stage during the past year. It is a plaintive mountain song, expressing wonder over what the singer will do when his money runs out. The synchronizing is perfect: Earnest Stoneman playing the guitar, the young matron the violin and a young mountaineer the banjo and the mouth harp. Bodies swaying, feet beating a perfect r[h]ythm, it is calculated to go over big when offered to the public.

of the Journal of Country Music, ed. Paul Kingsbury (Nashville and London: Country Music Foundation Press and Vanderbilt University Press, 1996), 2–19. All further citations of this piece will refer to the page numbers found in *The Country Reader*.

7. Of the nineteen acts who recorded during the Bristol sessions, five hailed from within twenty miles of Bristol, four from within fifty miles, five from within one hundred miles, and five from more than one hundred miles away (Wolfe, "The Bristol Syndrome," 210).

8. Wolfe, "The Legend that Peer Built," 6.

9. Wolfe estimates that as much as "60 percent of [Peer's]…time [was] already blocked out when arrived in Bristol" as a consequence of these preparations (Wolfe, "The Legend that Peer Built," 7–8).

AN OLD FAVORITE

Probably a number with which the citizens of this city and territory are better acquainted with is entitled, "Skip to Ma Lou My Darling["] by the same quartette. It has been one of the favorites at every country dance in this section for half a century, vieing [sic] with "Cripple Creek," and "Old Dan Tucker," "Sourwood Mountain," and other square dance numbers. This morning the management gave the number, following a rendition by the quartette, back over the record and it is a palpable hit.

"Yonder she comes, how do you do," and the ladies were honored all; "You've got money, and I have too," as the rights and lefts were exchanged; "All around the house and the pig pen too," as the birds flew into the cage and out again; "Pretty as a red bird—prettier too," as the ladies do, and the gents you know—through the entire gamut of the figures came trooping out of memory's hall and were re-enacted again as in the halycon [sic] days of yore.

The quartette costs the Victor company close to $200 per day—Stoneman receiving $100, and each of the assistants $25.[10] Stoneman is regarded as one of the finest banjoists in the country, his numbers selling rapidly. He is a carpenter and song leader at Galax. He received from the company $3,600 last year as his share of the proceeds on his records.

Source: "Mountain Songs Recorded Here by Victor Co.: Notable Performers of This Section at Work at Station in This City," *Bristol [Tenn.-Va.] News Bulletin*, 27 July 1927, p. 1.

FOR FURTHER READING

Tribe, Ivan M. *The Stonemans: An Appalachian Family and the Music that Shaped Their Lives.* Urbana and Chicago: University of Illinois Press, 1993.

Wolfe, Charles K., and Ted Olsen, eds. *The Bristol Sessions: Writings about the Big Bang of Country Music.* Contributions to Southern Appalachian Studies 12. Jefferson, NC, and London: McFarland, 2005.

10. Peer typically paid $25 to $50 per side. At that rate, the total income of $200 seems likely (Russell Sanjek and David Sanjek, *American Popular Music Business*, abridged ed. [New York: Oxford University Press, 1991], 22).

Ralph Peer

"Discovery of the 1st Hillbilly Great" (1953)

An innovator in the fields of recording and copyright,[1] Ralph S. Peer (1892–1960), who had supervised the seminal recording debut of Atlanta fiddler "Fiddlin'" John Carson for OKeh Records in 1923, moved to Victor Records in 1927, where he entered into an agreement that permitted him to own the copyrights of each song that he recorded in lieu of a salary.[2] This agreement placed Peer in control of one of the largest song libraries and made him a very wealthy man in a relatively brief time. Hillbilly music, which drew heavily on uncopyrighted traditional songs, was a viable field for Peer to explore in search of intellectual property.[3]

1. Russell Sanjek and David Sanjek, *American Popular Music Business in the 20th Century* (New York and Oxford: Oxford University Press, 1991), 21.
2. Nolan Porterfield, "Mr. Victor and Mr. Peer," *Journal of Country Music* 7, no. 3 (December 1978): 3–21.
3. Richard A. Peterson, in his influential study *Creating Country Music: Fabricating Authenticity* (Chicago and London: University of Chicago Press, 1997), has described the approach taken by Peer and later artist and repertoire (A&R) representatives as "strip mining" (30–32, 34–35).

Peer's work with Jimmie Rodgers (1897–1933) reveals who Peer capitalized on the work of the musicians who recorded for him. Born in Meridian, Mississippi, and influenced by the blues, vaudeville, and sentimental song, Rodgers made his debut recordings near the end of the Bristol sessions on 4 August 1927. A relatively unknown musician prior to the Bristol sessions, Rodgers went on to record more than one hundred sides for Victor over the span of only six years, including several variations on his trademark "blue yodels." Known as "the Singing Brakeman" and "America's Blue Yodeler," Rodgers's recordings encompassed a wide variety of musical styles and featured collaborations with leading jazz and Hawaiian musicians, as well as the other famous group to emerge from the Bristol sessions, the Carter Family. Although weakened from a lengthy battle with tuberculosis, Rodgers toured widely across the American South and Southwest, garnering fans from coast-to-coast and leading to generations of Rodgers impersonators.[4] By 1933, Rodgers's tuberculosis had taken a significant toll on his health, and within days of his final recording session in New York in late May 1933, he died in his hotel room.

The following reading, taken from the national entertainment industry magazine *Billboard*, was written to commemorate the twentieth anniversary of Rodgers's death and appeared alongside tributes from musicians Ernest Tubb and Hank Snow, both of whom were strongly influenced by Rodgers's recordings.[5] By the time Peer's recollections reached the pages of *Billboard*, the myths surrounding the Bristol sessions and Rodgers's career were already well-worn, and Peer situates himself as a heroic figure in this narrative. Although country music historians have suggested that some of the claims that Peer makes in this article are inflated at best, and incorrect at worst,[6] Peer's remembrance provides

4. Nolan Porterfield, *Jimmie Rodgers: The Life and Times of America's Blue Yodeler* (Urbana and Chicago: University of Illinois Press, 1979), 432–38; Joe W. Specht, "The Blue Yodeler is Coming to Town: A Week with Jimmie Rodgers in West Texas," *Journal of Texas Music History* 1, no. 2 (Fall 2001): 17–22.

Rodgers's influence on subsequent generations of musicians has been treated in a variety of sources, including Barry Mazor, *Meeting Jimmie Rodgers: How America's Original Roots Music Hero Changed the Pop Sounds of a Century* (New York and Oxford: Oxford University Press, 2009); Jocelyn R. Neal, *The Songs of Jimmie Rodgers: A Legacy in Country Music* (Bloomington and Indianapolis: Indiana University Press, 2009); and Travis D. Stimeling, *Cosmic Cowboys and New Hicks: The Countercultural Sounds of Austin's Progressive Country Music Scene* (New York and Oxford: Oxford University Press, 2011), 20–24.

5. Hank Snow and Ernest Tubb (as told to Bert Braun), "Rodgers' Influence on Country Music," *Billboard* (16 May 1953): 20, 35; Hank Snow with Jack Ownbey and Bob Burris, *The Hank Snow Story* (Urbana and Chicago: University Press of Chicago, 1994), 116–17, 352–58; Ronnie Pugh, *Ernest Tubb: The Texas Troubadour* (Durham, NC, and London: Duke University Press, 1996), 9–38, 185–88; Diane Pecknold, *The Selling Sound: The Rise of the Country Music Industry* (Durham, NC: Duke University Press, 2007), 71–72; Mazor, *Meeting Jimmie Rodgers*, 126–28, 138–39, 218–25.

6. Porterfield, *Jimmie Rodgers*, 108–109; Charles K. Wolfe, "The Legend That Peer Built: Reappraising the Bristol Sessions," *Journal of Country Music* 13, no. 2 [1989],

valuable details about his financial motivations for recording Rodgers and important details about the recording sessions themselves.

━━━━━━━

The best things in life seem to occur by pure accident. We strive to accomplish something worthwhile; success finally comes to us, but usually from an unexpected source.

In 1927, after serving as an executive of Okeh Records for a number of years, I decided to go into business for myself as a music publisher. At that time, a business alliance was started with the Victor Talking Machine Company[,] which continued for many years. The arrangement was that I would select the artists and material and supervise the hillbilly records for Victor. My publishing firm would own the copyrights, and thus I would be compensated by the royalties resulting from the compositions which I would select for recording purposes.[7]

During the spring of 1928 [*sic*, 1927] I made a survey of various Southern cities and determined to make initial recordings for Victor in Atlanta, Savannah, Bristol, Tenn., and Memphis. A recording crew of two men was assigned to me and I set about the business of finding talent and repertoire.

In Bristol, the problem was not easy because of the relatively small population in that area. The local broadcasting stations, music stores, record dealers, etc., helped me as much as possible, but few candidates appeared. I then appealed to the editor of a local newspaper, explaining to him the great advantages to the community of my enterprise. He thought that I had a good idea and ran a half column on his front page. This worked like dynamite and the very next day I was deluged with long-distance calls from the surrounding mountain region. Groups of singers who had not visited Bristol during their entire lifetime arrived by bus, horse and buggy, trains or on foot.

Jimmie Rodgers telephoned from Asheville [North Carolina]. He said that he was a singer with a string band. He had read the newspaper article and was quite sure that his group would be satisfactory. I told him to come on a certain day, and promised a try-out.

repr. in *The Bristol Sessions: Writings about the Big Bang of Country Music*, ed. Charles K. Wolfe and Ted Olsen, *Contributions to Southern Appalachian Studies* 12 [Jefferson, NC, and London: MacFarland, 2005], 12.

7. His agreement with Victor transferred rights to any music he recorded to Peer, generating reported single-quarter income of $250,000 from royalty payments alone. Through this arrangement, Peer controlled the rights to "more than one-third of all non-classical music recorded by Victor in 1928" (Sanjek and Sanjek, *American Popular Music Business*, 22–23; see also Porterfield, *Jimmie Rodgers*, 96–99).

FIRST MEETING

When I was alone with Jimmie in our recording studio (a very old warehouse which had not been in use for many years), I was elated when I heard him perform. It seemed to me that he had his own personal and peculiar style, and I thought that his yodel alone might spell success. Very definitely he was worth a trial. We ran into a snag almost immediately because, in order to earn a living in Asheville, he was singing mostly songs originated by the New York publishers—the current hits. Actually, he had only one song of his own, "Soldier's Sweetheart," written several years before. When I told Jimmie what I needed to put him over as a recording artist, his perennial optimism bubbled over. If I would give him a week he could have a dozen songs ready for recording. I let him record his own song, and as a coupling his unique version of "Rock All Our Babies to Sleep." This, I thought, would be a very good coupling, as "Soldier's Sweetheart" was a straight ballad and the other side gave him a chance to display his ability as a yodeler. In spite of the lack of original repertoire, I considered Rodgers to be one of my best bets.[8]

He was quite ill at the time, and decided that instead of trying to return to Asheville he would visit a relative in Washington, D.C. The money for his recording services was enough to pay for this trip.

TALENT OBVIOUS

A few weeks later, when I heard the test recordings made in Bristol, it was apparent that Jimmie Rodgers was tops as a yodeling singer, and I arranged to have his record issued quickly. The dealers ordered heavily and then re-ordered. It was obvious that Jimmie Rodgers was the best artist uncovered by the Bristol expedition. I had already written Jimmie about getting more new material ready, but had received no reply. Consequently, I located him by telephone and was pleased to have his assurance that he had a wealth of new songs. I arranged a recording date at the Victor studios in Camden [New Jersey]. Jimmie and I met for the second time when he stepped off the train in Philadelphia.

BLUE YODEL

We worked hard far into the night getting enough material in shape for the first recording session. Actually, we did not have enough material, and

---

8. Because Peer's agreement with Victor granted him ownership of the copyrights to the songs he recorded, he tried to record only original material. For a more detailed discussion of the impact of this approach to copyright on repertoire selection and art-ist livelihood in early country music, consult: Peterson, *Creating Country Music*, 37–48; Mark Zwonitzer with Charles Hirshberg, *Will You Miss Me When I'm Gone?: The Carter Family & Their Legacy in American Music* (New York: Simon & Schuster, 2002), 130.

I decided to use some of his blues songs to "fill in." When we recorded the first blues I had to supply a title, and the name "Blue Yodel" came out.[9] The other blue yodels made at the same time had titles suggested by the words, but when I witnessed the tremendous demand for the original, I decided to change these names to "Blue Yodel No. 2," "Blue Yodel No. 3," etc.

From this time until his death he was able to lead a new life because of his income from recordings and royalties. Unfortunately, he was generous to a fault, and when he received a large check he shared it with friends and relatives. The best doctors told him that he would not live because his tuberculosis was incurable. As a result of his fast-selling Victor records, Jimmie Rodgers quickly rose to the top as an entertainer. He began to earn good money working in night spots, traveling shows, etc., but his bad state of health was a great handicap.

This man really had "guts." He was fired with a great ambition to be successful, both as an artist and financially. Eventually he headed his own traveling show. As a guitarist he was an individualist; that is, he had his own way of selecting his chords, and was what can best be described as a "natural" guitar player. I remember that another artist, during the year 1931, spent a great deal of time learning one of Jimmie's "wrong" chords. Whatever he used always sounded right, but upon examination it was quite often not the chord which would ordinarily have been used. This provided individuality for all records in which his guitar playing predominated amongst the accompaniment, but quite often it was a problem to find musicians and other artists able to fall into the spirit of his recording style.

His recording of "Blue Yodel" skyrocketed Jimmie to fame in the amusement business. The once-poor Mississippi brakeman became the idol of the Southern and Western states. His fame developed through his record fans. Broadcasting stations were then comparatively infrequent, and only the radio chains had sufficient power to create nationwide propaganda. They adhered closely to a policy of using live artists, and almost invariably artists popular in the New York and Chicago areas. Jimmie was practically unknown north of the Mason-Dixon Line, but within a year he became the most important recording artist in the region where hillbilly music has always enjoyed greatest popularity.

9. Numerous writers have indicated that the title did not simply "come out." See, for instance, Porterfield, *Jimmie Rodgers*, 124; Neal, *The Songs of Jimmie Rodgers*, 207–209; Nick Tosches, "Jimmie Rodgers and 'The Famous Yodeling Blues Singer' of 1926," in *Waiting for a Train: Jimmie Rodgers's America*, ed. Mary Davis and Warren Zanes (Burlington, MA: Rounder Books, 2009), 40–41. Tosches also notes the prevalence of blackface minstrel songs in Rodgers's repertoire and his stint as a blackface performer in a medicine show in 1924–1925 as evidence that Rodgers was profoundly aware of the minstrel repertories and performance practices (37–38; see also Lynn Abbott and Doug Seroff, "America's Blue Yodel," Article MT193, *Musical Traditions* 11 [Late 1993], http://www.mustrad.org.uk/articles/b_yodel.htm; accessed 8 November 2011).

If his health had permitted, Jimmie would have become a top name in the theatrical world, but routine work on the stage was bad for him. His copyright royalties began to pile up, and eventually Victor gave him a royalty contract on a basis similar to a grand opera star. In an effort to extend the Rodgers popularity to our Northern states, I booked him on the Radio-Keith-Orpheum Circuit.[10] He was to appear as a single act in most of the leading vaudeville theaters. The salary, $1,000 weekly, was considered high at the time. Jimmie became ill, however, and we had to cancel the project.[11]

Rodgers liked working in "tent shows." He felt at home in the informal surroundings and greatly enjoyed his contacts with other performers. One of the highlights of his career was a tour through north Texas and Oklahoma as part of a charity Red Cross drive in which he was starred alongside of Will Rogers. They became fast friends.

In the spring of 1933, Jimmie and I corresponded about the possibility of additional recordings. Victor had about a year's supply of material already on hand. The record business in general was not good, and they did not think it wise to be too far ahead of the market. Jimmie Rodgers by this time had become "standard." There were one or two masters to be remade because of technical defects. There was also the necessity to negotiate a new agreement between Victor and Rodgers. Working with all of these factors, I arranged matters so that Jimmie could come to New York for a series of recordings, and after the first two dates it seemed best to delay further activities. He died May 26, 1933, in his hotel bedroom. It became my painful duty to send him back home to Meridian, Mississippi, for burial.

Today his distinctive style remains a goal for all new recording artists. Many of the compositions that he wrote wholly or in part have become perennial standards. His fame has spread to all countries of the English-speaking world. The impetus which he gave to so-called hillbilly music, in my opinion, set in motion the factors that resulted in making this sector of the amusement business into a matter of world-wide importance and a source for a high percentage of our popular hits.

Source: Ralph Peer, "Discovery of the 1st Hillbilly Great," *Billboard*, 16 May 1953, pp. 20–21. (Used with permission.)

10. The Radio-Keith-Orpheum Circuit was a product of widespread media conglomeration in the late 1920s. In 1928, the two largest vaudeville circuits, the Keith-Albee and Orpheum, merged to form the Keith-Albee-Orpheum, which the Radio Corporation of America (RCA) took control of in 1929 to form Radio-Keith-Orpheum, also known as RKO. The consolidation of these companies allowed RKO to cross-promote its artists on records, radio, film, and stage (Tino Balio, *The American Film Industry*, 2nd ed. [Madison: University of Wisconsin Press, 1985], 248–49; Sanjek and Sanjek, *American Popular Music Business*,11–12; Nick Tosches, *Where Dead Voices Gather* [New York: Back Bay Books, 2002], 175). See also Arthur Frank Wertheim, *Vaudeville Wars: How the Keith-Albee and Orpheum Circuits Controlled the Big Time and Its Performers* (Basingstoke: Palgrave MacMillan, 2006).

11. Porterfield, *Jimmie Rodgers*, 205–14.

FOR FURTHER READING

Davis, Mary E., and Warren Zanes. *Waiting for a Train: Jimmie Rodgers's America*. Burlington, MA: Rounder Books, 2009.

Mazor, Barry. *Meeting Jimmie Rodgers: How America's Original Roots Music Hero Changed the Pop Sounds of a Century*. New York and Oxford: Oxford University Press, 2009.

Neal, Jocelyn R. *The Songs of Jimmie Rodgers: A Legacy in Country Music*. Bloomington and Indianapolis: Indiana University Press, 2009.

Porterfield, Nolan. *Jimmie Rodgers: The Life and Times of America's Blue Yodeler*. Urbana and Chicago: University of Illinois Press, 1979.

Russell, Tony. "Country Music on Location: 'Field Recording' Before Bristol." *Popular Music* 26, no. 1 (2007): 23–31.

Wise, Timothy. "Yodel Species: A Typology of Falsetto Effects in Popular Music Vocal Styles." *Radical Musicology* 2 (2007), http://www.radical-musicology.org.uk/2007/Wise.htm; accessed 8 November 2011.

Wise, Timothy. "Jimmie Rodgers and the Semiosis of the Hillbilly Yodel." *The Musical Quarterly* 93, no. 1 (Spring 2010): 6–44.

7

Bill Williams

"Interview with Mother Maybelle Carter" (1968/1971)

The Carter Family, the second hit act that Ralph Peer recorded during the Bristol sessions, promoted a wholesome, family image that served as a valuable counterbalance to the rambling, rowdy image put forth by Jimmie Rodgers.[1] In a musical career stretching over sixteen years, husband-and-wife A.P. (Alvin Pleasant [1891–1960]) and Sara (Dougherty [1898–1979]) Carter and Sara's cousin Maybelle (Addington [1909–1978]) Carter promoted "morally good" concert and radio performances consisting of a wide array of sentimental songs, gospel numbers, ballads, and topical songs, many of which A.P. and his African American collecting partner Leslie Riddle gathered from people around their southwestern

---

1. John Atkins, "The Carter Family," in *Stars of Country Music: Uncle Dave Macon to Johnny Rodriguez*, ed. Bill C. Malone and Judith McCullough (Urbana and Chicago: University of Illinois Press, 1975; repr. New York: Da Capo Press, 1991), 100–101; Charles K. Wolfe, *Classic Country: Legends of Country Music* (New York and London: Routledge, 2001), 5; and Bill C. Malone, *Don't Get Above Your Raisin': Country Music and the Southern Working Class* (Urbana and Chicago: University of Illinois Press, 2002), 63–64. See also Bland Simpson, "The Carter Family," *Southern Cultures* 12, no. 4 (Winter 2006): 135.

Virginia home.[2] Many of the songs that the Carter Family recorded have become standards in country, old-time, and bluegrass music, including "Wildwood Flower," "Worried Man Blues," "Keep on the Sunny Side," and "Will the Circle Be Unbroken?"; and the Carter Family's distinctive three-part vocal harmonies and characteristic guitar and autoharp playing have been widely imitated since their earliest recordings were released. Although their records did not open the door for widespread touring, as had been the case with Jimmie Rodgers,[3] the Carter Family did make quite an impact on the radio, culminating in a lengthy stint on radio stations XERA, XEG, and ZENT—powerful stations located across the Texas-Mexico border that could be heard widely in the United States and in parts of Canada, between 1938 and 1941.[4]

2. Archie Green, "The Carter Family's 'Coal Miner's Blues,'" *Southern Folklore Quarterly* 25 (1961): 230–31, 233–34; Atkins, "The Carter Family," 97–100; Curtis Ellison, *Country Music Culture: From Hard Times to Heaven* (Jackson: University Press of Mississippi, 1995), 28; Wolfe, *Classic Country*, 6; Mark Zwonitzer, with Charles Hirschberg, *Will You Miss Me When I'm Gone: The Carter Family & Their Legacy in American Music* (New York: Simon & Schuster, 2002), 127–38; Colin Escott, "Water from an Ancient Well," *Journal of Country Music* 22, no. 1 (2001): 35; Katie Doman, "Something Old, Something New: The Carter Family's Bristol Sessions," in *The Bristol Sessions: Writings about the Big Bang of Country Music*, ed. Charles K. Wolfe and Ted Olsen (Jefferson, NC, and London: McFarland, 2005), 66–86; and Pamela Fox, *Natural Acts: Gender, Race, and Rusticity in Country Music* (Ann Arbor: University of Michigan Press, 2009), 175–78. Moreover, a thorough overview of the Carter Family's engagement with Appalachian balladry can be found in Peggy A. Bulger, "'Don't Forget This Song': Recorded Balladry of the A.P. Carter Family," *Mid-American Folklore* 10 (1982): 1–16.

3. Wolfe, *Classic Country*, 5, 7–12.

4. The Carter Family likely began performing on radio station XER (later, XERA), transmitting from Villa Acuña, Coahuila, Mexico, but with studios in Del Rio, Texas, during the winter of 1938–1939. The station, owned by Dr. John R. Brinkley (1885–1942), used a combination of hillbilly music, preaching, and persistent advertising to promote a number of products and services, including a surgery intended to cure male impotence. Having begun his radio work in Kansas, Brinkley moved his broadcast operations to the Villa Acuña in 1931, building one of the most powerful transmitters in North America. By 1939, the Carter Family moved to San Antonio, where they recorded one-hour transcriptions—pre-recorded programs recorded directly to 16-inch aluminum discs covered in a flexible acetate—for the so-called border radio station. Several of these transcription discs, collected by Carter Family scholar, anthropologist, and record collector Ed Kahn, are held in the Southern Folklife Collection at the University of North Carolina at Chapel Hill and have been reissued by Arhoolie Records as a three-volume set of compact discs (*The Carter Family on Border Radio, Volumes 1-3* [Arhoolie 411, 412, and 413, respectively]). For more discussion of the Carter Family's work on border radio, consult Ed Kahn, "The Carter Family on Border Radio," *American Music* 14, no. 2 (Summer 1996): 205–17; and Zwonitzer with Hirschberg, *Will You Miss Me When I'm Gone?*, 201–38.

For a more detailed discussion of John R. Brinkley's life and career, including discussion of his political ambitions, consult R. Alton Lee, *The Bizarre Careers of John R. Brinkley* (Lexington: University Press of Kentucky, 2002); Bruce Lenthall, *Radio's America: The Great Depression and the Rise of Modern Mass Culture* (Chicago and London: University of Chicago Press, 2007), 115–40; and Pope Brock,

A.P. and Sara were divorced in 1939 after several years of separation,[5] yet they continued to perform as a group until 1943, often featuring the second genera-tion of Carter musicians—their daughters.[6] After the group officially disbanded in 1943, Maybelle Carter formed the Carter Sisters with her daughters Helen, Anita, and June, recording occasionally and performing widely on radio,[7] while A.P. and Sara (who had married A.P.'s cousin) returned to relatively quiet private lives (despite A.P.'s failed efforts to emerge as a solo recording artist). During the urban folk revival of the early 1960s, the music of the Carter Family was in great demand, and Maybelle found herself performing the Carter Family's music at folk festivals across the United States. By the late 1960s, the Carter Sisters began performing with Johnny Cash, appearing on recordings and the nationally syn-dicated television program, *The Johnny Cash Show*. Inducted into the Country Music Hall of Fame in 1970, Maybelle's careful curation of the Carter Family rep-ertoire and legacy cemented the group's reputation as "the first family of country music."[8]

The following interview, conducted by *Billboard* magazine southern editor Bill Williams in 1968, is one of several interviews with Maybelle Carter from the 1960s and points to then-contemporary concerns about the preservation of country music history.[9] Carter, who seems reluctant to share many details in this interview, nonetheless provides useful background regarding the nature of the Carter Family's recording and radio careers, the musical environment in which she was raised, and the business of the early country music industry.

WILLIAMS: The date is February 1st, 1968. We are speaking from the Country Music Hall of Fame and Museum in Nashville, Tennessee. Our guest is Mother Maybelle Carter. Maybelle, we will begin by asking you to tell us as much about your early life as you can. What is your full name, including your maiden name, and when and where were you born? I hate to ask a lady that, but I will in this case.

Charlatan: America's Most Dangerous Huckster, the Man Who Pursued Him, and the Age of Flimflam (New York: Crown, 2008).

5. Mary A. Bufwack and Robert K. Oermann, *Finding Her Voice: Women in Country Music, 1800-2000* (Nashville: Vanderbilt University Press, 2003), 49.

6. Malone, *Don't Get Above Your Raisin'*, 64.

7. Wolfe, *Classic Country*, 12–18.

8. Ellison, *Country Music Culture*, 33.

9. For instance, Ed Kahn and Mike Seeger conducted several detailed interviews with Maybelle Carter in 1963. See, for instance, Maybelle Carter, interview with Ed Kahn, Ash Grove, 4 April 1963 and 19 April 1963, Southern Folklife Collection, Wilson Library, University of North Carolina at Chapel Hill Libraries, FT-12519; and Maybelle and Sara Carter, interview with Ed Kahn and Mike Seeger, 24 April 1963, Southern Folklife Collection, Wilson Library, University of North Carolina at Chapel Hill Libraries, FT-12520.

CARTER:	I was born in Scott County, Virginia, in 1909. My name was Maybelle Addington. I was married in 1926 to Ezra J. Carter, a brother of A.P. Carter.
WILLIAMS:	In your early life you grew up in Virginia, didn't you?
CARTER:	Yes, I lived in Virginia all my life till, I guess till, we came to Knoxville, Tennessee[,] in 1948 for the first time. No, North Carolina, in 1942. We were there for a year.
WILLIAMS:	Was music involved in your early childhood even before you became a Carter?
CARTER:	Oh, yes. We had an autoharp and a banjo when I was a little kid. I guess I was about three years old. And they kept the autoharp laying upon the table. I would have to pull it off down in the floor, and sit down in the floor to play it; 'cause I couldn't reach up there. Then I started to pick up the banjo[;] I guess I was about five years old when I started trying to play the banjo, and I played the banjo then till I was thirteen. In fact, I used to play for square dances, me and my other brother. My brother played the guitar with me. He finally gave up and gave me the guitar, so he just quit. I had a couple of brothers that played with me quite a bit.
WILLIAMS:	Did either of your parents play?
CARTER:	Yes, my mother played a five-string banjo. That's where I learned to play.
WILLIAMS:	Has this gone back into the family prior to that, to your grandparents, or do you know it?
CARTER:	No, I don't think my grandparents played any instruments. I can't remember. I was very young. I can only remember my grandmother, just seeing her sitting in a rocking chair, you know, on my mother's side, and my grandfather on my father's side. I can't remember my grandmother on my father's side, or my grandfather on my mother's side.
WILLIAMS:	Did your mother sing many of the old songs that came down through the years?
CARTER:	Yes, she did. She sang a lot of them, and her mother knew a lot of these old songs. Then I had an uncle who would play the fiddle, and his wife would beat on the strings with a knitting needle of all things.[10]

10. Also known as "fiddlesticks," this practice requires two players. The first plays the fiddle with the bow in the typical manner while the second taps rhythms on the strings with knitting needles, chopsticks, or other thin sticks. As old-time fiddling scholar Drew Beisswenger has noted, "dancers in previous generations would benefit from the rhythmic qualities added by the fiddlesticks player, but today the technique appears to be relegated to concert demonstrations" (Drew Beisswenger, *Fiddling Way Out Yonder: The Life and Music of Melvin Wine* [Jackson: University Press of Mississippi, 2002], 136).

WILLIAMS: That's a pretty good percussion instrument. What about school? Did you go to school there in Virginia, in the same town where you were born?

CARTER: Yes, what little I got I went in Virginia, and what little I got I had to walk for five miles in the snow, and the rain, and the sleet. I didn't get to finish school, which I regret very much. I wish I could have, but there was no way where we lived. It was so far to schools when we were small. Sometimes we had to cross a creek to get to the school house, and go up the side of a cliff when it was snowy, or icy, or bad; you just couldn't make it. There was no way.

WILLIAMS: What year did you leave school? Your sophomore or junior class?

CARTER: Yes. We moved to Bristol, Tennessee. I got married, and I got married before I was seventeen years old. I didn't start back to school when we moved to Bristol. I was sixteen, and I thought, well, I'll just get me a job. So I went to work in a hosiery mill, and I worked about three or four days. That done me.

WILLIAMS: Was this before or after you were married?

CARTER: That was before I married.

WILLIAMS: Where did you meet Mr. Carter?

CARTER: I went down to see Sara. She was married to A.P. Sara is my first cousin, and I went to see her; I went down on a train from Bristol to Maces Spring [Virginia], and that's where I met my husband.

WILLIAMS: What was he [Ezra] doing at this time?

CARTER: He was a railway mail clerk. He's almost eleven years older than I am. He was stating [starting?] a railway mail service for about twenty-three years, and his heart got kind of bad, so he retired. He hasn't done too much since.

WILLIAMS: When did the Original Carters begin singing?[11]

CARTER: We sang together for about, I guess, two years off and on before we recorded because I would go down to visit them, and they come up to our house in Bristol; and we would play. This particular time I went down to a show at the school. They were having a play at the school, and they wanted us to play for it. That's where I met my husband, the night I went down to do the show.

WILLIAMS: Your husband never did sing or play with the group, did he?

11.   The name "Original Carter Family" became used to describe the trio of A.P., Sara, and Maybelle after A.P.'s death in 1960, when Maybelle began using the Carter Family name to promote the group she had formed with her daughters (Wolfe, *Classic Country*, 17).

CARTER: No. He knows every chord on a guitar, a tenor guitar and a mandolin, but he has no sense of timing. He can't put 'em together very good, but he can play the chords.

WILLIAMS: How did the Original Carters decide to record, or did somebody contact you?

CARTER: Well, A.P. happened to be in Bristol, and he run into Mr. Peer, and he asked him. Of course, I think he found out he was there and he hunted him up. That's what I think he done; and just asked him [Mr. Peer]. He said, well come on up. So he came home, and the next day we went up to Bristol. We recorded six sides, six songs, our first recording. About six months later[,] we recorded in Camden, New Jersey, and we did six more about every six months.

WILLIAMS: Do you recall the very first song you recorded?

CARTER: Yes, very well. "Bury Me Under the Weeping Willow" was the first one.

WILLIAMS: What had A.P. done prior to this time?

CARTER: A.P. sold fruit trees and shrubbery. That is about all he ever done, a little farming.

WILLIAMS: Then it was just the cousins getting together and forming this group which ultimately was to become known as the Carter Family. Did you try to set a music[a]l style back then, or were you just concerned in singing in harmony?

CARTER: Well, I like to sing in harmony, but I also had to figure out tunes on the guitar to form some kind of a lead instrument. That was my problem, and that was what I had to stick with all the way through. I played with my thumb and finger—you know, picking the melody, because we only had the two instruments. Then Sara didn't play melody on the autoharp, she just strummed it. So I had to do it all on the guitar, and I didn't start on the guitar; and I didn't start playing autoharp until about twenty-five years ago.

WILLIAMS: Did A.P. play an instrument?

CARTER: He played guitar a little bit, and fiddle a little bit. Not very much. He was awfully nervous, and he played just enough to get by with.

WILLIAMS: In those early days, after you began recording, did you almost at once go out on personal appearances?

CARTER: Oh, yes. We played all the school buildings and some churches around in Virginia, and Tennessee, up in the eastern part of Tennessee, and Kentucky, and North Carolina.

WILLIAMS: What sort of money did you get for appearances back then?

CARTER: We charged fifteen and twenty-five cents at the door, and then you get about as much as you do now if you charge two or three dollars. You didn't have any taxes then.

WILLIAMS: How did you get booked? Did someone just contact you?

CARTER: A.P. went out and booked 'em himself. He just went around to the schools, and theaters, and places like that and booked them himself.[12]

WILLIAMS: Did he at this time become a full-time singer, and leave his job in the shrubbery business?

CARTER: Yes, he gave up his shrubbery business, and just devoted his time to singing and booking shows. He used to sing bass with his uncle who was a music teacher. In fact, I went to two music schools that he had held at our church from where I was born. I was ten or eleven years old, I guess, at the time. I learned quite a bit by going to those music schools. A.P. used to sing a lot with him. He used to sing bass, he was the main bass singer in the whole community up there.

WILLIAMS: Do you recall the first amount of money you received for singing professionally either as a personal appearance, or for records?

CARTER: I remember the records more than the personal appearances. I know we made six records and we got fifty dollars a side for making them, and we got our royalty of about one and a half percent—not hardly one and a half percent. That was it then. Then the next time, I think, we got seventy-five dollars a side.

WILLIAMS: Things were looking better already. Do you recall how well those early records sold?

CARTER: I think, they sold pretty good, or they wouldn't have called us back to make more. I had a first cousin and her husband that cut the same time we did, on the day after we did, and they made the one record. They never did make anymore. Mike Seeger sent me the tape on that record. He had it. I said, that was my first cousin. He said, you mean Jim Baker and Flora was your first cousin? I said, yes, she was my mother's sister's daughter. They live in Kingsport.[13]

WILLIAMS: Maybelle, do you remember when you first appeared on radio?

CARTER: Oh, let me see. The first radio appearance was in Bristol, Tennessee. I guess on WVOI, I believe, I don't know. I tell you, the things get away from me. You know how long it's been since Asher [Sizemore] and Little Jimmy were here? They were real small. Well, it was before that, and that was before we went to work in Texas, that was in '38; and I know it was before that.

12. After the Carter Family began recording, Ralph Peer served as their booking agent, likely seeing the correlations between personal appearances and record sales (Kahn, "The Carter Family on Border Radio," 208–209).

13. Jim (vocals and guitar) and Flora (vocals and autoharp) Baker, billed as "Mr. & Mrs. J. W. Baker," recorded two sides with fiddler J. E. Green and banjoist J. H. Holbrook on 3 August 1927, "The Newmarket Wreck" and "On the Banks of the Sunny Tennessee" (Victor 20863) (Tony Russell, Country Music Records: A Discography [New York: Oxford University Press, 2004], 90).

WILLIAMS: Yes, Asher and Little Jimmy [Sizemore] were here in about 1935-36 or along in that era.

CARTER: It was WOVI[14].... We were there. How I remember was because Asher and Little Jimmy were appearing there the next day, or the day before, and also Texas Ruby [Ruby Agnes Owens].

WILLIAMS: You later did your own radio series in Texas for a long time, didn't you?

CARTER: Yes, we did. We had a thirty minute show, no, an hour show. We had an hour in the morning, and an hour in the evening.

...

WILLIAMS: When you first started (going back to the Original Carter Family for a moment) did you ever dream, when you made that first recording in Bristol, that you would become nationally known and famous? Did you think along these lines at all?

CARTER: No, not at all.

WILLIAMS: What had you hoped to achieve from that first record?

CARTER: I hoped that we would be successful with our recordings and everything. But, of course, I didn't know how they [recordings] were going to turn out. I am very happy with everything the way it did turn out. I didn't think at all about ever making a record, to tell you the truth.

WILLIAMS: Despite the tremendous success you enjoy, there has been some adversity too. Did you, at any time along the way, ever consider giving it up?

CARTER: No, never. I just hung in there ever since I started. Sometimes one of the girls would drop out, and they would be gone, and I know I went through a lot trying to keep the family together. I had about ten different girls, I think, working with us time after time to take one of the other places. But finally (after June dropped out for awhile [sic]) me, Helen, and Anita decided that we would just go on, the three of us.[15] We worked that way till about a year ago. Since we all got back together again.[16]

14. The radio station that Carter is discussing here is likely WOPI, which went on the air on 15 June 1929 ("Bristol's New Broadcasting Station to Open Today," *The Bristol [Tenn.] News Bulletin* [15 June 1929]; see also: "History of WOPI-AM," http://www.wopi.com/history.html; accessed 19 November 2011).

15. At several points during their tenure on border radio, various Carter daughters—most frequently Maybelle and Eck's daughters, Helen (1927–1998), June (1929–2003), and Anita (1933–1999)—would perform with the Carter Family, contributing both solo and ensemble numbers (Kahn, "The Carter Family on Border Radio," 211–12).

16. June Carter began performing with Johnny Cash in December 1961 (Don Cusic, ed. *Johnny Cash, The Songs* [New York: Da Capo Press, 2004], xxvi), and Mother Maybelle and the Carter Sisters frequently contributed to Cash's mid-1960s recordings

WILLIAMS: Still, staying with the early days, was transportation a real problem getting around to various places?

CARTER: Yes, it was quite a problem. We had mostly old Model T Fords, you know. Many of a night I stood on the running board, and held a lantern to get home. We didn't have any lights on the car, or the lights would go out, or something would happen.

WILLIAMS: Playing these old school houses, and things of that sort, did you have a problem? Of course, there were probably no microphones, or speakers, or anything of that sort.

CARTER: No, lights—all kerosene lamps, and no microphones, or anything.

WILLIAMS: Did you just project a lot more?

CARTER: I guess so. I don't know. Of course, schools back then weren't too large and some of them were pretty good size, but they all [the crowds] seem to hear pretty good.

WILLIAMS: What would you consider a good crowd back then?

CARTER: Back then, if we had two hundred people we had a real good crowd in those little schools, because everyone had to walk to get there.

WILLIAMS: Did you ever play (in those early days) a large city, or was it all small, rural areas?

CARTER: We didn't play any large cities at all except it seems to me like back, no, that was after the girls started; we worked in Kansas City, Missouri. Nothing—only just the little towns such as Rogersville, Sneadville, and all the little places up in Tennessee and over in Kentucky.

WILLIAMS: When did you really feel that you were getting somewhere in the music industry? Was it when your first recording began to sell, or what really gave you confidence that you could do it?

CARTER: Well, I guess it was just the records selling like they did. I figured maybe we will get somewhere after all, and they have held on real good all through these forty-one years. I didn't ever think I'd be in it this long when I started.

and live performances. By 1968, the year that Cash and June Carter were married, Maybelle, June, Helen, and Anita were regularly featured in Cash's road show and on his ABC television variety show, *The Johnny Cash Show*. The Carters' contributions to Cash's work in this era is perhaps best represented in his *At San Quentin* (Columbia CS 9827, 1969). See also Johnny Cash with Patrick Carr, *Johnny Cash: The Autobiography* (New York: HarperCollins, 1997), 172–88; Michael Streissguth, *Johnny Cash: The Biography* (New York: Da Capo Press, 2006), 159–71; Leigh H. Edwards, *Johnny Cash and the Paradox of American Identity* (Bloomington: Indiana University Press, 2009), 92–94.

Source: Bill Williams, "Interview with Mother Maybelle Carter," *Country Music Foundation Newsletter* 2, no. 1 (March 1971): 4–12. (Courtesy of the Frist Library and Archive of the Country Music Hall of Fame and Museum.)

FOR FURTHER READING

Harrington, Beth. *The Winding Stream: An Oral History of the Carter and Cash Family.* Georgetown, MA: PFP, 2014.

Kahn, Edward A., II. *The Carter Family: A Reflection of Changes in Society.* Ph.D. dissertation, University of California at Los Angeles, 1970.

Medley, Mark. "The Eternal Guitar of Maybelle Carter." *Journal of Country Music* 20, no. 3 (1999): 3–5.

Rockwell, Joti. "Time on the Crooked Road: Isochrony, Meter, and Disruption in Old-Time Country and Bluegrass Music." *Ethnomusicology* 55, no. 1 (Winter 2011): 62–72.

Townsend, Thomas Carl. "The Carter Family's Rhythmic Asymmetry." In *Country Music Annual 2001,* ed. Charles K. Wolfe and James E. Akenson, 161–73. Lexington: University Press of Kentucky, 2001.

Zwonitzer, Mark, with Charles Hirschberg. *Will You Miss Me When I'm Gone: The Carter Family & Their Legacy in American Music.* New York: Simon & Schuster, 2002.

8

Harold A. Safford

"Bradley Kincaid" (1928)

Astar of both the *National Barn Dance* and the *Grand Ole Opry*, Bradley
Kincaid (1895–1989) was one of the most popular musicians of his gen-
eration.[1] A native of the Cumberland Mountains of Garrard County, Kentucky,
Kincaid represented a direct connection to the musical traditions of the Upland
South to many listeners, including the large immigrant populations of the Upper
Midwest.[2] Accompanied only by his "Houn' Dog Guitar,"[3] Kincaid performed,

1. Charles K. Wolfe, *Classic Country: Legends of Country Music* (New York and
London: Routledge, 2001), 126.
2. Tony Russell, *Country Music Originals: The Legends and the Lost* (New York and
Oxford: Oxford University Press, 2007), 171.
3. Loyal Jones notes that Kincaid kept "the little guitar throughout his career
(although he later performed with a Gibson and a fancier 1929 Martin 000-45) and
relinquished it only to the Country Music Hall of Fame" (Loyal Jones, *Radio's 'Kentucky
Mountain Boy' Bradley Kincaid* [Berea, KY: Appalachian Center, 1980], 13–14). Charles
Wolfe has indicated that Sears sold "a cheap copy (of the 'Houn' Dog Guitar') that was
sold by the thousands throughout the South and Midwest. In fact, there would come
a time when Bradley, going deep into the mountains to hunt up new songs, would be

recorded, and published dozens of ballads, sentimental songs, and minstrel tunes and, like many contemporary folklorists and ballad collectors, made it his personal mission to preserve the rich musical traditions of rural America.[4] As the biographical sketch excerpted below from Kincaid's immensely popular debut songbook, *Favorite Mountain Ballads and Old Time Songs as Sung by Bradley Kincaid, "The Mountain Boy,"* suggests, Kincaid was, like most of his radio colleagues, his professional vita revealed him to be a versatile musician who discovered that he possessed knowledge of a much-desired repertory that could catapult him to national and international fame.[5]

———

A BOY of the Kentucky mountains whose earliest experiences were associated with cows, cockleburs, razor-backed hogs, and fox hounds; a boy who lived and grew almost to manhood hidden away in these Kentucky mountains far from the advantages found in the centers of civilization; a young fellow who didn't have a chance to go to school until he was 19 years old, and then started in the sixth grade; a young fellow who plugged away despite these handicaps, earned an education for himself, married a sweetheart of his college days, and found his life's opportunity in the service of the Young Men's Christian Association[6]—that's a concise history of the life thus far of Bradley Kincaid, the young man who is known and loved by thousands of radio listeners in every section of the country as "The Mountain Boy with His Houn' Dog Guitar and Old Mountain Songs."

Bradley did his first singing over WLS with the Y.M.C.A. College quartet in 1926–27. It was by accident that Mr. Campbell, the director of the quartet, mentioned to Don Malin, musical director of WLS, that Bradley played and sang the old mountain ballads. Mr. Malin asked Bradley to come to the studio and give a program and the success of his first radio program is evidenced by the fact that "The Mountain Boy" has been on the National Barn Dance programs at WLS every Saturday night since, and on many of the other programs, too.

amazed to find one of his informants proudly holding a 'Houn' Dog Guitar'" (Wolfe, *Classic Country*, 125).

For a brief discussion of immigration's impact on country music in Chicago, consult Chad Berry, "Introduction: Assessing the National Barn Dance," in *The Hayloft Gang: The Story of the National Barn Dance* (Urbana: University of Illinois Press, 2008), 11–16.

4. Kristine M. McCusker, "Patriarchy and the Great Depression," in *The Hayloft Gang: The Story of the National Barn Dance*, ed. Chad Berry (Urbana and Chicago: University of Illinois Press, 2008), 156–57.

5. Jones, *Radio's "Kentucky Mountain Boy*, 64–65.

6. The Young Men's Christian Association, or YMCA, was a common site for young men and boys to gather, engage in a variety of activities, and as some social historians have suggested, be educated in the ways of middle-class manhood. See, for instance, Thomas Winter, *Making Men, Making Class: The YMCA and Workingmen, 1877-1920* (Chicago and London: University of Chicago Press, 2002); Emily Mieras, "Tales from the Other Side of the Bridge: YMCA Manhood, Social Class and Social Reform in Turn-of-the-Twentieth-Century Philadelphia," *Gender & History* 17, no. 2 (August 2005): 409–40.

Bradley Kincaid was born in Garrard County, Kentucky, in the edge of the mountains and very near the Blue Grass. His parents were both native Kentuckians. His great-grandfather was a full-blooded Scotchman, coming to Virginia from Scotland. So Bradley is Scotch, but he says he was born in this country to save transportation.

Bradley's father was a farmer, but was more fond of fox hunting. Often the father would come home after a hard day in the field, snatch a bit of supper, get his old fox horn from behind the door, blow up his two fox hounds and ride away to the hills, where he would spend the night fox hunting. It was on one of these fox hunting expeditions that the father traded one of his fox hounds to a Negro friend for an old dilapidated guitar. That explains the name "Houn' Dog Guitar."

That guitar was the first music box that any of the ten children in the Kincaid family had connected with in any way. It was not long, though, until all of them could strum a tune. Bradley, himself, would sit for hours and hours at a time with the guitar and sing the old ballads which he had heard his mother and father sing. When he was only four years old his father used to entertain friends by having Bradley sing for them.

Bradley's home was a part frame, part log house with four rooms and a loft. Being Scotch the family naturally kept pretty close company. The nearest school was two miles from Bradley's home and was only in session about three to five months out of the year. The teacher was often only an eighth grade graduate. Bradley had very little schooling until he was 19 years old, when he entered the sixth grade in the Foundation department of Berea College, Kentucky.[7] After going to school two years and having finished the sixth, seventh, and eighth grades, Bradley volunteered for army service at the age of 21 and spent two years in service during the World War,[8] one year of which was overseas in France.

Bradley returned to Berea College at the age of 23 and entered high school. He finished high school at the age of 26 and went to work for the State Y.M.C.A. of Kentucky. After two years in this work he came to Chicago and entered the Y.M.C.A. College, where he has been a student four years, getting his degree in June. Bradley found time to study voice and was active in musical affairs at college. Since coming to Chicago he has been a member of the Y.M.C.A. College Glee Club, of which he is tenor soloist; [sic] has directed glee clubs and church choirs, and organized a men's chorus at LaPorte, Ind[iana].

Mrs. Irma Forman Kincaid, whom Bradley met at Berea College, is a graduate of the Oberlin College Conservatory, and is very much interested in folk music. She has been especially attracted to the mountain ballads and has been very helpful in arranging the music for the booklet.

Bradley is particularly interested in Christian work and expects to spend his life in the service of the Young Men's Christian Association. Needless to say, he feels a debt of gratitude to Berea College that he can never pay and he says: "Had it not been for the advantages

---

7. Founded in 1855 as a racially integrated college, Berea College had, by 1911, revised its mission to "[focus] on the 'uplift' of southern mountain people" (Shannon H. Wilson, *Berea College: An Illustrated History* [Lexington: University Press of Kentucky, 2006], 1, 103).

8. World War I.

Berea College offers to mountain boys and girls[,] I probably would never have received any education."[9]

So, that's the story of "The Mountain Boy" of WLS, the Sears, Roebuck station, Chicago. And now you can know when you hear him strumming his "houn' dog" guitar and singing the old mountain ballads that have come down through the years that Bradley Kincaid is one fellow who is justly capable and has a real right to carry on these truly genuine American folk songs. And through this little booklet[,] he has made it possible for all of us to know and enjoy these famous old mountain songs and ballads.

Source: Harold A. Safford, "Bradley Kincaid," in Bradley Kincaid, *Favorite Mountain Ballads and Old Time Songs as Sung by Bradley Kincaid, "The Mountain Boy"* (Chicago: WLS, The Sears, Roebuck Radio Station, 1928).

FOR FURTHER READING

Berry, Chad, ed. *The Hayloft Gang: The Story of the National Barn Dance.* Urbana: University of Illinois Press, 2008.

Jones, Loyal. *Radio's "Kentucky Mountain Boy," Bradley Kincaid.* Berea, KY: Appalachian Center/Berea College, 1980.

9. An example of Kincaid's gratitude to Berea College can be found in Berea's Bradley Kincaid Collection, which houses his correspondence, business papers, and sheet music, among other things ("Guide to the Bradley Kincaid Collection," http://www.berea.edu/hutchinslibrary/specialcollections/saa13.asp; accessed 20 December 2011).

9

Paul Hobson

"Radio's Hillbilly King, Carson Robison, who is, with his Pioneers, a regular attraction for Oxydol every Sunday from Luxembourg, Lyons and Normandy, tells us in this interview how he writes his world-famous songs" (1938)

Kansas native Carson Robison subverts many of our stereotypes of the typical hillbilly musician. An accomplished guitarist who worked as a session musician on pop and jazz sessions in New York in the early 1920s, Robison partnered with the Texas-born light opera singer Vernon Dalhart to record some of the genre's biggest hits during the mid-1920s. He was a master of the topical ballad, contributing new songs about shipwrecks and railroad accidents, as well as the author of numerous western standards, including "When It's Springtime in the Rockies." Robison's songwriting career reveals the role that professional songwriters played in creating country music from its advent. Not all hillbilly songs were drawn from the oral tradition. While some songwriters utilized business models from New York's Tin Pan Alley to build large and lucrative song catalogues in the 1920s and 1930s, still other songwriters with interests in other genres of popular music capitalized on hillbilly music's popularity.[1]

Robison is also noteworthy because he was one of the first American country music artists to take the genre out of North America and to build a significant global audience for country music. As discographer and country music historian Tony Russell has noted, Robison traveled to Europe "three times in the 1930s...to tour and make records, and after he returned home[,] his fans tuned in to recorded programs beamed from Radio Luxembourg by 'Carson Robison and his Oxydol Pioneers.'"[2] At the same time, Russell is quick to point out that Robison was also quite a self-aggrandizer: "On his missionary trips to Europe and Australasia, when he was safely out of earshot of people who knew better, he talked himself up as a founder of country music."[3]

In the following 1938 interview with Robison, we get a sense of the professionalism that he worked to cultivate as a songwriter, singer, and bandleader, presaging many of the developments in the country music industry of the 1950s. With Robison working on his opulent 300-acre ranch, readers have the opportunity to see how this professionalism paid off for him. The interview also shows Robison negotiating a common problem in interviews of country musicians: how to maintain the common, working-class touch while living a life of great wealth. The interviewer notes that Robison claims that he "does all the work on the ranch," but Robison's consistent use of the third-person *they* to describe the people he writes for and about might reveal his own distance from that community.

═══════════════

IT'S been said that you can take the boy out of the country, but you can't take the country out of the boy[,] and that sums up the career of Carson Robison, often called the "father" of hillbillies, who broadcasts with his "Pioneers" for Oxydol regularly from Luxembourg, Normandy and Lyons.

Carson Robison has come a long way since he first saw the light of day in the mountains of Chepota, Kenses [sic]—but the more he has travelled the closer that little town has come to his heart. And that's why he can write such smash-hit songs based on the homely philosophy of the mountain folk. To prove his tune-assembling ability, he wrote "Carry me Back to the Old Prairie," which is played very often over the air, as you must already know.

His father was the champion cowboy fiddler of his state, and it was natural for Carson to follow in his footsteps. During his travels he gained the friendship of Wendall (It Ain't Gonna Rain No Mo') Hall, who brought him to New York and got him a job with the Victor Recording Company. That was in 1924.

1. Bill C. Malone and Jocelyn R. Neal, *Country Music, U.S.A.*, 3rd rev. ed. (Austin: University of Texas Press, 2010), 44–50.

2. Tony Russell, *Country Music Originals: The Legends and the Lost* (New York and Oxford: Oxford University Press, 2007), 145.

3. Russell, *Country Music Originals*, 149.

Inspired, Carson decided to form a regular troupe, which he called the "Buckaroos." In this group we find Pearl, John[,] and Bill Mitchell. In 1932[,] they came to England as the "Pioneers," which name has stuck ever since.

Carson's song hits include "Barnacle Bill, The Sailor" and "My Blue Ridge Mountain Home," and all in all he has composed more than 300 melodies. He has made a complete study of hillbilly songs, and contends that they are [the] only American folk music. Sales of his records have topped the twenty million mark, which seems to prove that he knows his stuff.

He is married and has two children. Donald, his 25-year-old son[,] is a real honest-to-goodness cowboy. He manages the "CR" Ranch, Carson's 300-acre place at Poughkeepsie, New York State, does all the work on the ranch (according to him)[,] and rides rings around his father's singing cowboys. Carson wants the boy to follow in his footsteps; for the girl, he prefers a general education and marriage.

Carson hates golf and bridge…likes poker and fishing…would rather watch games like baseball than play them. The outdoors is his workshop and playground. He's not superstitious…got his first contract on a Friday, the 13th.

Carson likes to stay out of doors all the time. He never takes a subway train in his frequent travels in merry Manhattan. He says, "I'm not going to get stuffed. I take trolley cars and buses. Can yo' imagine a cowboy in one of them contraptions? I wouldn't put a steer in them! I'm just a small town boy in a big city."

"Radio performers don't seem to have any of that fraternal spirit evidenced in other forms of entertainment," says Carson Robison. "I can remember when I played in vaudeville and most of the folks on a bill out of town lived in the same hotel, shared meals together[,] and had parties. In New York[,] they had a club house second [to none] and spent hours in each other's company."

Out on the coast, most of the film [words obscured] in Beverly Hills or Hollywood, and have many organisations [sic] and meeting places where they can get together.

"Perhaps I haven't gotten around enough, but as far as I know, there isn't any society of radio performers who meet in a specified place and discuss the problems of their profession and other constructive criticism now and then.

"I think it would be a good idea, for, after all, folks who have everything in common can get a lot done by pulling together, and I believe that it would benefit both the listeners and the performers themselves.

"Writing songs for the plain folks I know," says Robison, "is more than a professional study or hobby. It's a religion. You see, they don't seek perfection. It's sentiment and true emotion that counts with them. Hillbilly songs are their lives, their tales of romance, pathos and, perhaps, comedy. They don't sing them because they have good voices, but because it touches their hearts and strikes a real emotional note."

"Don't try too much for novelty," he continues. "It is more of an asset to be sincere. Every song I have written tells a story, a true story. Of course[,] it has to be dressed up, but the persons it concerns know it's about them.

"Hillbilly songs, especially, require the utmost in sincerity. The mountain folk aren't looking for any fanciful, imaginative tales. Their lives are colourful enough as it is, and fit right well into any lyric or music. Nature paints pictures pretty enough. Just telling about them with word pictures is enough for any man without his trying to gild the lily, as it were.

"Before you attempt to write songs, make an attempt to learn more about the people and the place you are going to write about. A song is like a story book. It may also be likened to a portrait—and you know that an artist studies his subject and keeps referring to it before he completes his picture."

And in [the] face of all this, it is strange to note that Robison created such a sensation when he performed recently in England. Observers asserted that such typical American music would not find a place in the heart of England. But after his initial showing, he was cheered lustily and was obliged to extend his tour.

Robison never pretends to be the big shot. He prefers to be as plain and simple as the folk he writes about, and perhaps that explains why his work has always remained so ringing true and typical.

Source: Paul Hobson, "Radio's Hillbilly King, Carson Robison, who is, with his Pioneers, a regular attraction for Oxydol every Sunday from Luxembourg, Lyons and Normandy, tells us in this interview how he writes his world-famous songs," unknown magazine, 28 March 1938, in the Carson Robison Name File (NF-1699), Southern Folklife Collection, Wilson Library, University of North Carolina at Chapel Hill Libraries. Used with permission.

10

John Wright

"J. E. Mainer" (1993)

Although many early historians of country music argued that the genre could be traced almost exclusively to the Appalachian Mountains, more recent scholarship has revealed that the Piedmont South also played a central role in the genre's development in the 1920s and 1930s.[1] For a few decades prior to the first hillbilly recordings, black and white southerners alike moved from rural farms to large towns and cities in search of work in the textile mills that had begun to spring up in the South during the late nineteenth century. Many early country musicians—including Fiddlin' John Carson, Charlie Poole, and Dorsey Dixon, among many others—worked in the cotton mills of such towns as Rockingham, North Carolina, and Spartanburg, South Carolina, and gained firsthand experience of

1. Pamela Grundy, "'We Always Tried to Be Good People': Respectability, Crazy Water Crystals, and Hillbilly Music on the Air," *Journal of American History* 81, no. 4 (March 1995): 1591–620; William F. Danaher and Vincent J. Riscigno, "Cultural Production, Media, and Meaning: Hillbilly Music and the Southern Textile Mills," *Poetrics* 32 (2004): 51–71; and Patrick Huber, *Linthead Stomp: The Creation of Country Music in the Piedmont South* (Chapel Hill: University of North Carolina Press, 2008).

the difficult and dangerous work conditions there as child laborers and as adults before taking up an instrument in order to avoid life in the mill.[2]

Not surprisingly, the towns and cities that were built around the Piedmont's textile mills were hotbeds for early country music. Musicians from different parts of the South came together to exchange repertoire and technique in informal jam sessions and built bands to support growing demand for dance musicians. As some bands became increasingly professionalized, they began working for radio stations and using the relatively new medium as a means to sell songbooks and to book personal appearances at social halls and schoolhouses within a reasonable drive of the station.[3] Some groups—including J. E. Mainer's Mountaineers, who are discussed in the excerpt that follows—were the beneficiaries of program sponsors who wished to leverage the popularity of individual musicians and the genre as a whole to market their products to the groups' fans. It should be no surprise, then, that country musicians were frequently sponsored by companies that manufactured household and farm products and any of a variety of medicinal potions, powders, and cures.

Hillbilly fiddler J. E. Mainer, who offers an oral history in the following excerpt, was one of the most successful country musicians of the 1930s. A native of western North Carolina, Mainer recounts his family's decision to move from the Appalachian Mountains to a Piedmont mill town to pay for farmland back home, his early performances in the many fiddle contests that sprung up around the region, and his first forays into radio. With his brother Wade (whose career reached into the twenty-first century),[4] J.E. formed a successful string band that played on radio stations in Charlotte and Raleigh, North Carolina, with the sponsorship of Crazy Water Crystals, a laxative company that sponsored many early stars of country radio.[5] After splitting with Wade in 1937, Mainer moved his band to San Antonio, Texas, and St. Louis, Missouri, revealing the broad appeal of country music in the 1930s and the expansive reach of radio and recordings during that time. Mainer's tale is far from extraordinary, however; rather, it is reflective of the typical career path of many of the genre's early radio and recording stars.

---

2. Patrick Huber's *Linthead Stomp* offers the most detailed study of these musicians. See also Kinney Rorrer, *Rambling Blues: The Life & Songs of Charlie Poole* (Danville, VA: McCain Printing, 1982).

For further discussion of labor conditions in southern textile mills, consult Cathy L. McHugh, *Mill Family: The Labor System in the Southern Cotton Textile Industry, 1880-1915* (New York: Oxford University Press, 1988).

3. Danaher and Roscigno, "Cultural Production, Media, and Meaning."

4. For more background on Wade Mainer, consult Dick Spottswood, *Banjo on the Mountain: Wade Mainer's First Hundred Years* (Jackson: University Press of Mississippi, 2010).

5. Grundy, " 'We Always Tried to Be Good People.' "

WELL, I'll get back on this story here that you wanted. I was borned and raised back in the Blue Ridge Mountains in Buncombe County, North Carolina, eighteen hundred and ninety-eight. And I stayed there till I was I reckon about eight or nine years old, and we moved out of the mountains back there to the cotton mills. Before we moved we lived in a little old one-room log cabin. They was six of us children and Dad and Mom.

And I remember they come up a rain there one night. Dad had dug a ditch down again the house. And they come up an awful storm and I work up way about two o'clock in the morning and I heard somebody a-pecking out there and beating and a-banging. And I raised up and looked over and Dad was out there out of the bed a-standing in water way up over his shoe tops and he had a axe there cutting a hole through the floor.

The rain had rained so hard it busted over that ditch and and [sic] knocked the front door in and was coming right on through the house. And Pa says, "You lay back down there and go to sleep." He said, "Don't you get up out of that bed now, boy, cause they's water down here." And I set there and watched him for I don't know how long while he got the hole cut through. When he got it cut through, why of course the water went on out through under the floor. The lower side of the house was a-setting I guess about eight or ten feet off of the ground. That's as how steep the side of the mountain was where we was living at this branch.

That old branch out there would get up, you know, and the water'd get so high and that branch out there would come in down that cove there so's logs and rocks would come down there and it'd make the awfullest fuss in the world. Go kindly like a freight train a-rumbling by your house these days.

Anyway, we finally moved out of that place there, moved across the mountain to a little place called the Peak Field. Moved over on an old sled my daddy had made. Had to cut a road through the woods to get over there. And Dad had a whole lot more field that he could work over there than where he was at.

Daddy never had no education in his life and he had to work hard all of his life. Back there in them mountains most people didn't make very much money. He could skin tan bark all day long, lay it out and let it try there three or four days, and then he'd take it to town. Drive fourteen miles to deliver it to the tannery. It would take him from mighty early in the morning till that night to get back to the house and he'd only make about ninety cents. I tell you, it was rougher back those days than people think here now. So Pa finally decided he'd move out of the mountains.

Well, he went down to a little town called Weaverville, North Carolina, and bought him a little farm down there. They was I believe about sixteen acres in it. Then we had to move to the cotton mill in Union, South Carolina, to pay for it. So we went on down there and we went to work in the mill. I went to work in the mill when I was eight years old. Now you can just imagine about how it was. They'd hire you. It didn't make no difference. All you had to do was just push a box and they'd hire you. Half the mills was closed anyway on account of help. Well, I went in that mill, I learned how to doff.[6] And you talk about a mean place, that was the meanest place ever I seed in my life. One day there were got done doffing and we had about twenty minutes' rest. And the old head doffer got Finley. That was my oldest brother. Got him

---

6. Doffers were responsible for changing the spindles and bobbins that fed the looms.

down on the floor under a big old oil tub and turned the faucet on him. And boy, he just got that boy all messed up with that old cylinder oil and stuff, you know.

Finley just went down in the heating shop and told Dad about it. Dad was a-working down there. Dad come up there and he grabbed that old head doffer in the collar and boy, he hit him hard. I bet he knocked him fifteen feet back across the spare floor there. And he told him, "If you ever lay your hands on one of my boys again," he says, "I've just started on you. I'll just finish it up."

Then Pa, he went down to see the superintendent about it. They all stayed in the same room, back them days, boss man, superintendent, all of them. Gone on up there and he telled the old man about it. He was wicked, oh man, he'd cuss every breath he'd draw. The old man come up there and asked the head doffer about it. Course they all stick together. They wasn't but a few words said about it so it was passed on off.

And we worked there till the next day, long about three o'clock—you see, you worked twelve hours—long about three o'clock, me and Finley, we slipped out of the mill. We shouldn't have done it but we did. They were just running over us so bad there in the mill that we just wasn't going to stay there. And the mill was five story high. We was working right in the top story and one of the section hands there grabbed Finley under the arms and held him out that window and he said, "Now boy, don't you believe I'll drop you?" Finley was crying, he was just crying his eyes out, and me a-standing back over there scared half to death too and crying, begged him not to turn him loose. And the other people standing around on the spare floor just dying laughing. Well, that fellow, he finally sets Finley back down there till the next day and me and Finley, we decided we would leave.

Well, we got out of that mill, we took up the railroad track. We didn't know where we was going. We was trying to get back home, we was trying to get back to Asheville. And it's a long ways, I don't know, sixty-five or seventy miles, and that's where we walked and walked and the sun begin to get down pretty low.

And I looked back down the railroad track and I seed somebody coming. I said, "Finley, yonder comes somebody." Finley says, "It walks kindly like Daddy, don't it?" I said, "Yeah, it do. We just better sit down here and wait and see." And sure enough, it was Daddy, and he come up and he had them whips in his hand. He was going to whup us. He was going to give us good and asked us, "How come that you run off and leave?" and Finley he just up and told him what that section hand had done, how he held him out the window there and things. Pa just throwed his hickory away. Said, "Well, you boys come on back. I'll go somewheres tomorrow and try to get a job somewhere else." We went on back to the house and the next day Pa, he come to Glendale, South Carolina. We stayed with Dad there and holp [sic] him till he got his place paid for and after he got his place paid for, why we moved back home.

There was a boy by the name of Roscoe Banks. He had married one of my older sisters and he come from back out of what they call the Table Top Mountains.[7] He wasn't that old at the time. He was just a young boy. They was just married and he played a fiddle and he'd bought the fiddle off of a hobo that'd come up there one time, got off the train there at Marshall and he was three days getting back there in them mountains where those fellows were working at, Roscoe and all of them.

7. A mountain range in the western Carolinas.

And he sold this fiddle to Roscoe and after we moved back up home up there, why I got to getting with Roscoe. And Pa, he'd bought me a little old banjo there and I'd get up early of a morning and I'd come just messing with that banjo trying to play it. And I got to where I could play it pretty good. I'd go up to that Roscoe every once in a while and sit down, him and Jim Bailey, an old fellow that lived there that picked the banjo to. Well, I'd get my banjo and I'd play with them. So I took up banjo playing and got pretty well with it there with them two.

Well, one day there I decided I'd leave home. I went and told Ma. I wouldn't tell my daddy cause I knowed he'd jump on me. I went and told Ma that I was going to leave and she said, "Well, where're you going to?" I said, "I don't know. I'm going off, see if I can't find me a job somewhere." So I went to Knoxville, Tennessee. I went to work in the Brookside Cotton Mill.

One Saturday when I come out of the mill there, about two o'clock, about two hours after the mill had stopped, they was a whole crowd of people out there standing around the railroad crossing. I decided I'd walk down there and see what it was. And when I got down there, they was an old man a-standing there on the railroad track. He was playing this fiddle and the poor fellow was drunk. And he was just a little fellow. I was standing back there watching him and I always did love a fiddle.

So he played a tune there—now this was in about 1913, '14, something like that. But anyway, he played a tune there that I've never forgotten. I don't guess I ever will forget it because when he got done playing this tune he turned around and started to cross the railroad tracks and Number Eleven hit him and killed him. And it just tore him all to pieces down that railroad track. Course the old fiddle busted and kindly went in the ditch, in the weeds. I went on back there to the boarding house where I was staying at.

The next day I decided I'd go back down there and maybe some—maybe they didn't find that fiddle. And I went down and got to looking around and I found it. Well, I went right to the mill and put in a week's notice and I worked the week's notice and I come back home. Hadn't been there too awfully long and whenever I got back home I was showing it to Roscoe and it was busted up pretty bad. Roscoe says, "That thing ain't worth fixing." I said, "Well, I believe I'll fix it anyway."

By the way, I didn't tell you what tune that old man was playing. He was playing an old tune called "The Drunkard's Hiccups." That's the tune he was playing. And I took that fiddle and had it fixed up and I've still got it today and I wouldn't part from that fiddle at all. Cause that was a real fiddle.

But anyway I came on back to the house and went back to playing my banjo with Roscoe and them. And we'd play around at square dances, we'd go out and visit people and play till away in the night, be entertaining people around, you know. Never did charge them anything for it. Just old country folks back there in them mountains. And there I got round to knowing my mind again. I decided I'd leave home again.

Well, sir, I caught a freight train—this was six years later, in nineteen hundred and twenty-two—I caught a freight train and come to Concord, North Carolina. Got off of the bus at Salisbury, walked through Salisbury and caught the train at a little old place about five mile this side of Salisbury and come on into Concord. And whenever I got into Concord I was broke. I didn't have but one twenty-five cent [piece] in my pocket's all I had and I was starved half to death.

Went up to a fellow's house there and asked him where I could get a boarding place at. "Well," he said, "I'll tell you. They's a lady right down here about the fourth house on the right." Says, "She runs a boarding place down there. If you'll go down there and see her, you might get a place to stay all night." I said, "All right, I believe I will." So I went on down there and knocked on the front door and boy, there was the biggest old stoutest looking woman come to the door you ever seed.

I introduced myself to her, told her that I was a-hunting for a job and I was broke and I didn't have no money. But if she'd let me stay all night with her, why, when I got the money I'd send it back to her. She said, "Well, you talk like a pretty honest boy. Come on in." So I went around in there and set around a while and they asked me if I ever worked in a mill. I told them, "Yeah." I told them I was a good doffer. So I went in the mill next morning and it just happened that I got a job.

This old lady's name was McDaniel. Flo McDaniel's mother, that's who it was. And she had a daughter there and I fell in love with the daughter and she did me, so after about a year after I come there we got married.

And I'd took up playing the fiddle through all that time and I wired to Asheville, didn't wire, wrote up there rather, and told Wade to come down there and get him a job in the mill and bring my banjo with him. And he did. So me and him, we went to playing together and after that, why, here come Daddy John Love along and he wanted to play with us. And me and Wade and Daddy John Love got to going to fiddlers' conventions. Yessir, we won just about every one that we went to. Just the fiddle and the banjo and the guitar. John Love was one of those types that sung kindly on the style of Jimmie Rodgers. He was a yodeler. And he was a good one, just like Jimmie Rodgers was. He was an old-timey.

They was a program started here in Charlotte called the Crazy Water Crystal program and they heard about me and Wade and John Love. So they sent one day for me to come over there and I went over there and they wanted me to take a job over there and broadcast, advertise for them, over at WBT in Charlotte.

Well, I come back and I tell the boss man about it and I told him, I said, "I don't want to leave my job." I said, "I might not make it, and if I didn't, I'd be out of a job." And he says, "J.E., you go on and take that. If you can't make it, your job will be here when you come back."

So I went on. And that was where we got started in, J.E. Mainer and the Mountaineers. They booked us out and we traveled just about everywhere. We traveled North Carolina, South Carolina, Georgia, Alabama, Kentucky. Played some in Tennessee, Virginia. Well, we went on that way for I reckon about thirty years. Playing nothing but schoolhouses. Didn't have nobody booking me out. People'd write in a-wanting us to come and make these personal appearances.

And I'll tell you, it was every night. Every night we was out somewhere or another. It didn't make no difference how it was a-raining or how it was a-snowing, anything like that, we was always on the road. Driving an old A-model Ford. You know about how one of them was. No heat in it and nothing else, snow on the ground, we went right on anyway. Well, I could tell you a lot if I just had time to, but I ain't got the time to, so—

Wade and Zeke Morris, they got to giving me a lot of trouble. They gone off and leave me and poor John there, we was on that fifty-thousand-watt station. Wade, I reckon he was like me, he'd get homesick and he'd want to go home. He wouldn't tell me where he was going or nothing. Come program time Wade and Zeke'd disappear. And me and John would have to take the program by ourselves, just the fiddle and the guitar. But we carried it on.

I went and told the boss man about it in the office down there. "Well, J.E., just find you somebody else," he said. "Where did they go to?" I said, "I don't know where they went to." And that was on one day at Saturday at dinner time. And I says, "I'm going up to Asheville tomorrow. Maybe Wade's up there." And sure enough, he was there, down in a well, helping Roscoe dig a well up there. He was pretty glad to see me, but he wouldn't let on like he was. So I brung him back to Charlotte with me. And we hadn't been on the air but a day or two, Zeke walked in the studio. And it was a sight in the world.

I can't think of all right now to tell you what really did happen. But anyway it was a sight in God's world how they worked us boys. I had a contract in California to go out there and make a movie with the Fox film company and I was tied up with the Crazy Water Crystal Company contract and they wouldn't turn me loose. So we left Charlotte and went to Raleigh, WPTF, and stayed up there for, I don't know, probably a couple of years together.

And you know how people is when they get—think that they're doing it all, why then, they just think that you ain't—they ain't got no more use for you. So that was the way Wade and Zeke was. See, I put them boys right on top. I held them up there for, well, all the time they was with me, and they got to where they thought I wasn't in it at all.

So I just decided one day I'd just quit them and leave. And that was where me and Wade and them boys split up at. I come back home here and stayed back here for three or four weeks. Decided I'd go back on the air. Well, I went to Harris, North Carolina, and I got Snuffy Jenkins,[8] went back to Old Fort where I got Zeke at and got George Morris, his brother, and I went down here at Richfield and got Leonard Stokes and went on the air over in Charlotte, over on WSOC.

We stayed there about two months, I reckon, and I got a call from WSPA in Spartanburg, wanting me to come down there and take a program. I went down there and took a program and we was getting along fine. People found out I was back on the air down in there and they got to writing in, wanting me to come out and put on a show. Well, I was booked up there, I don't know, oh, I'd say over a month ahead every night and I'd think to myself, "Well, it won't be long it'll be like it was before. I'll be on the road every night somewhere or another."

And I come off the air one day at 12:15 there and old man J. W. Fincher, the boss of the Crazy Water Crystals program from Charlotte, was out there in the yard sitting out there in his car. He says, "By golly, J.E., they just can't hold you down, can they?" I said, "No, I'm still going." He says, "That was a good program you boys had on in there. I really enjoyed you. I set out here and listened to that."

And he wanted me to go to Columbia, South Carolina, for him, down there on WIS. And I asked him, I said, "When do you want me to go?" He says, " I want you down there Monday morning." This was on Saturday at 12:15. "Well, Mr. Fincher," I said, "we are getting all the work we can do here. I kindly hate to leave here." I said, "They're so good to me, I hate to leave here." "Well," he says, "I'd sure like to have you down there. If there's any way of getting you," he said, "I'm going to get you. I'll give you sixty dollars a week. You take everything that you make on your personal appearances, sell your songbooks."

"But," he said, "I do want you to take the Old Hired Hand with you." That was a fellow that worked for Charlie and Bill Monroe. He was doing announcing for them and they had had a wreck in Blacksburg [Virginia] and I think a couple of them had to go to the hospital. Well, the others got out before he did and so they left Byron down there and Byron was out of a job

8. An early innovator of the three-finger banjo style later popularized by Earl Scruggs. For more, see Jim Mills, *Gibson Mastertone: Flathead 5-String Banjos of the 1930s and 1940s* (Anaheim Hills, CA; Centerstream, 2009), 35–41.

and he got to wanting to go down to Columbia with me down there if I'd take him and he'd do my announcing.

Well, that's where I just played you know what. Anyway, I took him on down there. He had a good education. He'd studied for a preacher and a lawyer both. Well, he got down there and we were just a-going fine. We was making plenty of money, booked out every night. And he got to rooting in ahead of me, rooting in ahead of me, and I seed he was going to take over the band down there and I just said, "Well, you can have it. I'm just quitting. I'm pulling out." So I come back home.

Went to Greensboro. Hadn't been up to Greensboro but about one week I reckon and got a long-distance call from San Antonio, Texas. Bensington Doyle from out of Chicago called me up and wanted me to go out there and take the program for them. So I asked them what they would pay me, and they said they'd pay me five hundred dollars a week and I could have all the money on the side I'd make.

But I didn't have as good a band as I'd been a-having. Them old-time musicians was hard to find. But I had one I thought I could get by with out there. They was playing my records all over the United States. You could be a-riding along at night and hear J.E. Mainer and his Mountaineers just most anywhere. And I went on out there and worked for them there in San Antonio, Texas. Worked for them out there six months.

And after the six months was up they sent me to KMOX in St. Louis, Missouri, and I stayed out there six months, and I decided then that I'd come home. So I come home here and they wanted me to go on WBT in Charlotte. So I went over there to see them about going on the program over there for Bensington Doyle from out of Chicago. And that man said to me, he said, "Have you got their address?" I said, "Yea, I've got it." And he said, "Give it to me, will you?" And that's where I made another mistake. I give him Bensington Doyle's address from out of Chicago.

Well, this fellow over there, was over this station, he had a string band on there called the Briarhoppers, Dick Hartman and the Briarhoppers. No, Tennessee Ramblers, that's who it was, Tennessee Ramblers. And they had to handle every program in the hillbilly line that the station took on over there. Well, he wrote this company a letter, Bensington Doyle from out of Chicago, and told them, says, "Ain't no use bringing J.E. Mainer and the Mountaineers over here, when we got musicians right here can handle it just as good as he can." Then he says, "It won't cost you not nearly as much it would if you'd had J.E. over here because they have to handle the program that we tell them to handle." He said, "We could just pay them a certain salary."

Well, you know what that done. That knocked me in the head going to Charlotte. But it wasn't long after that Bensington Doyle, he went off the air. I don't know what ever happened to him. He sure was a good company to work for.

I just about forget to tell you, Bensington Doyle sent me to Monterey, Mexico, one time. We crossed the Rio Grande down there going over from San Antonio, Texas. And we didn't have no pass. We got on the other side, they arrested us, put us in jail, for not having a passport. I told them, I said, "Mister, I'm supposed to go on the air up yonder in the morning, 6:15, for Bensington Doyle from out of Chicago." And I said, "I can't stay in this jail." "Oh yea," they said, "you will too." Course they didn't talk like that. They talked in a different kind of a language but I understood most of it. I knowed what they meant.

But anyway, I told them, I said, "You call the radio station up there and see if I ain't supposed to go on the air in the morning." So they did. They called up there and they told them,

Yeah, that J.E. Mainer was supposed to report there between 9 and 6:15 in the morning. So they said, No, they wasn't going to let J.E. Mainer out of jail.

Well, the radio station, they called Bensington Doyle in Chicago and told them about it. So Bensington Doyle told them, he says, "What's the phone number down there?"—where we crossed the Rio Grande at—and they got it and Bensington Doyle called up down there and told them to turn us boys loose. We had to go on the air up there the next morning. So they did. They turned us loose. And we ran on up there.

We didn't stay down there but about three weeks. Boy, I didn't like them Mexicans a bit no way. You couldn't turn around but you was scared to death of something. Afraid one'd throw a knife through you or something. Get one of their girls out there on the floor, sweetheart of a boy, and go to dancing with her, you sure were going to have a fight. That's all there was to it.

I've been on a hundred and ninety different radio stations throughout the United States. Been on the British Broadcasting Company across the water. In fact, I'm just known what you might say all over the world. And old J.E.'s going to quit before long. He ain't going to follow it up very much more. I'm getting too old to. Can't take it like I used to be any more.

Well, I'm going to say so long. If there's any more that I can do, why you let me know and I'll be mighty glad to do it for you. Wish you all the best of luck in the world and hope you uns have happy new years all the way through. And tell the Stanley boy I said hello when you see him.

Source: John Wright, *Traveling the High Way Home: Ralph Stanley and the World of Traditional Bluegrass Music* (Urbana and Chicago: University of Illinois Press, 1993), 24–33.
(From *Traveling the High Way Home: Ralph Stanley and the World of Traditional Bluegrass Music*. Copyright 1993 by the Board of Trustees of the University of Illinois. Used with permission of the University of Illinois Press.)

FOR FURTHER READING

Danaher, William F., and Vincent J. Roscigno. "Cultural Production, Media, and Meaning: Hillbilly Music and the Southern Textile Mills." *Poetics* 32 (2004): 51–71.

Grundy, Pamela. "'We Always Tried to Be Good People': Respectability, Crazy Water Crystals, and Hillbilly Music on the Air, 1933-1935." *Journal of American History* 81, no. 4 (March 1995): 1591–620.

Huber, Patrick. *Linthead Stomp: The Creation of Country Music in the Piedmont South*. Chapel Hill: University of North Carolina Press, 2008.

Spottswood, Dick, with Stephen Wade. *Banjo on the Mountain: Wade Mainer's First Hundred Years*. Jackson: University Press of Mississippi, 2010.

11

Virginia Seeds

"Back Stage Ramble: Cowboys and Cow Belles Enjoy the Barn Dance" (1936)

Within just a few years of the first commercial radio broadcasts in the United States, station managers across the country began producing "barn dance" programs that used rural music and comedic sketches to recreate the atmosphere of such pre-industrial rural entertainments as barn raisings, quilting bees, and corn shuckings. The first barn dance program was broadcast on Fort Worth station WBAP in 1922. The nation's most popular barn dances, though, were those that broadcast over "clear-channel" radio stations, which owned exclusive rights to a particular radio frequency. They included Chicago's *WLS Barn Dance* (later *The National Barn Dance*, first broadcast 19 April 1924), Nashville's *Grand Ole Opry* (first broadcast 28 November 1925 on station WSM), and Cincinnati's *The Renfro Valley Barn Dance*, first broadcast 9 October 1937 on station WLW).

Saturday-night radio barn dances exemplify what media studies scholar Susan H. Douglas has described as radio's "pivotal role...in helping us imagine ourselves and our relationships to other Americans differently. It constructed imagined communities...and thus cultivated both a sense of nationhood and a validation of subcultures, often simultaneously."[1] A popular pastime for many American families, these barn dances—which, ironically, replaced the very barn dances that had so characterized rural life in much of the United States and Canada—incorporated a live audience, fostered an atmosphere of controlled spontaneity, and created vivid characters with whom their audiences could relate so that listeners might feel as though they were actually attending the dance. Many barn dance performers adopted familial monikers (Cousin Emmy, Bashful Brother Oswald), were known only by their first names (Mac & Bob), or played out their romances on the air (Lulu Belle & Scotty); and, as seen in the following excerpt from the WLS newsletter *Stand By*, listeners were frequently offered behind-the-scenes insight into the production of the *National Barn Dance*. By depicting the radio stars as real people, the program invites listeners to imagine themselves as part of the community.

At the same time, these programs were reflective of and influenced regional conceptions of racial, ethnic, and gendered identity, as exemplified by the many references to the female performers' looks and the presence of "ethnic" white characters representing various ethnic groups in the upper Midwest (and simultaneous absence of African American and Jewish performers) on the *National Barn Dance* program.[2] The extraordinary number of performers named here gives a sense of the remarkable variety of musical styles that were presented on the *National Barn Dance*.[3] Consequently, by reaching out to a diverse and expansive audience, these programs exerted a significant and lasting impact on the daily lives of barn dance performers and their listeners.

A FAMILY picture typical of thousands of homes is sent to us by Mrs. I. C. Songs,[4] a Stand By reader, who lives in New Castle, Indiana.

"Saturday night finds Mother, Dad and the three kids with a big pan of popcorn, a dish of apples, and most important of all—the National Barn Dance. From seven until 12 o'clock on Saturday night are the shortest hours of the week."

1. Susan J. Douglas, *Listening In: Radio and the American Imagination* (Minneapolis: University of Minnesota Press, 2004), 11.

2. Michael Ann Williams, "Home to Renfro Valley: John Lair and the Women of Barn Dance Radio," in *The Women of Country Music: A Reader*, ed. Charles K. Wolfe and James E. Akenson (Lexington: University Press of Kentucky, 2003), 88–108; Kristine M. McCusker, *Lonesome Cowgirls and Honky-Tonk Angels: The Women of Barn Dance Radio* [Urbana and Chicago: University of Illinois Press, 2008], 28–49, especially 30–32; Stephanie Vander Wel, "*I Am a Honky-Tonk Girl*": Country Music, Gender, and Migration, Ph.D. dissertation, University of California at Los Angeles, 2008, 39–81.

3. Paul L. Tyler, "The Rise of Rural Rhythm," in *The Hayloft Gang: The Story of the National Barn Dance*, ed. Chad Berry (Urbana and Chicago: University of Illinois Press, 2008), 19–71.

4. Likely a false name published for comedic purposes.

That homey scene is one that is duplicated by barn dance fans all over the country, every Saturday night, while the boys and girls in the Old Hayloft are putting forth their very best efforts.

Backstage in the 8th Street Theatre, where most of the barn dance programs are broadcast, there is a hubbub of preparation just before seven o'clock, the official opening hour for the barn dance. Production Man Boyd rushes in with an arm-load of scripts. The [Prairie] Ramblers get tuned up and Patsy [Montana] practices a few yodels. The sodbusters play several bars of their first harmonica number. Henry stands offstage mumbling his lines.

"Stand by!" calls the production man. There is one hushed moment. Then the cowbells start ringing. The Saturday night barn dance is on the air. Yes, sir! and yes, ma'm! That means a good time for everybody.

And the good time includes the boys and girls behind the scenes, as well as the guests in the theatre and those listening in their own homes. I perched up on a rafter backstage in the Old Hayloft one Saturday night recently so I would really be able to tell you what goes on behind the scenes.

The two shows from seven o'clock to 7:30 are broadcast from the balcony studio of the theatre. By 7:30 the theatre is packed with more than 1,200 eager barn dance fans. While the cowbells ring out, the curtain is drawn and the barn dance crew is on the stage, singing "How do you do, everybody, how do you do?"

"SCOTTY BLUSHED"

That's really Lulu Belle's song, of course, but Scotty was doing a good job of singing it for her and for little Linda Lou that second Saturday night in January. Papa Scotty was blushingly receiving congratulations and undergoing a little good-natured teasing about his new state of parenthood, both on the stage and behind the scenes. The Hometowners even sang a special Rockabye Baby lullaby for his benefit.

Meanwhile, Christine,[5] blond, and lovely as the songs she sings, smooths out the lace apron of her barn dance dress and gives her curls a little pat. In just a minute she will be standing under a microphone, singing a song she has written herself, "A Swiss Mountain Girl's Dream."

Among all the interesting costumes worn by the boys and girls in the Old Hayloft, Christine's is outstanding. The dress of simple black velveteen has a tightly-laced basque and is worn over a red guimpe. Her starched white lace-trimmed apron is brought to each performance carefully wrapped in tissue paper so that it stays fresh and spotless. In the costume, she looks like a Swiss mountain boy's dream.

5. Christine Endeback, known as "the Little Swiss Miss" and "the Yodeling Swiss Miss," was born in the Netherlands (Tony Russell, *Country Music Originals: The Legends and the Lost* [New York: Oxford University Press, 2007], 205). James Leary has suggested that her musical style was representative of the upper Midwestern "polkabilly," which blended central and eastern European traditional musics with hillbilly styles in the upper Midwest (James P. Leary, *Polkabilly: How the Goose Island Ramblers Redefined American Folk Music* [New York and Oxford: Oxford University Press, 2006], 33).

OVERALLS IN STYLE

Most of the boys wear overalls to the barn dance party, although some prefer Western outfits. Tumble Weed's spurs click rhythmically as he strides across the stage and his carved belt is the envy of all the menfolks. The Ramblers, too, wear Western hats and cowboy regalia, except Salty who pours himself into tight, peg-leg trousers and wears a schoolboy straw hat. Arkie,[6] Ramblin' Red Foley and Scotty wear breeches and boots and open-necked shirts, typical of their native hill sections. Pat Buttram appears in a costume that could only have been rigged up in one spot, and that's Winston County, Alabama.

Verne, Lee and Mary look mighty pretty in brand-new costumes of full-sleeved white satin blouses and black satin jumpers with overall tops.

The Maple City Four this night impersonated Miss Minnie Scram, Miss Sulalia Stitchfiddle, Miss Libby Liddy and Miss Sara Scroveny, contestants in a bathing beauty contest. Attired in bathing suits of 30 or 40 years ago, the "beauties" with hair-rats piled high on their heads were each awarded 50 cents and a week's engagement at Station E-Z-R-A.

Winnie, Lou and Sally,[7] Evelyn Overstake, Sophia Germanich and Sally Foster all wear their "party dresses" of flowered muslin for the barn dance, with ribbons in their hair.

IT'S BUSY BACK STAGE

As the show goes on bus boys, in white coats[,] are backstage scurrying between "props" and screens, setting up a long table. The aroma of steaming coffee, ham, pickles, and cheese arises as the white-coated boys carry in the tray after tray of sandwiches and coffee.

Toddy DuMoulin, on the stage but hidden behind his cello, asks Verne to go out and snitch a sandwich for him. She shakes her golden curls and dubbing him, "Teddy Bear," tells him he'll have to go himself. Besides, she'll be on the air in just a few minutes. Of course, he can't go either and even the folks who are off the stage don't touch any of the food until the curtain of the first show is drawn at 9:30, and the Hayloft Drama goes on the air from the studios in the Prairie Farmer building.

Supper time!

There is a rush for the sandwich table and the barn dance crew enjoys a sociable half-hour while the 8th Street Theatre is emptying and filling up again.

"Anyone seen my chicken sandwich?" queries Bill Thall of the Tunetwisters. For an answer, Max Terhune "cock-a-doodle-doos" for him, as only Max can. The chicken sandwich joke seems to be one that comes up every Saturday night on account there aren't any chicken sandwiches.

6. Luther W. Ossenbrink (1907–1981), known as "Arkie the Arkansas Woodchopper."
7. A vocal trio named for WLS. At the time this article was published, the group consisted of Helen, Eileen, and Adele Jensen (Tyler, "The Rise of Rural Rhythm," 37; McCusker, *Lonesome Cowgirls and Honky-Tonk Angels*, 40; "Winnie, Lou and Sally: WLS National Barn Dance," http://www.hillbilly-music.com/groups/story/index.php?groupid=12199;accessed 5 January 2012).

IS PAUL REDUCING?

"What's the matter, Paul, aren't you eating?" Phil Kalar asks Paul Nettinga, the 213-pound tenor of the Hometowners quartet.

"Naw, I don't think I could eat a bite," Paul replies turning around to display two thick sandwiches bulging in the hip-pocket of his overalls, while he balances a cup and saucer.

Everyone sits on a step, leans up against the scenery or finds a chair to stretch out in until it's time for the second show to start at 10 o'clock.

Pat Petterson, having exchanged his bathing suit for the regulation overalls, finds himself next to Winnie. "Goin' North after the show, Winnie?" he asks.

"Yes, thank you just the same, but I have a ride," politely answers Winnie.

"But I need someone to take me home," mourns Pat. "It'll be 'way after midnight and awful dark. Don't you think you better escort me? It's leap year, you know." But Winnie is not to be inveigled into such an arrangement.

READY FOR 2ND SHOW

After the backstage spread, some of the boys and girls go up to the balcony studio for the barn dance frolic and the rest get ready for another performance of the National Barn Dance on the stage for the western network.

Known to his Prairie Farmer-WLS family as "The Chief," Burridge D. Butler, bronzed by the Arizona sun, was making his mid-winter visit to the Barn Dance. Although Mr. Butler is in Chicago for only a short time during the winter months, he always makes it [a] point to join the Barn Dance crew at least one Saturday night for the hayloft part.

Backstage, he was shaking hands and greeting the boys and girls he hadn't seen since he left in November. With a cheerful word for every member of the hayloft gang from the master of ceremonies to the property men, Mr. Butler skirted the stage and made his way out to one of the boxes in the theatre to join the fun of a real barn dance party.

> Source: Virginia Seeds, "Back Stage Ramble: Cowboys and Cow Belles Enjoy the Barn Dance," Stand By, 8 February 1936, pp. 5, 11.

FOR FURTHER READING

Berry, Chad, ed. The Hayloft Gang: The Story of the National Barn Dance. Urbana and Chicago: University of Illinois Press, 2008.

Biggar, George C. "The WLS National Barn Dance Story: The Early Years." JEMF Quarterly 6 (1971): 105–12.

Fox, Pamela. Natural Acts: Gender, Race, and Rusticity in Country Music. Ann Arbor: University of Michigan Press, 2009.

McCusker, Kristine M. Lonesome Cowgirls and Honky-Tonk Angels: The Women of Barn Dance Radio. Urbana and Chicago: University of Illinois Press, 2008.

12

"No Hill Billies in Radio:

Ballads Are Still Written, Says John Lair" (1935)

As many country music historians have observed, some radio barn dance producers were heavy-handed in their efforts to craft narratives and iconography that invoked familiar rural stereotypes—the noble mountaineer, the genteel mother, the hillbilly rube, and the caricatured blackface minstrel.[1] While clearly popular with many of the listeners to these programs, these stereotypical images perpetuated many commonly held biases about rural Americans—and "hill people," more specifically—that were inextricably linked with notions of

---

1. See, for instance: Richard A. Peterson and Paul DiMaggio, "The Early Opry: Its Hillbilly Image in Fact and Fancy," *Journal of Country Music* 4 (Summer 1973): 42–44; Lisa Krissoff Boehm, "Chicago as Forgotten Country Music Mecca," in *The Hayloft Gang: The Story of the National Barn Dance*, ed. Chad Berry (Urbana and Chicago: University of Illinois Press, 2008), 103–107; Kristine M. McCusker, *Lonesome Cowgirls and Honky-Tonk Angels: The Women of Barn Dance Radio* (Urbana and Chicago: University of Illinois Press, 2008); Pamela Fox, *Natural Acts: Gender, Race, and Rusticity in Country Music* (Ann Arbor: University of Michigan Press, 2009), 17–62.

rural ignorance, poverty, and simplicity found in popular culture and folklore alike.[2] At the same time, these programs were forged in the crucible of a rapidly changing American society. The 1930s witnessed dramatic cultural changes as rural migrants left their rural farms for economic opportunities in the emerging cities of the American South, Midwest, and Southwest; those who remained on the farm struggled through the Great Depression; and immigrants from eastern and southern Europe attempted to understand their new country. It is likely that the stereotypes presented through the radio barn dances of the 1930s and 1940s played an integral, if problematic, role in those transitions.[3]

Perhaps no one in the barn dance community was more influential on the iconography and sounds of the nation's radio barn dances than John Lair (1894–1985). A native of Rockcastle County, Kentucky, he moved to Chicago, where, by the late 1920s, he became involved as a talent scout for WLS's *National Barn Dance* program, bringing the Cumberland Ridge Runners, Linda Parker, Lulu Belle Wiseman, and Lily May Ledford to the program. Lair also served as WLS's music librarian, where, as folklorist Michael Ann Williams has pointed out, he "was instrumental in helping to promote barn dance entertainment as 'folk' rather than 'hillbilly' music."[4] In his regular "Notes from the Library" column, published in the WLS newsletter *Stand By*, Lair discussed the rich tapestry of mountain music and worked to disentangle Tin Pan Alley—which not only signified cosmopolitanism but also invoked the racial difference associated with jazz—from the presumably white culture of the Cumberland Plateau.[5] The following interview provides one example of how Lair used the familiar stereotype of the noble mountaineer to differentiate between the

2. For further discussion of the complex relationship between folklore and barn dance programs, consult Michael Ann Williams, *Staging Tradition: John Lair and Sarah Gertrude Knott* (Urbana and Chicago: University of Illinois Press, 2006).

3. Jeffrey J. Lange, *Smile When You Call Me a Hillbilly: Country Music's Struggle for Respectability, 1939-1954* (Athens: University of Georgia Press, 2004), 39–40; Chad Berry, "Introduction: Assessing the National Barn Dance," in *The Hayloft Gang: The Story of the National Barn Dance*, ed. Chad Berry (Urbana and Chicago: University of Illinois Press, 2008), 11–15; Boehm, "Chicago as Forgotten Country Music Mecca," 103; Michael T. Bertrand, "Race and Rural Identity," in *The Hayloft Gang: The Story of the National Barn Dance*, ed. Chad Berry (Urbana and Chicago: University of Illinois Press, 2008), 130–52.

4. Michael Ann Williams, "Lair, John Lee," in *The Grove Dictionary of American Music*, 2nd ed., ed. Charles Hiroshi Garrett (New York and Oxford: Oxford University Press, 2013). For further discussion of Lair's work with Parker, Wiseman, and Ledford, consult chaps. 2, 3, and 5, respectively, of McCusker, *Lonesome Cowgirls and Honky-Tonk Angels*.

5. Williams, *Staging Tradition*, 45–47. Such a mixture of popular and traditional styles was quite common throughout the country. See, for instance, Charles K. Wolfe and Richard A. Peterson's respective discussions of the influence of pop styles on the *Grand Ole Opry* (Charles K. Wolfe, "Country Radio, 1920-50," in *Country: The Music and the Musicians from the Beginnings to the '90s* (New York: Abbeville Press, 1994), 50; Richard A. Peterson, *Creating Country Music: Fabricating Authenticity* (Chicago and London: University of Chicago Press, 1997), 139–44.

hillbilly musicians with whom he worked and the more "authentic" hillbillies of his eastern Kentucky home.[6]

===

HILL billies in radio? They ain't no sich thing.
Mountaineers and folk from the hill country, maybe, but no hill billies.

That's the startling statement of John Lair, impressario [sic] of the Cumberland Ridge Runners[7] and a national authority on folk music and lore.

"Tin Pan Alley hung this name on certain types of music and entertainers," says John, "and it may well be that Tin Pan Alley will kill them off, too, as far as popularity goes.

"The term 'hill billy' has come to be associated with a manner of singing rather than with the songs themselves. You could take a number like 'Home on the Range' or 'Old Folks at Home' and nasalize it in what has come to be known as 'hill billy' style.

"The fact is that if a radio microphone actually could pick up a real hill billy singing back in the hill country of the south, most listeners probably would tune out. The typical mountaineer who has never been out of the hills sings because he likes to. He's not too much concerned with how it sounds.

"Many of the songs which we call folk or traditional songs really were published years ago.[8] I have traced several to original prints but as the generations went by and the songs were handed down, many of the words were changed to fit local conditions.

"In the cases of old English ballads which are still sung in the hill country, I have found that in general the older the song, the less the singer knows about the words and their real meaning.[9]

"If you ask a typical back-country mountaineer what he means by knights and ladies mentioned in some of the old ballads, the chances are he'll say, 'I don't know. That's the way the song goes.'

"Thus it is easy to see how the songs are changed and local words and characters substituted."

6. D. K. Wilgus, "Current Hillbilly Recordings: A Review Article," *Journal of American Folklore* 78, no. 309 (July-September 1965): 274; Lange, *Smile When You Call Me a Hillbilly*, 27–28.

7. The Cumberland Ridge Runners (Slim Miller, Karl Davis, Harty Taylor, and Red Foley) performed instrumental tunes and songs on the *National Barn Dance* (William E. Lightfoot, "Belle of the Barn Dance: Reminiscing with Lulu Belle Wiseman Stamey," *Journal of Country Music* 12, no. 1 [1987]: 8; Paul L. Tyler, "The Rise of Rural Rhythm," in *The Hayloft Gang: The Story of the National Barn Dance* [Urbana and Chicago: University of Illinois Press, 2008], 34).

8. Evidence of this phenomenon is well documented in a variety of sources, most notably Guthrie T. Meade with Dick Spottswood and Douglas S. Meade, *Country Music Sources: A Biblio-Discography of Commercially Recorded Traditional Music* (Chapel Hill: Southern Folklife Collection, 2002).

9. This supposition is borne out by numerous studies of the "Child ballads," collected by English folklorist Cecil Sharp and published in *The English and Scottish Popular Ballads*, 10 vols. (Boston: Houghton Mifflin, 1882–98).

John says he can recall hearing "hill billy" or back-country hill folks on the radio only once. That was during a program on which Mrs. Franklin D. Roosevelt appeared, together with several elderly women from the Carolina mountains.[10]

The women sang a number of old English ballads in true ballad style, sad, nasal and with a peculiar lift or wail at the end of a line of verse. The ballads had been brought across the water a century and a half or more ago.

Asked why it appears that the songs of the hill folks are so often sad, John said, "It takes important events to stir an old-fashioned mountaineer to the point where he will compose a ballad. And, unfortunately, perhaps, most of the important events in their lives have been tragic.

"That accounts for the tendency to write ballads about feuds, hangings, executions, prisons, shootings and ambuscades [ambushes]. The deaths of children also were favorite themes, as are train and ship wrecks and mine explosions.

"Mere lack of specific knowledge does not discourage a ballad writer. He hears something about an event and makes up a song about it, supplying his own details where necessary.

"Ballad writing is still going on today. Already I have received several songs sent in by persons who dealt with the recent wreck of the dirigible Macon. The Akron and Shenandoah[11] crashes and the wreck of the Morro Castle[12] also were duly celebrated in ballads while Floyd Collins trapped in the cave[13] and the kidnaping [sic] of the Lindbergh baby gave rise to a wealth of sad songs.

10. Perhaps a broadcast from the 1933 White Top Festival, held in southwestern Virginia in mid-August 1933. See David E. Whisnant, *All That Is Native & Fine: The Politics of Culture in an American Region* (Chapel Hill and London: University of North Carolina Press, 1983), 191–94.

11. The *Akron* and the USS *Shenandoah* were both dirigible airships. The USS *Shenandoah* crashed in Ava, Ohio, on 3 September 1925, killing fourteen people. Vernon Dalhart recorded Carson Robison's "Wreck of the Shenandoah" nine times for more than a dozen labels between 9 September and 23 October 1925. The *Akron*, a dirigible airship, crashed during a storm at sea on 3 April 1933, killing 74 people. Three songs—Frances Sims's "Crash of the Akron," Bob Miller's "The Akron Disaster," and Frank Welling's "The Ill Fated Akron"—were recorded 5–13 April 1933 (Meade, Spottswood, and Meade, *Country Music Sources*, 78–81).

12. Bob Miller's "The Morrow [sic] Castle Disaster" (recorded by Ray Whitley for the Banner label on 17 September 1934) and Buck Nation's "The Ill Fated Morrow [sic] Castle" (recorded but never issued for Decca on 22 January 1935) describe the burning of the SS *Morro Castle*, a cruise ship owned by the Ward Line, off the coast of New Jersey on 8 September 1934, killing 137 passengers and crew (Gordon Thomas and Max Morgan Witts, *Shipwreck: The Strange Fate of the Morro Castle* [New York: Dell Publishing, 1973]; Meade, Spottswood, and Meade, *Country Music Sources*, 72).

13. Floyd Collins captured news headlines in February 1925 after he became trapped while exploring Kentucky's Mammoth Cave. Fiddlin' John Carson recorded his "The Death of Floyd Collins" for OKeh on 15 April 1925, and it was soon covered by the popular "citybilly" singer Vernon Dalhart, who first recorded it for Columbia on 27 May 1925 and, according to Tony Russell, "had recordings of 'The Death of Floyd Collins' on twenty-six labels" in 1925–26, selling as many as 300,000 copies of the song in only the Columbia release (Tony Russell, *Country Music Originals: The Legends and the Lost* [New York: Oxford University Press, 2007], 15). See also: Oland D. Russell, "Floyd Collins in the Sand Cave," *The American Mercury* 42 (September 1937): 289–97; and Robert K. Murray and Roger W. Brucker, *Trapped!: The Story of Floyd Collins*, rev. ed. (Lexington: University Press of Kentucky, 1982).

"As for love songs, well, they're generally sad, too. Either the loved one dies or runs off with someone else. If true love runs smooth and the happy pair gets married, the ballad writer doesn't seem to think that worthy of notice and he just forgets about it.

"To hear a real, honest to goodness mountaineer singing is rather difficult. You'd just about have to sneak up on him as he sits singing in a hollow or in a cabin doorway at sundown.

"The citizen of the hills sings because he likes to. He may not sing beautifully but he sings sincerely and he sings loudly.

"I once saw a Kentucky mountaineer's band advertised down there as having the world's loudest 'Yee-hooer.'"

Source: "No Hill Billies in Radio: Ballads Are Still Written, Says John Lair." *Prairie Farmer's New WLS Weekly,* 16 March 1935, p. 7.

FOR FURTHER READING

Berry, Chad, ed. *The Hayloft Gang: The Story of the National Barn Dance.* Urbana: University of Illinois Press, 2008.

Williams, Michael Ann. *Staging Tradition: John Lair and Sarah Gertrude Knott.* Urbana and Chicago: University of Illinois Press, 2006.

13

Alva Johnston

"Tenor on Horseback" (1939)

Cowboys played a prominent role in the highly successful dime novels of the late nineteenth century, and recording and radio artists had performed cowboy songs since the 1920s.[1] But, while cowboy lore, songs, and silent films were immensely popular fare in American culture prior to the Great Depression, the early 1930s witnessed what many scholars and fans would consider to be a golden age in western films.[2] During the Great Depression, Hollywood

---

1. Archie Green, "Midnight and Other Cowboys," *JEMF Quarterly* 11, no. 3 (Autumn 1975): 138–43; Archie Green, "Austin's Cosmic Cowboys: Words in Collision," in *"And Other Neighborly Names": Social Process and Cultural Image in Texas Folklore*, ed. Richard Bauman and Roger Abrahams, repr. in Archie Green, *Torching the Fink Books & Other Essays on Vernacular Culture* (Chapel Hill: University of North Carolina Press, 2001), 68–73; Douglas B. Green, *Singing in the Saddle: The History of the Singing Cowboy* (Nashville, TN: Country Music Foundation Press and Vanderbilt University Press, 2002), 1–19; Peter Stanfield, *Horse Opera: The Strange History of the 1930s Singing Cowboy* (Urbana: University of Illinois Press, 2002), 9–25.
2. For a detailed discussion of silent cowboy films, consult Stanfield, *Horse Opera*, chap. 2.

studios—including, most notably, Republic Pictures—developed a new kind of cowboy hero: a singing cowboy who, like a modern-day Orpheus, won hearts and minds not through extreme violence but through the power of his song.[3] Singing songs that were drawn from both the cowboy songs published in John Lomax's *Singing Cowboys and Other Frontier Ballads* (see chapter 3) and newly composed songs that were heavily inspired by contemporary pop songwriting trends, the singing cowboys—played by handsome, clean-cut actors in white hats—were frequently pitted against unscrupulous businessmen and corrupt ranchers in stories that took place in contemporary settings.[4] Speaking to the anxieties of the Depression era, these films offered audiences the hope that good would triumph over evil and that their communities could be restored to their pre-Depression greatness through populist activism while providing songs that they could sing along to as they left the theater.[5]

One of the most popular singing cowboys of the 1930s was Gene Autry, a singer who had begun his career imitating the "blue yodels" of Jimmie Rodgers and eventually landed at WLS's *National Barn Dance*, where he rose to national prominence.[6] As the following article by *Saturday Evening Post* contributor Alva Johnston indicates, Autry's popularity as a singer and an actor transcended generation and gender, drawing thousands of moviegoers to his films each weekend. As musicologist Stephanie Vander Wel has convincingly demonstrated, Autry may have even developed a vocal approach that borrowed from such contemporary crooners as Bing Crosby and Frank Sinatra in an effort to reach out to housewives who dutifully tuned into his radio programs and attended his films.[7] At the same time, as Johnston's article suggests, screenwriters walked a fine line between appealing to boys, who spent their pocket change on movie tickets and cap pistols and wanted to see action sequences, and adult women, many of whom wanted to see romantic tales on the screen. In the process, Republic and other studios developed an approach to the singing cowboy films that transformed the songs into key plot devices that softened the edges of the offending plotlines.

Johnston also draws attention to the vast merchandising opportunities that the singing cowboy stars could capitalize upon. Although radio performers had been selling songbooks and hawking recordings on the air for more than a decade by the time the singing cowboys rose to fame, Autry and others frequently translated their on-screen success into great personal wealth by licensing their likenesses and names to manufacturers who produced everything from lunch boxes to toy pistols. Autry's clean-cut, domesticated image—which,

3. Stanfield, *Horse Opera*, chap. 4.

4. Green, *Singing in the Saddle*, 20–68; Don Cusic, "Cowboys in Chicago," in *The Hayloft Gang: The Story of the National Barn Dance* (Urbana: University of Illinois Press, 2008), 168–86.

5. Stanfield, *Horse Opera*, 128–47.

6. For a detailed biography, consult Holly George-Warren, *Public Cowboy No. 1: The Life and Times of Gene Autry* (New York: Oxford University Press, 2007).

7. Stephanie Vander Wel, "The Lavender Cowboy and 'The She Buckaroo': Gene Autry, Patsy Montana, and Depression-Era Gender Roles," *The Musical Quarterly* 95, nos. 2–3 (December 2012): 207–51. See also Stanfield, *Horse Opera*, 119–24.

Johnston notes, he maintained in real life as well as on the screen—made him an ideal candidate for such merchandising deals, as manufacturers could rest assured that his songs and occasional action sequences would create a demand for such things among the boys, while his image and romantic appeal would not discourage mothers from spending their much-needed Depression-era money on such frivolities.[8]

———

J. T. Flagg, of Florence, Alabama, started out last year to find a national hero. Mr. Flagg is a manufacturer of sweat shirts and needs national heroes in his business. For years his leading number was the Babe Ruth sweat shirt, with a portrait of the great home-run king on its bosom.[9] Mr. Flagg has to have new national heroes when the old ones fade.

The truth is that there has been a grave shortage of demigods in recent years. Mr. Flagg was compelled to use a synthetic hero on his Gang Buster sweat shirt—a composite picture of all the G-Men. But he learned that the hero business calls for an individual, not a type. Mr. Flagg had to find a hero or confess that America had run out of then. Last December he was about to give up the hunt when a national hero was suddenly deposited on his doorstep. Gene Autry, the Singing Cowboy, came to town. Florence went wild. Flagg was taken by surprise when he learned that his home town was celebrating the arrival of the man who put the West back on the map.

The sweat-shirt king was cautious. He checked up by following Autry from town to town. Mobs of hero-worshippers turned out everywhere. A ten-year-old barefoot boy walked fourteen miles to Birmingham, Alabama, to see Gene and his horse, Champion. Mr. Flagg learned that the Singing Cowboy's mail sometimes numbered more than 12,000 letters a week, exceeding the fan mail of any other star.[10] His annual audience is more than 40,000,000. Police chiefs boost their safety campaigns by using Autry's name in appeals to children to be careful in crossing the streets.

After trailing the cowboy star to Nashville, Mr. Flagg proposed the Gene Autry sweat shirt. "I'm afraid you're too late," said Gene. "I think they sold my sweat-shirt rights to a chap in New York."[11]

New York was called on the telephone. It was found that the contract had not been signed.

8. Autry would later translate that image into a successful career as a businessman and political leader (Peter LaChapelle, *Proud to Be an Okie: Cultural Politics, Country Music, and Migration to Southern California* [Berkeley: University of California Press, 2007], 140–43).

9. George Herman "Babe" Ruth Jr. (1895–1948) played baseball for the Boston Red Sox, New York Yankees, and Boston Braves between 1914 and 1935, amassing a total of 714 home runs during that time ("Babe Ruth Baseball Stats by Baseball Almanac," http://www.baseball-almanac.com/players/player.php?p=ruthba01; accessed 28 January 2014).

10. The popularity of media celebrities in the 1920s and 1930s was frequently measured by the number of letters and cards they received from their fans.

11. A licensing agent.

"I'll raise the New York man's bid!" exclaimed Flagg. Flagg's offer was accepted and the deal concluded.

"By the way," asked Flagg, "who was the New York chap?"

"I don't know his name," said Autry, "but he was the representative of a firm called the Gardiner-Warring Company."

"What?" cried Flagg. "That's my firm. That man is my agent. And he didn't know enough to close a deal like that. Wait. I'll get him on the phone now."

It hurt the sweat-shirt king to realize that he had outbid himself. His New York agent defended himself.

"Most people here never heard of Gene Autry," he said.

The agent was right. The Singing Cowboy is little known in New York and the other big backward cities. The idol of the towns and crossroads, he is just beginning to make inroads into the metropolises.

THE NEMESIS OF DOUBLE-DYED BUSINESSMEN

The Autry sweat shirt is only one of many Autry articles on the hero market. Another is the Autry cap pistol, which was the cause of a civic celebration at Kenton, Ohio. On August 8, 1938, the whole town turned out to greet Gene as its economic rescuer. Factories were closed or running part-time in neighboring towns, but the Kenton Hardware Company was operating night and day, turning out Autry cap pistols, of which 2,000,000 have been sold. The Singing Cowboy's fan mail has been increased by letters complaining that he has turned every day into Fourth of July.

Autry's domination of the cap-pistol industry is remarkable, as Autry is one Western star who makes little use of firearms. He has no notches on his revolver. His public includes millions of women, and they won't have their boyish-looking, light-haired, blue-eyed, singing, guitar-playing hero engaged in homicide, no matter how justifiable. He has to bring the villains back alive.

Those who have not seen a Western in ten or fifteen years are greatly surprised when they take in an Autry film. The old frontier is pretty well settled now. Bill Hart wouldn't recognize it. There are more dude ranches than cattle ranches in the new Westerns. Rustlers, horse thieves, desperadoes, half-breeds[12] and greasers[13] are almost extinct; the villains are mainly businessmen. Gene's life is spent, not in outshooting bad hombres but in outwitting capitalists. He is a combination of Sherlock Holmes in a ten-gallon hat, Don Quixote with common sense, and Bing Crosby on horseback.

The plots are as up-to-date as newsreels. One, for example, concerns helium wells; another, the hoof-and-mouth disease. In one Autry picture the businessmen are promoting a

12. The term "half-breed" was derogatory, used to describe a child of mixed Native American and European American ancestry. For a useful discussion of the ways that "half-breeds" were depicted in literature, consult Peter G. Beidler, "The Indian Half-Breed in Turn-of-the-Century Short Fiction," *American Indian Culture and Research Journal* 9, no. 1 (1985): 1–12.

13. The term "greaser" was also a derogatory one, used to describe Mexicans and Mexican Americans. For a discussion of the "greaser" in early films, consult Helen Delpar, "Goodbye to the 'Greaser': Mexico, the MPPDA, and Derogatory Films, 1922-1926," *Journal of Popular Film and Television* 12, no. 1 (Spring 1984): 34–41.

fake Sun Valley; in another they are exploiting the natives with fraudulent plans for a super Boulder Dam; in another, selling tractors and stealing them back from the farmers by trick contracts. The dude ranch opens the door for scenes which would have caused Tom Mix to tear up his contract in indignation. Through the device of a dude ranch anything can be introduced into a modern horse opera, from a fashion show to a pillow fight or a literary tea.

The Gran Gaucho,[14] as Gene is called in South America, is partly the church's gift to the movies. When he was five years old his grandfather, the Rev. William T. Autry, Baptist minister of Tioga Springs, Texas, taught him to sing in order to make him useful in the choir. Twenty years later the Legion of Decency, by boycotting the standard sex films, compelled Hollywood to get some new ideas, and the singing cowboy was one of them.[15] Autry credits his success to the guitar, the noblest of instruments.

MUSIC HAS CHARMS TO SOOTHE A SAVAGE WEST

On learning that Lee O'Daniel, with the help of a hillbilly band, had been elected governor of Texas, Autry said: "It proves you can get anywhere with a guitar."[16]

Nat Levine, the Hollywood producer, practically invented the singing cowboy. Levine had been watching the Legion of Decency. He foresaw that the flaming-youth pictures would soon be cooled off and that the Westerns were the one type of film that was certain to survive the moral wave. The weakness of the Western is homicide, but homicide is not so contagious as other frailties. But the trouble with the old Westerns was that they had nearly worn out their public. The shoot-'em-up-and-lay-'em-out formula had been repeated thousands of times. Westerns all looked alike and sounded like riveting machines. One day in 1934 it occurred to Levine that a tuneful cowpuncher might be the prescription for a sick industry. He considered hundreds of candidates. Finally the field narrowed to three.

No. 1 was a Broadway trouper who could sing and act, but couldn't ride.
No. 2 was a Hollywood man who could ride and act, but couldn't sing.
No. 3 was Gene Autry, who could sing and ride, but couldn't act.

14. Spanish for "the Great Cowboy."

15. Founded in 1934, the Legion of Decency was a Catholic organization that sought to root out immorality in popular culture. For a more detailed discussion, consult Una M. Cadegan, "Guardians of Democracy or Cultural Storm Troopers? American Catholics and the Control of Popular Media, 1934-1966," *Catholic Historical Review* 87, no. 2 (April 2001): 252–82.

16. "Pappy" Lee O'Daniel managed the Light Crust Doughboys, a popular western swing band (see chapter 14). For more on O'Daniel, consult Jean A. Boyd, *"We're the Light Crust Doughboys from Burrus Mill": An Oral History* (Austin: University of Texas Press, 2003), 25–42.

Similarly, Louisiana musician Jimmie Davis translated his musical fame into political success during the 1930s and 1940s. See, for instance, Kevin S. Fontenot, "You Can't Fight a Song: Country Music in the Campaigns of Jimmie Davis," *Journal of Country Music* 25, no. 2 (2007): 50–59; Kevin S. Fontenot, "Sing It Good, Sing It Strong, Sing It Loud: The Music of Governor Jimmie Davis," in *Shreveport Sounds in Black and White*, ed. Kip Lornell and Tracey E. W. Laird (Jackson: University Press of Mississippi, 2007), 46–57.

No. 1 was appearing on Broadway in Gilbert and Sullivan. The fact that he could not ride was not greatly to his disadvantage. In a couple of months he could be taught to stick in the saddle on a quiet horse, while doubles did the fancy riding for him.

No. 2 was a good actor and rider, and his inability to sing was not a fatal defect. He could fake lip motions and pretend to hack away at strings, while the music was dubbed in by real musicians.

Levine, however, decided on Autry. Gene already had a large radio and phonograph following. He was the country's most popular singer of cowboy ditties. The fact that he couldn't act was at first considered a negligible flaw, and later an asset. Like Gary Cooper and Jimmy Stewart, Autry has the kind of awkwardness and embarrassment that audiences like.

Gene was first tried out in a small part. Letters came to the Republic studio criticizing the picture because there was so little Autry in it. Levine next used Gene in a story called The Phantom Empire. In this the cowboy wandered a few thousand miles underground into a mythical kingdom and had some thrilling adventures with his lasso and guitar.

Levine then called in producer Armand Schaeffer and outlined the plan to star Autry in Westerns. Shaeffer went home and said to his wife, "I'm going to quit."

Schaeffer thought that his boss' idea was ridiculous. So did everybody else at the Republic studio. It was considered idiotic to try to turn a Western into a music festival. A Western was fifty or sixty minutes of furious action. How could it be interrupted four or five times for guitar recitals? Audiences asked for gunplay, and Levine wanted to give them crooning. As for Autry himself, he lacked the toughness of a Western star. The traditional Western hero was a bad man turned straight, while Autry was an attractive juvenile, soft-voiced and peaceful-looking.

Producer Schaeffer was dissuaded from quitting by Mrs. Schaeffer. He discovered later that Gene's liabilities could be converted into assets. The songs, instead of interrupting the story and making audiences lose interest, were written to push the plot forward. Autry ditties saw mobs like Mark Antony speeches. In one picture, Autry sings a message to a pal in prison, as Blondel did to Richard the Lionhearted. In other pictures Gene uses his ballads to unmask crooks. He sings good citizens into fury and villains into desperation.

In Mexicali Rose, the wicked businessmen are promoting fake oil stock. They hire radio time for Gene, and he sings of the millions of dollars to be made in black gold. Suspecting that his voice and guitar are being used for a bad purpose, he does his detective act, uncovers the fraud, and gets the money back for the suckers.

In Tumbling Tumbleweeds, a song was used to decoy and trap the villains. They had committed a murder. A wounded pal of Gene was the only witness against them, so they planned to kill Gene and his pal. They approach Gene's cabin and hear him singing to his wounded comrade. Under a partly drawn window curtain they see what appears to be a guitar player in a rocking chair. The heavies slip around to the door of the cabin and start shooting. The figure in the rock chair and another figure in a bunk take no notice as several bullets pass through them. The villains investigate. They find that Gene has arranged the blankets in the bunk to look like a man, and has rigged up a dummy with a guitar in the chair. As they make the discovery, they find themselves covered with the revolvers of Gene and others. Gene, hiding himself in a corner of the cabin, had kept the dummy rocking with a cord ties to his foot, while he played and sang. The song had played its usual double role as melody and incident, entertainment and plot construction.

The fact that women formed about one half of Autry's public dictated another revolution in the Westerns. The Battle-of-Gettysburg and the Custer's-Last-Stand effects had to be eliminated. This compelled a search for new plot material. The Wild West of Buffalo Bill's day and Billy the Kid's day disappeared. Crimes of cunning were largely substituted for crimes of violence. High-pressure salesmen and financial pirates became the villains, and Gene became a sort of one-man Better Business Bureau of the open spaces.

Jerry Geraghty, who writes most of the Autry scripts, watches the newspapers of the West for modern situations which can be used for the Singing Cowboy. A sensational development at Muroc Dry Lake near Barstow, California, is now being converted into an Autry picture. The United States Army acquired land in the Muroc Dry Lake region for use as a bombing field. In order to round out the tract, the Army needed to purchase tens of thousands of acres from farmers and others. Some of the private owners wanted ten times the price the Government offered, and formed an association to take the matter into court. The Army could not postpone the training of its flyers until the law had taken its course. It started dropping bombs while many farmers and other residents stuck to their properties. Cattle, which stampeded and ran for miles at every bombing, became skin and bones. Laying hens were killed when eggs broke inside of them. Children became nervous wrecks.

The facts had to be revised for picture purposes. The Army cannot be the villain. National defense is more important than the rights of individuals. Businessmen were naturally introduced for the dirty work. They discover great borax deposits in the properties the Government was seeking to buy. Autry foils the Borax Trust. He fixes it so that the Army gets the bombing field, the farmers get the borax, and the businessmen go to jail.

In The Man From Music Mountain, crooked businessmen exhibit blueprints indicating how they are going to transform a ghost town into a flourishing metropolis. They sell town lots to the natives. Gene discovers that it is a fraud. He stages a fake gold rush in the ghost town. Thinking the townsite is a bonanza, the crooked businessmen try to buy it back. At this point the fake gold strike turns into a real gold strike. The chase, which is still a feature of the modern Western, begins. Autry outrides the villains and causes the natives to hold on to their gold-bearing town lots.

THE IDEAL VILLAIN

Hollywood had nothing against businessmen, but it has to use them as villains, not only in the Autry pictures but in a large proportion of the film output. The picture magnates can't use foreigners as villains, because foreigners are sensitive. They can't recruit many villains from the professions, because the professions are sensitive. They try to avoid using politicians as villains, because politicians are sensitive. Hence the villain field has practically narrowed down to businessmen. It is even becoming necessary to pick businessmen with care. All minorities are sensitive. Hollywood quit heckling minorities twelve years ago, after riots greeted McFadden's Flats. The villainous businessman cannot belong to a sensitive minority. The ideal villain of today should be white, Protestant, native-born of native parents, of Anglo-Saxon stock, and engaged in business, preferably banking.

The love angle in the Autry pictures is handled with caution. Gene is the least demonstrative Romeo in the films. No clinches[17] are allowed in the Singing Cowboy pictures. He

17. Embraces.

can put his arm around the heroine's waist only if necessary to save her from falling over a cliff. Gene's romantic life is strictly chaperoned because of the large element of boys of grammar-school age in his audience. They cannot perceive what interest a real man like Autry can have in anything in skirts or jodhpurs.[18]

An Autry audience consists mainly of romance-loving women and romance-hating boys; it requires skillful compromises to please both. Gene can take out his guitar and sing a song to the heroine[;] he can't throw dying-calf looks in her direction. The love interest has to be laid on thick for the ladies; it has to be disguised as hate for the boys. It is absolutely necessary to placate Autry's young male public. An audience of 500 may be dying over a love scene; one raspberry causes 500 melting hearts to freeze.

One boy with a resounding hoot can change a mass emotional revel into a mass sneer. Every Autry scene has to be so written as to appease the raucous little woman haters.

HE TREATS DAMES ROUGH

Gene pleases his subadolescent fans when he is girl-shy. It strikes a sympathetic chord in them. They roar with understanding laughter when, after a sheepish moment in the presence of a glamour girl, he slinks for the nearest exit. On the other hand, they never like Gene better than when he is putting an insolent young thing in her place. They approve of their hero's policy of never letting a dame bully him. In Git Along, Little Dogies, the heroine drives her car through a pool of oil, splashes Gene from head to foot and then laughs at him. Gene jumps on Champion, chases the auto and brings it to a stop by shooting a tire. The heroine states that he is no gentleman. Gene puts a bullet through another tire. She attacks him. Gene picks her up and drops her into a brook. Gene cannot raise a hand to a girl by way of kindness, but he can toss her around to almost any extent in anger. After dropping her in the water, he is allowed to be slightly contrite. He lets the girl talk him into putting on the spare tires. While he is at work, she jumps on Champion and rides away. The girl-despising generation relishes all this, while the grownups see that the foundation is being laid for a beautiful romance.

In another picture the love interest starts with a misunderstanding and some cutting words between Gene and the gorgeous young postmistress. The exchange of insults is cut short by the whistle of the mail train. They run for it. Gene accidentally slams the door, so that the post-mistress' skirt is caught. A locksmith has to be summoned to release her in the presence of a giggling crowd. She thinks Gene did it a-purpose. This establishes hate which slowly changes to love.

Often circumstances lead Gene to think that the heroine is a spy, or she suspects him of being a businessman. Chivalry creeps in only when the heroine is in deadly peril. Reconciliation arrives in the last reel, but without hammer locks or half nelsons.[19] If Gene and the girl ride off together, Gene singing a song, that is the maximum concession to Cupid.

Plans were made once or twice to change Gene from a Western star to an all-around romantic. He would not listen to it. He said, "A cowboy, if he doesn't let his public down, is good until he is fifty years old. A matinee idol doesn't last five years."

18. Riding pants.
19. Wrestling maneuvers.

But if M-G-M has its way, it will move him into the big-leagues this fall, casting him in a remake of Will Rogers' best silent picture, Jubilo.[20]

Autry had been singing for twenty years before Hollywood picked him up. He made his first professional appearance in his teens, singing songs at a Tioga night spot, where he was paid by collections usually amounting to about fifty cents a night. His fame reached the ears of Professor Fields, of the Fields Brothers' Medicine Show. The boy obtained a three months' engagement at fifteen dollars a week to soften up audiences with pathetic ballads before the Professor began selling Fields' Pain Annihilator.

Gene's ambition was to sing and accompany himself on a saxophone, but it was years before he could acquire one of those expensive instruments. His father had taken a cattle ranch near Achille, Oklahoma. One of Gene's chores was driving cattle to the railroad station. Getting work as a roustabout at the station, he studied telegraphy and at seventeen years became a regular operator. Working the graveyard shift, from midnight until eight A.M., Gene found plenty of time to practice. He had bought a saxophone for seventy-five dollars on the installment plan, but the first time he tried it he met with a great disappointment. He had overlooked the point that it is a physical impossibility for a singer to accompany himself on a saxophone. Gene tried playing and singing alternately, but could not get the effect he desired. The turning point of his life came the day he traded the sax for a guitar. He soon became so good that he won an official rebuke from the division headquarters of the Frisco Railroad, because operators up and down the line were listening in while Gene played and sang into the telephone.

Autry worked at different stations all over the Frisco Lines—Tulsa, Sapulpa, Claremore, Catoosa, Afton, Vinita, among others. One night at Chelsea, Oklahoma, a man who came in with a telegram saw the guitar and asked Autry for ["]They Plowed the Old Trail Under.["] Gene obliged. Then the customer took the guitar and sang ["]Casey Jones.["] After the customer's departure Autry picked up the telegram, found it signed "Will Rogers," and had a belated attack of stage fright. Rogers came in with telegrams several times after that and stayed for hillbilly workouts. He gave Autry cautious encouragement.

"I think you have something," he said. "Work hard at it and you may get somewhere."

EX-"SIGNALER AND TELEPHONIST"

Nowadays, when Autry is on a tour of personal appearances, he is called on daily to appraise amateur talent. If he is really impressed, he gives cautious encouragement. His formula is about as follows:

"You may have something. Work hard at it. If you make good here, go to the next big town. Don't ever think of going to Hollywood. If you get to be good, Hollywood will find you."

For three years Gene was a telegrapher—"a signaler and telephonist," as the official organ of the British Gene Autry Fan Club described him. He later became a train dispatcher, a ticket agent and a yardmaster.

Autry knew Johnny Marvin, for years a famous radio and phonograph star. Inspired by Marvin, Gene went to New York in 1928 and called at the Victor offices. For a long time he sat in an anteroom without being able to get an audition. Finally he gave himself one. Taking his guitar out of the case, he began to play and sing. Nat Shilkret, a Victor official, happened to

---

20. Will Rogers (1879–1935) was a popular entertainer and comedian. For more information, consult Ben Yagoda, *Will Rogers: A Biography* (New York: Knopf, 1993).

walk through the anteroom and gave Gene a trial. Shilkret's verdict was: "You've got a voice, but you haven't had enough experience with the microphone. Go back and get on the radio. Work hard for a year and then come back here."

Shilkret gave Autry a to-whom-it-may-concern letter saying he had marvelous possibilities. Through this letter Gene's cowboy songs became a regular feature of the KVOO station at Tulsa. Gene had to get a job on the railroad to support himself; the idea of paying for radio talent had not at that time become popular in the Southwest.

Arthur Satherley, vice president of the American Record Corporation, picked Autry as a coming star and started making Autry records. In his last days on the railroad, Gene had been writing his own songs. During the Al Jolson, or Mammy Song, era, Gene had reversed the trend.[21] With the collaboration of Jimmy Long, a train dispatcher, he wrote ["]That Silver-Haired Daddy of Mine,["] a song which gave male parents some standing in the community. Thirty thousand records of Gene's rendition of this song were sold during the first month, and more than 300,000 all together. About seventy-five Autry records are on the market, and in total sales they have outsold Bing Crosby's. Autry has written, or collaborated in writing, more than 300 songs.

Gene made such a hit as an unpaid star at KVOO that WLS in Chicago drafted him at thirty-give dollars a week. From 1930 to 1934 he was a WLS headliner. He took his act, the National Barn Dance, on a tour of motion-picture theaters in the Middle West. He played the Tivoli Theater in Danville, Illinois, in 1932. Either in discouragement or playfulness, he wrote in big letters on his dressing-room door, "GENE AUTRY, AMERICA'S BIGGEST FLOP." Today the door, framed under glass, appears in the theater lobby with the legend:

"This is a door taken from a dressing room backstage of the Tivoli Theater, upon which Gene Autry painted the above inscription when he appeared with Jimmy Long in person on the Tivoli Theater stage, March 19-20, 1932."

Gene's fan mail has risen above 12,000 letters in a week and seldom drops below 2000. It spurts just after a picture comes out. The news that Autry, who does not smoke, had refused a $3000 offer to endorse a cigarette, filled the mailbags with letters of commendation. A grateful note came from Hugo R. Awtrey, of Richmond, Virginia, who has wasted most of his life in a vain effort to get people to pronounce his name right; his last name is pronounced the same as Gene's, and today he has no trouble. A Spokane woman wrote that she and her husband were considering divorce because they had no tastes in common, but they both went mad about Autry and now live in bliss. A mother wrote that the problem of getting her son to wash behind the ears had been solved when he saw Gene scrub his neck in one of his pictures. A letter of complaint came from L. R. Creason, proprietor of a picture house of Eufaula, Oklahoma, who wrote that the Autry pictures were a nuisance because children came at 10:30 A.M. and stayed for more than six hours.

When Autry went on strike for a higher salary,[22] one of his worshipers wrote to Congressman Jack Nichols, of Oklahoma, urging him to pass a law compelling the picture

21. Al Jolson (1886–1950) was an internationally renowned vaudeville and film actor and popular recording artist. For a detailed discussion of Jolson's career and its place within broader discourses about race in early twentieth-century America, consult Michael Rogin, *Blackface, White Noise: Jewish Immigrants in the Hollywood Melting Pot* (Berkeley: University of California Press, 1996).

22. Autry went on strike for a higher salary in 1938 (George-Warren, *Public Cowboy No. 1*, 169–73).

company to meet Autry's terms and put a stop to the terrible famine of Autry pictures. Gene's salary strikes resulted in compromises with substantial salary boosts. But today his salary is less than his income from Autry sweat shirts, cap pistols, holsters, spurs, hats, chaps, cartridge belts, games, comic strips, shaving creams, hair oils and toy balloons; not to mention papier-mâché statuettes and the Autry Stampede Suit, which is advertised as "Western Made for Western Men."

A HORSE GONE HOLLYWOOD

Autry has a gift for keeping his friendships in repair. He is the most famous telegrapher since Edison, but is still in touch with many of his Morse-code friends of the Frisco Lines. His greatest concentration of fans is in the territory served by the Frisco. Johnny Marvin, who encouraged Gene to turn professional, is today Gene's collaborator in writing Western songs. Smiley Burnette, originally the accordion player of Gene's radio outfit, has been the fat comic relief in every Autry picture and is today one of the funniest men in the Westerns. Smiley's genius has been recognized by the publication of his portrait on the lid of the Dixie ice-cream cup. In 1930 Gene received his first important write-up from George Goodale, a reporter on the Tulsa World; as soon as Gene began to get somewhere in Hollywood, he hired Goodale as his publicity man and manager.

Goodale found himself public-relations counselor to a horse. He has lodged Champion in the presidential suites in some of the best hotels in the country. Now and then Champion trots into a barber shop for a manicure. Autry himself has never had a chance to go Hollywood, because his pictures cost only $75,000 to make; Hollywood takes notices only of people in $1,000,000 productions. Gene's sensational Western costumes attract no attention in Hollywood, nearly everybody else being as fantastically garbed as he. The way to get stared at in Hollywood is to wear an ordinary business suit. Champion, on the other hand, has gone Hollywood. He knows that he is a distinguished horse. As the poet, Charles MacGregor, puts it in his ode to Champion in the British Gene Autry Fan Club Magazine:

> Who is this horse with kingly mien,
>
> Carrying proudly his master, Gene?

Champion, like a typical Hollywood star, burns up when a fuss is made over anybody else. If a stranger scratches another horse's nose in Autry's corral, Champion strides up and corrects the stranger's mistake by stretching out his own nose. On location and on personal-appearance tours, Champion travels in a big red truck; his personal attendant sleeps between him and the driver's seat. When he feels that it is high time for a fuss to be made over him, Champion picks up a mouthful of straw and drops it on his body servant, who has to wake up and tell Champion, by words or action, that he is the greatest equine star in the world. They say that Champion has the star psychology so developed that he likes to watch himself in the pictures.

Champion's menace is Pal, a horse with a brilliant metallic luster. Pal might have been dipped in Pactolus;[23] he looks like a solid gold horse with platinum nose and feet. Trotting over

---

23. A Turkish river where the legendary King Midas is thought to have lost his "golden touch" (Anna Baldwin, "Midas," in *Encyclopedia Mythica*, http://www.pantheon.org/articles/m/midas.html [accessed 9 Mary 2014]).

a distant hill in the sunlight, he gleams like the dome of a state capitol. Gene is reserving Pal for Technicolor.

Source: Alva Johnston, "Tenor on Horseback," *Saturday Evening Post* 212, no. 10 (2 September 1939): 18–19, 74–76. (*"Tenor on Horseback"* article © SEPS licensed by Curtis Licensing, Indianapolis, IN. All rights reserved.)

FOR FURTHER READING

Stanfield, Peter. *Horse Opera: The Strange History of the 1930s Singing Cowboy.* Urbana: University of Illinois Press, 2002.

Green, Douglas B. *Singing in the Saddle: The History of the Singing Cowboy.* Nashville, TN: Country Music Foundation Press and Vanderbilt University Press, 2002.

George-Warren, Holly. *Public Cowboy No. 1: The Life and Times of Gene Autry.* New York: Oxford University Press, 2007.

Vander Wel, Stephanie. "The Lavender Cowboy and 'The She Buckaroo': Gene Autry, Patsy Montana, and Depression-Era Gender Roles." *The Musical Quarterly* 95, nos. 2–3 (December 2012): 207–51.

14

George D. Hay

A Story of the Grand Old Opry (1945)

The longest-running radio barn dance program, WSM's *Grand Ole Opry*, made its broadcast debut in November 1925. Founded by former WLS staff announcer George D. Hay (known as the "Solemn Old Judge"), the *Opry* was conceived as a loosely formatted program that, as *Opry* historian Charles K. Wolfe has described, was intended to give listeners the impression "that every Saturday night a bunch of good ole boys would bring their fiddles and banjos into the big city and sit around picking tunes."[1] Whereas the staff of WLS's *National Barn Dance* frequently depicted their cast members as rural folks living in the big city, Hay emphasized the rusticity of the *Opry*'s acts, giving caricatured sobriquets to groups such as the Gully Jumpers and the Fruit Jar Drinkers and encouraging artists to adopt hillbilly attire for publicity photographs.[2] Yet, like Lair and Kincaid,

1. Charles K. Wolfe, *A Good-Natured Riot: The Birth of the Grand Ole Opry* (Nashville, TN: Country Music Foundation Press and Vanderbilt University Press, 1999), 15–16.
2. Wolfe, *Good-Natured Riot*, 15; Richard A. Peterson, *Creating Country Music: Fabricating Authenticity* (Chicago and London: University of Chicago Press,

Hay was also convinced that the music of rural Americans (and residents of the Appalachians and Ozarks, in particular) offered a point of connection between the modern world of radio, records, and automobiles and the agrarian lifestyles of nineteenth-century Americans. In the following excerpt, Hay relates a likely apocryphal story about a trip to the Missouri-Arkansas Ozarks that shaped his vision for the *Grand Ole Opry*.

═══════

HERE we are well past the middle of our story of the Opry and we haven't told how the idea came to us. Many times we do not realize just how ideas are unfolded. The Opry idea came from the blue and the green,—the blue of an Arkansas sky and the green of the Ozarks in midsummer. There is a little town that skirts the Missouri line, called Mammoth Spring. The spring itself, from which the town got its name, is really a small lake. It is said to be one of the largest open springs in the world. The water is almost icy cold. Near it there is a large country hotel, well appointed, where people of the old South came to spend the summers. They still do. Mammoth Spring is one of the most typical small towns in America. Perhaps that is why we got the idea out of the blue and put it on the green, because the Opry is a common denominator of all of the small communities in America—letting off steam on Saturday night.[3]

The Commercial Appeal, of Memphis, Tennessee, sent your reporter, who was one of its reporters, to the Ozarks to cover the funeral of one of America's World War One heroes. He was the son of a farmer, who was a one hundred percent American. We rode behind a mule team thirty miles up in the mountains from Mammoth Spring, leaving very early in the morning. It was a beautiful day. The neighbors came from miles around in respect to the memory of this United States Marine who gave his life to preserve their way of life. The young man's father welcomed them as he stood on the crude platform in the country churchyard, but closed his brief remarks in this manner: "Let all those who were against the government during the war pass on down the road."[4] We didn't see anyone leave. The minister conducted the services[,] and the neighbors drove their mules and cars silently down the road. It was a very impressive scene at the end of a day when rural Americans took the time out to check up on their lives.

1997), 67–94; Anthony Harkins, *Hillbilly: A Cultural History of an American Icon* (New York and London: Oxford University Press, 2004), 80–81.

3. The widespread acceptance of the *Grand Ole Opry* can likely be attributed to a variety of factors, ranging from the NBC network's broadcast of a selected live segments and WSM's status as a "clear-channel" radio station, which granted it sole national access to its frequency, 650 kHz.

4. The Missouri and Arkansas Ozarks were, as Ozarks historian Brooks Blevins has noted, "sharply divided between northern and southern sympathies" during the Civil War, transforming the region into "a dangerous, lawless land abandoned not only by the men going to war but also by scores of their families looking for safer homes free from the unofficial bands of Union and Confederate sympathizers who sought out their enemies and their enemies' families in the isolated backcountry" (Brooks Blevins, *Hill Folks: A History of Arkansas Ozarks and Their Image* [Chapel Hill and London: University of North Carolina Press, 2002], 31).

We lumbered back to Mammoth Spring and filed our story[,] which drew an editorial from the able pen of one of the South's greatest newspaper men, Col. C. P. J. Mooney.[5] One of Mr. Mooney's primary objects in life was to help improve the lives of farmers in the South.

We spent a day in Mammoth Spring. It is a beautiful spot for rest and quiet. In the afternoon[,] we sauntered around the town, at the edge of which hard by the Missouri line there lived a truck farmer[6] in an old railroad car. He had seven or eight children and his wife seemed to be very tired with the tremendous job of caring for them. We chatted for a few minutes[,] and the man went to his place of abode and brought forth a fiddle and a bow. He invited me to attend a "hoe-down" the neighbors were going to put on that night until "the crack o' dawn" in a log cabin about a mile up a muddy road. He and two other old time musicians furnished the earthy rhythm. About twenty people came. There was a coal oil lamp in one corner of the cabin and another one in the "kitty corner."[7] No one in the world has ever had more fun than those Ozark mountaineers did that night. It stuck with me until the idea became The Grand Ole Opry seven or eight years later. It is as fundamental as sunshine and rain, snow and wind[,] and the light of the moon peeping through the trees. Some folks like it and some dislike it very much, but it'll be there long after you and I have passed out of this picture for the next one.

Source: George D. Hay, *A Story of the Grand Old Opry* (Nashville: self-published, 1945), 35–37.

FOR FURTHER READING

Escott, Colin. *The Grand Ole Opry: The Making of an American Icon.* New York: Center Street Books, 2006.

Fox, Pamela. *Natural Acts: Gender, Race, and Rusticity in Country Music.* Ann Arbor: University of Michigan Press, 2009.

Peterson, Richard A. *Creating Country Music: Fabricating Authenticity.* Chicago and London: University of Chicago Press, 1997.

Wolfe, Charles K. *A Good-Natured Riot: The Birth of the Grand Ole Opry.* Nashville, TN: Country Music Foundation Press and Vanderbilt University Press, 1999.

5. Mooney was a long-time managing editor of the Memphis *Commercial-Appeal*, the newspaper for which Hay wrote. A brief biographical sketch of Mooney is available in Boyce House, *Cub Reporter, Being Mainly about Mr. Mooney and the Commercial Appeal* (Dallas: Hightower Press, 1947), 125–39.

6. A farmer who sells his/her wares from a truck alongside the road.

7. The opposite corner.

15

Janis Stout

"The Light Crust Doughboys Were on the
Air: A Memoir" (1996)

During the 1930s, swing music dominated the popular music landscape in
the United States, with such celebrated bands as those led by Chick Webb,
Duke Ellington, Count Basie, Jimmie Lunceford, and Benny Goodman transmitting regular broadcasts across recently established national radio networks.[1]
Much like rock and hip hop in later generations, the swing style manifested
itself in a variety of ways around the country, and many times, local swing musicians forged musical hybrids that blended swing with important local musical
practices.

Such was certainly the case with the western swing bands that flourished in
Texas, Oklahoma, and California during the 1930s and 1940s. Merging contemporary

---

1. For an in-depth discussion of the so-called Swing Era, consult George T. Simon,
The Big Bands, 4th ed. (New York: Schirmer Books, 1981); Gunther Schuller, *The Swing
Era: The Development of Jazz, 1930–1945* (New York: Oxford University Press, 1989);
and Thomas J. Hennessey, *From Jazz to Swing: African-American Jazz Musicians and
Their Music, 1890-1935* (Detroit, MI: Wayne State University Press, 1994).

swing and blues, traditional Anglo-American fiddling from Texas and Oklahoma, and the rich vernacular musics of Texas's Czech, German, Mexican, and Cajun communities, western swing bands catered to a predominantly working-class white audience that enjoyed dancing in large dancehalls.[2] Western swing bands frequently performed popular songs that originated in the jazz and blues domains, and musicians were commonly called upon to improvise solos, leading some musicians and scholars to argue that western swing should be considered the exclusive province of jazz history.[3] Yet, as Janis Stout's memoir of listening to the Light Crust Doughboys—the first and longest running western swing band—indicates, western swing musicians also played the same old-time tunes that were popular with hillbilly fans throughout the United States and Canada, suggesting that the musicians had at least some affinity for country music, as well.

The Light Crust Doughboys were founded in Fort Worth, Texas by Milton Brown, Herman Arnspiger, and Bob Wills, in 1931. Sponsored by Burris Mill, a flour company, and managed by future Texas governor W. Lee "Pappy" O'Daniel, the group made the first western swing recordings in 1932 and went on to great regional fame. The group went through numerous iterations over the years, often introducing new musical practices and repertories as the personnel of the band have changed over its more than eight-decade history, and the group continues to perform today.[4] Stout's memoir is noteworthy because it documents what it was like to spend her childhood watching her father, a fiddler with the Light Crust Doughboys, play in one of the most popular musical groups in Texas. Through the eyes of a child, it is possible to see the music-making she witnessed as a natural outgrowth of the unique multicultural environment of Texas.

THEY came on the airwaves at noon, first the theme song, "We're the Light Crust Doughboys...from Burris Mills," then the announcer booming out, "The Light Crust

2. See, for instance, Jean A. Boyd, *Jazz of the Southwest: An Oral History of Western Swing* (Austin: University of Texas Press, 1998), 1–2; Jean A. Boyd, *"We're the Light Crust Doughboys from Burrus Mill": An Oral History* (Austin: University of Texas Press, 2003), 2–12. For an extended discussion of the multicultural roots of Texas music, consult Lawrence Clayton and Joe W. Specht, eds., *The Roots of Texas Music* (College Station: Texas A&M University Press, 2003); and Gary Hartman, *The History of Texas Music* (College Station: Texas A&M University Press, 2008).

3. This belief is an undercurrent of much of Jean Boyd's work on western swing, especially in the musical analyses presented throughout her *Dance All Night: Those Other Southwestern Swing Bands, Past and Present* (College Station: Texas A&M University Press, 2012) and the oral histories collected in her *The Jazz of the Southwest*. Moreover, jazz historian Dave Oliphant treats the western swing band Milton Brown and His Musical Brownies in his *Jazz Mavericks of the Lone Star State* (Austin: University of Texas Press, 2007), 149–57.

4. The best history of the Light Crust Doughboys can be found in Boyd's *"We're the Light Crust Doughboys from Burrus Mill."*

Doughboys are on the air!" How many are left, I wonder, who remember tuning in every day and hearing that jingle?

Along with Bob Wills & the Texas Playboys, and the jazzier Milton Brown & the Musical Brownies, and incorporating along the way some of the straight western style of the Sons of the Pioneers, the Light Crust Doughboys originated what is known as western swing. My dad, Ken Pitts, was one of them. He played fiddle and did their arranging for about fifteen years, starting in the early thirties. My childhood was lived among echoes of that fact. And just a couple of years ago[,] four of the old Doughboys came to play at his funeral—"Riding Down the Canyon to Watch the Sun Go Down" and a fiddle breakdown like Dad used to play himself. It seemed fitting.

The Doughboys made recordings, personal appearances, and two movies. But their chief claim to fame was their daily fifteen-minute radio show broadcast in Texas, Louisiana, Arkansas, and Oklahoma. One of my early memories is of being on the show—sitting in the studio with my mother and seeing the yellow STAND BY light switch to the red ON THE AIR while they started playing the theme song and their announcer, Parker Wilson, came in with the intro above the music. Radio was live in those days.

Part of the formula for the Doughboys' enormous popularity was personalizing the band. Each player had an established personality, and they all had nicknames—Dad was "Abner," Marvin Montgomery "Zeke." People followed them like friends of the family. So it was not *quite* so ludicrous as it sounds that at the age of six, already a veteran of two years of piano lessons, I was brought on to play my recital piece.

I remember sitting there while they went through the show and being *real* quiet, then being hushed when I forgot—a fifteen-minute show seemed *so* long. And then settling myself on the piano bench and saying something into the microphone when Parker Wilson asked me a question, trying, no doubt, to make this cute. And then I played my little piece, and then there was the closing theme and the red ON THE AIR went off and I could talk again.

The Light Crust Doughboys came together in Fort Worth in the early thirties. The name, of course, was a pun evoking both the U.S. Expeditionary Force of World War I[5] and the fact that the band was a publicity device touting Light Crust flour for Fort Worth's Burrus Mills. "Bring on the biscuits, Pappy" became their familiar tag line—"Pappy" being W. Lee O'Daniel, their original impresario and announcer, who later rode the wave of the group's popularity into the governor's mansion and the U.S. Senate.

Dad was not one of the originals. I used to tell people he was, until I found out better from some jacket notes on a three-record set of LPs that Marvin and Knocky Parker, the group's phenomenal piano player, put together in later years. I found these when I was clearing out my parents' house, along with a discography also put together by Marvin, a rough memoir Dad had written, and one of his old Doughboys shirts, laundered, starched, and folded in a plastic bag.

When the band started in 1931 they were a threesome of Bob Wills, Milton Brown, and Herman Arnspiger. Wills left in '33 [sic] to form the even more successful Texas Playboys, working first in Waco and then up in Oklahoma.[6] Maybe being from Texas counted for more

5. The members of the U.S. Expeditionary Force were known as "doughboys."

6. Wills moved to Tulsa, Oklahoma, in 1934, where he and His Texas Playboys rose to prominence through their broadcasts on radio station KVOO and their performances at Cain's Dancing Academy. For more, consult chaps. 8–12 of Charles R. Townsend, *San Antonio Rose: The Life and Music of Bob Wills* (Urbana: University of Illinois Press, 1976).

in Oklahoma. How things developed during those years is a little sketchy, but by 1935 the Doughboys had grown to nine and "Abner" was one of them.

He was already an experienced radio musician, having played on the air, sometimes for pay and sometimes not, with a group of friends from high school calling themselves the Southern Melody Boys. This group—Dad, another fine violinist, Cecil Brower, a bass player named Hubert Barham, and a guitarist, Bob Wren—had played around town at house dances and in the parking lot of a root beer stand, making maybe a dollar a night. Hubert, our next door neighbor throughout my childhood, left the music business for good when he became a Fort Worth fireman. Cecil, who turns up in the family photo album as a skinny kid with a shock of blonde hair and a straw hat, was as good a violinist as Dad or better. As Southern Melody Boys, the two of them introduced the duet style that became popular with many stringbands.

In 1935[,] O'Daniel was abruptly let go. He came in one morning and found a note telling him to clear out. He was replaced by Eddie Dunn, who brought in Zeke Campbell, a fine lead guitarist, kept Clifford Gross and "Abner," and fired everybody else. Then he brought over three new players from Dallas: Dick Reinhart (vocal and guitar), Bert Dodson (vocal and bass), and Marvin Montgomery, a hot banjo player who would prove to be the longest-lasting Doughboy of them all. Dad says in his memoir that Marvin was probably the best banjo player in the country at the time. With these changes, the band jelled at six members. That number was important. It made possible their distinctive sound, a combination of light tonal texture and close harmonies.

In 1937[,] they added piano, in the person of an eighteen-year-old prodigy Marvin had first heard a couple of years earlier, from twenty miles south of Fort Worth. Knocky Parker had been so determined to join the Doughboys that when he came down with measles right before his audition date the family hid his shoes to keep him home in bed and he tried to walk it barefoot. They went after him and got him back and got him well, and he hit the Fort Worth musical scene full force. Later, Knocky became famous in folk and jazz circles, earned a doctorate in music, and served for many years as a professor at the University of Tampa. Right up until he died in 1986[,] he played a wild, rhythmic style so raunchy he sometimes hit the keys with his elbows, just as he had played when he joined the Doughboys. Marvin said in later years that he would travel anywhere anytime to play music with Knocky Parker—which tells you a lot about both of them.

The roster of personnel was always shifting. Take fiddle players, for instance. On the recordings done in the 1930s alone, the cast included Clifford Gross ("Doctor," who was kicked out for pulling a knife on Parker Wilson) and "Buck" Buchanan, besides Dad and Cecil Brower, back from a few years in the Midwest and once again joining Dad on close harmonies. In 1945, when the band came back together after the war, they brought in another fine violinist, a dark-haired clown named Carroll Hubbard. Shifts like that kept occurring as players went off to do something else and others took their place. A rhythm guitarist named J. B. Brinkley who came in in 1941 and again about the same time as Carroll broke his fist on the jaw of somebody who had made a crack about my dad. I remember him turning up at our door to borrow money during the time he couldn't work. But always there was the nucleus group—Dad, Marvin, Zeke—and the sound and format stayed pretty much the same until they broke up some after the advent of TV. Marvin says that Dad could make arrangements that would produce the Doughboys sound even when they used subs.

I've listened to that sound on the tapes I found at the house, and I can't figure how in the world they made such a hit. Maybe their music—thin, tinny, unsophisticated as to intros, bridges, and endings; music on a shoestring, you might say—caught for listeners the quality of life in the Depression. Music historians say it was a blend of border Mexican, cowboy, and gospel with blues and Louisiana jazz. I suspect Dad would have said they just tried things out and kept what worked. Whatever the roots, the crucial elements were their close harmonies, especially between the signature twin fiddles, and the swing rhythms they stitched them to.

Their repertoire consisted of a few regularly recurring types. There were traditional country numbers like "Goin' Up Cripple Creek" as well as fiddle breakdowns; hymns, like "In the Sweet Bye-and-Bye," too simply delivered to be called gospel; other sentimental pieces like "My Buddy"; western and neo-western ballads like "The Cattle Call" or "When It's Round-Up Time in Texas"; honky-tonk laments and blues like "All Because of Lovin' You"; and comic specialties like "Three Shif[']]less Skonks" and "Please Don't Help That Bear." Marvin did a falsetto little-girl character on some of these, "Rubber Dolly" for instance, and wrote some of the really silly stuff himself—"Cross-Eyed Cowboy from Abilene," "She Gave Me the Bird," and their big jukebox hit, "Pussy, Pussy, Pussy," an extended double entendre that couldn't be played on the air. As far as I can tell, the only money they made off this kind of stuff, or any of their records, was a fee for the recording session itself. If there were royalties, they couldn't have been much.

The Doughboys' list of recordings runs to 158 cuts. The first ones were made in 1936 in Fort Worth, with other sessions over the next few years in Dallas, in Saginaw, Texas (where a studio was built in the relocated flour mill), and in Los Angeles. A typical recording session was six to eight numbers, not all of which would be issued. They cut "My Buddy," for instance, on April 4, 1936, their very first session; but it was a remake, done on May 26 of that year in L.A., that was released. The longest single session was May 14, 1938, when they cut twenty-one numbers. The most memorable seems to have been June 14, 1939. It was fiercely hot, and the warehouse where they were set up had, of course, no air conditioning. They played with their shirts off, passing a bottle around (as Marvin's notes say) among "some of the band members as well as the boss-man—why hide it?"

I remember once—it must have been after the war—being taken along over to the Montgomerys' house, Marvin's and Kathleen's, on a Saturday or a Sunday afternoon when the boys got together to try out some numbers. I have a scratchy recording they made that afternoon on somebody's home equipment. There they are, talking over the numbers they were trying out, planning who would come in when for a solo, cutting up, laughing. Their sessions must all have been a good deal like that. I remember that they were drinking beer from long-neck bottles, and when the supply ran out[,] someone went out to get more. And my mother god mad and left, because she didn't hold with drinking.

Besides radio and recordings, there were also personal appearances. In the earliest years[,] they toured in an old junker of a bus, which meant that they sometimes had to go by train. On one of the train trips[,] a couple of the boys were playing cards and boozing and got into words with a passenger who took exception to having to step over the bass fiddle to get into the restroom. They had stowed it in the corridor rather than risk the baggage car. As they rolled into the station at whatever little Texas town it was, a fight erupted and Dad and a couple of the others jumped off the moving train and hightailed it before the cops got there.

By 1936, though, they were going around in a custom-made white bus with their name on the side, top-quality loudspeakers on top, and a platform on the back from which they could play parking lot appearances. They took that bus to Hollywood the year they got it and made their two Gene Autry movies, *Oh Susannah* and *The Big Show*. "Pappy" O'Daniel had ordered the bus but [had] been fired before it arrived.

Those few people who remember this stuff at all usually say that the Light Crust Doughboys campaigned for O'Daniel and won him the governorship. That isn't true. They never campaigned for him at all. It was another band that he'd formed after he was canned, called the Hillbilly Boys, who toured with him. One ex-Doughboy, Leon Huff, had gone along. A few times both groups hit town at the same time, and O'Daniel must have felt pretty low when he saw his wonderful bus sitting there inaccessible. One of those times, though, just one, when his own sound equipment failed, he got to use the bus.

I can remember, as a child, fingering the pegged wooden chessmen Dad had at the house, fitting them into the holes of the wooden chess board. Some of the bandmembers [sic] had had the set customized so they could play while riding, without the pieces sliding around. What could have happened, I wonder, to that chess set and board? It seems like a thing we would have kept.

It seems that some of the boys used the bus for other things, too, besides travel and chess-playing. Like rock musicians with their groupies, they would sometimes take girls down to the parked bus after night appearances. And Knocky, still just a kid and not understanding how such things would be regarded by wives, came back from one of their trips telling stories that caused severe domestic complications.

I can imagine, though I don't know, that Ramon DeArmon, a singer who was with the band until he suffered a shocking death that I heard about throughout my childhood, must have been one of the boys who had the most girls willing to make nighttime visits to the bus. DeArmon, called "Snub," either had the longest tenure of any of the singers during those years when the Doughboys enjoyed their fame or else he was one for whom my parents felt the most attachment, because he was the one they talked about the most. Mother always said he was so good-looking and had such a wonderful voice.

I have a memory, far back, of standing outside on one of the brick streets downtown, a very small child, my arm stretched up to where Mama holds my hand. It's cold, and my head is tilted back. I'm looking up at Daddy and the others, where they're playing up on some kind of platform. A man is singing "White Christmas" into a microphone: "May your days be merry and bright." A young, good-looking man with a pleasant, untrained tenor voice. Ramon DeArmon! my memory tells me.

Wrong.

For years[,] I thought I remembered Mother talking about how Ramon DeArmon sang "White Christmas." But it turns out he couldn't have sung it, not ever, not even once, because "White Christmas" didn't come out until 1942, in the Paramount picture *Holiday Inn*, with Bing Crosby, and by then[,] DeArmon was dead, killed in one of those horrible accidents people never forget. Doing some welding under his car one day—he was a young man, you understand, younger even than my father, who would have been twenty-seven at the time—Ramon ignited some spilled gasoline and was trapped under the burning car. Memories are such slippery things. What we think we remember we may only have heard about, and what we think we heard we may in fact have invented.

There's so much else I would like to know. Death is so final.

I've wondered sometimes if Dad really enjoyed playing. Wouldn't you think a musician would want to listen to music? But he was never one to listen. He never owned stereo equipment or records or, as far as I know, even listened to the radio. Music was his job, and he went about it with high standards of workmanship. But joy? I can't remember ever seeing him lean into the music when he played, [sic] or dance his feet. I never saw any body language.

I think of those pictures of Knocky looming over the keyboard, wild-eyed. I think of Marvin's statement that he would go anyplace anytime to play with Knocky Parker. Dad went if he had a job to play. After he died, when I found that set of LPs[7] Marvin had sent him of some of the old Doughboys back together, the shrink-wrap had never even been cut.

One more memory. This one I know is real.

The last time Dad rode in a car was one afternoon when we drove him across town for a radiation treatment. He was in a lot of pain in those days and pretty heavily doped up on morphine. His mind wandered. We were riding back that day after his treatment, and he was tired, and no one was talking, when suddenly he came out with an old Doughboys story.

Now, Dad was never one to use off-color language. Not around the family, anyway. I don't think I heard him say so much as a damn or a hell the whole time I was growing up. But out of the blue[,] he told us this:

"One time we had played a job out in West Texas. We had gone in two cars, and this square dance caller wanted a ride back to Fort Worth. So we let him get in the back seat between Ramon DeArmon and Zeke. He was hittin' the bottle hard, and after a while he got so drunk he started hugging up on Ramon, imagining that he was his girlfriend or something."

We looked at each other, my husband and I, and decided to take that at face value.

"He was really getting' all over him, you know. Well, Ramon took it for a while, and the he turns on this guy and he says, *Get your hands off me, you dog-assed bastard!*"

He didn't laugh, and he didn't say anything else. Just told the story. We got him home and helped him undress and got him into bed.

How many more stories like that did he have, I wonder, that I never heard? How much of his experience—how much of himself—did I never know?

Abner's gone now. Parker Willson is long gone. And Knocky and Snub and Bashful, and the white bus. And with them[,] those times and that special, silly, Depression-weary music they played when the Light Crust Doughboys were on the air.

Source: Janis Stout, "The Light Crust Doughboys Were on the Air: A Memoir," *Journal of Country Music* 18, no. 3 (1996): 5–9. (Reprinted with permission of Janis P. Stout and courtesy of the Country Music Foundation.)

FOR FURTHER READING

Boyd, Jean A. *Dance All Night: Those Other Southwestern Swing Bands.* College Station: Texas A&M University Press, 2012.

Boyd, Jean A. *The Jazz of the Southwest: An Oral History of Western Swing.* Austin: University of Texas Press, 1998.

Boyd, Jean A. *We're the Light Crust Doughboys from Burrus Mill": An Oral History.* Austin: University of Texas Press, 2003.

7. Long-playing records.

16

"Okies Reverse Order of Steinbeck's Tale" (1941)

During the middle of the 1930s, widespread drought and massive dust storms devastated the Great Plains states of Oklahoma, Texas, and Kansas, driving thousands of people from their homes as their farms failed and the banks repossessed their personal property. In the throes of the Great Depression, these people had little hope for gainful employment in their homes, so they set out for the lush farmlands and industrial developments of southern California. As fictionalized in John Steinbeck's famous novel *The Grapes of Wrath* and the songs of Oklahoman songwriter Woody Guthrie, the "Okies" endured great hardship on their journeys westward and faced intense discrimination when they began to settle in their new California homes. At the same time, Dust Bowl migrants fundamentally changed the cultural landscape of southern California, bringing with them fundamentalist religion, conservative cultural values, and country music.[1]

1. This narrative is expertly traced in James N. Gregory, *American Exodus: The Dust Bowl Migration and Okie Culture in California* (New York: Oxford University Press, 1989); and Peter LaChapelle, *Proud to Be An Okie: Cultural Politics, Country Music, and Migration to Southern California* (Berkeley: University of California Press, 2007).

One of the bands to follow the Dust Bowl migration westward was Bob Wills and His Texas Playboys. Wills, who was an original member of the Light Crust Doughboys, took his Texas Playboys to Tulsa in 1934, where they played for dances at Cain's Dancing Academy and broadcast over the powerful radio station KVOO. In 1940, he enjoyed a national hit with "New San Antonio Rose," a reworking of a song that he had previously recorded with the Texas Playboys in 1938.[2] As the band's audience in Oklahoma and Texas declined and their national star rose, Wills decided in 1943 to move the band to California, expanding the size of the group in the process.[3] Wills's stint in California was short-lived, however, as World War II decimated his band. Yet, the westward migration of western swing exerted a significant impact on the broader musical culture of southern California, prompting the formation of new bands to play dancehalls and radio stations throughout the Golden State and creating a dancehall culture there that rivaled that found in Texas and Oklahoma.[4]

The national attention afforded to western swing as a consequence of Wills's move to California also encouraged some observers to see the genre as a regional iteration of swing music, a belief held by many of the musicians who played in the genre. The uncredited author of this brief article for the jazz magazine *Metronome* draws favorable comparisons to musicians in bands led by the immensely popular bandleader Harry James and Benny Goodman, suggesting that western swing musicians were capable of playing with the same inventiveness, character, and verve as their better-known national counterparts and forcing us to consider further whether western swing should be brought into the country music tent.[5]

━━━━━━━

IF you have read the book or seen the movie, or just heard your educated girl friend rave about John Steinbeck's "Grapes of Wrath" [sic], you know that the theme of that sensational best-seller was the plight of migrants from Oklahoma, who had nothing where they came from, and found nothing where they got to (California). Comes now a band that lives and works and plays in Tulsa, Oklahoma, and it refuses to leave that fair city! And we thought that NOBODY stayed in Oklahoma by choice!

The band? Bob Wills and his Texas Playboys.

Who are they? A twelve-piece crew built around the hill-billy ministrations of leader Wills who wrote the very healthy *San Antonio Rose* [sic]. Confidentially, this here Bob Wills

2. For an extended discussion of the two versions of "San Antonio Rose," consult Charles R. Townsend, *San Antonio Rose: The Life and Music of Bob Wills* (Urbana: University of Illinois Press, 1976), 190–205.

3. For a more detailed discussion of Wills's career, consult Townsend, *San Antonio Rose*.

4. Gerald Haslam with Alexandra Haslam Russell and Richard Chon, *Workin' Man Blues: Country Music in California* (Berkeley: Heyday Books, 2005), 77–93.

5. For more discussion of the resonances between western swing and mainstream swing musicians, consult Part 1 of Jean A. Boyd, *Dance All Night: Those Other Southwestern Swing Bands* (College Station: Texas A&M University Press, 2012).

band is the best selling Columbia records band at the moment (on Okeh hill-billy label). *Rose* is climbing toward the quarter-million mark and the future looks *Rosy!*

So what, just another success story. Not at all, not at all. This band pockets within its well-oiled (that's what they grow in Oklahoma—oil) ranks some of the finest jazzmen you've ever heard when you hear them. There's a trumpeter, for instance, who plays a great deal like Harry James, but doesn't copy Ziggy Elman. There's a clarinetist who's got the purity of style and the melodic emphasis of a great musician, and there's a guitarist who comes closer than any other white plectrist to getting the solidity and swing and steady flow of ideas of Charlie Christian (also an Okie, by the by). Wait, that's not all. The rhythm section shields a drummer who gets a beat and keeps it, and therefore the rhythm, going. And it also keeps a pianist in the percussive, rhythmic style of a [Jess] Stacy. In other words—the band's got something, in no uncertain terms.

However, Wills is very suspicious of any approach to his band because he's afraid some big-city slicker from the east is going to steal away one of his precious bundles. And he's probably right. So the Texas Playboys go right on playing one-steps and the Oklahoma version of the shag at Cain's Dancing Academy in Tulsa (with hymns on Thursday at noon over a local radio station) and they resist all offers to leave the sacred precinct of the Okie.

Nonetheless, here's hoping they'll be enticed east. For one thing, that'll enable us to hear the band in person. For another, they'll give the boys a chance to hit the big-time they really deserve. And, for still another, they'll give some booker an attraction of real propor- tions: an all-around group that doubles on strings, plays first-rate hot[,] and carries a delightful hill-billy commercial tag.

Source: "Okies Reverse Order of Steinbeck's Tale," *Metronome* 57, no. 4 (April 1941).

FOR FURTHER READING

Haslam, Gerald, with Alexandra Haslam Russell and Russell Chon. *Workin' Man Blues: Country Music in California.* Berkeley: Heyday Books, 2005.

LaChapelle, Peter. *Proud to Be an Okie: Cultural Politics, Country Music, and Migration to Southern California.* Berkeley: University of California Press, 2007.

Townsend, Charles R. *San Antonio Rose: The Life and Music of Bob Wills.* Urbana: University of Illinois Press, 1976.

17

Maurice Zolotow

"Hillbilly Boom" (1944)

Throughout its nine-decade history, country music has periodically surprised national commentators who observe its immense popularity and its commercial success but struggle to understand how the genre's seemingly unsophisticated songs and stars could garner such acclaim. Observations such as those offered by *Saturday Evening Post* contributor Maurice Zolotow frequently reveal the elitist attitudes of the author, who looks down his or her nose at the genre while making farcical jabs at "pasture Paganinis" or "bayou Beethovens" and lays bare the class issues facing the nation at any given time.[1]

Such was the case near the end of World War II and the years immediately following its conclusion. Urban GIs who had little exposure to country music prior to their service were exposed to the genre through interactions with other

---

1. For a broader discussion of this history, consult Jeffrey J. Lange, *Smile When You Call Me a Hillbilly: Country Music's Struggle for Respectability, 1939-1954* (Athens: University of Georgia Press, 2004).

soldiers, the Armed Forces Radio Network, and the near constant influx of record-ings sent to the European and Pacific theatres. Furthermore, honky tonk juke-boxes and bands servicing the growing war industry centers on the West Coast also played music that addressed contemporary concerns: separation from loved ones, dancehall romance, and divorce.[2] Record sales and jukebox spins (one of the more lucrative revenue streams for recording artists and their labels during this time) skyrocketed as artists such as Al Dexter, Ernest Tubb, and Roy Acuff responded to the changing times. But, for observers like Zolotow, the wartime rise of country music merited attention not simply because the genre was taking the nation by storm but also because it ran counter to a classed understanding of musical genres that privileged the apparent sophistication of classical music and jazz over other, more popular forms of musical expression. It is noteworthy, however, that this period also witnessed the emergence of a movement, led by Tubb and others, to rename the genre in order to disassociate it with hillbilly stereotypes. This history is traced in Jeffrey J. Lange, *Smile When You Call Me a Hillbilly: Country Music's Struggle for Respectability, 1939–1954* (Athens: University of Georgia Press, 2004).

Zolotow's essay focuses on American Records Company A&R man Art Satherley, a British national who recorded hundreds of country, blues, and jazz art-ists during the 1930s and 1940s. Although much had changed in the national music industry between the 1920s and World War II, Satherley still followed the prac-tices of the early record producers, traveling thousands of miles each year to record regional favorites and emerging artists. As a consequence, Satherley was often on the cutting edge, discovering talent and musical styles that would later have a sig-nificant influence on the national popular music soundscape. Yet, for Zolotow, the southern cities that Satherley visited—which included such places as Dallas and New Orleans—were exotic lands with simple folks playing homemade instruments and speaking in dialect. Satherley's passion for the music and his efforts to engage with it on its own terms comes through in this piece, however, subtly pointing to Zolotow's biases and championing the music, its musicians, and its audiences.

———

IN March, 1942, Art Satherley, a courtly white-haired gentleman of fifty-two who is employed by the Columbia Recording Corporation for the sole purpose of roving around American and taking down on wax the homespun music of the hillbilly and cowboy troubadours, found himself in Dallas, Texas, while on his annual recording pilgrimage. Satherley had set up his portable recording apparatus in a suite in the Adolphus Hotel[,] and he was interviewing vari-ous talents from the Panhandle and the plains, when in strode a tall chunky chap attired in chaps, boots and a ten-gallon hat.

2. Peter LaChapelle, *Proud to Be an Okie: Cultural Politics, Country Music, and Migration to Southern California* (Berkeley: University of California Press, 2007), 76–110; Stephanie Vander Wel, *"I Am a Honky-Tonk Girl": Country Music, Gender, and Migration*, Ph.D. dissertation, University of California, Los Angeles, 2008, 139–96.

The newcomer was Albert Poindexter, a sometime house painter from Troup, Texas, who was convinced he had the gift of tongues. Poindexter brought along a six-piece band and also submitted thirty-five original ditties which he had composed in his spare time.

Like most of the Texas Tchaikowskys, Poindexter's lyrics were of a melancholy nature—dealing with the death of close friends, the desertions of cowboys by their sweethearts, conversations with herds of dogies, and the well-known fact that a cow hands [sic] band's friend, if not his only friend, is his faithful horse.

Now, Satherley had at various times recorded some of Poindexter's lamentable chansons, but they had not set on fire the world of hillbilly fandom, this world being a very enthusiastic and emotional group of some 25,000,000 admirers of the lonesome Texas plaint and of the mountain melancholy, which latter flourishes in the Southeastern States. The legion of admirers is headed by President [Franklin Delano] Roosevelt.

On that historic morning in March, Satherley, a scholarly and dignified man who speaks with a British accent and looks somewhat like an Oxford professor of Greek history, placed his pince-nez on his nose and patiently listened as Poindexter and his companions dreamily strummed and thrummed and twanged their way through the thirty-five lays of despair. Finally, Satherley selected twelve to be recorded. The best of the twelve, thought Satherley, was a lilting love song called Rosalita [sic]. Another of the twelve was a ballad having to do with the husband who is having a wild time in a night club in the company of a blonde when his wife catches him in *flagrante delicto*, she forthwith drawing a revolver, shooting out the lights and beating him gently about the face. Although he was not particularly impressed by this sage of marital infidelity, Satherley recorded it because he liked its steady, insistent rhythm. He was otherwise unimpressed, however, because he says that in hillbilly circles it is very common to hear songs about men and women who are unfaithful to each other, and who are always shooting it out with guns.

"To be honest about it," Satherley recently confided, "I never dreamed it would be the hit it turned out. We only released it because we needed a contrast to put on the other side of Rosalita."

Released in March, 1943, Rosalita [sic] was promptly forgotten. Instead, millions of Americans began to walk around advising [the] pistol-packin' mama to lay that pistol down. By June[,] it became one of the biggest-selling records in the history of American recording, and by December, 1943, it had sold 1,600,000 copies, and the manufacturer had orders on hand for 500,000 more which he could not fill because of the wartime shortages of labor and shellac.

On the black market, coin-machine phonograph operators were offering from three dollars up to as high as ten dollars for a copy of Pistol-Packin' Mama [sic] in good condition, because the jukebox cognoscenti preferred this record to all others. Even Bing Crosby was driven to recording it. The Hit Parade for a long time refused to recognize the existence of Pistol-Packin' Mama [sic] because the opening line went "Drinkin' beer in a cabaret," and the radio networks are not permitted to publicize people who look upon the malt when it is amber. This is a ruling of the Federal Communications Commission.[3] The publishers of Pistol-Packin' Mama [sic] hauled the Hit Parade into court and finally the lyric was altered to read "Singin' songs in a cabaret," and Pistol-Packin' Mama [sic] became No. 1 on the Hit Parade. Poindexter,

---

3. The Federal Communications Commission regulates broadcast communications in the United States.

who meanwhile had changed his name to Al Dexter, is now playing in vaudeville theaters at a salary of $3500 a week.

Satherley has a gloating air of triumph as he recites these and other statistics which prove that hillbilly music has come into its own. After Pistol-Packin' Mama [sic], among the biggest recordings of the past twelvemonth have been There's a Star-Spangled Banner Waving Somewhere [sic], by Elton Britt and his band, and No Letter Today [sic], by Ted Daffan and his Texans, and both of which have gone over the million mark. Six large radio stations now have gigantic programs devoted solely to hillbilly music, and WLS broadcasts five solid hours of the National Barn Dance [sic] every Saturday. In Nashville, Tennessee, the Grand Ole Op'ry [sic] is aired over WSM for four hours. NBC broadcasts portions of these two programs on a national hookup, and has a third sorghum show entitled The Hook 'n' Ladder Follies [sic].

Almost as remarkable are the grosses amassed by hillbilly units which play one-night stands all over the country in county auditoriums, schools, barns and theaters. Obscure performers playing in hamlets like Reeds Ferry, New Hampshire, will draw $5600 in a single night. On the road, hillbilly troupes will consistently outdraw legitimate Broadway plays, symphony concerts, sophisticated comedians and beautiful dancing girls. When a unit, say, like Roy Acuff and his Smoky Mountain Boys is scheduled to hit a town like Albany, Georgia, farmers will pour into Albany from a 200-mile radius, and night after night Acuff will play to audiences of 4000 in places where Betty Grable or Tommy Dorsey or Bob Hope would only succeed in drawing boll weevils. This is a great mystery to the clever strategists of show business who plan projects on Broadway and in Hollywood.

It is no mystery to Satherley, who, for some twenty-five years, has been crusading for hillbilly music among his cynical Broadway friends. Satherley dislikes the term "hillbilly," and he keeps talking about "folk music," "country music" or "mountain music." He says that the explanation of the hillbilly phenomenon is quite simple. He explains that most Americans either live on farms today or came from farms, and that the strains of a hoedown fiddle or a cowboy plaint are their own native folk music and the one they will always respond to, no matter how far they have gone from the farm. He also believes that the congregation of groups of young men in Army camps has much to do with the boom in hillbilly music.

Because much of the hillbilly talent is employed in farming or ranching, Satherley must seek out his talent in the bayous, the canebrakes, the cotton plantations, the tobacco regions. Every spring he departs from his home base in Los Angeles with the complete portable recording outfit—a set of six microphones, pickups, turntables, a truckload of blank disks[—] and he follows a trail from Dallas to Amarillo, Tulsa, Oklahoma City, Houston, San Antonio, Beaumont, working through New Orleans, around to Shreveport, up into Birmingham, Nashville and Columbia [South Carolina]. He makes about 400 recordings on each tour. He will record everyone from Gene Autry and Roy Acuff, the leaders in their respective fields of cowboy and mountain lament, to such lesser knowns as Bob Atcher and Bonnie Blue Eyes, Bob Wills, Memphis Minnie, Roosevelt Sykes, The Yas-Yas Girl, and Fisher Hendley and his Aristocratic Pigs, the latter being a very tempestuous hoedown fiddle band from South Carolina.[4]

4. It is worth noting that Zolotow here lumps African American blues singers Memphis Minnie and Roosevelt Sykes with country musicians, suggesting that Zolotow saw their southernness as a unifying factor that was stronger than their racial differences.

When word spreads that "Uncle Art" has arrived in a Southern town, dozens of folk geniuses will come trooping in from the mountains to attend the "recordin' jamboree." Homemade fiddles are dusted off, mandolins and guitars are taken off the shelf, as well as all the less conventional instrumentation of the hillbilly musician, which includes washboards, piepans, automobile horns, cowbells, train whistles, jew's-harps, combs, kazoos, harmonicas, sweet-potato fifes and carpenter's saws.[5] Satherley pays most of the semiprofessional artists twenty-five dollars per record side, while the luminaries receive a royalty of one half cent a side.[6]

When Satherley is told that there is somebody in an out-of-the-way place who has a very original ballad and that this native talent is too shy to come to town, he will pack his recording equipment into suitcases and head into regions where no city shoes have ever trod before. Traveling by plane, train and automobile, and on foot where there are no passable roads, he journeys 70,000 miles during a typical year.

Although all hillbilly music sounds monotonously alike to the urban eardrum, it includes many types of music.

The qualities Satherley says must always be present in fine hillbilly music are simplicity of language, an emotional depth in the music, sincerity in the rendition, and an indigenous genuineness of dialect and twang. "I would never think of hiring a Mississippi boy to play in a Texas band," he says. "Any Texan would know right off it was wrong."

The Wreck on the Highway [sic], a dirge-like opus composed and first sung by Roy Acuff, has all the qualities in perfection that Satherley looks for.[7] It is sung by a soloist and a chorus. The soloist, Mr. Acuff, has just returned from the scene of a dreadful automobile accident, and he asks, rhetorically, who was driving and who was killed. After pointing out that at the scene he saw whisky and blood running together, he inquires if they heard anyone pray. The chorus replies that they didn't hear nobody pray, dear brother. The lyric pursues its grim way, full of broken glass, more whisky, moans and screams, and death laying her hand in destruction, and the insistent refrain that nobody was heard to pray.

But, above all, sincerity, even if it is awkward unpolished sincerity, is the criterion used to judge the performer. "A true folk singer who is not synthetic can be recognized because he doesn't 'do' a song; he cries it out with his heart and soul," Satherley says. He remembers a sullen lean-jawed mountaineer whom he chanced upon in Hattiesburg, Mississippi, many years ago. The man sang railroad chants passably well, and he had a robust voice, but he lacked the note of sincerity. Nevertheless, Satherley recorded two of his numbers and gave him fifty dollars, a bottle of bourbon whisky and a straw hat. The following June, when Satherley returned

5. Although this may have been true in the early days of race and hillbilly recording, musicians who recorded for Satherley and other A&R men in the late 1930s and early 1940s were certainly more professional than the description here suggests. See, for instance, Elijah Wald's treatment of blues singer Robert Johnson's recordings in *Escaping the Delta: Robert Johnson and the Invention of the Blues* (New York: Amistad, 2004), 113–20.

6. Equating to one cent per record sold.

7. "Wreck on the Highway" was actually written by Rockingham, North Carolina, mill worker and radio star Dorsey Dixon, who recorded it with his brother Howard in January 1938. Acuff claimed credit for the song's composition until 1946. For more on this saga, consult Patrick Huber, *Linthead Stomp: The Creation of Country Music in the Piedmont South* (Chapel Hill: University of North Carolina Press, 2008), 237–40, 259–61.

to Mississippi, he found that the mountaineer had really acquired vocal sincerity. During the interim, the man and his wife had quarreled over the fifty dollars and he had blown out her brains. When Satherley greeted him again, he was languishing in jail waiting his turn to be hanged. He had also composed a new song, The Hangman Blues [sic], and this time he had really put his heart into it, and it was one of the most sincere Satherley ever recorded. In fact, he made the recording right in the condemned man's cell.

In his search for realistic sincerity, Satherley once happened upon a venerable and dignified colored preacher in Richmond, Virginia. He was holding a street revival. With him were two little blind boys playing on a dilapidated portable organ, held together only by ropes and prayers. The three sang Ezekiel Saw the Wheel [sic], and then the minister, smoothing his long black robes, began to preach a beautiful sermon, in which the words fell into spontaneous cadences and became a musical prose. It suddenly came to Satherley that it might be unusual to record a preachin', and he approached the minister and asked him for permission to record a sermon, which was steadfastly refused until Satherley argued that if the sermons were placed on records, then the flock in Richmond would derive spiritual comfort if their preacher had to visit another county or another state. The first preachin' records were released in 1930, and scored such a success that Satherley looked around for more suitable preachin' talent.

A few months later he was in Augusta, Georgia, and he passed the word around that he was looking for a good preacher. An immaculately dressed Negro in a reversed collar appeared, carrying a nickeled guitar, and said, "Ise a man of God and I hears you is looking for a sermon. I brung my flock with me." The flock sheepishly followed him in. The group sang a spiritual, and then the Negro launched into the most moving preachment Satherley had ever heard.

After the recording was completed, Satherley paid the prophet $100 for himself and his congregation. The following day the congregation appeared and asked for their payment. Satherley explained that he had paid their pastor.

"What pastor?" they cried. "He ain't our pastor. He picked us up on the corner and said he gwine gi' us two bits apiece iffn we he'p him sing the gospel. Why, he ain't even no churchgoin' man. He's blacker'n the devil hissel'. Why, he's the man who runs all our dens of 'niquity and 'bomination round her."

After sincerity, Satherley strives to project the meaning of the lyrics. "The person who listens to mountain music wants to hear a story," Satherley explains. "My singers must get the picture of the words. I've got to instill into them a picture of what they are singing about. If they're singing about a dead person, I impress on them that their best friend is lying dead and 'you'll never see him again.' I tell them, 'Sing it in the extreme.' In folk music, we don't care about trick ways of phrasing or hot licks; we concentrate on the emotions. The country people, these so-called hillbillies, are tremendously sensitive people, with deep emotions. Whereas the sophisticated city person likes these humbug boy-girl love songs, with everything pretty-pretty, the mountaineer is a realist. His songs deal with loneliness, misery, death, murder."

Art Satherley is very self-conscious about the fact that neither his physical appearance, his clothes nor his genteel British way of speaking is fitting to a talent scout for Texas and Tennessee minstrels. When he is on the road making recordings, he sometimes tries his best to look like and act like a hillbilly. He puts on a pair of corduroys and a sport shirt, and he goes squirrel hunting. He also tries to drink "cawn."[8] He pretends to be very understanding

8. Corn liquor, or moonshine.

when he runs into a mountaineering idiosyncracy, such as the tradition of putting one or more rattlesnake tails into a fiddle.

"These hoedown fiddlers say," relates Satherley, "that putting a couple of rattles into the fiddle makes it sound different from a classical-music fiddle. I have tried to argue with my boys on this point for very many years, but they are adamant. I tell them to try playing on a fiddle without any rattles inside, but they say they can't play hoedown without it. They give me all kinds of reasons[,] too. Some say the rattlesnakes keep the moisture out of the fiddle, others that it keeps spider webs and cobwebs out; some say it keeps dust out, others that it gives the fiddle the real vibration. The fiddler can only use rattlers he has killed himself. I am getting so I almost believe it myself."

Despite all his efforts, Satherley is becoming convinced that he will never be able to overcome the handicap of having been born in Bristol, England, in 1891. He was the son of an Episcopalian minister and was intended for a theological career. After he completed his education at Queen Elizabeth College, he became restless and served with the Somerset Yeomanry regiment of the British army for three and a half years. Thrown by a horse, he was deafened in his right ear, but says his left ear is now supersensitive, "like a microphone." He came to this country when he was twenty-two years old, and he got a job working in a factory, at Grafton, Wisconsin. When the firm went into the business of manufacturing phonographs and records, Satherley was placed in charge of production.[9] In 1925 he got tired of checking production sheets in an office, and asked to be transferred to an out-of-doors job, and ever since he has been traveling eleven months of the year in search of new folk music. In 1930 he discovered Gene Autry, a boy from Tioga, Texas, who was working as a railroad telegrapher near Ardmore, Oklahoma. In six months, Satherley made a national idol of Autry, and he has never been equaled in popularity in hillbilly circles.

Satherley discovered and recorded the cowboy music of United States Sen. W. Lee O'Daniel in the not-so-bygone days when O'Daniel was the conductor of a band called The Light Crust Doughboys and played such tunes as Please Pass the Biscuits, Pappy [sic]; Dirty Hang-over Blues [sic]; Peach-Pickin' Time in Georgia [sic]; There's Evil in Ye Children [sic].

He found Roy Acuff, today the most sensational personality in hillbilly music, in Nashville in 1938. Acuff is a quiet, shy person, who looks ten years younger than his thirty-nine years. He is married, and the father of a year-old son. He lives on a 150-acre farm about twelve miles out of Nashville. His income in 1943 was more than $200,000.

Like the pure hillbilly singer, Acuff hardly moves a muscle in his face when he sings. He sings mainly with his eyes closed, and now and then, as he feels a note deeply, tears will roll down his face.

In October, 1943, Acuff's program went on a coast-to-coast hookup of 129 stations, and to celebrate the event a party was given at the Ryman Auditorium in Nashville, where the Grand Ole Op'ry [sic] is performed to a regular Saturday night audience of 3500 who pay seventy-five-cents admission. Gov. Prentice Cooper was invited to grace the stage as guest of honor. Governor Cooper declined, stating that he would be no party to a "circus," and that

9. Satherley began his career with the now legendary Paramount Records, which recorded dozens of significant early blues musicians (Charles K. Wolfe and Patrick Huber, "Satherley, Art[hur Edward]," in *The Grove Dictionary of American Music*, 2nd ed., ed. Charles Hiroshi Garrett [New York: Oxford University Press, 2013], 348).

Acuff was bringing disgrace to Tennessee, by making Nashville the hillbilly capital of the United States.

Governor Cooper is supported by political boss Ed (Red Snapper) Crump, who is said to run Shelby County and Memphis with an ironclad grip. And thereby hangs a tale. It being an off-day for news in Nashville, Beazley Thompson, a reporter for the Nashville Tennessean [sic], decided to stir up a little excitement. He reported Governor Cooper's acid comment to Acuff, and said it would be a fitting revenge if Acuff were to run for governor. Acuff absently nodded, and this was all the encouragement Thompson needed. He immediately got up a petition, and now Acuff has been entered in the 1944 Democratic primaries. Boss Crump has been reported as much worried for the first time in his career. The Memphis Commercial Appeal [sic] pictorially demonstrated the crisis in Tennessee politics when it recently ran a cartoon showing a Capitol Hill politico standing outside a music shop and gazing pensively at a fiddle. The caption underneath read, "I wonder can you really learn in ten easy lessons?" Nobody in the South has forgotten how Lee O'Daniel successfully campaigned for governor of Texas by playing hillbilly music.

Art Satherley is convinced Acuff will be elected without any trouble, if he runs. As far as Satherley is concerned, it wouldn't be a bad idea if every state in the Union elected a hillbilly singer or fiddler as governor.

Source: Maurice Zolotow, "Hillbilly Boom," *The Saturday Evening Post* 216 (12 February 1944): 22–23, 36, 38. ("Hillbilly Boom" article © SEPS licensed by Curtis Licensing, Indianapolis, IN. All Rights Reserved.)

FOR FURTHER READING

Lange, Jeffrey J. *Smile When You Call Me a Hillbilly: Country Music's Struggle for Respectability, 1939-1954*. Athens: University of Georgia Press, 2004.

18

Nicholas Dawidoff

"Earl Scruggs: Three Fast Fingers" (1997)

By the mid-1940s, country music was a diverse genre that embraced Tin Pan Alley songwriting practices, electrified instruments and swing band arrangements, and crooning vocals, but the genre never lost sight of its string band roots. Rosine, Kentucky, native Bill Monroe, who with his brother Charlie had been one half of the popular Monroe Brothers in the 1930s, re-energized the string band tradition in 1939 with the formation of Bill Monroe and His Blue Grass Boys. Although Monroe and His Blue Grass Boys had achieved some success on the *Grand Ole Opry* in the early 1940s, it was not until he partnered with guitarist Lester Flatt and banjo player Earl Scruggs in 1945 that Monroe began to receive national attention for his work. Drawing from traditional fiddle tunes, early hillbilly recordings by Jimmie Rodgers and others, and blues and jazz improvisation, Monroe and his bandmates created a new country music subgenre that remains a vibrant force in American vernacular music and is still known by the same name as his band: bluegrass.[1]

1. For more on Monroe's contributions to country music, consult Tom Ewing, ed., *The Bill Monroe Reader* (Urbana: University of Illinois Press, 2000); and Neil V. Rosenburg and Charles K. Wolfe, *The Music of Bill Monroe* (Urbana: University of Illinois Press, 2007).

Although Scruggs is often credited with creating bluegrass's iconic rhythmic drive through his three-finger roll technique of banjo picking, he was actually the latest in a long line of North Carolina banjoists—including Snuffy Jenkins and Charlie Poole—to eschew the clawhammer style of playing favored by many string band musicians and heard ubiquitously on early hillbilly recordings.[2] With its constant pulse and ragtime rhythm, Scruggs's playing was a featured showpiece of the Blue Grass Boys and has influenced generations of banjoists since. Flatt and Scruggs left Monroe's band separately in 1948 and went on to form Flatt & Scruggs & The Foggy Mountain Boys, a wildly successful bluegrass band that toured college campuses during the folk revival of the 1950s and early 1960s, appeared on network television broadcasts of *The Beverly Hillbillies* in the mid-1960s, and helped to introduce the music of Bob Dylan to country audiences in the late 1960s. In that same time, Scruggs had revolutionized the banjo through the development of new tuner technologies that permitted the banjoist to adjust the tuning of the banjo while playing, banjo capos that allowed the instrument to play in any key, and a pedagogy book that remains a standard text for aspiring banjoists to the present day.[3]

In addition to providing insight into the many ways that Scruggs's career intersected with trends in country and mainstream popular music over the course of his then five-decade career, Nicholas Dawidoff's essay is particularly noteworthy because it works to contextualize bluegrass music within a broader history that includes the banjo's African origins, bluegrass's emergence as a commercial musical genre in the 1940s, and subsequent efforts to recast it as an authentic American folk music. Consequently, this essay challenges readers to reconsider how definitions of country music authenticity are influenced by the beliefs of those people ascribing authenticity to a musical style rather than representations of that style's inherent authenticity.[4]

———

Everybody was saying, "What is happening? What is that chord? How can he play it so fast? What is happening in this music?" It created an unbelievable sensation.

—*French Jazz critic Hugues Panassié, describing the scene at the Rue Chaptal in 1948, when the first Charlie Parker saxophone records reached Paris*

2. This style is well documented in the recordings presented on *American Banjo Three-Finger and Scruggs Style* (Folkways Records FA 2314 [1957]; reissued as Smithsonian/Folkways SF 40037 [1990]).

3. Earl Scruggs, *Earl Scruggs and the 5-String Banjo*, rev. ed. (Milwaukee: Hal Leonard, 2005).

4. For a general discussion of the ways that authenticity is culturally constructed, consult Allan Moore, "Authenticity as Authentication," *Popular Music* 21, no. 2 (2002): 209–23. See also Richard A. Peterson, *Creating Country Music: Fabricating Authenticity* (Chicago: University of Chicago Press, 1999); and Joli Jensen, *The Nashville Sound: Authenticity, Commercialization, and Country Music* (Nashville, TN: Country Music Foundation Press and Vanderbilt University Press, 1998).

The roads that lead into Boiling Spring, North Carolina, are lined with mossy gray Confederate memorials, Baptist church spires, and less sober institutions where strapping farmers compete in "Tuff Man" contests. There is always a tractor traveling along Highway 18 to slow up traffic, and a ramshackle building just around the curve selling pit-smoked pork barbeque tasty enough to stop it cold. Here in Cleveland County on the western fringe of the Piedmont, larger towns like Shelby are shady and peaceful and smaller ones can be even calmer. When I pulled in to a filling station to ask how much farther it was to Boiling Spring, a smiling man told me, "You're in the middle of it." It's a quiet place in a quiet part of the state, which makes it not terribly different from the way it was sixty years ago when a quiet local farmboy named Earl Scruggs spent his evenings teaching himself to play a banjo better than anybody ever had.

Scruggs lived his childhood in Flint Hill, a small community of wooden frame houses lying three miles south of the one stoplight in Boiling Spring. "It's really grown," Gretel Anthony, who has lived in Flint Hill for fifty-three years, told me. We were seated in her kitchen, which is two kitchens away from the one in the house where Scruggs lived from the time he was about seven. "His house and the one between it was the only ones," she said. "Well, there were three really. Now, well, there's about nine."

Flint Hill is folded into an angular ripple of hills and meadows dappled with cornflowers, and it's well tucked away on most other levels as well. The houses are scattered, the woods are silent, and unless you have lots of time and terribly strong legs—or access to a vehicle—your horizon is two or three houses down the road. Though I'd been in Nashville in the morning, as soon as I got out to Flint Hill I had a sense of being very far from other people, a kind of bucolic seclusion, so even the sight of a license plate from one state west immediately seemed exotic.

Almost every one of the nine houses in Flint Hill still has a garden full of squash, okra, butter beans, and cucumbers. Scruggs's father, George Elam Scruggs, was a cotton farmer. These days, the closest most people in the region get to bolls is down at the mill[,] where they turn them into socks or blue jeans. The weather here is, of course, the same as it ever was. "Gets a little foggy at times," Gretel Anthony said. "Between early spring and summer, that's the worst of it. I've had it so bad I've had to stop driving and pull over." When Earl Scruggs named his famous band The Foggy Mountain Boys, it was as much a tip of his hat to the old home as it was to A.P. Carter's song "Foggy Mountain Top."

Across the road from Earl Scruggs's former house is a forest of Carolina pines. Behind it is, Gretel Anthony says, "a big old tiny pear tree." Inside is twelve-year-old Tywaina Kennedy. Tywaina's mother and stepfather are textile-mill workers, just as Earl Scruggs was until it occurred to him that he could make a living doing something that pleased him more. Tywaina is thinking along the same lines. "I want to get me a real job," she said. "I couldn't work in a mill all my life." Tywaina hopes to become "a lawyer or a model." She asked me if there really were tall buildings in New York City. Later, I mailed her a packet with postcards of the Manhattan skyline and a tape of Earl Scruggs's music enclosed—he isn't played on the radio stations she hears—but the post office sent it back, making me wonder if perhaps they hadn't been able to find the house. Flint Hill is pretty isolated.

Earl Scruggs taught himself to play a banjo in part because he wanted the company. "I didn't have access to radio or cars," he said. "Maybe you could see another house or two. I played whenever I got a chance. In the wintertime[,] I'd build fires in the cookstove for my mother to cook breakfast. I took that job so I could play while the stove heated up and mother cooked."

The banjo came easily to him, especially after he experienced one of those rare, charged moments when a great musician discovers something for himself that will forever change the way other people think about an instrument. Many string musicians are precocious in acquitting their skills, but even by that standard Earl Scruggs was a quick study. He was ten, he thinks, when one day he and his brother Horace quarreled. Their mother sent them to opposite ends of the house. "I was sitting playing a tune called 'Reuben,'" said Scruggs. "Ever sit around daydreaming? Nobody knows the thoughts you are having. That's what I was doing. During that time I was suddenly playing the tune the way I do now. It sounds like a made-up story, but it's not. It actually happened that way. I was sitting in the living-room part of the house by myself. It turned me loose to play many different tunes because you can play a song like the words go. People can tell what I'm playing because it sounds like the words are said. You can pick out the syllables of the words."

What Scruggs had done was to begin playing a five-string banjo with three fingers. His thumb, middle, and index fingers were all picking, creating two strands of harmony to buttress the melody. In a sense, he could function as a trio all by himself. Because he alternated three fingers, Scruggs could play one note after another in rapid succession, giving the impression that he was playing his banjo at terrific speed. Later, when he joined Bill Monroe's band, Scruggs was introduced as "the boy who can make a banjo talk."[5]

He needed a companion. "I grew up in Depression days with nothing much for enjoyment and that helped me enjoy music more," he said. "I didn't have television or other distractions. Playing was something that made me feel good. Like my daddy. He had an old banjo, probably wasn't worth three dollars. He could play for himself. It makes me feel better so I'd think it made him feel better." Scruggs said that he came to depend upon the music, that it made him feel he had something to cheer him constantly even though he liked living in a place that he thinks first to describe by saying, "There were a lot of trees." Scruggs's father died when he was four. "I remember him, but not very well," Scruggs said. "I remember when he was sick. It really used to bother me growing up an awful lot."

The banjo became a staple on the American blackface minstrel-show circuit beginning early in the 1800s. For a brief time at the end of the century, it also enjoyed a vogue among well-to-do urban northeasterners, who played it in plush New York parlors and oak-paneled Philadelphia club rooms. Jazz bands like the New Orleans Rhythm Kings included a banjo, but it was strictly relegated to providing cadence. For rural working-class, twentieth-century Southern white audiences, the banjo served the function that it probably did for the Africans who invented its gourd prototype: it was used for entertainment and ceremony. In all cases[,] there was a recreational, casual attitude toward the banjo, a feeling that serious musicians could find something more versatile and challenging.[6]

---

5. For more on the intricacies of Scruggs's banjo style, consult Thomas Adler, "Manual Formulaic Composition: Innovation in Bluegrass Banjo Styles," *Journal of Country Music* 5, no. 2 (Summer 1974): 55–64; and Joti Rockwell, "Drive, Lonesomeness, and the Genre of Bluegrass Music," Ph.D. dissertation, University of Chicago, 2007, 181–219.

6. For more on the banjo's associations with minstrelsy, consult Karen Linn, *That Half-Barbaric Twang: The Banjo in American Popular Culture* (Urbana: University of Illinois Press, 1991), 40–80.

Up through the early 1940s, most country banjo players picked out songs by striking the strings of the instrument with a fingernail in a strum, note, strum, note rhythmic pattern. This downward motion was variously referred to as rapping, frailing, stroke, drop-thumb, and, as Ralph Stanley's mother played it, claw-hammer. Though you could certainly strum a tune on the ol' banjo, through World War II professional country musicians regarded the instrument primarily as a vaudeville prop. Famous banjo players like Dewitt "Snuffy" Jenkins, Marshall "Grandpa" Jones, David "Stringbean" Akeman, and especially "Uncle" Dave Macon earned their wages by cracking wise.[7] They might be skilled banjo pickers and bright men, but they were also comedians, and their instrument was, like Grandpa Jones's suspenders and knee boots, just another part of a hillbilly clown's wardrobe. It's not hard to see why. The clear, boinging tone you got when you plucked down on a chord punctuated a performer's slapstick hayseed stand-up, much as a drummer's rimshot might for a Borscht Belt comic[8] or a sheet whistle does for a circus clown.

Earl Scruggs never could tell jokes. He is a sober man, diffident when he is fresh to a situation and sweet-natured when he gets comfortable. Though his conversation is engaging, it is never witty. From the first[,] he was much too serious about his music to pass as a clown and he knew it. "I didn't know whether I'd be able to make it or not," he said. "I wasn't comedy oriented. Just didn't know whether I'd be accepted working for somebody when the only talent I had was playing the banjo."

Early in the 1940s, when he was a teenager, Scruggs played his banjo in local groups, like The Morris Brothers band across the South Carolina border in Spartanburg. In his later teens[,] he worked as a spare hand in a Shelby mill that made strong thread for sewing parachute cloth. "One reason I didn't leave the mill—it was only paying forty cents an hour—was I didn't want to leave home," he said. "The other was I didn't feel right leaving a job making thread for the Army during the war. They needed more help. A lot of guys were away fighting. After the war, that's when I left the mill."[9]

By the time Scruggs turned twenty-one in 1945, his musical tastes were already well-defined. Back when he was fourteen or so, he'd been trying out some up-tempo boogie-woogie numbers on his banjo and his mother overheard him. "She said to me, 'Earl, if you're gonna play something, play something that has a tune to it,' " he says. "That stuck in my

7. Several scholars have suggested that these performers represent a link to the nineteenth-century minstrel show. See, for instance, chap. 2 of Pamela Fox, *Natural Acts: Gender, Race, and Rusticity in Country Music* (Ann Arbor: University of Michigan Press, 2009).

8. The term "Borscht Belt" refers to a region in the Catskill Mountains of New York that became a center of Jewish tourism and a hotbed of Jewish comedy in the early decades of the twentieth century. See, for instance, Stefan Kanfer, *A Summer World: The Attempt to Build a Jewish Eden in the Catskills, from the Days of the Ghetto to the Rise and Decline of the Borscht Belt* (New York: Farrar, Straus, and Giroux, 1989).

9. For more on the connections between textile mills and early country music, consult Pamela Grundy, " 'We Always Tried to Be Good People': Respectability, Crazy Water Crystals, and Hillbilly Music on the Air, 1933-1935," *Journal of American History* 81, no. 4 (March 1995): 1591–620; William F. Danaher and Vincent J. Roscigno, "Cultural Production, Media, and Meaning: Hillbilly Music and the Southern Textile Mills," *Poetics* 32 (2004): 51–-71; and Patrick Huber, *Linthead Stomp: The Creation of Country Music in the Piedmont South* (Chapel Hill: University of North Carolina Press, 2008).

mind. She'd heard me play from the time I was five. I though, my goodness! If she can't tell what I'm playing[,] nobody else can. That got me interested in trying to play the tune. I'd hate to waste it, have nobody know what I'm playing. I have played with people like King Curtis, the great jazz saxophone man, and I do like to play around a tune—it's fun. But I don't like to play around a tune as much. I have to make it recognizable. So I've always tried to keep what would be the vocal a little louder than the rest."

Scruggs talks in a quiet, self-effacing way. He said now that he learned church songs from his neighbors in Flint Hill and through them he also picked up what he calls "the old songs": "Sally Goodin," "Cripple Creek," "Cumberland Gap," "John Henry," and the like. Many of them were Scotch, Irish, or English tunes that were now more popular in the southeastern American mountain country than they were in Britain. The Scruggs family acquired a Victrola[10] when Scruggs was very young, and then a radio several years later. Scruggs listened carefully to the records made by The Carter Family. "Simple" is Scruggs's word for Mother Maybelle's guitar playing, and he says that with admiration. After a while, he could play a melody on a banjo as clearly as she did it on her Gibson. The difference was that for all his love of melody, he simply couldn't contain his supernal fingers.

Late in 1945, Scruggs was working for a bandleader named Lost John Miller. Miller was based in Knoxville, but he traveled to Nashville every Friday night to do a Saturday-morning radio show. When in Nashville, the band stayed at the Tulane Hotel, and in the hotel coffee shop one Saturday, Scruggs met Jim Shumate, a North Carolina fiddle player who played with Bill Monroe's Blue Grass Boys. The Blue Grass Boys were in town for their weekly performance on *The Grand Ole Opry*. Shumate told Scruggs he thought he would make a fine addition to Monroe's band. Scruggs was happy in East Tennessee, but Shumate was persuasive; this would be a wonderful opportunity, he said, and offered to set up a time when Monroe might stop by Scruggs's room and listen to him play. Scruggs allowed himself to be cajoled into showing Monroe what he had.

Shumate knew that Bill Monroe could use a new lead musician. Until then[,] Monroe was running what amounted to a traveling carny show, a revue of sorts, which over the years had blended string music with a succession of novelty acts. When he breezed into town, besides a bass, guitar, and fiddle, under the tent with him he might have an accordion player, a jug blower, a harmonica player, an electric-guitar player, or a banjo player. Many of these men were comedians. Monroe had noproblem with that. He was a showman with profit on his mind[,] and he was always eager to find musicians who could keep pace with his boiling mandolin. (Monroe went so fast that the guitar player, Lester Flatt, took to clamping his middle fingers on the first and sixth strings to begin his famous time-setting scissors "G run," a syncopated riff that quietly accelerated until Flatt was on the third string in the key of G and cruising when he opened up and rejoined the others at full volume.) Monroe was skeptical about the idea of Scruggs, but not at all opposed to seeing if a man could play alongside him on a banjo. He agreed to meet Scruggs in his room at the Tulane.

On the appointed day, Monroe knocked on Scruggs's door at the hotel, came in, and sat down. Scruggs began to play. "When Bill came to my room to listen to me[,] I played two tunes, something familiar, 'Sally Goodin,' and something fast, 'Dear Old Dixie,'" said Scruggs. "He seemed very interested, but he seemed confused." Monroe didn't say much before he left

10. A brand of record player popular before World War II.

other than to tell Scruggs that he should come over to the *Opry* later and play a little with The Blue Grass Boys, Scruggs did that, and in just a few minutes he turned backstage at the *Opry* into the Rue Chaptal.

Monroe had mentioned Scruggs to Lester Flatt, and Flatt told Monroe that as far as he was concerned the kid could "leave the damn banjo in the case." A sharecropper's son and a former silk-mill hand from the central Tennessee town of Sparta, Flatt had been singing lead and playing guitar with Monroe for nearly a year. When "Stringbean" Akeman had been a Blue Grass Boy, he had vexed the other members of the band because they wanted to play fast and he couldn't keep up with them on his banjo. Flatt knew all about banjos. They were sand in the gears[,] and he didn't want them in any band that he was in. "Lester's whole way of thinking changed after we struck up a tune," says Scruggs.

"I was just dumbfounded," Flatt told a friend many years later. "I had never heard anybody pick a banjo like he did. He could go all over the neck and do things you couldn't hardly believe." Flatt had just seen a soft-eyed, bashful twenty-one-year-old kid transform the banjo into a different kind of instrument. Instead of the pluck, strum, pluck of the clawhammer, here was real melody. Scruggs played at a terpsichorean pace but with impeccable smoothness as he lent rich layers of texture to the songs. It was a little bit like watching a Model T take flight right in front of you. Monroe asked Flatt what he thought. Flatt said, "If you can hire him, get him, whatever it costs."

Another person sitting in on the *Opry* audition was a chubby old man who had stenciled "World's Greatest Banjoist" on the side of his instrument case. "Uncle" Dave Macon, "The Dixie Dewdrop," wore expensive suits, had fillets of gold in his teeth, a goatee, a thick watch chain, an infectious cackle, and a repertoire of songs with titles like "Keep My Skillet Good and Greasy," "Chewing Gum," and "Rabbit in the Pea Patch." He liked to announce that "Uncle Dave handles a banjo like a monkey handles a peanut," but that wasn't so. Uncle Dave was a beloved singer and a master sight-gag comedian. On a banjo, however, he was no more than a capable professional entertainer. Which he knew. "Shucks," Macon said when Scurggs finished the two songs. "He maybe can play in a band but I bet he can't sing a lick."

"He also said I wasn't a bit funny," says Scruggs. "He said that. I liked him. He was a proud old man. In essence he was saying that all I could do was pick. He had a lot going for him. He was funny and he could sing. I did sing, but I wasn't a featured singer. I wasn't trying to do what he was doing."

Scruggs wasn't sure he wanted to be a Blue Grass Boy. "I'd got enough of show business with the band I was with and I wanted to go back home," he said. "By nature I was a homeboy. I missed Carolina, missed my mother. I was tired of living in hotels. But at the time I didn't have a job back in the mill at Shelby, so I thought I'd try it for a few months and see. I was at the age when I enjoyed trying new things."

Soon after Scruggs joined Monroe, the tenor singer Curly Sechler [sic] paid a visit back to his home in China Grove, North Carolina. When he got there he found that "everybody was saying, 'What happened to Bill Monroe's music?'" What happened, Lester Flatt reflected later, was that with the inclusion of Scruggs, Monroe's band had moved their playing into a new realm. "When we got Earl, it was really the first time a sound like that had been heard," Flatt said. "There had been maybe a similar sound, but we then had what was to become known as bluegrass music."

Strictly speaking, Scruggs didn't invent a banjo technique so much as he refined a new style. Almost nothing in music comes straight out of the air. There had been men before him who could play banjo arpeggios with three fingers. Oddly enough, most of them came from the Carolinas. "After I left the Carolinas I learned that most good banjos were sold in North and South Carolina," says Scruggs. "I don't know why that is. Some parts of the country you go to, the woods are full of good fiddler players." Capable as men like Snuffy Jenkins, Hoke Jenkins, Johnny Whisnant, Don Reno, Wiley Birchfield, Charlie Poole, Smith Hammett, Rez Brooks, and Scruggs's own older brother, Junie, were with a five-string, the speed, agility, and personality with which Scruggs could play a banjo were beyond what anyone else was doing.

The banjo as a serious musical instrument was a source of incredulity in country music circles. People had to see and hear Scruggs for themselves. Once they did, most simply came away enthralled. "People really accepted it," Scruggs told me. "They'd come backstage and try to get me to explain what I was doing, ask me questions. Everything was fitting so well. He [Monroe] played a type of music that fit in for me."

Other banjo players immediately began to imitate Scruggs. When he was working with Monroe, The Stanley Brothers were playing a show on a radio station in Bristol, Virginia, and they sounded a lot like The Blue Grass Boys, in part because Ralph Stanley had taken up Scruggs-style banjo picking. "That was the greatest thing to happen in my career; that I could be playing well enough for somebody else to like," says Scruggs. Monroe didn't respond as gracefully. When he ran into the Stanleys, he accused them of ripping off his sound and stopped talking to them for a while.

Lester Flatt and Earl Scruggs were together with Monroe from 1945 to 1948, and many people consider that version of The Blue Grass Boys to be the seminal bluegrass band. The classic song of the period that reveals how much verve and grace Scruggs's picking brought to Monroe is the instrumental "Bluegrass Breakdown," in which Monroe on his mandolin, the fiddler, Chubby Wise, and Scruggs take turns speeding through an instrumental number that sounds a little like a bird being pursued by a pair of quick, eager dogs. Monroe, the bird, bursts out of the brush, madly fluttering his wings. Scruggs and then Wise each take a turn making a run at him, Monroe soaring away from them each time on his mandolin. Because Monroe takes the last break, it is fair to say that Scruggs and Wise don't catch him, but that they make a nice chase of it.

That was the way it was when you worked for Monroe: he was always out in front. The exception is "Molly and Tenbrooks (The Race Horse Song)," in which Scruggs has three solo breaks and sets the galloping pace for this musical account of a match race between two champion thoroughbreds. Generally Scruggs did not dominate the breaks in a tune any more than Chubby Wise did. In other words, with Monroe, Scruggs played the role of sideman, subordinating himself to his bandleader. All things being equal, for a time that was fine with him. Scruggs was only in his early twenties and he knew that everyone in Monroe's band was an unusually talented musician. Further, Scruggs happens to have been born with a sideman's disposition. Saying that Scruggs is modest is an understatement. He is humble; it comes naturally to him.

"You just get into a way of doing something," is how he describes his approach to music. "I don't have anything else to do. I'm concentrating quite a bit when I'm playing with somebody that's singing or a fiddle player. I spend most of my time trying to think of something to make him sound better. That's what I'm doing a lot of the time."

The fine young banjo player Alison Brown tells a story about Scruggs's self-effacing qualities. "I met Earl in the summer of 1990 with five Japanese banjo players," she said. "It was a big deal for me going to the master's house. The five Japanese guys had been to the Gibson banjo factory to buy five Scruggs model banjos and now they were on their way to Scruggs's house so that he could christen their banjos, so to speak. We got there, I sat down in a corner and watched. Here's these five Japanese guys and a couple of other players and Earl. We all had our banjos. We go around and kick off 'Fireball Mail,' one of those old Scruggs tunes. He played backup while everybody else took a solo. He didn't need to take a solo. It was such a selfless thing. He's the father figure for all banjo players. It's impossible to play bluegrass banjo without learning Earl Scruggs. People spend hours poring over the old recordings to get it right—just like Earl did it. Here, with us, he had nothing to prove. He was content to play backup in a style everybody knows he invented. He's kind of the opposite of Bill Monroe in that way."

Scruggs has received many compliments over the years for his playing, but the most resonant one is Robert Shelton's observation in his *New York Times* review of the 1959 Newport Folk Festival that Scruggs "bears about the same relationship to the banjo that Paganini does to the violin." Niccoló Paganini of Genoa was one of the great virtuoso [sic] of the nineteenth-century classical violin, a brilliant showman who could play a new concerto on sight, was a master of left-hand pizzicato, and specialized in pyrotechnic bowing, in which he ricocheted through a succession of notes on a single stroke. Paganini so thrilled to impress people that he would produce a scissors and cut every string on his violin but one and then pro-ceed through a piece working on that string while his audience gasped and applauded. Many people swore he was possessed, that "he had dedicated himself to the Evil One," as Franz Liszt excitedly said. When I asked Scruggs about Shelton's praise[,] he said, "Everybody likes a pat on the back, I guess," and looked like he wanted to crawl under his easy chair.

Not only did The Blue Grass Boys travel a relentless schedule of one-night stands across the South, they sped through the night in a converted limousine, taking turns driving and trying to sleep sitting up while the car passed over crooked, two-lane country roads. When they arrived in a town, they threw a baseball around to feel human again. "Monroe carried two or three baseball gloves and a ball with us," said Scruggs. "We'd be in the '41 Chevrolet all night and all day and we couldn't shift our legs, so we'd go out and play catch to loosen up our legs and have something to do until showtime."

Monroe's twin obsessions on the road appear to have been musical perfection and punctuality, as his salute to life with The Blue Grass Boys, "Heavy Traffic Ahead," makes clear. "We worked everything from coal camps in Kentucky and West Virginia, to farmland from Florida across the southeast," Scruggs said. "In those days they were all acquainted with the music." Besides playing his instrument, Scruggs was the Blue Grass Boy who sold tickets at shows and kept the books for Monroe. What he saw was that, given the daily take, Monroe was paying the band scantily. Flatt's biographer, Jake Lambert, says this income disparity bothered Flatt and Scruggs. Scruggs says not. He told Monroe's biographer, Jim Rooney, "I loved Bill like a brother and he was always good to me."

Of course[,] Scruggs spoke to Rooney well after 1948, the year he and Flatt gave their notice to Monroe and left him to form their own band. Flatt and Scruggs always publicly insisted that it was coincidence that they left at the same time. They claimed they had no plans to continue in music together. This account has been difficult for many people to believe—Jake Lambert says Flatt told him in confidence that it wasn't accurate—but Scruggs still adheres to it. "It's untrue," he protests whenever the more skeptical version of the events is presented to him. Scruggs is a civil man and has obvious distaste for unseemly behavior, which he would consider leaving his first employer in the lurch to be. Monroe asked him to stay on for an addi-tional two weeks and Scruggs readily agreed. He tried to please people. Still, he wanted out.

"I had got enough of music," Scruggs said. "With his [Monroe's] methods of operation we were traveling so much I was hardly going to bed. I had intended to go back to Shelby into a mill. When my notice was filled Lester turned in his notice; he was gonna leave. Lester called me and said he'd been thinking about it and we wouldn't be happy back in the mill. He suggested we get a job together at a radio station in Carolina, closer to home. We put a five-piece group together within a few weeks and we went to WCBY in Bristol, Virginia, and started making a living real quick. I've heard he [Monroe] felt we formed up to start a show, but that wasn't it. He went several years without speaking to us. That all went away. I consider Bill as my friend now."

It was precisely twenty-one years before they had a conversation. Monroe used his influence to keep Flatt and Scruggs off the *Opry* stage for several years, and even into the 1970s, whenever he talked about what he clearly considered this betrayal, Monroe seethed. Not that he lacked for a banjo player. Ralph Stanley was only one of many banjo players who quickly embraced Scruggs-style picking. Just as many distance runners began to complete a mile in less than four minutes once Roger Bannister had done it, banjo players began to play leads at warp speed as soon as Scruggs showed them how. Don Reno and later Rudy Lyle followed Scruggs in The Blue Grass Boys, and they handled Scruggs's old breaks with aplomb. Largely because of Scruggs, the banjo was now being accepted as an indispensable lead instrument in a bluegrass band. Meanwhile, Earl Scruggs and Lester Flatt thrived on their own.

FOR FURTHER READING

Cantwell, Robert. *Bluegrass Breakdown: The Making of the Old Southern Sound.* Urbana: University of Illinois Press, 1984.
Rosenburg, Neil V. *Bluegrass: A History.* Urbana: University of Illinois Press, 1985.

19

Rufus Jarman

"Country Music Goes to Town" (1953)

By the early 1950s, observers from around the United States were beginning to recognize country music's financial potential. Even prior to the development of Nashville as a major center for country music recording and publishing, the success of the *Grand Ole Opry* and the pioneering publishing enterprise Acuff-Rose—established by *Opry* star Roy Acuff and songwriter Fred Rose—drew interest from businessmen looking for new ways to invest their money. But it seems that they were often puzzled as to how such apparently "lowbrow" music could be so popular. In particular, the rise and tragic death of Hank Williams, who was both an *Opry* star and a member of the Acuff-Rose songwriting stable, attracted a great deal of attention.[1] Through national television appearances and crossover success as a songwriter, Williams demonstrated the broad popular and

---

1. The history of Acuff-Rose is traced in John W. Rumble, "'I'll Reap My Harvest in Heaven': Fred Rose's Acquaintance with Country Music," in *Reading Country Music: Steel Guitars, Opry Stars, and Honky-Tonk Bars,* ed. Cecelia Tichi (Durham, NC: Duke University Press, 1998), 350–77.

commercial appeal of country music.[2] Moreover, country music was increasingly important in Europe and Japan following its introduction during World War II and the constant infusions of new country recordings provided by American troops who have remained stationed around the world to the present day. Consequently, country music was no longer simply a rural music that had a small, devoted following, but was a music that had global potential on which label owners and publishers felt they needed to capitalize.

The following reading, which appeared in a magazine published by the U.S. Chamber of Commerce, shows the impact of American military involvement in Europe and Asia on country music in the years immediately following World War II. In the opening paragraphs of this essay, contributor Rufus Jarman offers a now clichéd discussion of the seemingly stark contrasts between the "highbrow" culture of European art music that had been exported to the United States and the "lowbrow" contributions of Opry stars who invoked minstrel tropes and described the difficulties of honky-tonk love affairs in song. Yet, Jarman later offers an explanation for the success of country music in Europe—and especially Germany, which continues to support a thriving country music culture—that may be found in musical and cultural affinities between European folk musics and contemporary country music.[3] Moreover, it is important to note that, while American record labels sent new product to record buyers in global markets, Jarman also noted the creation of new, syncretic country music practices that blended local vernacular traditions with global country music.[4]

═══════════

A N interesting new development has been observed recently in the musical tastes of the peoples of Western Europe, who have given to the world Brahms, Beethoven, Mendelssohn, Chopin, Wagner, Verdi and the waltzes of Johann Strauss. Now, it appears that

2. Williams has been the subject of extensive popular and academic study. See, for example, David Brackett, *Interpreting Popular Music* (Berkeley: University of California Press, 2000), 75–107; Bill Koon, *Hank Williams: So Lonesome* (Jackson: University Press of Mississippi, 2001); Colin Escott with George Merritt and William MacEwen, *Hank Williams: The Biography*, rev. ed. (New York: Back Bay Books, 2004); and Patrick Huber, Steve Goodson, and David Anderson, eds., *The Hank Williams Reader* (New York: Oxford University Press, 2014).

3. This narrative of cultural connections between Europe and the United States was invoked commonly in the world of early twentieth-century folksong collectors, but demands a much more nuanced consideration.

4. Several recent studies have traced the transnational flow of country music to Europe and Asia. See, for instance, Kristin Solli, "North of Nashville: Country Music, National Identity, and Class in Norway," Ph.D. dissertation, University of Iowa, 2006; Lee Bidgood, "America Is All Around Here": An Ethnography of Bluegrass Music in the Contemporary Czech Republic," Ph.D. dissertation, University of Virginia, 2011; and Michael Furmanovsky, "American Country Music in Japan: Lost Piece in the Popular Music History Puzzle," *Popular Music and Society* 31, no. 3 (July 2008): 357–72.

European musical culture has taken a surprising and ardent fancy to the works of a new school of composers and performers, who include:

> Roy Acuff and his Smoky Mountain Boys—including Grandpap who thumps a hillbilly bull fiddle (or doghouse),[5] while wearing a trick goatee and an old Confederate forager's cap—Lonzo and Oscar, a couple of bucolic comics who blow on jugs—a character known as "String Bean," who plays on a five-string banjo and wears his pants down around his knees[6]—and the late "Hank" Williams, a sort of "Irving Berlin[7] of the straw stack," among whose compositions are "Lovesick Blues," "Hey, Good Lookin'," and "Honky-Tonkin'."

In short, Europe has been exposed to—and has taken to—hillbilly and western (American) music. Until comparatively recent times, this form of musical expression had been confined to the fiddling "hoedowns" in the cabins and one-room schoolhouses of the Tennessee-Kentucky-Ozark hill country, and to the nasal wailings of cowboys on the lone prairie who, in song at least, are generally solitary and always sad.

Nowadays this homely artistry has gone international. American armed service personnel and this country's expanding participation in world affairs have made American "country music" almost as prominent in western Europe as the Marshall Plan.[8]

The same is true, maybe to a lesser degree, in Asia. Last spring, when a series of tornadoes hit areas of Tennessee, numerous Japanese sent inquiries from their native land to radio station WSM in Nashville, one of the greatest dispensers of mountain melody through its local and NBC network program, [the] Grand Ole Opry. The letter writers wanted to know if the elements had damaged the station or injured any of its hillbilly stars. Fortunately for culture and the international peace of mind, the station and the stars escaped damage.

Perhaps the greatest foreign hillbilly fan movement is in western German and the Germanic countries, long renowned as music lovers. In the beamed-and-plastered Teutonic beer gardens and brew houses, which for generations have resounded to Viennese waltzes and the umpah-ing of German bands, the high-pitched, scrappy fiddling of hoedown music now rings out, almost like Arkansas. Native bands, in some cases, have abandoned Strauss, and have taken names for themselves such as "Hank Schmitz and his Goober Growlers" or "Red Schmucker and his Mountain Boys."

Recently, some travelers from Nashville were astonished while visiting a café in old Vienna by the following event: A group of musicians, wearing Tyrolean hats and short leather pants, came out. The master of ceremonies announced in heavy, German-coated

---

5. The upright bass or string bass.

6. This is the same David "Stringbean" Akeman who played with Bill Monroe prior to Earl Scruggs's joining the band.

7. Berlin (1888–1989) was a Tin Pan Alley composer best known for his compositions "God Bless America" and "Alexander's Ragtime Band" (Jeffrey Magee, "Berlin, Irving," in *The Grove Dictionary of American Music*, 2nd ed., ed. Charles Hiroshi Garrett [New York: Oxford University Press, 2013], 440–44).

8. The Marshall Plan was a program intended to help rebuild Europe after World War II. For more background, consult Michael J. Hogan, *The Marshall Plan: America, Britain and the Reconstruction of Western Europe, 1947-1952* (Cambridge: Cambridge University Press, 1987).

English: "Ladies and Gentlemen: Eric (Grandpappy) Ritter and his Alpine Hillbilly Briar Hoppers will now perform. Their first selection will be: 'How Many Biscuits Kin You Eat This Mawnin',' followed by: 'Git Them Cold Feet Over On The Other Side.' "

Early last summer[,] a young man named Bill Carrigan returned to his home town of Columbia, Tenn., after a four-year hitch with the U.S. Army in Germany, where he was in charge of hillbilly music activities of the American Armed Forces (radio) Network, with head-quarters at Frankfurt. The network has stations, some of them three times as powerful as any in this country, at Munich, Stuttgart, Bremerhaven, Nuremberg, Berlin and Frankfurt. Calling himself "Uncle Willie," Bill Carrigan, a radio announcer before entering the Army, operated a daily hillbilly disc jockey show, "The Hillbilly Gast Haus." This program drew the starting total of 150,000 letters a year, not only from American personnel, but from European civilians in 22 countries, including Czechoslovakia, behind the Iron Curtain.

Somehow these letters and cards got past Russian censorship. "Please play George Morgan's 'Candy Kisses,' and think of us here now and then," the writers might say. Most letter from civilians, however, came from Germany. In German-belabored English, these often made such inquiries as "What ist meaning of the song 'Too Old To Cut The Mustard'?"

Hillbilly favorites, by countries, as best Mr. Carrigan could figure were: Germany, "Death On the Highway" (Roy Acuff); France, "My Daddy Is Only a Picture" (Eddie [sic] Arnold); England, "It Is No Secret What God Can Do" and "Peace In the Valley" (Red Foley); Belgium, "Let Old Mother Nature Have Her Way" (Carl Smith); Scandinavian countries, "Birth of the Blues" (Chet Atkins), while Hank Snow's "Moving On" was a general continental favorite.

As a special Saturday night feature, the "Hillbilly Gast Haus" broadcast transcrip-tions[9] of the WSM Grand Ole Opry radio program. Europeans and U.S. personnel took to this so avidly that a year or so ago[,] Mr. Carrigan organized a European version of the Opry, made up of Army hillbilly musicians. They performed every Saturday night to overflow audiences in the Frankfurt Palmgarden, seating 3,000. The hillbilly programs broke all Palmgarden atten-dance records, including appearances there of Bob Hope, Horace Heidt and other more sophis-ticated performers.

U.S. personnel and European civilians from as far away as Rome stood in line five and six hours to get in. Prim-faced ladies came over from London to applaud hillbilly renditions of homely religious hymns, and young women and men bicycled down from as far north as Denmark.

Later[,] the Army's Grand Ole Opry was put on the road. One of its duties came to be instructing local civilian musical groups in the mysteries of hillbilly music. German violinists, accustomed to rendering Viennese waltzes played with long, sweeping movements of the bow, had trouble grasping the hoedown technique, which is played with short, choppy strokes. It was amusing, witnesses report, to see Army hillbillies demonstrating the fiddling technique for such numbers as "Bile That Cabbage Down" to the frock-coated Germans, who carefully copied down these wild notes on paper.

Usually at the European performances, "Onkel Willi"—as the Germans addressed him—would begin the show by describing what was probably transpiring at the real Grand Ole Opry [sic], which has gone on the air out of Nashville every Saturday night since 1925. More

---

9. Pre-recorded programs.

than 5,000,000 hillbilly enthusiasts have visited the program, and more than 10,000,000 listen regularly to the program on the radio.

In a way, it is not surprising that Europeans should like American country music. This country's folk songs had their origins in the folk songs that early settlers brought over from Europe. The songs were changed to fit conditions and experiences in a new world that was rawer and cruder than Europe and filled with giants.

When the Scotch and English settlers came over the mountains into Tennessee, they brought their fiddles. That instrument has remained as important to the people of the ridges and valleys as bagpipes are to the Highland Scots. For generations[,] they have made the hollows resound to "Billy In the Low Ground" and "Ole Dan Tucker" and to such ballads as "You'll Never Miss Your Mother 'Till She's Gone."[10]

When I was a boy down in Tennessee, the audiences for these rustic troubadours were only country men and women. They gathered about store porches on Saturday nights. Sometimes they drove in buggies to lamp-lit rural schoolhouses. They paid for this entertainment by tossing dimes and quarters into sweat-stained black felt hats.

What brought this homely music out of the backroads and into great popularity nationally—and now internationally—was radio in general and in particular station WSM, owned by the National Life & Accident Insurance Company. Through country music, Nashville is now a phonograph-recording center comparable to New York and Hollywood. WSM has become the "big time" to country musicians, as the old Palace once was to vaudeville. The *Wall Street Journal* has estimated that country music in Nashville now amounts to a $25,000,000-a-year industry.

The whole picture adds up to an utterly astonishing phenomenon, and it all got started like this:

Not long after World War I, George D. Hay, a reporter for the Memphis *Commercial Appeal*, was sent to cover the funeral of a war hero in the Ozark foothills near Mammoth Spring, Ark. After filing his story, Mr. Hay attended a hoedown in a log cabin about a mile up a muddy road, "lighted by a coal oil lamp in one corner." He later recounted, "No one has ever had more fun than those Ozark mountains had that night. It stuck with me until the idea became the Grand Ole Opry seven or eight years later."

Mr. Hay was hired as station director by WSM in 1925, and on a Saturday night, Nov. 28 of that year, he launched the Opry. He called himself "The Solemn Old Judge." His first and only artist that night was a bearded, 80-year-old gentleman called "Uncle Jimmy" Thompson, who played an old-time fiddle and said he knew 1,000 tunes. He played an hour that first night, and didn't want to stop. Claimed he was just getting warmed up.[11]

The station was amazed at the response, and Uncle Jimmy was established as a regular Saturday night performer. The management was even more amazed within a few weeks by the droves of country musicians, inspired by Uncle Jimmy's example, who poured in to get into the act. As early as Friday afternoon[,] they would swarm about Memorial Square near the station—their ancient instruments in beat-up old cases and sometimes in flour sacks. There were fiddlers, guitar strummers, mandolin tinklers, harmonica moaners, banjo pickers and one woman with an old zither.

10. See also Charles K. Wolfe, *Tennessee Strings: The Story of Country Music in Tennessee* (Knoxville: University of Tennessee Press, 1977), 3–26.
11. See chapter 14.

Gradually[,] a large cast of country musical units was built up. There were almost no professional hillbilly musicians then. They were people who worked on farms, in stores, garages and blacksmith shops, who played for fun. Among the early WSM groups was Dr. Humphrey Bate, an Estill Springs, Tenn., physician, and his "Possum Hunters," made up of Dr. Bate on the harmonica[;] his son, Buster, his daughter, Alcyone, and Stanley Walton, guitars; Walter Liggett, banjo[;] and Oscar Stone, bass fiddle. Other early, similar groups were the Crook Brothers, the "Fruit Jar Drinkers" and "Fiddlin' Sid Harkreader and his Gully Jumpers."

Their renditions were almost entirely instrumental, with an occasional whoop and holler from one of the bandsmen when somebody hit a hot lick. But the show was really crying for a vocal star. It found one in a remarkable old character know as Uncle Dave Macon, "the Dixie Dewdrop."

Uncle Dave, who died last spring, lived at Readyville, Tenn. He wore a high wing collar, a bright red tie, a broad-brimmed hat of black felt, a double-breasted waistcoat, long sideburns, gold teeth and a sensational goatee. He used to play for quarters in a hat at the country school at Lascassas, Tenn., where I attended. He did wonderful things on a variety of banjos, and he sang in a voice you could hear a mile up the road on quiet nights.

Mules used to stir uneasily in their stalls halfway up the valley when they heard Uncle Dave squall:

As long as ole bacon stays at thutty cents a pound

I'm a-gonna eat a rabbit, if I haff-ta run him down...

Oh tell me how long....

I remember the first Saturday night, in 1926, when Uncle Dave made his debut on WSM. We had read about it in the paper, but we didn't mention it about Lascassas. We had one of the two radio sets in the community, and we were afraid everybody in that end of the county would swarm into our house to hear Uncle Dave, and trample us.

Nevertheless, the word got around and just about everybody did swarm into our house, except a few local sages who didn't believe in radio.

Except for Uncle Dave, who was mainly comedy, the Opry had no real vocal stars until 1938. Vocalists had contented themselves with singing the old favorites, "Rabbit In The Pea Patch" or "Clementine." Roy Acuff, with a string band from Maynardville, Tenn., was the first featured singer backed by a band. He was also first to identify himself with particular songs— "The Great Speckled Bird" and "The Wabash Cannon Ball."

These came to be identified with Acuff in somewhat the way "Cry" is with Johnny Ray. Later, Acuff began composing his own songs. He still performs on the Opry, which now has a whole stable of highly popular singers. Red Foley hit with "Smoke On The Water"; Ernest Tubb with "Walking The Floor Over You"; Cowboy Copas with "My Filipino Baby"; Hank Williams with "Lovesick Blues" and Little Jimmy Dickens with "Old Cold Tater." The most recent sensation is handsome Carl Smith of Maynardville, who sets rustic bobby soxers wild with "Let's Live A Little," and "Let Old Mother Nature Have Her Way."

These country music glamour boys are as big—sometimes bigger—in record sales and juke box popularity as Bing Crosby or Frank Sinatra. These men make up to $300,000 a year. They live in mansions with swimming pools attached in Nashville's fashionable suburbs, drive immense automobiles bearing their initials in gold, and wear expensive western get-ups—loud suits costing $300 each, $50 hats and $75 boots.

What baffles conservative Nashvillians are the crowds that swarm into town each week to see the program, which lasts four and a half hours. All of it is broadcast over WSM's powerful, clear-channel station, and 30 minutes of it has been broadcast for a dozen years over the NBC network, sponsored by Prince Albert Tobacco. Red Foley is the master of ceremonies. In addition to the music of bands and quartets, there are two immensely popular comedians, Red [sic] Brasfield[12] of Hohenwald, Tenn., and Cousin Minnie Pearl, a product of Centerville, Tenn.

Only the network portion of the show is rehearsed and that only once, for timing. About 125 stars and their "side men" take part in this whole jamboree, which is marked by great informality. Performers, some in outlandish costumes, stroll about the stage, join in with their instruments with units of the show other than their own, and occasionally toss one another playfully into a tub of iced drinks that is kept on the stage at all times.

Back when the Opry was new, people used to pack around a big plate glass window, like most studios had, to watch. The management began admitting as many as could get into the room, about 75, to sit around the musicians and cheer them on. Their applause and shouts added to the programs folksy flavor, and constituted one of the first of all audience-participation shows. Later, the station built an auditorium-studio that seated 500. Then about ten years ago, they moved into the Ryman Auditorium, which is about as colorful as the Opry is.

It was built in 1892 by subscriptions raised by Capt. Tom Ryman, owner of a line of river pleasure boats. He had gone to a tent meeting to jeer at a famous religious revivalist, the late Sam Jones of Cartersville, Ga. But that night[,] the preacher chose for his topic, "Mother," which hit Captain Ryman in a tender spot. He was converted then and there, and built a great tabernacle, "so Sam Jones wouldn't have to preach in a tent."

The old building has narrow pointed windows, a rostrum instead of a stage, primitive dressing rooms and old church pews that seat 3,572 persons. The 1,384 reserved seats, at 60 cents each, are taken weeks in advance. Often as many as 10,000 are turned from the door. The crows come from every state, averaging 485 miles per person to get there. More attend from Alabama and Illinois than from Tennessee. People as far away as Saudi Arabia have attended, writing ahead for seats. An ice storm a few years ago paralyzed the city but failed to stop the Opry crowd.

The audience ranges from a few people who think the term "Opry" means they should come formal and those who take off their shoes and nurse their babies during the show. Many of them come in trucks.

In Nashville hotels, they often bed down eight to a room, and bring along their food. They clean their hotel rooms, never having heard of maid service. Many of them never heard of tipping[,] either. Bellboys and elevator operators, when the management isn't looking, may make up for this oversight by charging ten cents per elevator ride.

Besides their radio programs and records, the Opry stars constantly manifest themselves to their followers through personal appearances, arranged by the WSM Artist Service Bureau, under Jim Denny.[13] Every night[,] one or more troupes of Opry stars are appearing in

12. Rod Brasfield.
13. The career of Jim Denny is traced in Albert Cuniff, "Muscle Behind the Music: The Life and Times of Jim Denny," *Journal of Country Music* 11: Part 1, no. 1 (1986): 39–48; Part 2, no. 2 (1986): 26–32; Part 3, no. 3 (1987): 22–32.

some city about the land. They have crammed Carnegie Hall in New York and played before sellout audiences in white ties and tails in Constitution Hall in Washington. More often[,] they appear on Sundays in picnic groves in Pennsylvania, Illinois or Ohio. Not long ago, one troupe played to 65,000 persons in four days in Texas.

To fill this schedule, the Opry stars live a hard life. They usually leave Nashville in their cars on Sundays, and drive hard from one engagement to another, heading back to Nashville in time for Saturday. Often they don't sleep in a bed for nights on end, but take turns driving.

They keep their car radios tuned to hillbilly broadcasts at all times, and when they hear some local rustic singer who sounds promising, they tip off Jack Stapp, the Opry's program director.

The touring stars have simple living tastes. One observer who has traveled with them reports that some stars, making hundreds of thousands of dollars a year, will eat the same meal three times a day—fried potatoes, fried eggs and fried pork chops. For, in spite of their fancy clothes, big cars and abundant money, the Opry stars remain simple people who "were raised hard and live hard," as one of them has said. Some of them do not know a note of music, but their great appeal as entertainers is in the rawness of their emotions and their sincerity in conveying them.

Hank Williams was discussing that shortly before his death in January. Williams was a lank, erratic countryman who learned to play a guitar from an old Negro named Teetot in his home village of Georgiana, Ala.

"You ask what makes our kind of music successful," Williams was saying. "I'll tell you. It can be explained in just one word: sincerity. When a hillbilly sings a crazy song, he feels crazy. When he sings, 'I Laid My Mother Away,' he sees her a-laying right there in the coffin.

"He sings more sincere than most entertainers because the hillbilly was raised rougher than most entertainers. You got to know a lot about hard work. You got to have smelt a lot of mule manure before you can sing like a hillbilly. The people who has been raised something like the way the hillbilly has knows what he is singing about and appreciates it.

"For what he is singing is the hopes and prayers and dreams and experiences of what some call the 'common people.' I call them the 'best people,' because they are the ones that the world is made up most of. They're really the ones who make things tick, wherever they are in this country or in any country.

"They're the ones who understand what we're singing about, and that's why our kind of music is sweeping the world. There ain't nothing strange about our popularity these days. It's just that there are more people who are like us than there are the educated cultured kind.

"There ain't nothing at all queer about them Europeans liking our kind of singing. It's liable to teach them more about what everyday Americans are really like than anything else."

Source: Rufus Jarman, "Country Music Goes to Town," *Nation's Business* 41 (February 1953): 44–46, 48, 51. (Originally published February 1953. Reprinted by permission, uschamber.com, January 2013. Copyright 1953, U.S. Chamber of Commerce.)

FOR FURTHER READING

Cohen, Sara. "Country at the Heart of the City: Music, Heritage, and Regeneration in Liverpool." *Ethnomusicology* 49, no. 1 (Winter 2005): 25–48.

Lange, Jeffrey J. *Smile When You Call Me a Hillbilly: Country Music's Struggle for Respectability, 1939-1954*. Athens: University of Georgia Press, 2004.

Johnny Cash on recording at Sun with Sam Phillips

Cash: The Autobiography (1997)

In the years following World War II, dozens of independent record labels sprung up in towns and cities throughout the United States, challenging the dominance of such major labels as RCA Victor and Decca.[1] Many of these labels, often run by enthusiastic entrepreneurs, directed their microphones toward local musicians, capturing sounds that were already popular with local audiences.[2] Such was the case with Memphis's Sun Records, which played a pivotal role in the early history of rock and roll. It was the site of what many scholars consider to be the first recording in the genre (although the recording—of Jackie Brenston's

1. The rise of independent labels was accelerated by the American Federation of Musicians' recording strike, which lasted from 1942 to 1944. For more on the recording ban, consult James P. Kraft, *Stage to Studio: Musicians and the Sound Revolution, 1890–1950* (Baltimore: Johns Hopkins University Press, 1996), 137–60.

2. Many of these entrepreneurs are discussed at length in John Broven, *Record Makers and Breakers: Voices of the Independent Rock 'n' Roll Pioneers* (Urbana: University of Illinois Press, 2009).

"Rocket 88"—was released on Chicago's Chess Records), and it helped to launch the careers of some of the biggest stars of early rock and roll, including Jerry Lee Lewis, Carl Perkins, Johnny Cash, and, most famously, Elvis Presley.

Sun Records was founded in 1952 by Sam Phillips, an enterprising entrepreneur who operated the Memphis Recording Service, a recording studio that made custom recordings for anyone who wished to document their musical efforts.[3] The best—and most marketable—of those musicians were frequently given the chance to sign a contract with Sun and have their recordings distributed to record stores, played on radio stations, and loaded into jukeboxes. A typical small businessman, Phillips assumed a great deal of risk by signing musicians who specialized in a wide variety of musical styles and, as a consequence, often took significant financial losses on artists whose recordings simply did not sell. At the same time, he was an astute judge of the market, often discouraging musicians from performing in styles that would not yield high record sales, radio airplay, and jukebox spins. Phillips later sold the contracts of some of his most successful artists in order to raise capital to continue issuing work by new artists.[4] In the process, musicians such as Cash and Presley found their ways to major labels that were capable of using their vast distribution networks and large production capacity to promote them to national and international audiences.

In the following excerpt from Johnny Cash's 1997 autobiography, Cash discusses what it was like to work for "Mr. Phillips" and reflects on Phillips's ability to select songs, develop arrangements, and to encourage the musicians on his label to sing in their own style. At the same time, as Cash's discussion of his royalty checks suggests, the musicians who recorded for Sun had little chance at getting rich from their work, a fact that would lead to some serious accusations against Phillips in later years.

———

WHEN I made my first move on Sun, I told Sam Phillips on the telephone that I was a gospel singer. That didn't work. The market for gospel records, he told me, wasn't big enough for him to make a living producing them. My next try didn't work, either—that time I told him I was a country singer. In the end[,] I just went down to the Memphis Recording Service one morning before anyone arrived for work and sat on the step and waited.

Sam was the first to appear. I stood up and introduced myself and said, "Mr. Phillips, sir, if you listen to me, you'll be glad you did."

That must have been the right thing to say. "Well, I like to hear a boy with confidence in him," he replied. "Come on in."

3. Colin Escott, *Sun Records: The Brief History of the Legendary Recording Label* (New York: Quick Fox, 1980), 25.

4. Most notably, Phillips sold Elvis Presley's contract to RCA Victor in 1955 for a reported $35,000 (Peter Guralnick, *Last Train to Memphis: The Rise of Elvis Presley* [Boston: Little, Brown, 1994], 231).

Once we were in the studio, I sang "I Was There When It Happened" and "It Don't Hurt Anymore" for him. I sang "Belshazzar." I sang Hank Snow songs, a Jimmie Rodgers song, a couple of Carter Family songs, whatever else I'd taken into my repertoire from among the popular country songs of the day. Sam kept directing me back to my own repertoire. "What else have you written?" Though I didn't think it was any good, I told him about "Hey, Porter," and he had me sing it for him.

That did it. "Come back tomorrow with those guys you've been making music with, and we'll put that song down," he told me.[5]

I was really nervous in the studio the next day, and the steel guitar player, Red Kernodle, another mechanic at the Automobile Sales Company, was even worse; he was so jittery he could hardly play at all. The results were predictable: the first track we recorded, "Wide Open Road," sounded awful, and it didn't get any better. After three or four songs, Red packed up his steel and left. "This music business is not for me," he said, and I didn't contest the point. After that[,] we settled down a little and managed to get a respectable take on "Hey, Porter."

Sam liked it. "That's going to be a single," he declared.

"What do you mean, a single?" I asked. I thought we were still auditioning.

"We're going to put out a record," Sam replied.

What a wonderful moment that was! I hadn't thought we had a chance, and now there I was, about to become a Sun recording artist.

"Now," Sam continued, "if we had another song, a love song we could put on the other side, we could release a record. D'you have a song like that?"

"I don't know," I said. "I'll have to think about it."

"Well, if you don't have one, go write one. Write a real weeper."

That's what I did. A couple of weeks later I called him with "Cry, Cry, Cry" in hand, and he had us come back in and cut that, too.

We had to do thirty-five takes before we got "Cry, Cry, Cry" right, mostly because Luther couldn't get his guitar part worked out. I kept changing the arrangement on him, and he kept messing it up. It was a comedy of errors until finally I told him to forget about the guitar break we were trying for and just chord his way through it. That worked out fine, I thought. The *boom-chicka-boom* instrumental style suited me, and it came naturally to us. Marshall Grant was mostly right when in later years he said that we didn't work to get that *boom-chicka-boom* sound—it's all we could play. But it served us well, and it was ours. You knew whose voice was coming when you heard it kick off.

Marshall and Luther limited me, it's true, especially in later years. Songs would come along that I'd want to record, but I didn't because I couldn't figure out the chords myself, and neither could anyone else in the studio. "City of New Orleans" by Steve Goodman was one of those. Kris Kristofferson sent it to me before anyone else got a shot at it, and if I'd taken the time and made the effort to learn it, I might just have had myself a major hit. Instead I let it pass and just kind of drifted along with Marshall and Luther (and, after '59, Fluke). I can't blame Marshall and Luther, of course. There were plenty of people I could have called to come in and show us what we needed to know, but I didn't bother (it's only in the last few years, in fact, that I've learned a couple of new chords). I took the easy way, and to an extent I regret that. Still,

5. Of course, Phillips was observing a long-held practice of preferring original compositions that could be copyrighted and could, therefore, ensure another revenue stream for the label.

though, the way we did it was honest. We played it and sang it the way we felt it, and there's a lot to be said for that.

My feelings about Sam Phillips are still mixed. I think he was another of those angels who appear in your life, but I'm not sure he treated me properly in a financial sense (I'm not sure that he didn't, either). Mainly, though, I'm still annoyed that he never gave me a Cadillac. He gave Carl Perkins one when Carl sold a million copies of "Blue Suede Shoes," but I never got one when "I Walk the Line" became such a huge hit. I don't know. Maybe it was because Sam saw Carl as his future in rock 'n' roll—he'd sold Elvis to RCA by then—whereas I was country, and you just don't give Cadillacs to country stars. It's a rock 'n' roll thing.

I still think I should have that Cadillac, though. I should just call Sam and tell him to send one over: black, with dark black trim and maybe a light black interior. I don't know what they cost now, but in 1956 you could get one that was top of the line for thirty-five hundred dollars.

I'm calling the man Sam, but back then I called him Mr. Phillips. We all did, even though he told us not to—he wasn't that much older than us, after all. I think it was Elvis, just nineteen when he signed with Sun, who got it started, and the rest of us who followed along. The women at Sun, Marion Keisger and Sally Wilburn, reinforced it. We'd take our questions and problems to them: Where were our royalty checks? Could we change the song we'd just recorded? They'd listen and then say, "We'll have to talk to Mr. Phillips about that." I was well into my forties before I changed my ways. I started worrying that if I kept calling him Mr. Phillips, he might start calling me Mr. Cash, and that would make me very uncomfortable. Mr. Cash was my daddy, not me.

Sam Phillips was a man of genuine vision. He saw the big picture, which was that the white youth of the 1950s would go crazy for music that incorporated the rhythms and style of the "race" records he produced for artists like Howlin' Wolf, Bobby Bland, B. B. King, Little Milton, James Cotton, Rufus Thomas, Junior Parker, and others (a list of names at least as impressive as those of the young white rockabillies with whom he is more famously associated). He also had a fine eye for talent and potential in individuals, even if it hasn't been pulled out of them before. In my case[,] he saw something nobody else had seen and I hadn't even realized myself.

He didn't run with the pack, either (which almost goes without saying, given the originality of his accomplishments). He wasn't one of those many music businessmen/producers who make their living forcing singers and musicians to sound like whatever is selling. He always encouraged me to do it *my* way, to use whatever other influences I wanted, but never to copy. That was a great, rare gift he gave me: belief in myself, right from the start of my recording career.

I liked working with him in the studio. He was very smart, with great instincts, and he had real enthusiasm; he was excitable, not at all laid-back. When we'd put something on tape he liked, he'd come bursting out of the control room into the studio, laughing and clapping his hands, yelling and hollering. "That was *great!* That was wonderful!" he'd say. "That's a rolling stone!" (by which he meant it was a hit). His enthusiasm was fun. It fired us up. And he really did have a genius for the commercial touch, the right way to twist or turn a song so that it really got across to people.

A case in point was "Big River," which I'd written in the backseat of a car in White Plains, New York, as a slow twelve-bar blues song and sung that way on stage a few times before I took it into the studio and sang it for Sam. His reaction was immediate: "No, no, we'll put a beat to that." He had Jack Clement get out his J200 Gibson, tune it open,[6] take a bottleneck,

6. Tuned so that it sounds a chord when none of the strings are stopped.

and play that big power chord all the way through, and that was just great. I thought it was fabulous. The groove he'd heard in his head was so much more powerful than mine, and I'll always be glad he felt at liberty to push ahead and make me hear it, too.

He did have strong ideas. Sometimes I didn't like it much when I felt that his mind was closed to something I wanted to do—he had a way of ruling out ideas, seemingly without even thinking about them—but ultimately I never had a real problem with that. I don't think it ever caused us to lose any good work, and anyway, he listened to me most of the time. By no means—that is, by no remote stretch of the imagination—was he one of those producers who like to impose their own "style" on artists who come into their studio. Sam's basic approach was to get you in there and say, "Just show me what you've got. Just sing me songs, and show me what you'd like to do."

And basically he and I saw eye to eye. We both knew up front that my music had to stay simple, uncomplicated, and unadorned, and we both felt that if the performance was really there at the heart of the song, it didn't matter if there was some little musical error or a glitch in the track somewhere. There are mistakes on several of my Sun records—Luther fumbling a guitar line, Marshall going off the beat, me singing sharp—and we all knew it. Sam just didn't care that much: he'd much rather have soul, fire, and heart than technical perfection. He did care when something I did challenged his notions of good and bad music, though. Then he was quite frank.

"That's awful," he'd tell me. "Don't do that."

I'd say, "All right, I won't," unless I disagreed strongly. Then we'd work it out between us.

It was truly a beautiful day when Marion Keisger handed me my first royalty check. The amount was tiny—$6.42, I believe—but to me it was like a million dollars. Maybe I wouldn't have to keep pretending to sell those refrigerators or get any other kind of job I really didn't want; maybe by the end of the year I could pay the rent on the little house I shared with Vivian and Roseanne; maybe, if I could keep borrowing from my father-in-law and George Bates at the Home Equipment Company, I could stay afloat until the end of the next royalty pay period, when Marion told me I might get a much bigger check. Maybe, just maybe, I could make a living at this! Elvis was doing okay, after all. He was running around buying his own Cadillacs.

The euphoria faded as I began to learn, slowly and often quite accidentally, how the business of music worked. It's embarrassing remembering how ignorant I was about business back then. It's even worse to admit that I'm not much better today. I've been forced to learn some basic rules during forty years on the job, but I've resisted fiercely and effectively; only the most unavoidable home truths have gotten through. I've always resented the time and energy business takes away from music—lawyers desperately needing decisions when the song in my head desperately needs to come out; accountants telling me I need to go there and sing that when I really want to stay here and sing this. The concepts don't match up. A businessman looks at a song and sees a pile of money surrounded by questions about its ownership; I see one of my babies. I remember how strange it felt sitting in a meeting in the '80s, looking down a long list of my own songs whose copyright was finally available for me to acquire, and seeing the title "Wide Open Road" among them. I was suddenly overwhelmed with a vivid memory of exactly how it felt thirty years before on the cold, rainy morning when I sat in the barracks in Germany with my five-dollar guitar and conjured that song up out of the air. How could anyone but me *own* that?

I don't know. I've canceled the vast majority of my meetings with lawyers and accountants, and whenever I've found myself forced into one, my strongest urge has always been to get out of it as quickly as possible, muttering something like, "I just want to sing and play my guitar."

I feel bad about not being fluent in music *and* money, and I look up to people who are. Jack Clement has no difficulty thinking and talking and doing business, but he still enjoys playing a G chord. He's been that way all the years I've loved and fought and worked with him, and I've always admired him for it.

Still, I've always tried to be straight with money and pay what I owe. After my very first tour as a Sun recording act[,] I walked into the Home Equipment Company office with the money I'd saved and paid George Bates every penny I owed him. And as I'd promised Vivian, I didn't buy a star car until we had our own house.

It wasn't a new Cadillac, either. It was Ferlin Husky's very slightly used Lincoln, the Car of the Year for 1956. That car was gorgeous, and just right for me: rock 'n' roll pink and Johnny Cash black.

I'm thinking now about Sam Phillips, concerned that I might have created an impression of discord between us. That's not so. Whatever differences I had with him, they've been long resolved. I bear no grudge against the man who did so much for me.

In 1984[,] the citizens of his hometown in Alabama held a dinner and roast for him, and Jack Clement and I drove down from Nashville and spoke. It was like a lovefest: a lot of hugging, a few tears, some old stories, and some struggles to get them right, the way they really happened.

I have so much respect for Sam. He worked so hard and did so much good for people like me. If there hadn't been a Sam Phillips, I might still be working in a cotton field.

Source: Johnny Cash with Patrick Carr, *Johnny Cash: The Autobiography* (New York: HarperCollins, 1997), 101–11. (Pages 101–111 from CASH: THE AUTOBIOGRAPHY by JOHNNY CASH and PATRICK CARR. Copyright (c) 1997 by John R. Cash. Reprinted by permission of HarperCollins Publishers.)

FOR FURTHER READING

Altschuler, Glenn C. *All Shook Up: How Rock 'n' Roll Changed America.* New York: Oxford University Press, 2003.

Bertrand, Michael T. *Race, Rock, and Elvis.* Urbana: University of Illinois Press, 2000.

Broven, John. *Record Makers and Breakers: Voices of the Independent Rock 'n' Roll Pioneers.* Urbana: University of Illinois Press, 2009.

Edwards, Leigh H. *Johnny Cash and the Paradox of American Identity.* Bloomington: Indiana University Press, 2009.

Hilburn, Robert. *Johnny Cash: The Life.* New York: Little, Brown, and Company, 2013.

21

Charlie Louvin

"Elvis" (2012)

Although he is best known as a rock and roll musician, Elvis Presley might just as easily be seen as a country musician. Like many contemporaneous rockabilly artists, he challenged conventional genre boundaries; and he used musical practices drawn from rhythm and blues, gospel (in the broadest sense of the term), and country music.[1] Moreover, after moving to RCA Victor in 1956, Presley frequently recorded with Nashville session musicians whose work transcended a variety of musical styles, and in the early stages of his career, he performed on Shreveport, Louisiana's *Louisiana Hayride* barn dance program and toured as a part of several "package shows" concerts that featured a variety of musical acts that, in many cases, could appeal to a wide audience.[2] Consequently, Presley

1. Craig Morrison offers the most thorough account of rockabilly to date. See Craig Morrison, *Go, Cat, Go!: Rockabilly and Its Makers* (Urbana: University of Illinois Press, 1996).

2. For a detailed discussion of the *Louisiana Hayride*, consult Tracey E. W. Laird, *Louisiana Hayrdie: Radio and Roots Music along the Red River* (New York: Oxford University Press, 2005).

shared the stage not only with such Sun Records labelmates as Johnny Cash, Carl Perkins, and Jerry Lee Lewis, but also with stars of the *Grand Ole Opry*, including Canadian singer-songwriter Hank Snow and the Louvin Brothers, a popular brother duet from Alabama.

Elvis's career was managed by Col. Tom Parker, a larger-than-life promoter who signed many of the top recording artists of the 1950s to his roster.[3] As Charlie Louvin recounts in the following excerpt from his memoirs,[4] Parker was quite the trickster, often devising elaborate stunts to draw media interest to his artists, which would, in turn, allow Parker to charge higher rates for their performances, recording contracts, and publishing rights and generating more income for Parker himself. At the same time, as Louvin alleges, Parker may have engaged in unethical business practices that made life on the road as part of a Parker package show not only difficult but also financially unsustainable.

Louvin also points to the challenges Presley faced as he embraced African American musical practices, slang, and attire for his predominantly white audiences. Racial comments delivered by an intoxicated Ira Louvin were not uncommon in the Jim Crow–era American South, revealing the complexities of the racial landscape of the 1950s.

BY 1956, we [the Louvin Brothers] had a few hits under our belt. There was "When I Stop Dreaming" and then "I Don't Believe You've Met My Baby," which was even bigger. We were as hot an act as they had on the Opry, and one day we got a call from Colonel Tom Parker to ask us if we wanted to tour with Elvis. Elvis hadn't become a phenomenon yet, but Parker knew he could if he could just get people to see him play. Once you get a true entertainer in front of people, they can entertain 'em. But you have to find a way to get the people seated first. If he'd have put Elvis' name up in lights, there might not be five people in the audience. So we were used to fill the seats, along with the Carter Family, Justin Tubb, and Benny Martin.

Elvis Presley was a true, honest-to-God Louvin Brothers fan, and so was his mother. Every time we'd have a new gospel record out, Betty[5] and I would swing by the Presley's house out there on Audubon Drive. Elvis never was there, the Colonel kept him pretty busy making his gambling money, but Mrs. Presley was always home, and we'd give the record to her. She was always cordial, and I think she really appreciated that we brought her the albums. Maybe that's why Elvis said that the Louvin Brothers were his all-time favorite duet.

I'll admit that I thought he was a fad. That he'd just caught on with a song or two, and probably wouldn't ever have another hit. But then there was this one time when Betty and

3. Journalist Alanna Nash has chronicled Parker's life and career in *The Colonel: The Extraordinary Story of Colonel Tom Parker and Elvis Presley* (New York: Simon & Schuster, 2003).

4. For background on the Louvin Brothers, also consult Charles K. Wolfe, *In Close Harmony: The Story of the Louvin Brothers* (Jackson: University Press of Missippi, 1996).

5. Charlie Louvin's wife.

I went to his home in Memphis to drop off one of our gospel albums for his mother, and I seen this middle-aged woman out there, down on her knees and reaching up under the wooden rail fence to pull grass. Just so she could take it home and say, "I took this from Elvis Presley's yard." And then I knew Elvis was no fad. He was loved by the old and the young, and everybody in between. He was simply a hit walking around just hunting for a place to happen. It took Chet Atkins' and Colonel Tom's help, but it did happen.

The funny thing was, after Elvis left Sun Records, it took Atkins and Parker six weeks in the studio to get the sound that Elvis had at Sun Records. They was trying everything they could to re-created it, but unlike Sun Records, they had real expensive equipment, and they couldn't get it right for the longest time. When they finally did find the magic button, that was it, though. I know two or three people that wrote songs Elvis recorded, and if that's all the money they had coming in, they could still make a living.

It didn't take us long to figure out what kind of man Colonel Tom Parker was on that tour. Mostly, we were scheduled in school auditoriums, and usually there were enough people there for a second show when we finished the first one. So Colonel Tom got in the habit of sending his gopher back to tell us in the dressing room that the next show would start in fifteen minutes, as soon as he could get the people in. And that we were expected to play it for free. Colonel Tom never tried to deal with the artists directly if he could help it. He always used a gopher. I always figured that was because he knew he was a fourteen-carat asshole, and that his being in front of an artist would likely cause an argument that would cost him money.

Anyway, after a few nights, everybody'd had about enough of doing two shows and only being paid for one. After all, the only person making any money on that second show was Colonel Tom Parker. So we all got together and decided to make a complaint. And we chose Ira as the one to deliver the complaint to Colonel Tom Parker's gopher.

So when the gopher came back the following night and told us that the next show started in fifteen minutes, Ira told him. "You tell Colonel Tom, if he wants to do a second show, he can come on back here with something green in his hand."

Well, the kid knew what that meant. But when Colonel Tom came back to see us, he didn't have anything green in his hand. Instead, he had a bunch of excuses. "I was gonna give everybody a bonus at the end of the tour," he whined. Which was bullshit, of course. He even bellyached to Justin Tubb. "Justin, you know I wouldn't try to screw you. I bought you your first poney when you was only a child."

He just had no shame. But it worked. Justin nodded. "Yessir, I remember that, Mr. Parker," and after Justin went, everybody started caving in. It began to look like Ira was the only one who had a problem playing two shows. But after that, if Parker advertised one show, we only did one show. I'm telling you, the man would turn down five thousand people standing out in the front yard just to keep from paying the artists for the work they did. That was the kind of man he was.

He was a potbellied pig. That's the best way to describe him. Maybe ten inches too much fat around the gut and a couple more hanging off his chin, just flabby all over. But he was a marketing genius along the lines of Smilin' Eddie Hill. One of the biggest shows we played on the Elvis tour was in an outside ball stadium. I doubt anyone who was there at that show would ever forget it, because at the end Elvis collapsed onstage. Fainted dead away, like with heat exhaustion. Lucky for him[,] there was an ambulance waiting only ten feet from the stage.

Well, back at the hotel, they'd been nice enough to hold the grill open so we could get short orders, and we were in the bar area laughing and shooting the shit when Elvis walked in after his ambulance ride. He ordered a cup of coffee and sat down with us.

"What happened to you out there?" I asked him.

"Aw, the Colonel put me up to that," he said. "The ambulance circled around a couple of times and then brought me straight back here."

"What'd he have you do that for?"

"He said it'd make the next show a big deal, but I don't see how." He smiled a little bit. "I told him I didn't want to break my guitar falling on it like that, but he told me he'd buy me a dozen guitars if it worked."

Well, there was a television in the bar, and right then somebody called out, "Look at that, Elvis, you're on TV."

Sure enough, there he was in his red sport coat, being loaded into the ambulance. And the announcer was saying they'd be updating fans all night on Elvis' condition, but it was expected he'd be just fine for the next night's show. We switched around the channels, and on all three networks, it was the same thing. That's how clever Parker was. He couldn't have bought Elvis that kind of publicity for a million bucks.

That tour was when he really caught on. Before that, nobody really knew what to do with him. I mean, he did some pretty wild stuff onstage, shaking around inside his clothes, and at first the audience didn't even know what he was doing. But the youth sure caught on, and before that tour was over, he was as hot as anybody in the United States.

Later, Elvis learned that there was a lot about Parker he didn't know. He was an illegal alien, for one thing. He came over from Holland, slid into Tampa, and created his own job to support himself. He walked down to the city offices and told the clerk he wanted to apply for the job of city dogcatcher. Well, she just looked at him funny and said, "We don't need a dogcatcher, sir. We don't have a dog problem."

So Parker got in his pickup truck, got himself a cage, and went out and picked up a load of the mangiest, ugliest dogs he could find, drove 'em to the best part of town, and turned 'em out. In a few days, all these uppity people in Tampa were calling the city to say that all these ugly strays were out here and somebody needs to do something. And sure enough, when Parker went back and applied for the job again, she hired him.

I don't know how he got hooked in with managing, but he managed a lot of people before he found Elvis. Eddy Arnold, Hank Snow, and Ernest Tubb, being three of them, and there were no country singers much bigger than them. Once he became your manager, he owned you, too. At least that's how he felt about it. Elvis' family had to sue him to get him to quit drawing money on Elvis after he died. Parker had been drawing his percentage, which was something like fifty percent, for a year after Elvis passed.

He was a big-time gambler, too. If he had fifty thousand dollars at nine o'clock at night, it'd be gone by midnight. He actually rented a place on the top floor of one of the biggest casinos in Vegas. That way, every time his money would come in from Elvis, all he had to do was get on the elevator for a few seconds to make it to the middle of the gambling district. He died broke, of course.

Unfortunately, Ira had one other run-in with Elvis and Colonel Parker on that tour. And the second one was a little more personal. See, Elvis closed every show, so when he'd get to the dressing room, we'd all be back there already sitting around. And this one time he came back, sat down at this old piano that was there, and started playing some old gospel song. When he finished the song, he spun around on the stool and said to everybody, "You know, that's the music I really love."

Well, Ira'd been drinking some. It was happening more and more by that time, now that we'd started to have a little success. "Well, you damn white nigger," he said to Elvis. "Why do you play that crap on the stage if that's what you love?"

Elvis just grinned at him. It wasn't the first time he'd been called a white nigger, I'm sure. A lot of people in Nashville felt the same way. "When I'm out there, I try to do what they want to hear," he said, easily. "When I'm back here, I can do what I want."

That was the end of it. And, if you think about it, what Elvis said made perfect sense. But, of course, a bunch of people spread it around that there was a big fistfight, and Ira had to be dragged off from trying to choke him. There was no punching or choking, though. People just added that in because it made things a little jucier.

Still, we never worked another date with Elvis after that tour. And Elvis never recorded a single Louvin Brothers song, even though he said we were his favorite duet, and we were known to be his Mama's favorite gospel singers. He recorded half a dozen Hank Williams songs, several Don Gibson songs, various other Acuff-Rose artists, but he never cut a Louvin Brothers song. Not one.

If I had to guess, I'd say that one statement by Ira cost the Louvin Brothers music catalog two or three million dollars. And I don't believe Elvis took offense, either. It was a stupid thing to say, but everybody knew how Ira was. I figure somebody had to have told Colonel Parker about it. Elvis Presley didn't hold a grudge, he was a good boy. But Parker sure as hell did. And he controlled everything Elvis did and didn't record.

I never saw Elvis after that tour, neither, though I did try once. I was working Memphis, and Elvis' stepmother was at my show. Well, my boy Sonny was with me, and he wanted to meet Elvis, so I went up to Elvis' stepmother after I got done playing and asked her if he was around. "Well, he's right over at the house," she said. "Why don't you just go on out there and meet him right now?"

I had a little time before my second show, and it was only four or five miles out to the house, so we got in the car and drove out. But when we got inside, the only person we found was Elvis' father. Elvis himself was sleeping. So I stood around talking to his father for a while hoping he'd wake up, and after about thirty or forty minutes, I finally asked, "What time does Elvis get out of bed?"

"Whenever he wakes up," his father said.

"Could you go on up and tell him I'm here?" I asked. "If he didn't want to come down, that's fine, but I'd like for him to know that I'm here and would like to see him."

His father just laughed. "I can't go up there."

"What do you mean you can't go up there?" I said. "You're his father."

"There's two guards between here and Elvis' door," he said. "They'd turn me right around."

Boy, this is wild, I thought. I'm probably twelve feet from the window to Elvis' room, and I'd have to go through two guards to get to him. Maybe I oughta get some small pebbles and throw 'em up against his window-glass.

I didn't, though. And we never did get to see him. We stayed as long as we could, but I had to get back for my second show. Of course, I doubt he would have looked forward to seeing Ira again, but he and I had always got along. I was just trying to get him out where I could shake his hand and maybe get a picture with him and my kid, but it didn't turn out that way.

It wasn't too long after than when he died. Which I expected to happen, of course. Elvis said all the time that he'd never live to be a day older than his mother was when she died. He was a real mama's boy, and, of course, if he had lived one more day[,] he would have been older than she was.

I've always believed he done it on purpose. That he snuffed himself. There wasn't nobody, even doctors, that knew anything more about dope than Elvis did. You can't convince me he accidentally killed himself that way. He knew exactly what you could mix and what you could not mix. He'd been managing it a good many years.

> *Source*: Charlie Louvin, with Benjamin Whitmer, *Satan Is Real: The Ballad of the Louvin Brothers* (New York: itbooks, 2012. 173–80). (Pages 173–80 from SATAN IS REAL by CHARLIE LOUVIN with BENJAMIN WHITMER. Copyright (c) 2012 by The Estate of Charlie Louvin, Sr. Reprinted by permission of HarperCollins Publishers.)

FOR FURTHER READING

Bertrand, Michael. *Race, Rock, and Elvis*. Urbana: University of Illinois Press, 2000.

Guralnick, Peter. *Last Train to Memphis: The Rise of Elvis Presley*. Boston: Little, Brown, 1994.

Nash, Alanna. *The Colonel: The Extraordinary Story of Colonel Tom Parker and Elvis Presley*. New York: Simon & Schuster, 2008.

Wolfe, Charles K. *In Close Harmony: The Story of the Louvin Brothers*. Jackson: University Press of Mississippi, 1996.

Murray Nash

"Miss Country Music and Her Family" (1955)

Women in country music have frequently been expected to demonstrate their domesticity even while singing songs about situations that take them far from home. Numerous women have pretended to be cousins and sisters of band members in order to avoid being seen as having loose morals, and musician mothers have often trotted their children on stage in an effort to demonstrate their maternal *bona fides*. Still others—such as Sara Carter of the Carter Family—continued to perform alongside ex-husbands to maintain a façade of domestic harmony for their fans.[1]

As country music historians Kristine McCusker and Stephanie Vander Wel have shown in their respective research on women in country music, these public images of domesticity frequently conflicted with the themes and musical

---

1. For a general introduction to the history of women's participation in country music, consult Mary A. Bufwack and Robert K. Oermann, *Finding Her Voice: Women in Country Music, 1800-2000* (Nashville, TN: Vanderbilt University Press and Country Music Foundation Press, 2003).

practices heard on their recordings and in their concert performances.[2] Such is the case with singer Kitty Wells, a long-time radio performer who came to national attention in the 1950s with her recordings of songs that expressed a distinctively female perspective on the hard-drinking and fast-loving life of the honky-tonk. Best known for her defense of honky-tonk women in 1952's "It Wasn't God Who Made Honky Tonk Angels," Wells is profiled in the article that follows and presented as "a busy housewife," the mother of three children, and "the best wife and mother in the business." Yet, as Vander Wel has noted, several of Wells's honky-tonk recordings subvert this domestic image by giving voice to the sexual desires of the women who inhabited the honky-tonks where her records were played on jukeboxes.[3] It is essential, then, that we read this piece not as simple reportage but as a deliberate effort to construct Wells as a domestic diva in order to counter her performances of honky-tonk desire.[4]

IF you ever saw her on the street you would take her for a busy housewife—which she is! If she had her children with her you would say to yourself, "There's a fine family"—which they are! And after you had seen them on the stage you would wonder how one woman could be wife and mother to this family and still hold the Number One spot in country music!

Yes, Miss Kitty Wells, as she is professionally known[,] is a fabulous young lady! In private life she is Mrs. Johnnie Wright, wife of the senior partner in the team of Johnnie and Jack. And to millions of fans all over the world she is Miss Country Music!

Few people know that she is a native Nashvillian and traveled all over the country only to return to her home town and there find fabulous success as a singer of country songs. August 30th is her birthday—her maiden name was Muriel Deason, and as a child she went about her school work and helped her mother keep house—much the same as all other Southern girls. No one particularly noticed her voice although her mother remembers that she used to be very fond of singing and her voice was very sweet and had a natural feeling.

In 1936 she teamed up with her cousin, Bessie Choates, as The Deason Sisters and began singing on a Saturday afternoon show from Nashville's WSIX called "The Old Country

2. Kristine M. McCusker, "'Bury Me Beneath the Willow': Linda Parker and Definitions of Tradition on the *National Barn Dance*, 1932-1935," in *A Boy Named Sue: Gender and Country Music*, ed. Kristine M. McCusker and Diane Pecknold (Jackson: University Press of Mississippi, 2004), 3–23; and Stephanie Vander Wel, "'I Am a Honky-Tonk Girl': Country Music, Gender, and Migration," Ph.D. dissertation, University of California, Los Angeles, 2008, 211–34. See also Pamela Fox, *Natural Acts: Gender, Race, and Rusticity in Country Music* (Ann Arbor: University of Michigan Press, 2009), 113–45.

3. Vander Wel, "'I Am a Honky-Tonk Girl,'" 224–25.

4. Barbara Ching and Aaron Fox, in their respective work on honky tonk culture, have examined these gendered and sexualized understandings of the honky-tonk in great detail. See, for instance: Barbara Ching, *Wrong's What I Do Best: Hard Country Music and Contemporary Culture* (New York: Oxford University Press, 2001), 26–46; Aaron A. Fox, *Real Country: Music and Language in Working-Class Culture* (Durham, NC: Duke University Press, 2004), 250–71.

Store." The girls were on the show for about a year[,] but since there was no pay involved they began thinking more seriously about the future. Here fate stepped in and made some changes.

A young lady named Louise Wright moved next door to the Deason home. Right away the two girls were singing together. Louise's brother, Johnnie Wright, came into the picture and Johnnie Wright and The Harmony Girls started appearing in the Tennessee area. It wasn't long until Muriel became Mrs. Johnnie Wright. Soon the team of Johnnie and Jack was formed and Louise dropped out of the group.

This combination showed definite promise and there was more and more traveling with Mrs. Wright going right along with her husband. 1942 found them making a name for themselves at WNOX in Knoxville, Tennessee. The young lady was singing a song or two on every show and needed a name of her own. "Kitty Wells" was a favorite old American folk song that seemed to fit—so from that time until now she has been known as Miss Kitty Wells.

After three years in Knoxville, they moved to WPTF in Raleigh, N.C.[,] and then on to the *Louisiana Hayride* at KWKH in Shreveport, La. Here they became nationally known through their broadcasts and RCA Victor records[,] which brought an invitation to WSM's *Grand Ole Opry*. They moved to Nashville and have been headliners all over the country ever since.

Kitty recorded eight songs for RCA Victor in 1949. Most of these were sacred numbers and didn't get very much attention. In 1952 she signed to record with Decca and her first release, *It Wasn't God Who Made Honky Tonk Angels*, was an immediate hit. She has had sixteen Decca records since and each has built Kitty Wells into the top country girl name of the country.

Johnnie and Kitty have three children—Ruby Jean who is 16, Johnny, Jr., 13, and Carol Sue who is 10. Ruby records by herself as "Ruby Wells" for RCA Victor and also is a part of the "Nita, Rita, and Ruby" trio. Johnny, Jr.[,] has taken the name of Bobby Wright on the Decca label and has several fine releases to his credit. Little Carol Sue is not to be left out and plans are being made for her recording in the near future. Unlike most family groups, the Wrights very seldom sing together since they each have solo voices.

But back to Kitty—the hub of attention in the Wright home. Being America's Number One Country Girl Singer has not changed her one bit.[5] She's still the same sweet, soft-spoken wife and mother she was before heading the country's music charts. She is one of the most attractive young ladies you'll find anywhere. She doesn't go in for gaudy dress but lets her winning smile and the twinkle in her eyes make her Miss Personality Plus. She is one the most willing in the signing of autographs and you'll never find her too busy for a friendly greeting. So fans and family alike all say that Miss Kitty Wells (or Mrs. Johnnie Wright) takes first place both as the best country singer and the best wife and mother in the business. And we might add that she heads one of the finest families you'll find in the country and five people that provide more good country entertainment through their appearances and records than any other we know of.

Source: Murray Nash, "Miss Country Music and Her Family," *Country & Western Jamboree* 1, no. 10 (December 1955): 7, 31. (Used with permission.)

5. Note the use of the diminuitive term "girl" here to describe Wells, who is—by virtue of her age, marital status, and motherhood—clearly an adult.

FOR FURTHER READING

Fox, Pamela. *Natural Acts: Gender, Race, and Rusticity in Country Music.* Ann Arbor: University of Michigan, 2009.

Vander Wel, Stephanie. "'I Am a Honky-Tonk Girl': Country Music, Gender, and Migration." Ph.D. dissertation, University of California, Los Angeles, 2008.

23

Linda Lamendola

"Steve Sholes—Star Maker" (1956)

Until the middle of the 1950s, Nashville was little more than a regional music center, famous more for being the source of the weekly *Grand Ole Opry* broadcasts than for being the international center of the country music industry. In fact, as several of the preceding chapters have shown, the production of country music was widely distributed prior to the mid-1950s. The first efforts to develop a music industry in Nashville were undertaken in the realm of publishing, when, in 1942, recording artist and *Opry* star Roy Acuff (1903–1992) joined with song-writer Fred Rose (1898–1954) to create Acuff-Rose Music Publishing.[1] Acuff-Rose was followed nearly a decade later by Tree Music, a collaboration between WSM program manager Jack Stapp (1912–1980) and New York broadcasting executive Louis Cowan (1910–1976) established in 1951, and Cedarwood Music, founded in 1953 by WSM talent agent Jim Denny (1911–1963) with financial support from honky-tonk star Webb Pierce (1921–1991).[2] Similarly, a number of small record

1. John Woodruff Rumble, "Fred Rose and the Development of the Nashville Music Industry, 1942–1954," Ph.D. dissertation, Vanderbilt University, 1980; Diane Pecknold, *The Selling Sound: The Rise of the Country Music Industry* (Durham, NC: Duke University Press, 2007), 57–58.

2. Albert Cunniff, "Muscle Behind the Music: The Life and Times of Jim Denny, Part 3: So Much to Do, So Little Time," *Journal of Country Music* 11, no. 3 (1987): 22–32,

labels flourished in the city during the decade following World War II, bringing a wealth of rhythm-and-blues, country, and gospel music to local and regional audiences, spurred in part by the growth of local recording studios and radio stations.[3]

First described as "Music City, U.S.A." in 1950,[4] several related industries began to coalesce in the city formerly known as "the Athens of the South" by the middle of the decade.[5] After the success of the 1953 WSM Disc Jockey Convention, the Country Music Disc Jockey Association (CMDJA) was organized to broaden the audience for country music, improve the quality of country music radio programs, and, most visibly, to continue organizing an annual disc jockey convention that brought thousands of disc jockeys to Nashville in support of the emergent all-country radio format.[6] The nation's three major record labels—RCA Victor, Columbia, and Decca—also established bases in Nashville; and, by 1957, RCA Victor built a regional office and a recording studio in the city.[7] By the end of the 1950s, Nashville was firmly established as a

41–46; Martin Hawkins, *A Shot in the Dark: Making Records in Nashville, 1945-1955* (Nashville, TN: Vanderbilt University Press and Country Music Foundation Press, 2006), 210–14.

3. The history of the early Nashville recording industry have been well documented in John W. Rumble, "The Emergence of Nashville as a Recording Center: Logbooks from the Castle Studio, 1952-1953," *Journal of Country Music* 7, no. 3 (December 1978): 22–41; Ted Jarrett with Ruth White, *You Can Make It If You Try: The Ted Jarrett Story of R&B in Nashville* (Nashville, TN: Hillsboro Press, 2005); Hawkins, *A Shot in the Dark*; Craig Havighurst, *Air Castle of the South: WSM and the Making of Music City* (Urbana and Chicago: University of Illinois Press, 2007), 144–47, 151–52; and John Broven, *Record Makers and Breakers: Voices of the Independent Rock 'n' Roll Pioneers* (Urbana and Chicago: University of Illinois Press, 2009), 93–115. Several of the recordings from Nashville's rhythm-and-blues labels were featured in the 2004–2005 Country Music Hall of Fame and Museum exhibit Night Train to Memphis and can be found in *Night Train to Memphis: Music City Rhythm & Blues, 1945-1970* (Nashville: Lost Highway, 2004) and *Night Train to Memphis: Music City Rhythm & Blues, 1945-1970, Volume 2* (Nashville: Lost Highway, 2005).

4. David Cobb, an announcer on Nashville radio station WSM, introduced an early 1950 *The Red Foley Show* with the following statement: "From Music City USA, Nashville, Tennessee, the National Broadcasting Company brings you the Red Foley Show" (quoted in Havighurst, *Air Castle of the South*, 156).

5. As William Henry McRaven noted in his mid-twentieth-century history of Nashville, "The 'Athens of the South' is the description given to Nashville by its early settlers in recognition of the educational and intellectual leadership manifest by its founders" (*Nashville: "Athens of the South"* [Chapel Hill, TN: Sheer & Jervis, 1949], vii). For further discussion of the influence of classical thinking on Nashville culture, consult Christine Kreyling, Wesley Paine, Charles W. Warterfield Jr., and Susan Ford Wiltshire, *Classical Nashville: Athens of the South* (Nashville, TN: Vanderbilt University Press, 1996); Martha Rivers Ingram and D. B. Kellogg, *Apollo's Struggle: A Performing Arts Odyssey in the Athens of the South, Nashville, Tennessee* (Franklin, TN: Hillsboro Press, 2004); and Mary Ellen Pethel, "Athens of the South: College Life in Nashville, a New South City, 1897-1917," Ph.D. dissertation, Georgia State University, 2008.

6. The WSM Disc Jockey Convention was first held in November 1952. See Havighurst, *Air Castle of the South*, 180–82; Pecknold, *The Selling Sound*, 73–75.

7. Hawkins, *A Shot in the Dark*, 221–38; Don Cusic, "Nashville Recording Industry," in *The Tennessee Encyclopedia of History and Culture*, http://tennesseeencyclopedia. net/entry.php?rec=1113; accessed 2 January 2013.

major musical center in the region, drawing a wide array of session musicians, singers, songwriters, and businesspersons to the city to create what was known as the "Nashville Sound," a pop-country hybrid that was the result of country sensibilities meeting pop and jazz arranging practices.[8]

The artists-and-repertoire representative, or "A&R man," was responsible for coordinating all of the personnel that were necessary to conduct a successful recording session, as well as for securing star talent and appropriate songs for that talent to record. Steve Sholes (1911–1968) climbed the ladder to great success at RCA Victor, first working on the factory floor in the 1930s and eventually apprenticing with several of the label's most successful record producers. In 1945, he became the head of A&R for the label's country and rhythm-and-blues departments, where he worked with such artists as Chet Atkins, Eddy Arnold, Pee Wee King, and Elvis Presley and played a key role in moving the label's country recording operations to Nashville in 1950. The reading that follows offers insight into many relationships that Sholes was required to maintain in order to create a successful recording session, as well as a look at the creative role that A&R representatives could often play in shaping the sound of the recording artists under their control.[9]

HAVE you ever found yourself wondering, as you flip a record on your phonograph, about the kind of fantastic world that is compressed into that whirling disc? If you'd like to believe that behind each hit lies an untold story, you can keep believing. There usually is.

The record business is one gigantic song stew, and the chef who throws in all the ingredients—singers, musicians, and song writers—and serves it all up to you in one heaping musical platter, is called an artists & repertoire man.

No one is more qualified to bring you the inside story of what goes into the making of your c&w [country & western] music record than Steve Sholes, the a&r man at RCA Victor and one of the top country music experts in the U.S.

Sholes handles more than 40 recording stars including Eddy Arnold, Hank Snow, Porter Wagoner, and Jim Reeves. He scouts the nation for new talent; hightails from his New York office every few weeks to Nashville, Tenn., for a business conference with Chet Atkins, who manages the RCA recording studio in Tennessee[;] arranges recording sessions in California one week and Chicago the next[;] and combs through an average of 40,000 songs a year in order to find his records.

8. William Ivey, "Commercialization and Tradition in the Nashville Sound," in *Folk Music and Modern Sound*, ed. William Ferris and Mary L. Hart (Jackson: University Press of Mississippi, 1982), 129–38; Joli Jensen, *Nashville Sound: Authenticity, Commercialization, and Country Music* (Nashville, TN: Country Music Foundation Press and Vanderbilt University Press, 1998), 62–88; Fabian Holt, *Genre in Popular Music* (Chicago and London: University of Chicago Press, 2007), 63–79.

9. Charles K. Wolfe and John W. Rumble, "Sholes, Steve [Stephen Henry]," in *The New Grove Dictionary of American Music*, 2nd ed., ed. Charles Hiroshi Garrett (New York and Oxford: Oxford University Press, 2013).

Occasionally, he finds it necessary to release an artist whose records aren't selling too well. "This," says Steve, "is almost like drowning one of my own children."

It almost happened to Wagoner.

When RCA signed him to a recording contract, his only professional experience had been gained while singing on a local radio station in West Plains, Mo., and he had recorded just two discs for another company.

Porter was with RCA for three years with nothing great happening. Even Porter's waxing of *Settin' the Woods on Fire* and *Company's Comin'* didn't sell as well as expected. So when Porter's contract became due for renewal, Sholes was confronted by a great big question mark. There was no questioning Porter's talents, but could his records sell?

One day Si Siman[,] who had brought Porter over to RCA, walked into Steve's office in New York and told him that he had found the song which would prove Porter's worth.

"This song will make him!" he prophesied.

You know the rest.

Satisfied Mind hit the No. 1 spot a few weeks after its release, and the public swung the pendulum that shifted Wagoner from near obscurity to the success he enjoys today.

"And it couldn't happen to a nicer guy," says Sholes. "Not only that, but in the meanwhile, Porter's contract had run out and when his record hit the top, he wasn't legally under contract to us. If Porter and his manager weren't honest gentlemen, we might have been left out in the cold without our star."

Steve is one of the men responsible for starting the word war between country music fans by coming up with the idea of having Eddy Arnold record with a city slicker musician like Hugo Winterhalter. While most of the c&w music professionals were shooting disagreeable adjectives at Sholes for committing such a crime, the public went out and bought the record.

What the public didn't know was that the plan for releasing a recording like *Cattle Call* and *The Kentuckian* had been brewing for two years with pros and cons flying thick and fast until finally, the record was released as a mere experiment.

The experiment proved so successful that Arnold's *Cattle Call* gets as much of a play from the pop disc jockeys as the pop records. It all adds up to shrewd c&w promotional work for country music.

When Arnold walked into the recording studio to record *Cattle Call*, he was startled to see the string section in Winterhalter's orchestra, which was backing him on that date for the first time.

Hugo said, "What's the matter, Eddy? Are you surprised to see this big string section?"

Eddy replied, "I've never seen so many fiddles all in tune at once!"

What goes into the making of your favorite record? This is the story.

It begins with a great performer like Arnold or Hank Snow, who, according to Sholes, "spends every waking minute thinking of new songs, looking for new songs, and practicing new songs. They walk, talk, and breathe music."

When the artist and Steve have decided which songs will be recorded, Sholes arranges the recording session.

A day or so before the recording session comes up, Sholes and the singer get together for a final tryout. Because some c&w musicians don't read music, they have to work twice as hard to give you a perfect recording.

As Sholes describes it, the song gets "kicked around," which simply means that the steel guitarist tries out his version; the fellows with the electric guitars chime in with their ideas of how the song should be played; the singer gives out with a couple of choruses. They keep gnashing their teeth, smashing their cigaret [sic] butts, and trying to song "just one more time." And finally, there is one last time and a new hit record is born.

"Well, anyway, we hope it will be a hit record," Sholes says.

One of Snow's most memorable recording sessions was the night that he didn't record. At 1 a.m. in the middle of a peaceful sleep, Hank was awakened by the phone. Would he please get down to the recording studio immediately? He [sic] was asked.

It was Anne Fulchino, the publicity girl at RCA. She needed some exclusive photographs of Snow in action while recording—for a story in *Jamboree*. It had to be done in a hurry because Anne had to be back in New York by 9 a.m. the next day.

So Snow rounded up the entire band at 1:30 in the morning, and they simulated a recording session while the photographer took the pictures.

Sholes' advice to those who dream of becoming record stars is to be darn positive that you possess plenty of talent. It's a long tough haul to success, and even with loads of talent, he says, "It can't be done overnight."

"Get as much professional experience as possible. Youngsters who have talent should try getting connected with local radio stations. The recording studios are always searching for new and different talent and are constantly signing new performers."

RCA Victor is almost Sholes' heritage. His father worked for the company back in 1920 in Camden, N.J. But Steve literally "worked his way up from the bottom."

When he was graduated from college in 1933, the record business was suffering in the [D]epression, so when Steve was offered a job in the factory division, he gladly took it.

When there finally was an opening in [the] record department, Sholes almost decided against taking the job. It meant a cut in salary. But it was the best decision he ever made. From a correspondence clerk, he worked his way up the ladder and today is recognized as one of the foremost experts on country music.

Source: Linda Lamendola, "Steve Sholes—Star Maker," *Country & Western Jamboree* 1, no. 11 (January 1956): 7, 27. (Used with permission.)

FOR FURTHER READING

Havighurst, Craig. *Air Castle of the South: WSM and the Making of Music City.* Urbana and Chicago: University of Illinois Press, 2007.

Ivey, William. "Commercialization and Tradition in the Nashville Sound." In *Folk Music and Modern Sound,* ed. William Ferris and Mary L. Hart, 129–38. Jackson: University Press of Mississippi, 1982.

Jensen, Joli. *Nashville Sound: Authenticity, Commercialization, and Country Music.* Nashville, TN: Country Music Foundation Press and Vanderbilt University Press, 1998.

Pecknold, Diane. *The Selling Sound: The Rise of the Country Music Industry.* Durham, NC: Duke University Press, 2007.

24

Ben A. Green

"Chet Makes Guitar Talk with Rhythm and Melody" (1957)

One of the keys to the success of the Nashville Sound was the talented group of session musicians and recording technicians—known as the "A List"—who performed on the dozens of recording sessions held each week, a group that included such remarkable musicians as guitarists Grady Martin (1929–2001), Hank Garland (1930–2004),[1] and Chet Atkins (1924–2011); bassists Bob Moore (b 1932) and Junior Husky (1928–1971); pianists Floyd Cramer (1933–1997) and Hargus "Pig" Robbins (b 1938); drummer Buddy Harman (1928–2008); and background singing groups the Jordanaires and the Anita Kerr Singers.[2] These

---

1. Rich Kienzle, "Grady Martin: Unsung and Unforgettable," *Journal of Country Music* 10, no. 2 (1985): 54–60; Rich Kienzle, "Hank Garland: Legendary Country-Jazz Artist," *Guitar Player* (January 1981): 76–86; Rich Kienzle, "The Forgotten Hank Garland," *Journal of Country Music* 9, no. 3 (1983): 28–32.

2. An engaging panel discussion with several A-list musicians can be found in John W. Rumble, "Let's Cut a Hit! Talking with A-Team Nashville Studio Musicians," *Journal of Country Music* 20, no. 2 (1998): 4–15.

musicians were called upon to produce simple "head arrangements" of the songs to be recorded on a given session and to minimize their mistakes in order to create clean, radio-ready recordings in an efficient manner.[3] Chet Atkins, one of the most celebrated of the "A List" musicians, was one of only a few Nashville session musicians to branch out into the realm of record production, eventually running RCA Victor's Nashville operations.

In the following profile, author Ben E. Green discusses the necessary skills of the session musician, the wide musical vocabularies that musicians such as Atkins brought to country music, and the growing national appeal of the Nashville Sound. Atkins was an innovator in the field of "fingerstyle guitar," in which the fingers of the right hand are used to play the melody, harmonies, and bass simultaneously. Although present in a wide variety of guitar-based styles, its origins in country music can be traced to the work of Merle Travis and other guitarists associated with the western Kentucky "Muhlenberg County" style, including Mose Rager, Ike Everly, and, more recently, Eddie Pennington. Atkins drew his influences from a broad range, especially jazz musicians such as George Barnes, Les Paul, and Django Reinhardt. Although the article here suggests that Atkins used his thumb, index finger, middle finger, and ring finger when playing, he more often used only his thumb, index finger, and middle finger.[4]

━━━━━━━━

NINE fingers are at work when Chet Atkins plays the electric guitar—bringing forth sounds that have won for him many followers and unusual honors. The work of these fingers, plus a personal devotion to Country Music and innate talent have placed this artist in a comprehensive key role held by few, despite a physical handicap that would have halted a weaker soul.

In fact, this handicap made somewhat of a wanderer out of Chet in his earlier days—as he went from climate to climate seeking relief from a pronounced asthmatic condition.[5]

Nowadays when he takes a position in center stage at the *Grand Ole Opry* to play a solo on the network show[,][6] listeners throughout the land are sure to hear something special and different. He regularly leads *Jamboree* disc jockey and reader polls as No. 1 instrumental soloist.

3. Morris S. Levy, "Nashville Sound-Era Studio Musicians," in *Country Music Annual 2000*, ed. Charles K. Wolfe and James E. Akenson (Lexington: University Press of Kentucky, 2000), 22–29.

4. For a more detailed discussion of Atkins's guitar style, consult Steve Waksman, *Instruments of Desire: The Electric Guitar and the Shaping of Musical Experience* (Cambridge and London: Harvard University Press, 1999), 88–94; Rich Kienzle, "Chet Atkins, Guitarist: The Sound, the Style, the Influence," in *Chet Atkins: Certified Guitar Player*, ed. John W. Rumble (Nashville, TN: Country Music Foundation Press, 2011), 30–33.

5. Michael Cochran, "American Icon: The Musical Journey of Chet Atkins," in *Chet Atkins: Certified Guitar Player*, ed. John W. Rumble (Nashville, TN: Country Music Foundation Press, 2011), 11.

6. *The Prince Albert Grand Ole Opry*, a thirty-minute broadcast on the NBC radio network.

Few probably can understand what makes the Atkins touch different. It's not just that he uses all fingers except the "little finger" on his right (the picking) hand.

The difference lies in the fact that Chet plays both the rhythm and melody simultaneously—something he couldn't possibly do if he were using a guitar bar or pick.

As Chet modestly explains, he figures the Lord gave him five fingers on each hand, and he thinks it only naturally [sic] to make the best use of all of them if he possibly can.

Chet plays an extremely active triple role in modern Country Music as a recording artist of note, a musical director for RCA Victor, and a free-lance accompanist. He also writes song melodies quickly and has done some song publishing, but now restricts his Athens Publishing Co. to his own songs.

In a day when singing artists largely dominate the stage, Chet has turned out big-selling instrumental records like *Blue Echo* this year, and *Poor People of Paris* and *Mr. Sand Man* previously. He was the first artist in America to record the *Paris* number.

Adding to his contribution to music generally, Chet also designed a guitar model for the Frederick Gret[s]ch Manufacturing Co. That firm recently introduced a third Chet Atkins model, and the artist personally demonstrated it at the National Association of Music Merchants convention held recently in Chicago.

When the Gret[s]ch people asked Chet to design a special model, it was not difficult. He had always "souped up" any guitar he bought, making various changes to meet his individual demands.[7]

Chet has been helpful to a number of artists, rising on the ladder...including the Everly Brothers (Don and Phil). He published two of Don's first songs, *Thou Shall Not Steal* and *Here We Are Again* and helped the boys get their first recording contract.

He also extended the helpful hand to Sonny James, then fresh out of the army, and the result was a Capitol recording contract for the promising young singer.

Since coming to Nashville in 1950[,] Chet has worked with many of the top singing stars in their recording sessions, including the late Hank Williams,[8] and such present-day stars as Webb Pierce, Eddy Arnold, and Elvis Presley.

Chet believes the modern trend to have background singing accompaniment is largely the result of Elvis Presley's remarkable success, and also in part to Sonny James' influence.

Steve Sholes, veteran artists and repertoire man for RCA Victor, said he wanted a quartet to be with Presley when he began his session for the sensational *Heartbreak Hotel*.

Chet called the Jordanaires and thus began a chain of events in which the Jordanaires have been closely linked with Presley's recordings, and also personal appearances.

Even so they did not sing on *Heartbreak Hotel*, but on *I Want You, I Need You, I Love You*, recorded at the same session.

7. Atkins's work with the Gretsch company to improve the hollow-body electric guitar is perhaps most evident in Gretsch's Country Gentleman (Model 6122), which was released in 1957. Atkins's tireless work in the improvement of his guitars has been documented in Waksman, *Instruments of Desire*, 96–100; Walter Carter, "Chet Atkins: Tinkerer Pursuing Perfection," in *Chet Atkins: Certified Guitar Player*, ed. John W. Rumble (Nashville, TN: Country Music Foundation Press, 2011), 51–67.

8. Williams, one of the most popular honky-tonk singers, died on December 31, 1953.

"I think the trend is now well established and will continue for some time," remarked Chet. "People are getting more musically educated[,] and they want to hear the best. They are what you might call 'beat conscious.' "

Chet attributes part of the phenomenal increase in Nashville song recording during the last year to the fact that many pop artists come in search of the "Country sound" for their own records. He traces this to the striking success of several Country artists in the pop field.[9]

"On sessions Country musicians play by ear," Chet explained. "Some of them read music but if they tried to play by the score they would do it mechanically.

"Here in Nashville are musicians who have 'good ears' for music. They can hear a song once and learn it. Depend upon them and yourself and you usually come up with a good arrangement. Occasionally I get with a singer prior to the session and get an idea about it, and once in a while we get a vocal arrangement written, but that's seldom."[10]

In addition to the two Presley hits mentioned, Chet was on the record session for Jim Reeves' *Four Walls* and the Everly Brothers' *Bye, Bye Love* and countless others.

9. Jeffrey J. Lange, *Smile When You Call Me a Hillbilly: Country Music's Struggle for Respectability, 1939–1954* (Athens, GA: University of Georgia Press, 2004), 207–20; Fabian Holt, *Genre in Popular Music* (Chicago and London: University of Chicago Press, 2007), 72–74; Albin J. Zak, III, *I Don't Sound Like Nobody: Remaking Music in 1950s America* (Ann Arbor: University of Michigan Press, 2010), 117–24.

10. Vocalist Anita Kerr, leader of the background singing group the Anita Kerr Singers, described the process of writing vocal arrangements for Nashville Sound-era singer Jim Reeves: "We sang on all of his sessions, and I arranged them for the vocal group and for the orchestra. I would get together with him and set the keys, and go home and write the arrangement. . . . Chet was always there, too. So it was the three of us talking about what we thought should be where and how the song would be treated. Once I got home and wrote it and got back the next day (Chet didn't ever give me too much notice), he [Reeves] would just breeze right through them" (quoted in "Anita Kerr: Arranger," in Michael Streissguth, *Voices of the Country: Interviews with Classic Country Performers* [New York and London: Routledge, 2004], 60). Atkins recalled that Kerr often wrote the arrangements even more quickly, recalling that "we'd decide that we wanted to add strings and I'd hire some fiddlers and she'd grab a pencil and write out lines for them to play" (quoted in "Chet Atkins: The Best I Could Do," in Michael Streissguth, *Voices of the Country: Interviews with Classic Country Performers* [New York and London: Routledge, 2004], 46).

Such forewarning was rare, however, as Morris S. Levy has noted that "the studio musicians only heard them [the songs] for the first time at the session. Sometimes the songs were played for the musicians on demonstration discs or tapes supplied by the publishing companies controlling the rights to the song or by the artist on the guitar or piano. The players would then sketch out the melody and song structure on scraps of paper and work out an arrangement between themselves, sometimes with input from the artist or producer. After a few run-throughs of the song to solidify the arrangement and allow the engineers to balance the sound levels, the song would be recorded" (Morris S. Levy, "Nashville Sound-Era Studio Musicians," in *Country Music Annual 2000*, ed. Charles K. Wolfe and James E. Akenson [Lexington: University Press of Kentucky, 2000], 23).

On August 6 this year, Chet played before 19,000 people in Milwaukee at an RCA Victor show. Included in the group were Julius LaRosa,[11] Pat O'Day,[12] and the Lain Brothers.[13] That is the largest audience Chet has ever appeared before. Another crowd in Milwaukee seven years ago numbered more than 10,000 at the Sportatorium, Chet recalled.

The Chet Atkins Fan Club, one of the most active in the country, held its fifth annual convention in Nashville during July. It is headed by Margaret Fields and her husband, Don, of Louisville. Approximately 75 attended the convention, some coming from distant states.

For years[,] the artist was known as Chester Atkins, but Si Simon [sic] of KWTO, Springfield [Missouri], cut it to Chet in 1946. The nickname stuck.

Chet was born on a farm in Union County near Knoxville, Tenn., but his father was a music teacher in piano and voice. Chet learned some music from him, and first played both the fiddle and the guitar.

He heard, however, that the most expert fiddlers started learning at age[s] 5 and 6, so he decided at age 13 to devote his life to the guitar. The electric guitar was new then and its vast potentialities had not been fully explored.[14]

After graduation from high school in Hamilton, Ga., Chet visited Knoxville and heard Bill Carlisle needed a guitar player at Station WNOX. Chet auditioned and got the job, and was also on the staff of the Dixieland Swingsters there.

Asthma continued to give him trouble, and Chet went successively to WLW in Cincinnati, WPTF in Raleigh, N.C., to Nashville on the network show with Red Foley, then for a month with the WRVA barn dance in Richmond, then to Springfield and later to Denver's KOA.

He cut his first instrumental number, *Guitar Blues*, for Bullet Records[15] when he was with the Red Foley group. Later in Denver[,] he signed with RCA Victor.

11. LaRosa (*b* 1930) was a popular Italian crooner who worked briefly for the popular radio and television host Arthur Godfrey (Whitney Balliett, "The Man Who Lost His Humility: Julius LaRosa," *American Singers: Twenty-Seven Portraits in Song* [Jackson: University Press of Mississippi, 2006], 161–67).

12. Born Paul Berg in 1934, Berg was a popular rock-and-roll disc jockey in the Pacific Northwest known for his sponsorship of teen dances (Peter Blecha, *Sonic Boom: The History of Northwest Rock, from "Louie Louie" to "Smells Like Teen Spirit"* [New York: Backbeat Books, 2009], 78–85; Pat O'Day with Jim Ojala, *It Was All Just Rock 'n' Roll: A Journey to the Center of the Radio & Concert Universe* [Seattle: R-n-R Press, 2002]).

13. Likely the Lane Brothers, a rock-and-roll group from Cambridge, Massachusetts, best known for their recording of "Boppin' in a Sack" (RCA Victor 47-7220, 1958) (Klaus Kettner with Tony Wilkinson, "The Lane Brothers," www.rockabilly.nl/references/messages/lane_brothers.htm; accessed December 6, 2011).

14. Although the first commercially manufactured electric guitar, the Rickenbacker "Frying Pan," debuted in 1932, technical problems with the instrument discouraged many musicians from engaging with it. Developments in the 1940s, particularly the efforts to build a solid-body electric guitar undertaken simultaneously by Les Paul and Leo Fender, encourage more musicians to take up the electric guitar in the 1950s. For a critical history of these developments, consult Waksman, *Instruments of Desire*, 14–74.

15. A Nashville-based record label founded by Jim Bulleit in 1946 that focused extensively on the recording of hillbilly music (Martin Hawkins, *A Shot in the Dark: Making Records in Nashville, 1945-1955* [Nashville: Vanderbilt University Press and Country Music Foundation Press, 2004], 24–38).

A session in New York followed the Denver visit, then he joined the Carter Sisters and Mother Maybelle in Knoxville. This group went to Springfield in 1949 and came to the *Opry* in 1950.[16]

Although with a group, Chet was fundamentally a soloist by nature, as there were no musicians within traveling distance when he was growing up with his guitar. He swapped an old pistol for the instrument.

Two older brothers, musically minded, had left home. They are Jimmy Atkins, now program director for Station KOA in Denver, and Lowell Atkins of Kokomo, Ind.[,] who operates an electric motor shop and plays music as a side-line.

Since becoming connected with RCA Victor, Chet has always worked with directors in record sessions. After a studio was established in Nashville[,] he took on added responsibilities, and he was made a musical director last May.

RCA Victor has announced plans for immediate construction of a new studio, modern in every detail, to supplant its present building in Nashville.[17]

With music so much in his soul, melodies come naturally to Chet. But he has great difficulty with the words. When he thinks he has some words to fit a melody[,] he calls on his good friend Boudleaux Bryant (*Bye, Bye Love* co-writer with his wife [Felice]). Chet and Boudleaux jointly wrote *Midnight* and *How's the World Treating You* that became hits.

Chet is married to Leona Johnson, formerly of Cincinnati. Their daughter, Merle, 10, is musically inclined but her daddy doesn't encourage her to go into it professionally. Maybe when she's 13[,] she'll make up her mind like he did.

Source: Ben A. Green, "Chet Makes Guitar Talk with Rhythm and Melody," *Country and Western Jamboree* 3, no. 7 (Winter 1957): 8–9. (Used with permission.)

FOR FURTHER READING

Chet Atkins: Certified Guitar Player. Nashville, TN: Country Music Foundation Press, 2012.
Waksman, Steve. *Instruments of Desire: The Electric Guitar and the Shaping of Musical Experience.* Cambridge, MA: Harvard University Press, 1999, 75–112.

16. Atkins joined the Mother Maybelle and the Carter Sisters in 1948 and moved to Springfield, Missouri, in 1949 (Mark Zwonitzer with Charles Hirschberg, *Will You Miss Me When I'm Gone?: The Carter Family & Their Legacy in American Music* [New York: Simon & Schuster, 2004], 266–81).

17. RCA Victor began recording at the Brown Brothers studio regularly in Nashville in 1950. In late 1954, RCA Victor began recording at the TRAFCO Building at 1525 McGavock, where Chet Atkins frequently supervised sessions. RCA Victor opened a Nashville studio at 17th and Hawkins in 1957 and opened a second studio on 17th Avenue South in 1964 (John W. Rumble, "Behind the Board: Talking with Studio Engineer Bill Porter, Part One," *Journal of Country Music* 18, no. 1 [1996]: 27–28; Hawkins, *A Shot in the Dark*, 230–31).

25

"Coast Country Biz Booms" (1957)

Country music thrived in California in the years following World War II as bands continued to cater to Dust Bowl migrants and their descendants. As Peter LaChapelle has demonstrated, for instance, dance halls featuring western swing bands flourished near the military bases and munitions factories of Los Angeles, and the large crowds of young people who flocked to them necessitated the electrification of instruments and the development of a loud, brash style that could compete with the revelers.[1]

Speaking to growing national interest in the business of country music, the following article demonstrates that entrepreneurs and promoters around the Los Angeles area developed novel ways to capitalize on the genre's popularity. Early

1. Peter LaChapelle, *Proud to Be an Okie: Cultural Politics, Country Music, and Migration to Southern California* (Berkeley: University of California Press, 2007), 76–110. See also Stephanie Vander Wel, "'I Am a Honky-Tonk Girl': Country Music, Gender, and Migration," Ph.D. dissertation, University of California, Los Angeles, 2008, 139–96; chaps. 7–10 of Gerald Haslam with Alexandra Haslam Russell and Richard Chon, *Workin' Man Blues: Country Music in California* (Berkeley: Heyday Books, 2005); and Rich Kienzle, *Southwest Shuffle: Pioneers of Honky-Tonk, Western Swing, and Country Jazz* (New York: Routledge, 2003).

television programs such as the *Town Hall Party* brought the excitement of the dance hall into the homes of young people in Compton, then a working-class neighborhood, and like *American Bandstand* in Philadelphia, encouraged audiences to participate in live broadcasts of the show.[2] Capitol Records, which was on its way to becoming a major player in the record industry, was also based in Los Angeles, and, as a consequence, it issued contracts to many of the most popular country musicians in southern California and, under the direction of producer Ken Nelson,[3] released hundreds of recordings. These recordings reflected the distinctive tastes of the region's country music fans, who preferred more pronounced dance rhythms, brighter timbres, tighter arrangements, and faster tempi than were heard in many contemporary country recordings from Nashville and other parts of the country. The following article—along with John Grissim Jr.'s piece (chapter 30) from a decade later—also challenges the prevailing country music industry narrative that places the center of creative and economic power in Nashville.

LOS ANGELES—COUNTRY MUSIC IS BIG BUSINESS ON THE WEST COAST

Measured by the number of shows, the size of their casts, the prominence of their artists, and the amount of air time, country music holds top rank as entertainment and its audience acceptance seems to be growing.

It would probably be misleading to compare one show with another in any of these particulars for each has its strong points, each its enthusiasts, and if there were any question of talent reserve, the shows need merely reach out into the nearby talent-rich Hollywood area and get all the guest stars they want, or the recording stars they can use—because so many artists have chosen this sunshine-laden land to make their homes.

Biggest shows in the southern California area now are:

- **Town Hall Party**, originating at Compton, Calif.[,] and
- **Hometown Jamboree**, originating at Annaheim [*sic*], Calif.[4]

Cliffie Stone of the Jamboree is a good man to start with. He's right in the middle of the mountain-size country music business as president of Central Songs, president of the Cliffie Stone Enterprises, jovial emcee, a Capitol recording star, C-W music promoter and personal manager for Tennessee Ernie Ford.

2. Many of the *Town Hall Show* broadcasts have been reissued on DVD by Bear Family Records.

3. For more background on Ken Nelson, consult his memoir, *My First 90 Years Plus 3* (Pittsburgh: Dorrance, 2007).

4. For more on Stone and the *Hometown Jamboree*, consult Kienzle, *Southwest Shuffle*, 101–108.

SAME SPONSOR 9 YEARS

His show, the Hometown Jamboree on KTLA-TV has just been picked up by a local furniture company for the ninth straight year of sponsorship, giving it the longest run of any such show on the Pacific coast. On KXLA, Cliffie's show runs five days a week, and is now in its twelfth year there.

Hometown Jamboree has top talent galore and Cliffie has geared it to a fast pace and to a program that has the largest appeal to the greatest number of people. The Jamboree runs from 7 to 8 p.m. but after 8:30 p.m. the lights are dimmed, the audience is free to stack the folding chairs against the walls and dance to their hearts' content to country music.

"We quickened the pace," Cliffie explains, "so that instead of doing 20 numbers in an hour as we used to do, we can now do 32.[5] That means that if somebody doesn't like a current number, he won't turn off his set, but will wait a minute for what comes next."

Cliffie finds he can best promote his show by promoting his artists. "A Show is only as good as its entertainers," he says, "and we try to get them out to mix with people by putting on personal appearances all over southern California, encouraging them to visit record stores, and to drop in at night clubs and other public places. We know this method works and we don't expect to change things when we've already got a successful operation."

Jamboree's talent now includes Tommy Sands, Billy Strange, Darla Daret, Merrill Moore, Harry Rodcay, Gene O'Quinn, Herman the Hermit who plays 160 novelty instruments, Dallas Frazier (Capitol), Molly Bee (Dot), Tennessee Ernie (daytime), Speedy West, Jimmy Bryant, and others in addition to a seven-piece band.

SANDS IS NEWEST

Newest addition is Tommy Sands who joined the Jamboree three months ago and who two weeks ago was recommended by Cliffie to the Krafts Food people to help them do a take-off show on a teen-age idol. This show was set for January 30 and the fast pace of the Jamboree is seen in the fact that Sands was recorded on a Monday and the records were in the hands of dee-jays the following Wednesday. Cliffie has also taken over the personal management of Sands.

Cliffie Stone has been in California 34 years and in country music most of his life. He summarizes the growth of country music on the West Coast this way:

"Country music has taken a jump in just the last three months. Our Saturday night crowds are getting bigger. There are two radio stations here—KRKD and KXLA, giving full time to country music. It seems pretty clear that the public wants this kind of entertainment."

The Town Hall Party of which Bill Wagnon is owner and producer, now in its fourth year, is still making tremendous strides audience-wise. It runs for three hours, starting at 10 p.m. Saturday nights on KTTV-TV (Los Angeles Times station) and whether folks are watching it in their living room or in person at the Town Hall, it's geared to bring everybody a good time.

---

5. With no commercial breaks, twenty songs per hour would result in an average of three minutes per song, or the standard length of a 45-rpm recording. Thirty-two songs per hour reduces the length of each song to under two minutes, a reduction by more than one-third.

The audience isn't seated at Town Hall—they gather round and dance and meet their friends and the artists when not on stage, while the music and hilarity pour forth, with almost everybody feeling he's in on it and contributing something to make it go.

All of it is sponsored—the first hour by a furniture company, the second hour by Rheingold Beer, and the third hour by Chevrolet—and there's a long waiting list of those who'd like to use it. It covers all of southern California. On Friday nights, the show is just for the audience, and it usually fills the Hall, big enough if people were seated, to accommodate 3,000.

10 TOP ARTISTS WEEKLY

Bill's present talent roster includes about 32 people and at least 10 top artists are on the program each week. Those most in demand include the Collins Kids, Tex Ritter, Johnny Bond, Joe and Rose Lee, Les (Carrot Top) Anderson, Skeets McDonald and Merle Travis. Newest addition to the roster is little Dorotha Boatright, age 11, picked up about three months ago in a talent contest, for whom several of the labels are vying for a recording contract. The Collins Kids, ages 12 and 14, were pre-empted for the Steve Allen show Jan. 27 and will be headliners at the San Antonio Livestock Expedition and rodeo starting Feb. 8.

So many of Townhall Party's talent roster are of national stature that Bill expects to expand the personal appearance tour side of his business this year, into all parts of the country.

Considerable new talent has been discovered on Town Hall party [sic] and Bill is always on the lookout for more.

Although both the Town Hall Party and the Hometown Jamboree originate in the same area, feature country music and are slanted to "please the greatest number," neither Bill Wagnon nor Cliffie Stone looks on the other as competition. That's probably because there is plenty of country music to go around, plenty of listeners ready and waiting, and as long as the two shows are scheduled for different hours, no country music lover need choose one show or the other. He can always have them both.

> Source: "Coast Country Biz Booms," *Country Music Reporter* 1, no. 11 (2 February 1957): 1, 7.

FOR FURTHER READING

Haslam, Gerald, with Alexandra Haslam Russell and Richard Chon. *Workin' Man Blues: Country Music in California*. Berkeley: Heyday Books, 2005.

Kienzle, Rich. *Southwest Shuffle: Pioneers of Honky-Tonk, Western Swing, and Country Jazz*. New York: Routledge, 2003.

LaChapelle, Peter. *Proud to Be an Okie: Cultural Politics, Country Music, and Migration to Southern California*. Berkeley: University of California Press, 2007.

Vander Wel, Stephanie. "'I Am a Honky-Tonk Girl'": Country music, Gender, and Migration." Ph.D. dissertation, University of California, Los Angeles, 2008.

Alan Lomax

"Bluegrass Background: Folk Music with Overdrive" (1959)

Mandolinist Bill Monroe's music had been heard on the *Opry* for nearly two decades by the time that Alan Lomax—son of folklorist John A. Lomax (see chapter 3) and himself a formidable scholar of vernacular musics—wrote the following article for *Esquire* magazine.[1] But, despite Monroe's national presence and the similar success of other major bluegrass bands, Lomax's essay seems to suggest that bluegrass music was a relatively recent development in 1959. Writing for a national audience, however, Lomax was not introducing bluegrass to country music fans. Rather, he was responding to a folk music revival that was beginning to take shape in Greenwich Village in New York and that was quickly spreading to college and university towns throughout the United States[2] Young people began

1. Lomax has been the subject of much recent study. See, for instance, John Szwed, *Alan Lomax: The Man Who Recorded the World, A Biography* (New York: Viking, 2010); and Ronald Cohen, ed., *Alan Lomax: Selected Writings, 1934-1997* (New York: Routledge, 2003).

2. For an overview of the folk revival movement, consult Ronald D. Cohen, *Rainbow Quest: The Folk Music Revival & American Society, 1940-1970* (Amherst: University of

to explore the rich variety of American vernacular musical styles that had been documented on the race and hillbilly recordings of the 1920s and 1930s, and many of them—including such luminaries as Mike Seeger and John Cohen—even took up instruments and traveled to meet older musicians in an effort to learn the nuances of early string band music and the blues.[3] By the late 1950s and early 1960s, commercial folk groups such as the Kingston Trio even topped the pop charts with their interpretations of early-twentieth-century vernacular musics.

As college students began playing banjos and singing traditional Appalachian songs and blues numbers, bluegrass music was transformed from a contemporary commercial country music subgenre into a seemingly authentic American traditional music.[4] Lomax is quick to draw parallels between bluegrass—"folk music with overdrive"—and Eastern European folk music and the jazz stylings of trumpeter Louis Armstrong in an effort to legitimize this position, and his description of bluegrass as a "clear-cut orchestral style" does similar work. At the same time, the similarities between Lomax's romanticization of bluegrass's "backwoods" style and early reportage on country music are striking in their consistent depiction of an idyllic rural past that never really existed in the first place.

Monroe and his protégés were quick to capitalize on the rhetoric of Lomax's article. Monroe often spoke of the "ancient tones" in his music, referring to the strains of string band music, traditional hymnody, and Scots-Irish traditions that filtered into his music,[5] while Flatt and Scruggs were frequent headliners on the college touring circuit and went on to record the songs of the folk revival's most celebrated and enigmatic exponent, Bob Dylan.

━━━━━

WHILE the aging voices along Tin Pan Alley grow every day more querulous, and jazzmen wander through the harmonic jungles of Schoenberg and Stravinsky,[6] grass-roots guitar and banjo pickers are playing on the heartstrings of America. Out of the torrent of folk music that is the backbone of the record business today, the freshest sound comes from the so-called Bluegrass band—a sort of mountain Dixieland combo in which the five-string banjo, America's

Massachusetts Press, 2002); Robert Cantwell, *When We Were Good: The Folk Revival* (Cambridge, MA: Harvard University Press, 1996); and David King Dunaway and Molly Beer, *Singing Out: An Oral History of America's Folk Revivals* (New York: Oxford University Press, 2010).

3. Ray Allen, *Gone to the Country: The New Lost City Ramblers & The Folk Music Revival* (Urbana: University of Illinois Press, 2010); Bill C. Malone, *Music from the True Vine: Mike Seeger's Life & Musical Journey* (Chapel Hill: University of North Carolina Press, 2011).

4. This history is traced in Neil V. Rosenberg, *Bluegrass: A History* (Urbana: University of Illinois Press, 1985), 166–202.

5. For a more nuanced discussion of Monroe's musical style, consult Neil V. Rosenberg and Charles K. Wolfe, *The Music of Bill Monroe* (Urbana: University of Illinois Press, 2007).

6. Modernist composers of art music Arnold Schoenberg and Igor Stravinsky.

only indigenous folk instrument,[7] carries the lead like a hot clarinet. The mandolin plays bursts reminiscent of jazz trumpet choruses; a heavily bowed fiddle supplies trombone-like hoedown solos; while a framed guitar and slapped base make up the rhythm section. Everything goes at top volume, with harmonized choruses behind a lead singer who hollers in the high, lonesome style beloved in the American backwoods. The result is folk music in overdrive with a silvery, rippling, pinging sound; the State Department should note that for virtuosity, fire and speed[,] our best Bluegrass bands can match any Slavic folk orchestra.

Bluegrass style began in 1945 when Bill Monroe, of the Monroe Brothers, recruited a quintet that included Earl Scruggs (who had perfected a three-finger banjo style now known as "picking scruggs [sic]") and Lester Flatt (a Tennessee guitar picker and singer); Bill led the group with mandolin and a countertenor voice that hits high notes with the impact of a Louis Armstrong trumpet. Playing the old-time mountain tunes, which most hillbilly pros had abandoned, he orchestrated them so brilliantly that the name of the outfit, "Bill Monroe and his Bluegrass [sic] Boys," became the permanent hallmark of this field. When Scruggs and Flatt left to form a powerful group of their own, Don Reno joined Monroe, learned Bluegrass, [and] departed to found his own fine orchestra, too. Most of the Bluegrass outfits on Southern radio and TV today have played with Monroe or one of his disciples—with the noteworthy exception of the Stanley Brothers, who play and sing in a more relaxed and gentle style.

Bluegrass is the first clear-cut orchestral style to appear in the British-American folk tradition in five hundred years; and entirely on its own it is turning back to the great heritage of older tunes that our ancestors brought into the mountains before the American Revolution. A century of isolation in the lonesome hollows of the Appalachians gave them time to combine strains from Scottish and English folk songs and to produce a vigorous pioneer music of their own. The hot Negro square-dance fiddle went early up the creek-bed roads into the hills; then in the mid-nineteenth century came the five-string banjo; early in the twentieth century[,] the guitar was absorbed into the developing tradition. By the time folk-song collectors headed into the mountains looking for ancient ballads, they found a husky, hard-to-kill musical culture as well. Finally, railroads and highways snaked into the backwoods, and mountain folk moved out into urban, industrialized, shook-up America; they were the last among us to experience the breakdown of traditional family patterns, and there ensued an endless stream of sad songs, from *On Top of Old Smoky* to *The Birmingham Jail*. Next in popularity were sacred songs and homiletic pieces warning listeners against drink and fast company; and in the late Thirties, the favorite theme for displaced hillbillies was *No Letter Today*.

Talented mountaineers who wanted to turn professional have had a guaranteed income since the day in 1923[,] when Ralph Peer skeptically waxed an Atlanta fiddler playing *The Old Hen Cackled and the Rooster's Going to Crow*, and Victor sold half-a-million copies to the ready-made white rural audience [see chapter 1]. Recording companies sent off field crews

---

7. The banjo is an instrument of African origins, but with a decidedly American history. For more background, consult Karen Linn, *That Half-Barbaric Twang: The Banjo in American Popular Culture* (Urbana: University of Illinois Press, 1991); Robert Cantwell, *Bluegrass Breakdown: The Making of the Old Southern Sound* (Urbana: University of Illinois Press, 1984), 91–114; and Cecelia Conway, *African Banjo Echoes in Appalachia: A Study of Folk Traditions* (Knoxville: University of Tennessee Press, 1995).

and made stars of such singers as Jimmie Rodgers, Uncle Dave Macon, Gid Tanner, the Carter family [*sic*] and Roy Acuff.

Countless combinations of hillbillies have coalesced and dispersed before radio microphones since WSB in Atlanta began beaming out mountainy music on its opening day. *Grand Ole Opry* has been broadcasting for thirty-three years; the WWVA Jamboree has gone on for twenty-seven.[8] In the beginning, performers sang solo or with one accompanying instrument; but before microphones they felt the need of orchestras, which, while originally crude, developed with the uncritical encouragement of local audiences.

By now there has grown up a generation of hillbilly musicians who can play anything in any key, and their crowning accomplishment is Bluegrass. When the fresh sound of New Orleans Dixieland combos hit the cities some fifty years ago, it made a musical revolution first in America, then the world. Today we have a new kind of orchestra suitable for accompanying the frontier tunes with which America has fallen in love. And now anything can happen.

> *Source:* Alan Lomax, "Bluegrass Background: Folk Music with Overdrive," *Esquire* 52 (October 1959): 108–109. (Courtesy of the Association for Cultural Equity.)

FOR FURTHER READING

Allen, Ray. *Gone to the Country: The New Lost City Ramblers & The Folk Music Revival.* Urbana: University of Illinois Press, 2010.

Cantwell, Robert. *Bluegrass Breakdown: The Making of the Old Southern Sound.* Urbana: University of Illinois Press, 1984.

Rosenberg, Neil V. *Bluegrass: A History.* Urbana: University of Illinois Press, 1985.

Szwed, John. *Alan Lomax: The Man Who Recorded the World, A Biography.* New York: Viking, 2010.

8. For more on the WWVA Jamboree, consult Ivan Tribe, *Mountaineer Jamboree: Country Music in West Virginia* (Lexington: University Press of Kentucky, 1984), 43–72.

Tom T. Hall

The Storyteller's Nashville, on Song Writing and
Song Plugging (1979)

Of course, developments in the recording studio were virtually meaningless without good songs for the musicians to record. Since the end of the nineteenth century, professional songwriters depended on a vast complex of publishers and song pluggers to convince popular performers to sing their songs and to collect print and performance royalties while continuing to write songs on a daily basis in the constant quest for a hit.[1] In the excerpt that follows, singer-songwriter Tom T. Hall describes the difficulties of convincing a popular recording artist to record someone else's song.

---

1. David Suisman, *Selling Sounds: The Commercial Revolution in American Music* (Cambridge, MA: Harvard University Press, 2009), 61–65.

D ESPITE the fact that "Harper Valley PTA" radically changed my career and status in Nashville, nearly three years went by from the time I wrote the song until its 1968 release.[2] Since a fellow can accumulate a lot of debts in that length of time, it should be obvious that Tom Hall (the "T" *still* hadn't been added) had to hustle up some options.

As he did several times during those years, Jimmy Key[3] subtly came up with an answer. His booking agency was hectic, successful, and "where the spotlights were directed." In contrast, his recording and publishing business was pretty dreary. Since a lot of my songs were around his files to be sold and since my garden and Miss Dixie[4] kept me fond of sticking extremely close to Nashville, Jimmy offered me regular office hours as his *song plugger*.

A song plugger is a person seeking to be abnormally abused because a song plugger carries a box of tapes, a ream of lyrics, and—in those days—walks up and down Music Row trying to get songs recorded. Sound easy? Consider one rather typical episode.

It was the general practice for an artist to arrive in town, check into a motel, then call all the song pluggers and songwriters to come and display their wares. This particular day Rex Allen was working out of a motel some distance from town. I had several of my songs and two or three of Roy Baham's songs which I thought would be good for Rex, as he had recorded a song for Lorene Mann[5] called "Don't Go Near the Indians"[6] and was looking for another hit.

When I arrived, Lorene Mann was there and several song pluggers from the major publishing companies. Rex was lying on his bed propped up by a couple of pillows and wearing a dressing gown. There were several empty bottles around the room as well as other signs that the auditions had been going on for several hours, or maybe several days. I waited in a corner, listening.

Rex demanded, "Where are Hank Cochran, Willie Nelson, and all the hot writers in town? I come all the way from California to listen to some songs, and I get them by everybody except the hit writers. I need a hit! If I just wanted *any* song, I could have stayed in California."

One of the song pluggers spoke up, "Rex, it's hard to get a song off one of Willie's or Hank's demos. These guys get most of their songs placed [with a recording artist] before they ever get out of the studio."

Rex was not sympathetic. "Well, why don't you-all go down and hang around one of their demo sessions. Play me something else and get to the good stuff."

There were reels of tape around the room, and I guess Rex had heard fifty songs by the time he got to mine. I handed him the lyrics and started playing the demos one after another, waiting for him to say, "Next song, please!" He was really short with me because I didn't know

2. Hall's "Harper Valley P.T.A." had been a hit for singer Jeannie C. Riley in 1968. Released as Plantation 3, the record spent three weeks in the number-one position on *Billboard*'s "Hot Country Singles" chart (Joel Whitburn, *Top Country Singles, 1944-2001* [Menomonee Falls, WI: Record Research, 2002], 294).

3. Co-owner of Hall's publishing company.

4. Hall's wife.

5. Mann (*b* 1937) was a songwriter and recording artist active in the 1960s and 1970s and perhaps best known for her duets with Justin Tubb (Mary A. Bufwack and Robert K. Oermann, *Finding Her Voice: Women in Country Music, 1800-2000* [Nashville: Vanderbilt University Press and Country Music Foundation Press, 2003], 327).

6. The recording (Mercury 71997) peaked at the number-four position on *Billboard*'s "Hot Country Singles" chart in the fall of 1962 (Whitburn, *Top Country Singles*, 7).

him, and, far as I know, he had never heard one of my tunes before. I played about four songs before he stopped me with another long speech about how he could not get anyone to bring him any material. I rewound my tape, took the lyrics, and said, as politely as I could manage, that I appreciated him listening. He then apologized for the outburst and asked me to continue, but I repeated my thanks and marched out the door while he continued explaining that he *really* did not want to hear the songs. Outside in the fresh air, I made myself a promise not to attend any more sessions like that one.

Somewhere along in the sixties, the practice of renting a motel and holding court went out of style, and I haven't noticed that the music business is any worse for it. However, I should mention that, while I didn't have the patience for it, there were some super song pluggers in Nashville at the time. When an artist would hit town, the pros would get a couple of cases of his favorite whiskey, a couple or three pretty girls, and at times would even pick up the motel tab for an artist who was selling records. A lot of songs...and hits...were recorded by artists who had been psychologically compromised by their acceptance of these luxury items and circumstances.

It was an art.

* * *

A S a song plugger for Newkeys Music, I was also a listener and evaluator of new songwriting talent as it came down the pike. One such new talent was a young man who had driven from Arkansas to break into the music business. He was a slim, blue-jeaned, cowboy-shirted young man of about twenty years. His guitar was of the catalogue variety,[7] but he had some pretty decent songs. Sometimes a song that is not all that great in itself can hint, to a trained ear, that a person could do better. I professed to having a trained ear since I had heard in the neighborhood of ten thousand songs in the past couple of years alone. So, while he didn't have anything that sounded like a hit song with him, I thought he had potential and a certain flair. I offered him a deal with Newkeys Music.

I explained that he would not get any money (a draw) and that he would be on the standard songwriter's rate of a penny a record, in addition to whatever BMI[8] would pay him for performances—all of which was a standard deal. But he had some questions.

"When do I get my money?"

"What money?"

"You're going to publish the songs, ain't you?"

"That's right."

"Where's my money?"

"What money?"

7. An entry-level or intermediate instrument, rather than a professional-quality instrument.

8. Broadcast Music, Inc., an American performing rights organization established in 1940 to collect royalties from radio stations that used songs written and/or published by affiliated songwriters and/or publishers (Russell Sanjek and David Sanjek, *American Popular Music Business in the 20th Century* [New York: Oxford University Press, 1991], 58–78).

"Let me get this straight now. You're going to publish my songs, and you ain't gonna give me now money?"

"There is no money to be had as yet. We don't make any money until someone either plays the songs on the radio or buys a record. Where do you expect us, as publishers, to get any money from anyone?"

"You must think I'm crazy. I am going to give you my songs and sign a contract, and you ain't gonna give me any of the money for the publishing or anything? Do you think I'm a damned fool? How do you figure I can write songs if I ain't got no sense?"

"Well, look," I say. "Where do you think we get money from your songs? Answer me that!"

"From publishing and demos and all of that. I ain't as dumb as I look."

"Let me tell you this much," I plead. "It doesn't make money when we publish an unrecorded song. It costs money. It takes lead sheets, demos, paper work, pitching, plugging, streetwalking, and sometimes politics to get a song recorded. When you finally have a record on the market by an established artist, we could have hundreds of dollars invested in it. Nobody, but nobody, sends us checks just because we live in Nashville and are in the music business. Someone has to use the song before we see any money, and that usually takes a year or more."

He picked up his tape, his guitar, and his lyrics, then said, "*I am telling you for the last time*—I am trying to give you a break with my songs. If I don't get some straight answers in a minute, I am taking these songs and walked out that door. I want my money, or I ain't signing a damned thing!"

I was completely exhausted, so I got out of my chair and *pleaded* with him not to take his songs to Jack "Cowboy" Clement. I got very confidential and said to him where no one could hear, "Jack Clement will probably give you a lot of money and make you a lot of promises, but money is not where it's at in this town. The thing to do is pursue your artistic goals and let the money go where it will. Jack has an office on Belmont Boulevard somewhere.... You got that? Belmont Boulevard...Jack Clement. Don't take your songs to him, or you'll wind up paying a lot of taxes and get into all kinds of trouble."

The Arkansas songwriter was studying the address he had written down the last time I ever saw him...and I didn't spend too much more time as a song plugger, either.

Source: Tom T. Hall, *The Storyteller's Nashville* (Garden City, NY: Doubleday, 1979), 97–101. (From THE STORYTELLER'S NASHVILLE by Tom T. Hall, copyright © 1979 by Tom T. Hall. Used by permission of Doubleday, a division of Random House, Inc. Any third party use of this material, outside of this publication, is prohibited. Interested parties must apply directly to Random House, Inc. for permission.)

FOR FURTHER READING

Adler, Thomas. "The Unplotted Narratives of Tom T. Hall." *Journal of Country Music* 4, no. 2 (Summer 1973): 52–69.

Chapman, Marshall. *They Came to Nashville.* Nashville, TN: Vanderbilt University Press and Country Music Foundation Press, 2010.

The Story of the Country Music
Association (1968)

The Country Music Association (CMA) was established in November 1958 following attempts to make the Country Music Disc Jockeys Association more representative of the diverse industry subgroups that functioned within Nashville. The CMA's principal goals were to gain greater airplay for country music on the nation's radio stations by providing comprehensive demographic research that offered detailed information about the country audience to radio stations and advertisers and, through its philanthropic arm, the Country Music Foundation, to document the genre's rich history and present it to the public. The following article, which commemorates the ten-year anniversary of the organization, comes on the heels of the opening of the Country Music Hall of Fame complex in 1967 and its first awards show, and reveals the tensions between the CMA's dual commercial and preservationist mandates.[1]

---

1. Diane Pecknold, *The Selling Sound: The Rise of the Country Music Industry* (Durham, NC: Duke University Press, 2007), 133–99.

*J*UST *what is* CMA? That's a familiar question from fans all over.

In dictionary terms, it is a country music, industry-wide association to promote country music in its entirety. The CMA's aggressive promotion of country music has resulted in a growing number of radio stations programming C&W[2] records, increased interest in country music for television and live shows, and greater acceptance of country music by people around the world. The Country Music Association has always felt country music is its own best salesman, and as a result has worked for greater exposure of country music to people everywhere.

The Country Music Association is also intent on encouraging the highest ethics in every phase throughout the industry, and it points with pride to its hundreds of outstanding members. The Country Music Association also serves as a sounding board for its members, encouraging and guiding the industry to continued healthy growth. Working with [singer-songwriter] Bill Anderson, a member of the Board, a Code of Ethics was established. The Code is a voluntary agreement to support and maintain the excellent relationships within the country music industry while exercising the consideration for others which is so typical of those who have built and grown with the trade. Large numbers of artists and performers have evidenced their earnest desire to support and improve the industry of country music by signing the Code.

The CMA seeks to insure that country music retains its individuality. The CMA has spearheaded a gigantic movement not only to preserve, but [also] to clarify the history of country music and to house valuable documents, recordings, and discographic material concerning the growth of America's most beloved music. Through special arrangements with the John Edwards Memorial Foundation at UCLA, the CMA has arranged for a special scholarship each year for the preservation of the many documents and memorabilia for study by both fans and serious students of country music.

The Country Music Association, known as "America's Most Active Trade Association," was organized in November 1958 by a group of hard-core Country & Western Music executives, and has been a team effort ever since. All of the 33 lifetime members and the 200 annual members of that initial year pitched in to nourish CMA to its current strength of more than 1,700 annual members, 120 active lifetime members, plus 150 organizational members representing the best of the C&W industry.

Originally there were nine Directors and five Officers. Connie B. Gay, broadcasting executive, served as CMA's president during the first two years. Wesley Rose [1918–1990], President of Acuff-Rose Publications, Inc., served as Chairman of the Board of Directors during that period. At the first annual meeting in November, 1959, the Board was extended to 18 Directors, and the slate of Officers was extended to nine. There are nine categories of membership, including Artist-Musician; Artist Manager, Booker, Promoter, Agent, and Ballroom Operator; Composer; Disc Jockey; Music Publisher; Radio-TV Personnel; Record Company Personnel; Trade Publication Representatives; and Non-Affiliated persons actively engaged in C&W. Rights Societies,[3] attorneys, record shop owners, etc.[,] belong to this category. The CMA

---

2. "Country & Western," the industry term to describe what we currently describe as "country" music.

3. Also known as Performing Rights Organizations, or PROs. There are three PROs in the United States: the American Society of Composers, Artists, and Performers (ASCAP), Broadcast Music, Inc. (BMI), and the Society of European State Authors & Composers (SESAC).

membership elects two Directors for each category. The Board of Directors elects the Officers. Directors, except the Directors-At-Large, serve for a period of two years and Officers serve for a period of one year. All Officers and Directors serve without pay and they pay their own expenses.

Following the first two-year period, Ken Nelson of Capitol Records served as CMA's President for two years and Steve Sholes of RCA Victor Records served the same period as Chairman of the Board. In November, 1962, Gene Autry was elected President and Wesley Rose was again elected Chairman of the Board. Then followed Tex Ritter, 1963–65; Bill [sic] Denny, 1966 and Paul Cohen, 1967. The current President is Hubert Long of Hubert Long Talent Agency. The Chairman of the Board is Jack Loetz who is Vice-President of Marketing Administration, Columbia Records. There are many other great people who have served CMA without whom the organization would be sorely lacking. Executive Director Mrs. Jo Walker has served CMA since its inception.

In 1961, CMA established the Country Music Hall of Fame.[4] Those people who have already been elected are Jimmy [sic] Rodgers, Fred Rose, Hank Williams, Roy Acuff, Tex Ritter, Ernest Tubb, Eddy Arnold, James R. Denny, Uncle Dave Macon, George D. Hay, Steve Sholes, Jim Reeves, Red Foley and J. L. Frank. This is the highest honor accorded to those who work in and contribute to the Country Music industry.

CMA proved to the industry that C&W is here to stay through its double-barreled study of the broadcasting industry. The radio survey revealed over 1500 stations programming C&W music from two to twenty-four hours per day. More than 400 radio stations program country and western music exclusively. CMA's survey of television revealed that more than one-half of the stations carry C&W and/or Gospel Music shows.

CMA has pressed into intangible areas. For instance, there is no measuring stick to determine CMA's role in the upsurge in C&W material being recorded by pop and jazz artists, and there's no scale to weigh CMA salesmanship in bringing more and more C&W acts before the national TV network eye.

In 1961, the CMA was instrumental in chartering the Country Music Foundation which had as its major task the fund-raising for and the building of the Country Music Hall of Fame and Museum. The Country Music Foundation is a non-profit corporation dedicated to the preservation of the histrionics of country music. From this group came plans for an international center where the men and women who built this great industry might be honored and their works preserved for research and study. Carefully planned around creative themes of "Sight and Sound," the Country Music Hall of Fame and Museum is designed to draw the serious, the curious, the dubious, the enthusiastic through a rich experience of past, present, and future. Symbolic of the rich heritage of rural America, the building expresses the strong influence of the growth and culture of our nation through country music. This was accomplished through the efforts of a vast number of country music related persons and organizations. The building opened on April 1, 1967 after expenditure of more than three quarters of a million dollars for the construction and upkeep.

This building also serves as international headquarters for the Association. It is located in the center of activity in Music City USA, at 16th Avenue South & Division Street. The

---

4. For further discussion of the Country Music Hall of Fame and Museum's formation, consult Pecknold, *The Selling Sound*, 194–99.

names of those firms and individuals who have contributed $10,000 to the fund are on a concrete plaque on the front of the building. Each of the contributing artists [is] honored with a star and his or her name in the Walkway in front of the building. This is an extra added attraction and other contributors to the building fund will also be honored.

Serving an average of 400 visitors a week during the summer months, the Hall of Fame and Museum, by the end of the year, had seen some 70,000 devoted fans and followers of Country Music come through the front doors, not counting tours of school children. During the holidays in bitter cold weather, over 800 visited.

In less than a year from the opening, all goals set by the Country Music Foundation had been surpassed. The auspicious opening on Saturday, April 1st, 1967 has led multitudes ranging from organized contingents from all over the world right through the doors into the sanctuary which houses not only a graphic history of the Country Music industry, but a view of its present expanse. A visual and aural demonstration of how a session is readied for recording greets the visitor as he leaves the auditorium where a motion picture presentation of the growth of country music runs continuously. The central hall is filled with the plaques and mementoes honoring those elected to the Hall of Fame. The north wing is filled with the artifacts from the many famous and near famous who have contributed to the elevation of country music to its present pinnacle in the hearts of the world.

Under the devoted and capable supervision of Mrs. Dorothy Gable, the energetic staff takes care of all questions from the littlest fan to the biggest star. She sees that groups are guided through the sights and sounds of the establishment. In addition, she is kept quite busy storing and placing the artifacts donated to the museum. Another of her tasks is to see that finances are taken care of and that the promotion of the Hall of Fame keeps pace with the ever changing industry.

Not only does the Hall of Fame and Museum house a wonderful exhibit unlike any found the world over, it also holds other activities which the tourist rarely, if ever, sees. The offices of the Country Music Association are found in the lower level suite along with suitable accommodations for the Country Music Foundation. In addition there are large basement rooms planned for future expansion when it becomes necessary. It is surprising that there have been so few traffic problems at the Hall of Fame, but the ample parking lot has served well. This, added to the gentle prodding from Dorothy to keep the visitors moving, assures that there is always room for more to visit the hallowed halls. The biggest problems are that visitors usually want to see the movie again and again. Often, they want to start the whole tour over again. To keep them moving along so there is room for the newer ones, Dorothy sees that they are led from exhibit to exhibit with little anecdotes drawing their attention to the next part of the program.

The prospects for the new year are greater than earlier imagined. There is room for more visitors than ever. Conservatively, Mrs. Gable expects 100,000.

The Country Music Association has assisted radio stations across the nation in conducting listening surveys, providing valuable sales information for prospective advertisers. The CMA co-ordinated a nationwide PULSE survey in over 24 markets that presented many eye-opening facts about the buying power of the country music listener.

It sees that members are kept alert to what goes on in the organization. Each month, the Country Music Association publishes an eight-page newsletter entitled "Close-Up" which is mailed to its entire membership and selected Advertising Agencies. The newsletter not only contains news of the CMA's activities, but also serves as a voice for the entire Country Music Industry reporting on important developments in all areas.

To draw public attention to its efforts, each year the CMA co-ordinates a nationwide "Country Music Month." Radio and television stations as well as Governors in many states participate in the month-long promotion, drawing attention to the Country Music Industry and its growing popularity.

The CMA in 1965 organized and held the first annual Music City U.S.A. Pro-Celebrity Golf Invitation in an effort to gain national attention to both country music and the country music artist. Top[-]name golf pros are invited to participate with country music artists in this festive event which has received nationwide publicity by sports writers.

The CMA, through the co-operation of various artists, record companies, publishers, and writers, in 1965, produced the first of the Hall of Fame Albums to raise money for the Country Music Association. Hundreds of hours of work went into the album and the result was one of the finest country music albums in history.

Jo Walker joined the organization in 1958 as office manager. Hired in December, she was an "unknown" to Country Music but convinced the membership that she not only was an accomplished manager but [also] a devotee of Country Music. She was elevated to the position of Executive Director in 1960. Through her hands have run the many plans for the future, the creative ideas for the growth of the CMA, the programs and plans for the major assist the CMA gives to the membership. Without her able and constant guidance, there might have been a few jolts along the way. Today, the future is in good hands as she steadily moves the office force and the driving gears of the CMA along the path to an even greater growth. With Country Music accounting for approximately one half of the record sales around the world, it is obvious that the CMA has in some measure helped in the growth, preservation and implementation of the heritage of America.

Source: "The Story of the Country Music Association," *Country*, March 1968, pp. 20–23.

FOR FURTHER READING

Pecknold, Diane. *The Selling Sound: The Rise of the Country Music Industry.* Durham, NC: Duke University Press, 2007.

"Ask Trina" (1968)

During the second half of the 1950s, country music fan clubs became increasingly powerful forces in the promotion of country music and the emergent all-country radio format. Members of fan clubs engaged in grassroots support for their favorite country artists, writing letters and making phone calls to local disc jockeys, publicizing appearances, and purchasing as many records as their household budgets might allow. Although country music fan clubs could boast both male and female membership, these organizations were predominantly the province of enterprising housewives who were expected to balance their fan club responsibilities (including replying to letters, collating press releases and newspaper articles, advocating for their artist, and compiling periodical newsletters) with their household duties.[1] As these organizations exerted a more powerful force upon the country music soundscape, Nashville executives often sought out the support of the fan clubs—inviting them to the annual WSM Disc Jockey Convention[2] and, beginning in 1972, the Country Music Association's Fan Fair,[3] providing promotional materials for newsletters and fan giveaways, and

1. Diane Pecknold, *The Selling Sound: The Rise of the Country Music Industry* (Durham, NC: Duke University Press, 2007), 130–32.
2. Pecknold, *The Selling Sound*, 73–75.
3. Pecknold, *The Selling Sound*, 211–18.

gaining free or reduced-cost publicity for their artists and the genre as a whole. Furthermore, as Diane Pecknold has observed, fan club newsletters frequently encouraged consumerism, asking fans to demonstrate their support for an artist and for the genre, more generally, through the purchase of recordings and concert tickets and their public support of local radio stations, requests that met with mixed reactions.[4]

Yet, just as fan clubs allowed many women to develop strong business skills and become leaders in the country music industry, industry insiders often denigrated the fan clubs at the same time they were using them to the industry's advantage, employing explicitly gendered terms to suggest that female fans were neglectful of their families and to cast aspersions on fans' marital fidelity.[5] Other artists, such as Bakersfield, California, musician and *Hee Haw* co-host Buck Owens (1929–2006) brought the fan clubs under the umbrella of their own corporate enterprises in order to control the discourse about their work and to capitalize economically, as well.[6] Although the relationship between fan clubs and the Nashville music industry was occasionally contentious, the following excerpt reveals the important role that fan clubs played in grooming artists, promoting their work, and launching the country music radio format.

With the assistance of a friend, Blanche "Trina" Trinajstick (1923–1997) founded *The K-Bar-T Country Roundup* in 1960, a newsletter that helped country fans connect with their favorite artists' fan clubs and assisted fan club officers in improving professional standards in their groups. Each issue featured an "Ask Trina" column, in which Trinajstick responded to letters from fans who inquired about the status of fan clubs and club officers who asked for her advice and expertise in relating to artists, negotiating conflict within their organizations, and making time for their fan club activities.[7] As the excerpts from this September 1968 column demonstrate, fan club officers willingly took on the time-consuming task of supporting "their" artists while negotiating an often tenuous relationship with the country music industry itself.

═══════

Q: What do we fan club presidents do about not hearing from some of the Reps. more than once or twice a year?

A: I don't know about you, but if it were me, I'd replace them! If you have Reps., you should give them a set of rules for carrying out their duties, and insist on them being followed.

4. Pecknold, *The Selling Sound*, 169–77, 201–18.
5. Pecknold, *The Selling Sound*, 207–209.
6. Such was the case with most of Owens's business efforts. Buck Owens Enterprises supervised Owens's bookings, promotions, and publishing, while Owens himself took charge of the producer's role in many of his Capitol Records recording sessions (Mark Fenster, "Buck Owens, Country Music, and the Struggle for Discursive Control," *Popular Music* 9, no. 3 [1990], 278).
7. Pecknold, *The Selling Sound*, 202–205.

Q: How do you find time for K-Bar-T, and housework too? I imagine you never have a spare moment!

A: Right! But that's the way I like it! I believe this question has been asked more than any other—over and over. I just don't feel like what I do is any more than other housewives who hold a job away from home. The difference being that mine is *in* my home, and it goes on ALL hours of the day and night! I DON'T belong to any women's clubs, nor do I join the "coffee and gossip" crowd who get together several times a week! I try to be a good neighbor, as well as a wife and mother, but K-Bar-T and country music are truly a vital part of me, and every minute I can spend with it is pure delight. As for housework—ugh! I try to get it out of the way as quickly as possible and get back to something enjoyable. Like Joan Rivers, the commedianne [sic], said, housework is futile—you work and clean and dust and mop, and two weeks later you have to do the same thing over again!!!

Q: When a president has a fan club, is the star supposed to give out application blanks, and run their own fan club?

A: There is [sic] two completely different questions here, which require completely different answers. It is definitely in your favor for the artist to give out application blanks for the club—this normally means that they are proud of you, and the job you are doing. As for the artist running their own club—I'm not sure just what you mean here. Any artist should take a sincere interest in the operation of his/her fan club[;] after all, it is their career you are promoting, and the operation of the club can have quite a bearing on the public's response to him. However, the club and it's [sic] operation should be discussed between artist and president, with agreement on both sides.

Q: Is there a graceful way to turn down requests for a star's phone number when people know you have it? I always say: "Sorry, that's privileged information." Am I right?

A: Yes, I would say so. There may be many ways to say it, but fans who insist on the artist's phone number will usually not take a "graceful" no for an answer, and sometimes you have to be a little emphatic. But of course you should never give in to 'em.

Q: Do you think an artist can change *completely* in his attitude toward his fans? Or do you think maybe we, as fans, expect too much of them?

A: No, I don't believe that an artist can change completely in his attitude toward his fans—I've always believed that when this appears to happen, the attitude and appearance you saw and admired at first was a front to hide the "real" person behind it, and the change is nothing but the REAL character showing through. As for the fans expecting too much of them—I'm sure there are instances when this is true, but I feel that one price of the fame and fortune they enjoy is time and effort to show appreciation to these fans who are actually responsible for their success.

* * *

Q: How old were you when you first started liking country music, and what singer was your favorite then?

A: I can't remember ever *not* liking and listening to country music! I was almost grown before I ever knew there *was* any other kind of music! My favorite, and my greatest inspiration for supporting country music in those days, was Texas Jim Robertson—who I wrote my first "fan" letter to! Jim was my favorite down through the years, although I lost contact with him for about 5 years at one time. (Jim passed away in November of 1966.)

Q: About how long does it take you to do your journals, printing, etc.[?]

A: This would be almost impossible to say, because I am doing preparation work on them for weeks in advance, and then come the deadline for material at the 15th of the month before publication, I *really* go at it, and every spare moment from then on is spent in stencil cutting, sorting and compiling material, mimeographing, assembling, addressing envelopes, licking stamps, etc.... right up until they go into the mail! From deadline to mailing date usually runs two to three weeks... sometimes more, depending on interruptions, other things that must be done, etc. But there is *no* way that I could tell you the amount of hours that goes into the preparation of a publication.

* * *

Q: How did you start and perform K-Bar-T?

A: Sorry, but the answer to this would take pages! A LOT of work & planning went into it—in fact about two year's [sic] worth!

Q: Do very many artists finance, or help finance, their fan club, for putting out journals, etc.?

A: I couldn't say how many do, and how many don't—I just know that many artists insist on helping with club finances, and others help little or none at all. It is more or less up to the artist, and his opinion on the benefits of a fan club, I suppose.

Q: Is there any risk for selling your own personal photos of the artists? This is snapshots you've taken yourself.

A: I'm not really smart on legal matters, and wouldn't want you to take my word on something like this without checking with someone who knows more about it than I do. But it seems to me that the photo's [sic] *you* take on your camera are your own personal property, and yours to do with as you wish. However, don't go by my opinion...best to find out for sure. Perhaps your local District Attorney could clarify this for you.

* * *

Q: Why do people think a person can run a fan club with no money? What do you think of the idea of people sending in stamps, maybe 20¢ a month? Maybe this would take some of the load off the club.

A: I realize that new clubs, and especially those for artists who are fairly new, has [sic] a hard time financing a club...but it would not be fair to ask your members to pay any more than the yearly dues, and you will drive away your members by the dozens if you try it! I'm sorry, I wish I had a solution for you, but this is one problem that should have been solved *before* the club was started.

Q: Is there a Ferlin Husky Fan Club?

A: No, not that I know of.

Q: Do you think an artist's chances of being on top for years will continue to be less? Will there always be security for such greats as Ernest Tubb and Kitty Wells?

A: You certainly do put me to the test, don't you??? Ha! Perhaps the stars of the future will have less chance of remaining on top for long periods of time, because as more and more country music artists come along, the competition is keener, and they have to be really outstanding talents to stay ahead of the competition. But for artists like Ernest and Kitty...or anyone else who endears themselves to so many people for so many years, there will never be any worry about future security.

Q: How does the National Committee for the Recording Artists[8] [sic] determine how much a singer, writer & publisher is [sic] paid for a tune?

A: Ooops! Here's where you've lost me again! I'll have to ask someone who knows more about this end of the business than I do! Will you hold the line, please?

* * *

8. The National Committee for the Recording Artist was formed in 1966 with the purpose of advocating legislation that would require that musicians receive payments any time their recorded work is played for profit, especially radios and jukeboxes (Leonard Feather, "Stan Kenton is Crusading for New Copyright Laws," *The Tuscaloosa News*, 19 July 1969, p. 3, http://news.google.com/newspapers?nid=1817&dat=1969 0717&id=lvQhAAAAIBAJ&sjid=CJwEAAAAIBAJ&pg=6333,3600037; accessed 16 January 2012); Russell Sanjek, *American Popular Music and Its Business: The First Four Hundred Years, Volume III: From 1900 to 1984* [New York and Oxford: Oxford University Press, 1988], 495).

Q: Does Stan Hitchcock have a fan club? And can you give me some information about him?

A: I have no information of a fan club for Stan Hitchcock, nor do I have any personal information about him. Will see what I can do.

* * *

Q: Do you think it is proper to remind a member more than once when his club membership expires?

A: Sometimes mail goes astray, as we all know, and sometimes the first notice is never received. I've had this happen to me a number of times. So I'd say a second casual reminder is okay.

Q: How do you find time to read all the material you get? And do you use items of news other than what is sent on the information sheet?

A: A minute here, a minute there! And often at night, I do a lot of reading of fan club material. Wish I were a speed reader, though! And yes, I do use occasional news items other than the ones sent on the information sheet—if they are sent on separate pieces of paper, and NOT included in a letter, or journal! They have to be clear and legible, and not something that I have to sort through and unscramble.

Q: Do most fan clubs pay for the pictures they use in journals, or do they ask the artist to supply these?

A: Definitely, the fan club takes care of this—except in a few (and VERY few!) cases where the artist provides professional photos for the journal. But unless the artist offers this help, it is the club's responsibility.

Q: Where can one buy a copy of The History & Encyclopedia of Country/ Western & Gospel Music [sic]?[9]

A: This book is published by Dr. Linnell Gentry, and a new and revised edition is due off the press currently, I understand, but I do not have the address to order it. If you take Music City News [sic], watch it's [sic] pages for the announcement, as they have been helping him to gather the up-dated material to revise the former edition.

Q: What is Buck Owens' real name?

A: Edgar Alvis Owens.

Q: Do you think it is really necessary to have a letter in every news letter or journal from the star! [sic]

9. First appearing in 1961, *A History and Encyclopedia of Country, Western, and Gospel Music* appeared in a second edition in 1969 (Nashville, TN: Clairmont, 1969).

A: YES! This is the most important part of *any* club publication to the fans, and without this contact from the artist, it is like eating dry cereal without the cream and sugar! In extreme cases, where it is impossible for the artist to get a letter to you, of course the members usually understand, but I think a personal touch from the artist is absolutely essential.

Q: Approximately how many pictures and biographies would be sufficient for the convention?

A: I always tell everyone that the need depends on a lot of different things, and we have no way of knowing. But I would say not less than 100, and not more than 200! If you send more than is picked up by the fans, we will try to get them back to you if you supply the postage, and if you are there, you should check the fan club room on Saturday, late, and take with you what is left.

Q: In all seven interesting pages on various bluegrass stars, why no mention of our club, and stars?

A: An over-sight, I am sure. It's hard to mention everyone in every issue.

Q: Does Billy Walker have a fan club?

A: I was contacted about one, but never did receive authorization on it, nor have I seen any material from one. I know a lot of fans would be glad to hear of a club for Billy, and I'll sure be telling you if I hear anything for sure.

Q: Is K-T Headquarters in your home?

A: Yes, in every room, all through the house, and in the basement! Seriously, you don't think the income from K-T would enable me to rent an "office," do you? It would be nice! No, everything is here in my home, and sometimes it looks like K-T will crowd us out of house and home!

Q: Do you prefer the present[-]day type of show with the spotlight on the "star," to the former way of having the whole stage lighted so you can see the entire band?

A: No, I do not! I like to see the whole band, and I don't think it is quite fair to them to be blacked-out on stage. After all, *they* are performing, too, and ofttimes without that band, the artist would sound pretty flat. So why not share the spotlight with them?

Q: Do you think the same fan clubs should win the awards every year?

A: If they did, it would get pretty monotonous, wouldn't it? Since you said 'at the convention,' I suppose you mean our K-T Club Awards...and our awards have been pretty well spaced, I think. We have only given awards to the same one TWICE, because it was earned, and no one else earned it. There is MUCH to consider in deciding who earns the awards, and we try to be as fair as we know how about it. But we don't give out awards unless we feel that a club has earned it.

Q: I had a little trouble with my electronic stencil running off solid black all the time—how do you prevent this?

A: I'd almost have to see the sketch you used to say for sure, because if you use a sketch you used to say for sure, because if you use a sketch or drawing with a lot of dark lines in it, this will happen—the trick is to learn the proper contrast in dark & light lines. But it sounds like you are inking too heavy for this kind of work. Electronic stencils take less inking than ordinary stencils. Try less ink, and if this fails to solve your problem, you'd better try a different sketch.

Q: How do you keep up with all your mail—I can't keep up with mine, and I'm sure you get lots more than I do.

A: I do fine reading it, but answering it is something else again! Each day at mailtime, EVERYTHING comes to a halt around our house while the mail is read, and sorted. I put it in two stacks...one to be answered at the first possible chance (this is subscriptions, renewals, convention mail, inquiries about clubs, etc....in other words, mail that demands an answer). In the second stack I put all the rest of the mail which I will answer as time permits...this is mail that actually does not require an answer, but I like to *get* mail, so I know the best way to do this is to *send* some!

Q: Is your son home from Service duty?

A: No, Mike is in Viet Nam, and will be there until spring. It will be the first time he's ever spent Christmas away from home! He is homesick, but feels like their job over there is necessary, and is considering extending his tour of duty there, so that he can stay until he finishes his service hitch. Of course 'Mom' had rather have him home, but we're proud of him.

Q: Last year at the convention I saw buttons or pins with K-BAR-T on them being worn by a lot of people—how are these buttons obtained, and are they given just to honoraries, or all members?

A: Last year we had Official Convention Badges made up (Metal—Pink, with brown printing) and these were the "pass" to the banquet...but this year we will have little plastic lapel pins available to everyone—just stop by the lobby of the Noel Hotel and pick one up.

Q: Do you know where one may purchase quite older recordings—even old 78's[10]?

10.   78-rpm records, commonly used for the recording of country music from 1922 until the advent of the long-playing 33 1/3-rpm record and the single-length 45-rpm disc in 1948 and 1949, respectively (Andre Millard, *America on Record: A History of Recorded Sound*, 2nd ed. [Cambridge: Cambridge University Press, 2005], 205–207.

A: I'm sure there must be such places—but off-hand I do not know of any. If anyone does, would they contact us?

Q: Are there other negro [sic] c/w artists besides Charley Pride? If so, who are they?

A: Probably more than we know about, but I have just received a news release from WWVA in Wheeling, West Virginia[,] telling about adding ni[n]e new members to the WWVA Jamboree, including a negro [sic] named Junior Norman.[11] I don't have any further news on him at this time but hope to have in the near future.

Q: Why must we sign our names on the K-T popularity poll ballots?

A: Because voting privileges are limited to members only, and this is the only way we can possibly know who sent the vote in. Also, if the decisions on the poll are ever challenged, we will have signed ballots from members to back us up. They never have been challenged, but if they were, and voting ballots were unsigned, there would be no way to prove that the ballots were filled out by our readers. (I'm surprised that anyone would object to signing a vote for their favorite—I'm PROUD of the artists I support!)

Q: Do you think a club president should ask for a specific amount of money for her artist's birthday?

A: NO! Not all members are able to give the same amount, while some may be able to give more. I think it should definitely be left up to the individual member how much they can give, and ONLY if they feel like they can, and want to.

Q: If our club arranges an out-door get-together at a park (for artists & members) with boat rides, or hay rides, could members be charged a small fee to help pay rental of boats, etc.?

A: Yes, but be sure to explain in your invitations or announcements how much the charge will be, and what it is for. This way, if a member don't [sic] want to pay the fee, he will know about it ahead of time.

Q: If someone you know to be a real troublemaker expresses to you an interest in representing a club run by someone you're acquainted with, would you warn the president about the person's trouble-making?

11. Claiming to be of mixed Indian, Dutch (likely Amish), and African American heritage, Silvey Dale "Junior" Norman Jr. (1933–1998) was a popular country singer in southeastern Ohio. With his band, The Fugitives, he played to white audiences throughout Ohio, West Virginia, and Pennsylvania before appearing on WWVA's *Jamboree USA* program in 1969 (Ivan Tribe, *Mountaineer Jamboree: Country Music in West Virginia* [Lexington: University Press of Kentucky, 1984], 69, 148; Rick Shriver, "Junior Norman and the Fugitives: African American Talent Meets the Hillbilly Genre," paper published at http://rickshriver.net/textfiles/Silvey%20Dale%20Norman.pdf; accessed 16 January 2012).

A: I think I would. Perhaps it won't do a lot of good, and the person may not act on your advice, but they will have been warned, and you will have done your part. I don't think it's right *not* to warn a friend of inevitable trouble—just as it wouldn't be right to stand by and watch a friend stumble over a rattle snake and not try to warn him.

Q: Do you feel that more significance is being placed on a star's personal image than actual talent and merit?

A: No, not really. I think the personal image is extremely important, and combined with the talent, make for greatness. I feel that one cannot exist without the other.

Q: How can a local artist make good? Or be discovered? Must the artist have an agent? Just how does he go about this?

A: I've heard this question asked of several artists, and always the answer is: Work, work, work; practice and strive for improvement; perform every chance you get, working always to perfect your performance—and have faith that you'll get that big BREAK someday!

Q: How do the DJ's get to answer the questions in the "Behind the Mike" feature?

A: For several years I have tried to come up with something to catch the interest of the disc jockeys…hoping to make them a part of *K-Bar-T*. Last year I made up and sent out several hundred of the questionnaires to DJ's all over the country. Up to now, I've received only about 20 of them back—which is about the usual percentage of cooperation I get from them! No offense intended, but they just aren't interested, and they are so busy that they haven't time to participate in this sort of thing. If I could find DJ's who would participate regularly in these discussions, I think it would be worthwhile, but I am[,] very frankly, ready to give up on them! (Sorry 'bout that, fellers!)

Source: "Ask Trina," *K-Bar-T Country Roundup*, September 1968, pp. 29–36.

FOR FURTHER READING

Pecknold, Diane. *The Selling Sound: The Rise of the Country Music Industry*. Durham, NC: Duke University Press, 2007.

John Grissim Jr.

"California White Man's Shit Kickin' Blues" (1969)

Although Nashville may have been synonymous with country music during the late 1950s and 1960s, Los Angeles continued to give Music Row a run for its money, promoting a hard-edged, honky-tonk–infused sound that, based on chart success and radio airplay, appealed to a broad segment of the country and pop audiences. The 1960s witnessed the development of the so-called Bakersfield Sound, spearheaded by second-generation Okie migrants Merle Haggard and Buck Owens and characterized by flashy electric guitar solos, a prominent dance beat, and lyrics bemoaning the struggles of the working-class men and women who populated the oil- and agriculture-rich San Joaquin Valley.[1]

Just as the Nashville Sound brought fans of mainstream pop music into the country music fold, the Bakersfield Sound's electrifying sound appealed widely to aspiring rock musicians, leading to the development of the first country-rock

1. For further background, consult chaps. 11–14 of Gerald W. Haslam with Alexandra Haslam Russell and Richard Chon, *Workin' Man Blues: Country Music in California* (Berkeley: Heyday Books, 2005); Buck Owens with Randy Poe, *Buck 'Em: The Autobiography of Buck Owens* (Milwaukee: Backbeat Books, 2013); David Cantwell, *Merle Haggard: The Running Kind* (Austin: University of Texas Press, 2013).

hybrids in the late 1960s. Many of the country-rock pioneers—including Chris Hillman and Clarence White—were active in the Los Angeles bluegrass scene in the early 1960s and drew freely from bluegrass, old-time, and honky-tonk music to forge a musical approach that blended the sensibilities of country and rock for their youthful, countercultural audiences. Most notably, the Byrds, an L.A.-based band best known for the jangly folk-rock sounds of their 1965 hit "Turn, Turn, Turn," began to incorporate the Bakersfield Sound into their work in 1968's *Sweetheart of the Rodeo*. The Byrds were inspired to do so by Gram Parsons, the heir to a Florida citrus fortune and leader of experimental country-rock bands The International Submarine Band and The Flying Burrito Brothers.[2] The California country-rock movement would eventually give birth to one of the most successful rock bands of all-time: the Eagles.[3] And, perhaps most notably, the Beatles covered Buck Owens's "Act Naturally" on their 1965 album *Help!*[4]

As historian Peter LaChapelle has noted, country music also played a central role in defining the increasingly conservative political outlooks of Okie migrants and their children. Looking at the countercultural movements of the 1960s, these people saw the countercultural protests against the Vietnam War and for civil rights as attacks on traditional white rural values. Haggard, who often wrote songs with a New Deal populist viewpoint, became an icon of this movement in the late 1960s with the release of "Okie from Muskogee," a searing indictment of the free love attitudes and poor hygiene of the hippie movement, and "Fightin' Side of Me," which reminded protestors that America did not need detractors. California country music, then, became a site for the negotiation of political ideologies and regional identity in an era of increasingly fraught intergenerational tensions.[5]

2. Parsons has been the subject of several biographical treatments, including Ben Fong-Torres, *Hickory Wind: the Life and Times of Gram Parsons*, rev. ed. (New York: St. Martin's Griffin, 1991); David N. Meyer, *Twenty-Thousand Roads: The Ballad of Gram Parsons and His Cosmic American Music* (New York: Villard Books, 2007); and Bob Kealing, *Calling Me Home: Gram Parsons and the Roots of Country Rock* (Gainesville: University Press of Florida, 2012). Musicologist Olivia Carter Mather has also addressed key elements of Parsons's vocal style in her essay " 'Regressive Country': The Voice of Gram Parsons," in *Old Roots, New Routes: The Cultural Politics of Alt.Country Music*, ed. Pamela Fox and Barbara Ching (Ann Arbor: University of Michigan Press, 2008), 154–74.

3. For more on the musical style of the Eagles, consult Olivia Carter Mather, "Taking It Easy in the Sunbelt: The Eagles and Country Rock's Regionalism," *American Music* 31, no. 1 (Spring 2013): 26–49. Diane Pecknold has also offered a compelling cultural analysis of the Eagles' place in country-rock in her essay "Holding Out Hope for the Creedence: Music and the Search for the Real Thing in *The Big Lebowski*," in *The Year's Work in Lebowski Studies* (Bloomington: Indiana University Press, 2009), 276–94.

4. The country-rock movement has been thoroughly chronicled in John Einarson, *Desperadoes: The Roots of Country Rock* (New York: Cooper Square Press, 2001). See also Olivia Carter Mather, " 'Cosmic American Music' ": Place and the Country Rock Movement, 1965-1974," Ph.D. dissertation, University of California, Los Angeles, 2006.

5. LaChapelle traces this history in chaps. 4–6 of *Proud to Be an Okie: Cultural Politics, Country Music, and Migration to Southern California* (Berkeley: University of California Press, 2007).

The following essay, excerpted from the rock magazine *Rolling Stone*, documents the changing cultural climate of California country music in the late 1960s. Although the title of the essay channels the anti-rural white anxieties frequently expressed by the youth counterculture and seen in the popular film *Easy Rider* (Columbia Pictures, 1969), journalist John Grissim offers a nuanced discussion of the ongoing development of the California music industry (which, as Diane Pecknold has demonstrated, played a key role in promoting the Nashville Sound and pioneering the all-country radio format during the 1960s).[6] Grissim, who built upon this article in his book *Country Music: White Man's Blues* (New York: Coronet Communications, 1970), also reveals the rich interplay between practitioners of country, rock, and pop that helped to energize the West Coast country movement. For instance, feature sections focusing on crossover songwriter Jimmy Webb and bluegrass and old-time musician-*cum*-pop icon John Hartford highlight the porous borders between musical genres during the late 1960s. Unlike Nashville's Music Row, which was consistently portrayed as an orderly, business-oriented place where recordings are made with great efficiency, Los Angeles is depicted here as a vibrant, creative place where (because of its distance from Nashville) innovation was valued and experimentation prized.[7]

———

"GEEMINY, it's amazing. Here is it Monday night, just terrible weather and here come the folks. And you know, if they like you, they really *like* you. One nice thing about it—they don't insult you, you know?"

Over 3,000 people had just driven through heavy rain and paid $10,000 to see America's number one country artist at the Circle Star Theatre near San Francisco. Mercy!

Buck Owens finishes his coffee and leans back on the dressing room couch, heels propped on the low Danish modern table before him. His tailored western suit is conservative, no silver studs, buckles or flashy buttons. Only the boots excel: black patent leather curving up to pencil-tip sharpness. His face has character. Smiles are real, the eyes now and again betraying a hint of shrewdness. Sandy blond hair, the barest suggestion of what-me-worry ears, a rich mid-western accent—he is authentic.

A response to a question about country music trends somehow turns into a rundown on recent Hooper ratings for Buck Owens-owned radio stations.[8] Before the morning in-traffic

---

6. Diane Pecknold, *The Selling Sound: The Rise of the Country Music Industry* (Durham, NC: Duke University Press, 2007), 133–67.

7. Yet, as Mark Fenster has convincingly demonstrated, West Coast musicians were quite proactive in the promotion of their business interests (Mark Fenster, "Buck Owens, Country Music, and the Struggle for Discursive Control," *Popular Music* 9, no. 3 (1990): 275–90.

8. Hooper ratings were one statistical method of tracking radio listenership (Hugh Malcolm Beville, Jr., *Audience Ratings: Radio, Television, and Cable*, rev. student ed. (Hillsdale, NJ: Psychology Press, 1988), 11–16.

sampling can be detailed, two women in their mid-thirties swoop into the room, shutting the door behind them.

"If you'll autograph my program, Mr. Owens, I'll give ya something." The shorter of the two, looking asexual in a sleeveless cocktail dress and a lacquered wig, offers a pen with an outstretched bowling arm. Her companion remains standing near the door, giggling, then sees herself in a mirror and instinctively checks her looks—wet-lipped smile, mini-skirt and piano legs. She giggles again.

"Well alright, girls, what're your names?" Owens obligingly takes the pen and signs the program, in return for which he is handed a bumper sticker for Sil's Club in Concord and a dirty joke cocktail napkin.

Everyone smiles, sort of. Piano legs moves forward and says she is related to a second cousin in the Owens clan and that "Billy Jean came here tonight, too, and she sends her best." Owens thanks them and allows the conversation to die a natural death. In short order he is back to the Hooper ratings, about which more later.

Several hundred feet away the lobby is crowded with late arrivals and pre-show tilters spilling out of the theatre's mammoth cocktail lounge. There is an abundance of Masonic lodge pins, cigars, spit curls, Eileen Feather high heels and Kinney casuals, shiny-seat pants, wide cuffs, short hair and large ears. A few servicemen in civvies lean against the wall, chewing gum, smoking, lonely. The atmosphere is boisterous and pungent, a blend of hair spray, after-shave lotion, cigarette smoke, Prairie Rose perfume and a whole lot of har-dee-har-har laughter.

A few turtlenecks and medallions radiate beneath double-breasted jackets (example—maroon over lime pastiche) but the dominant theme is dressy PTA.[9] The young marrieds, ten years out of high school, carry the residual look of Saturday night out with dad's car—Wildroot pompadours holding hands with VO-5 page boys.[10] On the whole the audience is middle-aged, affluent, a little overweight, and fiercely loyal to country music.

The program kicks off with Buddy Lane and the Wild West, a local fill-in doing a free gig for exposure. The rest of the bill—Rose Maddox, Sheb Wooley, Tommy Collins, and Freddy Hart—all work for Buck Owens' personal management corporation, a nice family package, which, along with Owens and the Buckaroos, sells for $7500 a concert.

Rose Maddox follows the opener, no longer fresh at fifty but still at it. A silver lame mini dress with full length sleeves and matching boots has replaced the leather skirt and western vest of 20 years ago. The klieg lights shine for a mercifully brief moment upon an aging cosmetic face. Her performance is perfunctory, a little desperate, but enough to bring applause for her pre-war hits.

It's like that with Country. Develop a following, keep singing, and you have equity for 30 years. Sheb Wooley follows Maddox with a string of Bible Belt jokes and novelty tunes (remember "Flying Purple People Eater"?). Freddy Hart and Tommy Collins—fading old favorites—wrap up the first half of the show with half-hour sets. They draw a good response but the house is clearly gearing up for the big moment.

Buck Owens is greeted with wild, foot stomping applause, cat calls, homemade signs ("Buck's Our Boy," "Buck is No. 1"), and half a dozen rebel yells. Except for respectful silence during slow-paced cheatin' songs, the boozy adulation continues with spontaneous yee-hahs

9. Parent-Teacher Association.
10. Both Wildroot and VO-5 were popular hair creams.

whenever the drummer for the Buckaroos gets heavy on the bass pedal during instrumental breaks.

The first two bars of virtually every number are greeted with noisy recognition.[11] Owens' tenor voice is clear and strong without a trace of resonance or vibrato, but it reeks with sincerity. Billie Jean and her friends are visibly moved when he breaks into "Togeeeather Agaain..." followed by "I Got the Hungries for Your Love [and] I'm Waitin' in Your Welfare Line." Everyone's a good'un in Buck's corral of country hits.

In the front row a happy teamster with a speck of toilet paper covering a shaving cut on his chin shifts his weight and stifles a belch while applauding.

The banter between Owens and his group is ritualistic and slow paced, roughly comparable to the Renfro Valley Barn Dance.[12] Sex jokes are out but pee-pee doo-doo one liners are in: "Yes sir, I bought some Ex Lax today...fastest moving product on the market." It's old stuff and in its own way an unspoken reaffirmation of the values which seemed to work so nicely in simpler, less dangerous times.

The program was morally good. The only sour moment came when the MC during intermission announced that "one of America's great folk singers is in the audience—Miss Joan Baez." The boos held sway over the applause.[13]

Why is Buck Owens the top draw in Country? "We try to generate some excitement and give them something to relate to. I think that's important to this class of people. On the whole, country music has not yet reached the point of providing that excitement because most of the performers feel that too much movin' and groovin' is an insult, that people won't understand it. Maybe some wouldn't, but gee, *I* don't feel that way."

"I've seen guys that didn't have record one go before all country audiences and just slay them. For instance these two boys that just started with some of my companies—The Hagers—they have a predominantly modern-rock-pop-Beatles sound although they do some country-western and blues. And gee whiz, they can just wreck the audience, knock 'em out....This speaks well for that kind of performance."

The country-rock-pop-Beatles and Western blues sound is not yet the national norm in California's cornucopia of bars and night clubs featuring live country and western music but something close to it seems to be packing them in, and on Saturday nights the avid shitkicker can whoop it up with such groups as Eddie Kanak and the Nashville Rejects, Curt's Oklahoma Cotton Pickers, Bob Blum and the Blenders, Toby Tyler and the Night Lifers, and Wanda Lee and Her Wanderers.

11.   Fenster has observed that Owens was not only astute in his creation of a business empire, but that he also was keenly aware of how his musical sound could convey an identifiable brand (Fenster, "Buck Owens, Country Music, and the Struggle for Discursive Control," 279–81).

12.   A radio barn dance founded by John Lair (see chapter 11) and broadcast on Cincinnati radio station WLW beginning in 1939. See Pete Stamper, *It All Happened in Renfro Valley* (Lexington: University Press of Kentucky, 1999), and chaps. 4, 5, and 7 of Michael Ann Williams, *Staging Tradition: John Lair and Sarah Gertrude Knott* (Urbana: University of Illinois Press, 2006).

13.   This anecdote highlights the tensions that LaChapelle has observed in Californian country music during the late 1960s and early 1970s (LaChapelle, *Proud to Be an Okie*, 180–207).

All this is possible in California because of the great Okie invasion which began in the Thirties and has continued unabated for over three decades. In truth the hundreds of thousands who migrated to the West Coast were from the South as much as the Midwest, but the vanguard consisted of refugees from the dustbowl of Oklahoma, eastern New Mexico and Texas. They were followed during the war by a huge influx of defense plant workers from the South.

No one really knew the magnitude of these demographic shifts until a post-war survey revealed that over 80 percent of the southern California population was from the South and the Midwest. And they had brought their music with them. Those who doubted needed only turn on their radio to find Roy Acuff's "Great Speckled Bird" being rammed everywhere. What had started out as an art form peculiar to the hills of the rural Southeast in the 1890's had somehow endured—even thrived—in a calamitous era of Depression, Dustbowl and World War.

Today country music on the West Coast is booming. Of the 650 AM radio stations with all-country programming in the U.S. and Canada, California leads with 24. Its tally of 258 Country clubs considerably exceeds that of any other state. Several country music television shows are videotaped in Los Angeles and San Francisco for national syndication. The top three country artists in 1968—Glen Campbell, Buck Owens and Merle Haggard—all live in southern California and record in Hollywood. At least a dozen other country and western artists record in Los Angeles. Two publishing houses—Blue Book and Central Songs—have Hollywood offices, as does the prestigious Academy of Country and Western Music. Further north in Bakersfield, Buck Owens' OMAC Artists Corporation is the third largest country booking agency in the nation with 21 acts. Recording studios are being constructed to serve two new country labels.

In fact Buck Owens is so popular that all 21 singles he has recorded (since 1963) have made No. one [sic] on the Country charts—without a miss. Now the inevitable has happened: Owens has recently been named by CBS to co-host with Roy Clark the replacement for the Smothers Brothers Show. Get ready. It's called *Hee Haw* and is billed as a country-western *Laugh-In* from Nashville. The announcement came shortly after Richard Nixon's first 100 days in office.

Country music has been hailed as America's great gift to people the world over. It has also been called shitkicker music and white man's blues and variously described as simplistic, unsophisticated, right wing, boring, bed-rock Baptist, red-neck, ignorant, and underneath it all, probably racist.[14] It is the only native American music which has been simultaneously damned as a fossilized art form and praised as the well-spring of modern folk music and rock.

Few people are more aware of this than Cliffie Stone, head of Central Songs, one of the five largest publishing houses in the country field. Stone is one of the few people who can locate his rambling one story headquarters in Los Angeles two blocks from Hollywood and Vine, furnish his offices with rocking chairs, ruffled curtains and ranch style couches with wooden arm rests and gingham slip covers—and get away with it.

14. See, for instance, Paul DiMaggio, R. Serge Denisoff, and Richard A. Peterson, "Country Music: Ballad of the Silent Majority," in *The Sounds of Social Change*, ed. R. Serge Denisoff and Richard A. Peterson (Chicago: Rand McNally, 1972), 38–55; and Jens Lund, "Fundamentalism, Racism, and Political Reaction in Country Music," in *The Sounds of Social Change*, ed. R. Serge Denisoff and Richard A. Peterson (Chicago: Rand McNally, 1972), 79–91.

A heavy, congenial man in his early fifties, Stone describes himself as a hard[-]core country music lover. He is also very bright and still likes to work. Leaving his desk to fill a substantial armchair upholstered in yellow leather with seam piping, he exudes the confidence born of right decisions in a successful career.

"Country music has an honesty and a sincerity that comes from the heart—the kind of thing that you just can't get in a pop song. It possesses the kind of emotionalism that sells, a thing that you can believe in."

"Women are the principal buyers of country music. If you can appeal to something they can relate to, that's what hits them. It can be a cheatin' song, or a drinkin' song, or a lonely song where they're home all day with the kids and they're doing the dishes and washing the clothes and doing the cooking and the old man is out drinkin' somewhere."

Stone has a keen sensitivity for the needs of that audience. The son of a long[-]haired banjo player whose name in the Twenties was Herman the Hermit, Stone started out during the Depression as a country bass player on the West Coast, got into publishing, then hooked up with Tennessee Ernie Ford as his manager for 15 years. While with Ford he set up Central Song's management arm to handle country and pop artists such as Molly Bee and Tommy Sands. In 1959 he began producing *Melody Ranch*, a syndicated television show from KTLA in Los Angeles featuring various country artists [see chapter 25].

Aside from Ernie Ford's bonanza years on television and the record charts, the primary money-maker for stone has been publishing. His success in that field hinged on an ability to mold the components of a country song into a shape that sells. Invariably this means telling a specific story about everyday people, something that "Tea for Two" never got around to.

While a country verse rhyme scheme is usually AABB or ABBA, greater emphasis is placed on fitting lyrics to a 4/4 or 3/4 metric structure. The song's title—often an involved punch line—emerges in a standard four-line chorus after verse I, followed by verse II, chorus, a short bridge, verse III and a final chorus. The pattern is identical to the pop ballads of the Fifties.

The difference shows up in the extraordinary character of the lyrics. Country writers have traditionally been able to elevate the most mundane circumstances to a level of near art. Witness Johnny Carver's "One More Night Together" (Reeklein Music, Inc.—BMI)[15]....The principal variation is the story song which goes on and on without chorus, usually ending up with last line irony which elicits either tears or laughter. A recent favorite in this genre is Porter Wagoner's "Carroll County Accident."[16]

These songs are heartfelt and sincere, not easily confused with such novelty hits as "Billie Broke My Heart at Walgreen's and I Cried All the Way to Sears" or "Does the Chewing Gum Lose Its Flavor on the Bedpost (Overnight)." But to someone unfamiliar with country music it is often difficult to distinguish between a deliberate self-lampoon of country manners and a dead serious ballad.

In the Twenties and Thirties, Christian temperance restricted love and sex to the insipid level of be-my-valentine (e.g. Carl Butler's "If Tears Were Pennies and Heartaches Were Gold"). This limitation was also true with pop music. After the war, however, Kitty Wells started telling it like it was with "It Wasn't God Who Made Honky Tonk Angels."

15. Lyrics of "One More Night Together" redacted for copyright reasons.
16. Story songs are also the subject of Thomas Adler's "The Unplotted Narratives of Tom T. Hall." *Journal of Country Music* 4, no. 2 (Summer 1973): 52–69.

With the lid off, country music was at last able to deal explicitly with alcoholism, marital woes and cheating with marvelous frankness. "Married by the Bible, Divorced by the Law" (circa 1950) started a new tradition which has been maintained by such offerings as "One Has My Name, the Other Has My Heart," "Who's Julie," and a popular number by Linda Manning who exhorts her errant husband to "put me in a high chair, tie a bib around my neck and Feed Me One More Lie." When several years ago wife-swapping showed signs of catching on nationally, "Let's Invite Them On Over" got a lot of air play on country stations.

Alcoholic songs such as "Losers Lounge" have always been popular, the latest example being Hank Snow's "Let's Get Drunk and Be Somebody"[17].... A 1967-68 favorite in this category was Hank Thompson's "What Made Milwaukee Famous Has Made a Loser Out of Me."

One of last year's top selling singles was "D-I-V-O-R-C-E" by Tammy Wynette, a tearful confession in which a mother tells how she and her ex-husband used to spell out the words they didn't want their little Joe to hear—the kicker being that little Joe thinks C-U-S-T-O-D-Y is fun and games. It's a classic weeper which has inspired Hollywood and Nashville to dredge up an old gag line appropriate for the title of Miss Wynette's next record: "Don't Say Fuck Around the K-I-D-S."

Lesser tragedies in the marriage/divorce genre are "Gotta Lotta Hen House Ways," "She May Be Sour Grapes to You But She's Sweet Wine to Me," and a real loser's lament by Jimmy Snyder with the vaguely obscene title "I Got Candy All Over My Face."

Satire and social comment has long been a staple crop for Country writers, the most recent success being "Harper Valley PTA," which crossed over to the pop field to sell six million records last year. Little Jimmy Dickens has done well in the past with "Where Were You When the Ship Hit the Sand" and "May the Bird of Paradise Fly Up Your Nose." Federal highway building programs come under attack in "I Got the Interstate Running Through My Outhouse," but top honors for social significance go to a new classic, Nat Stuckey's "Don't Give Me No Plastic Saddle (I Want to Feel that Leather When I Ride)."

What makes such far[-]out lyrics possible—even believable—is the music. The traditional country sound is characterized by guitar, fiddle and banjo, augmented by harmonica, zither, dobro or bass. It uses stock chord progressions, conventional leads and breaks, and a driving rhythm with no embellishment. Though in the past it has had a predictable sameness to it, the instrumental backing for a country song can evoke an incredibly broad emotional response, ideally suited to involved lyrics. Properly played, there is probably no instrument which is capable of making a sadder, more lonesome sound—or a happier one for that matter—than a fiddle. On that subject Jerry Ward, a former guitarist for Merle Haggard, put country fiddlers in an honored position: "Musicians tune fiddles, General Motors tunes violins."[18]

The majority of Country writers use a guitar for composition, generally choosing open keys (C, D, E, A and G) which allow the most resonant response from sounding board instruments. Song writing has changed little since Jimmie Rodgers wrote in the Twenties but today's added use of drums, pedal steel guitar, piano, choral backing, even harpsichord have made some arrangements far more complete, thus shifting much of the burden for hit-making to the producer.[19]

---

17. Lyrics of "Let's Get Drunk and Be Somebody" redacted for copyright reasons.

18. This may be a jab at the commercialization of the Nashville Sound. See chaps. 4–6 of Pecknold, *The Selling Sound*.

19. See, for instance, the discussion of Patsy Cline's relationship with producer Owen Bradley in Joli Jensen, *The Nashville Sound: Authenticity, Commercialization, and Country Music* (Nashville, TN: Country Music Foundation Press and Vanderbilt University Press, 1998), 89–117.

Scott Turner, head of country A&R for Imperial, writes and produces. In style of dress (two-button continental cardigans, ID bracelet, Italian slacks, flamboyant neck scarf) he is strictly L.A., but in his heart he's all country.

"I make my records for the farmer in the Ozarks who's been out there plowing his field all day and who comes in at night and turns on the radio. He doesn't want to have to think about 'the clouded blue haze through the canyons of the memories of your mind.' He doesn't want to think about what he's hearing, just feel the kind of direct relationship to a song that will make him say, 'Hey, that's me they're talking about.'"

Turner creates that grass roots, straight-from-the-soil response in a small, windowless office at Liberty Records on Sunset Boulevard, directly across from Hollywood High. Inside the crowded room two immense speaker cabinets tower on either side of a small upright piano ("for voicing only") which faces a desk, a wall[-]to[-]wall record library, and an elaborate sound system. The walls are covered with picture posters of recording artists, each captioned "Welcome to Imperial Country."

Imperial's country is largely Nashville. Turner had good reason to keep it that way.

"There are 100 places on the country chart. If you exclude Buck Owens and Merle Haggard, who have their own bands and record in Los Angeles, and Glen Campbell who's not really pure country, you've got 97 slots left. And with very few exceptions they're filled by artists who have recorded in Nashville. I just have to go with that 97 percent.

"For me the most effective combination for today's market is to take a song written by a West Coast writer, give it to an Arkansas-raised country artist who now lives in California and record it in Nashville."

The West Coast components to Turner's formula provide the touch of sophistication which he believes distinguishes a West Coast country song. As for the Nashville sound:

"It's six or eight guys who have been playing together for maybe ten years—people like Grady Martin, Chip Young, Jerry Reed. They're in that studio for one thing, to make a record they're proud of. Many times I've heard a take and said 'That's it, guys. I'm happy, it's great,' and they'll ask to do it one more time. That's taking an interest in my product. I can walk out of the studio with four...masterpieces. That's all I can call them."[20]

Included among his recent efforts is Johnny Carver's "One More Night Together." Turner records in Nashville once a month on the average, brings his product-masterpieces back to Hollywood and, when required, dubs in back-up vocals and/or violins using West Coast talent. He has the background to make it work. A former lead guitarist behind Tommy Sands and Guy Mitchel [sic], Turner at one time or another spent a year with Eddie Fisher trying to teach him to sing Country ("It was rough"), ran the publishing end of A&M Records during its fledgling phase, and worked two years for Cliffie Stone as a resident song writer.

While in the latter job he wrote or co-authored "Shutters and Board," "Hick Town" (an Ernie Ford hit), and altogether about 50 songs for most of the major country artists. Turner's compositions don't always ring a bell with Top 40 listeners but when someone the likes of hard driving Dave Dudley steps up to the mike in a Nashville studio to record "Trucker's Prayer," friend, you're talkin' 40,000 in sales at the very least.

20. Morris S. Levy, "Nashville Sound-Era Studio Musicians," in *Country Music Annual 2000*, ed. Charles K. Wolfe and James E. Akenson (Lexington: University Press of Kentucky, 2000), 22–29.

The remuneration for a song whose Country entry happens to cross over to the top field and really take off is substantial. Figuring a record royalty return of one cent per record, Tom T. Hall's "Harper Valley PTA" (six million sales) netted its author a minimum of $60,000, exclusive of income from BMI performance, sheet music, lyric rights, overseas revenues and miscellaneous uses. A more realistic figure for a single which sells well in both markets, say 200,000, would be a basic return of $2,000 compared to half that (or less) for Country alone.

A song which breaks into the Top Ten on both charts almost invariably becomes the title cut on a follow-up LP. With album sales currently equaling or exceeding those singles, an author can look forward to an additional $2,000, again based on 200,000 copies sold. If he performed as well as wrote the song, he is in an even better position. The combined song and record royalties add up to roughly five percent of the list price, in this case a return of $10,000.

Through revenue from performance societies (ASCAP and BMI)[21] var[ies] considerably, a hit song generally brings in $500-$1,000 from domestic airplay[;] however, the return can be much higher. Every time Glen Campbell sang "Gentle on My Mind" to open each edition of last year's Summer Brothers Smothers Show, author John Hartford and his publisher together pocketed around $500.

The obvious solution is to leave nothing to chance—write a pop-country song, record it using a heavy foot on the drums, and lush up the delivery with choral backing and fiddles (or violins, depending on which market one is discussing). The only drawback is the greater risk of ending up with a dud which satisfies neither market. But the potential for hitting it on the money explains why a good percentage of the 300 or so Country writers in California also write pop.

Charlie Williams, a country disc jockey for KFOX in Los Angeles, has written extensively for both Johnny Cash and Ray Charles. Don Robertson ("Happy Whistler," "Ninety MPH Down a Dead End Street") was responsible for a good chunk of Les Paul and Mary Ford's pop material in the early Fifties. (He can also lay claim to introducing "pedal piano" to Nashville—a keyboard style made so popular by Floyd Cramer that RCA, which had both Robertson and Cramer under contract, prohibited him from "copying Cramer's style" when recording his own songs). Others include Hal Blair ("Ringo"—which crossed into pop), James Hendricks ("Look to Your Soul," "Summer Rain") as well as writer-performer Jerry Wallace and Red Steagall, Billy Mise, Bobby George and Jerry Fuller.

One exception is Cy Coben, a former pop writer who 15 years ago got tired of "moon in June" lyrics and decided to try his hand at "Drinkin' and thinkin'." He has stayed in the Country field, written over 650 songs and has yet to get bored.

Cy Coben has been around country music so long that he can remember when Nashville wanted to "take WSM and the Grand Ole Opry and push them and their god-dam hillbilly music right into the Cumberland River."

That was twenty years ago, but the Athens of the South[22] eventually grew tolerant, even to the point of accepting a nice Jewish kid from New Jersey who claims he couldn't tell a

21. The American Society of Composers, Authors, and Publishers and Broadcast Music, Inc., respectively.

22. Nashville boosters hoped that the city would become a leader in the arts and highbrow culture during the nineteenth century, leading to the nickname "The Athens of the South" (Christine Kreyling, Wesley Paine, Charles W. Warterfield Jr., and Susan Ford Wiltshire, *Classical Nashville: Athens of the South* [Nashville, TN: Vanderbilt University Press, 1996]).

cow pasture from a corn field. Moreover, Coben belonged to ASCAP at a time when that organization considered country music and rhythm and blues (then called *race* music) a little less popular than slack key ukulele. The view was not entirely groundless.

"In those days country music was very loose in both meter and lyrics. You could throw in a half measure, even an extra measure, or hold a note if it sounded alright. There were no rules, no sophistication.... No one had ever heard of a ninth chord. But there was plenty of realism."

Coben first heard the direct realism of a country lyric while with a WWII construction battalion in the Solomon Islands. When he returned to New York to continue his career as a pop writer, he started writing country material on the side.

"I think I succeeded because I genuinely loved it, and I stuck by two rules: don't write about something you don't know and don't look down on country music."

Adherence to such maxims may not have made Coben a millionaire, but he has long been one of the top Country writers in the business, so much so that his songs are occasionally criticized for being too country. With a large home amidst a woodsy setting in the San Francisco Bay Area (he moved there in 1963) and permanent living quarters in Nashville where he spends four months of the year, he takes the carping in stride.

Coben looks like a diminutive Martin Balsam or a Keenan Wynn, an irrepressibly happy man whose conversation rolls on with guileless enthusiasm, full of anecdotes, unfinished sentences, hilarious digressions, bits and pieces of lyrics and rapid insights. He will regularly interrupt himself to pick up a guitar and sing a verse or two from songs he wrote for Eddy Arnold, Hank Snow or any of a score of Nashville regulars. There is not a trace of ego, only the excitement of sharing.

"I've written every kind of music there is. You name it, I've written it. All except one thing I couldn't do: rhythm and blues. I tried it but didn't have the feel for it. I guess it was strictly black and I couldn't travel in those circles. There again, being outside I couldn't write about it with sincerity."

Coben's ability to write almost anything was invaluable to RCA's Country pioneer Steve Scholes [sic]. In the early Fifties, Scholes [sic] would take Coben and a recording engineer out into the field to tape the music of the rural South, then return to N.Y. and have Coben write songs containing the same stylistic components.

"That's where my technical understanding paid off [Coben studied music theory and composition in the early Thirties]. I can write to order. It's not hack writing but a professional ability to shape an idea into a specific lyric structure."

He got so good at it that at one point, in September 1951, Coben had the No. One song on both the country and pop charts in Cash Box magazine. Since then he has had at least one song on either the domestic or overseas charts—somewhere. On the side he has written "Piano Roll Blues," "Nobody's Child" (recorded by the Beatles in antiquity), selections for Disney's *Alice in Wonderland*, a children's album of pet animal songs, space poetry for Leonard Nimroy [sic] (Star Trek's Dr. Spock), even "some Jewish material for Homer and Jethro for when they play Miami."

"Years ago you had to go through a long apprenticeship to get a solid professional grounding, but today everything is speeded up. Kids today can surround themselves with music—records, cassettes, guitars, radio and television. And they learn very fast.... Everywhere there are new musicians, writers and producers, all very young and very hot property."

Why are they beginning to listen to country music?

"What's happened is that young people today are realistic. They aren't the dreamers of yesterday. Because country music has that realism, because it tell sit as it really is, they can accept it.... Then again music today is becoming desegregated, it's all becoming one, reflecting our times."

"My advantage is that my background as a pop writer is very helpful to me now. For example, I did a song last year for Connie Smith called 'Burning a Hole in My Pocket.' It represents the trend in Country, but to me it's just a song I would have written during pop music days."

It is becoming fashionable in the trade to eschew such terms as pop-country, town and country, and contemporary-country, presumably because no two people agree on what they mean. A year ago the use of hyphenated hybrids had more validity, if only to distinguish Hollywood's country sound from that of Nashville, at least until Music City caught up. Now both cities have finally got it together: lyrics are a little more generalized—no "clouded blue haze" but neither are there such lines as "I would send you roses but they cost too much so I'm sending daffodils." Arrangements are plush, make full use of strings, horn, and vocal backing and seldom rely solely on standard chord progressions. Percussion is pronounced but rhythmic patterns with a 4/4 or 3/4 structure are often more complex than those favored in Nashville. The result is a blend of pop and country which has brought down on Hollywood the wrath of country purists and simultaneously made a great deal of money for Jimmy Webb, John Hartford, and Glen Campbell.

Webb, still in his twenties, has probably turned out more pop and pop-country songs that have sold more single records in a shorter period of time than anybody, anywhere. He wrote "Up, Up and Away" two years ago for the Fifth Dimension, later sold it to TWA[23] for a substantial six figure sum, and then came up with "MacArthur Park" (for Richard Harris). This was followed by a string of amazingly successful hits for Glen Campbell: "By the Time I Get to Phoenix," "Wichita Lineman," and "Galveston," all million-plus sellers. Though primarily a pop writer, he has almost single-handedly created a kind of suburban country sound.

Like Webb, John Hartford has been closely associated with Glen Campbell's success. A first-rate Nashville studio musician (guitar, banjo, and fiddle), he was already recording his own songs when he wrote "Gentle on My Mind" in 1967. A single release of the song was doing moderately well in the Country field when Campbell put out his own version which quickly sold over a million. Both artists prospered. Campbell became a super-star with his own network show and Hartford moved to Hollywood as a writer-performer with the Smothers Brothers. He now appears regularly on Campbell's program, and, among other things, collects songs royalties from "Gentle" recordings done by 183 artists to date.

Hartford recorded his first five albums in Nashville and has recently completed his sixth in Hollywood. He admits to a preference for West Coast production.

"I had a fight on my hands in Nashville. I was constantly being told to 'be careful you don't turn off that country audience.'... They didn't want me putting anything on a record that might not be aired on a country station.... I guess there was a certain amount of compromise on the first few albums, but then it got less and less.

"Out here on the Coast, you have a bigger palette to work with, because you can get people who can give you a strictly Nashville sound if you want it. But they can also digress with

23. Trans World Airlines.

you if you want. You have some of the best arrangers and horn and string people in the world to work with."

At 31, Harford [sic] is a comfortable amalgam of two cultures. His boots, rust brown leather pants and matching jacket are Laurel Canyon ranchy, yet when he speaks, the words start deep down in his throat and come chugging up past a magic twanger of an Adam's apple to emerge with marvelous resonance and the springiness of a new buggy whip. A full mane of dark hair covers ears formerly much in evidence on the record sleeves of early albums (Don't turn off, etc.). Long hair gives his angular face a darker, more interesting look. Still fond of Nashville, he has probably hung around too long with the brothers Smothers and their chief writer Mason Williams (L.A.'s answer to Renaissance man) to ever live there again.

In his early teens, Hartford played fiddle at square dances, but later "during the Blue Suede Shoes years," played rock guitar in honky tonks around East St. Louis and West Memphis.

"That was before you could get those slinky strings on your git-tar and we'd have to tune them way down low so you could push them half way off the next. Either that or put on all E and B strings."

The apprenticeship helped him develop a balanced outlook: "There's a lot of fantastically real country music, and there's a lot of bullshit."

While retaining his love for the former, Hartford got a degree in commercial art from Washington University (Missouri), then worked as a sign painter, Mississippi River deck hand, railroader and country DJ before he eventually crashed Nashville in 1965 to earn the dual distinction of being an A Team picker and the town hippie ("It was considered *in* to not understand me").

Having a liberal stance invited comparisons.

"Even though rock groups on the West Coast are very much into the bluegrass thing, there's a great difference in attitude. The Byrd's [sic] *Sweetheart of the Rodeo* is really liberal-left country music, both lyrically and in the way it's presented. It's very different from the same type of music put out by someone like Ferlin Husky or Bobby Lord....I tend to like the stuff the rock groups are doing because they're creative and original, and that's something I'm very much into."

Along parallel lines, a conservative approach to maintaining the Nashville sound could eventually backfire: "Nashville's got their one-sized string section, they've got two or three vocal background groups that work all the sessions, and they have some really fine sidemen, but the same guys are playing the same sessions all the time. And after a while there's a sameness to it. It's just too much....You've got to mix people around. And now they're putting vocal groups behind everything. The big word down there is *commercial*....I wouldn't be so hacked off about it if I didn't love country music.[24]

"I think, actually, the reason I left Nashville was I wanted more freedom—although I understand at the time I had as much or more freedom than anybody. But it's a relative thing. I wouldn't mind going back to record. They do have some incredible studios and some of the best guitar and banjo players in the world—more so than out here....Matter' fact, it might not

24. Hartford even recorded a biting criticism of the Nashville Sound on "I Reckon," the opening cut of his 1967 album *Looks at Life* (RCA Victor LSP-3687). Also, see the sleeve notes to *Looks at Life*, reprinted in Andrew Vaughan, *John Hartford: Pilot of a Steam Powered Aereo-Plain* (Franklin, TN: StuffWorks Press, 2013), 39–41.

be such a bad idea to do tracks back there and if you're going to do any sweetenin', do it on the Coast."

"Sweetenin'" has been around Nashville from the start, but somehow the idea of recording a solo voice and accompanying guitar and rhythm one day and then dubbing in a 30-piece ensemble with voices the next ran against the grain of country music. But Glen Campbell changed all that. Two years ago, working with Capitol producer Al DeLory, he developed an obviously successful approach to country music:

"For me to get the feel I want on a record, it would be pretty hard to go into a studio with a 21-piece band and get it all to sound solid. So on rhythm dates, I only do bass, drums, guitar, overdub the guitar, overdub whatever, and get the feel like I want, and the voice like I want it, and then Al overdubs the strings, the horns, or whatever."

Extensive overdubbing is basic to pop music, but what Campbell did was to use it to package "Gentle on My Mind" while preserving an identifiable country feeling. The combination was an enormous success, and has been sustained by Nashville, Jimmy Webb's songs, and Campbell's extraordinary popularity.

The hard part for Campbell was reaching the point where he had the flexibility to develop that combination. When he signed with Capitol in 1962, he was already an established studio musician and singer, but no one was sure what to do about it.

"I bounced around four or five producers before I said, 'But you don't understand, that's not what I want to do.' When you go with a company like Capitol, you tend to go along with what they say. No one ever seemed to ask me what I wanted to do. Finally, I worked out an arrangement with Al DeLory where I could do a couple of songs of my own on each session. . . . And if he wanted me to cut "Come to Jesus" in A-flat, I'd do it as long as I could get my lick in. It's worked out great so far."

Campbell finished up 1968 as the nation's top selling artist, outdistancing the Beatles by a comfortable margin. His last four albums have sold over a million copies. Last December alone, he accounted for over 4.5 million in LP sales. He picked up four Grammy awards, was named the Entertainer of the Year by Nashville's Country Music Association, and somehow ended up as the honorary chairman of the National Arthritis Foundation. Last month in Hollywood, the Academy of Country and Western Music named him the Best Male Vocalist of the Year and Top Television Personality, and presented him with an award for the Best Album (*Bobbie Gentry/Glen Campbell*).

This year will produce more of the same: television, movies, awards, state fairs, appearances, records, concerts, and a personal gross of around $3 million. His flack would have you believe he's still just a nice kid from Delight, Arkansas (pop. 450)[,] who learned to pick and sing on a Sears Roebuck guitar at the age of six, all of which is true.

Campbell grew up in Arkansas, absorbed the manners and mores of rural life, emerging unafflicted by racial prejudice. At 15, he decided to swap an uncertain future in school for a chance to play in his uncle's country-western band in Albuquerque, New Mexico. For the next eight years, he toured the Southwest, playing country bars six nights a week, five hours a night.

By 1960, he had a wife, his own band (The Champs), and was blowing more rock than country. Moving to Hollywood that same year, he played with several L.A.-based rock groups before starting work as a studio musician.

"I really got into studio playing in 1962 when I discovered I could make more doing that than running around trying to be a singin' star."

When he wasn't working studio dates (which at one point earned him $50,000 a year), Campbell did one night stands at both rock and country music shows up and down the Coast.

"I must have played arenas like the Cow Palace [San Francisco] three or four times. The bill was 'Chubby Checker, Sonny and Cher, the Byrds, and Many Others.' I was Many Others. That was back when I was doing *Shindig*. I did a lot of rock and roll on that show, everything from 'What's New Pussycat' to 'Cumberland Gap.'"

Campbell's appearances on *Shindig* may have been less memorable than that show's commercials for Stridex medicated pimple pads, but on the other had he had worked all the Beach Boys studio dates, knew their entire repertoire, and at one point substituted for Brian Wilson at a Houston concert. When Wilson subsequently had to bow out of a six-month tour in 1965, Campbell again took his place. In addition to raising his voice a tone and a half (from singing falsetto four nights a week), the tour was rewarding.

"I learned an awful lot about people. It showed me another side of the world I hadn't seen....I was actually a teen-age idol, so to speak. You know, I lost three or four shirts, a coupla wrist watches. I didn't know not to wear 'em. 'Cuz when you're running from the stage, they can really grab....

"Mike [Love] and the gang, they wanted me to go with them full time after that. I thought about it and decided I really didn't want to be a part of a group. I like being responsible for me....They didn't want to pay me what I wanted, but that's beside the point....It's like, 'The Beach Boys did so and so,' or 'Such and such a group done so and so.' I like to be me, not part of something that does something that, say, I wouldn't like, and then have it printed."

The decision was fortuitous. Campbell's mellifluous voice was ideally suited to a country lyric at a time when Jimmy Webb was changing the character of that lyric.

"Webb's stuff is a little bit country. But it's like Hartford says, they have quit writing' about "You broke my heart so now I'm gonna break your jaw' or 'You left me and now I'm gonna go down to the bar and put a nickel in the juke box and play A-11.' That's really one of the big reasons for the upsurge in country music....

"Actually I don't like to segregate music. To me it's like segregatin' people....People who say, 'That's Country and I don't like Country' gotta be pretty narrow minded. Either that or they don't know a damn thing about music. 'I don't like country music'—that's the dumbest remark I ever heard. Then you start naming off some country songs and they say, 'Is that Country? I didn't know that.' There's good in all music. It's like when I record, I don't aim at anything. I just find a good song and go do it like I want to. And if the country fans gripe or the pop fans grip, I can't help it."

Glen Campbell can't help it either if a good percentage of his public sees him as something more than an entertainer. In these troubled times, he has become for many the embodiment of those vanishing virtues tilled from the rich soil of the American earth. To them he is attractive, manly, self-effacing, honest, easy-going, inner-directed, and successful. Happily his private personality parallels his public image.

Ken Nelson—Capitol's A&R chief who has headed that company's enormously profitable Country area—looks like an amiable Midwestern dry goods dealer. He wears open collar shirts in simple pastels, usually has his sleeves rolled up half way, smokes and occasional cigar, and doesn't pay any mind if his calf shows when he crosses his legs.[25]

25. For more on Nelson, consult Ken Nelson, *My First 90 Years Plus 3* (Pittsburgh: Dorrance, 2007).

"I'm just a country boy m'self."

His is the smile of a man who hasn't been a country boy for 30 years but who does have over $350,000 in retirement benefits coming to him when he decides to relinquish his role as probably the best Country producer in the business.

Nelson has a prestige office on the top floor of the Capitol building but it isn't papered over with the expected plaques, pictures, citations and reassuring memorabilia. In his world the accoutrements of success are irrelevant. He lives outside fashion, a consummate practitioner of his craft, strangely at peace, and a benign presence in Studio A.

Ten minutes after the evening session is scheduled to begin, people are surprisingly set up and ready. The expected 45[-]minute prelude of instrument tuning and kit rattling standardized by the Jefferson Airplane is supplanted instead by a stirring andante rendition of "Tracks Run Through the City." The Hagers—Jim and John—have come to make Record One. They finish "Tracks" and run through a second song, "With Lonely," then a third, "Going Home to Your Mother." All agree "Tracks" should be the A side.[26] What about "Mother?" Nelson pauses.

"Well, it's a fine song and what it says may be true, but it knocks somebody's mother. You may eventually want to put it on an album, but with your first single you probably shouldn't knock anybody.... But it's your show. If you feel strongly about it, go ahead and use it."

Jim Hager looks at 21 years of experience and suggests they cut "With Lonely." No objections heard, the twins again run through "Tracks" for the benefit of sidemen on bass, two guitars, pedal steel, drums, and piano. The arrangement begins to come together as electric guitarist James Burton, replete in a white turtleneck and matching "tennis," puts together a lead. Here and there a few licks bring to mind his presence on Judy Collins' *Who Knows Where the Time Goes.*

Five bars into the first take, Nelson signals a halt.

"Is everyone in tune? Thought I heard a B flat somewhere."

The B string on the acoustic guitar is brought up to pitch, followed by two full takes, a playback, a reshuffling of the arrangement to cut 15 seconds off the time, and then a final take.

By this time the Hagers have transmitted the anxiety of a first recording session into a totally concentrated effort to sing well. Both watch and listen intently as Nelson suggests minor changes in phrasing, in emphasis. They're damn good, and they're hungry for that first record. Studio A has never been more efficiently used.

The character of this session—in fact of virtually all country music sessions—is significant only by comparison with the unstructured, sloppy and markedly unprofessional behavior of at least 50 percent of the rock groups who enter into a studio with the idea of making a record. A rock musician may only bring with him a fragmented vision of what he will eventually record (for him the studio *is* the instrument), but what is passed off as the machinations of the creative process is too often little more than an absurd indulgence of ego and a lack of technical competence, frequently manifested in the inability to put one's instrument properly in tune when the chips are down.

After a short break, during which Nelson explains to his charges the strictly commercial considerations of keeping singles short enough for use on radio stations and juke boxes,

26. 45-rpm singles were promoted as having an "A" side and a "B" side. The A side is thought to be the commercial hit, while the B side is often more novel.

the session resumes in a relaxed but purposeful mood. The group tackles "With Lonely" in several keys, settles for G, and completes a final take ten minutes short of the three hour mark. Everyone is pleased. The Hagers, potentially hot property, now have Record One.

For Nelson, the session wasn't much different from the studio work he originally did in the basement of Nashville's Tulane Hotel in 1948. At the time, however, production was only half the job. Finding the talent took up the rest of his time.

"I remember when I used to spend weeks driving all over the Midwest and the South scouting talent. I never ran into any miraculous performers, but I did get a good feel for country music and what people wanted to hear."

Nelson's judgment has been reliable. Since he took over the job from his predecessor Lee Gillette in 1950, he no longer cruises the boondocks. Between 40 and 50 demo records and tapes come into his office every month from three continents.

"Still, the record business today is no sure thing. A hit single sells between 25,000 and 50,000. Of course, if it crosses over into the pop field, it can go up to 200,000 or higher."

While 50,000 records sold is very good by today's standards, the figure is small by historical comparison. In the early Fifties, country boys like Hank Thompson and Eddy Arnold sold 500-600,000 records at a crack without going pop, primarily because only a few companies were turning out country records and these tended to be concentrated among relatively few artists. Ironically, the half-million sales mark for a strictly country record is a rarity today even though the audience is considerably larger.

According to Nelson, the present decline is in part due to the buying public's shift from singles to long-playing albums. Twenty years ago, 78[-]rpm records were the industry's staple commodity. Today the country fan more often waits for an LP release the title cut of which is a hit single. In other words, if you buy Carl Smith's latest Columbia release featuring his recent his "Faded Love and Winter Roses," you also get to hear "I Put the Blue in Her Eyes," "I Wish I Felt This Way at Home," and "Not In Front of the Kids."

If the LP buying trend continues at the present rate, 45[-]rpm singles within a matter of several years will be used almost exclusively as promotional devices for radio station air play.[27] Such a development could easily make a Program Director's job a long[-]term nightmare, but the changing nature of country music is already playing havoc in radioland, particularly in metropolitan areas. As middle-of-the-road and chicken-rock stations in Los Angeles, Fresno, and San Jose pick up the so-called town-and-country sound (Glen Campbell, Eddy Arnold and Hartford), the straight-out country stations are being forced to shift to more narrowly ethnic programming (i.e., hard[-]core country) to keep their audience and their advertisers.

The problem is transitional, however. The country audience in California growing and the stations serving it are starting to scramble for the ratings with the ardor of the more hyperbolic rockers. Promotion of country acts is increasingly important, but unlike Top 40, few country outlets are able to scare up a full house on their own. In the Los Angeles area, which receives as many as 45 AM-FM signals, country stations KFOX and KBBQ team together to cross-promote such attractions as the Jimmy Dean Show. In the Bay Area KSAY in Oakland and KEEN in San Jose have adopted the same practice.

27. This prediction did, in fact, come true, as albums dominated the sales landscape until the.mp3 era.

One station which has no problem packing the concert all on its own is KRAK in Sacramento, 100 miles north of San Francisco.[28] With a 50,000 watt easily covering Stockton, Modesto, and the upper half of the San Joaquin Valley, KRAK is the biggest country music station in the western states. Owned by the Hercules Broadcasting Company, KRAK is the largest of a small national chain which includes KKUA (690 AM) in Honolulu, a rocker which calls its DJs The Big 69 men (you can get away with a lot in Hawaii). KRAK's studios are buried in the Country Club Shopping Center, a mammoth retail complex which looks a little like the box in which Disneyland came.

While its audience is largely rural, the station can afford to buy quarter[-]page ads in the Wall Street Journal on a regular basis. One reason is that few country acts can successfully appear in and around Sacramento without KRAK's promotional backing (for a percentage). To prove the point the station recently acquired a large auditorium in an expansion move to grab a bigger share of area bookings.

The man responsible for producing country shows is Jay Hoffer, KRAK's program director. A thin, flat-chested executive in his late forties, Hoffer has clean, white hands, fastidiously neat desk and a philosophy of Americanism which conceivably would allow him to offer the use of the station's auditorium for a decency rally, for a percentage of the take. Having read about the groupies over lunch, Hoffer subsequently complained of objectionable language and advised *Rolling Stone* that "KRAK does not wish to be associated in any way with your magazine." He kept the issue.

In this spirit Hoffer has been careful to keep KRAK's programming traditional (no rockabilly) with a heavy stress on corn ("Now here's Freddy Hart with a streetsweeper's song for after the horse parade: 'Why Leave Something I Can't Use'"). Pee pee-doo doo again. KRAK's audience without doubt comprises the world's largest market for a commercial for ear wax softener offering a free ear trumpet ("TV listening device") with every bottle purchased.

Despite the domination of a large country audience, KRAK is a relative newcomer. During the war the thousands of shipyard and defense plant workers who had migrated from the Midwest to the San Francisco Bay area constituted a substantial market for country music. It was discovered—or rather stumbled upon—by DJ Cliff Johnson at KLX (now KNEW). Johnson, whose radio name was Cactus Jack, had always hated country music but that was before he was ordered to play it. Wally King, a contemporary of Johnson's (and since 1944 a newscaster with KSFO) recalls what happened:

"KLX's manager Ad Fried called all the staff announcers together (we weren't called DJs then) and said, 'I know you all hate the music but one of you guys is going to have to do a Western show—I don't care who does it.' The field narrowed down to a choice between me, Johnson and a third announcer, Everett Clayborne. Finally, Clayborne and I ganged up on Johnson and two days later 'Cactus Jack' started playing Western stuff off tapes from World Transcription Service (you couldn't get records because of the war shortage) and the few country-western records we had around the station.

"Cactus also worked a shift as a foreman at the Kaiser shipyard in Richmond where he met a lot of people from Oklahoma, Texas and Arkansas who kept asking him to play records by Bob Wills and his Texas Playboys. He'd never heard of him but they all insisted Wills was

---

28. LaChapelle, *Proud to Be an Okie*, 188–89; Pecknold, *The Selling Sound*, 148–50; Kim Simpson, "Country Radio's Growing Pains in the Music Trades, 1967-1977," *American Music* 27, no. 4 (Winter 2009), 501–502.

their little tin Jesus back there in the Southwest. One of his crew loaned him a cardboard box of Wills records to play and pretty soon the station was deluged with requests for more. Cactus asked his 'friends and neighbors' to send in Wills records and pretty soon he had a large collection. Then he got hooked on the stuff—you know, you listen to anything long enough and you get to like

When Wills himself heard about the response his records were receiving, he hooked up with Cactus for promotion and sold out the Oakland Civic Auditorium for a one-night Western Swing barn dance (there were no concerts in those days). Every few months for the next several years, Wills (with Cactus as MC) appeared somewhere in the area, often outdrawing the Dorsey, Miller, and Goodman bands.

Shortly after Cactus Jack uncovered the C&W audience, rival station KROW (now KABL) came up with Longhorn Joe (alias Wally Elliott) who managed to split the ratings. He, too, got into promotion and brought in Hank Williams, T. Texas Tyler, Hank Snow and, later on, the first Johnny Cash show.

By the early Fifties, a third cowboy—DJ-performer Blackjack Wayne (and his Country Ramblers)—had developed a local following. Wayne, who had been functioning as a country DJ on outlying stations, took Longhorn's split when the latter left KROW, but by that time Western Swing had ridden off into the sunset and the country audience had shrunk considerably.

Today, the largest audience for occasional-country are the 200,000 listeners to KSFO's immensely popular Don Sherwood. Roughly 20 percent of his songs on his A.M. commuter program are hefty-meaty-beefy trucker ballads and he-haw novelty numbers. Sherwood is in the enviable position of being able to play whatever material he happens to like regardless of whether the local country listener wants to hear it or not.

In any event, what a Country fan wants to hear is unclear, but as John Hartford's experience with "Gentle on My Mind" indicates, the character of the artist's voice often has the strongest bearing on a record's success. Hartford's trouble may be that he's too good. In country music, as in no other category, a voice that oozes sincerity and emotion is the most important requisite.[29] Cliffie Stone explains:

"There's an honesty to it. In fact, if I get a country artist who's got a good voice, I'm in trouble. It's gotta come from the heart. And if you listen to Buck Owens and Merle Haggard and Sonny James and all the others who really feel what they sing, you'll find an emotionalism that sells. It's not the fantastic voice. It's not the beautiful sound. It's that thing you can believe."

If a good voice lacks sincerity, one with a clear vibrato is downright dishonest. Historically, the emphasis is valid. Moreover, anything short of that would make a shambles of "You May Be Wild Bill Tonight But You'll Be Sweet William in the Morning."

Most country singers have, at one time or another, sung hillbilly, blue grass, folk, pop and even rock. Conway Twitty, Marty Robbins and Ferlin Husky all had pop hits during the Fifties. Jerry Lee Lewis spent a decade in rock before turning to Country. Of lesser importance was the brief rock career of Corky Jones, a young Bakersfield artist who in 1953 recorded "Hot Dog," a single which sold well locally. He toyed with the idea of adopting the Chuck Berry style and might even have cut "Johnny B. Goode," but he eventually decided to stick with country music.

Buck Owens never regretted the choice.

29. For more on this notion, consult Aaron A. Fox, *Real Country: Music and Language in Working-Class Culture* (Durham, NC: Duke University Press, 2004), 152–191.

The Drive from Los Angeles to Bakersfield 100 miles north is a fast two hours on Highway 99. The road rises to the lip of a teaming metropolitan bowl, over the lip and out of the smog, and into the barren Tehachapi Mountains. It winds through the top of 4,000 foot El Tejon Pass, then drops to the floor of the lower San Joaquin Valley down the Grapevine—a steep 14-mile grade populated day and night by huge diesel trucks grinding their way southward to the summit. On the valley floor gusts of hot, dry air spill on to the road from limitless flat farmlands.

Bakersfield does not have a skyline. The city arrives in the form of several exits from a 70[-]mph by-pass. Downtown is an area of two[-] and three-story buildings, surrounded by a sprawling patchwork of shopping centers, ranch style homes and asphalt streets flanked by service stations, tractor dealerships and drive-ins. A good number of its 60,000 citizens live off the nearby oil fields or the farmlands comprising the bulk of Kern County. The place is a dead ringer for Western Oklahoma: windmills, alfalfa, oil fields, humidity, horse flies, even a Republican congressman. Buck Owens doesn't own Bakersfield, yet, but if he has his way the town will be called Music City West in a year's time.

Hays Motors at 1805 South Chester Avenue is a small, tired used car lot and garage that isn't breaking any sales records. There's usually a few good old boys sitting inside the office passing time with manager Bill Woods, a stocky easy-going type who plays country-rock piano six nights a week at the Barrel House uptown. Wood's dual vocation is well suited to his leisure life loves: country music and stock car racing. The wall behind the office door is papered with a fading collage of dusty publicity photographs of country stars of the dim past, several business cards discolored with age, and an old pin-up calendar from an automotive supplier. On the cluttered desk is a stack of Grand Ole Opry brochures (c. 1955) with pictures of featured artists (Johnny Cash, looking like a sax player for the Wailers, is described as "a new member who sings and writes songs as well."

Bill figures he knows about as much about Buck Owens in the early days as anybody.

"Back in the early Fifties, I owned a club here called the Bill Woods Corral. Buck started out with my band playing take-off guitar. He was pretty good, even then. I called us 'Bill Woods and the Orange Blossom Playboys featuring Buck Owens.' Actually, you see, he didn't like to sing, but I encouraged him.... I had to force him to."

Woods pauses to tuck his shirt between a beer belly and a silver belt buckle.

"Buck stayed with me for about five years, even after I went over to another club—The Blackboard. Though we were a country-western band, we always played about 75 percent rock in clubs. Still do. That's why I'll put Buck up against any R&B or rock singer you ever heard, singing the same stuff."

Mercifully, Buck Owens chose country over R&B. He had more in common with Left Frizzel [sic] and Spade Cooley. Born in Sherman, Texas, in 1930, Owens grew up in Mesa, Arizona, got married at 16 and five years later moved to Bakersfield. There he worked as an Orange Blossom Playboy and starved along with most every other country musician except Ferlin Husky and Tommy Collins—two Bakersfield stars of the Fifties who developed a national following in that decade. About the same time the Owenses were amicably divorced. Ex-wife Bonnie Owens began her own career as a country singer and two years ago married Merle Haggard.

Woods was up on all the goings-on of the day:

"Ferlin Husky used to play in Tommy Collins' band. Then Buck took his place and changed the style a bit. He'd been signing and writing for a few years by that time and he first became known for 'Sweethearts in Heaven' and 'Down on the Corner of Love,' both which he recorded on the Pep label before owner Claude Caviness sold out to Ray Price in Nashville."

Owens' real break came in 1957 when he recorded his first album for Capitol. He left Bakersfield, traveled north to Washington and plugged to country club circuit, playing for whatever he could get at the door. After several records began to move, Owens moved back to California where he began operating out of Bakersfield and cutting more records with Ken Nelson at Capitol.

By the early Sixties, Owens had put together the Buckaroos, a solid back-up group (drums, pedal steel and two guitars) led by Don Rich, a lead guitarist who doubled with close harmony on vocals. In 1963, Owens met Jack McFadden, radio advertising manager for Sacramento's KRAK, and took him on as his personal manager. Soon after Buck Owens and his Buckaroos became big time. His career totals in record sales to date exceeds eight million.

What Buck Owens puts on those records is a flexible tenor voice (straight from the heart, naturally), his own imaginative songs and tight, clean arrangements with a lot of good picking and jumpy percussion. Its character differs from Nashville in its relative sparseness, and lacks the depth provided by the normal studio complement of six to eight musicians. But the result is a crisp and distinctive sound which rings true to the country ear. All this happens 100 miles north of Hollywood.

Today at 39[,] Owens prays he has played his last club date in buckets-of-blood saloons and shitkicker bars. With a $6,000 a night price tag he can relax. The new approach is one-nighters.

"Most of the time the crows are good just about ever-place. But of course California is awful good. It's the economics. The working people got more per capita income and more livin' margin. So I would say they rank with the best of them."

About the country orientation in pop music:

"I think it's something new to them. The rock-pop set is searching for a different sound, some simplicity, and country music has it.... But on the other hand, country-western is changing, too.... Now I recently had a record out that's a good example ['Who's Gonna Mow Your Grass'].[30] It's got drums and a bass passing tones, some coupla inner parts there and it has the fuzz tone for the lead part. Now we've found only one country-western disc jockey that didn't like it. In addition to that, Top 40 stations in Seattle, Portland, Dallas, Oklahoma City, and Desmoines [sic] played it. So you can see there's a definite fusion taking place.... The music as a whole is getting to sound more alike. The country-western artists are getting to where they sound more like today's pop-rock music."

Owens' latest single, "Johnny B. Goode," recorded live at the London Palladium, is straight out rock and has already broken into the pop charts.

What is happening to Country lyrics?

"The story song seems to be getting less and less and the modern lyric more popular. Like, gee, you know, I have some radio stations in Bakersfield. One on AM plays country-western and the other plays rockum-sockum type music on FM. You know, the underground sound. We play a lot of acid thangs. The only problem is that while the underground station pulls a good four or five rating none of the merchants will buy advertising. And let's face it, that's the name of the game. It's the economics."

It's the house hippie problem all over again.

"A while ago the gang told me one of the announcers was on marijuana so we had to get rid of him. You know, that kind of person can put the whole situation in a bad light. The

30. Interpolation in original.

music attracts the ten percent of undesirables, the ones with the outlook of, 'Gee, I'd rather take a dive than punch that eight to five,' you know."

Owens tells of another incident at one of his Phoenix rockers. A gaggle of micro-boppers set fire to a trash can to distract the security guard while they crashed the studio to reach the resident jock.

Leaning forward with sincere disapproval: "... Look, I'll be frank with you—I'm filthy rich. I don't have to put up with that kind of stuff."

Buck Owens is correct on both counts. As an enterprise, he is a poor man's Gene Autry with the personal drive to maintain an extraordinarily fast pace. Beneath his preoccupation with markets and ratings and "the economics" he's enjoying himself immensely. So is the better part of the Owens-McFadden clan.

The Bakersfield headquarters of Buck Owens' operations—principally OMAC Artists Corporation—is a plain-looking one-story office building on North Chester Street away from the center of town. It has the look of a formerly well[-]ordered business which suddenly expanded and had to find new space for Owens' son Mike (director of national promotion), Owens' sister Dorothy (Buck Owens Enterprises), his mother (help on the fan magazine), manager McFadden's son Joe (director of talent), and Joe's ex-school pal Jim Vaughn (formerly an assistant at Sears' fashion department) who took a pay cut to join the staff as number two man with the personal management arm.

The staff of 25 is close knit, hard working, young and promotionally oriented. Last fall OMAC's publicity department came out with issue No. 1 of *The All American*, a slick 12-page fan magazine. Claiming an instant club membership of 10,000 (motto: "Buck's Continued Fame Is Our Aim"), the publication contains the usual narcissistic adulation and at one point reminds its readers that "this country is strong because of a steadfast belief in God and that all-American music is for 'All Americans.'"

Any remaining doubts about the claim are sure to be cleared up before the end of the year. Plans are already in the works for a parade through downtown Bakersfield on the day the ribbon is cut on the soon-to-be-constructed Buck Owens Studios. The city will be officially declared the country music capital of the West and three dozen acts will appear throughout the day to prove it. Already invited to be present on the occasion: Governor Ronald Reagan and Vice President Spiro Agnew.[31]

The Bakersfield hype is not all that fanciful. An eight-track recording studio is already in operation on Merle Haggard's ranch. It was originally installed for his personal use, but Haggard, along with manager Fuzzy Owen, plans to resurrect the inactive Tally label in Bakersfield and open the studio for commercial use. If two recording operations can do a brisk business, additional facilities may be installed by one or more major labels. Then the ball would be rolling.

As for promoting country music and Bakersfield, Haggard speaks with characteristic frankness:

"Any time you build country music, you build yourself if you're involved. Right now I just cut records, but I'm interested in recording in other areas besides my own. As for

31. LaChapelle has documented the close connections between conservative politicians and Southern Californian country artists in his *Proud to Be an Okie*, 140–44.

promoting a town, I'm not really interested in that. Whatever I do that helps, well, I'm glad, but that's not really my intention, you dig what I mean?"

Merle Haggard's only connection with Buck Owens is that he married his ex-wife and books through OMAC. In several respects his career has paralleled Owens', but in character, style, and attitude Merle Haggard is clearly a man apart.

His voice is sweet water on parched earth, conjuring vistas of undulating wheatfields, dark soil and the rolling hills of the American heartland. His songs have the unmistakable feel of Jimmie Rodgers' classic blue yodels. And he sings country music in a way that communicates a sense of university felt experience.

Born in Bakersfield in 1937, Haggard was the third child of a Checotah, Oklahoma, fiddler who two years earlier had come west to escape the dust bowl. Young Merle's father died when he was nine, making an already hard life harder. He stayed in Bakersfield until his middle teens, then took off for several years of wandering through Texas and the Southwest where he worked on farms, drove potato trucks, hitch-hiked, hobo-ed and even did a stretch behind bars for something like car theft. Along the way he began to write and sing songs imbued with the authenticity of personal suffering and a sense of heritage instinctively grasped. Without knowing it, he had embraced and enriched the legacy of Woody Guthrie.

Returning to Bakersfield in 1961, Haggard fell in with the local country artists and began playing at the Barrel House, the Blackboard and other Country clubs. Then in 1964, with the help of fellow musician Fuzzy Owen, he landed a recording contract with Capitol. Things happened quickly thereafter. Haggard took on Fuzzy Owen as his manager, hooked up with OMAC in 1965, put together a fine back-up group (the Strangers) in 1966 and married Bonnie Owens in 1967. By the end of last year he had made nine albums which had sold nearly three million copies, written over 100 songs, and been voted the Best Male Vocalist in the Country field by Cash Box and several other trade magazines.

Like Buck Owens, Merle Haggard and the Strangers rent out for $6,000 a night. But Haggard is unique among country stars—he has a kind of "it-don't-make-no-difference" love for good country music. When he is home in Bakersfield, Haggard will occasionally wander into one of the clubs, borrow somebody's axe and sit on the edge of the stage, off to one side, next to a scotch and water, and jam with whoever happens to be playing.

With the Strangers for backing, Haggard has not had to rely on Nashville. He could record in a store-front church in the middle of Harlem and probably come up with a country sound more authentic than Floyd Cramer, Grady Martin, the Anita Kerr Singers, and eight of the best echo chambers on 16th Avenue South could together produce in any three sessions. However, for convenience he prefers to use Ken Nelson and Studio A for production and wife Bonnie and rhythm guitarist Gene Price for vocal backing. This parallels Buck Owens' use of the Buckaroos—up to a point.

"The Strangers are similar to the Buckaroos in that we have the same instrumentation, but anytime you have different musicians, it's going to sound different. We have a few style licks that we've come up with that Buck didn't have—identity licks I call them."

Does he see Nashville getting into difficulty by putting its "identity licks" behind every artist?

"Well anytime you limit the staff to a certain number of people, it's bound to start sounding commercial. By limiting I mean having the same studio musicians playing on all the sessions.... But then again it seems to me that the artists who get the most hits out of

Nashville—people like Johnny Cash—have their organizations. And that's why I'm interested in building up my own network here on the West Coast."

Like Cash, Haggard uses a bus for his U.S. and Canadian junkets, in this case a well-equipped Greyhound "Challenger" with separate quarters for all ten members of the tour. Life is thus a little less hectic and between stops Haggard can catch up on such tasks as reading a movie script.

"Bonnie and I and the Strangers had a small part in *Killers Three* but I think they played it up a bit too much. We might take the script we're looking over now. It's already been offered to Glen Campbell and Elvis Presley. Somebody said Glen wanted $400,000 to do it and Elvis wanted $800,000.... And [chuckling] now they come to me...."

About pop music's adaptation of country music?

"Well I think it's kinda like a fad. Rock and roll got strong for a while, and then the Beatles got strong. I wouldn't call them rock and roll...don't really know what you'd call them. And maybe Country is just the next thing in line. Then again it could be gospel music. You never know."

It may be a fad but without question a growing audience wants to hear more country music these days than ever before. In mid-April, Merle Haggard and the Strangers had a change to play for that audience in Hollywood, only the appearance was overshadowed by other events. He gave the inaugural performance at the V.I.S.—a new and lavish country-western club bankrolled by Dick Clark, the nation's top teenie impresario (305 rock/pop concert bookings last year). Clark had bought the old Cinnamon Cinder, a used teen night club (remember Dick Dale and the Del Tones?) and privately advertised $250 club memberships to Very Important Shitkickers in the Los Angeles area. Somebody was offended, a minor fuss ensued and Clark subsequently opted for a (probably anticipated) change to Very Important Shindiggers. Opening night was a boozy success, attended by a goodly number of the directors on the board of the Country Music Association who were in town for a quarterly meeting of industry big wigs at the Century Plaza.

The V.I.S. is aiming for an affluent urban clientele not embarrassed to be seen in a night club where the fellow onstage is wearing cowboy boots and has hair slicked back all funny. In truth the big acts in Country are fully on a par with the best pop groups, but their audience is characteristically fortyish, white, smokes less dope and drinks more. Like their counterparts in rock, however, the country acts attract their share of groupies.

Perhaps because there are less of them, full[-]time C&W groupies go by nicknames in the drag strip/race-horse category which are faithfully passed along the club circuit. Until recently the perennial favorite in Los Angeles was Hurricane Shirley, a good old gal who for the last ten years has serviced all the major acts on tour to the West Coast, including road managers, equipment men and relief bus drivers. Predictably her name has cropped up in Country songs over the years (Marty Robbins reportedly mentions her in one of his earlier, lesser hits).

Hurricane Shirley lately appears to have been put out to pasture by The Black Rider, a winsome lass of epic proportions who just loves them singin' cowboys.

The Country groupie tends to be older (sometimes much older) than her rock counterpart, wears shorter hair and seldom employs the direct "I'm-clean-I'm-over-18-let's-fuck" approach. But, as John Hartford opines: "They're the same as other groupies insofar as they all want to ball you."

On the same subject, Hartford sees a problem with pop music sounding more Country:

"Wouldn't it be something if all the categories of music broke down and all the groupies got confused because they didn't know who to ball?[32] ... The Plaster Casters would be going crazy. Everybody would be making music, man, they'd be plastering people in the streets."[33]

If the groupie phenomenon in country music is less widespread and less competitive than rock, it is in part due to the life styles of the majority of established Country artists. Most are in their middle thirties or older, live in the suburbs, mow the lawn on Sundays, and make enough money to send the wife to the beauty parlor once a week. Though he works in a show business environment as morally relaxed as any field of entertainment, the Country artist by contrast with his co-equal in the rock world is more beholden to the personal restraints imposed on a Christian family man away from home for a few weeks. Or, as Hartford puts it, "I don't think Stuart Hamblin is going to expose himself at his next concert."

No, the eroticism and the glorious indiscretion of rock are antithetical to the nature of country music. But this is as it should be. Rock and roll is instinctively revolutionary, whereas country music, not in a pejorative sense, reactionary. Perhaps it is historically significant that the most dynamics elements of each are being assimilated by American popular music.

Whether such assimilation will produce new vitality or new mediocrity in that music remains to be seen. But there is in the firmament of Country stars a performer whose approach to her music just might represent the wave of an uncertain future—Judy Lynn, Miss Show Business herself, a peach of a girl, a millionaire and consummate practitioner of what can only be called Gestalt Country.

Judy Lynn and her eight piece band ride the Silver Circuit, a chain of Nevada casino lounges in Las Vegas, Reno and Lake Tahoe. She's been doing it for six months out of the year for the last nine years and loving it. To each of her three nightly performances she brings one of the best Country bands in the business, a creditable voice (bothersome vibrato), the all-American beauty of a former Miss Idaho (1960), and the kind of tight-fitting super flashy Western clothes that only a $75,000 Nudie wardrobe can offer. For her trouble, Miss Lynn grosses $15,000 a week.

In a state where casino-Country acts draw terribly, the Judy Lynn Show is the longest running club act of any kind in Nevada. During that time the personable lass recorded 11 albums, became a top drawing card on the lucrative summer State Fair circuit, won Billboard's accolade as the Most Promising Country and Western Female Vocalist in 1967, and managed to keep her figure.

Miss Lynn and her producer/husband John Kelley recently spent a month in San Francisco taping 39 half-hour shows (with no guest artists) for national television syndication. Between Judy Lynn Shows No. 27 and 28, she paused to consider her past.

"When I first started out everyone told me not to wear pants, but to wear instead a gingham dress and be a pure little country girl and keep my mouth shut. Well, I had more ambition than that and with my husband's help, and the good Lord's we are succeeding.... Of

32. To have sex with.

33. A reference to famed group Cynthia Albritton, known as "Cynthia Plaster Caster" for her collection of plaster molds of rock musicians' penises (Jenny Sylvain, "'They Sure Broke the Mould...' Cynthia Plaster Caster: Groupie as Craft—Worker," in The Mammoth Book of Sex, Drugs & Rock 'n' Roll, rev. ed., ed. Jim Driver (Philadelphia: Running Press, 2010).

course, people today say any millionaire can have a big show, but they don't know how low me and my husband started."

The starting point was having their car repossessed in Nashville ten years ago. Times were doubtless hard. Miss Lynn was 21 at the time and only recently converted to the beauty and rich heritage of country music. Her idols of those halcyon pre-rock days were Doris Day and Rosemary Clooney. Somehow she took on the Doris Day mystique through the years, even as her interests broadened.

"I love rock...we do a lot of things on the show that are quite similar, like 'Downtown.' We want to appeal to city people and yet we're as hillbilly as you can get. We do songs like 'Good Old Mountain Dew' and 'Wabash Cannonball.' And yet we also do 'Moon Over Naples' and 'My Cup Runneth Over with Love.'"

They are all find songs. And Miss Lynn is a genuine, likeable person. But there is something about her—what she is doing—that pulls into focus the disparate elements of a terrible vision.

It all comes together in the persona of Judy Lynn as Miss Show Business. There she is, out there in limbo between California and Tennessee, orbiting a north-south axis past the Golden Nugget, Caesar's Palace and Harrah's Club. She is a native of Idaho; her band hails from California and the Midwest; she records in Nashville; her sparkle plenty outfits are made in Hollywood; her television shows are taped in San Francisco; she's beautiful, blonde, white, sacred, and sincere; and she is singing the songs of Jimmie Rodgers and Hank Williams, of Buck Owens and Merle Haggard, of Jimmy Webb, John Hartford, Johnny Cash, Bob Dylan and a thousand others. She is singing everybody's songs. Everybody's.

And they all sound the same.

Source: John Grissim Jr., "California White Man's Shit Kickin' Blues," *Rolling Stone* 36 (28 June 1969): 12–19, 22–30. (Used with permission of the author.)

FOR FURTHER READING

Fenster, Mark. "Buck Owens, Country Music, and the Struggle for Discursive Control." *Popular Music* 9, no. 3 (1990): 275–90.

Grissim, John. *Country Music: White Man's Blues.* New York: Coronet Communications, 1970.

LaChapelle, Peter. *Proud to Be an Okie: Cultural Politics, Country Music, and Migration to Southern California.* Berkeley: University of California Press, 2007.

Mather, Olivia Carter. *"Cosmic American Music": Place and the Country Rock Movement, 1965-1974.* Ph.D. dissertation, University of California, Los Angeles, 2006.

Haslam, Gerald W., with Alexandra Haslam Russell and Richard Chon. *Workin' Man Blues: Country Music in California.* Berkeley: Heyday Books, 2005.

31

Lee Arnold

"A DJ Tells Why—There's Country Music in the City Air" (1975)

By the late 1960s, radio stations devoted to the broadcast of the latest country recordings could be heard across the United States and Canada, spurred on in large part by the efforts of Connie B. Gay and the Country Music Association, which promoted country music audiences as modern consumers.[1] Although country music certainly had enjoyed long associations with rural America, it was increasingly becoming an urban music, as rural migrants moved in greater numbers to cities in search of industrial work, leading some adventurous station managers to try their hands at broadcasting country music. By the mid-1970s, stations flourished in Los Angeles, Chicago, and New York, although, as historian Kim Simpson has shown, country stations still struggled to achieve market parity with their pop and rock counterparts.[2]

As the public face of their local radio stations, disc jockeys—many of whom were long-time residents of the communities they served—played an important role

---

1. See chap. 4 of Diane Pecknold, *The Selling Sound: The Rise of the Country Music Industry* (Durham, NC: Duke University Press, 2007).

2. Kim Simpson, "Country Radio's Growing Pains in the Music Trades, 1967-1977," *American Music* 27, no. 4 (Winter 2009): 500–14.

in defining audience taste and developing programs that encouraged listeners to tune in to hear the advertisements that supported the stations' financial enterprise. As award-winning New York disc jockey Lee Arnold recounts in the following article[3], the development of a country station in the United States' largest city was far from an easy task, as on-air talent needed to be educated and audiences needed to be found.[4] Yet, as station WHN's eventual success as a top-five station in the New York market indicates, country music had become a national phenomenon by the 1970s.

━━━━━━━

MY involvement as a broadcaster in country music goes back further than I care to admit. But in just the past few years, I've watched country music grow and lately, blossom fully, here in New York. It didn't happen overnight and it was a painful struggle, but I'm delighted to have been a part of it.

I'm referring to country music's acceptance here both as live entertainment in clubs, and most important, as played by a major radio station. There's no quick way to know what a person likes musically than to play it on the air.

The first real breakthrough for country music as a potent radio force in the New York area came with WJRZ in Newark [New Jersey], when the format switched in 1965. It weathered many problems; however, in spite of all the shortcomings, it managed to evolve as a popular station with a respectable share of audience in the metropolitan New York area.

Just as the station was starting to "cook," it was sold to new owners who took country off the air and replaced it with a rock format. That was in 1971. There was a void on the air in the New York market for two years until February, 1973, when WHN went full-time country 24 hours a day. Since no country music had been heard in this area for so long, essentially we were a brand new station with a brand new format. So we were starting from scratch.

And I do mean scratch—that means the dj's too. I was the only one at the station who had a background in country; everybody else had experience in a different area. So I had to take each guy aside and give him a bit of advice. "Listen to the music, announce the songs, *but say nothing about the artists*," I told them all. I knew that country music fans would spot a phoney a mile away. They took my advice, and were patient students, eager to get their feet wet. I remember when one guy was just getting into it and was apparently just dying to say something about something he was *sure* he knew. So, after he played a particular record, he said: "That was Lynn Anderson. She's Bill Anderson's daughter...."[5] I laugh now, but we winced at the time.

After about three months, though, everybody had picked it up and they sounded like they'd been in it all their lives. They got involved with their music, with their audience, and,

3. Arnold was inducted into Country Radio Seminar's DJ Hall of Fame in 2002 ("Lee Arnold," http://countryradioseminar.com/lee-arnold; accessed 31 January 2014).

4. The northern and urban interest in country music was the subject of some sociological study during the 1970s, particularly in the work of Richard A. Peterson and Paul Dimaggio, "From Region to Class, the Changing Locus of Country Music: A Test of the Massification Hypothesis," *Social Forces* 53, no. 3 (March 1975): 497–506.

5. Lynn Anderson had several hit recordings during the 1970s, including "Rose Garden," and her mother Liz was a successful songwriter for several Bakersfield Sound musicians. Bill Anderson, on the other hand, was a star of the *Grand Ole Opry* from Georgia who broke through in the mid-1960s with such hits as "City Lights" and "Po' Folks." They are not related.

by getting out to any country show that came to town, they soon got involved with the artists themselves. I think most of the guys really became believers; they saw that this was music that people could relate to, and then they found that they themselves were relating to it.

I knew there was an immediate audience here who loved country music: those New Yorkers who had heard it on previous country stations, and the great number of people from other geographic areas originally—who had grown up with the Grand Ole Opry and who were now making New York their home. The other potential audience was a bonus. And that represented younger demographics—something country music stations never had before. These young people, who were into rock and recently became disenchanted with what it offered them, turned to country music. Everything in our lifestyle was geared for this type of audience, actually: our lifestyle of today, jeans, the way we feel about ecology and environment.

I know I'll be accused of being on an ego trip for what I'm about to say, but it is the truth: we were an instant success. Our ratings have proven that. Going from a dismal 16th in the market to a top-5 position and sometimes number one was most gratifying. WHN's success is based on many things: the music, the people who present it and what they say about it. It's involvement with the people—totally. If they believe the music they will believe you—it's that simple. Our air personalities are completely different from one another. That makes our total sound unique.

WHN has had some problems[,] naturally. There are still some sponsors who are reluctant to believe that our audience would react and buy their products. Their attitudes are based on old stereotypes about country music people. But we are ready to prove these few disbelievers wrong with the immense success we have had with other clients. The economic makeup of the country audience has changed. It's no longer the farmer in blue jeans, but every New York type you can find—professional and otherwise.[6]

The only major stumbling block we still have is in getting the record product. Our biggest complaint is from listeners who can't buy the country songs they hear on WHN. But this too is improving, thanks to the record companies' awareness of the problem.

Our success is felt in the fact that there are more country music nightclubs in New York than ever before, and new ones opening every month. Concert promoters are continually bringing in package shows and selling out the major concert centers in New York.

All I can say is that I'm glad it happened—and that I was able to have a hand in bringing it about.

> *Source:* Lee Arnold, "A DJ Tells Why—There's Country Music in the City Air," *Country Music Beat* 1, no. 1 (January 1975): 49. (Used with permission of the author.)

FOR FURTHER READING

Pecknold, Diane. *The Selling Sound: The Rise of the Country Music Industry.* Durham, NC: Duke University Press, 2007.

Simpson, Kim. "Country Radio's Growing Pains in the Music Trades, 1967-1977." *American Music* 27, no. 4 (Winter 2009): 500–14.

6. These are precisely the issues that Peterson and DiMaggio grapple with in "From Region to Class." A similar example might be found in Craig Maki with Keith Cady, *Detroit Country Music: Mountaineers, Cowboys, and Rockabillies* (Ann Arbor: University of Michigan Press, 2013).

Michael Bane

The Outlaws: Revolution in Country Music (1978)

In the early 1970s, the term "outlaw country" was used to describe the music of a group of country singers and songwriters who challenged the studio system that had dominated Nashville's Music Row since the 1950s.[1] The term "outlaw" was coined by publicist Hazel Smith, who used it to describe Waylon Jennings, Shel Silverstein, Kris Kristofferson, and other singers and songwriters who spent time at Tompall Glaser's "Hillbilly Central" recording studios in Nashville.[2] By the middle of the 1970s, the term "outlaw" was found in writings on Jennings, Willie Nelson, and other artists who negotiated new contracts for established country recording artists that allowed them to choose the songs that they recorded and the musicians they worked with.[3]

1. For a discussion of record production in the Outlaw era, consult Travis D. Stimeling, "Narrative, Vocal Staging and Masculinity in the 'Outlaw' Country Music of Waylon Jennings," *Popular Music* 32, no. 3 (2013): 343–58.

2. Michael Bane, *The Outlaws: Revolution in Country Music* (n.p.: Country Music Magazine/Doubleday/Dolphin, 1978), 6.

3. R. Serge Denisoff, *Waylon: A Biography* (Knoxville: University of Tennessee Press, 1983), 182–84; Willie Nelson with Bud Shrake, *Willie: An Autobiography,*

Michael Bane's 1978 book, *The Outlaws: Revolution in Country Music*, provides a useful postmortem of the Outlaw movement. While the release of *Wanted! The Outlaws* in 1976 marked, for many audiences, the debut of the Outlaw movement, the album could be more accurately described as its final chapter and, perhaps, little more than a promotional effort by RCA. Marred by bitter (and often drug- and alcohol-fuelled) disputes, the personal and business relationships that had permitted the building of the Outlaw movement were crumbling, and many of the industrial changes that Outlaw movement participants had desired did not come to fruition, despite their best efforts. In 1978, Waylon Jennings captured the movement's exhaustion in "Don't You Think This Outlaw Bit's Done Got Out of Hand." The following selection recounts the history of the Outlaw movement and offers insight into the difficulties that it faced as it challenged the production models of Nashville's Music Row. Moreover, Bane questions the motives of journalists who promoted the scene, suggesting a fundamental (if overstated) tension between commercialization and authenticity and problematizing the use of hillbilly imagery to describe the participants in the Outlaw movement.

━━━━━━━━━━

IT was all a mistake, really. Some New York writer came down to Nashville to feel out the scene, find out what these hillbillies were *really* like, and ended up—along with a whole bunch of pickers and singers and genuine certified one hundred percent redneck hillbillies—the Pancake Man at some terrible time in the not-so-wee hours of the morning.[4] The Pancake Man, in the Holiday Inn on West End Boulevard, sits astride the main drag which shuttles folks from the real Nashville across the Interstate to Music City Nashville, or Music Row.

So the writer and all these 'billies were sitting in there, and one of the 'billies—history has mislaid his specific identity—suggested that this Pancake Man was nothing short of pure Hillbilly Heaven; open all night, willing to admit just about anyone, and cheap. After a hard night cutting hits or playing pinball at J.J.'s Grocery or the Wooden Nickel or the Burger Boy, there's nothing like a big ole plate of greasy pancakes floating in an orgy of maple syrup to set

paperback ed. (New York: Cooper Square Press, 2000), 143–45; Chet Flippo, "From the Bump-Bump Room to the Barricades," in *Country: The Music and the Musicians*, ed. Paul Kingsbury, Alan Axelrod, and Susan Costello (New York: Abbeville, 1994), 318; Waylon Jennings with Lenny Kaye, *Waylon: An Autobiography* (New York: Warner Books, 1996), 187–91; Joe Nick Patoski, *Willie Nelson: An Epic Life* (New York: Little, Brown, and Company, 2008), 247–50.

4. Denisoff observed that Jennings credited Hickey's article with beginning the Outlaw movement in his song "Don't You Think This Outlaw Bit Has Done Got Out of Hand?", in which he observes that "someone called us outlaws in some ol' magazine....What started out to be a joke / The law don't understand" (Denisoff, *Waylon: A Biography*, 195).

the tone for the new day just beginning to creep up over the Interstate—sort of like dying and then discovering that the hereafter is all fresh strawberries and whipped cream. Besides, the Pancake Man was just about the only place open at five a.m.... Hillbilly Heaven.

But the New York writer took liberties. Hillbilly *Central*, like Grand *Central* Station, was the phrase that popped to mind, and by the time his copy appeared, he wasn't even talking about the Pancake Man anymore. He was talking about Tompall Glaser's studio/office building at 916 19th Avenue South. Like the Pancake Man, Tompall's place was open twenty-four hours a day, seven days a week, would let you in even if you had hair down to your ass, and was in the business of catering to dreams of one sort or another (though usually without the syrup). This is how, circa '74, Hillbilly Central got its name.

Actually, it's a pretty good name. Tompall's place is as close to Grand Central Station as anything in Nashville could be. Everybody—absolutely *everybody*—who was somebody, or wanted to be somebody, or just wanted to see somebody who was somebody, made their way to the stucco fortress on 19th, just far enough from Music Row to be fashionable (and, therefore, in an Outlaw scheme of things, very fashionable, indeed). Once inside they might find Waylon Jennings and Jessi Colter or Jack Clement or the inimitable Tompall himself. They might also find Kinky Friedman and his Texas Jewboys, Willie Nelson when in town, Dr. Hook and the Medicine Show, Shel Silverstein, or a baker's dozen of songwriters including people like Guy Clark ("Desperadoes Waiting for a Train"), Alex Harvey ("Delta Dawn"), Lee Fry ("The Hunger"), Billy Joe Shaver ("Honky Tonk Heroes"), Donnie Fritts ("My Life Would Make a Damn Good Country Song"), Lee Clayton ("Ladies Love Outlaws") and Billy Ray Reynolds ("It'll Be Her"). Not to mention the odd [Kris] Kristofferson or Mickey Newberry or Jimmy Buffett...the list is about as long as you want it to be, essentially a Who's Who of Outlawism. Hazel Smith, Hillbilly Central's promo person through those years, remembers the day when Marty Robbins' secretary dropped by—said she just *had* to see what kind of thing was going on in a building without windows—and that sort of sums up Hillbilly Central's curiosity value.

What's going on depends entirely on where you look. The ground floor is taken up by the hillbilly equivalent of offices, each of which is something of a cross between bedroom, conference room, junk store, and that closet you keep meaning to clear out. Two of these offices are occupied by Captain Midnight, the Man Friday and so-called "spiritual advisor" of Hillbilly Central, who lives there—it's cheaper than an apartment, and real homey if you don't mind the occasional crazed person or two stumbling through your bedroom at five a.m. In the back is Tompall's office, a gigantic mess composed of randomly stacked tapes ("The Tompall Glaser library of Music," says their owner with more than a trace of irony), loudspeakers the size of oil rigs perched on empty Jack Daniels whiskey kegs, tape and record players of various sizes and shapes, a desk whose top surface has yet to be exposed to the sight of anybody still alive, and various other fixtures and fittings lying around in the gloom.

Up the back steps of the building, however, are the real guts of Hillbilly Central, the recording studio itself, which looks like what lies beyond the average audiophile's Pearly Gates and is, according to Tompall, the state of the art in recording technology and only slightly less complicated than a good pinball machine. The studio itself—that is, the recording area—is almost as messy as the offices downstairs (it looks like someone threw a bomb into a cable factory)—but the control room is something else. The control room, where the producer and engineer do their stuff, is most definitely *not* hillbilly; this is where down-home values meet the Space Age, complete with all the phase shifters, digital delays and Dolby circuits[5] a simple songwriter/singer/producer/arranger/picker/businessman could possibly ever want or have time for. This is the home of all those records Nashville really didn't want to make. This is where the outlaws spent all those countless hours over their music.

Hillbilly Central was, in fact, intended that way. Tompall and his brothers built it for precisely that purpose, and once they'd got it built, what went on behind the salmon-colored walls and permanently closed shutters of the building was nothing short of a ticking time bomb in the heart of Nashville, a total revolution for a business that considered itself to be the most stable part of a notoriously unreliable industry.

There were two parts to that revolution, and it's hard to say which part mainstream Nashville considered the most threatening. The first part concerned money. Somebody told these Hillbilly Central people all about money in New York and Los Angeles terms, about how to wheel and deal and bargain and bluff until the stakes in the hillbilly music game took off through the roof. The second part concerned art. The Hillbilly Central people were gnawing away at the business of how an artist related to his music, forgetting the studio clock and the well-oiled production machine, and so Hillbilly Central became nothing more than a full-fledged musical laboratory, where new directions and new beginnings were considered the rule rather than the exception. The unorthodox took on a strange kind of orthodoxy all its own, and the word "hillbilly" became both a statement of identity and a war-cry against the middle-of-the-road monster that was eating Nashville's talent alive. Hillbillies, they said, and proud of it! Not slicked-up, sprayed-down, uptown countrypolitan smoothies, but pure-ass, down-home, straight-off-the-farm-out-of-jail-and-in-from-the-cold *hillbillies*! ("I called Tammy Wynette a hillbilly in my gossip column for *Country Music Magazine* once," says Hazel Smith, "and she called me up and was madder 'n a wet hen. 'Don't you call me a hillbilly!' she said. 'I'm not a hillbilly!' Well, I told her that *I was* a proud hillbilly, and over here at Glaser, well, we're proud of it. I told her it was a compliment.")

While all this was gearing up and getting going, two blocks away in the paneled recesses of the Music Row biggies, the powers-that-be at RCA and CBS and United Artists and all the others were shaking their heads. Whatever was going on at the Glaser fortress (and at Jack Clement's JMI Records studios), it didn't take much to see that all the long hair and blue jeans and staying up all night and swearwords and hard-ass business dealing wasn't [*sic*] what country music needed. These 'billies were a bunch of malcontents. More than that, though, they were a mystery. How come Tompall Glaser—of the Glaser Brothers, a fine, doing-nicely country act—was *doing* all this?

When Tompall Glaser came to Nashville in the late 1950's, the last thing in the world he planned to be was some sort of revolutionary. He came to be a star, and, being fresh from the Nebraska outback ("I didn't even see anybody except friends and family until I was twenty-one years old"), that task didn't seem so incredibly hard. After all, the exact same story was being acted out in Nashville every day—step off at the bus station one day, step into the Grand Ole Opry the next. And all the greats were still there, still working—Roy Acuff, Hank Snow, Lefty

---

5. "Dolby A," introduced by Dolby Laboratories in 1965, was designed to reduce extraneous noise in tape recordings (Doris Kilbane, "Ray Dolby: A Breaker of Sound Barriers," *Electronic Design* 53, no. 23 [20 October 2005], 84; "Dolby History," http://www.dolby.com/us/en/about-us/who-we-are/dolby-history/index.html; accessed 27 January 2012).

Frizzell, Eddy Arnold, Ernest Tubb, all reminders that the end of the rainbow was still very definitely there for the taking.

For a while it seemed that the sky was the limit. Within a few hard years, the Glaser Brothers—Tompall, Jim and Chuck—were one of the hottest groups in country music, the first group to tread that narrow line between pop and country with any consistent success. One of Tompall's early songs, "The Streets of Baltimore," had gone on to become a moderate hit for Bobby Bare, another of Nashville's new generation of singers. "They were good times," remembers Captain Midnight (otherwise known as Roger Schutt; he re-named himself after the Captain Midnight radio show).

"We both, Tompall and I, got to town about the same time, in the late Fifties," he says. "I went to work for WSM as a news writer in radio and television. The Opry used to have live shows that they did in the auditorium at the station, just down the hall from the newsroom, so I started hanging out with the hillbillies.

"I kept running into Tompall, and we'd hang out, and he has to be one of the best friends I've got. We'd keep running into each other—now, this was back when hardly anybody had offices. Everybody just roared, you know. Married hillbillies would come in off the road, and they'd just check into a hotel, you know; wouldn't even go home. Some of them would be out two or three days and wouldn't even check in at home. Everybody was hanging out at Tootsie's,[6] you know, for real. There wasn't a bunch of tourists...it was really loose. You could stay out and roar for two or three weeks, you know. Parties, very little rest."

If times were good, they were also naïve. Record production was simple and cheap—spend as little money as possible and crank the thing out. Do a couple of gigs on the Grand Ole Opry and peddle the records from the back of your bus, if you could afford a bus. Nobody was getting rich, but on the other hand, nobody was starving. Besides, there was something *funky* about being on the lunatic fringe of the music business.

Midnight continues: "It's really strange. When we first got here, the music business was like a brotherhood, you know, because everybody did hang out together and nobody did have offices and there was a certain pride. Like I say, it was like a brotherhood first of all, the city fathers couldn't give a shit less about the music industry at that time. Governor Frank Clement used to recognize the fact that there were records being made here, but that's about it. This was in the early 1960's, when being in the music business meant you paid a hundred dollars' deposit for a telephone instead of twenty-five like any other human being."

Even Wesley Rose, the head of the powerful Acuff-Rose publishing empire—they owned the incredibly lucrative rights to Hank Williams' work—was treated as if his feet were totally alien to the concept of shoes. "He used to tell about going to New York to talk business with MGM Records," says Midnight, "and the guy at the front desk would say, 'Hey, that hillbilly from Nashville's here.'"

It was right about the middle 1960's when, according to Tompall, everything started going to hell in a handbasket. Call it the rise of the Nashville Sound; call it the near-crippling effects of the birth of rock and roll; call it whatever you like—but things *changed*, and, from the vantage of people like Tompall Glaser and Captain Midnight, things changed for the worse.

6. Tootsie's Orchid Lounge, located next door to the Ryman Auditorium, home of the *Grand Ole Opry* until 1974. Because of its proximity to the *Opry*, it was a popular hangout for people involved in the Nashville music scene.

"Everybody got into this business thing," says Midnight, still sorrowful after all these years. "See, when this thing of offices started, people started when having office hours and secretaries and they started wearing coats and suits and things. They took the fun out of it, you know. You couldn't walk into somebody's office, jump up on somebody's desk, kick their fucking door in as a joke. Really took the fun out of it, 'cause they started taking that shit seriously."

The changes in country went a whole lot deeper than simply not being able to kick somebody's door in for a little recreation. Country music was becoming big business, and big business meant big money—for someone. The rock and roll scare had proved that if country was to survive, it had to be real sure of its power base—and to expand that power base if possible. A bunch of irresponsible hillbillies tuning into the Grand Ole Opry once a week doesn't translate into record sales. Crooners sell, so go with crooners. Keep the records as cheap as possible and try to get away from that "hillbilly" sound, steel guitars and stuff like that. Roy Acuff, Ernest Tubb, Hank Snow, Lefty Frizzell—scrap 'em. They're not commercial. Tompall and the Glaser Brothers—shelve 'em. They don't fit in.

There were other things, too, such as "The Streets of Baltimore" almost failing to get recorded because it talked about a country girl going to the big city, leaving her husband, and deciding—on her own—to "Walk the streets of Baltimore." *Real* country girls, Tompall was informed, would never go off and become *whores*. The same cold shoulder was waiting for John Hartford's recording of "Gentle on My Mind," a song discovered by Tompall and published by the Glaser Brothers' publishing company.[7] Filthy song:

"'Gentle on My Mind': everyone turned it down because it was too radical a song, 'cause it was about shacking up," says Tompall. He's been up for a long time now, several days, and he's getting just a little spooky around the edges. He storms around his cluttered office at Glaser Studios, turning the tape recorder off and on, playing records, playing the ukulele. He wants to go play pinball, and interviews have a way of falling apart after midnight. "But kids were shacking up. It touched a lot of chords. . . . When I wrote 'The Streets of Baltimore' in, uh, when was that?" he walks over to a framed plaque from Broadcast Music Incorporated, a songwriter's award for "The Streets of Baltimore," dated 1967. "Yea, 1967. I wrote the lyrics about what was happening to country girls then. When something becomes such an important part of society that it has its own definition and its own character, it must be faced.

"I married a woman who was a math major in college and minored in music and was a social worker from the word go. Her English textbooks used to fascinate me 'cause there she was in Memphis in college in the heart of the United Sates and in all the poetry and everything that was in that English lit book, there was nothing written by Americans. And they'd go to folk songs and shittier things that were not near as classic as some of our songs. Why don't they use real songs of the day? That people can identify with? So I always wanted to write a folk song, something that would have a relationship to a time in history.

"'The Streets of Baltimore' was written about the time that women were first realizing that they didn't have to take all that shit. In the Sixties, women were open about having babies and proud of it. A woman could actually say a lot of stuff and actually mean it. Women could actually get fucked without going to hell. So a lot of these little gals started showing up around the Grand Ole Opry, country chicks around nineteen who'd gotten married when they were

---

7. For more on "Gentle on My Mind," consult Andrew Vaughan, *Pilot of a Steam Powered Aereo-Plain* (Nashville, TN: StuffWorks Press, 2013), 42–47.

fourteen or fifteen, and now they had a little public sentiment going in their favor. And they had this poor old boy they was married to. This old boy, you could tell by looking at his hands that he'd worked his ass off, tell by his clothes that he didn't have much money left to spend on himself. And there was that little darlin' just eyeing every cowboy that came through."

When the point finally sank in, it was like swallowing a mouthful of castor oil. There were two things that Nashville didn't want any more: controversy and hillbillies. Controversy didn't sell to the middle-of-the-road market, and hillbillies were just plain embarrassing. If you like *country* country music, says Tompall, you were automatically provided with someone to harass and degrade you. It simply didn't matter that the previous year you and your brothers had been named the top vocal group in country music by the Country Music Association, or that your song, "Gentle on My Mind," had made a star out of an unknown called Glen Campbell and a cult hero of that guy who hung around all the time, John Hartford, and had then gone on to become the most-recorded song in the history of BMI.[8] It didn't mean a damn that you were *right*, only that you were out of step.

"You know how many times people use their musical taste for their social status," says Tompall. "For a long time, people who really like country music never had a socially sophisticated reason to. And there were some, when the old originals came along, there was a certain amount of pride in a hillbilly or a cowboy or a farmer living their own life. They owned themselves, y'know. People wouldn't give up that much to do that, but they liked looking at it, and the hillbilly singer represented that type of people.

"Then, though, it got shameful: people inventing life stories to go with the trade of country music. Made me ill. I found *myself* trying to do it at one point, and that was what *really* made me ill. I thought that was what was needed, but I just never could go far enough to please them"

The idea was slow in coming, but when it finally arrived, it exploded like the dawn over Interstate 40.[9] All right, goddamit, if the money men won't deal with an artist, Tompall reasoned, maybe they'll deal with a fellow *businessman*. It was one of those painfully simple ideas that tolled the end of an era.

"You didn't know what the hell went on," Tompall told interviewer Nelson Allen in 1976. "They wouldn't talk to the artist. They didn't have to. The artist didn't run the business. When independent productions got into it, it allowed me to form my own production company, so when I called a record company and said I was from Glaser Productions, I was the president, and I could talk to the president, but I could talk to nothing before that as an artist. I said, 'This is the fucking way to do it.' It's the same cowboy now, but I could say, 'I am the president of Glaser Productions and I am representing Tompall Glaser.' Then we could start talking money. Then I would just read rock magazines and get all those figures that they were giving all those unheard of rock stars they had. I just kept raising the ante and not signing a contract and they just kept getting more and more nervous."

The image would be ludicrous if it wasn't so painfully true—Tompall Glaser poring over *Rolling Stone*, trying to figure out how much he could get away with asking for the next

8. Broadcast Music, Inc., a performing rights organization that collects songwriting royalties.
9. Interstate 40, which connects Wilmington, North Carolina, and Barstow, California, runs through Nashville.

morning at negotiations. The amazing thing to Tompall was just exactly how much different [sic] being "the President" really did make.

"That was when I first began to know the power of business," he says, getting fired up on a subject that remains very near and dear to his heart. "I'd walk in to talk to people…went home, formed a production company, incorporated it, called myself president and went back and talked to the *same* motherfucker and got another $100,000. I thought, 'Whattaya mean? So *that's* what we've been missing.'

"Managers and people have been taking advantage of the hillbillies and the hillbilly music fans. There's been a lot of rip-offs going on. Imagine taking Hank Snow's and Lefty Frizzell's bands away from them when they recorded. Christ! They quit programming Ernest Tubb, so they made him obsolete. They put him on the scrap-pile before he died. But he's not obsolete. There's a market for him. See, this Outlaw thing turns a complete circle. Hillbillies thought we were leaving country music, but the plan was to bring it back to where it was. As I said in that song, bring it all back home. That's what it was."

The other thing that the businessman Tompall discovered, something that the artist Tompall had been seeking for years without success, was that a businessman can negotiate what no artist could demand—complete artistic freedom. The businessman Tompall, the more he played the game, discovered some literally amazing facts: Rather than accept a company producer—the sure path to stagnation—he could stipulate just who the producer would be. "Sign as a production company," says Tompall, "then you have to pay the producer, and you produce yourself." He laughs. "Then you put in your agreement that *you* get to choose the material that is released. They can't make me put *nothin'* out."

From this delightful subject, Tompall proceeds to musical philosophy. "Country music is very close to the people who listen to it," he says, "and they need to hear the sincerity and the reality of it. A man can only create music like that by taking the time to make it. It changes your attitude when you start shelling out four songs in three hours, then taking the money and putting it in your pocket. The label gave you the money to make records, and you shouldn't just cut the shit fast and put it out. Well, there's no reason why country music can't be just as big a music as rock was. I mean, there's as much opportunity, as much freedom for creating, and it's on an earthier level. Why should we take a back seat? I've asked myself that question a million times, and the answer is that we shouldn't. But the first thing we've got to do is make great records."

It started out a tiny germ of an idea, just a hint that there might be a different way, and that's very important to a farm boy like Tompall Glaser who came to town to be a star and found, in his own words, "all this shit." It is important to have a better way, because, again in his own words, "if you haven't got an alternative, then shut the fuck up." Nine years ago, he and his brothers built Glaser Studios. It took him a while, he says, to figure out that he was right and everybody else was wrong, but once it clicked there was no stopping him. Tompall is one *determined* hillbilly.

Of all the people labeled "Outlaws," Tompall fits the bill better than most. On one front, his name around Nashville is synonymous with the word "asshole"—and a hard-nosed asshole at that; a man who, when the chips are down, will not give an inch; a mean little man with crafty, shifty eyes, who gets nasty around strangers (especially journalists—on our first meeting, he suggested that I not come around again. The second time, he threw me out of the studio). He blusters and postures, stays up for days and is incapable of leaving any pinball machine unplayed ("It's a kick. Really a kick. Lights flashing, and things move. It seems like you're really doing something important—until you crash"). On another front, just when you think there's nothing there but this guy who keeps tossing you out of the studio, you discover that he had extra platinum records made up for everyone in his office after he and Waylon's and Willie's *Wanted: The Outlaws!* [sic] album became the biggest seller in country music's history. He's the guy who, when Hazel Smith had a car wreck an hour outside of Nashville at three in the morning, hopped into his Lincoln, picked her up and proceeded to make her so mad at him that she snapped out of shock, then laughed. During our last interview, Tompall spent several hours of his time in the studio mixing a Lone Star Beer commercial for an up-and-coming singer, then offered to have *his* band come in and overdub the instrumental tracks—and then refused to log the time in the studio book. No charge. And every so often, in between the posturing and the lecturing and the blustering and all the necessary hype that surrounds any recording star—and Tompall Glaser is a star—there are these strange flashes of a genuinely nice guy; a gruff cowboy with a heart of gold, a man who chose to stay and fight the System and, surprisingly enough, won—and paid a price for that victory.

With this kind of approach to life and music and this kind of setup in the heart of Music City, it was inevitable that Tompall would eventually attract the attention of a similarly inclined cowboy, Waylon Jennings. Nashville just wasn't big enough to keep those two apart. The only catch was that at first they both thought (as they do now) that they hated each other. But Captain Midnight figured that deep down Waylon and Tompall had a lot more in common than they were willing to admit, and so he kept chipping away. Any two people so totally obsessed with pinball, he figured, couldn't remain enemies for too long. Midnight was right, and pretty soon you could hang around places like the Burger Boy and J.J.'s and watch the boys in action together—sweaty hair hanging in matted strings, dirty jeans and black leather vests over what may or may not have once been white shirts, silver-banded cowboy hats, fists smashing those gambling machines (and not them sissy things that only pay off in a bunch of numbers and maybe some good feeling, either, but the real thing, the ones that pay off in *money*).

"I wasn't there when this happened," says Hazel Smith, "but I remember hearing both of them tell it. Both of them—Waylon and Tompall—were playing pinball one night and were discussing how to record a certain song. It was, like, ten p.m. and on the spur of the moment, they quit playing pinball, got pickers in, had them there by midnight and Waylon started recording. Tompall helped him produce that album, I believe, *Honkytonk Heroes* [sic]."

It was the pinball machines that did it, Tompall remembers.

"I got stoned once playing those things, and I said to Waylon, 'Ain't no reason you can't do "Loving Her Was Easier" right now.' I went over to the phone and put a dime in and set it up. We went over and did the session, and he'd never touched the red button before. They wouldn't let him produce before. He said, 'That's nice. That's awfully nice. Just pick up the phone and call a session.' And it didn't cost near as much to produce yourself. They take a percentage of everything. They keep about five artists hot and the other forty-seven cheap. So I said, 'I'm gonna get the fuck out of this; I ain't gonna be just filling a shelf. I ain't good enough to be terribly big anyway, but that ain't what I want. I just want to be terribly good.' So Waylon wanted to fight 'em too. So Chuck and Jim [the other Glaser brothers] and I were in business, so I said, 'Well, Waylon, you're gonna have to hang around.'"

Waylon did hang around, uprooting other Hillbilly Central characters until he had carved out his own little niche in the stucco fortress on 19th Avenue South. He and Tompall became workmates, playmates, and brothers.

"Waylon had given Tompall an Ovation guitar," remembers Hazel Smith, drawing from her reservoir of Waylon/Tompall stories. "Well, Waylon had a Cadillac and Tompall had just bought a new Lincoln Continental Mark IV. Waylon is not the most coordinated person in the world, not the best driver. He's a wonderful guy and I love him, but he did go out and get in the car, and promptly backed into Tompall's Mark IV—brand new. Waylon walked back in the building and said, 'Tompall, who's the best friend you've got in the world?' Tompall said, 'You are, Waylon.' He said, 'Tompall, who just gave you a brand new Ovation guitar?' Tompall said, 'You did, Waylon.' And he said, 'Tompall, who just backed into your new Mark IV?' And Tompall said, 'You son of a bitch.' That's a true story."

Then there was the time, shortly after Waylon moved in, when he walked into the door. It seems that Tompall put up an extra door to give Waylon more privacy, but what it actually did was block Waylon's original door from opening all the way. That was no big problem, Midnight remembers, except that Waylon was in the habit of jumping up and running out the door. The first time he tried, he ran smack into the partially open door, triggering a string of profanity that melted candles for blocks and confirmed beyond a shadow of a doubt the horror stories of the legendary Jennings temper. The second time he jumped up and smashed into the door, he didn't say a thing. He stalked through the studio, gathered up a hammer, a hacksaw and big knife, and headed back to the door. After a few tentative licks with the saw, it became painfully obvious that the door just wasn't going to *respond* the way Waylon had in mind, so he took the big knife (actually a sharpened tire tool, a gift to Midnight from Donnie Fritts after his trip to Mexico to film *Bring Me the Head of Alfredo Garcia*[10] with buddy Kristofferson) and began whacking away on the door, venting his rage like some berserk woodsman. When he was finished—and everyone else in the studio was suitably terrified—Waylon took the door to Tompall's office, where he proceeded to nail it over the only functioning window in Glaser Studios. It's still there, and the whole incident is referred to as When Waylon Chopped Up the Door.

Then there was the pinball—those pinball machines were a constant temptation, especially when the damn things weren't where they were supposed to be.

"One night they was playing this pinball machine over at the Burger Boy in the back room, and when I walked in I never thought a thing about it, because the office at Glaser were always in an uproar," says Hazel. "Well, the pinball machine was in the middle of the floor and Tompall was playing it and they were having a good time and Captain Midnight was there. In a little while the gentleman who owned the pinball machine had been called, and he was pissed off. What had happened was that Tompall had moved the pinball machine from the front of the Burger Boy through this long, slender hall, then turned it around and moved it up the steps into the back room, because he wanted to play pinball in the room with Waylon and Captain Midnight. It was his favorite machine, and he had knocked the roof out of the room and broke the glass on the machine. It cost him, oh, I don't know, several hundred dollars getting that repaired. But that was about the biggest *outlaw* thing they ever did."

Naturally enough, stories like this circulated around Nashville very quickly, and soon an image had formed. These boys, it seemed, really *were* outlaws—weirdo dope-smoking cussing swearing lunatic pinball-crazy *outlaws*. One day the boys were "cowboys" or "assholes," the

10. *Bring Me the Head of Alfredo Garcia*, dir. Sam Peckinpah (Estudios Churubosco Azteca S.A., Optimus Films, 1974) ("Bring Me the Head of Alfredo Garcia," http://www.imdb.com/title/tt0071249/; accessed 26 January 2012).

next day they were all-number-one, solid-gold-soul "Outlaws." From friends it became a term of endearment; from enemies, a curse. In either case, it was a handy way of explaining almost anything. Tompall been up all night playing pinball? What do you expect—he's an outlaw. Waylon been knocking down doors? Outlaws again. Tompall and Waylon cut a song nobody in their right mind would touch? That's Outlaw music. Outlaw Chic had arrived. Cowboy hats and boots began springing up around Nashville like mushrooms after a spring rain, and one critic described the "new" Nashville as "Dodge City East." Swapping Waylon 'n Tompall stories became a favorite pastime, and the more hip you were, the closer to the flame you could claim to be. If you were *really* hip, you could actually be an eyewitness.

At first, the Outlaws' reaction to their new name was mixed. Waylon was less than enthusiastic when Hazel, after her talk with the North Carolina disc jockey, told him. When she told Tompall, though, something clicked. He didn't like labels, but he could put up with one if it helped him make a point. If being the "President of Glaser Productions, Inc." helped him in his dealings with the money men, maybe being an Outlaw would help him deal with the burgeoning new young audience, a goal he had long cherished. Wait, he cautioned Waylon, and just remember that a label means only as much as you want it to mean—and *this* label might help us both make a million dollars. Tompall, of course, was right. It worked. Waylon and Tompall together were *contenders*, and these hillbillies weren't uneducated and dumb anymore. Under Tompall's business tutelage, he and Waylon's publishing company, Baron Music, went from a bunch of songs in a shoebox to a million-dollar concern, easily the hottest of Nashville's heavily competitive publishing houses. In the loose atmosphere of Glaser Studios, Waylon's music flourished as it never had before, and suddenly Waylon Jennings was the star everyone thought he should be. And Tompall, who idolized Waylon, stood by like a proud father.

"When the [brothers] group broke up, I needed a brother and I went with Waylon," Tompall said in 1976. "We're fighting now and I don't know if we'll stay together, but that doesn't matter. We did a little thing together. We're both individuals and it works out that way. We had a good shot, but the point that I wanted to prove was that a unit of people working together, banding together, can show strength. Waylon and I together had twice the strength that we had as individuals. Maybe twenty times. People who wouldn't listen to him before suddenly listened to him. He could back it up legally. He had an ally."

The relationship between Tompall and Waylon had its problems, both internal and external, but Tompall fought to keep it together. Twice he refused to leave Nashville—once when Waylon suggested moving to Austin, Texas, and closing ranks with Willie Nelson, who seemed to be on the verge of forming a music empire to rival Nashville, and once when Tompall's record company was suggesting a move to Los Angeles for a clearer shot at the "pop" market. Damn it, Tompall told them (and Waylon), the fight isn't in Austin and it isn't in Los Angeles. It's right here in Nashville, right here two blocks away from Music Row, and if we win—and if our winning is ever going to amount to anything in the long run—we've got to beat them on their own turf.

"A good decision is like a good song. It's perfected simplicity," says Tompall. "There was a long list of guys who wished something could be done [about Nashville]. Willie was very important to this thing that Waylon and I did because Willie even made the old purist Nashvillians ashamed of themselves that he would walk away. He didn't walk away in violence, and he wasn't run out—he just shucked it all. And it made it look to everybody else, as it did to me, that the great illusion that everybody's been trying to sell in the music world, in country music...Willie Nelson found out it wasn't worth it. It just diminished the importance of it so much that what Waylon and I did worked."

Tompall Glaser still has a dream, and Tompall Glaser loves Nashville and country music almost more than life itself. It's a dream he articulates often, and towards which much of his life is geared.

"I want to walk down the street someday and see young people coming here, writing good songs, proud to be here again," he says, once again storming around his cluttered offices. "See, when I first came here, a lot of people were proud to be here. It was a good feeling. It gave you pride. You didn't give a shit whether the rest of the world liked you or not. And we were the underdogs and the niggers of the music business. Our music was the least respected of popular music, but we had our pride among ourselves. It was like a family suddenly going sour, and I want to have that same pride again. The public can sense—an individual can sense—when something is real and when it isn't. The people know.

"When we started, people thought we were going to destroy Nashville. Who wants to destroy Nashville? It's a long way from my mind. But if a guy can't offer a good, decent alternative, he should shut the fuck up. But if he's got a good, decent alternative, all he's got to do is keep doing it, and pretty soon the whole fucking industry will be doing it, because there are too few people in this town that know what the fuck to do. Because they don't love it; they're doing it for the fucking salary. Professional vice-presidents, that's what I mean."

Working with Waylon had an even greater benefit for Tompall—the benefit of Waylon's musicianship, of Waylon's ear. Since the breakup of the Glaser Brothers, Tompall had been driven to perform again, to prove to the music community that he was more than just a businessman who happened to put out a couple of records every now and then. But Tompall's vision went beyond just becoming another Nashville singer-songwriter. He was searching for that elusive fusion of blues and country, a fusion that has provided the central theme for popular music in the South for most of this century. He didn't see himself as another Elvis, singing bluegrass songs with a bluesman's shout, nor did he see himself as a white Ray Charles, crooning country ballads in his own distinct vocal style, a deep, whiskey-flavored baritone drawl. Tompall's voice was unique, but it was not strong; it should be used as one element in a musical package—and that package, he realized, would just *have* to be a new step in the marriage of blues and country. That's what he really wanted to do. What he needed was a *band*.

All this was running around in his mind one night in Atlanta when he dropped in to catch a show by Bobby Blue Bland, one of the finest interpreters of the blues, and was knocked flat by Bland's firebrand guitarist, Mel Brown. The huge Mississippian utterly dominated the stage, twisting licks out of his guitar that Tompall had heard in his mind—and nowhere else—for years. This, then[,] was the connection he needed in order to take a people's music like country and blend it with a people's music like blues and see what comes out. After the show, he went backstage, told Mel Brown what he had in mind, and suggested that the next time he was in Nashville he should head straight for Glaser Studios. Mel was surprised, but interested. Definitely interested.

"Then Mel came to town," Tompall says. This is his favorite part of the story. "I'd met him three years before, and I'd asked him for an autograph. I told him that if he was ever in Nashville to look me up. Two years later he was there. He called me and said, 'Still want to cut that album?' I said, 'Yea, let's go.'"

For Nashville, it was revolutionary. Elvis had made it all right for a white singer to sound like a black singer, and Charley Pride had made the reverse true. But a living, breathing blues guitarist—a living, breathing, *black* blues guitarist who brought along Bobby Blue Bland's drummer, also black—that was something to set the country club atwitter. What *would* these Outlaws do next?

Tompall's vision had come true. The arrival of Mel Brown and Charles Polk provided the nucleus of his hillbilly blues band, and to this hard core he added Ted Reynolds on bass, Ben Keith on steel ("I knew he was the best steel player alive, but I didn't know if he'd ever come back to Nashville"), Red Young on keyboards, and Fred Newell on electric guitar. The results were spectacular. The music was tight, and it was *intense*, more like the music made in Memphis and Fort Worth bars than on the stage of the Grand Ole Opry. It was a new step in people's music, and it was very good indeed.

"It just made good sense," Mel Brown told interviewer Frye Gaillard before one of the band's first shows in Atlanta. "The roots, you know, are the same—hard times on both sides. It's just that he [Tompall] is the only cat with nerve enough to do it this way. Instead of a white cat playing the blues licks, he has me and Charles."

"That's the band, boy, and it is great," says Tompall. "They dress like who they are. I dress like who I am. We each try to play our natures, and I believe that's how the sound is going to be. A natural blend of the people who helped create rhythm and blues, who helped create country music, and some great contemporary musicians. That's why you feel a little influence of jazz, a little feel of gospel, a little bit of blues."

A good example of this kind of music is "Put Another Log on the Fire," which was written by Shel Silverstein and recorded by Tompall (and was, incidentally, MGM Records' best-selling country single of 1976 with no promotion on their part).... "That song is more fun every time you do it," says Tompall, "and it always will be. I let the band clown around and *I* keep it straight. It's always fun. It's a fun song. It's not a dumb song. It's a delicately intellectual song. Dumb-ass people misread it completely and intellectuals won't touch it with a ten-foot pole."

This leads him, once again, into musical philosophy. "Progressive jazz,[11] for instance, is only *appreciated*," he says. "It doesn't give you goosebumps. In order to get goosebumps, you've got to strike a basic chord."

This, in turn, leads him back to himself, and a very important Tompall statement: "Most people are afraid to try to make a living at what they love because they think that life must be rottener than that, but I wasn't educated. I was from so far back in the sticks that I didn't know I couldn't make it. I still don't. And I hear things, and I want it right, and I won't settle for anything else."

This is the philosophy—or just the plain fact of life—which created Hillbilly Central, and it was the lack of such a philosophy that created the Nashville Sound, a fluke which turned into a system. Groups (like the Glaser Brothers) which were ready to evolve were not allowed to—and when music is not moving forward, it begins to slide back. Thanks to Tompall and

---

11.   It is difficult to discern if Glaser is describing what most scholars and critics would identify as progressive jazz—the classically influenced big bands of the 1940s and 1950s—or, more likely, "modern jazz" (Max Harrison, "Progressive Jazz," in *The New Grove Dictionary of Jazz*, 2nd ed., ed. Barry Kernfeld, *Grove Music Online, Oxford Music Online*, http://www.oxfordmusiconline.com/subscriber/article/grove/music/J364200; accessed 27 January 2012).

his Hillbilly Central cohorts, the logjam has been broken and the music is flowing again. The beginning of the revolution is over, and the fortress on 19th Avenue South is still standing.

"That building *was* a fortress," says Hazel Smith. "It was a place where they could go hide. It was a home to them, and there were no Picassos on the wall. I remember someone once suggested that there was a black cloud over that building, but I never did really feel that. I felt like it was a building that housed a lot of love for a lot of people. Both Waylon and Tompall felt that, somehow or other, the world was against them, you know. And honestly, as far as the music establishment was concerned, they didn't have that many friends in the business. Not really, and I don't know that they do now. They were almost like hillbilly stepchildren, and, by God, that's how they were treated, too. And regardless of whether they sell pop or what the hell they sell, both of them will tell you they're hillbillies, and they are."

Late in 1976, after *The Outlaws* album had made Waylon and Tompall (and Willie Nelson) the hottest-ever properties in country music, Tompall and Waylon had a falling out. Ostensibly, it was over money, but more likely it was due to all sorts of factors rising out of the strains and stresses of stardom, the inflations and deflations of ego which happen in such situations. Neither Tompall nor Waylon is voluble on the subject, and it has become impossible, in a town which thrives on gossip and half-truths and downright lies, to discern what really happened. The result was clear enough, however: Waylon left his niche at Hillbilly Central and set up his own offices, and legal papers flew back and forth. Tompall stayed where he was, and among other things he wrote a song with the message: "And I wonder if I'll find / The cowboy heroes that I left behind / Come back, Shane." He also wrote a poem which he prefers to keep private; it is a sad, bitter poem about losing friends, about being too old to make lifelong friends all over again.

Hillbilly Central, though, continues, and Tompall still rules the roost, and the action still goes on all night. It is on one of those nights that I have my final session with him.

It is two a.m. and we have been out driving—Tompall cruising down the highway in his Lincoln, playing his ukulele and steering with his knees—and now we are back in his office with the stereo cranking out the second Tompall Glaser and The Outlaw Band album at permanent ear damage level. Tompall is almost wound down after the evening's cruising and pinball. He has been talking for about two hours, and we're both strung out to where it's all starting to make some kind of strange sense. Tompall is walking around his office, throwing tapes down, picking up his ukulele and breaking into song, picking up an out-of-tune guitar and doing his damnedest to get it into shape, playing a tape at god-awful volume to emphasize a point. He wants you to understand, see, but he's not going to be vulnerable any more. Tompall Glaser wants you to care, but if you don't, fuck you. He watches like a hawk to see if his visitors give a shit. At one point I glance casually at the tape recorder, and before I can say a word, Tompall jumps up and shuts it off. "All right!" he shouts at the top of his lungs. "So you don't want to hear the goddamned tape! I saw you looking at the machine!" Nothing I can say will convince him otherwise. He talks in bursts, sentences that never seem to be finished and thoughts that have a way of wandering all over the globe.

"Say there was a hundred different emotions that each human being could experience, and say that there were a hundred, no, a thousand different variations to each emotion. Now, see what the complication is, how difficult it is to think that you really understand somebody? And I worked that little formula out for myself because I think it describes simply and accurately why people don't understand each other. They know that we all have different emotions and that we all feel them to different degrees, and yet how many people have you met who think they got you figured out completely? And they don't pay a fucking bit of attention to you when you're trying to tell them what you feel. It sounds the same when you're telling them the truth or telling them a lie.

"It's that other thing you sense about people…you sense it from entertainers when they're on stage. You sense it from your family, your brothers and sisters. You feel compelled to love by the laws of society, but you still know the ones who like you and the ones who don't. Now, you can tell yourself that they all love you and all that horseshit like we all do, but you know which ones like you best and which ones don't.

"It's like stray dogs in a parking lot, sniffing around. They'll either fight to the death or walk up to each other, sniff around a little and go off looking for pussy.…

"Music is based upon human emotion, that's all it's based on. And human emotion is basic. It's so simple. There are a few major emotions that all of us must go through. To different degrees, of course, but we do. And those finer points are songs. A song is a reflection on a moment—a moment's reflection on a period of time, a period of heartache or joy.…"

So it goes; Tompall on music, Tompall on life, Tompall on life and music. He really *is* beginning to run out of steam now. He is sitting on a ratty old couch whose springs have seen much better days. All the blustering and posturing have gone, and he is sitting there with a dopey grin, eyes twinkling like some kind of strange combination of pirate chief and leprechaun. "Just listen," he says dreamily while his new album thunders on. "Just listen to that fucking *band*."

Source: Michael Bane, *The Outlaws: Revolution in Country Music* (New York: Country Music Magazine Press, 1978). (Used with permission of author.)

FOR FURTHER READING

Reid, Jan. *The Improbable Rise of Redneck Rock.* New ed. Austin: University of Texas Press, 2004.
Stimeling, Travis D. "Narrative, Vocal Staging and Masculinity in the 'Outlaw' Country Music of Waylon Jennings." *Popular Music* 32, no. 3 (2013): 343–58.
Streissguth, Michael. *Outlaw: Waylon, Willie, Kris, and the Renegades of Nashville.* New York: itbooks, 2013.

Rex Rutkoski

"The Pill: Should It Be Banned from Airplay?" (1975)

Since the advent of commercial country music, singers and songwriters have often addressed the political and cultural issues of the day.[1] In the early 1970s, one of the more pressing cultural issues was the women's liberation movement, a social movement that pressed for growing recognition of women's economic, political, and reproductive rights. Concurrent with the rise of what is often described as "second-wave feminism" was the marketing of the first pharmacological contraceptive: the birth control pill.[2] "The pill," as it was known, offered women the opportunity to exercise control over their reproductive health. Perhaps not surprisingly, as more and more women embraced the birth

1. Robert Van Sickel has argued that country musicians have remained largely apolitical in their songs, but such flash points of political activity highlight the genre's engagement around key issues ("A World without Citizenship: On [the Absence of] Politics and Ideology in Country Music Lyrics, 1960-2000," *Popular Music and Society* 28, no. 5 [July 2005]: 313–31).

2. For a history of the contraceptive pill, consult Lara V. Marks, *Sexual Chemistry: A History of the Contraceptive Pill* (New Haven, CT: Yale University Press, 2010).

control pill, there was also a significant backlash against the new contraceptive, as detractors suggested the pill would allow women to be promiscuous and engage in sexual intercourse outside of the confines of marriage.[3]

In 1975, honky-tonk singer Loretta Lynn, who was already well known for singing songs about outspoken women, recorded "The Pill," which presented the first-person perspective of a woman who intended to take the birth control pill to stop a life of endless pregnancy. Although her song was widely acclaimed and reached number five on the *Billboard* country singles chart,[4] many radio station owners and program directors refused to add the song to their playlists, often citing the song's challenges to conservative morality as a primary reason for their decisions. As is often the case when music is censored, however, audiences showed increasing interest in the song, granting greater exposure for Lynn and the song's message than would have been possible without efforts to censor it.[5]

In the following piece from the Pittsburgh-based *Country Music News*, contributor Rex Rutkoski reveals the key role that local publications played in determining local audience attitudes, functioning in similar ways to today's social media. *Country Music News* followed this brief piece with an extended interview in its June issue, allowing Lynn to explain her work to local audiences, noting that she had had six children and five grandchildren in her relatively short life. Although she distanced herself from the women's liberation movement, she also remarked that "the pill is the best thing that ever happened to a woman when she's having one baby after another." Furthermore, despite public criticism, Lynn noted that she had "gained fans because I've sold more copies of that record. 'The Pill' ain't hurt me a bit."[6]

═══════

YEARS after creating its initial controversy, the birth control pill, with help from Loretta Lynn, is stirring debate again.

"The Pill," credited to the authorship of Lorene Allen, Don McHan and T. D. Bayless, is the opening track of Loretta's new MCA album, "Back to the Country."

3. Susan Faludi, in her widely celebrated book *Backlash: The Undeclared War against American Women*, 15th anniversary ed. (New York: Broadway Books, 2006), has discussed the broader response to the women's liberation movement in great detail.

4. Joel Whitburn, *Top Country Singles, 1944-2001*, 5th ed. (Menomonee Falls, WI: Record Research, Inc., 2002), 206.

5. Stephanie Vander Wel discusses broader concerns about gendered representations in Lynn's career in *"I Am a Honky-Tonk Girl": Country Music, Gender, and Migration*, Ph.D. dissertation, University of California at Los Angeles, 2008, 248–50.

6. Rex Rutkoski, "Backing Pill Doesn't Mean She's a Libber," *Country Music News* 2, no. 1 (June 1975): 3.

The song is a lively number in which the singer portrays a newly liberated woman, tired of having her lifestyle cramped by a man who cheats on her, while keeping her wardrobe stocked with maternity dresses.

"This old maternity dress I've got is goin' in the garbage," the artist defiantly declares, adding, "The clothes I'm wearin' from now on, won't take up so much yardage."

In case anyone missed her message, she then explains:

"Yeah, I'm makin' up for all those years, since I've got the pill."

In the final stanza she gives her cheating lover this mock assurance:

"It's getting' dark, it's roosting time, tonight's to good to be real / And daddy, don't you worry none, 'cause mama's got the pill."

The song rapidly is moving up on the charts, picking up people on both sides of the debate as it goes along.

Some are saying "The Pill," because of its content, shouldn't be on the airwaves.

Others are maintaining that its healthy country music is keeping pace with contemporary subjects, and not taking the "if you don't talk about it, it will go away" approach.

Country Music News is interested in hearing the opinion of its readers on the matter. If would be good, also, to receive response from longtime Loretta Lynn fans.

Also, we would like to know your feelings about the move by the owner of the Midwest country radio stations (see Country Music News, Feb., 1975) to establish a review board to screen songs.

The owner, Mark Sanders, said he wants to combat "suggestiveness and obscenity which is creeping into country and western music."

Do we need someone to make a decision on song content for us, or should we be permitted to continue to have the option of turning off a radio if we aren't happy with a tune?

Write Country Music News, Suite 300, Jonnet Building, 4047 William Penn Highway, Pittsburgh, Pa. 15146.

Readers whose letters are received by March 26 will become eligible for one of three country albums to be given away. Names will be pulled out of a hat.

Source: Rex Rutkoski, "The Pill: Should It Be Banned from Airplay?" Country Music News 1, no. 10 (March 1975): 12. (Used with permission of the author.)

FOR FURTHER READING

Bufwack, Mary A., and Robert K. Oermann. Finding Her Voice: Women in Country Music, 1800-2000. Nashville, TN: Country Music Foundation Press and Vanderbilt University Press, 2003, 263–79.

Faludi, Susan. Backlash: The Undeclared War against American Women, 15th Anniversary ed. New York: Broadway Books, 2006.

Lynn, Loretta, with George Vecsey. Coal Miner's Daughter. New York: Warner Books, 1976.

34

George F. Will

"Of Pride and Country Music" (1975)

Many Americans—including the most diehard of country music fans—often perceive the genre as the exclusive domain of white artists and audiences. Yet, there is no doubt that African American musicians played key roles as backing musicians and songwriters from the earliest hillbilly recordings to the present day, albeit in roles that have been, in the words of Diane Pecknold, "hidden in the mix." The overwhelming presence of white faces on television broadcasts, album jackets, and fan publications reinforced such perceptions, drawing attention to the rare moments when black musicians stepped into the foreground as recording artists. The history of African American participation in country music is frequently told as a set of exceptions to an otherwise hard-and-fast rule: country music is and has always been exclusively white but for a small handful of figures: *Grand Ole Opry* harmonica virtuoso Deford Bailey, Nashville Sound-era singers Charley Pride and O. B. McClinton, "hick-hop" artist Cowboy Troy, and contemporary star Darius Rucker. However, such a narrative only works to obscure the genre's rich and complex racial history.[1]

1. For a more nuanced discussion of this phenomenon, consult Jeffrey T. Manuel, "The Sound of the Plain White Folk? Creating Country Music's Social Origins,"

The following essay by long-time *Washington Post* columnist George F. Will grapples with this history in light of the remarkable success experienced by Charley Pride, an African American recording artist from Sledge, Mississippi, who broke into the country charts during the height of the civil rights movement. As the American South became the focus of increasing news coverage, the idea that a black musician would embrace such a seemingly white genre—*and* enjoy success on the *Billboard* charts and the *Grand Ole Opry*—made little sense. Yet, as Will's article indicates, Pride claimed an artistic lineage that was traced back to some of the most significant contributors to the country music repertory, including such iconic figures as Hank Williams and Ernest Tubb. In so doing, Pride could allay criticism of his seeming inauthenticity by establishing himself as a logical heir to country music's legacies. Pride's embrace of country music—and the public's widespread embrace of his work—may also have served as a powerful symbol of racial tolerance for whites at a time when such symbols were increasingly important, even if, as some scholars have recently posited, his participation in the genre may have forced him into the role of "token" black and consequently absolved country music of its racist public image.[2] At the same time, Will vividly describes the racialized ways in which Pride's voice was initially received, pointing to just how pervasive such viewpoints were in the music industry and illustrating the success of the industry's early racialized marketing plans.

OVER SOUTHERN OHIO—TWA Flight 83 is at 39,000 feet, out of Washington, heading for Phoenix. The passengers are drinking little bottles of ready-made martinis, eating war surplus food, breathing canned air and listening to canned music through plastic headsets.

TWA has provided an hour of Charley Pride—that "Country Charley," hoss. He is a spectacularly successful country music singer. And he is black. And thereby hangs a tale.

When the history of our racial troubles is written, there should be a chapter on Pride. But there probably won't be, because the people who write history don't listen to country music on transistor radios hung next to lever-action 30-30s on the rifle racks of pick-up trucks.

Your basic country music audience is white, and disproportionately rural and southern. You would not think of it as a promising audience for a black man. Remember, in the 1920s and 1930s, country music lyrics contained twangy references to "niggers" and "coons."

Popular Music and Society 31, no. 4 (October 2008): 417–31; Karl Hagstrom Miller, *Segregating Sound: Inventing Folk and Pop Music in the Age of Jim Crow* (Durham, NC: Duke University Press, 2010); Diane Pecknold, "Travel with Me: Country Music, Race, and Remembrance," in *Pop When the World Falls Apart: Music in the Shadow of Doubt*, ed. Eric Weisbard (Durham, NC: Duke University Press, 202), 185–200; Diane Pecknold, ed., *Hidden in the Mix: The African American Presence in Country Music* (Durham, NC: Duke University Press, 2013); Rebecca Thomas, "There's a Whole Lot o' Color in the 'White Man's Blues': Country Music's Selective Memory and the Challenge of Identity," *Midwest Quarterly* 38 (1996): 73–89.

2. Thomas, "There's a Whole Lot o' Color in the 'White Man's Blues,'" 82.

That's the way it was when Pride was born in Sledge, Miss., in 1938, the year Marian Anderson was barred by the Daughters of the American Revolution from singing in Washington's Constitution Hall. Pride grew up liking the music of Ernest Tubbs [*sic*], Roy Acuff, Tex Ritter, Hank Williams, Eddie [*sic*] Arnold. All white.

Soon Jackie Robinson was playing second base in Brooklyn and Larry Doby was playing outfield in Cleveland, so Pride decided he'd become a ballplayer.

But just to keep his options open[,] he ordered a Silvertone guitar from Sears and practiced picking when he wasn't playing ball.

In the early 1960s[,] he was in Helena, Mont., playing semi-pro ball, working at a smelter in a zinc factory and singing in a roadhouse. He was discovered there by a man with Nashville connections. So on his way back to Montana from flanking a Florida tryout with the New York Mets, Pride stopped in Nashville for an audition.

Pride sang "Heartaches by the Number"—sang it like a good ol' boy from Mississippi and Montana, and his auditioner leaned back, bemused, and said: "O.K., now sing in your natural voice."

Pride: "What do you mean?"

Auditioner (after a pregnant pause): "Sing another song."

Pride sang "Cheating Heart" and the auditioner said: "How do they take you in Montana when they see you?" Pride: "About the way you're taking me."

Auditioner: "We're going to have to give you another name, something like George Washington W. Jones III." Pride: "Hold it. If we're going to do business [,] it will be under my real name."

Face it: The name Pride sounded uppity. And anyone familiar with country music even just a dozen years ago knew it would be easier for a black person to become a Supreme Court Justice or Secretary of Transportation than to be voted (as Pride soon was) the top male singer in country music.

But when country music businessmen heard Pride sing, they saw green, not black. He has perfect pitch when it comes to delivering the oddly cheerful country music lyrics about highways, domestic disasters, and humble origins.... He has sold and is selling umpteen jillion records, is making millions of dollars and is standard fare on the airlines.

More important, Pride is big with the listeners of radio station WWVA, Wheeling, W.VA. [*sic*]—the men knocking back cans of Iron City Beer before trucking to Richmond and points south.

If the country music audience is becoming color-blind, the country cannot be far behind.

Source: George F. Will, "Of Pride and Country Music," *Washington Post*, 2 May 1975, p. A23. (Used with permission.)

FOR FURTHER READING

Pecknold, Diane, ed. *Hidden in the Mix: The African American Presence in Country Music*. Durham, NC: Duke University Press, 2013.

Pecknold, Diane. "Travel with Me: Country Music, Race, and Remembrance." In *Pop When the World Falls Apart: Music in the Shadow of Doubt*, ed. Eric Weisbard, 185–200. Durham, NC: Duke University Press, 2012.

Thomas, Rebecca. "There's a Whole Lot o' Color in the 'White Man's Blues': Country Music's Selective Memory and the Challenge of Identity." *Midwest Quarterly* 38 (1996): 73–89.

Aaron Latham

"The Ballad of the Urban Cowboy: America's Search for True Grit" (1978)

Dance hall culture has been an essential part of working-class Texas life since the middle of the nineteenth century, when German and Czech immigrants began to construct large buildings to host community dances and other social gatherings, and continues well to the present day, as honky-tonk, western swing, and conjunto bands accompany the shuffling and spinning of dancers every weekend.[1] Similarly, the Cajun country of Louisiana, which borders East Texas, also boasts a long-held tradition of social dancing in community dance halls and providing a venue for local Cajun, zydeco, and western swing musicians to ply their wares.[2] Not surprisingly, then, the Houston area, which is situated in

1. Gail Folkins, *Texas Dance Halls: A Two-Step Circuit* (Lubbock: Texas Tech University Press, 2007).

2. Malcolm L. Comeaux, "The Cajun Dancehall," in *Accordions, Fiddles, Two Step & Swing: A Cajun Music Reader*, ed. Ryan A. Brasseaux and Kevin S. Fontenot (Lafayette: Center for Louisiana Studies, 2006), 139–51. For a general history of Cajun music, consult Ryan André Brasseaux, *Cajun Breakdown: The Emergence of an American-Made Music* (New York: Oxford University Press, 2009).

the heart of dance hall territory, has been an important center for dancers and musicians since the middle of the twentieth century.[3]

By the late 1970s, Houston was undergoing rapid change. The petrochemical industry, which had been a key part of the Houston economy since World War II, was expanding, drawing more and more workers to the city to support refineries, chemical plants, and offshore drilling operations.[4] The vast majority of these workers came from working-class backgrounds, and not surprisingly, many of them sought out dancing, drinks, and women in local bars and dance halls. Located just outside of Houston in the town of Pasadena, Gilley's, a club owned by country music luminary Mickey Gilley, provided the ideal venue for dancing with a large dance floor, top-notch country music, and, in a nod to the modernization of cowboy culture, a mechanical bull that allowed men to demonstrate their physical strength and women to put on sensuous displays.

Journalist Aaron Latham, writing for *Esquire* magazine, documented life at Gilley's through the troubled romance of two patrons, Dew Westbrook and his partner, Betty. Dew and Betty's relationship unfolds at Gilley's, reenacting the lives of such common honky-tonk characters as the emotionally distant man and the flirtatious and habitually jealous honky-tonk angel. Calling Dew an "urban cowboy," Latham points to what many observers deemed to be a masculinity crisis faced by working-class white men in the face of the increasing mechanization and technologization of American industry, as well as the challenges to patriarchal values put forward by the ongoing women's liberation movement. Gilley's here becomes, in a sense, both an authentic Texas dance hall and a poor modern substitute for the real thing. Latham's story took on even greater significance when, in 1980, John Travolta and Debra Winger starred in a feature film based on the article, *Urban Cowboy*, and the successful double-album soundtrack featuring the modern country sounds of Mickey Gilley, Johnny Lee, and Charlie Daniels, among others, led to the establishment of *Urban Cowboy*-style dance halls all across the United States.[5]

DEW Westbrook is a big-city cowboy. The range he rides is a Houston honky-tonk saloon called Gilley's, which is as big as a ranch inside. The animal that carries him is a bucking bull. He straddles this dangerous beat right there in the saloon's south forty where the landscape is dotted with long necked beer bottles (in place of sagebrush) and verdant pool tables (in place of pastures). The bull is mechanized, but it bucks as hard as a real one, breaking an occasional arm, leg, or collarbone. Sometimes it crushes something worse. A honky-tonk cowboy has to risk his manhood in order to prove it.

3. For but one example of Houston's musical significance, consult Andy Bradley and Roger Wood, *House of Hits: The Story of Houston's Gold Star/SugarHill Recording Studios* (Austin: University of Texas Press, 2010).

4. Much of the history of Houston's development as a petrochemical and shipping center is discussed in Martin V. Melosi and Joseph A. Pratt, eds., *Energy Metropolis: An Environmental History of Houston and the Gulf Coast* (Pittsburgh: University of Pittsburgh Press, 2007).

5. For more detailed analysis, consult chapter 5 of Jason Mellard, *Progressive Country: How the 1970s Transformed the Texan in Popular Culture* (Austin: University of Texas Press, 2013).

Dew, the beer joint bull rider, is as uncertain about where his life is going as America is confused about where it wants to go. And when America is confused, it turns to its most durable myth: the cowboy. As the country grows more and more complex, it seems to need simpler and simpler values: something like the Cowboy Code.[6] According to this code, a cowboy is independent, self-reliant, brave, strong, direct, and open. All of which he can demonstrate by dancing the cotton-eyed Joe with the cowgirls, punching the punching bag, and riding the bull at Gilley's. In these anxious days, some Americans have turned for salvation to God, others have turned to fad prophets, but more and more people are turning to the cowboy hat. Dew paid $35 for his on sale.

One way the Cowboy Code is transmitted to the new urban cowboy is through country-and-western music. How Dew sees his world is shaped by the songs he hears on the radio and the lyrics sung by the band at Gilley's. Country music is the city cowboy's Bible, his literature, his self-help book, his culture. It tells him how to live and what to expect.

Actually, the life story of Dew, the urban cowboy, sounds as if it should be set to twangy music and sung as a country-and-western ballad. Dew met Betty at Gilley's, *twang-twang*. They had their wedding reception at Gilley's, *twang-twang*. But they quarreled over the bull at Gilley's, *twang-twang*. And then Dew met somebody new at Gilley's, *twaaaang*.

A few months after the breakup. I made a date to go to Gilley's with Dew and his new girl friend. I know his ex-wife would be there too. When the three of them met at the bullring, it might be like Frankie and Johnny.

HONKY-TONK SATURDAY NIGHT

Before we could go to Gilley's, Dew had to change clothes. He had curly hair the color of the beach at Galveston, worn a little long for a cowboy. His nose had a slight bump in it like a bull's back. And he had pale-blue eyes that squinted. He was a good-looking cowboy who had had a hard un-cowboy day.

"The foam glass is eating me up," Dew complained. "It'll take the hide off you real quick."

---

6. Discussions of the cowboy code and its persistence in country music culture can be found in Michael Allen, "'I Just Want to Be a Cosmic Cowboy': Hippies, Cowboy Code, and the Culture of a Counterculture," *Western Historical Quarterly* 36, no. 3 (Autumn 2005): 275–99.

For more discussion of the competing uses of cowboy iconography during the 1970s and early 1980s, consult Archie Green, "Austin's Cosmic Cowboys: Words in Collision," in *"And Other Neighborly Names": Social Process and Cultural Image in Texas Folklore*, ed. Richard Bauman and Roger Abrahams, repr. in Archie Green, *Torching the Fink Books & Other Essays on Vernacular Culture* (Chapel Hill: University of North Carolina Press, 2001), 68–73; Barry Shank, *Dissonant Identities: The Rock 'n' Roll Scene in Austin, Texas* (Middletown, CT: Wesleyan University Press/University Press of New England, 1994); Travis D. Stimeling, *Cosmic Cowboys and New Hicks: The Countercultural Sounds of Austin's Progressive Country Music Scene* (New York: Oxford University Press, 2011); Jason Mellard, *Progressive Country*; Cory Lock, "Counterculture Cowboys: Progressive Texas Country of the 1970s & 1980s," *Journal of Texas Music History* 3, no. 1 (Spring 2003): 14–23.

Dew, who works six days a week, had spent his Saturday sawing foam glass, a form of insulation, with a saw at Texas City Refining. All of the maze of pipes and towers at the refinery needed insulation. At twenty-two, Dew has already spent over three years insulating petrochemical plants. It is hard, boring work. All assholes and elbows, as he puts it.

After work, the big-city cowboy had come home to his covered wagon: a mobile home. He lives in a trailer park that is built in a circle, so at dusk all the mobile homes really do look a little like a wagon train circled up for the night.

"I'll just be a minute," Dew said.

He was ready to turn into an urban cowboy. He exchanged his hard hat for a black felt cowboy hat with toothpicks stuck in the band and his name spelled out in small gold letters stuck in the back. (No country cowboy ever decorated his hat with gilt lettering.) He traded dirty bell-bottom blue jeans for clean bell-bottom blue jeans that had just been ironed. (No country cowboy ever wore anything but unironed, straight-legged jeans.) Then he swapped his work sneakers for cowboy boots with a flat, rubber heel designed for a range made up mostly of asphalt, sidewalks, and linoleum. (No country cowboy ever wore anything but high, pointed, leather heels designed to let a cowboy dig in his heels if he roped something mean.) And his workingman's T-shirt was replaced by a cowboy shirt with mother-of-pearl snaps and short sleeves. (If a country cowboy wore short sleeves, his arms would be scratched off the first time he passed a mesquite tree.) Now the urban cowboy was ready to mount his pickup truck and ride forth to Gilley's in search of adventure. He had his armor on. The cowboy has always been America's knight-errant. During the Middle Ages, dressing a knight in his armor was a solemnly important ritual. The dressing of the urban cowboy is no less so.

When a city cowboy dons his cowboy clothes, he dons more than garments. He dons cowboy values. These values evolved among people who lived fifty miles apart. While they were away from everyone else, they *had* to be independent and self-reliant. And when these people did occasionally see one another, they could not afford to waste time being anything but open and direct. And now these values, forged by people who lived too far apart, are serving people who live too close together.

When Dew puts on his cowboy hat, it temporarily drives from his head the memory of his job at the refinery. When he pulls on his cowboy boots, he can temporarily forget that he is a member of insulators union local 22 which ties him to the city that he is always saying he is going to leave. His life is divided into hard hat days and cowboy hat nights. It is a way of coping. It may sound crazy, but it works. Or, as the band down at Gilley's sings....[7]

On the way to Gilley's, Dew drove his orange-and-white pickup fast and loose. He made it buck. Beside Dew on the pickup seat sat Jan Day, twenty-four, with whom he has lived ever since he broke up with his wife, *twang-twang*. Auburn-haired Jan possessed a porcelain beauty that made men want to save her from breaking. She was so fragile, in fact, that she sometimes fainted at Gilley's, which is no place for the porcelain hearted. She wore cowboy boots, flared jeans, and a transparent top with nothing underneath. (No cowboy cowgirl could afford to let her breasts roam free as doggies.)

---

7. Excerpt from Waylon Jennings's "I've Always Been Crazy," redacted for copyright reasons.

"I'd never go to the Nesadel," Dew said of a joint down the road from Gilley's. "It's a rock place. A different set goes there. Sometimes there's tension between the two groups. I'd never go in the Nesadel without twenty ol' cowboys to back me up."

From the road, Gilley's Club looks like a little old shack. But when you walk through the door, you see that it is a great deal more. It's just a honky-tonk, but it looks about as big as the MGM Grand Hotel or St. Patrick's Cathedral. It has about forty pool tables which makes it roughly equal to forty bars under one roof. On a busy night, this capital of the urban-cowboy culture has a population greater than most state capitals had during the heyday of the Old West. When Willie Nelson played Gilley's, 4,500 people crowded inside.

On our way to the dance floor, we passed a gang of downtown cowboys gathered to pay a quarter to smash the punching bag just to prove how hard they could hit. A dial measured the force of each punch. If the honky-tonk cowpokes slugged hard enough, a siren went off. And most of them did hit hard enough. That part of Gilley's sounded like a firehouse. When the saloon cowgirls are watching, the saloon cowboys often hit the bag until their hands bleed and their knuckles break. At the end of an evening, there is often blood on the bag.

Jan and Dew tried to teach me how to dance the cotton-eyed Joe. You make a line and kick a lot. And every time you kick you yell: "Bullshit! Bullshit!" It is a perfect shit kickers' dance.

Then everyone danced the Shotess, which was followed by a crow's step, which was followed by a polka, which was followed by the whip. All the cowboys danced with their hats on. When they danced slowly, the cowgirls hooked the cowboys' belt loops with the fingers of their left hands. And the cowboys held onto the cowgirls' hair with their right hands.

When the band took a break, everyone headed for the bullring. It costs two dollars to ride the bull, and you have to sign a waiver saying you won't sue no matter how bad you get hurt. A cowboy on the sidelines runs the bull by remote control, making it buck according to his whim. One cowboy got so good at running the bull that he claimed he could throw off a cowboy's hat, turn the cowboy around, and then throw him on his hat.

Dew, who hadn't ridden the bull for some time, was apprehensive. He had brought two ace bandages from home. He used one to wrap his right knee and the other to saddle his left wrist. Then he pulled a bull-riding glove onto his left hand.

"Why do you ride left-handed?" I asked. "I thought you were right-handed."

"I am," Dew said, "but that's what I make my living with." He held up his right first. "I'm crazy to ride, but I'm smart."

He placed his cowboy hat on a chair in front of Jan like a votive offering. Then he climbed aboard the big, bad bull.

As the bull started to buck and spin, Jan took in a deep breath and looked worried. As I scanned the bullring, I noticed another intent face. It belonged to Betty, Dew's ex-wife. I knew she was still in love with the bull rider, *twang-twang*.

BETTY AND EDDIE WERE LOVERS

Dew's real name is Donald Edward Westbrook. The cowboys at Gilley's made a nickname out of his initials. Everybody at Gilley's has a nickname. There's Gaiter and the Hippie and Armadillo.... But Dew's family calls him Eddie. One night a couple of years ago, Eddie met Betty Jo Helmer at Gilley's. At the time, he was nineteen and she was eighteen. Betty and Eddie like each other right away. It seemed like destiny. After all, their names rhymed the way the names of lovers in a good country song should. At the time, it didn't occur to them that all country songs have unhappy endings.

On that first night, Betty came to Gilley's with her girl friends. She wore pants, not having worn or even owned a dress for years. She had a turned-up nose, an adolescent pout, and long brown hair. She wasn't quite beautiful, but she was as cute as a picture on a T-shirt. Dew came up and asked her to dance. She accepted.

"Now you're stuck with him," one of her girl friends said.

But that was all fine with Betty. She had been watching him dance, and she liked what she saw. An urban cowboy doesn't have to know how to brand or rope or hog tie or bull-dog…but he does have to know how to dance. Eddie took hold of Betty's hair, and she hooked her finger through his belt loop. They danced until closing time as the band sang good old honky-tonk lyrics like….[8]

The next night, Betty and Eddie came to Gilley's together. And the next. And the next. Betty and Eddie were lovers.

One night after two a.m. closing time, Betty and Eddie went from Gilley's to Granny's all-night omelet joint. (There are more nicknames ending in "y" and "ie" in Texas than there are at an Eastern girls' boarding school.) At Granny's, Eddie tickled Betty until she pinched his leg. He got mad and hit her right there in front of everybody. But Betty loved Eddie in spite of the pain, *twang-twang*.

They decided to get married. Eddied wanted to have the wedding at Gilley's. (Actually, there have been several marriages performed in the saloon. Judge West, a colorful old-time justice of the peace, comes over and joins the couples in matrimony.) But Betty refused to get married in a honky-tonk. She wanted a Baptist minister to perform the ceremony in church. So they compromised, agreeing to get married in church but to have the wedding reception at Gilley's.

The only dress Betty ever wore at Gilley's was her wedding dress. And she didn't want to wear it. She wanted to change right after the exchange of vows so she could go to her wedding reception in her Levi's. But her father insisted that he wanted pictures of his daughter dancing in her wedding dress. So another compromise was in order. Betty went to her Gilley's wedding reception in her wedding dress and danced just long enough for the photographer to snap a few pictures. Then she went into the ladies' room and took off her wedding dress. When she emerged to enjoy the rest of her wedding reception, the eighteen-year-old bride wore pants.

Betty had expected Eddie to want to stay until closing time. She was shocked when he suggested leaving early. They spent their honeymoon at the Roadway Inn, which is only about a mile from Gilley's. There was no place to stay any closer. The Roadway is built in the shape of a tower. Because the building is round, all the rooms are triangular. When they ordered breakfast on the morning after their wedding night, room service brought it up on a tray with plastic silverware.

BULL RIDING SATURDAY NIGHT

Dew spurred the bull even though he didn't really have spurs on his boots. He slammed his heels again and again into the machine between his legs. The mechanical bull bucked and

---

8. Excerpt from Kris Kristofferson's "Help Me Make It through the Night," redacted for copyright reasons.

spun. Dew was getting bruised and dizzy. He came up off the bull's back as though he was headed for the mattresses, which surround the bull, stacked two layers thick. But somehow Dew saved himself. He crashed back onto the bull's back, his sexual organs taking a beating. Dew winced in pain.

A honky-tonk cowboy named Steve Strange was manning the bull's remote controls. He made it spin first one way and then the other. Cowboys who have ridden real bulls say that in some ways the mechanical bull is harder to ride because you can't watch its head and tell which way it is going to turn. The treachery of the bull depends upon the treachery of the man at the controls. Steve, who was once badly hurt by a real bull, is treacherous indeed. He seems to believe that everyone should get mangled as badly as he did when a real bull gored him in the chute. He told me that as a result of his injuries he has a plastic bone in his leg, a plastic plate in his head, and a plastic testicle. I was not sure whether to believe him, so he knocked on his leg. It sounded like plastic. Then he knocked on his head. It sounded like plastic too. I was afraid he was going to keep on knocking, so I stopped him. Bragging about your injuries is another important part of being an urban cowboy. The more banged up you are, the more of a man you are.

Dew pitched forward on the bull, which is how you can get hurt the worst. I knew what he going though because I had tried riding the bull myself a couple of days earlier. When I asked for instructions, one of the cowboys told me: "Put your left nut in your right hand and hang on." Armed with this advice, I crawled aboard. When the bull started bucking, I desperately wished I could think of some way to do what the cowboy had told me to do. I kept crashing into the rigging which was supposed to hold me on but which had become a hammer banging between my legs. A bell tied to the bull clanged maddeningly in my ears. I was frightened. Deciding it was time to get off, I began to wonder how you let go of a tiger. I looked for a good place to land. Then I felt myself flying horizontally through the air. I hit the mattresses with my right shoulder first. Stumbling to the sidelines, I sat down to record my impressions, but my hand was shaking so much I couldn't write.

Dew pressed himself back up into a sitting position, somehow staying aboard. The bull on which he rode had the heart of a pickup truck. A piston rather than sinews made it buck. The urban cowboy was trying to tame a wild, wooly machine. Which was as it should be because the urban cowboy knows a lot more about horsepower than about horses. He lives in a world where machines have replaced every animal but himself, and he is threatened. In his boots and jeans, the urban cowboy tries to get a grip on and ride an America that, like his bull, is mechanized. He can never tame it, but he has the illusion of doing so.

BETTY AND EDDIE WERE BULL RIDERS

Betty and Eddie spent much of their marriage at Gilley's. When they weren't honky-tonking, they both worked. Betty worked in construction, putting hardware in houses. Eddie insulated petrochemical plants and moonlighted at an auto racetrack.

Betty and Eddie are both second-generation noncountry cowboys. Betty's father works in construction like his daughter. And Eddie's father is an insulator like his son. Way back, one of Betty's grandfathers did have a trading post, but it doubled as a wrecking yard.

Eddie was born in a small Texas town named Longview. But he lived there only seven years before moving to the Houston area.

"I lived in a town on top of a mountain," Dew reminisced one evening in his trailer. "That's how the town got its name. I'd like to get back to Longview someday. Have my own insulation shop."

All the urban cowboys talk about going back to the great good country. In the meantime, they keep going to Gilley's or some other honky-tonk. "It's like Peyton Place out here,"[9] Betty said one night at Gilley's. "Everybody's been with everybody." She even told me which cowgirls had given venereal disease to which cowboys and vice versa. Gilley's is a *very* small town in the middle of one of America's biggest cities.

While the Gilley's cowboys keep saying they are going home to a real small town someday, they grow more tightly bound to the big city, the union, and the petrochemical plant every day. They are ready to move at a moment's notice, but they don't move. They live in mobile homes that aren't mobile. Dew would need a semi to move his trailer. He lives in a home on wheels that has never rolled an inch since he moved in.

Dew has two pickups and used to have even more vehicles before he smashed up several cars. The driveways of the homes in his neighborhood are overrun with cars and trucks and campers. Everyone seems to have a herd of cars in his front yard. These car pokes have stored up all this potential mobility without going anywhere. As the band at Gilley's sings....[10]

Betty was born in the Houston area. The closest she ever came to real cowboy life was gathering eggs on a relative's farm. But if she is not part of a long cowboy tradition, she is part of a long Gilley's tradition. Back in the alleged good old days, her mother used to run around with Mickey Gilley and Sherwood Cryer, the creators of Gilley's Club. Gilley, the country canary who sings "A Room Full of Roses," gave his name to the honky-tonk, but he owns only a piece of it. The principle [sic] owner and real boss is Cryer. This king of the urban cowboy business never wears anything but mechanic's coveralls. Betty's mother knew the two partners many, many dollars ago. Which makes Betty second-generation Gilley's.

Both Gilley's Club and Gilley's career started doing pretty well. The honky-tonk went from a place that would hold 500 to one that would hold almost ten times that many. Cryer kept tacking on tacky additions. As Gilley became better known, he started coming to the club less often because he was touring more. Now Gilley plays Gilley's only a couple of times a year.

When George Jones was playing Gilley's, the president of his fan club was murdered after she left the saloon. She was raped and beaten to death with a tire iron. The police suspected all the Gilley's regulars. Even Cryer had to take a lie detector test. The case was written up in *True Detective*. Eventually, the cops arrested a local auto mechanic who seemed to fancy his tire iron as a six-shooter.

When Jerry Lee Lewis was playing Gilley's, Cryer himself got hurt. A woman hit a man over the head with a bottle of V.O. When Cryer went to the man's rescue, she cut the back

9. Originally a 1956 best-selling novel by Grace Metalious about small-town life in a fictional New Hampshire town, *Peyton Place* was also a popular soap opera that broadcast on ABC television from 1964 to 1969 ("*Peyton Place* [novel]," http://en.wikipedia.org/wiki/Peyton_Place_(novel); accessed 27 May 2014; "*Peyton Place* [TV series]," http://en.wikipedia.org/wiki/Peyton_Place_%28TV_series%29; accessed 31 January 2014).

10. Excerpt from Ronnie Milsap's "Only One Love in My Life," redacted for copyright reasons.

of his head and neck with the broken bottle. His white shirt suddenly turned red, and he was terrified. The next day, he ran into the woman in a liquor store buying another bottle of V.O.

"She looked at me like she knew me," Cryer remembered, "but couldn't place me."

There is a local Monopoly-like game with a card that says not "go directly to jail" but "go to Gilley's and get stomped."

Cryer began to think of ways to cut down on the violence. So he put in the punching bag to give the honky-tonk cowboys something to hit besides one another. When the cowboys started lavishing more attention on the bag than on the cowgirls, the women cut the cord. But Cryer had it fixed. And he says the number of fights has gone down.

Then Cryer heard about the mechanical practice bulls used on the rodeo circuit. He thought a bull would go over in his shit-kicking honky-tonk. The bull was installed shortly after Betty and Eddie's wedding. The merciless machine was rough on the marriage. At first, Eddie did not want Betty to ride the bull. He said she would get hurt, but perhaps he was already worried she could out-buck him. Eddie even went so far as to order the man who ran the bull not to let Betty ride.

"I don't like anyone to tell me I can't do something," Betty told me one night at Gilley's. "To me, it's them saying I can't because I'm a girl. And I've got to show them I can."

She and her husband quarreled about whether she would be allowed to ride the bull. In the end, she decided she would have to show him. She had a drink to fuel her courage and to kill the pain. But when she got on the bull's back, she felt all too sober. When she got off, she was drunk.

The bull can be adjusted to buck hard, harder, or hardest. Betty kept riding it at higher and higher and higher speeds. Eddie rode the bull too, but he had a hard time keeping up. After all, a woman has an advantage over a man when it comes to bull riding. As the cowboys around the bullring put it: "A woman has nothing to lose." As strange as it may seem, bull riding is really woman's work. Poor Eddie.

Soon Betty wasn't only riding at higher and higher speeds, she actually started trick riding on the bull. She learned to stand up on the bucking bull's back. While Eddie had to hang on just to keep his seat, Betty was riding the bull like it was a surfboard.

Eddie found himself married to a honky-tonk Annie Oakley whose theme song seemed to be:

Anything you can do, I can do better...

Cowgirls' Saturday Night

After about eight seconds on the bull's back—long enough to qualify in a rodeo—Dew yelled that he had had enough. Steve pressed the bull's off switch. Sliding down, Dew staggered to the sidelines. He had lived up to the Cowboy Code, proving himself brave and strong, but it made him walk funny.

"That's the longest eight seconds I've ever seen," Dew said. "I'm shaking like a—ing leaf. Stand still, leg. My insides are going everywhere."

Jan handed him his hat.

"Were you worried?" he asked her.

"Just a little bit," Jan said.

Then the women took over the bullring. Jessie LaRue, a nineteen-year-old barmaid at a pool hall, rode the bull wearing jeans and a braless halter. Her breasts bucked along with the animal. Standing up on the heaving back, she taunted all the men who had gathered to watch.

"Get up here and ride," Jessie challenged. "It's tame. I done tamed it. I'll ride with you. That's bad, letting' a girl outride you. If I can ride with no hands, you can ride with one."

When she finally jumped down, Jessie came over to the cowboy running the bull. She had a favor to ask.

"Would you put this on my ass?"

She held out a Band-Aid. He agreed to help her out, and she lowered her jeans partway. The bull had rubbed a blister.

The next rider was Rita Sharp, a twenty-six-year-old waitress at the Red Lobster. She too challenged the men. If she could ride it, why couldn't they?

"I can ride her," called out one honky-tonk cowboy.

"I'll bet you can't stay on," she called back. "If you've got $100, we'll see."

"Can't I help it," said the cowboy running the bull, "if the girls are better at riding on top than we are?"

Then Debbie Welburn, a nineteen-year-old waitress at the Pizza Hut, rode the bucking bull so well it seemed she could have ridden and carried a pizza on a tray at the same time. She is something of a legend around the bullring because she rode last fall right after her feet were operated on. She came to the bullring on crutches with her feet encased in soft casts. Cowboys had to carry her out to the bull and set her on its back. If she had been thrown, she would have ripped out all her stitches or worse. She might have been crippled. No male rider ever did anything that brave or that crazy. The honky-tonk cowgirls keep putting more and more pressure on the honky-tonk cowboys.

After Debbie's impressive ride, two cowgirls got on the bull and rode it together. They faced one another, bending, swaying, bouncing, moving together in a rhythm which was almost sexual. They were the queens of the mountain.

Then a woman mounted the bull who had never ridden it before. With the speed turned down, she rode the bucking machine easily.

"Throw her," begged her boyfriend, "or I'll never hear the last of it."

But she wasn't thrown.

Several cowboys responded to the cowgirls' challenges. They paid their two dollars and took their chances playing Gilley's roulette with their sex lives. One by one, they were thrown. And one by one, they crawled off the mattresses with their hands between their legs.

"I just busted two nuts," Steve bragged after throwing one cowboy. "He won't get none tonight."

The lot of the urban cowboy becomes harder and harder. He tries to escape from the overwhelming complexities of his petrochemical days into the simplicity of his honky-tonk nights. But then Gilley's turns out to be a complicated world too. Once the bullring was the simplest of the simple entertainment at Gilley's. Either you rode the bull or you got bucked off. You beat the bull or it beat you. It was perfect for an urban cowboy who never beat anything beyond the walls of the saloon. But then Eve entered the bullring. The cowboys were no longer simply measured against the bull, they were measured against the cowgirls.

And yet the values represented by the cowboy hat prevailed. The cowboys did not try to exclude the cowgirls from the bullring, for that would have violated the code of openness.

The cowboys didn't tell the cowgirls that a woman's place wasn't on the back of a bull. No, the cowboys just tried to keep up with the cowgirls as well as they could. I could tell, though, that they weren't happy with the way things were turning out.

"My favorite thing," said Betty, who had come up to talk to me, "is to watch all the guys fall off. Then I get up and ride it."

Dew decided to ride again. He got on the bull a little stiffly. He braced himself, leaned back, and raised his right working hand. He was ready. The bullring master put the bull into a dead spin. It turned about a half a dozen circles in a row. Dew did not sit the bull very prettily, but he sat it.

"I think," Betty said, "I can ride it better than he can."

HE DONE HER WRONG

Betty and Eddie's marriage turned out to be a rough ride. They quarreled about the bull and many other things too. He didn't want her to ride the bull, so she rode it. He told her not to do other things, so she did them. Soon Eddie was going to Gilley's without Betty, *twang-twang.*

On Friday night, February 10, 1978, Dew met Jan. He felt her watching him on the bull. Actually, he had sensed her studying him for two months. But now he decided to do something about it. When Dew got down off the bull, he walked over to chat with the bullring master. The woman came closer. They continued to circle each other warily for a while, like beginners approaching the bull.

Then Dew spoke his first words to Jan, "When are you going to take me home and rape me?"

Reminiscing about his opening line later on, Dew explained that he was a "direct" person. He said meeting someone was like driving a car. He didn't want to "piddle around." He wanted to get where he was going. Directness is one of the cardinal cowboy virtues. Dew had his cowboy hat on so he could say what was on his mind.

Jan answered, "Whenever you get ready."

Sometime after they had agreed to sleep together, they got around to introducing themselves. But these introductions were not really necessary. After all, they both had their names clearly tooled on their belts. Everyone at Gilley's does. It is part of the Cowboy Code of openness. The belt goes with the hat.

Dew and Jan stayed until closing time. He showed off by riding the bull again for her. And then Jan took Dew home and raped him.

They stayed together all night Friday and all day Saturday. Then they went back to Gilley's Saturday night. Sunday night they went back to Gilley's again. Monday night they went bowling.

On Tuesday, Dew started work insulating an offshore drilling rig. That meant working a twelve-hour shift from noon until midnight. Jan would drive down to the dock, pick him up, and whisk him back to Gilley's. They would get there just before closing time, but they would get there.

Betty obviously must have known something was going on, but she didn't know just want or with whom until she came home and found Eddie ironing his blue jeans. She asked him why he was ironing. He said he was going riding with Jan. Which was bad enough. What made it worse was that Eddie was going riding with Jan on Betty's horse. As the band at Gilley's sings....[11]

Betty went home to live with her parents in a little house on Peach Street with a herd of cars out front. But Betty, who still loved Eddie, was so unhappy that she wanted to get out of town completely for a while. She decided to visit her sister in San Antonio for a couple of weeks.

Betty was happy to get away to San Antonio, perhaps the most beautiful city in Texas. But when the sun went down, she missed Gilley's. The later it got, the more she pined for her saloon. She missed the music and the dancing and the friends. And perhaps most of all she missed the bull. The next morning, Betty called Les Walker, one of the bull masters, and asked him to come get her. Les drove to San Antonio and picked her up. Betty lasted exactly one night away from Gilley's.

But Betty still did not know herself. A short while later, she decided she had to get away again. She went to visit a girl friend who lived in Huntsville, home of the prison rodeo. This time she didn't even last the night. At eleven p.m., Betty told her girl friend that she had to get back to Gilley's. They drove to Houston together. Without even stopping by Betty's home, they went straight to the saloon. The two cowgirls arrived at Gilley's at one-thirty a.m., a half hour before closing time. The night was saved, Betty could ride the bull before she went to sleep.

Meanwhile, two months after they met, Jan agreed to move in with Dew on one condition. She wanted him to give up riding the bull at Gilley's. She didn't want the man she slept with to get hurt. They had a big fight. He would ride the bull if he damned well wanted to. Not if he wanted to sleep with her, he wouldn't. He was threatened with a kind of sexual strike unless he gave up his violent ways. It was *Lysistrata*[12] in cowboy clothes. Dew chose loving over bull riding. And Jan moved in.

GREEN-EYED SATURDAY NIGHT

Dew kept his promise. He didn't ride the bull again until I came into his life. And I brought a photographer with me. The old bull rider could not resist riding for the camera, but his bull riding days are really behind him now. At least, they are behind him as long as he stays with Jan. When a real cowboy rides a bucking animal, he is trying to break it, to tame it, but Dew could never break the mechanical bull. A motor doesn't get tired. But an urban cowboy can be broken. Jan has broken Dew.

After Eddie's ride, Betty walked up to him and said hello. But Jan was there, so Eddie did not return the greeting. This scene has been repeated at Gilley's ever since Betty and Eddie broke up. It usually ends with Betty going to the far side of the bullring and crying. The worst night was back in May, when Betty saw Eddie at Gilley's and tried to tell him that their divorce had come through that day. But Jan wouldn't let him talk to her. Betty went in the cowgirls' room and cried for a long time, *twang-twang*.

11. Excerpt from Mel Tillis and A. R. Peddy's "Honky Tonk Song," redacted for copyright reasons.
12. A play by the Greek playwright Aristophanes, in which the women of the city withhold sex from their husbands to force them to end a war. For a full text of *Lysistrata*, see http://www.gutenberg.org/files/7700/7700-h/7700-h.htm; accessed 31 January 2014.

But Betty didn't cry this Saturday night. She decided to make Eddie jealous instead. Walking up to Steve, the head bull master, she asked him to put his hands up in the air. He looked like a badman caught by the sheriff in a western movie. With her victim now properly positioned, Betty reached out, grabbed the front of his cowboy shirt, and popped open all his mother-of-pearl snaps with one motion. Steve just stood there for a moment, more or less topless, with his shirt gaping open from his navel to his throat.

Then he counterattacked. Steve grabbed Betty and started trying to pull her knit halter off. The honky-tonk cowboy bulldogged the cowgirl to the floor and kept trying to do to her what she had done to him. They rolled together on the bottom of the saloon with the cigarette butts and the expectorated chewing tobacco. Steve got Betty's top partway off, but then she pulled away from him.

Dew and Jan tried to ignore this whole scene. They moved off toward the dance floor. If Betty had expected her ex-husband to come to her rescue, she was disappointed.

Steve got up and resnapped his cowboy shirt, but by then the urge to unsnap had become infectious. Another cowgirl came up and popped open his shirt. This time Steve's counterattack was more fruitful. Since his new assailant wore a cowboy shirt, Steve reached out and unsnapped her from top to bottom. She had nothing on underneath.

Betty stood by calmly combing her hair. When she finished, she returned to her favorite toy. Jan had gotten Dew, but Betty had gotten the bull. She crawled up on its bucking back and played. She stood up, moved from one end to the other, sat down, turned around, and rode backwards.

HARD-HAT MONDAY

Dew had to get up at six-thirty Monday morning to go to work. After getting dressed hurriedly, he drove his pickup thirty-eight miles to Texas City Refining. That is a long commute for someone who lives in a mobile home. He could move his trailer closer to the refinery, but then he would be farther from Gilley's. He would rather commute to his hard hat days than to his cowboy hat nights.

Pulling into the refinery's dusty parking lot. Dew got out of his truck with his tape measure strapped to his hip like a six-gun. He walked into the plant a little stiffly. He was still feeling the aftereffects of his bull ride.

Inside the refinery, Dew found himself swallowed up by one of the most denatured landscapes on the face of the earth. The petrochemical cowboy works on a giant spread crowded with metal trees (oil derricks and cracking towers), with metal underbrush (valves and pipelines), and with metal lakes (giant oil tanks). This is petrochemical pastoral. It is a barren landscape.

Taking hold of his saw, Dew cut into the foam glass, which in turn dug its teeth into him. And as he worked, he remembered the band at Gilley's singing....[13]

It is one of Dew's favorite songs. After a day spent working inside the refinery, no wonder Gilley's seems like the great good place. When Dew talks about his saloon, he sounds idealistic. But when he talks about his job, he sounds sullen, complaining about Mexicans who,

13. Excerpt from Johnny Paycheck's "Take This Job and Shove It," redacted for copyright reasons.

he says, will work so cheap they are taking away union jobs. At work, the urban cowboy is a small, threatened creature, but at the honky-tonk, he rides tall in the saddle.

A mechanized refinery can actually be a lot more dangerous to ride than a mechanize bull. On May 30, an explosion killed seven workers at Texas City Refinery. Luckily, Dew was home asleep at the time. Back in 1947, almost all of Texas City blew up. Close to 550 people were killed.

One workday at the killer refinery, a valve near Dew caught on fire. He dropped everything and ran as fast as he could in his track shoes. He doesn't wear boots on the job. He wouldn't be able to run fast enough. This time someone put the fire out before the killer refinery went up again.

Dew has had much worse falls on the job than he ever had in the bullring. He once fell off a scaffold 200 feet in the air, but he landed half on and half off a grating ten feet below. Somehow he hung on.

Right now, Dew works in the shop sawing and sawing. When all the foam glass is cut in just the right curving shapes, like pieces of a giant girdle, Dew will help fit these pieces around towers soaring hundreds of feet in the air. Some days, he will work on scaffolds high over the dead earth. Other days, he will labor suspended at the end of the rope, like a spider.

Dew makes $9.60 an hour and time and a half on Saturday—a forty-eight-hour week. But he pays 25 cents an hour to his union. Theoretically, he earns $460 a week, but he only takes home $250. he wants to save up to move to Longview, but so far he has not been able to save anything. He says he hopes his little brother stays out of the refineries.

Quitting time is four p.m. After work, the refinery parking lot is full of men in pickups taking off hard hats and putting on cowboy hats. Some of the pickups have bucking broncos painted on them.

When Dew reached his mobile home Monday evening at five o'clock, he found an unexpected note waiting for him. It had not come in the mail. It had been hand delivered and tucked under the windshield wiper of his second pickup. It was a request for money to pay for a vacuum cleaner. Eddie had given Betty a vacuum cleaner as a Christmas present, then later he insisted she trade it in for a better one. He never made any payments on the expensive model after the marriage broke up. Now Betty was convinced she was going to jail. So she carried the bill over to the trailer park. It was more than a bill, it was also a love letter. On the back, Betty had written in huge block letters: "I LOVE YOU."

A love letter on the back of a bill . . . it sounded like a honky-tonk song.

Dew looked up from the love bill and said, "Bein' a cowboy ain't easy."

He didn't go to Gilley's that night. He stayed home and saved his money.

BETTY AND THE BULL

At six p.m. Monday evening, Betty started getting ready, as she does almost every day of her life. She took her time. She washed her hair, and she dried it while she watched some television. In all, she spent almost four hours getting ready. At ten p.m., right on time, according to her rigid internalized schedule, she walked through the door at Gilley's.

As always, Betty headed right for the bullring. On the way, she looked for Eddie, but she didn't see him. She hoped he would come later, but even if he did, he wouldn't come back to the bull. The bull was all hers now.

Entering the ring she vaulted onto the back of the beast. She stood, she sat, she jumped back and forth over the rigging. From on high, Betty surveyed the saloon again, looking for Eddie. But he still wasn't there. Oh, well. She clung to the bull, which pounded her harder than any man had ever been able to.

Wrung out, she slid off the bull and came to the sidelines. She would take a break and then ride again. She would ride over and over all night long.

"I've got people to tell me," Betty said, "that I care more about this bull than anything else."

Source: Aaron Latham, "The Ballad of the Urban Cowboy: America's Search for True Grit," *Esquire* 90 (12 September 1978): 21–30. (Reprinted by permission of SLL/Sterling Lord Literistic, Inc. Copyright by Aaron Latham.)

FOR FURTHER READING

Mellard, Jason. *Progressive Country: How the 1970s Transformed the Texan in Popular Culture.* Austin: University of Texas Press, 2013.

Morris, Mitchell. *The Persistence of Sentiment: Display and Feeling in Popular Music of the 1970s.* Berkeley: University of California Press, 2013.

36

Tom Anthony

"Kenny Rogers: Drawing Full Houses" (1981)

The "urban cowboy" phenomenon was the mid-point of country music's decade-long flirtation with pop in the late 1970s and early 1980s. During this time, musicians with pop recording credits began to venture into country music, including Olivia Newton-John, the Osmonds, and John Denver, among others, bringing national attention to an increasingly celebrity-oriented country music culture. Concurrently, some established country recording artists—including, most notably, Dolly Parton—began to branch out beyond country music and the Nashville city limits to incorporate the sounds of disco and R&B into their music, play shows in Las Vegas, San Francisco, and Hollywood, and develop acting careers that brought them national fame.[1] Country record sales skyrocketed during this period as country recordings found their way onto Top 40 radio, and country singers became national celebrities.[2]

1. See Mitchell Morris, *The Persistence of Sentiment: Display and Feeling in Popular Music of the 1970s* (Berkeley: University of California Press, 2013), 173–208.
2. This history is also traced in Ken Tucker, "9 to 5: How Dolly Parton and Willie Nelson Qualified for 'Lifestyles of the Rich and Famous,'" in *Country: The*

Among the singers who capitalized on these trends was Kenny Rogers, one of the most widely celebrated and best-selling country artists of the 1970s and 1980s. By the time he launched his country career in the mid-1970s, the Texas-born Rogers had been a professional musician for more than a decade, working in a wide array of popular genres. But, as the following essay by Tom Anthony indicates, Rogers had found only middling success as a member of the New Christy Minstrels and Kenny Rogers and the First Edition and was in desperate need of a career revitalization. Country music—which by the late 1970s was a decidedly adult genre—provided such a venue;[3] by 1985, Rogers was selling out concert arenas across the United States, starring in made-for-television movies that were based on songs that he had recorded, and making chart-topping country recordings of songs by such songwriters as former disco superstar Barry Gibb.

With the help of a Harvard-educated business manager, Rogers's success represented the latest developments in a country music industry that had become increasingly professionalized and that represented the latest trends in marketing strategy and brand management. At the same time, we see in this article familiar efforts to establish Rogers's down-home country credibility as Anthony points to Rogers's Texas upbringing and "humility" in the face of fame, while Rogers himself suggests that he "always thought the country story song was...[his] strength."

THE story's always the same, from Los Angeles to Toronto, from Du Quoin, Illinois, to Sikeston, Missouri—the audience is a study in contradictions. They come in cowboy hats and blue jeans, three-piece suits and leisure suits, wearing cowboy boots, dress shoes, or Adidas. When it's time to meet the press and assorted VIPs backstage, the clothing clash is jarring. Everyone is sporting authentic (i.e., expensive) Western footwear or fashionable Guccis. The star is the only one wearing loafers.

While autographing and gladhanding continues [sic] behind the scenes, attendance records that were set by the king of capacity, Elvis Presley, are being broken out front. Kenny Rogers' tour promoter and look-alike, C. R. Spurlock, admits, "What pleases me more than the numbers is the mix. The fans are evenly divided between old and young, male and female." Looking out across a concert audience, you can see 12- to 60-year-olds lip sync to the hits.

The TV monitors backstage in Cedar Rapids, Iowa, show an audience that looks very familiar. This time, however, the fans will serve as ambassadors to the world representing all the audiences who have gone before. A CBS film crew is working on the "Kenny Rogers' America" television special; an NBC crew is compiling a report for "David Brinkley's Magazine"; and another team is preparing a special to be seen around the world. There's an electricity in the

Music and the Musicians, ed. Paul Kingsbury, Alan Axelrod, and Susan Costello (New York: Abbeville Press, 1994), 256–79.

3. For more on the adult nature of country music in the 1970s, consult Rosa Ainley, "I Was a Teenage Country Fan: A Tale of Two Soundtracks," in *Girls! Girls! Girls!: Critical Essays on Women and Music,* ed. Sarah Cooper (New York: New York University Press, 1996), 116–21.

dressing room that is even felt by the old pros who've been this way dozens of times before. Everyone feels it, with one exception: Sitting on a folding chair in a large room of some two dozen people, Kenny Rogers nonchalantly strums a guitar to himself.

It is at first uncomfortable referring to a grown many as "Kenny." Fortunately, he's a willing talker with a reassuring, soft Texas drawl. His humility impressed me. In fact, someone once noted that if Guinness[4] ever had a world's record for modesty, Kenny Rogers might win. However, it wasn't always that way. Kenny's roller-coaster career has carried him into a land of vain glory, followed inevitably by a crash into reality. Of his younger days, he's the first to admit, "I was down that egotistical road before, and although I'm not proud of it, that's what happened. Now I have learned an important lesson, and I can be very careful to see to it I never follow that road again."

He credits his success largely to two uncontrollable variables—luck and timing— although that may not be giving enough credit where it's rightfully due. Some of his family's earliest recollections of little Kenny involved his fervent conviction that he was going to be a star. This was wild talk coming from a Houston tenement where this little boy was going to have enough problems just getting through school with astigmatism in one eye, which caused his pupils to dance around, making it difficult to focus.

One of eight children, Rogers denies that being poor bothered him: "There may not have been much money, but there was a lot of love." To this day, he claims that money is merely a gauge of success. He contends, "The more money I make, the more things I know I'm doing right." As a child[,] he wanted to be a star; he never said anything about being rich.

During his teen years, those childhood dreams were not forgotten. He reasoned that there were two roads on which to search for his dream: sports and music. Those were areas he enjoyed, and they offered the added benefit of being the two best arenas from which to attract girls. He admits, "I wasn't a great athlete, and eventually I realized I couldn't wreck my knees playing music, so I left sports."

The first Kenny Rogers' hit was recorded when he was 19. He appeared with his high school group on American Bandstand to perform "Crazy Feeling." You don't remember the song? Don't feel bad. About the only thing Kenny remembers is that "it was the most obscure million-selling record of all time."

About those early days, Kenny's mother Lucille says, "He never worked a day in his life. All that boy ever knew was singing."

Kenny grimaces when he hears those words; then, with a smile, he reminds her, "That's not strictly true; I sold office supplies once." There is a pause and a loud laugh as he remembers, "I got fired for taking long lunch breaks to play my guitar."

Since musical longevity usually comes from dues-paying and since his high school group didn't have a follow-up record, Kenny quietly slipped from million-selling obscurity into the Bobby Doyle Trio. The Kenny Rogers' story begins in earnest with this group, and it reads like a history of music for the last 20 years: jazz, folk, psychedelic rock, country/pop. He even recorded some disco music (never released) before "Lucille" finally made its way to the top of the charts.

As jazz lost its appeal, Kenny cashed in on the last of the folk-music craze with the New Christy Minstrels in 1966. A little over a year later, he left to form The First Edition, initially a

---

4. *The Guinness Book of World Records.*

psychedelic act, then a "hip" soft-rock act. After almost a decade, the group was spinning at the end of the record; Kenny decided to hit the reject button and try a solo career. He left the Edition with memories, a lot of practice performing before large audiences and a debt of $65,000.

In a $300-a-month apartment in Encino, California, a depressed Kenny Rogers sat and wondered how he was going to pay the rent. Music was all he knew, but the prospects of continuing that career seemed dim. It's a hard fact of music life that it's frequently tougher for someone who has had a string of hits to return to the top of the charts than it is for a new artist to barrel his way to the top. A long-time radio programmer admits there's a "has-been" stigma attached to an "old pro," and there is little support from DJs for these "fallen" artists. There's infinitely more prestige involved in helping a new act explode into the spotlight than there is in spinning the latest disc from an established artist.

Ken Kragen, who had handled the business matters of The First Edition, worked out a strategy to get his client back on top. The key was country. At first it might appear that country music would be quite a culture shock for someone who popularized one of the classic psyche-delic songs of the '60s. However, appearances can be quite deceiving in the entertainment industry.

Surprisingly enough, "Just Dropped In (To See What Condition My Condition Is In)" was written by one of Nashville's best songwriters, Mickey Newberry. Later, the roots of coun-try sprouted the biggest First Edition hit; "Ruby (Don't Take Your Love to Town)" was written by Mel Tillis. Thus it's understandable when Kenny explains, "Almost every singer can do several different types of music, but there's usually only one he does best. I always thought the country story song was my strength.

"I've always done country music. I've done exactly the same thing for 15 years. It just wasn't merchandised as country before. 'Reuben James' and 'Ruby' were really country songs. The First Edition just happened to be merchandised as a pop group—a pop group doing coun-try songs. Now I'm a country artist who does songs salable in the pop market."

The trail was a long one, but his jazz, folk and rock successes were merely the qualify-ing prizes for the Grand Prize awaiting him in country music. Kenny Rogers learned quickly that familiarity breeds success. There may be no better ears in the music world today than his for recognizing hit records ("those songs that sound familiar the first time you hear them"). Another familiar sound has carried him through all those changes in music. "I have one basic common denominator that has connected all my songs[,] from 'Something's Burning' to 'You Decorated My Life'—and that is my voice."

That voice link with the past means a fan of The First Edition can walk into a Kenny Rogers' concert and feel right at home. His stage presence evokes a special intimacy.

Whenever possible, he walks off the stage and strolls into the audience, shaking hands or accepting a kiss. He loves that personal touch. Of course, it may also be a little devil in the man; a member of the crew chuckles, "It drives the lighting and sound men nuts!"

After "The Gambler" ran up the charts like a runaway train,[5] Rogers admitted he has always felt a little like a frustrated group singer ever since his early days. He claims it took a

5. Written by Don Schlitz, "The Gambler" reached number one on the *Billboard* country charts and number sixteen on the *Billboard Top 40* charts in 1978 (Joel Whitburn, *Top Country Singles, 1944-2001*, 5th ed. [Menomonee Falls, WI: Record Research, 2002], 301; Joel Whitburn, *The Billboard Book of Top 40 Hits*, 9th ed. [New York: Billboard Books, 2010], 556). The song was also adapted into a successful series of made-for-TV movies.

while to assimilate the proper stage actions that allow for the naturalness onstage that is now a Kenny Rogers concert trademark. He told Johnny Carson[6] that today his stage shows are laid back: "I kinda go out onstage and hang around for an hour." However, he admits with a smile. "The hardest thing I ever had to do was learn to walk and sing at the same time. If you sing in a fast tempo, you can't walk in the same tempo or you'd be running back and forth across the stage. My toes used to curl up, and I felt like I was going to trip every time I stepped on a mike cord. I had to learn to walk gracefully."

The lessons learned early in his road career are very apparent today. I have twice accompanied the Rogers' entourage and have found that there are not a lot of rules—but those that do exist must be strictly observed. A little beer won't get anyone into trouble, but hard liquor had better be kept off the premises, and no one should even *think* of drugs on tour. Any drug use is grounds for immediate dismissal.

Road life is a "floating tennis game," since everyone in Kenny's band, Bloodline, plays tennis. (In fact, he has been teased for hiring musicians less for their music than for their backhand.)[7] There are certain variables when traveling from town to town, but the general ingredients are much the same: makeshift dressing rooms and missed meals; reservation errors and ever-changing schedules; long days, short nights and few chances to catch your breath; press by the busload and problems by the ton.

The rigors of road life are also a necessary evil. Touring is one aspect, although an integral one, of an overall strategy. It's the further evolution of that same game plan which first established the blend of mainstream pop and country music into a style that refuted any suggestion that never the twang shall meet. Kenny Rogers is simply as much a businessman as an entertainer. The line he sings with such ease is merely the means toward an end bottom line that would make a blue-chip stock turn green with envy. In the last two years, Kenny has made about $50,000,000. During the last five months of 1979, while the rest of the music industry was singing the blues, his records sold a total of 10 million copies. Nevertheless, even those figures pale in light of his latest album, *Kenny Rogers' Greatest Hits*, which alone sold over 10 million copies in five months. It could conceivably become the largest-selling album ever by an American artist.

Such favorable financial figures didn't just materialize one day on an accountant's ledger. Kenny's business-like and thoroughly intelligent approach to the music industry is best evidenced by his own admission that since becoming a solo artist he's followed a "game plan." "We knew exactly what we wanted to do and have not had to veer from that plan once."

The "we" is Kenny and Ken Kragen, a Harvard Business School graduate (B.A.) and former producer of "The Smothers Brothers Comedy Hour."[8] The youthful-looking Kragen has been the driving force behind an extension to the original plan—acting.

For more background on "The Gambler," consult Rick Moore, "Behind the Song: 'the Gambler,' *American Songwriter*, 2 May 2011, http://www.americansong writer.com/2011/05/behind-the-song-the-gambler/; accessed 31 January 2014.

6. Host of NBC's *The Tonight Show.*

7. This is not an uncommon phenomenon in country music. Bill Monroe, for instance, was known for hiring sidemen as much for their baseball skills as for their musicianship. See Bill Hardwig, "Cocks, Balls, Bats, and Banjos: Masculinity and Competition in the Bluegrass Music of Bill Monroe," *Southern Quarterly* 39, no. 4 (Summer 2001): 35–49.

8. For more on the connections between *The Smothers Brothers Comedy Hour* and country music, consult Andrew Vaughan, *Pilot of a Steam Powered Aereo-Plain*

Before the tremendous ratings success of "The Gambler" (the highest-rated TV movie in two years), skeptics dismissed such screen interest as a self-serving bout with "play-acting." However, Kenny Rogers didn't accept the role for a little ego exercising. In fact, according to Kragen, it wasn't at all easy to convince his client to even step in front of the camera.

While on the set for their next TV movie, "The Coward of the County," the manager/producer recalled what Kenny kept saying even after such remarkable initial success: "Kenny told people that 'The Gambler' would probably be the only thing he would do moviewise, since he was doing fine in concerts and didn't think he wanted to change that."

Obviously, with Kenny only 200 feet away shooting a movie scene, that opinion had changed. "It took me two years of work," says Kragen, "but Kenny's finally getting excited about acting."

The initial reluctance was partly due to the lesson he learned while filming "The Gambler"; a lot of acting is sitting around, barely enduring ennui while lights are set, scenery arranged and lines delivered for the 15th time. Rogers says, "Yeah, I feel more comfortable with that. I still don't think I'm a great actor, but I'm much more comfortable."

Since the country term for modesty has practically become "Kenny Rogers," there's a need to look elsewhere for an assessment of just what to expect in mid-fall when CBS presents "The Coward of the County." The man in the director's chair, Dick Lowry, acknowledges that the star has been doing his homework quite faithfully since they worked together on "The Gambler." "Kenny has obviously been paying a lot of attention to performances; he's been going to movies, watching television and studying what he sees."

"The Coward of the County" features Kenny as the uncle to Tommy, the coward. Based on the gold record that told the story of Tommy, his girl, Becky, and their run-in with the Gatlin boys, the movie fleshes out the character of Matthew Spencer (Kenny Rogers), the man into whose care Tommy is left after his father dies in prison. Fans are likely to be surprised at more than the quality of the acting in "Coward," since a lot of people may be expecting a western. "So was I," says Rogers, laughing. "I do feel more comfortable in the Old West, but this takes place in 1941, so it's period, but not Old West.

"This whole thing came about because I told Ken Kragen that if I was going to do another movie, I would want to do something a little different from myself," Kenny explains. "I really love the idea of playing an evangelist preacher, kind of an Elmer Gantry[9] character."

Viewing the dailies (the developed film from the preceding day's shooting), it's apparent that "Coward" is something different. Dick Lowry and Steve Poster, the director of photography, have captured a visual warmth and cinematographic texture that carry the movie beyond regular TV fare. It's representative of the thorough professionalism that Kragen and Company have developed a reputation for achieving in all of their endeavors.

Kenny is understandably proud of all his accomplishments. However, his proudest nonmusical contribution to society gets very little press coverage. Two years ago[,] the Kenny

(Nashville, TN: StuffWorks Press, 2013), 53–61. For more background on *The Smothers Brothers Comedy Hour* more generally, consult David Bianculli, *Dangerously Funny: The Uncensored Story of "The Smothers Brothers Comedy Hour"* (New York: Simon & Schuster, 2009).

9. Elmer Gantry, a corrupt Kansas City minister, was the main character in Sinclair Lewis's 1926 novel of the same name ("*Elmer Gantry*," http://en.wikipedia.org/wiki/Elmer_Gantry, accessed 27 May 2014).

Rogers Cerebral Palsy Center opened in Sikeston, Missouri. This, plus an above-average share of charity concerts and activities, doesn't get much publicity because Rogers fidgets and moves nervously in his seat whenever the topic is broached. He fears people will believe he is out after praise and personal glory, so he doesn't talk about it much; he just states quietly, "I try to give back as much as I get out of this business." It appears in this he is successful, too.

Kenny and his wife, Marianne, have recently been single-handedly propping up the Southern California housing industry; the Rogers[es] recently moved from their thoroughly renovated Italian Renaissance home in Bel-Air into a $15 million estate in Beverly Hills formerly owned by movie producer Dino de Laurentiis. At least one room (maybe one wing) will be set aside for some of the dozens of awards Kenny has gathered during the last few years. But he still insists his finest prize is his fourth wife, Marianne Gordon, a regular on the long-running TV series featuring country singers Roy Clark and Buck Owens, "Hee Haw."

They met during the deep slump following the folding of The First Edition. Kenny couldn't have been much more emotionally and financially drained. Marianne admits, "I was more concerned with his three marriages than I was with his financial position, but I think our relationship would not be nearly what it is now if it weren't for those marriages."

"Marianne taught me that success isn't everything," Kenny explains, "but having someone to share your ups and downs with is." Ironically, after he adopted this philosophy, he succeeded.

The achievements of Kenny Rogers are now largely history. He'll continue to evolve as an entertainer, but the imprint he has made on the music industry is already clear. In June of 1980, the banjos and fiddles broke out in celebration of the announcement that for the first time ever, country music sales outdistanced pop, disco and soul to pull in behind rock and roll in popularity.

Critics may decry the urbanization of country music, and purists may weep over the homogenization of its sound, but the figures—which represent the listeners, the ones who really count—tend to support Kenny, who claims, "I think it's the best thing that's ever happened to country music. It's brought a lot of people into the fold who otherwise wouldn't have listened to country music. It used to be you either liked country music or you didn't, because it all sounded alike. Now, it's no longer one dimensional, and I think that's great."

Source: Tom Anthony, "Kenny Rogers: Drawing Full Houses," *The Saturday Evening Post,* July-August 1981, pp. 50–53, 102. ("Kenny Rogers: Drawing Full Houses" article © SEPS licensed by Curtis Licensing, Indianapolis, IN. All rights reserved.)

FOR FURTHER READING

Morris, Mitchell. *The Persistence of Sentiment: Display and Feeling in Popular Music of the 1970s.* Berkeley: University of California Press, 2013.

Tucker, Ken. "How Dolly Parton and Willie Nelson Qualified for 'Lifestyles of the Rich and Famous.'" In *Country: The Music and the Musicians,* ed. Paul Kingsbury, Alan Axelrod, and Susan Costello, 256–79. New York: Abbeville Press, 1994.

37

Alanna Nash

"Emmylou Harris" (1988)

Since its advent in the era of 78-rpm discs, country music has favored the single as the predominant form of recording distribution. Whether the two-sided releases of the 78- and 45-rpm era or the single-song format of contemporary. mp3 downloads, record companies have preferred to distribute singles because they work better than their album-length counterparts in radio broadcasts and jukebox play. Even following the development of the long-playing (LP) album in the late 1940s, country record labels have seldom used albums for anything other than compiling a recording artist's recent singles. Yet, in the wake of rock music's embrace of the concept album—a full-length album that combines several songs to tell a story or to explore a broad theme—in the mid-1960s, several country recording artists whose work straddled the domains of country and rock began to explore the LP's musical and storytelling potential.[1]

---

1. For but one example of the concept album's use in country music, consult Travis D. Stimeling, "'Phases and Stages, Circles and Cycles': Willie Nelson and the Concept Album," *Popular Music* 30, no. 3 (2011): 389–408.

At the same time, many of those same musicians were beginning to demand the opportunity to hand-select the musicians who would join them in the recording studio, challenging the Nashville studio system that had dominated country record production since the 1950s. In the process, some country musicians established artistic identities that transcended their individual performances, channeling the respectability that had begun to be associated with rock musicians such as the Beatles, who came to control every aspect of their musical output.

Singer-songwriter Emmylou Harris was among the musicians associated with this movement, and over the course of her more than four-decade career, she has taken full advantage of these changing production and distribution practices to forge an identity as a high-caliber musician.[2] After beginning her career with the mysterious singer-songwriter Gram Parsons,[3] Harris formed The Hot Band, a group of virtuosic musicians who provided unprecedented accompaniment to her unorthodox ethereal singing.[4] Working with producer and then-husband Brian Ahern, Harris drew freely from a wealth of traditional country music, including songs from the Carter Family and the Louvin Brothers, among others, while contributing numerous autobiographical and quasi-autobiographical songs that also established her reputation as a strong songwriter. In the following extended interview with music journalist Alanna Nash, Harris reflects on the process of writing and recording her 1985 concept album *The Ballad of Sally Rose*, her insecurities as a singer and songwriter, and her efforts to build a distinct artistic identity in the wake of duet partner Gram Parsons's untimely death in 1973. At the same time, this interview highlights the creative freedom that was granted to more marginal major-label country recording artists during the seemingly overcommercialized 1980s.

EMMYLOU Harris shifted the shiny black guitar and cupped her hand to her forehead, screening out a beam of the television lights that separated her from the audience. "This is for all you Marys out there, myself included," she said, launching the downbeat on the big Gibson and sailing into the vocal with hillbilly vengeance....[5]

2. See also Marshall Chapman, *The Came to Nashville* (Nashville, TN: Country Music Foundation Press and Vanderbilt University Press, 2010), 59–78.

3. For more on Parsons, consult Ben Fong-Torres, *Hickory Wind: the Life and Times of Gram Parsons*, rev. ed. (New York: St. Martin's Griffin, 1991); David N. Meyer, *Twenty-Thousand Roads: The Ballad of Gram Parsons and His Cosmic American Music* (New York: Villard Books, 2007); Bob Kealing, *Calling Me Home: Gram Parsons and the Roots of Country Rock* (Gainesville: University Press of Florida, 2012); Olivia Carter Mather, "'Regressive Country': The Voice of Gram Parsons," in *Old Roots, New Routes: The Cultural Politics of Alt.Country Music,* ed. Pamela Fox and Barbara Ching (Ann Arbor: University of Michigan Press, 2008), 154–74.

4. For more on The Hot Band, consult Ricky Skaggs with Eddie Dean, *Ricky Skaggs: My Life in Music* (New York: itbooks, 2013), 180–96.

5. Lyrical reference to Rodney Crowell's "Leaving Louisiana in the Broad Daylight," redacted for copyright reasons.

It's been fifteen years now since Harris first began rolling on between the ditches in earnest, serving her redneck apprenticeship "in the better hippie honky-tonks of the nation," as she recalls, with the patron saint of country-rock, Gram Parsons.

Parsons, who rode his sorrowful crown to glory on a combination of morphine and booze in 1973, didn't stick around long enough to see the full effect of his musical hybrid. But if Parsons was an original, Harris, 41, has nearly matched him in carving out an identity for herself unique in all of country music. Not only has she carried on Parsons' mission of taking pure, traditional country to a broader audience,[6] but through her own artistry and integrity, she has helped raise the music to a new position of respectability and grace. In the meantime, she established herself as one of country music's premier voices, winning the Country Music Association's Female Vocalist of the Year award in 1980.

Alabama-born, but California-cured, Harris was initially perceived as less hillbilly than hippie, since she came to appreciate country music only in her twenties. Nevertheless, she had a number one country album with her first major-label release, *Pieces of the Sky*, and all along has managed to convey an authenticity above reproach while balancing stalwart country standards with brilliant, and sometimes esoteric, contemporary country-rock. Much as Judy Collins once pushed the work of Joni Mitchell and Leonard Cohen to the forefront of the folk-pop consciousness, Harris and her former husband, producer Brian Ahern, unearthed a treasure trove of offbeat songs and maverick songwriters—Rodney Crowell, Townes van Zandt, Guy and Susanna Clark among them—to provide her with some of the most haunting original and intelligent country material of the '70s and '80s.[7]

Aside from an almost innate sense of good song selection, however, Harris has a voice that, it has been said, would melt an all-day Sugar Daddy. In many ways, she is the consummate country artist, as adept with a plaintive country ballad as she is with hard-muscle rock 'n' roll, displaying a distinctive tonality and gift for emotional phrasing with both.

The daughter of a Marine officer, Harris grew up in various parts of the country, mostly North Carolina and Virginia. In high school, she went the cheerleader route, played alto sax in the marching band, and eventually became class valedictorian. While her Woodbridge, Virginia, classmates regarded her as something of a prig, Harris desperately wanted to be "hip and cool," and started singing at parties to gain acceptance. At sixteen, she thought about quitting school "to become Woody Guthrie."

At the time she met Parsons in 1971, Harris was feeling her life had been "relatively uneventful." Then 24, she was a college dropout and the divorced mother of a one-year-old girl. Behind her lay an abysmal first album (*Gliding Bird*), made during a folkie stint in New York City, an aborted attempt to sing country in Nashville, and a brief, decidedly un-hip career as a model home hostess in Columbia, Maryland.

6. Parsons described his musical vision as "Cosmic American Music."

7. Several of these songwriters are profiled in Kathleen Hudson, *Telling Stories, Writing Songs: An Album of Texas Songwriters* (Austin: University of Texas Press, 2001). Moreover, Van Zandt's biography and music are treated in John Kruth, *To Live's To Fly: The Ballad of the Late, Great Townes Van Zandt* (New York: Da Capo Press, 2007); Robert Earl Hardy, *A Deeper Blue: The Life and Music of Townes Van Zandt* (Denton: University of North Texas Press, 2008); and Brian T. Atkinson, *I'll Be here in the Morning: The Songwriting Legacy of Townes Van Zandt* (College Station: Texas A&M University Press, 2011).

Hearing her sing in a club in Washington, D.C., Parsons, formerly of the Byrds and the Flying Burrito Brothers, thought Harris had a natural feel for country music, and later sent her a plane ticket to L.A. to help with his first solo album, *GP*. A tour and a second album, *Grievous Angel*, followed before Parsons went on to Hillbilly Heaven in a perfect Hank Williams fantasy. He was twenty-six.

From the beginning of her solo recording career, Harris had a hardcore following, culled primarily from Parsons' small, but loyal, country-rock audience. Soon, though, the urgency, intensity, and purity of her recordings won over both the Old Guard Nashville and the mainstream country fans—diverse groups that nevertheless stayed with her through forays into more contemporary material (*Quarter Moon in a Ten Cent Town*), as well as side trips into acoustic, bluegrass-flavored work (*Roses in the Snow*) and rock 'n' roll (*White Shoes*).

Early in the '80s, however, the frustrations of a failing marriage and worries about creativity threatened to overwhelm her, especially when critics judged several of her later albums to be somewhat below her usual standards. In 1984, in what amounted to not only a commercial risk but a creative and artistic rebirth, Harris quit the road and separated from Ahern, leaving their California home to relocate in Nashville. She then began work, with songwriter Paul Kennerley, on her first major composing project, *The Ballad of Sally Rose*, a concept album that stands as a tour de force of writing, singing, playing, and even production.

Based somewhat on Harris' own life, *The Ballad of Sally Rose* is, in effect, a country opera. In the course of thirteen songs, it traces the life of a young woman who opens a show for the Singer, whom she falls in love with, marries, and eventually leaves for her own career. As with any great romance, it incorporates the elements of fate, tragedy, and success tempered by heartbreak and elusive peace of mind. The album, her first without Ahern, the first she co-produced, and the greatest challenge of her career, rivals *Roses in the Snow* as her masterpiece.

The following interview took place at Warner Bros. Records in Nashville in January 1985. It also contains comments from other interviews we did in a Nashville hotel room in October 1981, before an April 1978 club date in Chicago, and backstage at the Grand Ole Opry in October 1975. Since the most recent interview, Harris has married her *Sally Rose* collaborator, Paul Kennerley.

Q   Your new album, *The Ballad of Sally Rose*, which you co-wrote and co-produced, must have taken a staggering amount of work—more than any of your previous records.

A   A lot of work, yes. It had to be written, which was hard enough in itself, and then I had to actually do [co-produce] the album, so it was kind of like a double-backed project. I mean, I never had to deal with *that* end of it before. No album is a piece of cake. They're all a lot of work. But to have to write the material, too... I mean, I had the ideas for the body of the material, giving the nucleus of a story there. But after those songs were written, then there was the problem of filling in the gaps with segues to tell the story, and other songs that also had to be good.

Q   This album must have been a catharsis for you, since it got you writing again after a long spell.

A   Well, yeah. The reason you write is because there's something you want to say that is important to you—enough to go through all the torture of writing. (Laughter) Because I don't find it a pleasant thing. I *really* don't. I'm glad I don't have to make my living that way. So, yes, it was.

Q   The kernel for the story actually came from an experience you and the band had at Mount Rushmore, right?

A   Yeah, well, seeing Mount Rushmore is a pretty interesting experience! (Laughter) I mean, it's an amazing thing to think that somebody actually did that. But then, on the other hand, it's just an odd sight. And yes, the character of Sally Rose came from being there. We had a night off, and we were in a bar. It was the night before we played, so we were kind of enjoying the fact that we were in town as just a bunch of people going out to a bar and enjoying ourselves. And Phil [Phil Kaufman, her former road manager], being very protective of me, told somebody who thought they recognized me that no, I wasn't Emmylou, I was Sally Rose. And then we started taking it that she was my sister, or she was a background singer in my band, and between us, she just got to be one of these imaginary characters who became a part of the jargon of the road. I mean, there was a certain point where we called ourselves "Sally Rose and the Buds." (Laughter) But shortly after that, I got the chorus for that song, "The Ballad of Sally Rose," with, you know, "Through the valley of the shadow of Roosevelt's nose," from the Mount Rushmore thing. And then I started thinking, "Well, here's this character," and I had some other song ideas, so I started thinking of approaching it as a story, in order to finish songs, or as a crutch to help me write, if nothing else. I mean, I had some songs that were fictitious, and some songs that were very personal to me, and I just thought of combining them into something else—a concept, an opera, whatever you want to call it.

Q   Most people think of this as being extremely autobiographical, with the inside allusions to Gram Parsons. You're probably tired of this question.

A   Well, on the other hand, I'm asking for it. I know I am. And obviously, there are autobiographical references. But on the other hand, it *isn't* the story of my life. Some of those things happened to me, and some of them didn't. So I can't call it an autobiography, even if I wanted to, which I don't. But, obviously, Gram is the inspiration, was *always* the inspiration for it. But it is more than the story of my relationship with Gram. First of all, a lot of those things didn't happen, and then it goes into a futuristic thing. I mean, I tried to make Sally Rose a sort of timeless character. You don't really think about when this is happening, or how old she is when she ends up. It could be anything at any time in any place. But that's all, really, that I can say about it. I think anytime anybody writes anything— or, at least, the way I am…anything I would write has to be drawn a little bit from something I've at least thought about, or had a limited experience with. A song like "Woman Walk the Line" is much more fictitious. I got the idea for the song, but it's actually based on somebody that I know who had more experiences than that. And Sally Rose's character and the things that happened to her came out of combinations of friends and people that I don't even know very well. But obviously one of those people is *me*. (Chuckling)

A   Is she almost a real person for you now?

Q   Yeah, she really is. Well, she definitely was when I first got the idea, or rather after I got the three characters, because I had to make definite characterizations in my mind, in order to say, "This song is about this character, and this is what she went through, and why she did this." But then later on, when I realized that the only way the story could really make sense was through one character, I changed the story line around a little because the characters had been a bit one-dimensional, and because of how limited you are in the space of one album to tell the story of three people. So she was able to go through more things, mature a little bit more, and be a little more complicated personality. But obviously, she is still pretty one-dimensional. I mean, it *is* just a record. But I'm just saying from my point of view, all the incarnations and all the process of writing and creating that went into it, all of a sudden, there she is. But I have to admit that I'm still haunted by the ghosts of the other two characters. They were so important in creating Sally. They're almost like her alter egos.

Q   What were they like? Did they have names, too?

A   No, not really. The names weren't nearly as interesting as Sally Rose. But one of them was an older woman who had had a really hard life, and was a very close character to me, because she was based on a couple of people who are very close to me. And she was the most wonderful—I mean, *wonderful* character. I loved her. Then another one was a little more contemporary, based on a couple of friends of mine. It's hard to explain, because when it got time to really develop them and do the project, they were discarded, but they actually helped put Sally together. They helped her become who she was.

Q   *Roses in the Snow* is generally considered your masterwork, and yet in a way, this is equal to it. Would you agree?

A   Well, it's been a long time coming, and it's a good feeling that it's done. Because sometimes it was the only seed that kept me going when I was feeling overwhelmed by a lot of things. You know, trying to be creative, but on the other hand, just being a working person who keeps twenty-five or fifty people on a payroll. So you've got all that pressure, all the time. But in the back of my mind I was thinking, "I do have an idea, and I know it's something I want to do, and someday I'm going to do it." But what finally happened was, I realized that it wasn't going to happen by itself, that it was going to take leaving the road, letting my band go, and breaking out of a lot of routines which at one point had been very creative, and had become almost destructive. And even *then* I tried to procrastinate. Because we wrote half the album, let's say, and I put it on the back burner and started another album. (Laughter) Which is also, I think, going to be a good album. I mean, I'm still basically a singer of country songs. And that still is a nourishing part for me. But I started it, and it was [pedal steel player and songwriter] Hank De Vito, bless his heart, who is a good friend, who pushed me to go ahead with it. He had heard the songs Paul and I had written, and then I played him the stuff that we had not done tracks on, and then I played him the tracks I had cut [for another album], which I think are very good tracks, and he was very supportive. But at one point, he talked to Paul about it, and he said, "You know, this stuff that you all are writing is the most important thing she's done in a long time, and I really wish you guys would finish it." And, of course, Paul was in agreement, too, but he didn't want to pressure me, because he was a part of the writing of it. So the two of them really sort of approached me and said, "We think that you should go ahead and finish it." And it was that kind of positive, loving concern and pressure that made me put everything aside, once again, but even more seriously. And Paul put his own writing and personal work aside, too. It was just a complete, constant…I can't tell you how constant it was. Because we were writing, and going right into the sessions, even to the point of…we had written one verse to "Bad News," because it was just going to be a segue, and after we got into cutting it, we realized that it was so exciting that we wanted another verse. So we just cut the verse without even having the words.

Q   So you don't want to compare it with *Roses in the Snow*?

A   Well, I mean, it's special to me. And I'm hoping that it's special to other people. But it ultimately was done because it was so personal, and I wanted to do it. And you do take a chance that it won't make any sense to anybody else. I think anytime you do something that's persona, you take that risk.

Q   The reference to "columbine," which actually I mistook for "common vine"…

A   That's all right. It's me and my enunciation, which has always been bad.

Q   I thought it might be part of the same reasoning for bringing in strains from "Ring of Fire," "Wildwood Flower," "You Are My Flower," and "Six Days on the Road"—that those were classic references to earlier works, and you used the columbine image as a reference to "Barbara Allen," the old folk song, where the "rose grew 'round the briar."

A   Well, I wasn't thinking of "Barbara Allen," but you're right, in the sense that a lot of my images do come from that, consciously and unconsciously. Because even though I used the word "columbine," it was the same kind of idea, of that image of something entwining around something else.

Because I've always been intrigued by those old songs, and I love the poetry of the songs that we don't even know who wrote them, the poetry that became the language of the mountain people, or the folk people everywhere. And then, of course, that led into "You Are My Flower." That just fell out one day. Those words fell out. And then when it says, "You are my flower," and then it just goes into that instrumental…that was almost like an accident. But on the other hand it's because I love that old [Carter Family] song, "You Are My Flower," and because I'd had the idea of the fact that "He used to call me sunshine." And then the idea of "You *are* my sunshine." Referring. I love the idea of referring to a line from another song, or referring to a title. Because it brings in kind of a double meaning. It brings in memory and nostalgia, and it sometimes gives me ideas for songs—just what another song might mean to me will give me a feeling for another song that I would write.

Q   How did you decide who you wanted on the album, as far as Dolly Parton, Linda Ronstadt, Gail Davies, and Waylon Jennings, for example?

A   Well, when I first got the idea for the project, I decided that either I was going to do all the harmonies myself or I was going to ask Dolly and Linda to do all of it, or a majority of it. Because there's just a certain sound that we have that is just *real* good. It's a real strong female sound. I definitely wanted to have women singing on it. It's not a feminist thing. It's just a *sound* that you're going for. Women singing with women sound different from women singing with men. That's all there is to it. And of course, there are certain songs that I really felt it was important to have Dolly and Linda on to get a certain sound, and then I was going to do the rest of the harmonies myself. But there were a couple of killers that were *so* high, and my voice just sounded really thin. So I called Gail and said, "Help!" (Laughter) She has a wonderful high "head" voice—real strong. And she came in and just did a great job on a few of those things. And also we have a real good blend. We've been talking about doing a duet together. I think it would be great. And as far as Waylon, there was one song that was written from having been inspired by his particular feel…

Q   Was that "Rhythm Guitar"?

A   Yeah. And we felt that even with everybody who had played on it, the song was still missing something. So we had him come in. And actually, he's really only on that one song, but we just wanted to list everybody who had played. It was going to get so enormous to list everybody who played on every song, because there were quite a lot of people playing on every track. Sometimes we'd have somebody come in just to play a few chords on one chorus. But it adds just that little texture that was needed. It's a very layered album. There are lots of textures, lots of little invisible things that Paul put on there. So it might be misleading to have Waylon's name on there, but he is on the records. It's just that he's really on the one track.

Q   Had you wanted your previous records to have these kinds of textures and layers?

A   Well, I think of this album as having a certain sound, but I don't think it's that far from the other records. I mean, I have worked with a very brilliant record producer [her ex-husband, Brian Ahern], who I think is one of the best, and who's responsible for bringing certain sounds to country music which had never been heard before. And I think Paul and I both owe a tremendous debt to Brian. So it's not like it's that different. To me, the main difference is that it is original material, so it's more cohesive as a work. That's the difference that I see.

Q   When you were with Brian, what did you two aim for when you went into the studio?

A   Well, basically it was real simple. I mean, I picked a song, or Brian and I together came up with tunes that we wanted to do, and we came in for the best feel for the track—that thing that's really hard to describe, but when you hear it, you go, "*That's* what I wanted to get." And basically, I worked with the same bunch of musicians for a long time, and we were able to communicate in a special way. Like, John Ware, the drummer— even though I play in and around the beat, and he keeps perfect time, over the years we developed a style of playing together that was kind of creative in a way. (Laughter) So we were able to come up with a song that pulsated with a heartbeat of its own. And from there, Brian and I decided what overdubs we wanted, or who I wanted to sing harmony. We decided later what finishing touches we wanted to put on it. As I say, doing this album was in many ways not that different. I've always been used to that kind of collaboration. But I think sometimes a song tells you what it wants. You just have to learn to listen.

Q   You've been quoted as saying that you made records for people who don't particularly like country music.

A   Well, I've been told that that's what I have accomplished on a certain level. I make records, basically, for myself, or that my point of progression is a love of country music. I've never really known who my audience is. They've just always been there, thank goodness. But I do think country music is appealing to more people, and it's reaching young kids and on into older people. There don't seem to be the boundaries anymore. I suppose that's good. Somehow I've ended up making certain people who maybe were not country music fans listen, and from there, hopefully, decide to listen to George Jones and Merle Haggard, and get into the real hardcore, nitty-gritty country performers, of which I don't really... I wish I could say I was, but I am what I am. And I progress from the point of "I love this country song, and I'm gonna do it with as much care for the tradition as I can." And somewhere along the line I come up with whatever it is I come up with, or that they give a lot of labels to but I don't concern myself with. (Laughter) I mean, I really am trying to do this thing right. I believe that I'm a country musician, and that I do as [much] root country music as I can. Sometimes what I do shows that the roots are extending, in that in our live show we do straight country, and we don't water it down, but well, we do old George Jones stuff and Louvin Brothers stuff, and bluegrass and maybe end with some rock 'n' roll so they can dance. There are nights when no matter what I do, I can't seem to break through. And I blame myself. I feel like "Well, maybe if I'd danced a little bit," but maybe I didn't feel like doing it. So I just retreat into my little shell, and it doesn't work. But the whole show is a collection of songs, done by what I feel is a real traditional country band. This band is a very important part of who I am musically and as an artist. Because I think it's really important to get up onstage and play country music and make it exciting. With some of the songs, the music is sweet and pretty, too. So it's not afraid to be the two extremes—this band is capable of playing a waltz as well as rocking out. And I think that's what I want my audience to get out of it—to really enjoy being able to listen to the sweet, pretty sad songs, and to really get up with the up material, too. I always loved a lot of different kinds of music.

Q   But people buy your records and go to your concerts who wouldn't go to see Roy Clark, for example.[8]

A   Well, that may be true, but that doesn't really make me happy. Because in a sense, I'm influenced by the real Old Guard country—George Jones and the Louvin Brothers and Webb Pierce and the real stone-hard country. But I can't pretend to be that kind of an artist. I think I'm trying to be true to myself. I'm definitely influenced by those people, and I think it shows up in my records and in the material that I do, but there's no way that I can pretend to be Kitty Wells. But if people could get turned on to Kitty Walls, perhaps, through the fact that she influenced my music, and they could like that music and appreciate it as much as I do, that would be great. But I've learned that you can't hit people over the head with it and say, "You *have* to listen to this, and you *have* to like it." You either love country music or you hate it. I don't think there's any middle ground, as far as that hard-core country. Country music is white blues. I mean, to me, Ray Charles is the father of [modern] black blues, and George Jones is the country singer of the white blues. It's that sound. They're completely different, but they strike the same kind of chord, to me.

Q   I'd like to talk about specific albums that you recorded with Brian. *Cimarron* is an album that failed to get your usual glowing reviews. How do you feel about that album?

8. Clark is a singer-songwriter and multi-instrumentalist, and he was a long-time host of the television program *Hee Haw*.

A   *Cimarron* was, I think, a very country album for me. And I say that
       because *Evangeline* was purposely not one, only because we had collected
       these bizarre, left-field songs that I liked a lot and wanted to do. But
       instead of spreading one or two of them in basically a country album, we
       decided to put them all on one album, and do something that was sort of
       a sideline for me. It was fun, and it was very different for me. But with
       Cimarron, I got back to … well, I did a version of "Last Cheater's Waltz,"
       and I did a Bruce Springsteen song ["The Price You Pay"]. But to me,
       the way we did it, and with the lyrics, it's a country song. And I know
       I can't explain that, and it may not even be true, but in my mind it is, so
       therefore it becomes my reality. I say, "This is what it is, on my record, to
       me."

Q   *Evangeline* contains the famous Dolly-Linda-Emmylou[9] version of
       "Mr. Sandman." How did you think that up?

A   Well, it was Brian's idea to do it. I was horrified. I said, "I'm a serious
       singer. I can't do a song like *that*," you know. (Chuckling) Now, I love it.
       It's fun. But it was incredibly difficult. It's a very hard song for a singer
       like me. I have a hard enough time hearing certain simple harmony parts,
       much less something that doesn't even sound remotely like a melody to
       my ear—you know, those kinds of harmonies. I really admire people who
       can do it, but it never occurred to me that I would be able to do it. Those
       kinds of parts are like road maps to me. They just make no sense. And
       the way I learned them was to literally sit down with them, and note for
       note, just chisel them into my brain until I could sing them in my sleep.
       And now I know all the parts. Because not only did I do it with Dolly and
       Linda, and struggled to learn one part, but then they wanted to do the
       video and put it out as a single, and I had to learn all the harmonies. And
       now that we do it onstage with the guys, I have to sing all the high parts,
       which requires a change in the actual structure of the song. [She also sang
       it with Pam Rose and Mary Ann Kennedy on the *Sally Rose* tour.] So it's
       fun, but it's so hard that I sort of pat myself on the back every time I get
       through it.

Q   Did Dolly and Linda have trouble with their parts?

A   No. (Laughter) I have to say that I think Linda probably knew the parts.
       I think she probably taught me and Dolly our parts. Dolly got hers right
       away, while I was sweating off in the back room, where nobody could
       hear me, just trying to get those intervals I could *not* hear. I would just
       guess, just *leap* for them and hope that I would make them. And I finally
       learned them. The "bum-bums" were a bit difficult, because not only were
       they sometimes strange intervals, but we did them in such a way that
       they came at different timings. It's like patting your head and rubbing

9. Dolly Parton and Linda Ronstadt.

your stomach. It requires mental and vocal coordination that is above and beyond the call of duty. For me. (Laughter) But now that I've sort of got it under my belt, it's fun, but it was hard.

Q You have a talent for collecting left-field songs.

A Well, I look in left field. I spend a lot of time out there. (Laughter) When I used to do four shows a night in bars, I refused to do anything on the hit parade. (Laughter) Which made it kind of hard to make a living, but I managed. I would do them after they'd been *off* the hit parade for several years, but it was just the idea that I was always digging around for relatively obscure material. And I found it.

Q Where do you find it.

A Well, let's see. Give me an example.

Q Well, of course, you were lucky enough to have Rodney Crowell in your band, and he wrote a number of them.

A Right, I was very lucky there. It was like owning my own candy store. I mean, just all these wonderful songs, and nobody knew who he was. I'm really fortunate to have been able to have that experience. He was in my band, and he'd say, "Listen to this, Lou," and all of a sudden, there was "Even Cowgirls Get the Blues." Or he'd say, "Well, here's one, and it was "Leaving Louisiana in the Broad Daylight." And "['Til I] Gain Control [Again]," of course, devastated me, and I'm still recovering from that one. I think it's one of the finest songs ever written.

Q When Rodney left the band to pursue a solo career, Ricky Skaggs replaced him. And then Ricky left for the same reason.[10] Did their leaving cause big problems?

A No, I've been fortunate again, in that I've been able to find people who don't... I'm not looking to duplicate, to clone the Hot Band, only in the sense of musical excellence, and being able to duplicate what's gone on in previous records and other performances, what I look for with any new member is whether he's going to add a certain, different texture. I mean, Ricky was totally different from Rodney. Ricky added a bluegrass edge, in addition to being able to play a multitude of instruments. We did a different kind of harmony singing. It had a lot more of a bluegrass edge, and there were a lot more specific parts. I learned an incredible amount from him. *Roses in the Snow* was a product of learning how to stick to the right part, instead of doing a duet kind of thing, where you can wander around. I mean, I had to learn, "You sing *this* note, and not that note." I benefited a great deal from having Ricky in the band. But when he left, I didn't look to find another Ricky. Not just because there

10. For more on Skaggs's departure, consult Skaggs with Dean, *Kentucky Traveler*, 196–206.

isn't another Ricky around, but I wasn't really sure what I was looking for. I was looking for a kind of "What's next?" in a sense, although part of me wanted to go back to that Rodney Crowell type of honky-tonk thing that the Hot Band started as. And I happened upon an old friend of mine, Barry Tashian. He and I had done the first Gram Parsons record together. In fact, we had discussed starting a band in 1973, after Gram's death, and it was just totally out of the blue that we happened to run into each other. It was almost like a sign that this is what should happen. And Barry joined the group, and it's been really wonderful.

Q   He used to play rock 'n' roll.

A   Yeah, he had a group in Boston, called Barry and the Remains, that was sort of the quintessential Boston rock group. They opened for the Beatles on that Shea Stadium tour. I mean, he goes back a ways. Well, we all go back a ways.

Q   You said it was "almost like a sign." Do you have a sense of fate or purpose about what you're doing?

A   Yes, I do. (Hesitantly) And it's something that's just there, and I don't take credit for it. What happened to me and what affected me in my life [are] what determines a lot of what I do. And you are the bystander, and the bolt of lightning just happens to come up and give you a direction or a sense of what you want to do. Even though you still spend most of your time in the dark, it's a movement toward something. You're not really sure, but at least you're using your instincts to progress.

Q   Do you ever think, "I wonder if Gram knows what I'm doing now?" or "I wonder what he would think about it?"

A   Well, it's not something I think you can really answer, or that I even concern myself with. The fact that he had a tremendous effect—in fact, he probably had *the* effect—that made me decide what it was that I should do with my time and energy, is really the only response that I can make to that. It doesn't matter whether he knows or not. The fact is, I'm grateful, almost, in a sense, for what awareness I was given through him, and being able to be affected by something very strongly in the sense that I never question at least what I'm trying to do. Maybe sometimes I question whether I'm doing it as well as I should, or what to do, but not the actual content.

Q   I read that you said, "When Gram died, I felt like I'd been amputated, like my life had just been whacked off. I'd only been with Gram a short time, but…I never realized what kind of music was inside me…until I met him. It's amazing how much he changed me, and it's impossible for me to talk about my music, or myself as a person, without talking about Gram to some extent."

A   Well, obviously, his death had a big impact on my music, because I had pretty much geared myself to being a harmony singer. I was very happy with being kind of an apprentice, in a sense that we had a very good partnership. We had a natural vocal duet, and we got along very well. He was a very close friend, so his death made me work very hard. I had to make a decision. I had to go on doing a lot of things that before I had depended on him to do. He picked the material, and he did this, and that, and I sort of learned and put whatever ideas I had into it. So it was kind of like being thrown into the water when you don't know how to swim. And I started immediately with the help of very close friends in Washington, D.C., to get together the kind of band that we had had on the road. I had a lot to learn. I mean, I'm still learning, you know. Still working on what I'm doing, trying to find the right songs, do the right kind of arrangements, and learn the right harmonies. It never ends, I don't guess.

Q   You have a success that doesn't seem to follow any particular formula, even if some of the early albums had a hint of formula to them, with a traditional classic or two, some Gram Parsons material, a handful of contemporary left-field songs, and a Beatles tune, maybe. Is there a key to this larger success of yours?

A   Doing what I want. But I also have to admit that I was fortunate enough to be allowed to do it, in the sense that, for some reason, the records sold enough to give me enough credibility to where even though my records don't go platinum, and I'm not a household word, I can do basically what I want, and get the same number of people to buy the records. That gives me a leverage to be able to experiment, and be able to do what I want. I'm very grateful for that. I really am aware of how important that is, to be able to enjoy what I do.

Q   Is there any other woman in country music who has that position?

A   Well, it's hard to say. Because it's obviously a personal point of view. It depends. There may be others out there who feel they are as at peace with what they're doing as I am. I don't think you can look at someone on the surface and say, "This is what's happening with them."

Q   As a lot of country music gets more pop-oriented, yours continues to stay pure.

A   Well, it's interesting, because to me it's obvious that that's what's pop about my music. People say, "She's a pop artist," and somebody else will say, "No, she's a country artist," you know. What turns me on about the music I do is the purity of it. And the traditionalness about it is what is pop about it.

Q   I think Warner Brothers doubted that there was anything pop about either *Blue Kentucky Girl* or *Roses in the Snow*, particularly. Was there any actual opposition from them, though?

A   No, there's never been any opposition, in the sense that we've never told them what we were doing. It's not like we were secretive or anything.

But basically, they've sort of given us a free rein. I admit that they were a bit mystified by it, considering that I was—quote—"successful" on that pop level that we're talking about. Not that I'd had a pop hit. I've never had a pop hit, even though "Mr. Sandman" was played on the Top 40 stations [and went to #37 on the *Billboard* charts]. But the record company assumed that I was heavy crossover potential, which is an understandable assumption to make, in a way. So with *Blue Kentucky Girl*, I gave them what appeared to be an album that had absolutely no chance of crossover, let's say, like *Elite Hotel* might have had a chance, or *Luxury Liner* might have had. But *Blue Kentucky Girl* appeared to have no chance. But once again, I get back to my theory that the more pure and obviously left field, in a sense, you make an album, the more pop it is. To me, *Blue Kentucky Girl* was very cut-and-dried. It had a purity to it that gave it a pop quality. But this is another case of not being able to see the forest for the trees. And even I have to admit that I didn't realize that about it. But it was really clear-cut. Much more clear-cut than *Luxury Liner*, in that there's no way you could call anything on it pop or rock 'n' roll. But they didn't resist it. And with *Roses in the Snow*, I admit there were people who thought it was a disastrous thing to do. To the point of coming out and telling me, you know, because of the way the market was. And they knew I had things in the can that later appeared on *Evangeline* and *Cimarron* that they felt would make a stronger album, a kind of *Elite Hotel* album, that was something for everyone, in a sense. Rather than do something that was basically restricting myself, even more so than on *Blue Kentucky Girl*. But we did that for a reason, you know. We were really trying to make a point, that instead of diversification, we were putting on an even bigger set of blinders, and keeping it in an extremely narrow range. A lot of the reasons were personal, for me. They were clarification reasons. And I have to admit that I was astounded at the success of *Roses*. It's not like I set out to do a failure album, but I was surprised that it seemed to do even better than *Blue Kentucky Girl* or *Luxury Liner*. I still don't understand it, other than the fact that there is an incredible audience out there for bluegrass music that no major record company has capitalized on. I believe that there's an enormous market for bluegrass music. And *Roses* was kind of a tribute to that form of music.

Q   "Poor Wayfaring Stranger," from that album, is an extremely evocative track.

A   Well, thank you. But I can't take any credit for that at all, and I'm one who isn't ashamed to take credit. But Brian insisted I do the song. I didn't want to do it. I didn't feel I could sing it. And I felt that it had been done, because it's been done very well by much more authentic singers. Ralph Stanley is one of them, of course. So I didn't want to do it. And it was Brian's arrangement, and it turned out to be a live vocal, with everything recorded live. I don't think I could have gone in the studio and overdubbed it, because I didn't believe I could sing it. Therefore, they caught me. Brian sort of set me in a situation where he knew he could get what he wanted, in spite of the fact that I didn't think that I would be able to do it. And I have come to love that arrangement and everything about it. But that is totally his record.

Q   There were no overdubs at all?

A   Well, there were some overdubs, but basically, I mean, that's Tony Rice's guitar solo, and that's my live vocal. Brian is really able to get the sound of instruments. He really knows how to record voices and instruments and put it all together. So that album was acoustically, to the ear, a real masterpiece of engineering and mixing.

Q   How would you characterize the upcoming album [*Thirteen*]?

A   It's just a collection of what I think are pretty basic country songs. But I have to use the word "austere" in a way. Paul called it "blow-down miserable love songs" (laughter), because I mean every one of them was just...ohhh! Anyway, I love that kind of song. I always will.

Q   But you have another album in mind, too, don't you?

A   Oh, yeah, I've always got a few projects in mind. Basically, I'll probably continue to just do albums of country songs, and hopefully there might be one or two that I've written. My only sort of distant hill—longing to do it someday, setting a goal for myself—is my Celtic album, which I do much more talking about than anything else. Except for listening to a lot of Bothy Band records, and Chieftains, and collecting songs that I know, if I knew how to do it, could be done in that style. If I *just* knew how to do it. I don't think it's the kind of thing where you can just go into the studio with a bunch of those really good musicians who play on those records. It's gonna take a lot more homework on my part.

Q   How easy will it be for the average country music fan to get into that, do you think?

A   Well, it doesn't matter. I mean, I love that music so much. It's also so close to the mountain music that a lot of the real good country music comes from, you know, because of the sound of those instruments. It's more folk music than it is anything else. So I don't think it would be that hard for them to get into. And I think I do have some interesting ideas as far as material. I mean, there's no point of doing it for the sake of doing it. But I can see where it would be an exciting musical project, which is why I'd want to do it. [Other projects recorded since this interview include the aware-winning *Trio*, with Dolly Parton and Linda Ronstadt, and *Angel Band*, a collection of gospel songs.]

Q   What do you think of your singing these days? *The Ballad of Sally Rose* is probably the strongest vocal performance you've done in a long time.

A   Well, it is the strongest. My voice is stronger than it's been in a few years. I'm a lot healthier than I've been. I'm taking a lot better care of myself. But you always think you can do better. You're never satisfied. I don't know anybody who's ever done a record who's completely happy with it. On the other hand, it's funny. Because I'd written the songs, I didn't put as much pressure on myself for the vocals for some reason. I was more concerned with every aspect of the record—the production, the writing, you know. But on the other hand, I guess I do feel all right about the singing.

Q   Why is your voice stronger now?

A   Well, two years ago, I got nodes on my throat, and I started going to…well, not a vocal coach, but somebody who gave me an exercise routine to do. And so on the road, I do it three times a day, and I do regular exercise, too. I just think there's a certain point in your life where you have to start taking better care of yourself, or every aspect of your life is going to suffer. And you don't think of your voice as being a muscle, but it is. And you do have to exercise it and take care of it, and feed it properly and give it enough rest.

Q   What about that edge you get to your voice sometimes? Is that something you can control and use for effect?

A   I think it's probably gotten to be something that I *can* call up at will. But I'm not sure I really know when to use it and when not to use it. I'm an untrained singer, so if I had to think about what I was singing, or technique, I would just clam up. I don't think I would be able to do it. Once again, I think it's just muscles. You know, the more time you spend in the studio, the more chance you have of knowing what you're supposed to be doing. There are times I think I want to sing with a little harder edge when I hear it back. I say, "I really meeked out on that." Sometimes I accept it and go with it. And then there are times when I say, "Well, I have to go back and try it one more time." But we may be talking about two different things here. Are you talking about the real gravelly sound that has sort of come in my higher register?

Q   The way you deliver the phrase "two more bottles of wine" at the end of that song, for instance?

A   Yeah. But that was really forced. Now I can get it more…even when I'm singing something soft and high, I can get.…That's much more natural than hitting a kind of rock-'n'-roll thing. I'm not a rock-'n'-roll singer. I love rock 'n' roll. It's great to play, but it doesn't come natural for me to sing it, and I do tend to hurt my voice for the higher registers and the more delicate sounds when I consistently try to hit it really hard. So it's more than kind of…I get kind of a raspy sound in it. But that has to be on the more raspy songs, really. Something like "Drivin' Wheel" is pretty easy for me, but straight-out rock 'n' roll is just.... I'm too old for it now, anyway. So I don't have to worry about it anymore. (Chuckling)

Q   Do you really think that way?

A   I think I'm talking more psychologically. (Laughter) No, I shouldn't really say that, because when I'm talking about rock 'n' roll, I'm talking, I suppose, about how we used to think of it as teenagers. Rock 'n' roll has definitely grown up. I mean, if rock 'n' roll is Bruce Springsteen, we can be rock-'n'-rollin' when we're eighty-five. Because that's definitely a very mature music, lyrically and in every other way.

Q   Most critics found your rock-'n'-roll album, *White Shoes*[,] to be quite strong and effective.

A   That was sort of a side trip for me, as far as having any, perhaps, cohesiveness. But on the other hand, as just a collection of songs, and the recording of the songs, I thought it was a good album. I thought Brian's production on it was brilliant. "On the Radio" almost made *me* cry, and I don't listen to my records that way. But just the *sound* of that record—the sound of that particular track... and, of course, Sandy Denny's song, "Like an Old-Fashioned Waltz," has always torn me up—before she died, even. When I first heard the song, I cried. So I had always wanted to do the song, and then after her death.... I didn't even know Sandy Denny, but on the other hand, you can't help feeling a certain connection there—your vulnerability and everything else comes in to give another dimension to the song. So there are special moments on that album for me. But on the other hand, I don't consider it a country album, but I think that I have the right, if I want to, to do a side [rock-and-roll] album.[11] I'm not trying to pull the wool over anybody's eyes. I'm just making a record.

Q   The title cut—where you talk to yourself, with "Lou, you gotta start new"—showed a sense of humor that you display in person, but not very often in your music.

A   We've worked that up in the show, because it's great having Pam [Rose] and Mary Ann [Kennedy] to do all those Bonnie Bramlett "woah, woahs."[12]

Q   Bonnie's one of the great ones.

A   Oh, gosh, yeah, she *is* great. I'd love to see her in the mainstream, recording. I don't know why somebody doesn't do a country-blues album with her. A lot of us just sort of play at that kind of sound. But nobody can really sing it like Bonnie can.

11.   Interpolation in original.
12.   Interpolations in original. Bonnie Bramlett is a well-known soul singer from Alton, Illinois who is best known for her work as half of the duo Delaney & Bonnie during the 1970s.

Q   Why don't you produce it? That would be a good stretch for you, wouldn't
     it?

A   Well, I don't know that I would be the one to produce something like
     that. But if my involvement in the project was, let's say, executive
     producer, whatever that is, to get something going, I would certainly
     lend my endorsement and any energy that I might have toward that. As
     far as whoever could pull that off, I would think maybe there would be
     somebody who would be a better producer for it. But there are a lot of
     good people out there who are tried and true, and who have been through
     a lot of the bullshit, and who should be taking advantage of the country
     market. Sometimes that can be a bad thing, because it loses some of its
     definition. On the other hand, you can look on it as a positive thing, to
     where maybe a lot of the people who had some pop success, since pop
     is so closed right now, could take advantage of having the visibility that
     county music and country radio and country sales can give an artist. It's
     a much more staying, lasting thing. I think it would be great. They've got
     Nicolette [Larson] making a country record. I'd just love to see somebody
     like Bonnie come back, if she wanted to do it.

Q   With a project such as that, and especially the Delia Bell album you
     produced [*Delia Bell*], do you see yourself in the role now of being able to
     foster worthwhile projects and help artists who maybe couldn't get on a
     big label without your endorsement?

A   Well, I don't know how much help I can be. It's just like, I don't know
     that I helped Delia. I did one album, and now you can't even buy it, you
     know? Actually, I guess I'm being pessimistic. But eventually that will
     happen, I'm sure. I mean, I think it's a good record, and I'm glad I got to
     showcase Delia, because I think she's *the* classic woman country singer of
     that genre. I think the material was good, but I made certain mistakes on
     the album that if I did another album with her I wouldn't make. Certain
     material wasn't suited for her that really *I* wanted to do, but I think that
     happened on only one or maybe two songs, and the rest of the material
     was very well suited for her. So I feel that I was a good producer for Delia,
     but I don't think I would be a good producer for Bonnie. I can almost
     visualize the kind of record she could make, though.

Q   You've just recently moved back to Nashville after living many years in
     California. But you lived here before, when you were trying to get started.
     What was it like for you here then? Somebody told me you worked as a
     waitress across the street from the Greyhound bus station. Is that right?

A   It was a very short time. It sounds more colorful than it actually was.
     I came here in the early summer of 1970. My daughter [Hallie] was
     about two months old. My [first] husband [songwriter Tom Slocum] and
     I didn't have very much money, and I had been singing in New York
     unsuccessfully, doing some local TV, doing a few jobs. The pregnancy

kind of hampered that, of course, although I did work right up until my daughter was born. It's actually a lot easier to work before you have the baby than afterwards, so it was very difficult for me to find work singing. And a few times when the cash got really low, I was forced into my only other skill, which is waiting tables. And so I did wait there for a while. Isn't there a Polynesian restaurant, the Mai-Mai, or the Mai-Tai, in town? Every time I mention it to somebody, they say, "I never heard of it." So I wonder if I made it up.

Q   Why did you come here? Because you thought you had a better chance to break into country music here than in New York?

A   Well, I had been doing some country music in New York, although I was working purely as a solo performer with just myself and my guitar. It seemed to me that there wasn't really room for any country music in New York, although my decision was partly that and partly that it was very depressing in New York. It was very hard. My career was at a standstill, and I guess I just wanted to make a change. And Nashville seemed a lot easier than going out to Los Angeles. But circumstances being what they were, it was really impossible for me to give it a chance. Perhaps if I'd stayed, things would have worked out. But I was only here for way less than a year. Maybe six months.

Q   Did you get any singing work here?

A   I worked at one concert at Vanderbilt, at their coffeehouse there, and I did a couple of weeks playing a Happy Hour thing at the Red Lion Pub at one of those big motor inns out there on Murfreesboro Road, I think. (Short laugh) It seems like fifty years ago. I went to Washington, D.C., after that. This was the end of '70, around Christmastime. My parents have a farm outside of Washington, in Maryland, and seeing as how I was broke and at the same time my marriage had broken up, I really didn't know what to do at that point. My parents were really concerned about me, and asked me to come home and just collect my thoughts. My family and I are very close, and I went back there and discovered, much to my surprise, a really nice little musical community in Washington. A lot of bluegrass.

Q   And then in early '71 you started working the Washington clubs, which is where you met Gram Parsons.

A   Yeah. I had a job working as a hostess in model homes in a housing development in Columbia, Maryland, during the day, and then I would go in a few nights a week and sing in these few bars where you would get a young crowd, mostly college students. And I sort of got back into music. Being in New York and going through some hard times had taken the music out of the music, if you know what I mean. Those years I spent in Washington were very good for me. I was able to get back to the reason I went into music in the first place.

Q   Originally, though, you did folk music. That Jubilee album you cut in
      New York [*Gliding Bird*] was more folk than country.

A   (Uncomfortable laughter) That was kind of disastrous. But yeah, in
      college, a guy by the name of Mike Williams and I were like an Ian and
      Sylvia duet. This was in '66, I think. And I became real dissatisfied
      with college and quit school and went to Virginia Beach. My plan was
      to earn enough money to go to a real good drama school. So I worked
      as a waitress and at night I worked in coffeehouses and sang. In the
      meantime, I got more and more into music and less and less into drama.
      And at the end of '67, I went to New York to seek my fame and fortune.
      (Laughter) And I worked the coffeehouses, although the folk scene at
      that point was really dying out. So I didn't get a whole lot of work. And
      finally after a couple of years and the birth of my daughter, I just had had
      enough, and I left for Nashville.

Q   So you were obviously interested in country music before you met Gram.
      But where did that interest come from?

A   I listened to country music when I was growing up. I mean, I wasn't
      raised on a farm in Tennessee, you know, one of twelve children, or
      anything. I was from Alabama, but we traveled around all my life, because
      my father was in the Marine Corps. So I have no roots anywhere, but we
      lived all over the place—North Carolina, Virginia. And we made a lot of
      family trips from wherever we were stationed at the time to my mother's
      family in Birmingham. We'd always travel at night, and that's when you
      get WWVA the best, so that's a sound from my childhood. But I really
      found a deep love and appreciation for country music. I don't know if it's
      because I'm originally from the South, and just latently found my roots,
      or what it is. But it's just a sound, and a feeling that's in the music. And
      you either hear it and appreciate it, or you don't. It's just a matter of taste.
      My brother is a country music fanatic, and he was long, long before it was
      hip for his contemporaries to be into it. He's just a couple of years older
      than me. So I heard it from him, but it was really my association with
      Gram that set me in one direction. Believe it or not, I had never heard
      of the Louvin Brothers, and he turned me on to them, and to George
      Jones—to all the hard-core country. And he taught me so much about
      harmony singing. I would say he is responsible for ninety percent of my
      style. But I had had influences from people like Jerry Jeff Walker, who was
      in New York at the same time I was,[13] and Paul Siebel, who has written
      some really fine country songs. And David Bromberg, who does all sorts
      of material, of course, and has an incredible mind for material. He turned
      me on to a lot of bluegrass Some other roots were very, very varied. But

13.   For more background on Walker, consult chap. 4 of Travis D. Stimeling, *Cosmic
Cowboys and New Hicks: The Countercultural Sounds of Austin's Progressive Country
Music Scene* (New York: Oxford University Press, 2011).

country music just makes simple, clear-cut statements in a poetic way. That's why I think country songs are so hard to write. Because you can't use anything extraneous. It has to come right to the point.

Q   I own a couple of copies of the Byrds' *Sweetheart of the Rodeo* album, but I can't hear Gram on any of them. Why is that?

A   Because they took his vocals off. There was some kind of contract hassle, I think. But if you listen real close in the headset, you can hear him, because his phrasing is so different from Roger McGuinn's. It's so strange. It's like hearing a ghost, because his phrasing is the real traditional, Louvin Brothers phrasing, and Roger McGuinn sang it like, you know, Roger McGuinn. And there's such an overlapping that you can hear him in the spaces where Roger doesn't sing, because Gram elongates his phrasing. But there are albums that were released before the injunction where you can actually hear Gram, because you can't miss Gram's voice. I mean, things like "The Christian Life." Obviously Gram found that, because he was the one who really brought the Louvin Brothers to the attention of all of us non-knowing, non-believing people. (Short chuckle)

Q   The first time I interviewed you—in 1975 backstage at the Opry for a TV special for the Opry's fiftieth birthday—was the first time you had ever even been to the Grand Ole Opry. In other words, the first time you ever saw any kind of Opry performance, you were on it.

A   Yeah, the first time. I regret that I never got to see a show at the Ryman. I kept meaning to go when I lived here, but all of a sudden, I didn't live here anymore. It happens, you know. I never saw the Statue of Liberty in New York, and I lived there for two years.

Q   And then five years later, in 1980, you were named the CMA Female Vocalist of the Year.

A   Right. But I was up for it so many times when I didn't get it that it was almost like they took away my amateur standing when they gave it to me. (Laughter) It was almost like "Oh, no!" And I started to not even go. I was on the road, and I actually did have a day off, but I was way the hell up in Milwaukee or someplace, so I figured I had an excuse. I mean, you know, I didn't think I was going to win. But Eddie [Ed Tickner], my [former] manager, said, "I got a new tuxedo, Emmy, and I'd like you to come to the CMA with me." And I said, "Well, Eddie, you've never asked me to do anything, so if you really want me to go, I will." It was really, *really* exciting. It really was.

Q   Have you had any embarrassing moments onstage, on your road show?

A   Um, sure. (Laughter) There's the classic one, of falling on my derriere in front of seven thousand people, holding my guitar. This was in the middle of "C'est la Vie," because I stepped in a crack on the stage and went flying up and just landed right on my rear, and, you know, everybody saw it. But as embarrassing as it is, what are you going to do? I got up and I finished the song. (Laughter)

Q   You mentioned Hallie, but you have another daughter, Meghann, from your marriage to Brian Ahern. And during that marriage, you also had a stepdaughter, Shannon. How have you been able to balance the nomadic life of an entertainer with a home and children?

A   That's something that I have had a bit of difficulty with, and something I've had to work on. I would never take them on the road, and I don't feel guilty about that. And I don't feel guilty about my work and what I do. But sometimes I spend way too much time in the studio getting things exactly the way I want it, and that doesn't leave me much quality time with the family. And instead of accepting that, I feel a great deal of dissatisfaction and almost guilt about it. It's just a matter of cutting yourself off at a certain point and organizing your time a little better. Because it really is possible to do it. I think it's important that you set an example for your children that you work hard at what you do, even though maybe when the kids are younger, no matter how hard you try, they might get a distorted view and think you're just having a party all the time. They don't understand how much work is involved. That's something I can't help. There's no way I can enlighten them to that. I can just hope that eventually, as they reach adulthood and figure out exactly what everything is all about, they're going to gain something from it.

Q   In many ways, *The Ballad of Sally Rose* is a much meatier album than you've done in some time. A lot of your hard-core following was frustrated that you hadn't delivered something like this earlier.

A   Well, there was no way I could....I was at the point where I was feeling those frustrations, too, but it was really traumatic to make the changes I had to make to get to the point where I could even *approach* doing anything like this.

Q   Before we turned on the tape recorder, you said you suffered from writer's block for seven years. Has this album gotten you out of it?

A   I don't think so. (Laughter) Because, first of all, I haven't really had time to write anything else. I *am* going to approach it again. Obviously not this kind of project, but I have had several ideas since that have been logged in the way that they're always logged, which means the first available piece of paper that I come across. You know, the ideas are jotted down, and then they're carefully preserved and put in a certain notebook where I keep all of my bits and pieces of paper. And at some point after this tour is over, and hopefully before I do the next album—or finish it, I should say, 'cause I have started it—I will hit it again. At least I can see the possibility, because all these songs at one point were just pieces of paper in a notebook. I have nothing but admiration for Paul and other real good songwriters who can write about anything and everything, and do. Because I'll never be able to write that way. I can't imagine just sitting down and having to stare at a blank piece of paper. Writing is not the kind of thing I look forward to doing. But at least I feel like I have a start on something. It would be really pathetic for me to never write again just because I happened to do this album. Unless, of course, I stop getting ideas. If *that* happens...

Source: Alanna Nash, *Behind Closed Doors: Talking with the Legends of Country Music* (New York: Cooper Square Press, 2002), 198–221. (Used with permission.)

FOR FURTHER READING

Chapman, Marshall. *They Came to Nashville*. Nashville, TN: Country Music Foundation Press and Vanderbilt University Press, 2010.

Skaggs, Ricky, with Eddie Dean. *Kentucky Traveler: My Life in Music*. New York: itbooks, 2013.

Holly G. Miller

"Randy Travis: Nice Guy Finishes First" (1988)

The "urban cowboy" craze promulgated country music into the national consciousness in the early 1980s, but by the middle of the decade the genre was ready for one of its periodic swings back toward traditional sounds and imagery.[1] If the pop-oriented sounds of Alabama, Janie Fricke, and other urban cowboy–era artists and bands brought new audiences to country dance halls, record stores, and radio stations, country fans seeking the sounds of postwar honky-tonk and western swing were left with few new artists to satisfy their tastes. That is, until 1986, when three male recording artists—Randy Travis, Dwight Yoakam, and Ricky Van Shelton—broke into country radio and challenged longstanding records for country album sales. Known as "the class of '86" or the "new traditionalists,"[2]

1. For more on these periodic swings, consult Richard A. Peterson, "The Dialectic of Hard-Core and Soft-Shell Country Music," in *Reading Country Music: Steel Guitars, Opry Stars, and Honky-Tonk Bars,* ed. Cecelia Tichi (Durham, NC: Duke University Press, 1998), 234–55.

2. See, for instance, Don McLeese, *Dwight Yoakam: A Thousand Miles from Nowhere* (Austin: University of Texas Press, 2012); Ricky Skaggs with Eddie Dean, *Kentucky Traveler: My Life in Music* (New York: itbooks, 2013), 207–76.

these men—all of whom were in their twenties—channeled the sounds of Ernest Tubb, Buck Owens, and Hank Williams in their choice of new compositions, their own songwriting, and their selection of classic songs to re-record for a contemporary audience. By the end of the decade, Nashville had signed dozens of traditionalist recording artists who would have been passed over for more cosmopolitan musicians only a few years earlier, but Travis and Yoakam proved to have staying power on the charts that others simply did not have. In this feature article, published in the *Saturday Evening Post*, author Holly Miller presents a portrait of Travis's path to "overnight success," a path that took him from juvenile delinquency to the heights of country superstardom over the course of a decade.

───────────

Lib Hatcher remembers the lean days—all 3,650 of them. She wouldn't trade them, she says, but that doesn't mean she wants 'em back, either. Those were the days when she almost missed making payroll, when she hocked her diamonds and pooled her cash to buy a mechanical bull just to keep her nightclub open long enough for someone to discover what she had discovered in 1976, the voice of Randy Travis. For ten years it was like that—she, promoting her protégé; he, frying catfish and washing dishes when he wasn't singing on stage. Then it happened; everything clicked. There was a hit single, an album contact, an offer for a tour, even a movie deal. He was hot. Finally.

And everyone was calling him an overnight success.

In Nashville, success is a matter of record: how many you sell over the counter and how many you break at the gate. It's not important how you get to the top, but only that you travel in style. Since 1986, Randy Travis has tallied a phenomenal 5 million in record sales, played to S.R.O.[3] audiences at about 180 concerts each year, and traded up from a converted bread truck to a $400,000 luxury bus, complete with full kitchen, whirlpool, and an entertainment center stocked with his favorite collection of "Mayberry" reruns.[4]

In the competitive world of country music, everyone is applauding Travis as the nice guy who has finished first. More than just down-home roots and western boots, he's a back-to-basics artist who's steering the Nashville sound away from crossover pop and back for its future—to the twang, dang, and wailing fiddles of the past. In the process, he's picked up every major music award that the industry gives to its stars, including two platinum albums; a

---

3. Standing room only.

4. *The Andy Griffith Show*, a television program about a fictional small town in North Carolina, which aired on CBS from 1960 to 1968. For a broader discussion of the program's place in 1960s popular culture, consult Allison Graham, *Framing the South: Hollywood, Television, and Race during the Civil Rights Struggle* (Baltimore: Johns Hopkins University Press, 2001), 154–64.

Grammy; male vocalist of the year honors from the Country Music Association; and American Music Awards for best country single, album, video, and country male vocalist of 1988.

"I'll tell you, the whole thing has been a big surprise," Travis says, shaking his head in disbelief. "When we got in the business, the type of music I'm doing just wasn't selling or drawing many people to shows. I never expected to have a gold album. I can honestly say it never entered my mind. Now the first two albums have sold more than 5 million. *Incredible*. And from what I understand from Warner Brothers, the orders have been real good for the third album."

Real good. In fact, according to his New York publicist, Evelyn Shriver, Travis' third album, called *Old 8x10*, was *shipped* platinum.

If all this fuss has mystified the artist, it has caused a scramble in Music City. Opening acts that have always drawn their best applause with impersonations of Hank Sr., Willie, and Waylon are now integrating Travis tunes into their medleys. Talent scouts are haunting honky-tonks and looking for no-frills stylists to replace the rhinestone wowboys of the early '80s. Sound-alikes may surface, but more than music is at play here. Travis is patient. He's picky about his material: he has been known to record as many as 20 songs in order to choose the best 10 for an album, and he's such a purist that he politely refuses to sing anything that smacks of pop.

The result of all this patience has been a string of hits and sold-out concerts that has earned him rave reviews in publications that rarely recognize country-western efforts. The *Wall Street Journal* says his songs are "so softly compelling they could gentle down the boisterous clientele" of any honky-tonk. The *New Yorker* claims Travis possesses "a quavering, bottomless voice that often overwhelms the songs he sings." And the normally staid *New York Times* gushes: "He imbues every lyric with an aura of deep, serious nostalgia for a picture-perfect rustic never-never land of social and romantic harmony."

The "rustic never-never land" of his youth was never that picture perfect. He grew up on a turkey farm in Marshville, North Carolina, the second oldest in a family of six children. By the age of nine, he was singing professionally at fiddlers' conventions, private parties, and VFW halls.

"My parents are big country-music fans," he explains. "Daddy, especially. He had quite a collection of 78s[5]—Gene Autry, Roy Rogers, Tex Ritter, Lefty [Frizzell], Hank [Williams], and the others. He pushed me and my brother Ricky to do this since I was about eight. He bought us guitars, drums, and a piano; then he'd take us to lessons and always insisted that we practice. Ricky and I had bands together from the time we were nine. We even got paid for some of the jobs."

When he was 16, he entered a talent contest at a Charlotte club called Country City USA. He was so shy that he never said a word to the audience, just sang his song, then hurried off stage. Still, he made an impression.

"I had owned the club for about three months," recalls Lib Hatcher, now his mentor, his manager, and the mastermind of his career. "I loved country music, so I started a talent contest to generate business. It lasted eight weeks, and sometime during that period Randy came in. I remember I had a little table near the stage where I always did my paperwork. I never paid much attention to the talent contest because the performers were so bad. But when Randy

5. 78-rpm records.

started singing that night I dropped the papers I was holding and thought, *This is something special.*"

Lib had a good ear. She had been a closet country collector since high school, when she owned one set of pop records for friends who dropped by and another set just for her. She hired Randy as the club's regular entertainment and then devised ways to make him a star.

"I started booking Nashville acts in the club every month," she says. "We really couldn't afford it, but I kept hoping somebody would come along who would help. I never doubted what I thought Randy could do, but I wondered why other people weren't hearing what I thought I was hearing." She admits there were hard times. "Some weeks I didn't know how we were going to make it," she continues. "Then the *Urban Cowboy* craze came along, and I hired a boy with a pickup truck to take me to Texas to buy a mechanical bull. There was a long list of people waiting to get the things, but I managed to get ahead of them. We brought it back, and within a few months I was able to buy a new club."

As shy as Randy was, he could always talk to Lib. One night, she recalls, he told her more than she was ready to hear. He confessed he was in trouble—drinking, fighting, and some skirmishes with the police. She went with him to court and explained to the judge that he had a full-time job, was under the supervision of her and her husband, and had learned his lesson. The judge agreed to give him a second chance and released him to Lib. They've been together ever since. When her husband tired of the time Lib was dedicating to Randy's career, they divorced. Travis-Hatcher romantic rumors persist in spite of the age difference, but each speaks of the other only in glowing, professional terms.

"She's a great business lady," he says of her. "I don't know if it's a gift, a talent, or what, but she has the knack of making the right decisions. I trust her so much that if there's a meeting to discuss my career, I feel fine not being there."

She returns the compliment: "He's a sweetheart. All I want him to worry about is his music. I try to keep him informed on everything else, but sometimes I wonder if he's listening."

It was Lib's business sense that prompted them to move closer to the action. That meant Nashville, where she took a job managing the Nashville Palace nightclub and he became the full-time house singer and part-time cook and dishwasher. The onstage exposure finally led to his discovery by a Warner Brothers vice president.

"We were turned down more than once by every label in town," Travis says. "But I'm kind of one to believe if you work at something long enough and keep believing, sooner or later it will happen."

Now their goal is to make it last.

The pace they've set for themselves is grueling, but it's paying off. Literally. His style may be pure country, but he's managed to cross over and pull from audiences usually not drawn by mournful lyrics about cheatin' husbands and hurtin' hearts. He recently sold out a performance at [the Royal] Albert Hall in London and did three encores in Paris. At stateside concerts, young girls line up to hand him long-stemmed roses, and written proposals of marriage arrive daily. Albums are released at one-year intervals, although when the third one arrived at music stores in July, the first two were still on the charts and the second was selling at a clip of 6,000 a day. A recent Christmas album is expected to be a perennial seller.

"We don't want to put records out too fast because they might hurt the stuff that's already doing so well," Lib says. "But the old fans are always begging for new things. Country fans look on you as part of the family, and they want to know everything about you. You get familiar with their faces because you see them so often. When we go to a certain town[,] we expect to see this one or that one because they're always there. They bring cakes and other things."

In Nashville, Randy has become so recognizable that Lib had to figure out how he could come and go from their Music Row office building without being cornered by tour buses and swarmed by fans. Now he drives into a back garage and enters a workout room (he lifts weights) that connects directly to their second-floor suite. She says such protection is necessary because he has a hard time saying no to requests for one more picture or one more autograph. If anything, she says, success has made him more humble.

At age 29, Travis leads a squeaky-clean life and demands that the 24 people who travel with him do the same. That doesn't mean, however, that he's above pulling a good prank from time to time. He likes to tease Lib about her nonstop work habits and looks for ways to make her laugh. On a recent pass through Bristol, Tennessee, she slipped into a phone booth to place her usual myriad of phone calls to the network of people involved in making Randy's career go.

"I had my back to the door," she explains. "And when I was done, I couldn't get out. The guys had wrapped the phone booth in duct tape. It was O.K., though; I had lots of dimes."

Source: Holly G. Miller, "Randy Travis: Nice Guy Finishes First," *Saturday Evening Post*, 1 October 1988, pp. 60, 90–91. (Used with permission of the author.)

FOR FURTHER READING

Cusic, Don. *Randy Travis: The King of the New Country Traditionalists*. New York: St. Martin's Griffin, 1990.
"The Old Sound of New Country." *Journal of Country Music* 11, no. 1 (1996): 2–24.

39

Bruce Feiler

Dreaming Out Loud: Garth Brooks, Wynonna Judd, Wade Hayes, and the Changing Face of Nashville (1998)

Country music once again achieved crossover success on the pop charts during the early 1990s with the rise of what came to be known as the "hot country" style, an approach that added the theatrics of stadium rock to the new traditionalist country music that had flourished at the end of the 1980s. Bolstered by the development of SoundScan, a technology that more accurately tracked record sales, advertisers began to see the widespread appeal of hot country, and radio stations quickly responded by reconfiguring their formats to accommodate an increasingly narrow corpus of music by contemporary country artists. Concert performances moved beyond the municipal auditoriums and fairgrounds that had sustained country music since the 1950s, as musicians began to book sold-out performances at sports stadiums, some of which were televised on national networks.

Although the following reading depicts him at an ebb moment in his career, Garth Brooks was the undeniable leader of the hot country movement of the 1990s. With roots in the rodeo and honky-tonk culture of his native Oklahoma and a passion for rock and pop of the 1970s, Brooks topped the country charts and sold out arenas across the United States for most of the decade. A dynamic performer known for flying onstage from a high wire and his fashionable geometric western shirts, Brooks's performances spoke to an adult generation that had been reared on the rock shows of Boston and Journey, not the heartbreaking recordings of Tammy Wynette and George Jones. Yet, Brooks also channeled traditional honky-tonk themes of heartbreak, deceit, and revenge in songs such as "Longneck Bottle" and "Thunder Rolls" and the class-conscious boasting of hard country in songs such as "Friends in Low Places."[1]

The following excerpt from journalist Bruce Feiler's chronicle of the country music industry of the 1990s focuses on the audacity of Brooks's concert performances. Brooks's concerts were symbols of excess and consumerism, requiring a fleet of tractor trailers and dozens of crew members to build the elaborate stages, rig complex lighting designs, and create a high-fidelity sonic experience. Brooks is presented here as an insecure showman, obsessively tweaking every element of the concert experience in order to provide the best experience for his fans and to allow him to remain in the limelight—the place where he feels most alive. It should not be surprising, however, that, even as Brooks himself obsesses about his country music authenticity, he had nearly as many detractors as fans; Texas songwriter Kinky Friedman, for instance, called him "the anti-Hank."[2]

━━━━━

IT was just before three o'clock in the morning when the giant corrugated metal door of Atlanta's Omni Coliseum opened onto the foggy night. Outside, the first of ten brand-new hospital[-]white tractor trailers was idling with its back panels facing the auditorium. Minutes later, the Peterbilt thirty-eight-foot truck inched its way into the building and a team of several dozen men swarmed around its doors. A few of the men did warm-ups. A handful smoked. One drank coffee. They were dressed in blue jeans, torn sweats, and shorts, with Lynyrd Skynyrd T-shirts and Oakland Raiders parkas. They had on black Nike hightops, workboots, sandals. Each was sporting a well-used pair of gloves—woolen, stretched leather, canvas, mesh. And all

1. For more on class in hard country music, consult Barbara Ching, *Wrong's What I Do Best: Hard Country Music and Contemporary Culture* (New York: Oxford University Press, 2001); Aaron A. Fox, *Real Country: Music and Language in Working-Class Culture* (Durham, NC: Duke University Press, 2004). Bill C. Malone has treated the subject of class in country music more generally in *Don't Get Above Your Raisin': Country Music and the Southern Working Class* (Urbana: University of Illinois Press, 2002).

Brooks's career is thoroughly treated in Patsi Bale Cox, *The Garth Factor: The Career Behind Country's Big Boom* (New York: Center Street, 2009). Later career decisions, including the creation of an alter ego persona, are the subject of Heather Maclachlan, "The Greatest Rock Star Who Never Was: Garth Brooks, Chris Gaines, and Modern America," *American Music* 26, no. 2 (Summer 2008): 196–222; Elina Shatkin, "The Strange Case of Chris Gaines and Garth Brooks," *Journal of Popular Music* 25, no. 3 (September 2013): 389–97.

2. Kinky Friedman, "A Tribute to Me," *Texas Monthly*, February 1999, http://www.texasmonthly.com/content/tribute-me; accessed 31 January 2014.

were wearing a drop-dead I'm-a-professional expression as they freed the locks that turned the handles that opened the doors that were adorned with a frank admonition: NOT FOR HIRE. The only hint of celebrity on the trailers was a lavender circle on the back of each door inside of which was painted an understated purple g.

By the time his platoon of "g-trucks" arrived in downtown Atlanta, Garth Brooks's once meteoric career seemed to be in total free fall. The new album on which he had pinned so many hopes, *Fresh Horses*, had failed to keep pace with his previous releases. Though it had sold 3 million copies in its first three months, it had failed to hold the top position on even the country album charts—a far cry from several years earlier when he held that position for well over a year. Instead, by early March, he was down to a mere 15,000 units a week on the SoundScan chart that once had signaled his rise to prominence and that just a year earlier had calculated his weekly sales at ten times that amount. To add to his troubles, Garth had been roundly pilloried—then ridiculed—for his actions at the American Music Awards. At the Grammy Awards several weeks later, Vince Gill walked to the podium after winning an award for Song of the Year and announced that, unlike Garth, he planned to accept his trophy. At the Nashville Music Awards, a good barometer of industry attitudes, host Gerry House, a prominent DJ, declared that if anyone offered him an award, he wouldn't be fool enough [to] leave it behind.

Then, to add to the growing perception that he was losing his flawless touch, the video Garth released for "The Change" consisted entirely of footage of rescue workers at the site of the Oklahoma City bombing.[3] As a native son of the region, Garth had intended the video to pay tribute to the valor of the rescue workers. Instead, it was widely viewed, particularly in Oklahoma, as exploiting the tragedy for his own financial gain. Irate viewers deluged CMT with requests to pull the video. Garth worsened the situation by trying to strong-arm his label into sending a CD of the song to *every* radio station in America—not just country—and asking them to play it at 9:02 CST on the anniversary of the bombing. When the label refused, saying he'd be mocked for his Jesus complex, Garth took out a full-page ad in *Billboard* on his own letterhead[,] inviting radio stations to telephone his office and coordinate a tribute. Faced with such stubbornness by the still reigning if weakened king of the genre, CMT and hundreds of radio stations did honor his request, though the following week many stations quietly dropped the song from their playlists, making "The Change" the second single from *Fresh Horses* to die a premature death. "Spend any time in Nashville and it's clear that Brooks just baffles the hell out of the local music industry," Melinda Newman, his friend and confidante, wrote in *Billboard*. "People speculate on everything: 'How does he handle his fame so well?' 'Why doesn't he just go ahead and quit while he's at the top?' 'Why on earth does he keep talking about being forgotten?'"

The start of Garth's new world tour, if nothing else, was giving him a reason to stop worrying—or, at least, getting him out of the house for a while. But even when the show started setting records (80,000 tickets in Atlanta in two and a half hours, more than Elvis; 88,000 tickets in Washington, D.C., a venue record; 60,000 tickets in Miami, the most since the Grateful Dead), Garth began fearing that deep inside he might even be losing enthusiasm for

---

3. The Alfred P. Murrah Federal Building in Oklahoma City was bombed on April 19, 1995. For more background, consult Edward T. Lintenhal, *The Unfinished Bombing: Oklahoma City in American Memory* (New York: Oxford University Press, 2001).

the one thing he'd always enjoyed in his career: his performances. After two years of waiting, tonight he would find out.

Once the back doors of the Omni were opened, the crew went to work. The forklift driver, nicknamed "Grumpy Old Man," started removing giant cases of equipment. A team of riggers—"Go-Go," "Charlie," and "The Abomination"—sidled up the twin aluminum ramps and began rolling out silver fiberglass boxes. As soon as the boxes hit the ground, a new crew of workers took over from the first and shepherded the equipment—banded lights, grid motors, spansets, ratchets—onto the floor of the auditorium. The floor was covered in a patchwork of thick cardboard panels that sat directly on top of the ice hockey rink.

Within minutes, the entire crew was working. A few men arranged the portable silver cases along one side of the floor. A few more carried the first of the light trusses—giant rectangular scaffolding structures—and put them on the cardboard floor. Occasionally one would shout or burst into song. A few tripped over a stray cord or patch of exposed ice ("Hey, Mack, get some tape over here before somebody kills *his*self... "). A steady chorus of loud metallic clanks accompanied the scene. But mostly everyone did his job with quiet determination and a few commands from the small tea of roadies who traveled full-time with the show.

"Opening a tour like this is a major deal," explained Debbie Diana, a thirty-something lighting specialist who, along with other members of the Atlanta crew, was making ten dollars an hour for her work, with no guarantee that she would even get to see the show. "We look forward to it. We don't know what the stage is going to look like. In six hours, though, we'll see."

"Is there something special about this particular show?" I asked.

"Well, since Garth started touring a couple of years ago, most country acts are as large, if not larger, than the rock tours going out. Five years ago, country was not like this, with lots of vari-lights and sophisticated equipment. Garth came along and was so influenced by rock 'n' roll that he did country with rock production. I've heard that in this new show there's movable parts up in the truss, with motors and stuff. They've got forty-two motors—that's a lot. They're moving something up in the sky. We'll have to wait and... ooh, look," she cooed, "a giant mirrored ball. I think we have our first clue."

By the end of the first hour, the shape of the rigging was beginning to unfold. The eight-foot trusses were laid out in a giant octagon, with a smaller octagon truss inside it, connected with four-foot-long crossbars as spokes. The whole rigging looked like a giant oven burner, roughly twenty-five feet in diameter, that in time would be raised to the ceiling of the building and used to suspend the lights. This rigging would be the first thing constructed, followed by the speakers, and ultimately by the stage itself, which would rise from the floor and spread its wings from one side of the arena to the other.

At 4:45 A.M., a team of men who had found their way to the ceiling began lowering strands of one-inch garden chain to the floor. One by one, the chains were hooked to the motors that had been affixed to the various joints of the double octagon. As the chains were being attached, the rest of the crew worked furiously. Two men set about attaching strobes to the giant truss. Several more strung bundles of cable around the perimeter. And one lone man with a pair of black jeans that sagged, plumberlike, down his backside had the all-important job of affixing two F-100 Performance Smoke Generators, a machine about the size of a portable vacuum cleaner that contained a heater, a pump, and a tiny fan, into which water and mineral oil were poured and out of which spurted artificial fog. "The ones on the floor go pretty much all the time," he explained. "The ones up in the air we just give a blast every now and then and they produce just fine."

With the rig now pieced together, the pace seemed to quicken. At a quarter after five, one of the riggers started the computer that would run the lights. Minutes later, one of the electricians arrived with a silk-screen frame and a bucket of purple paint, which he used to paint Garth's signature g on both ends of each light rack. And just before six, the first rack of several dozen lights was bolted to the rig. "There are five hundred pars, or fixed lights," the head electrician explained. "Another hundred and fifty varis, or moving lights. All together, about a thousand."

"Any particular color scheme?" I asked.

"The truth is, there are so many moving lights. Everything changes color, changes focus, changes position. It's pretty much the case where your imagination is the only limit."

By half past six, the rig was ready to be raised, but production manager John McBride, who had met his wife Martina [see chapter 49] when she opened for Garth, decided to hold the ascension until seven, when Mark McEwen would be doing the national weather report for "CBS This Morning" live from the Omni floor. Jolly, friendly, almost giddy in his early morning element, Mark positioned himself at the edge of the floor, and, at precisely 7:01, received his cue from New York: "I wonder if I might quote a Garth Brooks song," he said, " 'I'm much too young to look this damn old.…' " He chuckled at his happy TV pun. "So here we are, getting it all together. Garth is going to open his first tour in two years right here at the Omni tonight. We'll be talking to Garth later on this morning, but shall we take a look at the weather.…" Mark was not two words into his speech when McBride gave the word and the giant rig, with cables dangling and lights shivering, slowly began climbing to the sky. A burst of applause went up from the crew. Mark himself glanced briefly at the creation. And fifty feet away, to no one's particular notice, a bleary-faced man with sleep in his eyes walked underneath the giant metal door, past the last truck waiting to be unloaded, and gave a simple, satisfied salute to the stage. "Okay, folks, here we go."

It was a little past 7:30 A.M. when Garth ambled into the backstage holding room. He had changed clothes in his dressing room, then lumbered across the hall to where the rest of us were waiting: his two publicists, his brother, and the makeup lady who had been hired for the day by CBS. He was not in a good mood.

"I knew I never should have touched it," he said to no one in particular. He greeted everyone with hugs and shakes, then plopped down in the chair. "It'll probably be a year now before I'm normal again. I wanted to surprise my wife. And look what happened.…"

He removed his black GARTH BROOKS WORLD TOUR baseball cap. His hair, normally graying and thin, was a vivid peanut butter color—a little bit darker on the top, a little bit orange around his ears.

"Oh…? No…" The makeup lady was fumbling. "It doesn't look…bad," she finally said. She was lying.

"I cut it close to my head," Garth said, not buying it for a second. "You get out in the sunlight and this thing takes off like it's on fire."

"Who did it for you?" the makeup lady asked.

"Somebody who does Sandy's hair. When she finished, she said, 'Oh[,] my God. It's red…!' And to think, Sandy loved the gray."

"And what was wrong with that?" she said.

"I don't know. Ten-year anniversary. I look at those wedding pictures. Sandy looks the same. I thought I would try to do something. That week she was gone, I thought I would surprise her. And now look…"

With his makeup applied, Garth stepped outside to examine the rigging. Immediately his executive instincts took over. "You got your ratchet up?" he asked one of the workers. "How 'bout those plugs?" It was that side of Garth, his Barnum-esque showmanship combined with his Bailey-like business savvy, that had forever changed the dynamics of country stage shows. In the early years of Nashville, country artists rarely traveled outside the South. Performers would play the Opry on the weekend, then drive to small-scale venues within a day's commute of Music Row. In time promoters began packaging Opry legends and taking them on the road, like the tour with Minnie Pearl that played Carnegie Hall in 1947. By the late 1960s, country music had grown to a level where some name performers—like Johnny Cash—could begin to venture into larger arenas, but for the most part country artists were unable to compete with pop artists. All that began to change in the late 1970s with the emergence of country as a mass-appeal music. Though most country artists still made the bulk of their money playing state fairs and annual rattlesnake jamborees, a handful of stars—Kenny Rogers [see chapter 37], John Denver, the Oak Ridge Boys—were beginning to show real clout in drawing fans to arenas. Unlike outdoor festivals, which are known as "soft tickets" since fans get the added lure of the fair or the carnival, arena sales are considered "hard tickets" since all you get is concert.

One reason fans had long been reluctant to see country artists in concert is that they didn't do much onstage. For generations, country singers were simply that: singers. They stood in front of a microphone and sang. While rock shows had been remade in the 1970s by everyone from the Rolling Stones to Kiss [sic], country artists were content to plant their feet, lower their hats, and drip their tears into their proverbial beer. More than anyone else, Garth Brooks recognized this disparity and set about designing a show that would mix the best of the arena acts he remembered seeing as a child with the country acts he so desperately wanted to emulate. Simply put, he yanked country into the age of the arena.

"Originally I was scared to move around too much onstage," Garth told me, "I remember one night in 1989 we were opening for Chris LeDoux, this real cowboy, and I told my guys that we would have to curtail what we normally did onstage because we didn't want to overwhelm the people. We went out there and put on this nice, quiet, gentlemanly show. Then all of [a] sudden Chris LeDoux comes out. They turn out the lights and—*boom!*—he comes catapulting over this hay bale and lands in the middle of the stage. I said, 'Geez! Look at that!' From then on, I started understanding that whatever the audience does out there, I can do back to them, and they'll send it back to me ten times bigger."

Within a year, Garth had moved from being an opening act to headlining his own gigs, and he quickly began adding more elaborate stunts to his act: catapulting from trapdoors, swinging from ropes, even dangling from ladders he had suspended from the rigging. As with so many other areas of his career, he managed to combine pop pyrotechnics with country sincerity. Following the lead of Madonna and Michael Jackson, for example, he employed a headset microphone, but in his case he suspended it from the brim of his hat[.] ("What people don't realize," Garth told me, "is that the hat actually blocks out the light and makes it easier to see the fans.")[4] More importantly, Garth realized that these theatrics would work even better on television. In 1992, he began what would become a series of televised specials on NBC—in

---

4. Madonna and Michael Jackson deployed headsets to facilitate the performance of complex dance choreographies.

effect, hour-long commercials—that brought his stage show to millions of fans who had never had to leave their living rooms. Having successfully moved from "soft ticket" to "hard ticket," he then rewrote the rules even further by moving to *no ticket*: All you had to do was sit at home and watch. Instead of diminishing sales, though, the exposure made Garth's show a must-see. Not just in the South, but in cities from Miami to Seattle to San Diego, and, beginning in 1994, abroad: Australia, Germany, Spain, the Netherlands, Ireland, England, and Scotland. It was that tour, his most recent, which was foremost in Garth's mind that morning in Atlanta.

"To me, this isn't the first day at all," Garth said when I asked him if he had any opening[-]day rituals. He was wearing a black jumpsuit and, to cover his errant hair dye, a black baseball cap from the current tour. The makeup had removed most of the weariness from his face. A few drops of Visine had eliminated most of the puffiness from his eyes. "As soon as I got in the dressing room," he continued, "the same thing was happening as in Aberdeen, Scotland. There's no hot water, no food. It's freezing. I got in there and felt that cold water and thought, 'This ain't the first day, it's just the next day.'"

The only thing this was the first day for, he said, was the stage and the show. And even the show was similar to the past, though without many of the pyrotechnics he had used in his television specials.

"You've got to remember," Garth said, "if you've seen us on TV, you haven't seen us live. TV is what [Arnold] Schwarzenegger does.[5] You do things you don't do elsewhere. You burn things. You toss cymbals. You fly. We did that once. It was in Dallas, at Texas Stadium, and it cost us 1.7 million dollars to film three nights. We couldn't afford to do that every night. I wouldn't *want* to do it every night."

In fact, they almost didn't get a chance to do it at all. That famous show in Dallas, taped and broadcast as the second of Garth's NBC specials, proved almost deadly. In his typical shoot-for-the-rafters style, Garth decided he wanted to fly above the audience. In order to pull it off, though, his tour managers were forced to come up with an elaborate rigging that stretched from the floor of Texas Stadium to the roof. On paper, the scheme worked fine, but no one had tested it. Several days before the taping, while his team was installing the equipment, the rigging buckled. "Everybody panicked," Garth said. "When the thing started snapping, people started jumping. I had friends who were up on it, and they have never been so scared in their lives. There were seventeen we took to the hospital." But still he had a show to do. "So I made this speech to my guys," Garth continued. "I said, 'Look, I've got to go down there and clean it off. Nobody here has to go.' There was this big box of hard hats sitting there. I grabbed one and started going down to the stage. And I turned around, man, and here comes just this trail of those white hard hats, following right down. I see my wife with a hard hat. My crew. It was a good day. Of course it was a bad day—but it was a good day, too."

Garth had that dreamy look in his eyes again—the one he develops when he starts talking about certain moments in his career. It was that part of him that often made him seem on the verge of falling into a trance.

"So as I was saying...." He returned to the present. "I'm not sure different is the thing. People come to a concert like this to have fun. They come to forget, they come to scream as loud as they want, they come just to sit and watch. Whatever they want to do. That's what we

5. Austrian bodybuilder and actor Arnold Schwarzenegger starred in the wildly successful *Terminator* franchise from 1984 to 2003 ("Terminator [franchise]," http://en.wikipedia.org/wiki/Terminator_%28franchise%29; accessed 31 January 2014).

do. We'll play the old stuff. We'll do some of the old gags. We keep the pit cables down in case we want to swing on those. And we'll see what the people like."

By a little after 4 P.M., the stage was nearing completion as Garth returned to the coliseum for a preshow run-through. Eschewing the stairs, he scampered up the stage as if it was a jungle gym and started prancing from one side to the other. "Look at this baby!" After all the attention paid to the lights, the stage itself was clearly the dominant part of this creation. The heaping piles of steel and metal that earlier had looked like pots and pans had been transformed in the previous twelve hours into a giant elevated stage the size of half a basketball court. Unlike most stages, with their bundles of sound monitors and towering ramps, this construction, which cost $300,000, was surprisingly flat. All the bells and whistles had been suspended underneath the rostrum, along with a series of scrims, trapdoors, and assorted platforms that would come rising out of the floor with a simple glance from Garth (and the press of a button underneath).

To add to this futuristic feel, the stage itself was made of corrugated mesh, like a high-tech freezer shelf. "It's an ample mesh," Garth explained. "Stretched. We've taken the regular mesh and stretched it even further. Then we went and put the monitors underneath it. We had fifty-something monitors last time on a stage that was seventy percent of this size. This year we have thirty monitors, but we cover more ground."

At the center of this massive plateau—and clearly its focal point—was a giant Plexiglas capsule about the size of the Apollo command module that contained the fifteen-piece drum set. Made with half-inch Plexiglas designed for use in 747s[6] and christened the "U.S. Hope" by Garth, the capsule was mounted on a giant hydraulic piston that gave it the ability to rise periscopelike into the air and spin itself around like a giant robotic ventriloquist's dummy gone horribly out of control. "Houston, we have a problem: The drum set is leading a coup." To accept this galactic theme, the capsule had been decorated with a single decal of the American flag that Garth had received from NASA, along with some navy blue spacesuits for the crew to wear. "There are all sorts of names for the capsule," said drummer Tommy Johnson, "the 'egg,' the 'drum dome.' I prefer 'boy in the bubble.'"

Garth liked the "boy in the bubble" for different reasons. From a practical point of view, the bubble, by preventing the drums from bleeding into other instruments, allowed him to record each show on a forty-eight-track recorder for use in a "live" album later. From a showman's point of view, the bubble gave him a toy to play with in his own private playground.

"So what kind of soles do you have on those shoes?" Garth asked.

"Rubber," I said cautiously. After months of hanging around him, I had learned to be wary of such outbursts.

"Then go ahead, run up there," he said. For a second, I thought he was talking about one of the risers that had been raised from the floor. But before I had the chance to decide, he wiped the bottom of his Nike hightops and darted up the bubble in three rapid-fire steps. I followed (though, unlike him, I had to balance myself so I wouldn't fall off). "Now you can see what I've been talking about," Garth said. Indeed, from atop the pod, the view of the stage was stunning. The cold layer of cardboard on the coliseum floor had grown into a glacier of technology. The stage itself—cool, flat, accented with bursts of artificial fog—seemed like something out of a sci-fi opera. The fiddle player was warming up in one corner. A soundman was testing

6. Boeing 747 airliners.

the board in another. With musicians popping in and out of trapdoors, the whole scene began to feel like an audience participatory game of "Chutes and Ladders."

"There's two things I would say about this stage," Garth said. "It's smart, and it's flexible. First of all, the money we'll save because we don't have seat kills"—those seats in the front several rows that usually go unsold because they have obstructed views—"will pay for this stage in the first month alone. Then the whole front section can be removed when we go to Europe, since their venues are smaller. We're just really proud of it."

Proud is an understatement. Earlier, Garth had introduced me to the head of his film crew, whom he had flown in from Ireland to record the show. I asked him the difference between a Garth show and a U2 show, since he had worked with both. He didn't hesitate. "The amount of time Garth spends thinking about it," the man said. "He's obsessed with it."

Indeed. "I hope this show tonight will be the worst one we give all year," Garth said, "but that it will still be a pretty good show. What I hope most is that people walk out of here saying, 'I came here four years ago for seventeen bucks. I had the time of my life. I screamed. I laughed. And I came here again tonight for seventeen bucks. I had the time of my life. I screamed. I laughed.'"

What Garth was most worried about, though, was perception. "One of the big questions that will be in everyone's mind when they sit down here is: 'Has he forgotten country music?'" Garth said. "That's why the second song out of the holster is 'Two of a Kind.' We want to tell them we're still country. We want to make sure these people sit there and go, 'All right, it's the same guy I knew.' And then they're open to new stuff. But if you just bomb them with stuff, they say, 'Ah, well, he's forgotten.'"

Though his show was only a few hours away, Garth could not escape the central worry that had consumed him for so long—what did the audience think of him, did they still like him, would they still enjoy his show? Even given the notorious insecurity of artists, it would be hard to imagine Mick Jagger, say, or Elvis, or the Beatles giving in to such anxiety about whether the public thought they were too pop, too rock, too crossover, too successful. Yet despite Nashville's leap into the American mainstream (or maybe because of it), country artists, more than those in any other genre, are obsessed with this definitional question. For Garth, it was a near-religion. "Our message is this," he had said at a preshow press conference. "We are not country music. We are a *part* of country music. We represent the best we can what we feel our brand of country music is. And we take that all over the world with us."

What he didn't say at the press conference was that having spread that message as far as it could go, he now doubted his own fitness to be its chief evangelist.

"You want to know the thing that scares me most?" he asked me. "It's pretty heavy." He squatted on top of the drum capsule and slid down to the stage floor. "What scares me most has to do with Katharine Hepburn. She made a wonderful speech about 'it' in one of her movies. She said, 'There's just a thing that some women have. And if you don't have it—no matter what else you've got—it's not enough.' That's what I'm worried about. I'm worried about getting on top of that piano and going, 'Where is he? Is GB going to show up or not?' And I'll know as soon as I jump off the piano and hit the grating. That's my biggest fear. Sitting on the farm for two years going, 'Is it still there?'"

By just before showtime, that fear had become almost palpable. A funereal hush had come over everyone backstage. The only person the least bit upbeat was Garth's mother, Colleen, who had just driven in with her husband Troyal on the bus Garth bought them for Christmas.

"The only thing I'm worried about tonight is some of his antics," she said. A sprightly women in a purple jumpsuit and freshly upswept Martha Washington white hair (actually, she could have passed for Hazel)[7], she looked like the biggest bettor—and the one with the saltiest tongue—at the local ladies' auxiliary bridge club. "He always runs up that drum thing in tennis shoes. He's going up there with ropers tonight. He could slip. Or fall. If he does, his finger will go through that stage. That stage is like razors."

Colleen had her own opinions about why her son, the one she claimed to be her spitting image ("He's bullheaded like his father. Other than that, I see nothing but his mother . . . "), continued to be so insecure.

"All males are weak," she said. "It doesn't make any difference who they are. It takes Jesus Christ, or a woman, or a parent to make them realize that they're not. I think all males truly want to be a hero. What Garth wants to be is what he thinks every man should be: a person of complete strength, a man of his own mind. I think he'll be perfectly happy with himself when he knows he is a good man."

"And is he there yet?" I asked her.

"I think he is so close. But I think he doesn't feel it yet. When I talk to him I say, 'I'm so proud of you. You're such a good man.' And this means all the world to him. What Garth needs to do is stop and say, 'It's not what I've done, but who I am,' and realize he can only do so much. I don't care who you are—John Wayne or anyone—life only offers you a certain level. Garth's reached it. He just doesn't realize it yet. If I could give him any advice, it would be: 'Son, you're there. Be happy and enjoy it.'"

At 8:45, Garth emerged from his dressing room. To ease his surreptitious entrance underneath the stage, he was wearing a navy blue NASA jumpsuit over his traditional cowboy garb. On his shoulder, he balanced his black plastic hatbox. Ten minutes later, the hatbox was empty and the mammoth light rig, which had been lowered from the ceiling to cover the stage, started rising in a cloud of artificial smoke. After several minutes, a white grand piano rose up from the stage. At the keys was a man in a white tuxedo and a white cowboy hat. It was a perfect tableau of Garth's last video, "The Red Strokes," and it elicited an explosion of flashbulbs. But the scene was artificial. Minutes later, the real Garth Brooks, looking like a postage stamp in red, white, and blue, emerged hydraulically from inside the fake piano, sang the line he had written especially for this moment, "Oh, I said a little prayer tonight / Before I came onstage . . ." and opened his arms to the crowd.

Source: Bruce Feiler, *Dreaming Out Loud: Garth Brooks, Wynonna Judd, Wade Hayes, and the Changing Face of Nashville* (New York: William Morrow, 1998), 257–68. (Pages 257–68 from DREAMING OUT LOUD by BRUCE FEILER. COPYRIGHT © 1998 by BRUCE FEILER. Reprinted by permission of HarperCollins Publishers.)

FOR FURTHER READING

Cox, Patsi Bale. *The Garth Factor: The Career behind Country's Big Boom.* New York: Center Street, 2009.

Maclachlan, Heather. "The Greatest Rock Star Who Never Was: Garth Brooks, Chris Gaines, and Modern America." *American Music* 26, no. 2 (Summer 2008): 196–222.

Shatkin, Elina. "The Strange Case of Chris Gaines and Garth Brooks." *Journal of Popular Music Studies* 25, no. 3 (September 2013): 389–97.

7. Played by actress Shirley Booth, the title character in a situation comedy about a maid and the family that employed her. The show aired from 1961 to 1966 ("*Hazel* [TV series]," http://en.wikipedia.org/wiki/Hazel_(TV_series), accessed 27 May 2014).

40

Debbie Holley

"Country Dancing Sparks Club Growth: New
Nightclubs, Remixes Target Trend" (1992)

Although dance hall culture has been an important part of country music
since its advent, audiences outside of Texas, Oklahoma, Louisiana, and
California have often shown only sporadic interest in dancing. The early 1990s
witnessed another national boom in country dancing with the advent of the "line
dancing" craze that filled nightclubs and dance halls and spawned line-dancing
fitness groups and social clubs in small towns and big cities across the United
States.[1] Line dances have been popular in the United States for centuries and
can be traced to the popularity of contra dances that arrived in the New World
with immigrants from the British Isles in the seventeenth century, and as anyone
attending a wedding reception might notice, the "Electric Slide" is one of the
nation's most popular line dances.

With the chart success of Billy Ray Cyrus's "Achy Breaky Heart" and the
subsequent choreography of a line dance to accompany it, several country artists

1. Ralph G. Giordano has traced this history in *Country & Western Dance* (Santa
Barbara, CA: ABC-CLIO, 2010), 91–138.

recorded songs expressly for the line-dance circuit, labels often hired professional choreographers to create special dances for their new hits and created special dance remixes for play over club sound systems, and clubs hired professional dance instructors to teach their patrons the latest dances.[2] For dancers who lived in areas without access to face-to-face instruction, The Nashville Network's *Club Dance* program—broadcast from the Wildhorse Saloon in Nashville—allowed viewers to learn the newest dances, participate in aerobic exercise in the comfort of their living rooms, and join in the broader line-dance culture. Moreover, line dances were designed to permit dancers with a wide range of skill levels to participate, and because the dances did not require partners, the dance clubs were popular among the single set. As a consequence, line dancing took the nation by storm in the early to mid-1990s, breathing new life into dance clubs around the United States at a time when social dancing was in decline.[3]

THE number of dance clubs featuring country music is on the rise as consumers "Come on Over to Country," as Hank Williams Jr. invites them to in his current single.

New country-oriented clubs are popping up from coast to coast, and clubs that are not strictly country are adding more music in this format, responding to customer demand. Existing country dance halls say business is better than ever.

Club managers say younger crowds are coming out to dance—a factor that is involving record labels more heavily than before in this alternative market. Sony, Arista, and Capricorn have lately been turning out dance remixes to cater to potential record buyers at country music clubs, and other labels are considering doing the same.

Jeff Walker, president of Nashville-based Aristo Media, which services videoclips and dance mixes to clubs, says club marketing began 12-15 months ago. However, he maintains that the video success of Mercury's Billy Ray Cyrus has caused labels to take a more aggressive look at marketing to clubs. Other executives point to the Brooks & Dunn "Boot Scootin' Boogie" dance remix (Arista) and the recently released, four-song remix sampler from Hank Williams Jr.'s "Maverick" album (Capricorn) as evidence of a new marketing opportunity in the clubs.

Walker notes that the increase in the number of clubs using country music is "the natural extension to what is happening with the media. Country music is now hip."

Although there are no reliable data, he calculates that the number of clubs has increased by 50-60% over the past 18 months to about 1,200. This figure, he says, includes chains and independent clubs and those that use live as well as recorded music.

In addition to the growth of country-only clubs, there has been an increase in the number of clubs that feature country one or two nights a week or show country videos, says

2. In fact, the Wildhorse Saloon, located in downtown Nashville, continues to offer instruction for line dancers at the time of this writing.

3. In addition to Giordano's history of line dancing, a nuanced study of country line dancing can be found in Jocelyn R. Neal, "Dancing around the Subject: Race in Country Fan Culture," *The Musical Quarterly* 89, no. 4 (2006): 555–79.

Walker. But, amid all the changes, he adds, there is still an element of caution lingering from the "Urban Cowboy" overkill [see chapter 35].

Club owners, managers, and DJs, meanwhile, report plans for additional clubs, changes in programming and décor, and more uses of country videos. Some clubs are even dusting off the mechanical bulls that were a craze during the "Urban Cowboy" fury of the early '80s.

There are clubs that play music videos on big-screen TVs. One club in Florida has a camera on its mechanical bull in the "rodeo room" so people in other rooms can watch the bull riders. Most clubs add top 40 into the country mix later in the evenings.

While a number of clubs offer live music, most of those venues feature local bands. At least for now, the circuit for country acts signed to labels is fairly limited. The big thing happening at country-oriented clubs is dancing, and patrons don't seem to mind dancing to records.

FREE DANCE LESSONS

For those just getting into the scene, several clubs offer free dances lessons, including Mr. Lucky's in Phoenix, the Texas-based Midnight Rodeo chain, and Denim & Diamonds in Santa Monica, Calif., which is the big new country nightspot in the Los Angeles area.[4]

There are two other Denim & Diamonds locations in California—the original in Sacramento, which opened in March 1991, and a new one in Huntington Beach, which debuted April 22. Denim & Diamonds are the former Bentley's nightclubs, which played top 40 music. GM[5] Joe Esposito says the chain owners are "looking at three to four more clubs by the end of the year."

Other Los Angeles-area country-music clubs include the Palomino, the Longhorn Saloon, and the Crazy Horse Saloon.

In New York, meanwhile, a new 15,000-square-foot country dance hall called Do Da's American Country opened May 20. Operated by Ken Cameron and Bonnie Kay Ziegler, who own the 6-year-old Do Da's in Fort Lauderdale, Fla., Do Da's plans to offer live, name entertainment five nights a week. The programming between sets will be a mix of 90% country and 10% country-flavored rock.

Do Da's subscribes to a video service for the latest and classic country videos, which are shown on a large screen visible from both levels. Often they run with no sound. Do Da's offers dance lessons by professional dancers and is developing a dance team to compete on the national level.

If that sounds like shades of the disco era, it's no surprise. Reg Moreau, a partner in the Hollywood/Fort Lauderdale club Desperado, says the site had been a disco in the '80s until he and his partners "changed it into a country club to fit the country trend."

His club also uses videos, records, and live bands as well as a mechanical bull to lure customers. But Moreau says, "There is more dancing being done to the video and DJs." He says there are other new country clubs in South Miami and West Palm Beach, Fla.

4. See, for instance, the professional resume of dance instructor Gloria Johnson (http://www.gloriajohnson.us/bio.htm; accessed 31 January 2014). Thanks to Jocelyn Neal for this reference.

5. General manager.

LIVE ENTERTAINMENT

Mark McDevitt, GM of J. David's Mr. Lucky's in Phoenix, says his club features live entertainment on both floors. One floor is top 40 and one is 100% country. "We have a house band Tuesday through Saturday, and we try to book the up-and-coming new acts," he says. DJs play music between live sets. Little video is used.

McDevitt says, "It's obvious country is going back to a younger crowd." He says there are plans to expand the club within the next month.

Likewise, Roger Gearhart, GM of eight country clubs in the Southwest, says, "I'm definitely seeing an increase in the number of country clubs in every market we're in." Among the venues run by Gearhart are Graham's in Oklahoma City, Okla., Cactus Moon in Abilene, Texas, and Graham Central Station in Phoenix.

Also seeing growth potential in country-music clubs is Mark Easterling, promotions director of Associates Club Management, which works with the Midnight Rodeo chain and also oversees Wild West in Houston and the Dallas club in San Antonio, Texas. "Ideally we'd like to add three to four clubs a year over the next several years," he says. "We hope to stay in the South and Southwest."

Regarding the Midnight Rodeo chain, he adds, "We're one of the originals. We have two [clubs] that have been open for 11 years." The chain has clubs in Amarillo, Lubbock, San Antonio, and Houston, Texas, and is constructing another one in Birmingham, Ala., he says.

Easterling's clubs use live acts an average of twice a month in each property—including some national acts—and also show video sparingly.

NEW MARKET EXPOSURE

Nashville executives note that the new wave of country-oriented clubs offers them a chance to get exposure for their product in markets where their artists might never otherwise be heard.

"If you can't get a record on a radio station in a market, and the video channels don't penetrate that market," says Walker, "the club may give you an opportunity to play that product in its audio mix."

Alan Butler, VP of promotion and artist development at Arista, says the Brooks & Dunn remix and video came about after he and others from the label visited clubs and noticed that "when the band would take a break, the DJs would throw on these long dance mixes of Madonna, Hammer, and Michael Jackson—and these were country clubs. These are the new discos where all the young people hang out on Friday and Saturday."

Rick Rockhill, national director of country promotion for Capricorn, says a consultant suggested he target clubs for Williams' new release. "We took the idea a step further and remixed four different cuts," he says. "It's just a monster." CD-X, a Nashville firm that services CDs to clubs and radio, distributed the Williams sampler to clubs only, while the label serviced it to key radio outlets. He says the added costs of remixing are insignificant "if we see an increase in sales."

Rick Blackburn, VP/GM, Atlantic/Nashville, says he is considering a club mix on some of Confederate Railroad's material. But he adds that Ray Kennedy's next album will probably be the label's first dance remix project.

Eddie Mascolo, VP of national country promotion at RCA Records/Nashville, says he will service clubs with remixed product if he has a record that is "suitable," such as an Aaron

Tippin cut. He says he has noticed that some clubs have switched their programming emphasis to "playing country with some pop music in the mix instead of playing pop music with a country song in the mix."

BOWEN INTERESTED

Jimmy Bowen, president of Liberty, says he has assigned an A&R person to research clubs to see what kind of mixes, if any, need to be done. "There are a half-dozen dances they do in these clubs," Bowen points out. "If your music doesn't fit those dances, why waste your time doing a special mix?" Bowen is looking toward remixes on David Lynn Jones, Jason, Pirates of the Mississippi, and Garth Brooks "if the music fits."

Mike Martinovich, VP of marketing for Sony Music in Nashville, says his label was the first to release a dance remix on Mary-Chapin Carpenter's "Down at the Twist and Shout" last year. "We've done probably five or six since that time, and we service them ourselves." Martinovich says he has noticed an increase in the number of requests from people "from Connecticut to Arizona" who say they are programming country music: "We certainly consider clubs as part of our marketing mix now."

He says Sony's next club focus will be on Stacy Dean Campbell, a youth-oriented 24-year-old "who will lend himself beautifully to the club strategy," says Martinovich. He says he is working on other club ideas related to some of his artists, "but nothing concrete now."

Source: Debbie Holley, "Country Dancing Sparks Club Growth: New Nightclubs, Remixes Target Trend," *Billboard* 104 (6 June 1992): 1, 76. (Used with permission.)

FOR FURTHER READING

Giordano, Ralph G. *Country & Western Dance*. Santa Barbara, CA: ABC-CLIO, 2010.
Neal, Jocelyn R. "Dancing around the Subject: Race in Country Fan Culture." *The Musical Quarterly* 89, no. 4 (2006): 555–79.

41

Eric Boehlert

"Classic Country Stations Fill Niche: Claim Fans of Currents, Standards Mix" (1993)

With the rise of such "hot country" artists as Garth Brooks and Shania Twain in the early 1990s, recording artists who had been mainstays of country radio for a decade or more began to find it increasingly difficult to get their music on radio playlists. The audience for country music was growing exponentially with the rise of hot country's pop- and rock-oriented country sounds, and radio station program directors began to become reluctant to play recordings that did not conform to the new sonic standards, fearing that their hard-won new audiences would be turned away by the sounds of steel guitars and fiddles. As a consequence, many long-time fans of the genre felt as though the stations that they had supported for many years had abandoned them and their musical tastes in favor of quick profits.

Consequently, as the following report from *Billboard* indicates, some radio station groups developed an alternative programming format that showcased "classic country" recordings, commonly using the AM frequencies that they had largely abandoned during the rise of commercial FM radio in the late

295

1970s and early 1980s.[1] These changing programming practices had two significant impacts on contemporary country music culture: (1) the segregation of country music audiences into those who support a seemingly more authentic traditional
country; and (2) the continued neglect of popular hits from previous years on contemporary FM country radio stations.[2]

———

W HEN country great Roy Acuff died last year, some commentators took mainstream
country radio to task, complaining that, in its current rush to be contemporary, the
format had turned its back on Acuff and other Nashville legends.

For the most part, that charge is accurate. But if those critics had looked, or listened,
more closely, they would have discovered that while mainstream and burgeoning hot country
stations battle over the musical direction of country radio, more and more traditional outlets—
spinning plenty of Marty Robbins, Loretta Lynn, and Roger Miller—are quietly staking out
niches for themselves.

"It's stuff you really don't hear on country radio anymore," says KYGO-AM Denver PD
Chuck St. John, describing the station, which has been classic country for the last five years.

Exact figures on numbers of traditional stations are not available, partly because defining traditional playlists and rotations is open to interpretation. Their numbers are increasing,
though, simply because the subcategory did not exist until recently. After all, before traditional
and hot country, there was simply country. But as the format's audience ballooned and frag-
mentation began, broadcasters looked to superserve more specific audiences.

Those aiming for younger listeners have received plenty of press and industry attention mostly due to the stations' FM homes and their ability to break new artists (Billboard, Oct.
31, 1992).

The traditional stations, thought, often on AM, appeal to a smaller and less glamorous demographic: 35-plus. That audience is made up of listeners who "don't understand why
they don't hear Conway Twitty on the radio anymore," says Jim Murphy, PD of Satellite Music
Network's traditional "Real Country" format, which is heard on more than 100 stations.

It's those type of listeners, say several programmers, who welcome familiar artists and
are turned off by some of the increasingly pop-sounding records coming out of Nashville. "I'd
call it a backlash," says Murphy.

1. For a discussion of FM radio's rise to dominance, consult Christopher H. Sterling
and Michael C. Keith, *Sounds of Change: A History of FM Broadcasting in America*
(Chapel Hill: University of North Carolina Press, 2008). Kim Simpson has also offered
an in-depth discussion of market segmentation and the growth of specialized radio
formats in *Early '70s Radio: The American Format Revolution* (New York: Continuum,
2011).

2. This history is traced more deliberately in George H. Lewis, "Lap Dancer or
Hillbilly Deluxe? The Cultural Constructions of Modern Country Music," *Journal of
Popular Culture* 31, no. 3 (Winter 1997): 163–73.

Charlie Connor, PD at KOWA (The Cow) Las Vegas, says his listeners "are turned off by what radio and record companies are trying to push off as country music today. There is a lot of good new country music. But a lot of it, too, I consider frustrated rock music."

As Connor claims, along with those testing the pop waters, just as many Nashville artists are embracing traditional sounds. "Real Country's" Murphy points to the music of Alan Jackson, Randy Travis, and Mark Chesnutt as examples. "A lot of that sounds good next to Patsy Cline," agrees KYGO's St. John, who mentions that recent ballads such as Trisha Yearwood's "Walkaway Joe," translate best for his format.

Programmers are quick to point out that, unlike oldies and classic rock formats, traditional country does not exist in a time warp. Current releases make up between 15% and 35% of traditional rotations, depending on the station.

Programmers say that's because listeners tell them, through research, that they like the old standards but they don't want to hear them exclusively. "Real Country" has cut back on the number of Grand Ole Opry acts it plays over the last three years to avoid burnout. KOWA's playlist is much looser. PD Connor tries not to play the same song more than once every three days.

Just as rotations vary within traditional country, so, too, do the tags used to describe the stations. SMN's "Real Country" was first known as "Traditional Country," but research showed that listeners instantly associated that name with "old," not the overall image the network was shooting for. For Connor in Las Vegas, "Country and Western" best describes the sound of KOWA. And "Country Classics" is the moniker St. John opts for in Denver.

For label promotion executives, who are always trying to break new acts and new singles from established stars (and who are no fans of classic rock), the slow but steady growth of traditional outlets is not necessarily a drawback. Scott Borchetta, VP [of] field promotion at MCA Nashville, says he welcomes the older-skewing country stations because they allow mainstream ones to open up their playlists and become more current.

The relationship between mainstream and traditional stations is often a close one. In several markets, including Denver and its KYGO-AM-FM, the two stations make up broad-based AM/FM country partnerships. And with the growth of local marketing agreements and duopoly situations, the trend is likely to continue as broadcasters try to sew up chunks of the country audience rather than duplicating a competitor's listenership. "Two or three formats doing exactly the same thing is too many formats in any market," says Murphy.

Source: Eric Boehlert, "Classic Country Stations Fill Niche: Claim Fans of Currents, Standards Mix." *Billboard* 105 (6 March 1993): 75, 79. (Used with permission.)

FOR FURTHER READING

Jensen, Joli. "Taking Country Music Serious: Coverage of the 1990s Boom." In *Pop Music and the Press*, ed. Steve Jones, 183–201. Philadelphia: Temple University Press, 2002.

White, Billy D., and Frederick A. Day. "Country Music Radio and Culture Regions." *Journal of Cultural Geography* 16, no. 2 (1997): 21–35.

Peter Cronin

"Nashville's Studio Boom Alters Musical Landscape" (1993)

Although it is perhaps best known as a center of country music recording, Nashville has also enjoyed a long history as an important center of rock and pop recording, playing host to Elvis Presley, Roy Orbison, Perry Como, and others in the 1950s and early 1960s and, quite famously, Bob Dylan in the late 1960s. However, while Nashville had been on the cutting edge of many trends in the recording industry, many music industry insiders still viewed the city as a southern backwater that was too far removed from New York and Los Angeles to make sustained efforts to record pop and rock acts there.

As "hot country" was taking over the airwaves in the early 1990s and major label recording budgets grew exponentially, Nashville became an increasingly attractive place to make pop and rock recordings. The city's greatest liability—its distance from L.A. and New York—became one of its strengths as studio owners, engineers, and musicians alike sought respite from the fast-paced, high-stress life of the nation's largest cities, and Nashville's comparatively cheap real estate prices encouraged record growth in the construction of recording studios.

In the following report from *Billboard*'s Peter Cronin, the impact of this growth on the national popular music landscape becomes increasingly clear. It is obvious that music industry executives, constantly looking to capitalize on the next big trend, were willing to completely overhaul the industry to chase the ever-changing tastes of audiences. Also apparent are the impending changes to Nashville itself, whose residents in the late 1980s still viewed it as something of a small town and close-knit community. The influx of new residents, new capital, and new ideas would challenge the status quo, often resulting in tense public conflicts about musical aesthetics and business ethics.

C OUNTRY music's unprecedented growth is pumping new life into Nashville's thriving studio scene. As musicians, producers, engineers, and investors pour in from both coasts, many industry observers feel this city, with its easy pace and low cost of living, could become the recording capital of America.

Several fundamental changes are taking place in the Nashville studio market, including a rise in producer-owned facilities and an increase in the number of new studio owners hailing from Los Angeles and other cities, looking to lure their pop clients to Nashville's pleasant environs.

While most insiders agree growth is inevitable, the biggest questions around town are whether the country boom can sustain increased studio competition, whether an increase in the number of new, state-of-the-art studios can convince major pop acts to come to Nashville and make records, and what effect that kind of influx of out-of-towners would have on the special chemistry that has long characterized the market.

With plans to concentrate on country music, producer Garth Fundis recently purchased the Sound Emporium, and producers Richard Landis and James Stroud are opening Loud Recording.

Meanwhile, Alan Sides, owner of L.A.'s Ocean Way and Record One Studios, David and Dee Mancini, owners of L.A.'s Devonshire Recording, and producer Chas Sanford are preparing to open Nashville facilities.

Many Music City studio pros seem ambivalent about the likelihood of pop ever gaining a strong foothold here. But Landis, a former VP of A&R[1] at BNA Records, is not alone in his fervent belief that there will be no major groundswell of noncountry music in Nashville.

Sides echoes the sentiments of many in country music when he points out that music audiences are giving up on the canned perfection of pop and turning to country "for its lyric and melodic value."

Sides, along with partner/engineer Bill Schnee and other investors, has purchased the abandoned Alamo Church in the center of this city's Music Row district. In addition, they're converting another 63,000-square-foot building nearby into a multistudio facility that will offer the first large rock 'n' roll-type tracking rooms in Nashville.

While Sides feels country music will make up a substantial portion of his business, he is sure that many of his L.A.-based clients "will enjoy coming to Nashville and using the musicians in town."

1. Vice-president of artists and repertoire.

The Mancinis are less reticent in their quest to bring pop to Music City. They've chosen the pastoral setting of nearby Franklin for a lavish, L.A.-style studio complex. The proposed $13 million, multi-acre complex will feature four complete recording studios and a huge, 400-seat soundstage for shooting videos and television. The Mancinis feel pop stars and television people will be willing to travel to Tennessee to escape the urban rat race. And they plan to be ready for them, with such lavish amenities as a swimming pool, tennis courts, and a nine-hole putting green.

For the "high echelon" stars that visit Devonshire, the Mancinis promise living quarters, fax machines, phones, and futuristic video tie-lines into the studio from offices in the facilities so artists can look in on their sessions, or do a vocal from an office. David Mancini has been involved in the design and construction of major studios from the Record Plant and Larrabee Sound in L.A. to Wally Heider's in San Francisco, and owns or co-owns six West Coast studios.

Nashville's lively music industry and reputation as the "Third Coast" can sound appealing to many in the recording industry. Producer Chas Sandford, former owner of a home studio in L.A. that was used by Def Leppard, Rod Stewart, and producer Bob Clearmountain, among others, was all but forced to get his business out of that city in the wake of the much-publicized home-studio zoning controversy (Billboard, May 9, 1992).

Now living in Franklin, Sanford plans to open a multistudio commercial facility in the Music Row area within a year.

While it hasn't always been the case, as country music has grown over the past decade into today's multimillion-dollar industry, Nashville finally has begun to embrace its reputation as Music City, and maintains an open-arms policy toward incoming music-related business.

Motown CEO Jheryl Busby and COO Harry Anger were recently guests of honor at a BMI luncheon attended by representatives of the Mayor's office and the City Council, as well as several leaders from Nashville's black community. Joyce Rice, BMI's director of writer/publisher relations, says the pair were here to talk about starting a country label in Nashville "because of the city's reputation for having the facilities and the artists, but, more than anything, they were attracted by the openness of the people."

However, many view Nashville's newfound attention to be a mixed blessing. Don Was hopes Nashville doesn't become victimized by the "carpetbagger syndrome." The L.A.-based producer, in town co-producing Kelly Willis' new MCA record with Tony Brown, echoes a common fear when he warns that "if you're coming to Nashville looking for some pot of gold at the end of the Garth rainbow, you just insult the people who are making great country records, and delude yourself."

Garth Brooks' producer, Allen Reynolds, theorizes that people coming to town with a different perspective might impact the way things are done here. But, like most Nashville producers, he doesn't plan to change the way he works, relying on "the live performance, and getting that magic moment in the studio." He relates the tale of out-of-towners from the pop world visiting Jack's Tracks, his Music Row studio, and being incredulous that he put a singer in the studio at the same time as the musicians. "I thought to myself, 'How else?'," Reynolds says, laughing.

Still, Reynolds feels it could be beneficial to all if new studios bring new talent. "Within the industry there are a lot of talented people who are not getting memorable songs elsewhere, and are seeing songs that they respect coming out of Nashville. It's not all hillbilly, barroom stuff."

ATMOSPHERE FOR SONGWRITERS

Nashville songwriters are indeed working with a wider stylistic palette than ever before, reflecting a widening definition of "country." In fact, much of what is being written sounds more like James Taylor than George Jones. The constant need for quality songs to feed the growing number of country artists has created an atmosphere for songwriters that Thom Schuyler, RCA's VP of operations, has compared with Paris' artist community in the '20s. With constant demo sessions and expanding country-division artist rosters, Nashville studios are indeed reporting that business is up approximately 15% over the previous year.

But, with new facilities on the horizon, many local studio pros wonder how long they can stay busy.

Ron Treat, manager of Soundstage, one of the premier rooms in town, says that, even with his recording rooms booked solid, he is beginning to wonder if studios in town will ever really see the big payoff. "The labels are keeping all the money," he says. "In terms of budgets, their people are still nickel-and-diming us to death."

Like most studio people in town, Jake Nicely, manager of Woodland Digital, isn't intimidated by the idea of new facilities opening up. "Good competition is always good," he says. "If it's a qualified bunch of people who know the industry, which I imagine these people will be, then it will help everybody in general."

Most insiders don't expect country recording budgets to increase dramatically, mainly because Nashville producers, working quickly and efficiently with budgets in the $100,000-$150,000 range, have been turning out records that sound as good as or better than anything in the more extravagant world of pop.

RATE ROLE REVERSAL

A self-described "pop producer who moved to Nashville," Landis sees a role reversal taking place, with rates rising in Nashville as they fall in L.A. In the mid-'80s, Nashville was the place in which to record very cheaply, and L.A. was "arrogantly expensive," with studios getting about $2,000-$3,000 per day. Rates in L.A. have come down, "with rare exceptions" to $1,000-$1,300 per day, says Landis, while some industry observers in Nashville note that studios here are averaging $1,500-$1,800 per day.

Emerald Sound manager Anthony Little wishes incoming studios well but feels they will "have a real tough time calling a rate of over $1,500 per day."

Landis warns against coming to Nashville just to take advantage of the boom, pointing out that producers and engineers can't expect to waltz in and make country records without some sense of the music's history and some of the special expertise this kind of recording requires.

Rather than any particular recording techniques, most of which he says are not exclusive to country music, Landis points to a "sensibility" and "passion for the music," as the things that distinguish a good country producer. "I just don't see a bunch of guys moving in and having the industry trust them," he says. "People want to come to Nashville because country is hot, and other formats are not, and that does not make for success."

Landis, Stroud, and Fundis are among an elite group of Nashville music executives that also includes MCA's Tony Brown, Liberty's Jimmy Bowen, Mercury's Harold Shedd, Arista's Tim DuBois, and Asylum's Kyle Lehning, who move easily from mixing board to boardroom.

That tradition, dating back to the days when consummate "song people" like Chet Atkins [see chapter 24] and Owen Bradley were calling the shots, has always been at the heart of this city's appeal and success as a recording center.

Some, like Bowen and Lehning, believe that pop can flourish here, and that these new studios may be just the beginning. MCA Publishing president Jerry Crutchfield, who has been writing and producing hit records here for more than 25 years, feels there's definitely a need for more top-notch studios in town.

According to the latest figures from Music Row magazine, there are about 140 commercial recording facilities in Nashville. But, like the hi-tech gear that keeps these studios on the competitive cutting edge, that figure is constantly being updated and revised. If one were to include very visible recording room in town—from top-of-the-line, world-class rooms, to demo studios packed into old houses along Music Row,[2] to professional-quality home studios all over the outlying hills—that number probably would double.

Still, when it comes to cutting basic tracks, Crutchfield, like any top producer, is quite fussy. Only a short list of Nashville studios, including Soundstage, Masterfonics, Emerald Sound, and the Music Mill are considered consistently up to par by many of these producers.

POP HISTORY

Popular music has always had some presence in Nashville. For years, some of the biggest names in pop—including Rosemary Clooney, Perry Como, Elvis Presley, Bob Dylan, and Bob Seger—have quietly come here to take advantage of the technical expertise, musicianship, and great songwriters.

Was jumps at the opportunity to tap that tradition. "There are guys in Nashville doing strictly country music who have strong R&B backgrounds, and to be able to combine the two is a very significant thing," Was says. "The best example would be a guitar player like Reggie Young, who comes from a Memphis/Muscle Shoals background,[3] but it's not like he plays R&B or country. It's hard to put your finger on the origin of his licks. Is it Smokey Robinson or Hank Williams?"

At his Bennett House Studios in Franklin, producer Keith Thomas has been sculpting pop hits, most notably for Vanessa Williams and Amy Grant, that are a lot closer to Smokey than Hank. The track for Williams' Grammy-winning "Save the Best for Last" was created largely by the producer working alone in his MIDI[4] room.

Cynics point out that his MIDI-based records could have been recorded anywhere, and have nothing to do with Nashville. But Thomas feels technology may be one of the keys to Nashville's future in pop. As recording equipment has evolved, it no longer is necessary for a

2. "Demo studios" are low-cost recording facilities that cater to aspiring artists and songwriters who are hoping to have their songs recorded.

3. Memphis, Tennessee, and Muscle Shoals, Alabama, were centers for soul and rhythm and blues production during the 1960s and 1970s. For more background, see Rob Bowman, *Soulsville, U.S.A.: The Story of Stax Records* (New York: Schirmer, 2003); Peter Guralnick, *Sweet Soul Music: Rhythm and Blues and the Southern Dream of Freedom* (Boston: Back Bay Books, 1999); and Robert Gordon, *Respect Yourself: Stax Records and the Soul Explosion* (New York: Bloomsbury USA, 2013).

4. MIDI (Musical Input, Digital Interface) is a computer technology that allows musicians to create sounds using computer software.

producer to go where the pop players are, and Thomas, like an increasing number of recording pros, decided that the Tennessee lifestyle was simply more conducive to creativity. "After working several years, it has really started to pay off," he says. In addition to Williams and Grant, Bennett House has recently played host to James Ingram, Peabo Bryson, Trey Lorenz, and Michael W. Smith.

Source: Peter Cronin, "Nashville's Studio Boom Alters Musical Landscape," *Billboard* 105 (19 June 1993): 1, 66. (Used with permission.)

FOR FURTHER READING

Cox, Patsi Bale. *The Garth Factor: The Career Behind Country's Big Boom.* New York: Center Street, 2009.

Kosser, Michael. *How Nashville Became Music City, U.S.A.: 50 Years of Music Row.* Milwaukee: Hal Leonard, 2006.

43

Kyle Ryan

"Any Kind of Music But Country: A Decade of Indie Country, Punk Rock, and the Struggle for Country's Soul" (2005)

Inspired by the countercultural ethos, rough timbres and textures, and political engagement of punk music and the raw sounds of honky-tonk, the alternative country movement emerged during the early 1990s around young bands in the American Midwest, Texas, and California who struck a decidedly anti-Nashville stance in their songwriting and rhetoric.[1] Arguing that contemporary country music had abandoned its working-class heritage and created music that spoke to the concerns of the suburban middle class, many alternative country artists reclaimed such country artists as the Carter Family, Hank Williams, and Merle Haggard and used revisionist histories to reposition them as punk icons.[2]

1. For a timeline of alternative country music's history, consult Kelly Burchfield and Barbara Ching, "Alt.Country Chronology," in *Old Roots and New Routes: The Cultural Politics of Alt.Country Music*, ed. Pamela Fox and Barbara Ching (Ann Arbor: University of Michigan Press, 2008), 233–39.
2. Aaron Smithers offers a useful discussion of the connections between alternative country and punk in "Old Time Punk," in *Old Roots and New Routes: The Cultural*

Some artists—including, most notably, the Belleville, Illinois-based band Uncle Tupelo—often reworked classic country songs into high-octane punk statements of cultural disaffection and revitalized country styles that had fallen out of the country music mainstream, including western swing, honky-tonk, and bluegrass.[3] Still others, such as singer-songwriter Robbie Fulks, wrote songs that were highly critical of the Nashville music industry's image and financial obsessions and the compromises that the industry had made to reach the large audiences that the genre enjoyed in the 1980s and 1990s.

The following essay by Kyle Ryan was published in the magazine *Punk Planet*, a national publication directed at the national punk audience. This piece, which serves as an introduction to a country subgenre that had been around for more than a decade, lays bare the central ideologies of the alternative country movement. Although other publications—especially *No Depression*, which adopted a nonchalant attitude toward defining the genre in the first place[4]—had worked to articulate the genre's constantly changing boundaries and its ideological concerns for its audience, this introductory essay offers the benefit of hindsight, exploring some of the genre's successes as well as its failures. Moreover, whereas *No Depression* frequently celebrates the genre's country roots, Ryan highlights here the punk underpinnings of a marginal subgenre. In particular, alternative country is presented as a more ethical form of country music, one that does not support the bombastic consumerism of a Garth Brooks concert and that respects the rich traditions of American vernacular musics.

———

THE phrase "alt-country" is the "emo"[5] of the country world: No artist or label espouses it, but everyone sort of grudgingly co-exists with it.

Politics of Alt.Country Music, ed. Pamela Fox and Barbara Ching (Ann Arbor: University of Michigan Press, 2008), 175–94.

3. For more on Uncle Tupelo, consult chaps. 1–6 of Greg Kot, *Wilco: Learning How to Die* (New York: Broadway Books, 2004); S. Renee Dechert, "'Oh, What a Life a Mess Can Be': Uncle Tupelo, Bahktin, and the Dialogue of Alternative Country Music," in *Country Music Annual 2001*, ed. Charles K. Wolfe and James E. Akenson (Lexington: University Press of Kentucky, 2001), 70–91.

4. *No Depression* is best known for touting a tag line defining alternative country music as "whatever that is." For a sense of the attitudes and musical styles championed by the alternative country music scene, consult Grant Alden and Peter Blackstock, eds., *The Best of* No Depression: *Writing about American Music* (Austin: University of Texas Press, 2005).

5. Short for "emotional," the term "emo" was used to describe the music of such bands as My Chemical Romance. For more background, consult Karen Tongson, "Tickle Me Emo: Lesbian Balladeering, Straight-Boy Emo, and the Politics of Affect," in *Queering the Popular Pitch*, ed. Sheila Whiteley and Jennifer Ryncenga (New York: Routledge, 2006), 55–66; Sarah F. Williams, "'A Walking Open Wound': Emo Rock and the 'Crisis of Masculinity in America," in *Oh Boy! Masculinities and Popular Music*, ed. Freya Jarman-Ivens (New York: Routledge, 2007), 145–60; and Andy R. Brown,

"If I never hear that term again, it would be too soon," says singer Neko Case. She has it a little tougher, though, as critics often refer to her as an alt-country "chanteuse." Other artists have found ways around it. Singer Sally Timms half-seriously refers to her work as "art country." Singer-songwriter Robbie Fulks uses "descriptive country," mostly because if confuses people.

"After a while it's a non-answer answer," he says. " 'We play descriptive country.' And then they just stop talking about it." He laughs, but he adds that he can see the validity in the dreaded alt-country moniker.

"I think there are a lot of bad people in that category," Fulks says, "But I think it makes sense to have a category like that, something that says, 'I'm country, but I'm not totally evil.' "

Convincing people of that, particularly those who grew up listening to punk, has gotten easier during the past decade. It's been 10 years since alt-country pioneers Uncle Tupelo broke up. Bloodshot Records produced its first release (a compilation of Chicago underground country called *For a Life of Sin*) and nearly 10 years since *No Depression*, the bi-monthly magazine of the alt-country scene, published its first issue. That the genre has lasted that long is a surprise to even those who were there at the start.

"It was like we put on a dance to save the teen center, but now we've got to run the fucking thing," says Bloodshot Records co-owner Rob Miller of the label's unexpected success.

That Bloodshot was founded by punks is just one of the numerous parallels between the alt-country and punk-rock worlds, and the line separating them has occasionally grown blurry. And that, critics say, is precisely the problem. As alt-country grows in popularity and fans and performers with no history in country music come into the scene, some worry about the genre's purity. More than a decade after the rise of alt-country, a debate rages about what it means, what it's done to country music, and just who is allowed to play it.

FUCK THIS TOWN: THE DECLINE OF COUNTRY MUSIC

While many may debate the merits and failings of alt-country, there's one thing the fans of the genre can agree on: that contemporary mainstream country music is no good. Fulks suggests its current state is part of a decline that began more than 30 years ago, though its atrophy isn't unique.

"It's the same thing that makes Beyoncé music bad or Tom Petty music bad," he explains. "The evolution of the music and the people that make the music is technology-driven. It's human performance giving way to edited performances and to the values of an engineering man. Also, I think country music in particular is too market-driven and too dependent on that narrow window of program directors on commercial radio—that's what totally drives country music."

He knows firsthand. In addition to releasing a record on Geffen Records in 1998 (*Let's Kill Saturday Night*), Fulks moved to Nashville in 1993 to work in music publishing after a friend scored a hit for Garth Brooks. At his job, he wrote songs in the hopes someone on Music Row, the city's music-industry hub, would pick them up. The experience proved to be both exhausting and humiliating, and it inspired perhaps his best-known song, "Fuck This Town,"

"Suicide Solutions? Or, How the Emo Class of 2008 Were Able to Contest Their Media Demonization, Whereas the Headbangers, Burnouts or 'Children of ZoSo' Generation Were Not," *Popular Music History* 6, nos. 1–2 (2011): 19–37.

from 1997's *Southmouth* (Bloodshot). In Nashville, Fulks "shook a lotta hands / ate a lotta lunch / wrote a lotta dumbass songs."

Dumbass songs were *exactly* what label executives and program directors at radio stations wanted—just not, apparently, what Fulks wrote. At this point in the '90s, with the success of Garth Brooks, country radio found success with songs that were country, but not *too* country.

"I remember there was a big push in the early '90s to rid country music of any lingering Hank Williams feelings that it had," Case says. "There were ads like 'All Country, No Bumpkin!' or 'Not the Country Your Grandparents Listened To!' or 'Noboby'd Dog Is Gonna Die!' It was really stupid."

But, Case concedes, stupid sells.

"I don't think it's country's fault, but bad music apparently sells a lot of ads—which makes me sad because I think people really miss out," she says. "I'm sure they don't know they do, but they do. I don't really mourn the death of access to mainstream radio for mainstream folks, though, you know? You could be in the company of great independent bands, or you could [be] in the company of Toby Keith. Which would you choose?"

Few people besides executives of large broadcasting corporations would argue that radio has improved over the years. Fulks thinks their days could be numbered, as the Internet and satellite radio challenge the corporate radio model. But the sound of commercial radio and the process by which songs are created for it won't change. Fulks calls it "the hegemony of the machine."

"They're naturally deferential—a lot of producers are—to this idea that a record is a collage of finessed measures," Fulks says, "and the measures are finessed by this outside party that's on this 40-channel board working a lot of arcane and intimidating buttons. The more it has to do with that, the less it has to do with people rehearsing the songs and coming in and giving it all you got."[6]

Not that Fulks shuns what the studio magicians create—the man who wrote "Fuck This Town" also confesses to enjoying Shania Twain, the archetype of what that song refers to as "soft-rock feminist crap."

"It's the total apotheosis of what I was just saying about music put together at a bar at a time by engineering nerds, so I wouldn't go see Shania in concert," Fulks says. "I'm not interested in that, but as marvels of engineering, the records are really required listening for anybody in country."

Many would argue that the technical wonder that helps make artists like Twain sound sparkingly clean also makes the songs seem more generic and removed from the everyday lives of listeners. And it's because of this that while Bloodshot co-owner Nan Warshaw may run a country label, the overlap between Bloodshot's and mainstream country's audiences is virtually nonexistent.

6. Of course, such arguments around the value and limits of technological mediation are quite common throughout contemporary popular music. See, for instance, Leslie C. Gay Jr., "Acting Up, Talking Tech: New York Rock Musicians and Their Metaphors of Technology," *Ethnomusicology* 42, no. 1 (Winter 1998): 81–98; Thomas Porcello, "Music Mediated as Live in Austin: Sound, Technology, and Recording Practice," in *Wired for Sound: Engineering and Technologies in Sonic Cultures*, ed. Paul D. Green and Thomas Porcello (Middletown, CT: Wesleyan University Press, 2004), 103–17; and Joseph G. Schloss, *Making Beats: The Art of Sample-Based Hip-Hop* (Middletown, CT: Wesleyan University Press, 2004), 63–78.

"The more I talk to people and think about people who are listening and buying country music today, compared to who the fans of our bands are, it's completely different audiences," Warshaw says. "Commercial country is suburban mall music. It has, I think, less to do with traditional country than what our bands are doing."

Therein lies the great paradox of so-called alt-country: It's more traditional than mainstream country music, yet labeled "alternative." While radio programmers, artists and label executives pay lip service to the legacies of Johnny Cash, Hank Williams, or Merle Haggard, they push songs like Shania Twain's "That Don't Impress Me Much," which has as much to do with Johnny Cash as Madonna's "Holiday."

Current country music is "actually a kind of fantasy," says musician Jon Langford. "They might as well be singing about elves and wizards. It's completely irrelevant to people's everyday lives."

His bandmate in the Mekons, and fellow solo artist, Sally Timms agrees.

"The more traditional kind of country music that came out in the '60s and '70s—it was just grittier," Timms says. "But then again, most contemporary music now isn't very interesting. It's so packaged that I don't think any of those forms, aside from some kind of kitsch value, will be very highly regarded in 20 years' time."

While Shania Twain may represent country's crossover-minded excess, Toby Keith's shit-kickin' anthems draw the most contempt from the alt-country world. Keith was relatively successful in the 1990s with his sort of neotraditionalist country, but never had a massive commercial breakthrough. He found it after the September 11 attacks with his album *Unleashed*. It featured the time-to-kick-some-ass track called "Courtesy of The Red, White, And Blue (The Angry American) [....]"[7]

Jingoistic anthems turned out to be extremely lucrative, and Keith followed up *Unleashed* with 2003's *Shock'n Y'all*, featuring songs such as the saccharine "American Soldier," the bizarrely messianic "If I Was Jesus," and, classiest of all, "The Taliban Song." It's about a "middle-eastern camel-herdin' man" who hates the Taliban and dreams of escaping Afghanistan on his camel (check the refrain "ride camel ride") [....][8]

THREE CHORDS AND THE TRUTH: PUNK AND COUNTRY

Although he probably couldn't have anticipated what someone like Toby Keith would do with it, legendary country songwriter Harlan Howard famously referred to country music as "three chords and the truth." Not surprisingly, that sentiment plays well in the world of punk rock.

"Hank Williams Sr. was as punk as anybody," says Jon Snodgrass, singer-guitarist of the alt-country band Drag the River. "A lot of that stuff was just so bare-bones and raw and full of life, you know? It's got a lot of the same things that made me enjoy punk rock."

Jon Langford made a similar discovery when listening to a mixtape a DJ friend made for him called *Honky Tonk Classics*. Having grown up in Wales (the "Mississippi of the UK," according to Miller), Langford didn't have a terribly favorable impression of country music.

7. Excerpt from "Courtesy of the Red, White, and Blue (The Angry American)" redacted for copyright reasons.
8. Excerpt from "The Taliban Song" redacted for copyright purposes.

"I thought country was rubbish, just right-wing crap that wouldn't possible be interesting," he says. "It was old man's music."

But Langford became obsessed with the artists on the mixtape and preached the country gospel to his bandmates in the Mekons, though it wasn't the music that attracted him as much as the subject matter, he says. "There was a kind of language that came in it—a playfulness, but also a seriousness to the topics and the actual engagement with everyday life—which seemed remarkably similar to our daily lives at that point."

Not long after, the Mekons released *Fear & Whiskey*, arguably the first record that had an identifiable alt-country sound. Timms, who joined the Mekons around that time, had the same kind of epiphany Langford did about country.

"It is blue-collar music; so was punk," Timms says. "It deals with the same things; it could be political music, it could be difficult music, it could take on subject matter that affected people's regular lives, but did it in a way that people still enjoyed listening to and might dance to and might just absorb as they dance."

The message and themes weren't the only attractions; the music itself proved to be equally gripping for Dallas Good, singer/guitarist of country-psychedelic band the Sadies. He and his brother, Travis, who's also in the Sadies, grew up in a country household. Their father, Bruce, played in legendary Canadian bluegrass band The Good Brothers. The boys were fans of punk rock, but they didn't grow up despising country music.

"There's very, very aggressive styles within every category of music," Dallas Good says. "Of course that's going to appeal to people that enjoy aggressive music. It didn't take too much time to realize that bluegrass is much faster than the fastest hardcore music."

Rob Miller made a similar discovery in high school when he stole a record from his girlfriend's mother by bluegrass legends Flatt & Scruggs. The duo were perhaps most famous for "The Ballad of Jed Clampett," the theme song to *The Beverly Hillbillies*. Miller brought the record to practice for his punk-rock band as a joke one night.

"I was like, 'Hey look at what I stole,' and we played it, and it was the fastest music we'd ever heard," Miller says. "Could we play this fast? We couldn't. We just listened to the musicians, and it just floored us."

Jon Snodgrass had been a fan of old country music growing up, but Uncle Tupelo really inspired him, along with a legion of other fans. Uncle Tupelo had punk-rock roots, and to Snodgrass, they sounded like a country version of his favorite band Hüsker Dü. He avoided playing a similar style, though, because he lived in St. Louis, practically Uncle Tupelo's hometown. He eventually started playing in the punk band Armchair Martian and moved to Colorado.

There, he met another Uncle Tupelo fan named Chad Price, who had been singing for punk legends All. Together they formed Drag the River as a side project, enlisting the help of fellow punk rocker JJ Nobody from the Nobodys. Their punk-rock pedigree made for some surprised fans once Drag the River began playing. During their first tour, promoters enthusiastically touted them as members of All and Armchair Martian.

"When we first started touring, we would get like a lot of All fans at the shows having no idea what we were," Price says, "but surprisingly, everybody was really cool with it."

Other bands embrace their punk backgrounds more directly. "High Life," the first track on the self-titled debut by Whiskey & Co., actually lifts a verse from "Start Today" by Gorilla Biscuits. It's one way the Florida band has tried to bring punk to country.

"As long as you're writing music, part of your soul is going to come through," says vocalist Jim Helm. "It doesn't really matter what genre you're in."

Whiskey & Co. have stayed pretty close to their punk roots; No Idea Records, home to bands like Planes Mistaken For Stars and J Church, released their album last year, though Whiskey & Co. is the lone country band on the roster.

"When Var [Thelin, co-owner] decided to put out the record, I was a little worried," says Helm, who also works at No Idea while attending grad school in Gainesville. "I mean, I was glad he was putting it out, but we are unlike anything that ever comes off of No Idea, and we did get a lot of people that were like 'What?'

"We're not a punk-rock band on a punk-rock label, which is sad in a way because I don't think there should be any reason why you can't be a punk-rock country band," Helm says.

When Whiskey & Co. toured with Hot Water Music and Against Me!, they were met with many blank stares, but they also received compliments from some people—usually the older ones—after the show. That's no fluke; it seems that most people rediscover country music once they hit their mid-to-late 20s, particularly if they grew up with punk rock.

"Time went from being 19-year-old fresh-faced punk rockers to being 28-year-old guys who have relationships that have broken up and actively drank too much and spent a lot of time sitting around in bars," Jon Langford says. "We were kind of world-weary. It's funny to think about it now; at that age—26, 27—we had gotten a bit old mannish. We felt like we had been through the wringer."

Punk rock tends to change how its proponents see the world; as punk rockers age, it becomes more of an idea and less tied to a specific sound. At 15, country music is heresy; at 25, it's a mirror of the foundation of punk rock. Langford puts it simply: "Country is punk music for old people."[9]

"When you grow up in that scene, when you get older, and you no longer want to burn down the governor's mansion or destroy the world or whatever," Miller says, "you are seeing this other kind of music that is also very simple, very straightforward, very direct. It has an immediate connection with the audience.

"People will pick up a Robbie record or a Bobbie [Bare Jr.] record and say, 'I don't hear any punk in here,'" Miller continues. "It's more in the ethos and the way that we run the business."

WHO'S [SIC] COUNTRY IS THIS, ANYWAY?

While Bloodshot's artist-friendly ethos makes them attractive to performers, others—sometimes their own bands—have criticized what the label represents. When Bloodshot released *Cockadoodledon't* by Th'Legendary Shack Shakers in 2003, vocalist Colonel JD Wilkes felt apprehensive about the association.

"We knew we would be kind of damned into a world that was sort of dying as far as hip factor and sex appeal is concerned," Wilkes says. "But I see the alt-country thing as kind of the neofolk scare that's mostly guys that appreciate country music but are masquerading as

9. Trent Hill has problematized country music's relationship with youth culture in his essay "Why Isn't Country Music 'Youth' Culture?," in *Rock Over the Edge: Transformations in Popular Music Culture*, ed. Roger Beebe, Denise Fulbrook, and Ben Saunders (Durham, NC: Duke University Press, 2002), 161–90.

farmers when they're really sort of socialist intellectuals, and that's foreign to my experience as a guy from sub-rural Kentucky.

"Most of the people that I know from that area, you know, they like having guns, and they're not for gay marriage," Wilkes continues. "It's all these issues that Bloodshot and *No Depression* magazine support that don't really reflect the attitude of the red states. That just seems a little strange to me."

Not surprisingly, the band left Bloodshot (located in blue Illinois)[10] after *Cockadoodledon't* and released their latest, *Believe*, last year on Yep Rock Records (located in red North Carolina). The blue-versus-red analysis is a bit faulty here, though, as Chicago served as the nation's hub of country music for a healthy chunk of the 20th century. That status came from the mostly forgotten National Barn Dance, broadcast by radio station WLS. It ran from 1924 to 1960, and during that time it was *the* end-all/be-all of country music.

Regardless, the question of country "authenticity" is one that Miller doesn't take lightly. "It's an argument that, depending on when you catch me, I'll either just kindly dismiss," Miller says, "or if we go to a bar right now, I can go on a one-hour rant about how intellectually flimsy an argument it is, because who belongs to country? Is there going to be some sort of arbiter of genetic authenticity of who can do this music? It's just not valid."

To placate critics, he rattles off the Southern home states of 12 of the bands that have been integral to the label's development, from Ryan Adams to Trailer Bride to the Old 97s (North Carolina, Mississippi and Texas, respectively). "It's not really a John Kerry-ish Northeastern cabal of intellectuals," he says.

Are people in Maine not allowed to play country music simply because of their home state? The argument goes. Or is country only for people from a rural area? Why not cities? The same authenticity argument rages in every genre. Who's punk rock? Do white people have a place in hip-hop?

Jamie Barrier of The Pine Hill Haints can see both Miller and Wilkes' points. Barrier grew up in Alabama and now lives just across the state line in rural Tennessee. The Haint's sound doesn't quite fit a particular classification; it's a mix of bluegrass, folk and country, all of it distinctly Southern. But he concedes that country music has no "home"; it just happened to be popularized in the South.

"In a lot of ways I agree with JD Shack Shaker regarding 'Northern' people taking an old Southern tradition and giving it rules, running the show, calling the shots, executing artists and all that," Barrier says. "Like sometimes the Haints will play with a 'country' band from Europe or New York City or the Northeast, then we'll meet them, and they treat us like Alabama morons who don't get it."

If anyone "gets it," Barrier does. As a child, his grandfather took him to community hootenannies out in the country where people gathered to sing songs all night long. The tradition continues today, and Barrier still participates when he's not on tour.

10. "Blue" in this instance refers to Democratic; Illinois frequently votes Democratic in presidential elections. Yet, it should be noted that, while Illinois as a whole tends to favor Democratic candidates in national elections, it is largely a consequence of Chicago's influence on electoral politics. Downstate Illinois—where Uncle Tupelo was founded—tends to favor Republican candidates in local and state elections. For more background, consult James D. Nowlan, Samuel K. Gove, and Richard J. Winkel Jr., *Illinois Politics: A Citizen's Guide* (Urbana: University of Illinois Press, 2010), 12–20.

"That's more than just music, more than Uncle Tupelo," Barrier says. "It's like pumping gas at a random catfish house and hearing old men talk. It's a poetry; it's a distinct way that the community in the rural South phrases things and words; the way people choose to express being broke or hungry or stoned, the way they cook their greens and grits, and the music is an extension. It's not a solo artist who was a Hank fan. It's part of the culture."

For Bloodshot, it was never about Uncle Tupelo either (neither Warshaw nor Miller were fans) or a mere fondness for country icons. The label has also strenuously avoided anything resembling shtick.

"The bands that made me insane are bands that we've got a dumpster full of demos of people that are like the Tractor King Howdy Boys and the Pitchfork Trio and all that shit," Miller says. "They're throwing hay around on stage and wearing straw hats. And it is shtick—shtick I can't stand."

Unfortunately, there are hundreds of bands or musicians for whom shtick is an innate part of their conception of country music. Maybe thousands of them. Jon Langford and Robbie Fulks felt like they've played with all of them.

"The promoter will say[,] 'We gotta band that sounds just like you, and they're opening for you tonight,'" Fulks says. "'You're gonna love 'em. They're like the Knoxville equivalent of Robbie Fulks.' Just because this has happened like 50 times. I'm like, 'Oh my god, I can't wait to see what this person thinks sounds like me.'" He laughs. "It's always something really horrible, you know? It's a bunch of people pretending to be hillbillies in overalls and screaming, and they can't play their banjos, and it's all a theatrical presentation. That's really obsessed me over the years: Is that what people hear when I'm playing?"

Barrier has had few run-ins with such *Hee-Haw* [sic] types on the Haints' many tours, though he tends to encounter snotty traditionalists who critique his playing style or dismiss him as an "Alabama moron." For the jokey country bands, the presentation may just be their shield.

"A lot of those country bands, it almost seems like they're making fun of it," Snodgrass says. "Or maybe they kind of liked it, but they didn't really know how to write it, and they didn't know how people would take it if they did write country songs, so they'd do it tongue-in-cheek."

Listening to Drag The River's album *Closed* might make listeners wonder if Snodgrass and Price's tongues are there, too. Nearly all of the 14 songs talk about cirrhosis-inducing amounts of drinking (practically a country-music cliché). There's also a sort of religious ballad, "Life of Ruin," where Price begs Jesus to save him from himself, though to cynical ears it may sound like a parody of that old country staple, the spiritual ballad. But Price insists there's no irony involved. Yes, they drink that much, and "Life of Ruin" isn't just their take on what a redemption song would sound like; it *is* a redemption song. "I'm not writing anything just to draw people into like, 'Oh yeah, they're country,' you know?" Price says. "It's all real."

Whiskey & Co. have numerous tales of hard drinking and hard living on their debut album, but there are also songs obviously written from a male point of view, which Helm's bandmates wrote before she joined the band. "Barroom Women" talks about having "$15 for a whore" before the refrain of "all you barroom women I like you best."

"That's another thing we get a lot of flack for because people say it doesn't sound authentic to have a woman singing songs from a male point of view, which I can agree with," Helm says. Whiskey & Co. wrote all their new material together, so Helm is anxious to record new songs without the personal disconnect.

Langford and Timms, being native Europeans, have to answer for a lot more when the authenticity argument comes their way. Timms has made two country records, and her latest album, *In the World of Him* (Touch & Go), features songs written by Langford and Ryan Adams.

"When I made a country record, some people would very occasionally go, 'You don't really have the credentials to be able to sing a country record," Timms says. "But I'm not singing in a fake American accent and pretending I grew up in the Appalachians.

"I always thought of myself more as a singer and an interpreter, so I don't see why I should be contained in one genre. Why can't I make a country record if I want to.?"

Langford's made more than a few of them; the Bloodshot catalogue would be missing a sizeable chunk without his contributions as a solo artist and with the bands the Waco Brothers and the Pine Valley Cosmonauts. He also paints portraits of country-music icons based on their old publicity photos, though he's taken to blindfolding them, scratching their faces, or replacing their heads with skulls in his paintings. He also once took headstones he created with the names of country-music legends and placed them in front of the headquarters of various record labels in Nashville. That a European would pull such shenanigans is more than enough to rile traditionalists.

But Langford also had a habit of irking Europeans. After he became obsessed with country music, Langford and friends would perform songs by legendary country singer Buck Owens at shows in Leeds, much to the confusion—or outright irritation—of the locals.

People in Chicago, where he eventually moved, celebrated him for it. The city had a popular country-western club called the R&R Ranch near downtown, home of the long-running local country band the Sundowners.

"I'd get up on stage on a Saturday night with the Sundowners and do all these songs with a room full of drunken urban Appalachians dancing smoking, and drinking and giving me the time of day," Langford says. "It was sort of trial by fire because they could have been like, 'We know you're from Wales! You're not country! Go away!' If they had said that to me, I would have never, ever played that again."

Instead, he's performed twice at the Grand Ole Opry with the Waco Brothers. At his core, though, Langford says he's a punk rocker, and he has his own qualms with inauthentic alt-country.

"You know, the whiney singer-songwriters with their friggin' acoustic guitars perpetuating fucking myths about the wind blowing in their hair," he says. "[Those] were the people we were trying to destroy, you know?"

Somewhere, there's an acoustic singer-songwriter writing about the breeze on the plains and thinking that Langford doesn't have a clue. Just like in every other genre, fans of country music will endlessly debate who's real and who's a poser: too country, not country enough, too jokey, too serious, too Northern to be authentic, too Southern to be worldly.

In alt-country, where genres mix and match, steady footing can be hard to find. A decade after releasing their first album, Bloodshot's Warshaw and Miller not only understand that, but expect it.

"We may be the standard bearers of the alt-country music from the punk perspective," Warshaw says, "but from the Americana perspective, we're still the red-headed stepchild."

"Yeah, we can't do anything right," Miller adds. "You get the alt-country fascists hating the record because it doesn't fit within their parameters, then everybody else who's already made up their mind about the whole spectrum of alt-country going, 'Oh that's alt-country.

I don't like that.' With a genre that rides musical boundaries, we're riding a fence that's on top of a smaller fence."

Source: Kyle Ryan, "Any Kind of Music But Country: A Decade of Indie Country, Punk Rock, and the Struggle for Country's Soul," *Punk Planet* 66 (March-April 2005): 78–82. (Used with permission of the author.)

FOR FURTHER READING

Alden, Grant, and Peter Blackstock, eds. *The Best of No Depression: Writing about American Music.* Austin: University of Texas Press, 2005.

Fox, Pamela, and Barbara Ching, eds. *Old Roots, New Routes: The Cultural Politics of Alt.Country Music.* Ann Arbor: University of Michigan Press, 2008.

Lee, Steve S., and Richard A. Peterson. "Internet-based Virtual Music Scenes: The Case of P@ in Alt.Country Music." In *Music Scenes: Local, Translocal, and Virtual,* ed. Andy Bennett and Richard A. Peterson, 187–204. Nashville: Vanderbilt University Press, 2004.

Russell, Robert Allen. "Looking for a Way Out: The Politics and Places of Alternative Country Music." Ph.D. dissertation, University of Iowa, 2009.

Rich Kienzle

Review of *BR5-49* (1996)

Not everyone was enamored with the rise of the alternative country movement. For some critics, the tongue-in-cheek attitudes of some alternative country bands struck them as disingenuous parodies of older country
music. Also, the efforts on the part of some alternative country musicians to
revive the musical practices associated with honky-tonk, western swing, and
the Bakersfield Sound were cast, on the one hand, as great tributes to country music traditions or, on the other, as evidence that alternative country had
been creatively stifled by its revivalist tendencies. Whereas many proponents
of alternative country music saw the movement as a valiant resistance to the
overt commercialism of the "hot new country" that dominated radio airplay,
the frequently outspoken critic and country music historian Rich Kienzle, in
the following review of BR-549's debut album, pointedly questions whether
such self-conscious appropriations of country music tradition were sufficient to
bring country music back to its roots. At the same time, Kienzle also chastises
his colleagues in the music press for championing a band that, in his opinion,
was simply going through the motions and not expressing a distinctive creative

vision, in the process implying that music journalism had failed to remain objective in its assessment of contemporary trends.

———

L AST year, based on their gigs at Robert's Western World, a downtown Nashville honky tonk/boot shop, the local country intelligentsia clasped this neo-honky-tonk quintet to its collective bosom. Seen as a homegrown alternative to the arid musical climate there, the group attracted additional hype from various journalists, both old Nashville hands who know the music and younger wanna-be scribes who understand the differences between Pearl Jam and R.E.M. better than those between Hank Williams Sr. and Jr. The band name, if you don't know, comes from the late Junior Samples' "Used Cars" skits of *Hee Haw*, portraying ol' Junior as a moronic car salesman holding up a sign (often upside down) emblazoned with the fictitious phone number "BR-549" (the band moved the hyphen.

I was impressed that Arista signed BR5-49, remaining openminded even when friends who saw them in Austin were underwhelmed. But an ominous sign came with their *Live at Robert's* EP, the disc and press kit packaged by Arista in a burlap sack (hillbilly, y'know). Dumb originals like "Bettie, Bettie," celebrating 50's pinup girl Bettie Page, and "Me 'N Opie Down by the Duck Pond," a witless tale of TV's *Andy Griffith Show* gang getting high, might be a barrel of fun at Robert's. But building an entire act based on 50's iconography, *Andy Griffith* reruns and oldies seems a pretty shaky premise. Several 5-49 boosters, aware of my misgivings, counseled me to judge them not by the EP, but by their forthcoming studio album. And that's what I've done.

It's true that the 5-49ers sincerely love the old stuff, but the problems begin on track one, on "Even If It's Wrong," where someone got the dumb idea to remind everyone of the fact by including four seconds off the scratchy surface noise heard on old 45's or 78's. That's not all. For a seemingly non-mainstream set, they're quite willing to follow certain Music Row dictums. Consider singer-guitarist Chuck Mead's original "Little Ramona (Gone Hillbilly Nuts)." Its lyrics may jab line dancers, but the song percolates with boot-scooting rhythms that could still land it on *Club Dance*.[1] Those same beats drive Moon Mullican's "Cherokee Boogie" (based on Johnny Horton's 1959 version) and their chugging, but ill-sung versions of two Webb Pierce standards: "Honky Tonk Song" and "I Ain't Never."

Over 20 years ago, Commander Cody and His Lost Planet Airmen and Asleep at the Wheel created memorable music from older styles and placed their own stamp on various oldies.[2] 5-49 haven't done that. Sure, they capably re-create Ray Price's "Crazy Arms" and Gram Parsons' "Hickory Wind," but add nothing new or fresh. Even on singer Gary Bennett's original "Even If It's Wrong," the guitar break recycles part of Paul Burlison's famous solo on Johnny Burnette's rockabilly classic "The Train Kept a-Rollin'." Studio musicians re-create country and rock oldies for Karaoke albums all the time, but no one calls that artistry.

1. See chapter 42.
2. For more background on Asleep at the Wheel's western swing revivalism, consult chap. 5 of Travis D. Stimeling, *Cosmic Cowboys and New Hicks: The Countercultural Sounds of Austin's Progressive Country Music Scene* (New York: Oxford University Press, 2011).

As for other originals, Mead's ballad, "Lifetime to Prove," could be filler on a Billy Ray Cyrus album, and the Latin beat of "Chains of This Town" falls flat. If the shallow rockabilly posturing of "One Long Saturday Night" isn't bad enough, "Baby Are You Gettin' Tired of Me" sounds like Lester "Roadhog" Moran with the guitars in tune. "Little Ramona," a tale of a punk rocker turned country, might apply to certain of their boosters, given its shallow, name-dropping focus ("ol' Hank," "Manuel suits," etc.). Even their musicianship would win few awards, particularly Don Herran's hyperactive steel and fiddle and "Hawk" Shaw Wilson's mechanical drumming.

According to the August 29th USA Today, 1996 has seen flat country record sales and declining concert revenues. The troubling question: are we so Garthed, Shaniaed, McGrawed and Faithed out that we'll embrace anything that sounds different? Perhaps a drastic change is due, one that will sweep aside the worst of today's prepackaged crap as New Traditionalism vanquished Urban Country ten years ago.[3] But are new ideas, true creativity and musical excellence so scarce that people who should know better will champion this very ordinary retro act as the next new thing? If so, perhaps things, as George Jones once sang, have truly gone to pieces.

Source: Rich Kienzle, Review of BR-549, Country Music (1996): 28–29. (Used with permission of the author.)

FOR FURTHER READING

Alden, Grant, and Peter Blackstock, eds. The Best of No Depression: Writing about American Music. Austin: University of Texas Press, 2005.

Fox, Pamela, and Barbara Ching, eds. Old Roots, New Routes: The Cultural Politics of Alt.Country Music. Ann Arbor: University Press of Michigan, 2008.

3. See, for instance, "The Old Sound of New Country," Journal of Country Music 11, no. 1 (1986): 2–24; Don McLeese, Dwight Yoakam: A Thousand Miles from Nowhere (Austin: University of Texas Press, 2012).

45

Deborah Evans Price

"Has There Been 'Murder On Music Row'? Key Players
Speak Out" (2000) and "Is There 'Murder On Music
Row'? Debate Continues" (2000)

The rise of "hot country" in the 1990s highlighted key musical and cultural
tensions that have shaped country music culture almost since its emergence in the early 1920s. As musicians, engineers, and producers capitalized on
a national fascination with country music by incorporating pop and rock practices into country music, musicians, industry insiders, and fans who adopted a
traditionalist attitude toward their work took a defensive posture toward these
new developments. After nearly a decade of hot country's success as a radio format, unprecedented country record sales, and extraordinary tour profits, country
music seemed to some to be in a battle for its soul.[1]

In 1999, Nashville songwriter and bluegrass bandleader Larry Cordle penned
a song that captured some of these concerns. "Murder on Music Row" accused

---

1. Joli Jensen, "Taking Country Music Seriously: Coverage of the 1990s Boom,"
in *Pop Music and the Press*, ed. Steve Jones (Philadelphia: Temple University Press,
2002), 183–201.

Music Row of forsaking the heartbreak songs, steel guitars, and fiddles of the honky-tonk tradition in search of money and fame gained by the inclusion of loud drums and rock guitar styles. Much as Waylon Jennings had done in his 1975 hit "Are You Sure Hank Done It This Way?," Cordle also suggests that Hank Williams and George Jones, those touchstones of honky-tonk authenticity, would not be taken seriously in the contemporary country music environment. Cordle's song, which received airplay on bluegrass radio and won the International Bluegrass Music Association's Song of the Year award, became a national sensation when top country stars George Strait and Alan Jackson performed it on the 1999 Country Music Association awards program and recorded the song in 2000; ironically, although the two musicians were heavily influenced by honky-tonk, they also had been two of the greatest beneficiaries of country music's growth in the 1990s.

As the following interviews compiled for *Billboard* in the weeks following the release of Strait and Jackson's recording indicate, Nashville insiders debated the merits of the charges leveled in "Murder on Music Row" and, in the process, clearly articulated the key issues at stake in the rise and commercial success of hot country: the neglect of "classic" country artists and their fans, the power of radio program directors and disc jockeys to make or break an emerging artist's career, and the struggle between the need for record labels to turn a profit and the needs of artists who sought opportunities for professional development and self-expression.

Some of the figures interviewed here—including Brad Paisley, whose career was just beginning to get off the ground—clearly used this as a platform to situate their own work within a traditionalist vein and to link themselves to a particular subset of the country music audience. On the other hand, some of these interviews reveal a more nuanced approach to the problems outlined in "Murder on Music Row," suggesting that—as the historical record indicates—hot country was simply another iteration in a long line of country music subgenres and the commercialization of the genre.[2]

———

NASHVILLE—The longstanding debate over traditional country music vs. pop music seems to be reaching a crescendo these days, as George Strait and Alan Jackson cling to Billboard's Hot Country Singles & Tracks chart with the controversial album cut "Murder on Music Row."

The song was penned by Larry Cordle, leader of the venerable bluegrass outfit Lonesome Standard Time, and writer/producer Larry Shell. Cordle's version of the song surfaced last year in Nashville when an anonymous copy of the tune wrapped in crime-scene tape was delivered to WKDF (Music City 103) Nashville. Lonnie Napier, executive producer of Carl P. Mayfield's morning show, recalls playing the song and getting immediate response. "Carl thought it had merit and deserved to be played," he says. "People were blown away when they heard it."

In the weeks that followed, Napier says, the song drew "thousands" of comments on the station's Web site and request lines. Mayfield proceeded to appoint Waylon Jennings a detective to investigate the "murder."

Later recorded by superstars Strait and Jackson for Strait's "Latest Greatest Straitest Hits" album (MCA Nashville), the song, although never released as a single, has been generating both airplay and controversy, thanks to lyrics about how Music Row killed country music in favor of pop. The song even aims a few direct shots at radio.

Everyone seems to have strong opinions on the case. Billboard talked to key players on and off music Row and posed these questions: Has traditional country music been murdered, and if so, who's to blame?

BRAD PAISLEY: "I don't think it's been murdered. I think somebody had stuck it away in a closet or locked it in a cell somewhere, and it's awaiting execution at this point [laughs]. That's how I see it. And it's up to us to get it paroled."

JOE GALANTE,   chairman, RCA Label Group: "In each decade, the definition of 'traditional' country would change. I believe you still have singers and songs that are traditional for this decade. If you compare our music to what is really pop, you will hear and feel the difference. Our songs are still about adults and their joys, hopes, dreams, and sorrows. The heart and soul are still in the music. It hasn't been murdered, but it has changed with the audience tastes."

CHARLIE DANIELS: "I don't believe that traditional country is dead. I just think it's being held captive by an industry which seems to be bent on self-destruction. It's very obvious that the people who consult radio don't get past their telephones when they do their research. There are people from coast to coast who are saying, 'I just can't listen to country radio anymore.'"Not that there's anything wrong with their formats; they're just not broad enough," Daniels says. "Country music has become much too big for just one format. If it is to survive, somebody has got to start playing some more music, get on back to the roots, so to speak."

DONNA HILLEY,   president/CEO, Sony/ATV Tree Publishing: "I don't think it's dead or that anybody has killed it. I think every decade everything changes, including music. It's just as in life—nothing stays the same. Music is cyclic, and country music is enjoying some of the greatest successes we have ever had, i.e. Garth [Brooks], Shania [Twain], Dixie Chicks, Faith [Hill], and Martina [McBride]. Who is to say these acts are not country? I certainly feel they are, but they have a broad range of acceptance. So, perhaps definitions are changing in country music, but it certainly is not dying."It is all about perception," Hilley continues. "For example, if you used the word 'grass' 30 years ago, it was about something on your lawn that you walked on and played in. Today that same word could have a different meaning, but there is still grass."³

ALLEN BUTLER,
president, Sony Music Nashville: "We have not murdered country music at all. There's still great country music on the radio. There are still artists being signed every day in this town that are traditional country acts, but it has become a little more difficult to get some of that music, especially by newer artists, on the radio. "The artists that come in here now are all in their 20s, and some of them have a great respect for traditional country music," Butler says. "Fortunately or unfortunately, depending on how you want to look at it, a lot of these kids have grown up with many different musical influences, which of course impacts how they make their own music. "It's nothing for a new artist to say their musical influences are Alan Jackson, George Jones, and also artists in pop music," he says. "People don't just listen to one kind of music anymore. They push buttons and listen to whatever they like. Consequently, music has a lot of different flavors to it right now. You can argue that's good or bad. Some people think it's not good. Others think it takes us to a broader audience."

SCOTT LINDY,
PD of WPOC Baltimore: "We decided not to play ["Murder"] for the lyrical content. We also decided not to run any liners that say, 'We're screwing all the artists you love, and we want to be taken off the air for being so lame!' This song, a bitter tale of hanging on to the past, is good for no one. How do you think the major country acts of the '50s and '60s felt when Hag,⁴ Waylon [Jennings], and Conway [Twitty] pushed them off the radio? Get a grip, people. Times move on, and so does our format. "If country radio had the equivalent format that rock does in classic rock, or that pop does with the oldies format, everyone would stop bitchin'," Lindy says. "The fact is, I love Merle, Waylon, Conway, and most of the heroes of that era, but my job is to get ratings. Those songs and artist will drop our ratings in two [Arbitron] books."

MIKE CURB,
CEO, Curb Records: "I don't think country music has been killed. I think it is one hit record away from re-emerging."

CONNIE BRADLEY,
ASCAP senior VP: "I don' think traditional country music has been murdered. Life is all about change. Nothing stays the same, including music. With acts such as George Jones, George Strait, Alan Jackson, and Lee Ann Womack, traditional country will always be represented well."

KYLE YOUNG,
executive director, Country Music Hall of Fame: "Like songs about the Vietnam War or unfaithful spouses, 'Murder On Music Row' is the kind of social commentary that has colored the country music continuum since the beginning. The tension between 'traditional' and what at the

3. A reference to marijuana.
4. Merle Haggard.

moment is defined as 'not traditional' has also been there from the beginning. And, whichever way the wind blows, the 'Grand Ole Opry' is still on the radio every Saturday night."

DARREN DAVIS,   PD at KIKK (Young Country) Houston: "I wouldn't play that song if it was No. 1 in the country 17 weeks in a row, because all I play on this station is songs from the last two years. We don't play anything older than 1998. Wouldn't it be hypocritical of me to put on a song, no matter who's singing it—I don't care if the pope is singing it—that makes fun of everything that this station is all about? That's a song that's never going to see the light of day here. "Already I've gotten E-mails from as far away as Sweden," Davis says. "How they found out I'm not playing it, I don't know…I've gotten the most livid E-mails saying bastards like me are what has killed country music and they are going to report my form of radio piracy to the FCC.[5] Country music has been the slowest-evolving format of any music format, always with an urge to cling to 20 years ago, and it hasn't done the format any favors. That's why it's had its problems over the last several years."

Source: Deborah Evans Price, "Has There Been 'Murder On Music Row'? Key Players Speak Out," Billboard no. 112 (29 April 2000): 58, 60. (Used with permission.)

NASHVILLE—In the last issue, Billboard queried a cross section of the country music industry to get opinions on "Murder On Music Row," the George Strait/Alan Jackson duet that charges that "the almighty dollar and lust for worldwide fame" have killed traditional country music.

Strait and Jackson will continue to fan the flames of controversy when they perform the song as the opening number on the upcoming Academy of Country Music Awards show Wednesday (3). In the final installment of this two-part piece, other industry professionals offer their views on the perennial traditional country vs. pop debate.

Once again, we asked, Has traditional country music been murdered, and, if so, who's to blame?

LEE ANN WOMACK,   MCA Nashville recording artist: "I don't think it can be killed, and I'm one of the artists who intends to see that it's not. I think there are hopefully going to be artists who are going to take care of the music. If it's done right and done well, people love it…. It's more about making great music than it is whether or not it's swimming in fiddles and steel guitars. My intention is to take care of the music and preserve it, and hopefully 20 years from now we'll look back and there will have been other people [doing] it too. Country is not going to die. It can't. It's an art form. It will be preserved."

LUKE LEWIS,   president, Mercury Nashville: "Is anyone certain that there is a wide audience for traditional country music out there, or are those of us who love it a dwindling minority? If there is a market for it, we need

5. The Federal Communications Commission, a federal agency that regulates the broadcasting industry.

to find a new or different way to reach the fans. Country radio has a different agenda. Their core and target audience is middle-age women who, a lot of research says, prefer audio Prozac[6] and sentimental sap to those messages so inherent in 'traditional' songs that might deal with the darker side of life. True enough that trains and life on the range have become irrelevant in contemporary times, but drinkin', leavin', cheatin, and lying are, unfortunately, still very much a part of most of our lives, and those themes have proven over the years to be OK [with], if not preferred by, many music fans."Nashville is still loaded with great songwriters who can deal with those provocative themes and create compelling music which will stir the hears, ring the cash registers, and cause more listeners to tune in rather than tune out. Traditional country music has not been murdered by anyone. It's just wandering around in the dark trying to find a way back to its audience."

REBECCA BROWN,   associate V.P., writer/publisher relations, SESAC: "Real, traditional country music will never die. It's just too beautiful and to universal and too ornery a form to be killed off that easily. But, I'd say the same thing about the blues, and that radio format isn't doing so well right now, is it? A lot of the blame for the current state of country music and country radio comes from too many people looking for someone to blame and not enough people working together to preserve and perpetuate what makes the format so unique and, hopefully, so endearing."

MITCH MAHAN,   PD, WIRK West Palm Beach, Fla.: "There's no way I'll play ["Murder"]. Why would I want to let two of the format's superstars rip me to shreds on my own station? Alan, love ya. George, you're a god. But which of the legends you're singing about didn't get a chance to sing 'I Cross My Heart' or 'Chattahoochee' because you had taken their place? There may have been murder on Music Row, but Alan and George are still accomplices."

CRAIG MORGAN,   Atlantic recording artist: "I don't think country music has been murdered. I think we tried to broaden our horizons so much we maybe got a little bit away from what made country music what it is. And it's not just the style—there are multiple styles in country music, and that's what's so great about this format—but we got away from who country music is. As a country music artist, I'm an approachable guy. That's what country music has always been to me. It's the guy you can walk up and talk to that you see at the local store pumping gas. It's people who don't get away from who they are and their roots."

RALPH EMERY,   veteran radio broadcast and former host of TNN's "Nashville Now": "Traditional country music has always been the 'mother's milk' of our genre. At this moment, it seems like the mother is out of town. If the only reason to succeed is money, then our poets have little meaning.

6. An antidepressant marketed widely during the 1990s.

It is dead? Not if we realize in time the uniqueness of its mission.... If it continues in the present fashion, then country music as a separately defined art form will cease to exist. Those of us who took on the fight with rock 'n' roll when it threatened our extermination some years ago would hate to see this happen. Who's to blame? Perhaps the question should be: What's to blame? The fear of failure?"

GARY OVERTON,

executive VP/GM, EMI Music Nashville: "I don't think traditional country music is dead. I don't think the format has ever had a lot of real traditional country music on radio, even during the gold rush of the last 10 years. At the end of the day, the real artists break through, and that's what's important."

BARRY COBURN,

president, Atlantic Records Nashville: "I can go along the dial and I can hear 'Stairway to Heaven' and I can hear 'Hotel California.'[7] I can hear all the great pop songs from 15 to 25 years ago. In country music, you can't. We've discarded those people and thrown them out with the water. I have a problem that we as an industry overall don't provide a place for those people."

WES MCSHAY,

PD, WKDF (Music City 103) Nashville: "I don't think [traditional country has] been totally killed. I thank God for people like Alan Jackson and George Strait. There are some really strong country music voices. So country [has] not been killed, but there has been an attempted murder on Music Row because of greed and the desire to sell records to younger people. As for the blame, there's plenty of guilt to be spread around."

BRUCE HINTON,

chairman, MCA Records Nashville: "George and Alan dueting is a major event that can only help country radio. To the extent it's a little controversial I think is a plus. If we're not careful as an industry, we could find ourselves homogenizing a playlist down to audio wallpaper, and ultimately you can't grow an audience for the long term that way."

Source: Deborah Evans Price, "Is There 'Murder On Music Row'? Debate Continues," Billboard no. 112 (6 May 2000): 36, 133. (Used with permission.)

FOR FURTHER READING

Cox, Patsi Bale. The Garth Factor: The Career Behind Country's Big Boom. New York: Center Street, 2009.

Jensen, Joli. "Taking Country Music Seriously: Coverage of the 1990s Boom." In Pop Music and the Press, ed. Steve Jones, 183–201. Philadelphia: Temple University Press, 2002.

Feiler, Bruce. Dreaming Out Loud: Garth Brooks, Wynonna Judd, Wade Hayes, and the Changing Face of Nashville. New York: HarperCollins, 1998.

Kosser, Michael. How Nashville Became Music City, U.S.A: 50 Years of Music Row. Milwaukee: Hal Leonard, 2006.

7. FM radio hits by 1970s rock icons Led Zeppelin and the Eagles, respectively.

46

Scott Galupo

"The Critical Rockist and Gretchen" (2005)

One response to the so-called "Murder on Music Row" (see chapter 45) was the rise of the MuzikMafia, a collective of musicians who embraced a variety of musical styles from country to hip hop that took Nashville by storm in the mid-2000s. From their home base at the Fontenelle mansion and a bar called "3rd and Lindsley," the MuzikMafia promoted an aesthetic that championed "music without prejudice," and the shows that they staged could be free-for-alls in which musicians moved fluidly from one genre to another while singers, rappers, and avant-garde painters worked their magic. The MuzikMafia espoused a decidedly uncorporate ideology in its infancy, challenging the dominance of Music Row by celebrating the artists who had been marginalized by the city's music industry. Yet, as ethnomusicologist David Pruett has demonstrated, the MuzikMafia was led by four business-savvy "godfathers," including former Lonestar bassist John Rich, songwriter Jon Nicholson, and publisher Cory Gierman, and quickly worked to establish the MuzikMafia as a dominant force in the Nashville music industry, forming record labels, promoting concerts, and even producing a short-lived reality television show.[1]

1. The MuzikMafia has been documented in David B. Pruett, *MuzikMafia: From the Local Nashville Scene to the National Mainstream* (Jackson: University Press of

Although the MuzikMafia claimed to promote "music without prejudice," it is best known for its advocacy of country musicians, generating such successful acts as Big & Rich (led by Rich and fellow godfather "Big Kenny" Alphin), Cowboy Troy, and Gretchen Wilson. As the following essay, published in the *Washington Times* at the height of the MuzikMafia's success, indicates, Wilson's work addressed the concerns of many observers who were afraid that country music had lost its way in the wake of a decade of hot country success. Critic Scott Galupo positions Wilson's work within the context of "rockism," a critical viewpoint developed in the 1970s that celebrates those musicians who write their own songs, play a direct role in the production of their recordings, and seems to embody the characters who speak in their songs.[2] As musicologist Nadine Hubbs has argued, Wilson's songs—especially her successful debut single, "Redneck Woman"—challenged dominant portrayals of women in contemporary country music by embracing a decidedly working-class, "virile" femininity that encompassed a love for outdoor activities and an overt sexuality.[3] Galupo's essay—although attempting to use aesthetic arguments to bait a political argument—points to the ongoing processes by which country musicians define their authenticity.

WHAT should a proper rockist make of country singer Gretchen Wilson?
Before we answer that, we'd better define terms. "Rockism" is a critical theory that holds that popular music was good for about five minutes in the late 1960s. Art and commerce then were in some kind of magical synchronicity; the public's tastes were as refined as those of critics. Alas, the theory goes, things slid inexorably downhill until the horrors of disco, Madonna and hip-hop made a mockery of all that was holy about rock.

Mississippi, 2010); David B. Pruett, "When the Tribe Goes Triple Platinum: A Case Study Toward an Ethnomusicology of Mainstream Popular Music in the U.S.," *Ethnomusicology* 55, no. 1 (Winter 2011): 1–30.

2. Rockism has been thoroughly treated in recent popular music studies literature and popular criticism. See, for instance, Robert Christgau, "Rockism Faces the World," *The Village Voice* 35 (2 January 1990), 67; Kalefa Senneh, "The Rap Against Rockism," *New York Times* (31 October 2004), http://www.nytimes.com/2004/10/31/arts/music/31sann.html; accessed 9 November 2012; Douglas Wolk, "Thinking about Rockism," *Seattle Weekly* (4 May 2005), http://www.seattleweekly.com/2005-05-04/music/thinking-about-rockism.php/; accessed 9 November 2012; Michael J. Kramer, "Rocktimism?: Pop Music Writing in the Age of Rock Criticism," *Journal of Popular Music Studies* 24, no. 4 (December 2012): 590–92; Miles Parks Grier, "Said the Hooker to the Thief: 'Some Way Out' of Rockism," *Journal of Popular Music Studies* 25, no. 1 (March 2013): 31–55.

3. Nadine Hubbs, "'Redneck Woman' and the Gendered Politics of Class Rebellion," *Southern Cultures* 17, no. 4 (Winter 2011): 44–70.

Rockists disapprove of, in no special order, drum machines, sampling,[4] lip-syncing[5] and synthesizers—basically any form of prestidigitation that distorts the direct expression of guitar, drums, bass and voice.

For a long while, rockists also have taken it upon themselves to monitor the health of country music, a genre whose simple virtues are easy to lionize as well as to caricature.

The structure and instrumentation of an authentic country song are seemingly as set in stone as religious liturgy. (Country artists themselves are often as jealously protective of their music as rockists are of rock—witness Alan Jackson's hits "Gone Country," which lampoons venue-shopping country poseurs, and "Don't Rock the Jukebox," on which a heartbroken hillbilly can't bear to hear non[-]country noise.)

Thus, it's a truism in the rock press that any music that emanates from Nashville today is by definition impure, inauthentic and patently commercial (an unforgivable vice among rockists). To differentiate it from the country they purport to cherish, it's often dismissed as "pop" country.

Music critic Sasha Frere-Jones defined the rockist attack on pop this way in the online magazine *Slate*: "Pop music isn't made by people, but by bands of hired guns on assembly lines, working to rationalized standards established by technocratic committees maximizing shareholder investment. The emphasis of pop songs is on transitory physical pleasures, instead of the eternal truths that rock protects."

And, the kicker: "Pop is also consumed by lots of women and kids, and what do they know?"

In the lesser country category are crossover commodities such as Kenny Chesney, Faith Hill, Tim McGraw and Shania Twain. (The least generous rockists tend also to overlook arguably "authentic" country stars such as Toby Keith and Brad Paisley.)

The pure typically include: Hank Williams I and III, but never II; old soldiers such as George Jones, Merle Haggard, Willie Nelson and the late Johnny Cash; and the late Gram Parsons.

It's curious, is it not, that Mr. Cash, Mr. Nelson and Mr. Parsons weren't strictly country singers; they were themselves "crossover" artists, albeit of a rebellious sort more acceptable to rockists.[6]

As a short-lived member of the Byrds and later as a solo artist, Mr. Parsons, indeed, is often credited with inventing country rock before there was a name for it—a movement that has seen various permutations (the Eagles, Charlie Daniels, Alabama), none much favored by

4. A digital technology that allows producers to manipulate snippets of pre-recorded sound. For more information on sampling's use in another form of popular music, consult Joseph G. Schloss, *Making Beats: The Art of Sample-Based Hip-Hop* (Middletown, CT: Wesleyan University Press, 2004).

5. The act of pretending to sing while a recorded vocal track is played in place of a singer's live voice. For a broader discussion of this phenomenon, consult chap. 3 of Philip Auslander, *Liveness: Performance in a Mediatized Culture* (New York: Routledge, 1999).

6. For more background, consult Robert Hilburn, *Johnny Cash: The Life* (New York: Little, Brown, 2013); Joe Nick Patoski, *Willie Nelson: An Epic Life* (New York: Little, Brown, 2008); and Ben Fong-Torres, *Hickory Wind: The Life and Times of Gram Parsons*, rev. ed. (New York: St. Martin's Griffin, 1998).

rockists until the arrival of so-called alternative country, which, through an unusual critical inversion, has come to be seen as more country than country itself.

The magazine *No Depression*, which chronicles the fortunes of alt-country bands, is celebrating its 10th anniversary this year. Its name comes from the 1990s debut album of Uncle Tupelo, a seminal St. Louis band that spawned Son Volt and Wilco, outfits that are still active today.[7]

Again, the genre catholicity is striking: Neither Son Volt nor Wilco ever claimed to be anything other than rock bands—and with each new album, it's become increasingly difficult to categorize the experimentally-minded Wilco.[8]

None of this is to defend artists like Miss Hill or Mr. Chesney or the nine-to-five song-writing fabrication that's so common on Music Row. It is, rather, to question whether rockists like country music at all.

Which brings us back, at last, to Miss Wilson, who this week released "All Jacked Up," her lively follow-up to last year's quadruple-platinum "Here for the Party." Miss Wilson is the traditionalist in a group of recently emerged artists—including the duo Big & Rich and "hick-hop" rapper Cowboy Troy[9]—that has given Nashville a much-needed draft of fresh air.

With her rough-hewn, tobacco-chewing "Redneck Woman" persona—a persona well-matched by her songs, some of which were crafted by John Rich of Big & Rich—Miss Wilson should have plenty of cred to pass muster with rockists. Barroom stomps such as "California Girls" and "Skoal Ring" are blessedly free of pop impurities, as are the album's teary-beery ballads, "I Don't Feel Like Loving You Today" and "Raining on Me."

The one thing that may discredit Miss Wilson in the eyes of rockists is her unapologetic embrace of red-state values. On "Jacked," she sings of the unappreciated merits of stay-at-home motherhood ("Full Time Job") and makes an anthem of lyrics such as "I'm for the Bible / I'm for the flat" on "Politically Uncorrect." Such Everywoman sentiments will no doubt endear her to country fans—but not to rockists, whose celebration of all things primitive and working class stops at the edge of Republican politics.

One hesitates, however, to politicize the aesthetic standards of rockists. They are narrow enough as it is.

7. See also Grant Alden and Peter Blackstock, *No Depression: Writing about American Music* (Austin: University of Texas Press, 2005).

8. For more on Uncle Tupelo, Son Volt, and Wilco, consult S. Renee Dechert, "'Oh, What a Life a Mess Can Be': Uncle Tupelo, Bahktin, and the Dialogue of Alternative Country Music," in *Country Music Annual 2001*, ed. Charles K. Wolfe and James E. Akenson (Lexington: University Press of Kentucky, 2001), 70–91; Stevie Simkin, "'The Burden Is Passed On': Son Volt, Tradition, and Authenticity," in *Old Roots, New Routes: The Cultural Politics of Alt.Country Music*, ed. Pamela Fox and Barbara Ching (Ann Arbor: University of Michigan Press, 2008), 192–221; and Greg Kot, *Wilco: Learning How to Die* (New York: Broadway Books, 2004).

9. "Hick-hop" was, as the name might suggest, an effort to blend elements of country music and hip hop. For more background and criticism of the style, consult Adam Gussow, "Playing Chicken with the Train: Cowboy Troy's Hick-Hop and the Transracial Country West," *Southern Cultures* 16, no. 4 (Winter 2010): 41–70; David Morris, "Hick-Hop Hooray? 'Honky Tonk Badonkadonk,' Musical Genre, and the Misrecognitions of Hybridity," *Critical Studies in Media Communication* 28, no. 5 (December 2011): 466–88.

Source: Scott Galupo, "The Critical Rockist and Gretchen: Gretchen Wilson's Traditional Country May Have Too Red State a Tilt," *Washington Times*, 30 September 2005, p. D1. (Copyright © 2013 The Washington Times LLC. This reprint does not constitute or imply any endorsement or sponsorship of any product, service, company or organization. License #39163.)

FOR FURTHER READING

Hubbs, Nadine. "'Redneck Woman' and the Gendered Politics of Class Rebellion." *Southern Cultures* 17, no. 4 (Winter 2011): 44–70.
Pruett, David. *MuzikMafia: From the Local Nashville Scene to the National Mainstream.* Jackson: University Press of Mississippi, 2010.

Craig Havighurst

"Scenes from a Rose Garden" (2006)

In the wake of the hot country juggernaut of the 1990s, many country musicians began to broaden their horizons beyond the walls of the honky-tonk and to write and record songs that engaged with broader social issues, including the legacy of the civil rights movement, LGBT rights, and the AIDS epidemic. One of the more interesting bodies of songs to emerge from country music's increasing social consciousness were those addressing domestic violence. Whereas much country music prior to the mid-1990s had alluded to physical, mental, and sexual violence in the home, hot country artists often chose to address domestic directly, following a national trend to bring domestic conflict out of the privacy of the home and into the public square. Songs such as Garth Brooks's "The Thunder Rolls" (1991) and the Dixie Chicks' "Goodbye, Earl" (2000) were accompanied by videos that depicted spousal abuse and the women who turned the tables on the men who abused them. These songs and videos were not without controversy but, much like the contemporary anti-domestic violence movement, they addressed uncomfortable subjects and brought practices that were often hidden from view into the public eye.[1]

One of the more powerful songs to arise from this movement was Martina McBride's "Independence Day" (1994). Written by songwriter Gretchen Peters, the song presents the perspective of a daughter who had witnessed domestic abuse during her childhood, reminding listeners that domestic violence negatively effects more than the person who is directly abused. Rather than taking the abuse passively, however, the speaker's mother—who becomes the talk of the small town where she lives because of the marks on her face—burns down her home (presumably with her husband still inside) on the Fourth of July, declaring her independence from abuse in a massive public spectacle. With an empowering chorus that prays for the "weak [to] be strong," the song became an anthem for the anti-domestic abuse movement in the 1990s, and McBride became an important symbol for abused women and men across the nation.

In the following essay by Nashville journalist and country music historian Craig Havighurst, we see McBride not only as the voice of female empowerment but also as a self-assured businesswoman who, with her husband John, owns the most sophisticated recording studio in Nashville, a supremely talented vocalist who is capable of recording pop tunes and classic country songs in an equally convincing manner, and a creative mind who is constantly seeking ways to improve her craft and reach new audiences.

═══════════

EVEN in the recording hotbed that is Nashville's Berry Hill neighborhood, Blackbird Studio is dressed to impress the audiophile. It catacombs from room to state-of-the-art room through doors that seal like air-locks. Parallel walls and square corners are scarce, giving the place a post-modern angularity, a three-dimensional metaphor for creativity that never travels in straight lines. In keeping with the name, Blackbird owner and mastermind John McBride has on display his large collection of Beatles memorabilia: movie posters, old newspapers, Rickenbacker guitars and, apparently, the actual console used to master *Abbey Road*. In one tracking room, a grand piano sits on a slab of polished black granite etched with Paul McCartney's lines in billboard size letters: "Blackbird singing in the dead of night. Take these broken wings and learn to fly..."

It's a pleasant surprise to realize that one of Martina McBride's biggest hit song titles, "A Broken Wing," is secreted within that lyric, because the indulgence and solidity symbolized by the Blackbird floor is something she and John have earned since moving to Nashville as newlyweds in 1990. And because McBride has spent much of her fourteen years on RCA Records looking for crafty ways to fold pop conventions into her own rooted but ecumenical

---

1. Consider, for instance, the detailed analysis that Lori Burns and Jada Watson have offered of the Dixie Chicks' video for "Top of the World" in "Subjective Perspectives through Word, Image, and Sound: Temporality, Narrative Agency, and Embodiment in the Dixie Chicks' Video 'Top of the World,'" *Music and the Moving Image* 4, no. 1 (2010): 3–37.

vision of country music. There's more than a little Beatles woven into the jangle and crackle of her hit "Happy Girl" or the polyphonic "Beyond the Blue" from her *Wild Angels* album. She's nurtured a social conscience with her popular songs "Independence Day" and "Love's the Only House." And yet, she's defined one of the most identifiable and popular sounds in contemporary country music with a diva roar that has few equals.

The complexities of McBride's music have been lost on some who choose to hear only her most polished singles and her sometimes over-earnest identification with angels, waifs, and fellow "girls." Though "Independence Day" might be the most important women's anthem of the 1990s, McBride's prairie-state straightforwardness has perhaps made it difficult for some to believe that she is a searching artist who thinks hard before she cuts a new record or bends the tradition. But conventionality can be deceiving; she has anticipated trends in subject matter and production that would blossom across the industry, from girl-power to generous use of mandolins. Indeed, the singer, who turned forty in July of 2006, said that one main motivation for *Timeless*, her new CD of classic country music covers, was a certain ennui that she recognized during the making of her previous release, the self-titled *Martina*.

"I was feeling a little bit like I'm making the same record again," McBride said in an interview at Blackbird in December 2005. "And I never felt like that with any other record. I always felt like this is a new sound, this is a new direction. I wouldn't have put (*Martina*) out if I didn't feel like it was a great piece of work, but I felt at the time like I'm not saying anything new here. It was the least creative piece of work that I've done."

Other artists with career statistics like McBride's might well be tempted to repeat themselves. She has taken home four Country Music Association Female Vocalist of the Year trophies, a record she shares with Reba McEntire. At radio, she's earned eighteen Top Ten hits and five #1 singles. All but her first album have achieved platinum status. She was one of a handful of artists invited to play the Grand Ole Opry's third-ever visit to Carnegie Hall in November 2005, and she was the first Opry cast member ever to be afforded an entire hour slot on the Saturday night show, during which she performed most of the songs off *Timeless*.

McBride's career coincided with a period of rapid change in country music, sometimes leading and sometimes following the shift from early 1990s New Traditionalism to turn-of-the-millennium therapy songs. Men in cowboy hats gave way to women with looks and attitude. When McBride arrived, the typical country protagonist might have proffered a quarter, so an ex could "call someone who cares."[2] By the time she really hit her stride in the late 1990s, McBride had helped define an Oprah[3] generation brand of country, in which everyday heroines love themselves and empathize with others. Along the way, she's even seen changes in how women are regarded on Music Row. When she auditioned, RCA Records still had a quota system on female artists ("there are four or five other girls that we're looking at, and we can only sign one," she was told by a label official), but her songs of female strength haven't confronted discrimination head-on so much as bolstered the morale of the sisterhood.

"I think (women) have come so far, that we have the luxury of not knowing—I don't even know if I'm a feminist or not," she said last fall in an interview with cable channel A&E. "So many things I take for granted, that I don't have to worry about because somebody before

2. A reference to "Here's a Quarter (Call Someone Who Cares)," recorded by Travis Tritt in 1991.

3. Oprah Winfrey, a media mogul and taste maker known for promoting positive living.

me worried about that. I'm just a person that wants everybody to just be fair. If that's a feminist, then, yeah, I guess I am."

Ardent feminists might take issue with McBride accepting an offer that speaks volumes about her identity, her popularity, and her wholesome reputation. In 2005, she consulted on the Martina McBride Barbie, which, according to its promotional copy, "features a recreation of the glamorous gown she wore to the 39th annual ACM Awards[4]...a real winner in white deserving of a standing ovation. Includes a collectible poster and keepsake bracelet!" About this, the singer said, "The first thought through my mind was that there were so many girls who would make a prettier Barbie. You know Faith, Shania. I'm thinking, 'Are you sure they know what they're doing?'"

That said, McBride's doll-like qualities have served her as well as her tours and albums. She's more than comfortable in front of a camera, and she meticulously guards her image. On her 1998 Christmas album, she posed with fake snowflakes on her upturned nose, while thousands of watts of expertly diffused white light flooded her arresting eyes. Years before that, she turned her hair into a brand impression when she chopped it off in a pixie 'do between her first and second albums.

The gloss and glamour, not to mention her improbably petite physique, only serve to heighten the marvel that is her voice, a complex alto that projects without bludgeoning, a force she uses with honesty and restraint, while divas all around her find new ways to torture money-notes.[5] Its twang-free Kansan flatness may contribute to the idea that she's less "country" than, say Reba McEntire, but McBride's voice is not at all featureless, with a velvety smoke in the middle registers, a throaty purr when she steps on the accelerator, and a catch that hints at a yodel when she turns corners. She resists audio compression in favor of lung-based dynamic control, and she disdains electronic pitch correction. Initially, critics noticed her nuance, not her power, but of course that has evolved with songs like "Independence Day" and "Where Would You Be," which she said is the hardest vocal workout she's ever cut.

"You know I think it took a long time for people to get a handle on what I was all about, as far as my singing ability," she said. "I remember singing 'Independence Day' at the CMAs[6] and I think that got some people's attention. But it took a long time before I got sort of a reputation for what I worked up to, which is being really well respected as a singer, and that's really my proudest thing."

McBride's hometown of Sharon is square—literally—a tidy, six-by-six grid of streets in remote south-central Kansas, a dozen miles south of a burg called Nashville. "I had thirty-two people in four grades of high school," she told me for a 2001 interview with *The Tennessean*. "It's so small and untouched by commerce—by everything, really. We go back there, the land is still the same. There are no subdivisions. There are no malls. The other little town of 1,200 barely hangs on to a grocery store and a hospital. So it's just timeless, and the people are the same, and I feel like I'm the same. Obviously I've traveled and been exposed to a lot of different things. But what I took away from that upbringing was you're just who you are. You never put on airs for anybody."

She was born Martina Mariea Schiff on July 29, 1966, the same summer the Beatles released *Revolver* and defended John Lennon's remark about being more popular than Jesus.

4. Academy of Country Music.
5. Notes that are difficult to reach because of their high or low range.
6. Country Music Association awards.

Mother Jeanne and father Daryl owned a wheat and cattle farm. Daryl had always been a musician. His family band, The Schiffters, welcomed Martina into the fold as soon as she could sing. From the time she was ten until she left home after high school, classic country music was a regular weekend commitment.

"We would rent an armory or an old school and throw a dance," she remembered. "And from miles around, all ages, everybody from little kids to senior citizens, would come and they'd bring their coolers. It was bring your own bottle. And we would play a four-hour dance, everything from Ernest Tubb to ZZ Top to whatever was popular on country Top Forty radio. And it was really a big part of a lot of people's childhood."

After high school, McBride moved to Hutchinson, a veritable Kansas metropolis of 40,000, where she worked in a Dairy Queen and sang in a rock band. It was part of a four-year musical sojourn that wound up back at its starting point.

"I spent several years trying to figure out what kind of music I wanted to sing," McBride recalled. "Growing up singing country music, I knew I loved that, but it's only natural to explore other kinds of music and other kinds of singing. That's for me what it was—looking around."

The bars and the ballads hurt her voice, and the Aretha Franklin and Whitney Houston covers became as much work as fun. She scaled back to working as a backup singer in a country band in Wichita. About that time, she met John McBride, owner of a sound company. They were married in 1988. The following year, Martin's father called and asked her to join him for a local battle of the bands. That night proved to be the "light-bulb moment" that set her career in motion.

"I'll never forget it," she said. "John was mixing the show, and he taped it, and he goes, 'Let's go out to the car and listen to the tape.' So as I was sitting in the car with him and I said, 'You know what? I want to sing country music. I don't want to sit around and sing in clubs and be in Wichita anymore. I want to go to Nashville." John didn't hesitate. He was in. Martina went inside. "I talked to my mom, like, five minutes later. We went to the ladies room together. And I said, 'I've made a decision. I want to sing country music. I've just figured it out.' And she said, 'Well that'll sure make your dad happy.'"

The McBrides arrived in Nashville in January of 1990, just as the Randy Travis-inspired boomlet was priming Music Row's Garth Brooks explosion. John, bearing truckloads of live sound gear, was in a splendid position to take advantage [see chapter 41]. In 1991, his company landed the sound engineering job for Brooks on his first headlining tour. And when Martina got bored and lonely waiting tables and singing demos, the Brooks tour found a slot for her working a merchandise table so she could be with John on the road. Opening the show was newcomer Trisha Yearwood, who by the end of the tour had securely launched her career.

John's industry contacts helped more than Martina's retail career. He had worked for John Kay of Steppenwolf, who made a meeting with Nashville music publisher Kevin Lamb. Lamb suggested McBride improve her demo tape (she'd sung "Crazy" in a warehouse recording) and recommended some pickers to help. She met drummer Lonnie Wilson and other future members of her studio band that way. She met her one and only producer, Paul Worley, when he was still an executive for Sony/Tree publishing [sic], and she remembers him as one of the first major leaguers to help her out.

But she hadn't met anybody at powerful RCA Records. When she and John got word that the label was looking for a solo female artist, they took a chance with the demo tape and a now-famous purple envelope with "Requested Material" written on the outside. Three weeks later, RCA asked her to audition. When she was signed, A&R executive Josh Leo looked across his desk and asked what kind of artist she wanted to be.

"I was completely taken aback," McBride recalled. "I hadn't really given that any kind of thought. I can't remember what I said—a wishy[-]washer [*sic*] answer." That wasn't good enough, he told her. "So I said I want to be a traditional country artist, like Alan Jackson and Clint Black. He said OK. He was cool with that as long as I had a direction. I think that was really important looking back—that he made me focus. So I walked out of the room going, OK that's what I want to do. That was my guideline for finding songs."

She was underwhelmed with what she heard in the new world of pitch meetings.[7] "I can remember looking for songs and hearing all these average, fluffy kind of nothing-songs, and I kept going back and back and saying, 'Nope, didn't hear it.'" She remembered sitting at EMI with two of its song pluggers. "I'd been there several times. And they were probably thinking, 'God, this girl, does she ever give up? Who is she? She doesn't even have an album."

She made what must have seemed an immodest proposal from a newcomer. "I remember saying, 'play me what you'd play Alan Jackson if he walked in the door.... I want something that has some substance to it and is COUNTRY.'" Someone in the room had the good sense to play her "Cheap Whiskey" by Emory Gordy Jr. and Jim Rushing (though not without the apparently important qualifier that it was "more of a guy's song"). The boldly traditional lament, in a slow waltz tempo, told the story of a person who "traded her love for a drink" and went down in flames. It "set a tone," McBride said, for *The Time Has Come*, her first album. "True Blue Fool" caressed its chorus with mournful yodels nearly as arresting as those of LeAnn Rimes on "Blue" a few years later. "The Rope" was a buoyant, gospel-leaning tune with a folk-sweet melody. Reviewers were largely impressed, and one observed that if the artist hadn't yet completely found herself, at least she wasn't driving in the middle of the road.

Two weeks after release, in April 1992, McBride rejoined the Garth Brooks tour, this time as the opening act. It was a huge career break and a graduate course in what it meant to be a headliner. "Seeing him perform and his philosophy and how he related to his fans and how he was on stage, I think that was a big influence on me," McBride said. However, it didn't produce the same rush of success that it had for Yearwood. McBride's title track, an uptempo leaving song, peaked only at #23 on the *Billboard* country chart. The follow-ups, "That's Me," a ballad, and then "Cheap Whiskey," only made it into the forties.

McBride still loves *The Time Has Come*. "I didn't say, 'That didn't work; I need to try something else.' That wasn't it at all," she remembers today. But at the time[,] she told reporters she thought it felt "inhibited," and whether consciously or not, she had her ears open for different kinds of material on album number two. She told herself to loosen up. She chopped her auburn tresses off into the shock she's now famous for. She appealed to [producer] Paul Worley to spend more time with her in the studio. And she latched onto two career-changing songs by Gretchen Peters.

"When I found 'My Baby Loves Me,' I think that was probably the song that kicked off the sound that my style evolved into," said McBride. She knew it wasn't the country music she'd grown up on, but she was drawn to its melody and its message. "High heels or sneakers, he don't give a damn," sang the brassy narrator. "My baby loves me just the way that I am." Lonnie

---

7. See Tom T. Hall's discussion of the song plugger's work in chapter 27.

Wilson's insistent snare drum, and McBride's self-assured, woman-to-woman delivery pushed "My Baby Loves Me" to #2 in early December 1993, just three spins shy, nationwide, of #1.

McBride and Worley confess to some calculation behind the even less conventional follow-up single, "Life #9," by Kostas and Tony Perez. It was thought to have line-dance potential at a time when that was driving a lot of hits. They even made a dance mix that Worley hopes never resurfaces. It clawed to #6, but it set up McBride's big breakthrough.

Worley played Peters's "Independence Day" for McBride in his office. She heard a multi-layered lyric, a home run chorus, and a vivid as daylight story about an abused wife, an observant daughter, and a fiery play for justice. "I just had an instant reaction," she said. "That was MY song. I didn't want anybody else to record it." The record, rippling with emotion and kissed by Worley's idea of struck chimes in the chorus, stands as one of the most moving singles of the 1990s. McBride maintains that nobody imagined it would be a controversial song until after it was released as a single on May 7, 1994. But to her surprise, a significant number of stations wouldn't play it. "I was so passionate about that song," said McBride, "that my immediate reaction was, 'Well, let me talk to them.' So I got a list of radio stations and I called up the program director personally and would say, 'This is Martina McBride. Let's talk about why you're not playing "Independence Day." ' " Some said it was too graphic, or that it risked alienating listeners. She countered that it was no more challenging than what they were airing on the news. And then, suddenly, the news was imitating art.

Five weeks after the single came out, Nicole Brown Simpson and Ronald Goldman were found stabbed to death in Los Angeles. O. J. Simpson's history with his murdered wife appeared to include spousal abuse, and suddenly it was the nation's hottest topic. "They started playing the song. And I got attention," said McBride. Officially, it never cracked the Top Ten, peaking at #12, but the video, which acted out Peters's ambiguous and dark lyrics with a real burning house, and the self-evident impact of the record itself, transcended chart position. McBride sang the song while eight months pregnant with her first daughter, Delaney, at the 1994 CMA Awards and sold her industry peers on her voice, her charm, and her star stature. "She brought the house down," Paul Worley recalled. "Standing ovation. People were just shocked at this little wisp of a girl, eight months pregnant, just laying it out there. No smoke, no mirrors. It definitely made people start to pay attention."

Except then came "Heart Trouble" and "Where I Used to Have a Heart," which flared out at #21 and #49, respectively. It's a shame that the latter wasn't better received or worked to other adult formats; Bonnie Raitt had taken the world with similar material just a few years before, and not sung as well. McBride said in the liner notes of her 2001 *Greatest Hits* album that "Strangers" should have been the next single. It was, she said, the only argument she ever had with RCA. "I think I'd have had a different career. I think it would have kept the momentum going a little bit." As it was, she was a famous name with too-few hits in her shows. For a couple of years she'd get back on the bus thinking, "Thank God for 'Independence Day'!"

Her signature song notwithstanding, the trio of albums that McBride released between October 1995 and October 1999 may best reflect her vision as a forward-thinking country artist. Her role as producer, always substantial, expanded. "I would bring in examples of things, and I would try to express how I wanted this record to sound and what I wanted the instrumentation to be like," she said. And Worley remembered that "it took a journey of several albums to find the sound that was anything like what we now have. Starting with the second album, and more and more, she really insisted that she had to be there and I had to be there for anything to be going on. Because she definitely had her own opinions and tastes about what licks were played, she evolved into a co-producer." Beginning with *Wild Angels*, she was credited as such, a rarity for women in Nashville in any era. "That was my idea," Worley said. "She never asked for it. But it seemed to be accurate and to honestly express what was going on with the music. The consumers needed to understand that about her."

One only need bask in the warmth and daring of "Safe in the Arms of Love" to understand Worley's ability to execute McBride's vision of marketable earthiness. The swooping stereo pan of background vocals could have been copped from the Beatles, while the prominent use of fiddle against mandolin, in an almost Celtic instrumental break, anticipated sounds Worley would nurture as a signature of the Dixie Chicks a few years later. The song reached #4, and "Wild Angels," the title track, with its big chorus and big-hearted message, became McBride's first #1 hit.

Then, more chart disappointment, including a lukewarm reception of the perfectly fantastic "Cry on the Shoulder of the Road," written by Matraca Berg. Sung in harmonic union with The Band's Levon Helm, the song achieved an Emmylou Harris-stature conjunction of performance and lyric. Elsewhere on the album, McBride even tackled an important Harris cover, Delbert McClinton's "Two More Bottles of Wine," with even more gusto and after-hours abandon.

Nearly two years elapsed before McBride's next big hit, "A Broken Wing," reached #1 in January 1998. The song dealt with some of the same feminist subject matter as "Independence Day," leavened with a gospel choir. Then, in stark contrast, she soon followed with the apple-crisp "Happy Girl," a Beth Nielsen Chapman and Annie Roboff tune that reached #2. Those came from *Evolution*, which was not misnamed. McBride didn't even look like herself on the cover. The songs ranged all over the place.

"I've always let the music dictate the album and what direction it takes," McBride said. "I can remember several times along the way hearing songs and looking at Paul and going, 'Is that country? Is that country music?' I'll never forget hearing 'Happy Girl' and thinking, I don't even think that's a country song, but I like it. So I've always kind of had an issue straddling that fence. I've always questioned myself: Is that country enough? I definitely remember asking that question a lot on *Emotion* and then sort of after that I just kind of accepted that it is country enough—because we're having hits and people seem to like it—and stop analyzing it."

Emotion came in late 1999, after McBride had taken time during a couple of summers to join up with Lilith Fair, Sarah McLachlan's moveable feast of musical feminism, which helped push a wave of new female singer-songwriters. McBride may have been one of the only country artists there, but she discovered that most of the fans in the audience knew the words to "Independence Day." When she scouted songs for *Emotion*, she brought some of what she called the tour's "alternative reference point" along. She tackled a Matraca Berg–Randy Scruggs thera-pop[8] number called "Anything's Better Than Feeling the Blues," and Patty Griffin's mesmerizing "Good Bye." And she found another Gretchen Peters song, "This Uncivil War." The album's settings are spare; McBride's voice is plain and in the foreground. Her social conscience bubbled through in the unusual "Love's the Only House," a Tom Douglas–Buzz Cason song that finds the narrator trying to break through barriers separating her and her world

---

8. Short for "therapy-pop," a term used here to denote songs that with themes of empowerment.

of comfort from the poor and America's "teenagers walking around in darkness." The song reached #3 in April 2000.

"That record really scared me to release it," McBride said. "I can remember sitting with John on the back deck and saying[,] 'I don't know. I think I've really done it this time.' And he said, 'What?' And I said, 'It's just not country at all.' He said, 'You've got time, go back in and do something.' And I said, 'No, it feels like the right record. It just scares me because it's just so different.' And you know it wasn't as well received as our other albums, fan-wise or radio-wise. But I go back and listen to it now and I still am so proud of it."

All three of those late 1990s CDs achieved platinum status, indicating a million copies sold, *Evolution* triply so. McBride's *White Christmas*, released in late 1998, also sold a million and earned kudos as one of the most tastefully produced and beautifully sung holiday albums in a world full of obligatory chestnut roasters. She landed her first CMA Female Vocalist of the Year trophy in 1999, and she helped conceive the well-received "Girls Night Out Tour" with Reba McEntire, one of her heroes from her teenage years.

A decade into the business, it seemed a good time for a *Greatest Hits* album—to the label anyway. McBride had a funny reaction. "I give a lot of credit to (RCA Label Group Chairman) Joe Galante, because it was his idea. I kind of balked at it," she said, because she couldn't shake the feeling that artists only did hits packages when they were past their prime. But it turned out to be much more than an obligatory release. McBride added four new songs for a total of nineteen tracks. All four new songs became Top Ten hits, including the #1 "Blessed." The album sold three million copies, reinforcing McBride's stature as one of modern country's major stars.

We're at Blackbird Studio, just a few feet from where McBride recorded *Timeless*, and she is talking about the gulf between the world she knew growing up and the world of the now. Many country singers have journeyed from isolated lives of modest means to busy lives of riches, but McBride seems more acutely aware of the gulf between the Kansas calm of her youth and the broadband cacophony her girls are about to inherit. "You know, with Dolly and Loretta and Tammy, they just WERE," she said. "Now, there's just so much competition for celebrity status and for media. It's constant, twenty-four-hours-a-day of entertainment. How do you fill that?"

She's speaking even more as a mother than as an entertainer. She was pleased with John[, who] recently made a point of taking Delaney and Emma to a record store for a tangible alternative to the point-and-click interface of iTunes. McBride even related a story about help-ing Delaney, now twelve, comprehend the whole idea of artistry in a new, digital, track-by-track world.

"She wanted to download a song, and I said, 'Don't you want to hear what the other songs on the record are—what else she has to say?' And I could tell she hadn't thought of that. I said, 'For instance[,] on my last album my singles were "This One's for the Girls" and "My Daughter's Eyes." Do you really think those were THE best songs on the record and that noth-ing else on there was worth hearing?' And she said, 'Well, no.' So that's the thing: we're raising a generation of people that just are interested in this single, that single. And they don't really care about the artist. And I just really think that's a shame."

So Martina McBride, embodiment of crossover 1990s country music, may be more old-school than some give her credit [for]. And, in this, one senses yet another motivation for recording *Timeless*. She's been singing some of the songs on the new album since she was young. She learned some of them from her mother. There can be little doubt that, at some level, this one's for the girls, so to speak.

She went to her label head, Galante, with the idea for *Timeless*, expecting him agree to the idea as a concept album, but not as a regular album fulfilling her contract. Albums by current stars covering large numbers of hit songs used to be a norm in Nashville, but for at least a decade, such exercises have been limited to tribute albums. But to her surprise, Galante said it sounded like a great idea all around. He'd market it. He'd work singles to radio. McBride related that, "He turned to me one time when we were listening to some roughs. And he said, 'You know this is kind of a risk, don't ya?' And I said, 'Well, yeah, it probably is.' And that was pretty much it. He just really embraced it."

The Blackbird studio became what Worley and others who spend time there called "Planet McBride." The girls came over after school, hung out and did homework. Martina and John worked together in the studio for the first time as creative partners. He indulged his long-held desire to mix Martina in the studio more like he mixes her live, with space and clean tones. The band played pre-1970s instruments through vintage gear to analog tape. Martina was increasingly pregnant with her third daughter, making it difficult for her to get as close as she wanted to John's hand-picked and immense 1939 bottle microphone. She cut "Satin Sheets" and "Once a Day," [and] "You Win Again," which had been on her first Nashville demo tape, and "You Ain't Woman Enough to Take My Man." Arrangements were largely borrowed from the hit records, including a lush, countrypolitan "Rose Garden," which was released as a single. And she sent picker after picker out of the studio until she found enough intimacy and space to sing a breathtaking, album-closing "Help Me Make It through the Night."

Martina gave birth to her third daughter, Ava Rose, on June 20, 2005, just as the album was being finished. She's come away from the whole experience reflectively. "I thought, even though I grew up singing like this, this is a style that I have not done for a long time. I wondered how it was going to be," she said. "And what I realized is that songs like 'Blessed' and all these songs I'm known for are work. I have to really figure out how I want to sing those songs. I have to really spend a lot of time working with the delivery. This, by comparison, was maybe the kind of music I'm supposed to be singing, and all that other stuff I've done for the past few years, that I'm known for, is kind of out of character for me really. It was a weird discovery process."

Her assertion that she doesn't know what kind of music she'll make next is positively Kansan in sincerity. But Worley's willing to speculate a little. *Timeless*, he said, "freed her from the bonds of having to create those big pop tracks. My guess is she won't go back to the pop tracks. My guess is she won't go back to the pop stuff she was doing. I think it'll be more earthy and organic." After all[,] she's not in Kansas anymore, and roads are long and winding, so there will likely be more weird discoveries for Martina McBride. They've helped her fly pretty high so far.

Source: Craig Havighurst, "Scenes from a Rose Garden," *Journal of Country Music* 25, no. 1 (2006): 22–27, 32–36. (Reprinted with permission of Craig Havighurst and courtesy of the Country Music Foundation.)

FOR FURTHER READING

Burns, Lori, and Jada Watson. "Subjective Perspectives through Word, Image, and Sound: Temporality, Narrative Agency, and Embodiment in the Dixie Chicks' Video 'Top of the World,'" *Music and the Moving Image* 4, no. 1 (2010): 3–37.

48

Jill Sobule

"Searching for the Republican Artist" (2008)

The first decade of the new millennium witnessed one of the worst periods of political polarization in the United States since the late 1960s, as the nation struggled to cope with the devastation of the terrorist attacks of September 11, 2001, an ongoing "Global War on Terror" that involved American troops in Afghanistan and Iraq, and the continued threat of further terrorist activity on American soil. Although musicians rallied around the flag in the days immediately following 9/11, it did not take long for them to articulate their increasingly divided political beliefs in music.

In contrast to Alan Jackson's song of somber reflection "Where Were You (When the World Stopped Turning)?," the release of Toby Keith's "Courtesy of the Red, White, and Blue (The Angry American)" (2002) and Darryl Worley's "Have You Forgotten?" (2003), which expressed the anger of many hawkish Americans, presented country music as the voice of the conservative, pro-war Right.[1]

---

1. For more background on this moment, please consult Peter J. Schmelz, "'Have You Forgotten?': Darryl Worley and the Musical Politics of Operation Iraqi Freedom," in *Music in the Post-9/11 World*, ed. Jonathan Ritter and J. Martin Daughtry

Furthermore, when Dixie Chicks lead singer Natalie Maines proclaimed at a 2003 London concert that she was "embarrassed" that U.S. president George W. Bush claimed Texas as his home, radio stations removed their recordings from playlists and communities held public events to destroy Dixie Chicks recordings.[2] By the 2008 presidential election, the political ideology of mainstream commercial country music was firmly conservative, with many artists performing at the Republican National Convention in Minneapolis and endorsing Republican candidate John McCain.

In the following essay, songwriter Jill Sobule—known for her 1995 song "I Kissed a Girl"—interrogates the political leanings of popular musicians, noting that the vast majority of them espouse political beliefs that are left of center. Curious, though, are Sobule's observations regarding country music's strong presence in Republican politics. Noting that "Democrats have way more musical options to chose from" than their Republican counterparts, Sobule's remarks point to country music's historical role in depicting the perspectives of whites who feel marginalized by contemporary society—attitudes that Republican supporters made clear during the 2008 election cycle, as voters expressed anxieties about the nation's increasing diversity, concern about its financial solvency, and fears about apparent government intrusion into the personal decisions of its citizens.[3]

═══

JOHN Rich, of the country duo Big & Rich, was the big music star at the Republican National Convention in Minneapolis. He sang his new anthem, "Raisin' McCain." I was actually surprised that he was a Republican (maybe because I had him confused with the Fu

(New York: Routledge, 2007), 123–54. See also Lesley Pruitt, "Real Men Kill and a Lady Never Talks Back: Gender Goes to War in Country Music," *International Journal on World Peace* 24, no. 4 (December 2007): 85–106; and Andrew Boulton, "The Popular Geopolitical Wor(l)ds of Post-9/11 Country Music," *Popular Music and Society* 31, no. 3 (July 2008): 373–87.

Robert Van Sickel has argued that, over a forty-year period extending from 1960 to 2000, country music was largely apolitical, but this example provides a valuable exception to his findings (Robert W. Van Sickel, "A World without Citizenship: On (the Absence of) Politics and Ideology in Country Music Lyrics, 1960-2000," *Popular Music and Society* 28, no. 5 (July 2005): 313–31.

2. Several authors have discussed the fallout from Natalie Maines's comments. Consult Jada Watson and Lori Burns, "Resisting Exile and Asserting Musical Voice: The Dixie Chicks are *Not Ready to Make Nice*," *Popular Music* 29, no. 4 (2010): 325–50; Molly Brost, "Post-Dixie Chicks Country: Carrie Underwood and the Negotiation of Feminist Country Identity," in *The Politics of Post-9/11 Music: Sound, Trauma, and the Music Industry in the Time of Terror*, ed. Joseph P. Fisher and Brian Flota (Farnham: Ashgate, 2011), 161–72.

3. See, for example, Daniel Geary, "'The Way I Would Feel about San Quentin': Johnny Cash & the Politics of Country Music," *Dædalus, the Journal of the American Academy of Arts & Sciences* 142, no. 4 (Fall 2013): 64–72.

Manchu-mustached cowboy from the Village People). The only other musicians I saw on the televised coverage of the proceedings were fellow Muzik Mafia [*sic*] members Cowboy Troy and Gretchen Wilson.

Now, no matter what your politics are—or your musical tastes—you have to admit that the Democrats have way more musical options to choose from.

Just think of the Democratic National Convention in Denver's Mile High Stadium, where Stevie Wonder, will.i.am, John Legend, Michael McDonald, and Sheryl Crow sang between the speeches. Other major pop stars (Moby, Death Cab for Cutie, Kanye West, Bono, Randy Newman and more) were flown in to perform at various events and parties during the week.

It's not that Republicans don't try. They have, for instance, used songs by John Mellencamp, Jackson Browne and Van Halen during the campaign—that's until those artists told them to…stop it. Sarah Palin may be a barracuda, but Heart's Ann and Nancy Wilson didn't let her sing it.

Which brings me to the question: Why are there more acclaimed and varied artists on the left than on the right? And that's not to say that there aren't plenty of sucky liberal songwriters out there—someone just sent me their un-ironic song about Sarah Palin, rhyming whalin' and sailin'.

Maybe there are great Republican artists out there of whom I am not aware, so I Googled "republican musicians songwriters." What I first found was the MySpace[4] page for some guy from Orlando. He made a list of Republic notables. First among the "Republican rock stars" mentioned were Alice Cooper, Gene Simmons and Marilyn Manson. How awesome would that have been to have them together doing a medley of their hits on the convention-hall floor? I would have tuned in, for sure.

Then I saw a recent magazine article on the "5 Biggest Democratic Musicians and 5 Biggest Republican Musicians." Number one for the Dems was Bruce Springsteen. Number one for the other side was '70s gay cowboy look-alike John Rich. I will admit ignorance of his song catalogue—he could be great—but how could you compare him to the Boss?

The Nuge (Ted Nugent) was No. 2 on the Republican lineup. Of course, that was no surprise. But No. 3 did take me aback: the late Johnny Ramone. I have always thought of punk rock as rather left-leaning (unless it's of the white supremacist variety). I connect it with the Clash, Billy Bragg, Dead Kennedys and later-generation bands like Green Day. Could this be the same guitar player who performed the anti-Reagan song "Bonzo Goes to Bitburg"? I wonder, though, if alive today and after the last four years of the Bush administration, he would have still stuck to his guns (at least the metal variety, as he was a big NRA guy).

Kid Rock was No. 4 (again, no surprise) and a favorite of Sarah Palin's, according to Meghan McCain, John's daughter. Meghan said of Palin, "She's totally hip with music." Pam Anderson, Rock's ex, by the way, is for Obama. *People* magazine told me.

Number five was country great Ricky Skaggs. You can say that country artists, in general, lean Republican. But classics like Willie Nelson and Kris Kristofferson are Dems who have also been very outspoken against the war. If I am not mistaken, Obama, on that Mile High night, closed his speech with Brooks and Dunn's "Only in America." The duo has not asked Barack to stop using their song—ironically, the same song George W. Bush used at his last

4. A social networking site popular in the mid-2000s.

convention. Kix Brooks said it's "very flattering to know our song crossed parties and potentially inspires all Americans." Even that archenemy of the Dixie Chicks, Toby Keith, says he is a Democrat (albeit a very conservative one who twice voted for Bush). Also, Nashville-based Music Row Democrats are my MySpace friends.

Oops, I just read, as I was editing this, that the Music Row Democrats, which started as a political-action committee for 2004 nominee John Kerry, disbanded last February. No wonder they haven't answered my emails. I did see, however, a new political group called Music Row for McCain.

Disclosure: Yes, I am a Democrat (surprise). And I was one of those "progressive" artists who volunteered to play in Denver for their convention week. Yet I am open when it comes to talent and the arts. For instance, I do not let the politics of former Tennessee Senator Fred Thompson get in the way of my *Law & Order* enjoyment. I like Skynyrd. And if and when I finally dig into the songs of John Rich, I will try not to be biased.

But I would guess many people do let their party affiliation or "world view" affect their iTunes purchases (or free downloads). In fact, I am friends with a fine singer-songwriter who happens to be really, really conservative. I have to admit that is a bit of a rarity in these circles. Because of that, he has been somewhat paranoid that his career would be in jeopardy if he came out of his political closet. It's not right, but he may be correct. So it got me wondering if there are more secret Republican pop or alternative artists out there. And conversely, are there modern country and Christian recording artists who are afraid to show their support for Obama? To be "Dixie-Chicked" is now in our vocabulary.

And what about Republican hip-hop and R&B artists? I tried Googling that one, but came up totally empty—although James Brown became a Republican, Ray Charles might have been, and Sammy Davis Jr. got in hot water for hugging Richard Nixon in 1973. I didn't even waste my time looking up gay Republican musicians.

So again, why do people in the arts tend to be more liberal? That's a huge and complicated question. Could it be a left brain/right brain thing? One person goes to business school, while the other majors in creative writing or feminist art history—you know, the "liberal arts." Maybe it's the spirit of rebellion and danger—Rage Against the Machine vs. Amy Grant. I know that growing up I was influenced by the politically charged songs of the late '60s and early '70s, as well as early punk. There is a lot more passion and possibility in lyrics that deal with social injustice as opposed to, say, tax cuts. Music comes out of the underdog, the oppressed or those who empathize with the underdog and the oppressed. However, I guess that could also include the white working-class stiffs who somehow feel snubbed by what they perceive as the unpatriotic, Christian-bashing, gay-loving elite. So I really don't know the answer. All I know is good music is good, no matter the party affiliation of the artist or writer. Maybe I'll download a John Rich song and give it a try. It just won't be "Raisin' McCain."

Source: Jill Sobule, "Searching for the Republican Artist," *Performing Songwriter*, November 2008, pp. 86–87. (Used with permission of the author.)

FOR FURTHER READING

Brost, Molly. "Post-Dixie Chicks Country: Carrie Underwood and the Negotiation of Feminist Country Identity." In *The Politics of Post-9/11 Music: Sound, Trauma, and the Music Industry in the Time of Terror*, ed. Joseph P. Fisher and Brian Flota, 161–72. Farnham: Ashgate, 2011.

Boulton, Andrew. "The Popular Geopolitical Wor(l)ds of Post-9/11 Country Music." *Popular Music and Society* 31, no. 3 (July 2008): 373–87.

Schmelz, Peter J. "'Have You Forgotten?': Darryl Worley and the Musical Politics of Operation Iraqi Freedom." In *Music of the Post-9/11 World*, ed. Jonathan Ritter and J. Martin Daughtry, 123–54. New York: Routledge, 2007.

Watson, Jada, and Lori Burns. "Resisting Exile and Asserting Musical Voice: The Dixie Chicks Are *Not Ready to Make Nice*." *Popular Music* 29, no. 4 (2010): 325–50.

49

Vanessa Grigoriadis

"The Very Pink, Very Perfect Life of
Taylor Swift" (2009)

Country music has seldom included the voices of young people.[1] Despite such
notable exceptions as the precocious instrumental virtuosity of guitarist Larry
Collins, steel guitarist Barbara Mandrell, and mandolinist Ricky Skaggs, and
chart-topping singers Brenda Lee, Tanya Tucker, and LeAnn Rimes, country music
has predominantly been the domain of adults, especially since the end of World War
II. The widespread success of teenage country recording artist Taylor Swift in the late
2000s, therefore, necessitated an increasing attention to teenagers and the newly
emergent "tween" market.[2]

1. This phenomenon is discussed at some length in Trent Hill, "Why Isn't Country
Music 'Youth' Culture?," in *Rock Over the Edge: Transformations in Popular Music
Culture*, ed. Roger Beebe, Denise Fulbrook, and Ben Saunders (Durham, NC: Duke
University Press, 2002), 161–90.

2. On "tween" music, consult Tyler Bickford, "The New 'Tween' Music Industry: The
Disney Channel, Kidz Bop, and an Emerging Childhood Counterpublic," *Popular
Music* 31, no. 3 (2012): 417–36.

Swift, whose professional songwriting and recording careers began while she was still in high school, broke numerous sales records not only for country music but in the broader popular music marketplace as well. Her songs, which document the daily challenges faced by teen and "tween" girls and address them as a peer, and her clean-cut, "good girl" image, allowed her to reach a wide audience of young women, while boys and men often saw her as the attractive "girl next door," further adding to her appeal. Swift's popularity among the youth set took her places where few country recording artists have had the opportunity to go: opening a network broadcast of the annual Grammy Awards, opportunities to serve as the spokeperson for national advertising campaigns, and the attention of tabloids that document the ins and outs of her romantic affairs.

Like most women in country music, Swift has had to devote a great deal of energy to presenting an image that is saleable to the country audience.[3] At the same time, her pop aspirations have forced her to strike a balance between playing to her country roots and looking beyond the demands of a limited audience. As Vanessa Grigoriadis's 2009 feature article from *Rolling Stone* indicates, Swift has skillfully used the media to her advantage as she has worked to articulate an artistic and personal identity to her fans and potential audiences. The image that she presents here—of a cute, "indecisive" young girl who is playing house in her multi-million-dollar mansion—runs counter to the impressive business acumen that Grigoriadis is quick to point out. One might see this essay as a quintessential study in the ways of the modern country music publicity machine, skillfully blending "downhome" and "uptown," "hard core" with "soft shell."[4]

═══════════

ON a bright Sunday afternoon in Los Angeles, Taylor Swift is on good behavior, as usual. In high school, she had a 4.0 average; when she was home-schooled during her junior and senior years, she finished both years of course work in 12 months. She has never changed her hair color, won't engage in any remotely dangerous type of physical activity and bites her nails

---

3. For further discussion of this phenomenon, consult Pamela Fox, *Natural Acts: Gender, Race, and Rusticity in Country Music* (Ann Arbor: University of Michigan Press, 2009), 113–44; Kristine M. McCusker, "'Bury Me Beneath the Willow': Linda Parker and Definitions of Tradition on the *National Barn Dance*, 1932-1935," in *A Boy Named Sue: Gender and Country Music* (Jackson: University Press of Mississippi, 2004), 3–23.

4. These terms are taken from Joli Jensen, *The Nashville Sound: Authenticity, Commercialization, and Country Music* (Nashville, TN: Country Music Foundation Press and Vanderbilt University Press, 1998), 21–38; and Richard A. Peterson, "The Dialectic of Hard-Core and Soft-Shell Country Music," in *Reading Country Music: Steel Guitars, Opry Stars, and Honky-Tonk Bars*, ed. Cecelia Tichi (Durham, NC: Duke University Press, 1998), 234–55, respectively.

to the quick. At 19 years old, she says she has never had a cigarette. She says she has never had a drop of alcohol. "I have no interest in drinking," she says, her blue eyes focused and intent beneath kohl liner and liberally applied eye shadow. "I always want to be responsible for the things I say and do." Then she adds, "Also, I would have a problem lying to my parents about that." Swift has gotten far playing Little Miss Perfect—not only was her second album, Fearless, at Number One for eight weeks this winter, but she's enjoyed numerous perks, like a 10-day stay at the West Coast home of her childhood idols, Faith Hill and Tim McGraw, which is where she is today. The couple, who befriended Swift in Nashville, offered the use of their house while she is in L.A. appearing on an episode of her favorite show, CSI. The fact that Swift's first hit single is called "Tim McGraw"—a wistful, gimmicky ballad about a separated couple who recall each other by their favorite McGraw song—is a clue to her feelings about them. "I love Tim and Faith," she says, dashing about the house, which is utterly enormous, filled with gilt crosses and life-size Grecian statues, and worth about $14 million (Eddie Murphy is a neighbor, in a house "the size of a country," says Swift). "I think I like the bright colors in here better than the lighter ones," she says, critiquing the rooms, which seem to go on endlessly, like galleries in a museum. "I don't know. I go back and forth. You know when you walk into a furniture store, and you're like, 'Oh, that's how I'm going to decorate my house,' and then the next one you're like, 'No, that's going to be the way I decorate my house'?" She giggles. "I think when I do it, I'm going to be so indecisive."

Swift lives at home with her parents in a suburb outside of Nashville, in a big house overlooking a lake. The family was wealthy before she became a star—both of Swift's parents have had careers in finance, which makes them particularly good advisers, and they aren't interested in their daughter's cash. One of them usually travels with her, and her father, a kind and friendly stockbroker, has just arrived, a stack of business documents in tow. Swift seems to have three gears—giggly and dorky; worrying about boys and pouring that emotion into song; and insanely driven, hyper self-controlled perfectionism—and, as she embarks on a wholesome afternoon activity, the third aspect of her personality comes into play. In Hill and McGraw's white-marble kitchen, she attacks the task of baking mocha chocolate-chip cookies with a single-mindedness rarely seen outside a graduate-level chemistry class, measuring and sifting and whipping with sharp, expert movements, while her father keeps up a patter about her career.

It takes superhuman strength for a teenager to listen to her father talk at length about her personal life, and even Swift—the goodiest goody-goody in the nation—struggles to remain polite. She's constantly worried about saying something that could be construed as offensive to her fans, and even sways away at a question about her political preferences before conceding that she supports the president: "I've never seen this country so happy about a political decision in my entire time of being alive," she says. "I'm so glad this was my first election." Her eyes dart around like a cornered cat as her dad runs on about the tour bus on which she travels with her mom: "We call it the 'Estrogen Express,'" he says. "That's not what we call it," counters Swift. Then her dad talks about the treadmill he got for her, because she didn't want to deal with sign-ing autographs at the gym. "That's not why!" yelps Swift. "I just don't want to look nasty and sweaty when people are taking pictures of me."

But these are momentary distractions in an otherwise pleasant afternoon. Within 45 minutes, Swift produces two dozen perfect, chewy cookies, which she offers around with a glass bottle of milk. Suddenly, she squints at the jar, [sic] and shrieks a little: eggnog. She scours the fridge but comes up empty-handed, irritated by the foolishness of her mother, whom she surmises was shopping absent-mindedly. This cannot be. Snack time is ruined. Then she blinks rapidly and composes herself.

"I didn't do that," she says, shaking her head firmly. "Mom did that."

Swift likes to do everything the right way, and most of the time that means she likes to do everything herself. She may be a five-foot-11-inch blonde, but she does not have the carefree soul that usually goes along with that physiognomy, and her back is starting to hunch a little from stress. Swift writes or co-writes all of her songs: She's been a working songwriter since the age of 13, when she landed a development deal with RCA Records. "Taylor earned the respect of the big writers in Nashville," says Big and Rich's John Rich, a hot Nashville producer. "You can hear great pop sensibilities in her writing as well as great storytelling, which is the trademark of old-school country song-crafting." At 14, Swift walked away from RCA's offer of another one-year contract—"I didn't want to be somewhere where they were sure that they kind of wanted me maybe," she deadpans—and put herself on the open market. She received interest from major labels but held out for Scott Borchetta, a well-regarded executive at Universal who left the company to start his own label, Big Machine Records. "I base a lot of decisions on my gut, and going with an independent label was a good one," she says. "I thought, 'What's a once-in-a-lifetime opportunity? What's been done a million times?'" Says Borchetta, "Taylor and I made an aggressive deal on the back end." He chuckles. "I've written her some very big checks," he says.

Swift has sold 6 million of her first and second albums, making her the bestselling artist of 2008. Now she is preparing to launch her first headlining arena tour of 52 cities in April (a date at the Staples Center in L.A. sold out in two minutes). She's benefited from a broad demographic appeal: The "Taylor Nation" ranges from country to indie-music fans to the Disney generation, particularly the good gifts. Her impeccably crafted songs easily translate to pop radio, and Swift is clearly taken with the notion of crossing over, though she's nervous about alienating her core audience. "You can't forget who brought you to the part, and that's country radio," she insists. She's very savvy: It was her decision to sing "Fifteen," her song about the innocence of that age, with Miley Cyrus at the Grammys. "I think it's cool, because when she was 15 she had a lot of things going on," says Swift. "Lessons learned." (This is how savvy she is: When she was starting out in music, she used her spare time to paint canvases—"I'm interested in Jackson Pollack's kind of art, where art is beautiful but it's nothing and yet it's incredible"—which she then sent to country-radio managers as gifts.)

For all her high-minded business acumen, as an artist Swift is primarily interested in the emotional life of 15-year-olds: the time of dances and dates with guys you don't like, humiliating crying jags about guys who don't like you, and those few transcendent experiences when a girl's and a boy's feelings finally line up. You can't go anywhere without your best friend. You still tell you mom everything. Real sexuality hasn't kicked in yet. Swift won't reveal anything on that topic herself. "I feel like whatever you say about whether you do or don't it makes people picture you naked," she says, self-assuredly. "And as much as possible, I'm going to avoid that. It's self-preservation, really."

Self-preservation is one of Swift's favorite phrases, and she uses it in reference to both her professional and personal lives. She wants to have a long career, not get tossed away like most teen stars. "I've not seen many people work as hard as Taylor," says Kellie Pickler, a good friend. "She's a very competitive girl, and those people go far." Along with the Jonas Brothers and a gaggle of young Disney stars like her pals Miley Cyrus, Selena

Gomez and Demi Lovato, she's part of a backlash against the pantyless TMZ[5] culture of earlier in this decade, which proved to be a career-killer for Lindsay Lohan and her clique. Swift admits that she was fascinated by girls like Paris Hilton when she was younger—in a rare moment of prurience, she notes that her high school football team was named the Commandos, then laughs wryly—but says that she never though the gossip about these women was true. "You should never judge a person until you know the full story," she explains, matter-of-factly.

Swift is certain she would never let herself get caught up in such shenanigans. "When you lose someone's trust, it's lost, and there are a lot of people out there who are counting on me right now," Swift says. She cocks her head. "Rebellion is what you make of it," she says. "When you've been on a tour bus for two months straight, and then you get in your car and drive wherever you want, that can feel rebellious."

If face [sic], it must be tattooed on, because it never drops during hours of press on a recent weekday in New York, a day that includes mind-numbing patter on Sirius XM[6] and Clear Channel,[7] a voiceover for a new style show on MTV and a sickeningly saccharine luncheon for her L.e.i. sundress line sold at Walmart. It's a tour de force: Swift engages easily with the teen-fashion journalists following her around, bantering about blow-dryers and bachelorette parties; then, she's gracious to the misshapen radio hosts, calling everyone by their names and administering warm hugs by the dozen. But there's a moment, at the Walmart luncheon, when she gets a little testy with a young fan—Swift asks the fan where she's from, and when the girl answers, "New Jersey," Swift makes fun of her accent—but this is literally the only sin against a human she commits during a 10-hour day in which she's barely fed, never stops smiling and signs hundreds of autographs with a pink Sharpie pen.

This politesse is part of Swift's character, a way of treating others taught by her loving family. Her parents intentionally raised their kids in the country, on a Christmas-tree farm with a grape arbor and seven horses, in eastern Pennsylvania, while Swift's father commuted to work. "I had the most magical childhood, running free and going anywhere I wanted to in my head," says Swift. But her parents also prized success in the real world: They even gave her an androgynous name, on the assumption that she would later climb the corporate ladder. "My mom thought it was cool that if you got a business card that said 'Taylor' you wouldn't know if it was a guy or a girl," says Swift. "She wanted me to be a business person in a business world."

Swift rode horses competitively as a child, but her main hobby was making up fairy tales and singing the songs from Disney movies by heart. At six, she discovered a LeAnn Rimes record, which she began to listen to compulsively. "All I wanted to hear from then on was country," she says. "I loved the amazing female country artists of the Nineties—Faith, Shania, the Dixie Chicks—each with an incredible sound and standing for incredible things." She began to act in a children's musical-theater company but found that she preferred the cast parties, which featured a karaoke machine, to the stage. "Singing country music on that karaoke machine was my favorite thing in the world," she says. As is the Swift-ian way, even at 11 she was determined to "pursue other venues" where she could perform, and soon found the Pat Garrett Roadhouse, which had a weekly karaoke contest. "I sang every single week for a year and a half until I won," she says. Her prize: opening for Charlie Daniels at 10:30 a.m.; he played at 8:30 at night.

5. TMZ is a popular website chronicling celebrity gossip in the United States. It is noted for publishing inappropriate candid photographs of celebrities.
6. A satellite radio service in North America.
7. The largest holder of radio stations in the United States during the 2000s.

Newly emboldened, Swift began to perform the national anthem at local sports games, and even landed a gig with her favorite team, the Philadelphia 76ers. But tragedy soon befell our young songstress. It seems that her classmates did not agree that country music was cool. "Anything that makes you different in middle school makes you weird," she says. "My friends turned into the girls who would stand in the corner and make fun of me." She was abandoned at the lunch table. She was accused of possessing frizzy hair. She tried to fit in by joining teams but proved to be horrible at every sport. Then redemption came in the form of a 12-string guitar. "When I picked up the guitar, I could not stop," she says. "I would literally play until my fingers bled—my mom had to tape them up, and you can imagine how popular that made me: 'Look at her fingers, so weird.'" She takes a deep breath. "But for the first time, I could sit in class and those girls could say anything they wanted about me, because after school I was going to go home and write a song about it."

This is Swift's tale of triumph, and she likes to tell it a lot when she's interviewed. It sounds canned, in a way—who hasn't been made fun of in middle school?—but she's managed to keep the feelings raw, and access to them is part of her appeal. The sun is starting to set as Swift heads downtown, near the World Trade Center site, to play a live acoustic set on the radio station Z100 for about 50 "Caller 100s"—a group that happens to be almost exclusively plain, primly dressed girls between 12 and 17. The fans listen raptly as Swift chats about bad-hair days and ex-boyfriends. They hold up their camera phones, sometimes with a Sidekick in the other hand. Swift keeps insisting that they sing along with her, and at first they're shy, but soon the scene resembles a teenage-girl "Kumbaya" session, all the alienation and hurt that they feel in their real lives melting away, replaced by a deep sense of peace. "Taylor is so down-to-earth," gushes Darlane Shala, a ninth-grader from Manhattan. "She's just such a good person."

Afterward, Swift takes more photos with the girls and looks at her fan letters. The girls write about feeling like outsiders, about getting ostracized by girlfriends over misunderstandings with boys, about hating girls who make fun of other girls and not understanding why some people enjoy being so cruel. "When I first discovered your music a few years ago, something in me opened up," says a meticulously crafted two-page letter from a high school sophomore, who included a picture of herself at the beach. "I had been feeling upset, and you told me that I'm not alone," she continues. "Your lyrics mean the world to me, and I swear they are the narration of my life." She adds that Swift has given her a path for the future: "I wish more than anything that I could change a teenager's perspective," she writes, "the way you have done for me."

This is Swift's primary hope for her music: She wants to help adolescent girls everywhere feel better about themselves, and in the process heal her younger self. "In school, I loved reading To Kill a Mockingbird, and I'm very interested in any writing from a child's perspective," she says. At high school in Henderson, Tennessee, a suburb of Nashville—her parents agreed to move when she landed her RCA contract, at the beginning of her freshman year—Swift's interest in country music was obviously considered normal, but she still wasn't popular. She may be pretty now, and she eventually might have abused the power that comes with being a beautiful senior girl, but when she left high school, at 16, she was still a gangly sophomore. "There were queen bees and attendants, and I was maybe the friend of one of the attendants," she says. "I was the girl who didn't get invited to parties, but if I did happen to go, you know, no one would throw a bottle at my head."

In a way, Swift's emotional state seems to be stuck at the time when she left school. She says that she has only a half-dozen friends now—"and that's a lot for me"—and she talks constantly about her best friend, Abigail, a competitive swimmer and freshman at Kansas State, with a new nose ring and a new pet snake, doubtlessly having many experiences that Swift may not be ready for. In fact, Swift is a very young 19-year-old. "I feel like Miley, Selena and Demi are my age," she says at one point, acknowledging the fast-paced lives of her Los Angeles-based contemporaries. "It's crazy, I always forget that they're 16."

And in her love life, Swift admits to being mighty inexperienced. She says that she's had her heart broken, but she's not sure if she's ever really been in love. She had a boyfriend her freshman year, a senior hockey player: "We weren't an It couple," she drawls. But there really haven't been many guys since then except for Joe Jonas, who famously broke up with her over the phone for another girl. Swift wrote a song on her second album, called "Forever & Always," about Jonas, then filmed a MySpace video with a Joe Jonas doll, during which she remarks, "This one even comes with a phone so it can break up with other dolls!" Jonas later insinuated that she hung up on him. "I did not hang up on him," she says now, then mouths, "Omigod."

The illogic of love is unsettling to Swift, who has a hard time understanding it with her supremely rational mind. Music, for her, is a way of expressing feelings that are largely repressed or absent. She maintains that marriage is something she would "only do if I find the person I absolutely can't live without" and "it's not my ultimate goal in life." In fact, the first two singles on Fearless—"Love Story" and "White Horse"—are about a guy that she considered dating but never even kissed. Many of her songs are not about her own personal experiences with love—about half are inspired by her friends' relationships. "I'm fascinated by love rather than the principle of 'Oh, does this guy like me?'" she says. "I love love. I love studying it and watching it. I love thinking about how we treat each other, and the crazy way that one person can feel one thing and another can feel totally different," she says. "It just doesn't take much for me to be inspired to write a song about a person, but I'm much more likely to write that song than do anything about it. You know, self-preservation."

A couple of weeks ago, Swift started four days of rehearsal at a studio on the outskirts of Nashville for her upcoming tour. She picks the alfalfa sprouts out of a sandwich—Swift avoids vegetables, hates sushi and in general gravitates away [sic] from anything healthy—and straps on her guitar, strumming as she gives her tour manager instructions on the set list. As much as she engages in good-natured banter with her band, she's clearly in charge of this show: With a faintly sex-kitten stage presence—punctuated by many pumps of her very long arms in the air—she cues fiddle licks, restages a number and shuffles the orchestration in a mash-up. Then she stops. "Omigod," she giggles. "For 'Love Story,' the stage is going to become a church, and I'm going to get into a white dress." She bites her lip. "There's so many cool sets," she says later. "We're going to have a giant castle!"

After rehearsal, she returns to her parents' home, which is set on a promontory over Old Hickory Lake. "In the summer, people fish off the dock," says Swift, then deadpans, "More people now. Apparently, there are more fish now." The mantle of their living room is crammed with bulky glass awards, and posters of Swift line the hallways; a large sitting room is devoted to racks of clothes that Swift has worn in performance or public, with a sign affixed that reads, "Please go through: Keep or give to Goodwill." Her younger brother Austin, a 16-year-old lacrosse player and academic overachiever, has moved into a room on the garage level, doubtless to have some space away from the Taylor Nation, but Swift still lives in her childhood bedroom.

It's a small room, decorated almost exclusively in pink and purple. Her closet is itty-bitty, with clothes organized in neat rows above her shoes and a drawer of padded bras.

Any sign of her life as a superstar has been scrubbed, with the exception of a postcard from Reba McEntire. She rifles around in her armoire—careful not to show its contents, which she considers too messy for guests—and pulls out a cardboard box of colored wax, which she uses to seal envelopes. "I wrote my Valentine's Day cards yesterday," she says, holding up a thick stack. "It's not going to be a big shindig for me. I didn't have that one person." She smiles. "So I had to write 30."

It's almost 8 p.m., and Swift is planning to work on her set lists for a few hours tonight, but first she needs a Frappuccino. She hasn't started her car, a champagne-colored Lexus, in a couple of months—her brother has to jump-start it—and when she finally pulls out onto the road, she seems a little less perfect. She's an unsure, semi-reckless driver, hitting the brake too hard, pointing the car this way and that at various intersections like she's tacking a boat. She screams, "Five-oh!" as she spots a cop, then pulls into a drive-through Starbucks. "I've been in three accidents, but none of them were my fault," she walls.

Soon she comes to a stop, pointing to an expanse of lawn. "This summer, the guy from the 'Fifteen' song came back into Abigail's life," she says. "He got me to bring her here, and while we were on the way he texted her, 'We need to talk.' "When they arrived, the guy was standing in the center of this field in a big heart made of candles, holding a bunch of roses. "It was so romantic," she says, smiling dreamily. "I love that kind of stuff." Then she starts pulling away. "You know, I totally burned a CD for him to play that night, because he wouldn't have known Abigail's favorite songs otherwise," she says, tapping the steering wheel. "And as usual, I had to clean up the mess the next day." She sighs. "But that's OK," she says. "I didn't mind."

Chet Flippo

"Why the Term 'Country Music' May Disappear: Marketers of the Future May Dissolve Music Genre Labels" (2010)

The first decade of the twenty-first century witnessed a revolution in the way that consumers engaged with the recorded work of their favorite musicians. Unlike any time during the century or more that record labels had been issuing recordings, the new millennium brought with it a technological shift that removed the need for the production and sale of physical recordings: the Internet. Beginning with Napster in the late 1990s and continuing to such popular streaming services as Rhapsody, Spotify, and YouTube today, the Internet has made it increasingly easy for listeners to obtain recordings, leading many commentators to lament the impending collapse of the global music industry.[1]

1. Many of these trends have been documented in Mark Katz, *Capturing Sound: How Technology Has Changed Music*, rev. ed. (Berkeley: University of California Press, 2010), 177–210; Kiri Miller, *Playing Along: Digital Games, YouTube, and Virtual Performance* (New York: Oxford University Press, 2012); and Jonathan Sterne, *mp3: The Meaning of a Format* (Durham, NC: Duke University Press, 2013).

The Internet and the many personal audio devices that are connected to it (mp3 players, tablet computers, and smartphones) have allowed listeners to fashion personalized playlists that transcend traditional genre boundaries and to discover music that might fly under the radar of their local radio stations. At the same time, record labels, radio stations (both terrestrial and satellite), and the marketing companies that have risen to prominence in the last decade have attempted to identify smaller generic niches that cater to more focused demographics and allow advertisers to reach their target audience with greater ease.[2]

The hot country format that was developed in the early 1990s continues to dominate terrestrial radio airplay, and the few outlets that continue to stock physical recordings (including, most notably, big box retailers) still carry the latest releases from the artists who are heard on those stations. But the increasingly diverse musical tastes of the country music audience—and of those people who mix country sounds into their otherwise rock, pop, and hip hop playlists—has led to something of a crisis for music industry marketers who must rely on remarkably specific adjectives to describe the sounds of new bands, to get their music into the playlists of potential listeners, and to encourage those listeners to attend lucrative concert performances.

Country music journalist Chet Flippo, writing in his *Nashvile Skyline* blog in 2010, describes some of these challenges, offering a long view of country music's generic nomenclature and offering some predictions for the genre's future in the Internet age.

NOW, as that enterprise dwindles and transforms into a song-dominated download industry, genre distinctions are becoming blurred and even non-existent for many listeners. As songs trump the notion of artists, artist loyalty may become eroded as well.

If you look at a cross section of what's generally considered to be current country music, you see a large array of many genres and sub-genres: from traditional country to classic country, old-timey music, modern trad, rockabilly, Western swing, cowboy, current classic contemporary trad, contemporary Texas, Red Dirt, mainstream country, recurrent contemporary mainstream, Southern rock, Americana, splinter Americana, alt-country, folk-country and country punk. Plus some other even smaller areas where its artists defy any labeling. And then there's bluegrass, with its own sub-genres. And there's no doubt some niche areas I've left out.

Some people regard all of that as country music—and some don't. Some like all or many parts or sub-genres of it—and some like only one or two or three areas. Many fans of '70s rock have discovered that today's mainstream country *is* '70s rock. And some bluegrass is actually closer to jazz than to country.

---

2. See, for instance, the proliferation of channels available on satellite radio and streaming audio services.

So, will those genres continue to exist as genres or even sub-genres if all the artists therein will be regarded mainly as providers of songs (or "tracks") to be downloaded? As albums increasingly cease to be a dominant factor, which areas of country will fade and blur into some other area or simply disappear altogether?

The hardcore physical genre/music-labeling separation itself dates from the beginnings of the retail sales of records. In retail stores, they were separated by a loose system of labels. Rack jobbers serviced the racks in stores by genres, and the stores demanded a premium for racking the records that sold the most to get the most prominent racks. You paid to get your records racked up front and in the end-caps because it paid off in sales. Over the years, the big sellers have been rock and pop and country and rap and hip-hop and R&B.

Radio and the music trade charts long ago put labels on music. In those earlier days, all black music was labeled "race music." Jerry Wexler changed "race music" to "R&B"—for rhythm & blues—in the 1940s when he was at *Billboard*, before he became a genre-changing record company producer and executive in rock, country and R&B.[3]

In its earliest days, country was called "hillbilly music." It originally came from the hills of England and Scotland and Ireland, after all, and then from the hills of Appalachia. But as far as I can tell, the word "hillbilly" was first used in print in 1900 in the *New York Journal*, which wrote, "a Hill-Billie is a free and untrammeled white citizen of Alabama, who lives in the hills, has no means to speak of, dresses as he can, talks as he pleases, drinks whiskey when he gets it and fires off his revolver as the fancy takes him."[4]

So, commercial country music came to be called "hillbilly music," a name given to it by country pianist Al Hopkins in the 1920s. The term "country & western" was used in the heyday of the singing cowboys and Western swing and is now only used by people who don't know any better.

When the Country Music Association was formed in 1958, the term "country music" finally began to replace "hillbilly," with a huge amount of urging from the late Ernest Tubb, who said, " 'Hillbilly,' that's what the press use to call it, 'hillbilly music.' Now, I always said, 'You can call me a hillbilly if you got a smile on your face.' We let the record companies know that they were producing country music 'cause we all come from the country."[5]

Now that such big-box stores as Wal-Mart and Target have cut their CD rack space down to an absolute minimum, whatever racks remain are reserved for supposed guaranteed big sellers, period. No more racks for catalog CDs. And no more stores for large-scale catalog racking, such as the late Tower chain of brick-and-mortar stores.

I suspect it's pretty much a given that when albums finally disappear, so will genres, as genres. Except probably for such clearly defined (and low-selling) genres as jazz and classical. Pop music with all its bastardizations long ago became a dumping ground for whatever didn't make it up off the butcher shop floor to be made into the latest brand of sausage.

3. Jerry Wexler with David Ritz, *Rhythm and the Blues: A Life in American Music* (New York: Knopf, 1993), 62.

4. This history is traced in greater detail in Archie Green, "Hillbilly Music: Source and Symbol," *Journal of American Folklore* 78, no. 309 (July-September 1965): 204–28; and Anthony Harkins, *Hillbilly: A Cultural History of an American Icon* (New York: Oxford University Press, 2004).

5. For more on the formation of the Country Music Association, consult Diane Pecknold, *The Selling Sound: The Rise of the Country Music Industry* (Durham, NC: Duke University Press, 2007), 133–67.

But what has been defined as country will be a free-for-all. Then what, for staunch country music fans? The downloaders will seek out their tracks by their favorite artist and will find others largely by word of mouth and by the Internet. The CD fan holdouts will still search out and find what remains. I suspect the vinyl LP audience will continue to grow, as that album audience becomes a larger cult of true devotees of music fidelity and music integrity. And what about the future of country radio? They will find a way to survive. However devious it may be. They always do.

Source: Chet Flippo, "Why the Term 'Country Music' May Disappear: Marketers of the Future May Dissolve Music Genre Labels," *Nashville Skyline*, 14 January 2010. http://www.cmt.com/news/nashville-skyline/1629745/nashville-skyline-why-the-term-country-music-may-disappear.jhtml; accessed 23 March 2012). (Used with permission of the author.)

FOR FURTHER READING

Sterne, Jonathan. *mp3: The Meaning of a Format*. Durham, NC: Duke University Press, 2013.

51

Skip Hollandsworth

"The Girl Who Played with Firearms" (2011)

During the first decade of the twenty-first century, broadcast television net-works and their cable counterparts revived and revised the talent show, a long-time staple of radio and television broadcasting in the United States. Mobilizing new mobile technologies to involve viewers directly and indirectly in the selection of winning contestants, programs such as *American Idol* and *Nashville Star*, among others, brought dozens of new artists to radio and record-ings, each with a fan base that had been carefully cultivated through the shows' audience participation models.[1]

These programs were particularly beneficial to the country music world, gen-erating such country radio mainstays as Kelly Pickler, Scotty McCreery, Carrie Underwood, Blake Shelton, and Miranda Lambert, among many others. Yet, some observers—including professional critics and average television viewers alike—were skeptical of the talent show format, arguing that such programs catered to

1. For a nuanced discussion of the *American Idol* phenomenon, consult Katherine Meizel, *Idolized: Music, Media, and Identity in American Idol* (Bloomington: Indiana University Press, 2011).

the lowest common denominator and generated sound-alike artists who simply lubricated the gears of a profit-seeking and talent-blind popular music industry.

Reading Skip Hollandsworth's *Texas Monthly* feature on *Nashville Star* contestant Miranda Lambert through that lens, we can see a concerted effort to present the award-winning, multi-platinum Lambert as a product of her impoverished and danger-filled childhood, a recording artist with a distinctive voice as a songwriter, a powerful and self-sufficient businesswoman, and a domestic diva.[2] By the same token, Hollandsworth is quick to point to Lambert's powerful feminism, an attitude that empowers women to escape from abusive relationships and take control of their lives. Like her contemporary Gretchen Wilson, Lambert channels a distinctive working-class feminism that simultaneously embraces a "bad-ass" attitude and glamour, violence and domesticity.[3] Situating her work in a lineage that extends back to Wells and Lynn, Hollandsworth presents Lambert in much the same way as her musical foremothers: as a tough woman who is at home in the honky-tonk and the household.[4]

FOUR hours before Miranda Lambert is scheduled to perform in front of five thousand fans in Corbin, Kentucky, she's making a beeline for the commissary that has just been set up by her road crew. "I'm sorry, but if I don't start eating right now, I'm literally going to die of starvation," she says to no one in particular as she fills up a plate of food. She sits down at a table, spears an entire chicken breast with her fork, lifts it toward her mouth, and then notices me sitting across the table, notebook in hand, ready to write down what will happen next. For several seconds the chicken breast hangs in the air, quivering on her fork. Miranda tosses back her magnificent mane of blond hair and stares at me with one eyebrow raised. She shifts in her seat, sliding one leg underneath the other.

More seconds pass.

"Well, crap, there goes my ladylike image," she finally says as she leans forward and rips into the chicken. After a few seconds of high-speed chewing, she takes another equally giant bite.

"Pretty impressive," I murmur.

"Thank you," she replies. "People think you can only enjoy food if you eat it slowly. Well, I'm here to tell you that it tastes just as good when you eat fast. And I like eating fast. I've got things to do."

Since arriving in Corbin earlier this July day, Miranda has run laps in the parking lot of the local arena, with her ragtag parade of small dogs—Cher, Delta, and Delilah—trotting

2. Compare this depiction to Murray Nash's treatment of Kitty Wells in chapter 22.

3. This approach is similar to what Hubbs has discovered in her analysis of Gretchen Wilson (Nadine Hubbs, "'Redneck Woman' and the Gendered Politics of Class Rebellion," *Southern Cultures* 17, no. 4 (Winter 2011): 44–70.

4. Pamela Fox has discussed this phenomenon in greater detail in *Natural Acts: Gender, Race, and Rusticity in Country Music* (Ann Arbor: University of Michigan Press, 2009), 113–45.

diligently behind her. She has performed a series of lunges next to her tour bus, and inside, she has whipped through a few dozen push-ups and sit-ups. She's met with her manager to talk about her new album, *Four the Record*, which will be released in November, and she's talked to her publicist about her newest venture, an all-female band called the Pistol Annies, which she formed last year with two of her friends and whose self-titled debut album is coming out in less than a month. And as soon as she finishes eating, she's scheduled to meet with some New York advertising executives who have come to Kentucky to try to persuade her to become the national spokesperson for one of their products.

The dinner is over in less than five minutes. Miranda stands up and brushes a few crumbs off her tank top and low-slung blue jeans. "Holy crap!" she says, giving me a dazzling smile, the dimples in her cheeks so deep they could hold water. "I've got to get moving."

For nearly a decade, she has been a blur of activity. It wasn't long ago that she was just another small-town Texas teenager who dreamed of becoming a country music star. She lived in Lindale, outside Tyler [Texas], and she was so determined to get her career started that she entered a program in high school called Operation Graduation—"made up of a bunch of pregnant girls and druggies and me," she recalls—so she could finish early.

There was no question she could belt out a song: in 2003, at the age of nineteen, she placed third on *Nashville Star*, a country music talent show that aired on the USA cable network. But it was hard to imagine her becoming one of country music's next big things. In no time, the leggy, high-heeled Carrie Underwood would win *American Idol*, singing glossy pop-country songs that had been crafted to appeal to a mainstream audience. Her first hit, "Inside Your Heaven," was about a woman hopelessly in love with a man. "You're all I've got," Carrie sang. "You lift me up.... All my dreams are in your eyes."[5]

Miranda insisted on doing songs she had written or co-written, and her lyrics were about as mushy as a Cormac McCarthy novel. One of her songs celebrated a vindictive woman who had decided to burn down the house of her cheating lover. Another told the story of a lady sitting by the door with a gun, waiting for her abusive man to come home from jail. Miranda wrote about girls who cussed, drank too much, packed pistols, and raised hell. Her gals didn't have time to pine over their two-timing men. They were too busy plotting to get even.

Nashville insiders were mystified by this pillow-lipped little teenager, just five feet four inches tall. "Light 'em up and watch them burn," Miranda would sing about no-good dudes in her country twang. "Teach them what they need to learn.... I'm givin' up on love, 'cause love's given up on me." Only one word could describe her consonant-dropping, take-no-prisoners style: "twangry."

Today those Nashville insiders are falling all over themselves to have their photos taken with her. In the words of *Rolling Stone* magazine critic Will Hermes, Miranda, who's now 27, is "the most gifted woman to hit country's mainstream in a decade." The three albums she has released since 2005 (*Kerosene*, *Crazy Ex-Girlfriend*, and *Revolution*) have all gone platinum, selling at least a million copies each. Three of her singles from *Revolution* alone went to number one on the *Billboard* country music charts. And in the past year, she has won a Grammy, three Country Music Association Awards (in addition to being named female vocalist of the year), and four Academy of Country Music Awards.

What's most remarkable is that Miranda has achieved such commercial success without sacrificing what Jon Caramanica, the country music writer for the *New York Times*[,]

5. Hubbs, " 'Redneck Woman' " also offers this comparison.

describes as her "sharp tongue, a penchant for flamboyant lyrical gesture, and a cooing voice that only barely sugarcoats deeply acidic thoughts." Indeed, Miranda is still relentlessly knocking out one song after another about rowdy women who, when wronged, don't think for a second about standing by their men. The first single released from *Four the Record*, "Baggage Claim," is about a girl who trashes her wayward beau's worldly goods.

Also on the album is a duet that she recorded with her new husband, Blake Shelton, the popular good-old-boy country singer from Oklahoma and celebrity judge on NBC's *The Voice*. And what, in her newly married bliss, did she choose for her and Blake to record? A song called "Better in the long Run," about a couple who's breaking up.

"What can I tell you? It's a heck of a good song," Miranda says. "And let's face it, isn't the dark side a lot more interesting? Seriously, if all I did was sing about all the really nice things that happen to women, I'd be bored to death."

Since country music began, female singers have wailed over the plight of fellow women caught in relationships with no-good men. "Most every heart that's ever been broken was because there always was a man to blame," sang Kitty Wells in her 1952 classic "It Wasn't God Who Made Honky Tonk Angels," the first song by a female artist to hit number one on the *Billboard* country charts. Two decades later, in "I Wanna Be Free," Loretta Lynn reveled in the possibilities a divorce from a hard-drinking husband might bring ("I'm gonna take this chain from around my finger and throw it just as far as I can sling'er"), and in 2000's "Goodbye Earl," the Dixie Chicks had an abusive husband unabashedly murdered and dumped in a lake by his wife and her best friend. Even Carrie Underwood released the single "Before He Cheats," about a woman taking revenge on an unfaithful boyfriend by keying his truck and smashing the headlights with a baseball bat (of course, in her music video, Underwood carries out the vandalism while wearing high heels).

But no one has sung these kinds of songs as often and with such relish as Miranda Lambert. She is part blond babe and part saucy shitkicker, the kind of gal who's pretty enough to win a beauty contest but tough enough to crack open someone's head with a beer bottle. "Look right here," she tells me, pointing to an elaborate tattoo spread across her left arm of two intertwined revolvers graced by angel wings. "That defines who I am. The wings are my way of saying, 'I'm a nice, down-home, small-town girl.'" Then she points to the pistols, and for a moment her eyes narrow. "But if you do me wrong, you better watch out, because I won't take any of your crap."

That philosophy, as simple as it is, has become a call to arms for a loyal, growing fan base, made up mostly of women under the age of forty. When Miranda heads off to her post-dinner meeting, I walk out to the parking lot, where a few dozen fervent "Ran Fans" are already gathered behind a security fence, holding cameras, desperate to get a shot of their heroine. One young woman, who's wearing a straw cowboy hat, a flowered dress with spaghetti straps, and cowboy boots, tells me how the hit song "Gunpowder and Lead"—a seething tune about a woman lashing out at a punishing ex-boyfriend that Miranda dreamed up while taking a concealed-handgun class—changed her life. "That song helped give me the courage to break up with my own boyfriend, who treated me like dog meat," exults the young woman.

When I remark that "Gunpowder and Lead" seems to suggest that firearms, not diamonds, should be a girl's best friend—"He'll find out when I pull the trigger!" is one of the more memorable lines—another Ran Fan, in a midriff-baring shirt, Daisy Dukes, and boots, jubilantly shouts, "Hell, yeah!"

I then bring up "Kerosene," the song that first made Miranda famous—yes, the one about a girl wanting to burn down the two-timing boyfriend's house—and more Ran Fans chime in with such comments as "You know that every girl fantasizes about doing something like that." I ask if any of them have ever gotten out of control like the girl in another Miranda single, "Crazy Ex-Girlfriend," who threatens to beat up an old boyfriend's new girlfriend in a pool hall, and they all just look at me as though I'm one more clueless man. "Miranda puts into words what we're all thinking," someone says from the back of the crowd, which sets off a group cheer.

"Women love her badass attitude," says Miranda's mother, Bev, who helps handle Miranda's merchandising from her home in Lindale. "Last year we started selling a camouflage hoodie with a line from one of her songs printed on the back that read 'Time to Get a Gun.' And it sold like crazy. Wearing that hoodie was her fans' way of saying that they were badasses too."

Miranda's father, Rick, estimates that her merchandise sales are now "easily ten times higher than they were a year and a half ago." Rick oversees the Miranda Lambert Store and Red 55 Winery (named after Miranda's favorite truck, a red '55 Chevy) in downtown Lindale. That's right, Miranda now has her own private wine label, with the wine coming from the Lou Viney Vineyards, in nearby Sulphur Springs. "They must be like an aphrodisiac to her fans, because they're buying them by the case," Rick notes. "For these women, it's all Miranda, all the time."

Men, on the other hand, are a little bewildered. In 2008, after listening to "Gunpowder and Lead," the editors of *Esquire* named her Terrifying Woman of the Year in their annual music awards issue, concluding, "It's tough to tell where the insanely violent characters begin and the real Miranda Lambert leaves off."

"I remember when Miranda first came out with her 'Kerosene' video," chuckles her husband, who called me from his tour bus in Michigan, where he's promoting his new album, *Red River Blue*, which hit number one on the *Billboard* country charts in late July. "You'd see all these guys doing double takes. Here she was, walking down this dirt road, so unbelievably hot-looking in these tight jeans and tight T-shirt and with all her blond hair bouncing around,. And she gave the camera this nonstop sexy look with those damn sexy eyes of hers. You could just hear guys saying, 'Oh, man, who is that?' But all the while she was walking, she was pouring kerosene leading out of her boyfriend's house, and at the end of the song, she threw a match. And those guys who were getting so worked up were suddenly saying, 'Run for your life!' "

A man is likely to become only more bewildered when he meets Miranda in person. She not only has the perfect teardrop face but her voice is as buttery as a biscuit. "I'm sorry I say 'crap' so much when I talk, but I do like the word," she tells me during one of our conversations, popping out some lip gloss, as she does every ten minutes or so, and touching up her lips. She is also utterly unpretentious. She will happily spend an hour talking about all the abandoned dogs she and her mom have adopted (Miranda now owns seven but takes only Cher, Delta, and Delilah with her on tour). Or she'll chat about the books she's reading (*The Help* and *Hunger Games*). Or that she likes to bake chocolate-chip cookies.

"Oh, listen, she's a complete, one-hundred-percent sweetie," Blake says.

"Always?" I ask.

"Always," he replies. There's a silence, and then he laughs again. "But come on now. Do you think I'm dumb enough to risk getting in any trouble with her? Do you think I'm that stupid?"

For most of the Seventies, Miranda's father was a cop for the Dallas Police Department, assigned to the patrol division, then to undercover narcotics, and then homicide. He also sang in a country band named Contraband, which played at all the country-and-western joints along Greenville Avenue. "It was a good way to meet drug dealers and make undercover buys and get them off the streets," says Rick, a stocky, good-looking man who loves to tell stories. "And by the way, it was also a good way to meet Dallas stewardesses." Then he met Bev, a former junior college cheerleader from East Texas who was working in Dallas as a leotard-wearing fitness instructor at an Elaine Powers Figure Salon, a gym for women. "Lights out," he says. "That girl had it all."

After Miranda was born, the Lamberts moved to Van Alstyne, north of Dallas, and opened a small detective agency. At one point, when business slumped, they lost everything, moved to Lindale to live with Bev's brother, and later rented a ramshackle house that was about to be bulldozed. The Lamberts planted a garden, and they raised chickens, pigs, rabbits, and goats. "If I saw a deer in the pasture, I'd run out and try to shoot it, whether it was deer season or not," says Rick. "We were that flat-out poor."

In 1997[,] the Lamberts got back on their feet when they were hired by the lawyers of Paula Jones, a former Arkansas state employee, to look into allegations that she had been sexually harassed by Bill Clinton when he was Arkansas' governor. Rick finally got his family out of the rent house and moved them into a 4,800-square-foot home in Lindale. A few months later, when the preacher at their church saw how big the house was, he asked the Lamberts if they would mind taking in a woman who was being beaten up by her husband. Soon, another abused woman arrived, with her children. "I told the women that we would clothe them and feed them as long as they told their husbands not to step foot on our property, because if they did I would ask no questions," Rick says. "I would get out my gun and drop them in the front yard."

By then, Miranda was fourteen years old. When she'd get home from school, she'd sit in the den and listen to one of the abused women, tears streaming down her face, talk about what she'd endured. Some nights, she'd sleep on the floor in her parents' bedroom while a woman slept in her bed. Other nights, when it was just the family at the house, she would sit with her little brother at the dinner table and listen to her parents talk about their investigations. "We talked about who was cheating on who[m] or who was shacking up at some motel, and she'd quietly take it all in," says Rick. "She heard about some gal who had been left dead-broke by her husband, who had walked out on her and the kids. She heard about some other gal who was so down on her luck she started drinking and getting in trouble. And she'd say, 'Daddy, it isn't right what those men are doing.' When I look back on those years, I realize she was getting a clinic in how to write a country song."

Throughout her childhood, Miranda had sung along with Rick when he had "picking parties" on his front porch for his neighbors and hunting buddies. At the age of sixteen, she competed in a country music talent show in Longview. Although she lost in the second round—she was the only teenager competing—she was hooked. Rick put together a little backup band for her, and he and Bev began driving her to honky-tonks, where she performed a lot of Tanya Tucker and Rusty Weir covers, mostly in front of drunk rednecks. One night, in Dallas, while she sang in a railroad car that had been converted into a bar, a bloody fight broke out involving five or six patrons. Undeterred, Miranda kept singing, not missing a note, not even when everyone in the bar spilled out to the parking lot to keep the fight going.

At another Dallas hole-in-the-wall, some guy asked her if she wanted to smoke pot. She promptly told Rick, who put him in a choke hold. "Miranda started yelling, 'Kill him,

Daddy! Kill him!" says Rick. "She was trying to get ready to sing, and she was pissed that some-one was trying to mess her up."

"No, that isn't exactly what she said," sighs Bev. "She only yelled, 'Kick his ass, Daddy! Kick his ass!'"

When she wasn't touring honky-tonks, Miranda would sit with her guitar on the floor of her bathroom, where the acoustics were good, and, using the five chords her father taught her, knock out one song after another. None of them were about kissing boys or cruising around the town square with her girlfriends. In one song, she described a desperately unhappy woman falling in love with Jack Daniel's [sic]. "He's the best kind of lover that there is," wrote Miranda, who was still years away from legal drinking age. "I can have him when I please, he always satisfied my needs." In another, she described a woman driving down Highway 65, try-ing to escape her life. "Wanna feel my freedom blowin' through my hair," wrote Miranda, who had only recently gotten her driver's license. "Throw my troubles to the wind and scream out, I don't care."

"One day," recalls Rick, "she walked into my room while I was strumming some chords on my guitar, and she suddenly sang to the melody I was playing, 'Rain on the window makes me lonely.' We both came up with some more lines, and in an hour and a half, we had a song about a woman sitting on a bus, devastated by the end of an affair with a married man. We played it for Bev, and when Miranda sang, 'I'm gonna find someplace I can ease my mind and try to heal my wounded pride,' we both shook our heads. Miranda had this eerie ability to take on someone else's story and make it her own."

Miranda sang that particular song, "Greyhound Bound for Nowhere," in the finals of *Nashville Star*. Later, she met with executives from Sony BMG in Nashville. "We walked into a room filled with about twenty people," says her agent, Joey Lee, "and they started going through their thing, saying, 'We need you to write with this person and work with this producer so that we can produce a great record.' And Miranda basically stopped everyone in their tracks and said, 'Have y'all listened to my songs? Because that's who I am and that's what I'm going to keep doing, and if I can't do it my way, I'll go home and come back when you're ready for me.' She was eighteen years old and walking away from a major record deal. And right then, to his credit, the president of the label said, 'Okay, Miranda, go make your record.'"

When that first record, *Kerosene* was released, in 2005, the programming directors for country music stations were put off by the songs' straight-talking females. Not one of Miranda's four singles from the album cracked the top ten of the *Billboard* country singles chart (which is heavily determined by radio play). But the album itself went to number one on the *Billboard* country album chart. So did her second album, *Crazy Ex-Girlfriend*. Clearly, as the great coun-try singer Kenny Chesney would later say, Miranda "was singing to an audience that wasn't being sung to."

By 2009, when she released *Revolution*, country radio was waiting for her with open arms. Three singles from that album went to number one: "White Liar," whose character warns devious dudes that she'll get the last word if they mess around on her; "Heart Like Mine," about a frisky female who declares, "I heard Jesus, he drank wine, and I bet we'd get along just fine"; and "The House That Built Me," a heartbreaking elegy to a young woman making one last visit to her childhood home, still trying to deal with some unnamed loss.

Revolution earned Miranda so many awards she didn't know where to put them. Yet she never took a break. She went straight back to work writing new songs for *Four the Record*, and she formed the Pistol Annies. (If you think they aren't created in Miranda's image, consider their first single, "Hell on Heels," about a group of women who swindle righteously from bad men.) Country Music Television's Chet Flippo, the dean of Nashville critics, is already calling the Pistol Annies' debut album, which came out in August, "one of the best albums of 2011."

Meanwhile, she never stopped touring, performing eighty to a hundred concerts a year, many of them in smaller cities like Corbin so that her rural fans—"who could use some cheering up these days," she says—could get a chance to see her. She was so determined to keep performing that she gave herself only eight days off for her wedding and honeymoon. The celebrity-packed affair was held at a ranch near San Antonio. Miranda and Blake exchanged vows on a cowhide rug beneath an arch decorated with deer antlers, and they walked back up the aisle after the ceremony to the classic Roy Rogers tune "Happy Trails." At the reception, the guests ate venison from deer that had been shot by the newlyweds.

"The whole things sounds both gloriously regal and gloriously redneck," I tell her. She gives me a look, and I realize I have said the wrong thing.

"I don't think there was anything redneck about it," she says indignantly. "It was just us."

The next day, the newlyweds went back to Blake's Oklahoma ranch, finished opening their presents (among their favorite gifts: matching shotguns and his-and-her flasks), and went fishing. Miranda tweeted a photo of herself during the honeymoon, holding a bass she had caught. Then they flew to Reba McEntire's vacation home in Cancún, where Blake says he drank the water and got diarrhea.

On their days off from their separate tours—usually Monday through Wednesday—Miranda and Blake fly in private planes to Oklahoma and meet up at Blake's 1,200-acre ranch near Tishomingo (population 3,293). "We piddle around, go back-roading, build brush fires, shoot targets with our hunting bows. You know, the usual," Miranda says. "Sometimes I get him to go to the Walmart with me over in Ada. Or sometimes we go into town and hit the Dairy Queen."

After dinner, they curl up on the couch and watch true-crime shows on television (when I ask Miranda why she likes true crime, she says, "Dude, really? Have you heard my songs?"). Then, after downing a couple of "Rana-ritas"—a drink she created that's made up of Crystal Light Raspberry Lemonade, a shot of Bacardi, and a splash of Sprite Zero—they pull out their guitars and start singing. "Whenever we sing together, I try to outsing her and make her sound sucky," says Blake, "and she does everything she can to make me look bad, and this goes on and on, all night long, like two dogs fighting for a bone."

Blake, who's a good six feet five before he puts on his boots, and Miranda are a country music version of Nick and Nora, the always bantering married couple from the classic old film *The Thin Man*. They can't go five minutes without getting into some comic exchange about each other's flaws. Blake calls Miranda "the most damn hardheaded and uncompromising woman on the face of the earth. Once she makes up her mind about something, that's how it is, no matter how wrong she might be." Miranda, in turn, calls Blake, who used to wear a mullet, "a big old Oklahoma blowhard."

Blake and Miranda even keep up their needling through their Twitter accounts. In early July, Blake was booked to sing on NBC's *Today* show on exactly the same day and at exactly the same time that Miranda was booked to sing on ABC's *Good Morning America*. Blake began tweeting his fans, exhorting them to watch him. Miranda shot back in her own tweet, "They won't be watching you. They will be watching me!" Later she reminded Blake that she had a secret weapon to get more people to tune into her show. "I have boobs," she wrote. Blake replied, "True, but only two." Miranda quickly wrote, "Well, if you count Pistol Annies, I have six!"

Blake admits that Miranda jumps on him when he has a little too much to drink and starts tweeting things that get him in trouble. "And if I ever tweet something about another girl being hot," he says, "or if some female fan tweets me saying, 'Blake, I love you,' Miranda sees it immediately and she's on my ass, going, 'What is that about?' When Miranda marks her territory, it's marked, and I love her for that. I love knowing she's that passionate about me."

But during my conversation with Miranda, she makes it clear that that love goes only so far beyond the border of Texas. She told Blake in no uncertain terms that when she's pregnant and goes into labor, "I'm jumping in the car and hauling ass to Texas. It takes exactly forty-two minutes to get from the ranch to a hospital I've picked out right on the other side of the border, and that's where I'm going to be. Our child is going to be born a Texan."

"I told you, she's her own girl, and she always will be," says Blake. "But if you ask me, that's what sets Miranda apart from all the other female country artists who are out there. She's done it exactly her way, singing the songs that are important to her. Hell, the way her career is going, I'm soon going to be able to retire and hang out on the ranch and hunt deer and drink some beer. I'm telling you, Miranda is awesome!"

Although she still doesn't sell as many records as the other two female country stars who are under the age of thirty—Underwood and Taylor Swift—there are signs that the rest of America is getting to know Miranda. *Us Weekly*, the celebrity magazine of record, put her and Blake's wedding photo on its cover. And the ABC Family Network is developing a TV series based on Lambert's family: the drama follows two private investigators whose children, one of whom is a budding country singer, assist in solving crimes. "It's sort of like Nancy Drew meets *Hee Haw*," says Rick.

What will really make Miranda take off, of course, is a crossover hit that even non-country music fans want to hear. She came close with "The House That Build Me." "And I did record a song for the new album that's the first genuine love song I've ever written in my life," Miranda tells me. "It's called 'Safe.' It's about a woman feeling safe with a man, and I wrote it in thirty minutes while sitting on Blake's bus. He was onstage performing, and I was supposed to be watching him, but this idea hit me and I started writing, and boom, I had it."

"Give me one of your best lines from the song," I say.

She squinches her eyebrows together. "Well, okay, this doesn't sound like me, but one line goes, 'You walk in front of me to make sure I don't fall and break my own heart.'"

"That doesn't sound like the typical Miranda song. Maybe you're changing."

Her eyebrows rise, almost mischievously. "Don't count on it," she says. "I still got a lot of attitude left."

It's now nine o'clock in Corbin, and Miranda is backstage in her concert attire: a T-shirt made by Haute hippie, a blue-jean vest, a tiny blue sparkly shirt, and cowboy boots with fringe. She's wearing a necklace she bought at Junk Gypsy (a funky knickknack shop in College Station), with a pendant reading "You gonna pull them pistols or whistle Dixie?" And she's got on hoop earrings the size of basketball rims. Her hair is huge—she always does her own hair and makeup before concerts—and, predictably, there's a tube of lip gloss in her hand.

"Let's go," says Miranda, downing a Rana-rita, and at precisely 9:10, she and her band hit the stage. The sound that comes from the audience can only be described as a sort of high-pitched primal scream. Miranda launches into "Only Prettier," about a woman staring down a snooty woman from the good side of town. "Well, I'll keep drinkin' and you'll keep getting' skinnier," she sings. "Hey, I'm just like you, only prettier." She then goes straight into "Kerosene," and at the end of the song, she raises her microphone stand into the air: it's in the shape of a shotgun (the microphone itself, by the way, is a bright girly-girl pink). "I'm here to tell you, I'm a redneck chick," Miranda shouts, her outlaw persona in full bloom. "I'm a hell-raising, deer-killing, chicken-fried-steak-eating redneck, and I don't take crap off of anybody!" The primal scream in the audience becomes a full-throated roar.

The *New York Times*' Jon Caramanica describes a Miranda concert as a "theater of rural feminism." It's doubtful any of the women in the audience have actually picked up a pistol and aimed it at a man. Miranda herself told me that she's never gotten so pissed off at a guy that she resorted to violence. "There was one time in high school when I was talking on the phone to my boyfriend, and he said he couldn't go out with me that night," she says. "But then he mentioned he was ironing a shirt, so I knew something was up. I drove with my friend to a bar in Tyler where I thought he might be and saw his car in the parking lot. I turned around and went home. Then, the next day, I looked as pretty as I had ever looked going to high school, and a couple days after that it was his high school graduation, and I looked as pretty as I could again. That's when I broke up with him, right then on graduation night."

"That's it?"

"It really wasn't very nice," she says. "I mean, his whole family was there."

Still, Miranda knows that the women in her audience—heck, maybe all women—love the fantasy of letting loose and throwing all the frustration of their lives back into men's faces. The last song of her ninety-minute concert, "Gunpowder and Lead," is easily the highlight of the night, with the entire audience bellowing along to lyrics that one would think would be more appropriate for a rap song. Miranda stomps across the stage, whips around in a frenzied circle, claps her hands, tosses her hair back and forth, and lets out a half-crazed whoop on the final chord. Just before the lights come up, she gives her fans her famous beautiful smile and shouts, "I love you!"

I notice, to my surprise, a number of men scattered throughout the audience, starting at her in rapt fascination. Perhaps they are at the concert because their girlfriends have dragged them there. Or perhaps they figure the concert is going to be a perfect place to meet hordes of single women. "Or maybe they were there because they secretly love Miranda," Blake later suggested. "Why wouldn't they? She lets you know she's a real woman. I think, deep down, guys look at Miranda and say, 'I wish I had somebody like that.'"

After the concert, Miranda calls for her dogs and then heads for an Airstream trailer parked next to her tour bus. "My little getaway," she calls the Airstream, which comes along on all her tours and has been renovated to look like a miniature lounge, complete with several small couches, a television, and a bar. She sips another Rana-rita and chats with friends and band members. For some reason, she starts talking about her favorite fast foods: the ten-piece Chicken McNuggets at McDonald's, the burger meal at Sonic, the crispy-chicken sandwich from Burger King. "It's terrible for me, but I love all that damn food," she says, unpretentious as ever.

Soon she's off to her tour bus, her three dogs trotting behind her. She's got to call a couple of girlfriends—she's planning a girls' float trip down a Hill Country river for later in the summer—and she wants to call Blake to tell him she loves him and "to let him know that I'm sure I sang better tonight than he did."

In the distance, a few last Ran Fans are still standing behind the security fence. When they get a glimpse of Miranda, they let out a cheer. Miranda turns and gives them a fist pump, and they cheer again. At least for a moment, all is right in their world.

Source: Skip Hollandsworth, "The Girl Who Played with Fiarearms," *Texas Monthly* 39, no. 10 (October 2011): 102–78. (Used with permission.)

FOR FURTHER READING

Brost, Molly. "Post-Dixie Chicks Country: Carrie Underwood and the Negotiation of Feminist Country Identity." In *The Politics of Post-9/11 Music: Sound, Trauma, and the Music Industry in the Time of Terror*, ed. Joseph P. Fisher and Brian Flota, 161–72. Farnham and Burlington: Ashgate, 2011.

Index

A&E (television network) 332
Academy of Country Music Awards 322, 359
Academy of Country and Western Music 184, 192
Acuff, Roy 100, 102, 103, 105, 117, 119, 120, 122,
    141, 159, 166, 184, 211, 213, 228, 296
Acuff-Rose Music Publishing 117, 135, 141, 165, 212
Adams, Ryan 311, 313
Agnew, Spiro 200
Ahern, Brian 252, 253, 254, 259, 273
Akeman, David "Stringbean" 111, 113, 119,
Alice In Wonderland (film) 189
The All American (magazine) 200
Allen, Lorene 224
Allen, Nelson 214
Allen, Rex 161
Allen, Steve 155
Alphin, "Big Kenny" 326
American Bandstand (television series) 153, 246
American Idol (television series) 357, 359
American Music Awards 277, 282
American Society of Composers, Artists, and
    Performers (ASCAP) 165n3, 188, 189, 321
Anderson, Bill 165, 206,
Anderson, Les (Carrot Top) 155
Anderson, Liz 206n5
Anderson, Lynn 206
Anderson, Marian 228
Anderson, Pamela 342
Andy Griffith Show (television series) 276n4, 316
Anger, Harry 300
Anglin, Jack
    See Johnnie and Jack
The Anita Kerr Singers 146, 149n10, 201
Anthony, Gretel 109
Arkie the Arkansas Woodchopper 67
Armed Forces Radio Network 100, 120
Armstrong, Louis 157, 158
Arnold, Eddy 120, 134, 143, 144, 148, 166, 189,
    195, 212, 228
Arnold, Lee 205–7
Arnspiger, Herman 90, 91
Atcher, Bob 102
Asleep at the Wheel 316
Atkins, Chet 120, 133, 143, 146–51, 302
Atkins, Jimmy 151
Atkins, Lowell 151
Atkins, Merle 151
Autry, Gene 74–85, 93, 102, 105, 162, 166, 200, 277
Awtrey, Hugo R. 83

Baez, Joan 183
Baham, Roy 161
Bailey, Deford 226
Baker, Flora 43
Baker, Jim 43
Balsam, Martin 189
The Band 337
Banks, Roscoe 58–9, 61
Bannister, Roger 116
Bare, Bobby 212
Barham, Hubert 92
Barnes, George 147
Barrier, Jamie 311
Basie, William James "Count" 89
Bate, Alcyone 122
Bate, Buster 122
Bate, Dr. Humphrey 122
Bates, George 129–30
Bayless, T.D. 224
The Beach Boys 193
The Beatles 180, 183, 189, 192, 202, 252, 263,
    264, 288, 331, 332, 333, 337
Bee, Molly 154, 185
Beethoven, Ludwig van 99, 118
Bennett, Gary 316
Beowulf 19
Berg, Matraca 337
Berry, Chuck 197
The Beverly Hillbillies (television series) 108, 309
Beyoncé 306
Big & Rich 326, 328, 341
Birchfield, Wiley 114
Black, Clint 335
Blackburn, Rick 293
Blackjack Wayne and his Country Ramblers 197
Blair, Hal 188
Bland, Bobby "Blue" 128, 219, 220
Blum, Bob, and the Blenders 183 Blum, Bob, and
    the Blenders 183
Boatright, Dorotha 155
The Bobby Doyle Trio 246
Bond, Johnny 155
Bonnie Blue Eyes 102
Bono 342
Borchetta, Scott 297, 348
Boston (band) 281
Bothy Band 266
Bowen, Jimmy 294, 301
BR5-49 315–749

Bradley, Connie 321
Bradley, Owen 186n19, 302
Bragg, Billy 342
Brahms, Johannes 118
Bramlett, Bonnie 268
Brasfield, Rod 123
Brenston, Jackie 125–6
Brinkley, J.B. 92
Brinkley, John R. 38n4
British Broadcasting Company (BBC) 63
Britt, Elton 102
Broadcast Music, Inc. (BMI) 162, 165n3, 188, 213, 214, 300
Brockman, Polk 3
Bromberg, David 271–2
Brooks & Dunn 291, 293
Brooks, Colleen 288–9
Brooks, Garth 280–9, 294, 295, 300, 305, 306, 307, 330, 334, 335
Brooks, Kix 343
    See also Brooks & Dunn
Brooks, Rez 114
Brooks, Troyal 288
Brower, Cecil 92
Brown, Alison 114–5
Brown, Mel 219–20
Brown, Milton 90, 91
Brown, Rebecca 323
Brown, Tony 300, 301
Browne, Jackson 342
Browning, Robert 17
Bryant, Boudleaux 151
Bryant, Felice 151
Bryant, Jimmy 154
Bryson, Peabo 303
Buchanan, Robert "Buck" 92
The Buckaroos
    See Owens, Buck
Buffett, Jimmy 210
Burlison, Paul 316
Burnette, Smiley 84
Burnette, Johnny 316
Burton, James 194
Busby, Jheryl 300
Bush, George W. 341, 342–3
Butler, Alan 293
Butler, Burridge D. 68
Butler, Carl 185
Buttram, Pat 67
The Byrds 180, 193, 254, 272, 327

Cameron, Ken 292
Campbell, Glen 184, 187, 188, 190, 192, 195, 202, 214

Campbell, John C. 10
Campbell, Olive Dame 8
Campbell, Stacy Dean 294
Campbell, Zeke 92
Carpenter, Mary-Chapin 294
Carrigan, Bill 120
Carson, "Fiddlin'" John 2–6, 30, 55, 72n13
Carson, Johnny 248
Carter, A.P. (Alvin Pleasant) 27, 37, 39–43, 109
Carter, Anita 39, 44
Carter, Ezra J. 40, 41
The Carter Family 27, 31, 37–46, 112, 127, 132, 137, 159, 252, 258, 304
Carter, Helen 39, 44
Carter, June 39, 44, 44n16
Carter, Maybelle (Addington) 27, 37–46, 112, 151
Carter, Sara (Dougherty) 27, 37, 39, 41, 42, 137
The Carter Sisters 39, 44, 151
Caramanica, Jon 359–60, 366
Carver, Johnny 185, 187
Case, Neko 306
Cash Box (magazine) 189, 201
Cash, Johnny 39, 44n16, 125–30, 132, 188, 197, 198, 202, 204, 285, 308, 327
Cason, Buzz 337
Caviness, Claude 199
Cedarwood Music 141
Central Songs 153, 184
The Champs 192
Chapman, Beth Nielsen 337
Charles, Ray 188, 219, 260, 343
Checker, Chubby 193
Chesney, Kenny 327–8, 363
Chesnutt, Mark 297
The Chieftains 266
Child, Francis James 8–9, 17
Choates, Bessie 138
Chopin, Frédéric 118
Christian, Charlie 98
Clark, Dick 202
Clark, Guy 210
Clark, Roy 184, 250, 260
Clark, Susanna 253
The Clash 342
Clayborne, Everett 196
Clayton, Lee 210
Clear Channel (corporation) 349
Clearmountain, Bob 300
Clement, Frank 212
Clement, "Cowboy" Jack 128–30, 163, 210, 211
Cline, Patsy (Virginia Patterson Hensley) 186n19, 290
Clinton, Bill 362
Clooney, Rosemary 204, 302

Club Dance (television series) 291, 316
Coben, Cy 188–90
Coburn, Barry 324
Cochran, Hank 161
Cohen, Leonard 253
Cohen, Paul 166
Collins, Floyd 23, 72
Collins, Judy 194, 253
The Collins Kids 155
Collins, Larry 345
   See also The Collins Kids
Collins, Tommy 182, 198
Colter, Jessi 210
Commander Cody and His Lost Planet
   Airmen 316
Como, Perry 298, 302
Connor, Charlie 297
Cooley, Spade 198
Cooper, Alice 342
Cooper, Gary 79
Cooper, Prentice 105–6
Copas, Lloyd "Cowboy" 122
Copland, Aaron 17
Cordle, Larry 318–9
Cotton, James 128
Country Music Association (organization)
   164–168, 192, 202, 205, 214, 277, 355
Country Music Foundation 164, 166, 167
Country Music Hall of Fame 39, 164, 166–7,
   321
Country Music Television (CMT) 282, 364
Cowan, Louis 141
Cowboy Troy (Troy Coleman III) 226, 326,
   328, 342
Craft, Edwin Arthur 5
Cramer, Floyd 146, 188, 201
Creason, L.R. 83
The Crook Brothers 122
Crosby, Bing 75, 77, 83, 94 101, 122
Crow, Sheryl 342
Crowell, Rodney 252n5, 253, 262–3
Crump, Ed "Red Snapper" 106
Crutchfield, Jerry 302
Cryer, Sherwood 236
Cumberland Ridge Runners 70, 71
Curb, Mike 321
Curt's Oklahoma Cotton Pickers 183
Cyrus, Billy Ray 290, 291, 317
Cyrus, Miley 348, 351

Daffan, Ted 102
Dale, Dick, and the Del Tones 202
Dalhart, Vernon 51, 72n11, 72n13
Daniels, Charlie 230, 320, 327, 349

Daret, Darla 154
Davies, Gail 258
Davis, Darren 322
Davis, Karl 71n7
Davis, Sammy, Jr. 343
Day, Doris 204
de Laurentiis, Dino 250
De Vito, Hank 257
The Dead Kennedys 342
DeArmon, Ramon 94–5
The Deason Sisters
   See Wells, Kitty (Muriel Deason)
Death Cab for Cutie 342
Def Leppard 300
DeLory, Al 192
Denny, Jim 123, 141, 166
Denny, Sandy 268
Denver, John 244, 285
Dexter, Al 100, 101–2
Diana, Debbie 283
Dickens, Little Jimmy 122, 186
Dixie Chicks 320, 330, 337, 341, 343, 349,
   360
Dixieland Swingsters 150
Dixon, Dorsey 55, 103n7
Doby, Larry 228
Dodson, Bert 92
Dorsey, Tommy 102, 197
Douglas, Tom 337
Doyle, Bensington 62–3
Dr. Hook and the Medicine Show 210
Drag the River 308, 309, 312
DuBois, Tim 301
Dudley, Dave 187
Dunford, Eck 28
DuMoulin, Toddy 67
Dunn, Eddie 92
Dylan, Bob 108, 157, 204, 298, 302

The Eagles 180, 324n7, 327
Easterling, Mark 293
Easy Rider (film) 181
Ellington, Edward Kennedy "Duke" 89
Elliott, Wally "Longhorn Joe" 197
Elman, Ziggy 98
Emery, Ralph 323–4
Endeback, Christine 66n5
Esposito, Joe 292
The Everly Brothers 148, 149
Everly, Don
   See The Everly Brothers
Everly, Ike 147
Everly, Phil
   See The Everly Brothers

Fender, Leo 150n14
Fields, Don 150
Fields, Margaret 150
The Fifth Dimension 190
Fisher, Eddie 187
Flagg, J.T. 76–7
Flatt, Lester 107, 112, 113, 114, 116, 158
The Flying Burrito Brothers 180, 254
Foley, Red 67, 71n7, 120, 122, 123, 150, 166
Ford, Mary 188
Ford, "Tennessee" Ernie 153, 154, 185, 187
Foster, Sally 67
Frank, Buddy
Frank, J.L. 166
Frank, Leo M. 2–3
Franklin, Aretha 334
Frazier, Dallas 154
Fricke, Janie 275
Fried, Ad 196
Friedman, Kinky 210, 281
Fritts, Donnie 210, 217,
Frizzell, Lefty 211–2, 213, 215, 277
Fruit Jar Drinkers 86, 122
Fry, Lee 210
Fulchino, Anne 145
Fulks, Robbie 305, 306–7, 312
Fuller, Jerry 188
Fundis, Garth 299

Gable, Dorothy 167
Gaillard, Frye 220
Galante, Joe 320, 338, 339
Garland, Hank 146
Gay, Connie B. 165, 205
Gearhart, Roger 293
Gentry, Linnell 174
George, Bobby 188
Geraghty, Jerry 80
Germanich, Sophia 67
Gibb, Barry 245
Gibson, Don 135
Gierman, Cory 325
Gill, Vince 282
Gillette, Lee 195
Gilley, Mickey 230, 236
The Glaser Brothers 212–3
Glaser, Chuck
    See The Glaser Brothers
Glaser, Jim
    See The Glaser Brothers
Glaser, Tompall 208, 210–22
    See also The Glaser Brothers
Godfrey, Arthur 150n11
Goldman, Ronald 336

Gomez, Selena 348–9, 351
The Good Brothers 309
Good, Bruce
    See The Good Brothers
Good, Dallas 309
Good, Travis 309
Goodale, George 84
Goodman, Benny 89, 97
Goodman, Steve 127
Gordon, Marianne 250
Gordy, Emory, Jr. 335
Gorilla Biscuits 309
Grable, Betty 102
Grand Ole Opry (radio program) 47, 64, 86–8, 102, 105, 107, 112–3, 116–24, 132, 139, 141, 147, 151, 156, 159, 188, 198, 206n5, 207, 211, 212, 220, 226, 227, 254, 272, 285, 297, 313, 322, 332
Grant, Amy 302, 343
The Grateful Dead 282
Green Day 342
Gretsch, Frederick, Manufacturing Co. 148
Griffin, Patty 337
Gross, Clifford 92
Gully Jumpers 86, 122
Guthrie, Woodie 96, 201, 253

The Hagers 183, 194–5
Hager, Jim
    See The Hagers
Hager, John
    See The Hagers
Haggard, Merle 179, 184, 186, 187, 197, 198, 200–2, 204, 259, 304, 308, 321, 327
Hall, Tom T. 160–3, 188, 335n7
Hall, Wendal (It Ain't Gonna Rain No Mo') 52
Hamblin, Stuart 203
Hammett, Smith 114
Harman, Buddy 146
Harkreader, Sid 122
Harris, Emmylou 251–74, 337
Harris, Richard 190
Hart, Freddy 182, 196
Hartford, John 181, 188, 190–2, 193, 195, 197, 202–3, 204, 213, 214
Hartman, Dick 62
Harvey, Alex 210
Hatcher, Lib 276, 277, 278
Hawkins, Hawkshaw
Hay, George D. 86–8, 121, 166
Heart 342
Hee Haw (television series) 170, 184, 250, 260n8, 312, 316, 365
Heidt, Horace 120

Helm, Levon 337
Hendley, Fisher 102
Hendricks, James 188
Hepburn, Katharine 288
Herman the Hermit 154, 185
Hermes, Will 359
Herran, Don 317
Heider, Wally 300
Hill, Faith 320, 327, 333, 347, 349
The Hillbilly Gast Haus (radio broadcast) 120
Hilley, Donna 320–1
Hillman, Chris 180
Hilton, Paris 349
Hinton, Bruce 324
Hitchcock, Stan 174
Hoffer, Jay 196
The Hometowners 66, 68
Hope, Bob 102, 120
Hopkins, Al 355
Horton, Johnny 316
House, Gerry 282
Houston, Whitney 334
Howard, Harlan 308
Howlin' Wolf 128
Hubbard, Carroll 92
Hubert Long Talent Agency
    See Long, Hubert
Huff, Leon 94
Hurricane Shirley 202
Hüsker Dü 309
Husky, Ferlin 130, 173, 191, 197, 198
Husky, Junior 146

Ingram, James 303
International Bluegrass Music Association 319
The International Submarine Band 180
iTunes 338, 343

J Church 310
Jackson, Alan 297, 319, 321, 322, 324, 327, 335,
    340
Jackson, Michael 285, 293
Jagger, Mick 288
James, Harry 97, 98
James, Sonny 148, 197
Jefferson Airplane 194
Jenkins, Dewitt "Snuffy" 61, 108, 111, 114
Jenkins, Hoke 114
Jennings, Waylon 208–9, 210, 216, 217, 218,
    232n6, 258, 319, 320, 321
Jensen, Adele
    See Winnie, Lou, and Sally
Jensen, Eileen
    See Winnie, Lou, and Sally

Jensen, Helen
    See Winnie, Lou, and Sally
Jimmy Dean Show (television series) 195
John Edwards Memorial Foundation 165
Johnnie and Jack 139
The Johnny Cash Show (television series) 39,
    44–5n16, 197
Johnson, Cliff "Cactus Jack" 196–7
Johnson, Leona 151
Johnson, Tommy 287
Jolson, Al 83
Jonas Brothers 348
Jonas, Joe 351
    See also Jonas Brothers
Jones, Corky 197
Jones, David Lynn 294
Jones, George 236, 259–60, 271, 281, 301, 317,
    319, 321, 327
Jones, Marshall "Grandpa" 111
Jones, Paula 362
Jones, Sam 123
The Jordanaires 146, 148
Journey 281

Kalar, Phil 68
Kanak, Eddie 183
Karpeles, Maud 10
Kaufman, Phil 255
Kay, John 334
Keisger, Marion 128, 129
Keith, Ben 220
Keith, Toby 307, 308, 327, 340, 343
Kelley, John 203
Kennedy, Mary Ann 261
Kennedy, Ray 293
Kennedy, Tywaina 109
Kennerley, Paul 254
Kernodle, Red 127
Kerr, Anita
    See The Anita Kerr Singers
Kerry, John 311, 343
Key, Jimmy 161
Kid Rock 342
Kincaid, Bradley 47–50, 86–7
Kincaid, Irma Forman 49
King, B.B. 128
King Curtis 112
King, Pee Wee 143
King, Wally 196
Kirby, Beecher "Bashful Brother Oswald" 65
KISS 285
Kragen, Ken 247, 248, 249
Kristofferson, Kris 127, 208, 210, 217, 234n7,
    342

The Lain Brothers 150
Lair, John 48 69–73
Lamb, Kevin 334
Lambert, Miranda 357–67
Lambert, Jake 115
Landis, Richard 299
Lane, Buddy, and the Wild West 182
Langford, Jon 308–9, 310, 312, 313
Lanier, Sydney 21
LaRosa, Julius 150
Larson, Nicolette 269
Laugh-In (television series) 184
Lawson, "Red-Necked" Jim 5
Ledford, Lily May 70
LeDoux, Chris 285
Lee, Brenda 345
Lee, Joey 363
Lee, Johnny 230
Legend, John 342
The Legendary Shack Shakers 310–1
Lehning, Kyle 301–2
Lennon, John 333
Levine, Nat 78
Lewis, Jerry Lee 126, 132, 197, 236
Lewis, Luke 322–3
The Lickskillet Orchestra 4
Liggett, Walter 122
The Light Crust Doughboys 78n16, 89–95, 97, 105
Lilith Fair 337
Linda Lou 66
Lindy, Scott 321
Liszt, Franz 115
Little, Anthony 301
Loetz, Jack 166
Lohan, Lindsay 349
Lomax, John A. 16–7, 23, 75, 156
Lonesome Standard Time 319
Long, Hubert 166
Long, Jimmy 83
Lord, Bobby 191
Lorenz, Trey 303
Louisiana Hayride (radio program) 131, 139
Louvin Brothers 131–6, 252, 260, 271–2
Louvin, Charlie
    See Louvin Brothers
Louvin, Ira
    See Louvin Brothers
Lovato, Demi 349, 351
Love, "Daddy" John 60
Lowry, Dick 249
Lulu Belle & Scotty 65, 66
Lunceford, Jimmie 89
Lyle, Rudy 116

Lynn, Judy 203–4
Lynn, Loretta 224–5, 296, 360

MacGregor, Charles 84
Macon, "Uncle" Dave 111, 113, 122, 159, 166
Maddox, Rose 182
Madonna 285, 293, 308, 326
Mahan, Mitch 323
Mainer, J.E. 55–63
Mainer, Wade 56
Maines, Natalie 341
Mancini, David 300
Mancini, Dee 299
Mandrell, Barbara 345
Mann, Lorene 161
Manning, Linda 186
Manson, Marilyn 342
Maphis, Joe 155
Maphis, Rose Lee 155
Martin, Benny 132
Martin, Grady 146, 187, 201
Martinovich, Mike 294
Marvin, Johnny 82, 84
Mascolo, Eddie 293–4
Mayfield, Carl P. 320
MC Hammer 293
McBride, John 284, 331, 334
McBride, Martina 320, 330–9
McCain, John 341
McCain, Meghan 342
McCarthy, Cormac 359
McCartney, Paul 331
McCreery, Scotty 357
McClinton, Delbert 337
McClinton, O.B. 226
McDevitt, Mark 293
McDonald, Michael 342
McDonald, Skeets 155
McEntire, Reba 332, 333, 338, 352, 364
McEwen, Mark 284
McGraw, Tim 327, 347
McGuinn, Roger 272
McHan, Don 224
McLachlan, Sarah 337
McLister, Cecil 28
McShay, Wes 324
Mead, Chuck 316
The Mekons 308, 309
Mellencamp, John 342
Melody Ranch (television series) 185
Memphis Minnie 102
Memphis Recording Service 126
Mendelssohn, Felix 118
MIDI (Musical Input, Digital Interface) 302

Miller, Bob 72n11
Miller, Rob 306, 309
Miller, Roger 296
Miller, Slim 71n7
Milton, Little 128
Mise, Billy 188
Mitchell, Bill 53
Mitchell, Guy 187
Mitchell, Joni 253
Moby 342
Monroe, Bill 61, 107, 110, 112, 113, 115, 119n6, 156–7,
    158, 248n7
Monroe, Charlie 61
Montgomery, Kathleen 93
Montgomery, Marvin "Zeke" 91, 92, 93
Mooney, Col. C.P.J. 88
Moore, Bob 146
Moore, Merrill 154
Moran, Lester "Roadhog" 317
Moreau, Reg 292
Morgan, Craig 323
Morgan, George 120
The Morris Brothers 111
Morris, George
    See The Morris Brothers
Morris, Zeke
    See The Morris Brothers
MTV 349
Mullican, Moon 316
Murphy, Eddie 347
Murphy, Jim 296
MuzikMafia 325–6
MySpace 342–3, 351

Napier, Lonnie 320
Napster 353
The Nashville Network (television network) 291
Nashville Now (television series) 323
Nashville Star (television series) 357–8, 359, 363
Nation, Buck 72n11
National Association of Music Merchants 148
National Barn Dance (radio program) 47, 64–8,
    70–3, 75, 83, 86, 102, 311
National Life & Accident Insurance Company 121
Nelson, Ken 153, 166, 193–5, 199, 201
Nelson, Willie 161, 208, 210, 218, 219, 221, 233,
    327, 342
Nettinga, Paul 68
New Christy Minstrels 245, 246
New Orleans Rhythm Kings 110
Newport Folk Festival 115
Newberry, Mickey 210, 247
Newell, Fred 220
Newman, Melinda 282

Newman, Randy 342
Newton-John, Olivia 244
Nicely, Jake 301
Nichols, Jack 83–84
Nicholson, Jon 325
Nimoy, Leonard 189
Nita, Rita, and Ruby
    See Ruby Wells
Nixon, Richard 184, 343
Nobody, JJ 309
The Nobodys 309
Norman, Silvey Dale "Junior' 177
Nugent, Ted 342

Oak Ridge Boys 285
Oakley, Annie 237
Obama, Barack 342, 343
O'Daniel, W. Lee "Pappy" 78, 90–4, 105–6
O'Day, Pat 150
Old 97s 311
O'Quinn, Gene 154
Orbison, Roy 298
Ossenbrink, Luther W.
    See Arkie the Arkansas Woodchopper
The Osmonds 244
Overstake, Evelyn 67
Owen, Fuzzy 200, 201
Owens, Alvis Edgar "Buck" 170, 174, 179, 180,
    181–2, 183, 184, 187, 197, 198–201, 204, 250,
    276, 313
Owens, Bonnie 198, 201
Owens, "Texas Ruby" Agnes 44

Paisley, Brad 319, 320, 327
Paganini, Niccoló 115
Palin, Sarah 342
Parker, Charlie 108
Parker, Junior 128
Parker, John William "Knocky," II 91, 92, 94, 95
Parker, Linda 70
Parker, Col. Tom 132–3
Parsons, Gram 180, 252, 253, 255, 263–4,
    270–2, 316, 327
Parton, Dolly 244, 258, 261n9, 266
Paul, Les 147, 150n14, 188
Payne, Rufus "Teetot" 124
Pearl, Minnie 123, 285
Pearl Jam 316
Peel, William Lawson 5
Peer, Ralph 3, 27–8, 29n10, 30–6, 37, 43n12, 158
Pennington, Eddie 147
Perkins, Carl 126, 128, 132
Perkins, Luther 127, 129
Peters, Gretchen 331, 335–7

Petterson, Pat 68
Petty, Tom 306
Phillips, Sam 125–30
Pickler, Kellie 348–9, 357
Pierce, Webb 141, 148, 260, 316
The Pine Hill Haints 311
Pine Valley Cosmonauts 313
Pirates of the Mississippi 294
Pistol Annies 359, 363, 365
Pitchfork Trio 312
Pitts, Ken 91–5
Poindexter, Albert
    See Dexter, Al
Polk, Charles 220
Pollock, Jackson 348
Poole, Charlie 55, 108, 114
Poster, Stephen 249
The Prairie Ramblers 66
Presley, Elvis 126, 128, 129, 131–6, 143, 148, 202,
    219, 245, 282, 288, 298, 302
Price, Chad 309
Price, Ray 199, 316
Pride, Charley 177, 226–8
The Prince Albert Grand Old Opry (radio program)
    See Grand Ole Opry

Rager, Mose 147
Raitt, Bonnie 336
Ramone, Johnny 342
Ray, Johnny 122
Reagan, Ronald 200, 342
Reed, Blind Alfred 28
Reeves, Jim 143, 149, 166
Reinhardt, Django 147
Reinhart, Dick 92
R.E.M. 316
The Renfro Valley Barn Dance (radio program)
    64, 183
Reno, Don 158
Republic Pictures 75, 79
Reynolds, Allen 300
Reynolds, Billy Ray 210
Reynolds, Ted 220
Rhapsody 353
Rice, Joyce 300
Rice, Tony 266
Rich, Don 199
Rich, John 325, 328, 341, 342, 343, 348
Riddle, Leslie 37–8
Riley, Jeannie C. 161n2
Rimes, LeAnn 335, 345, 349
Ritter, Eric (Grandpappy) 120
Ritter, Tex 17, 155, 166, 228, 277
Rivers, Joan 171

Robbins, Hargus "Pig" 146
Robbins, Marty 197, 202, 210, 296
Robertson, Don 188
Robertson, Texas Jim 172
Robinson, Jackie 228
Robinson, Smokey 302
Robison, Carson 51–4, 72n11
Roboff, Annie 337
Rockhill, Rick 293
Rodcay, Harry 154
Rodgers, Jimmie 30–6, 37, 38, 60, 75, 107, 127,
    159, 166, 186, 201, 204,
The Rolling Stones 285
Ronstadt, Linda 258, 261n9, 266
Roosevelt, Eleanor 72
Roosevelt, Franklin D. 101, 255
Rogers, Kenny 244–50, 285
Rogers, Roy 277, 364
Rogers, Will 35, 82
Rose, Fred 117, 141, 166
Rose, Pam 261
Rose, Wesley 165, 166, 212
Rucker, Darius 226
Rushing, Jim 335
Russell, Richard 5
Ryman, Capt. Tom 123

The Sadies 309
Samples, Junior 316
Sanders, Mark 225
Sands, Tommy 154, 185, 187
Sanford, Chas 299, 300
Satherley, Arthur 83, 100–6
Schmitz, Hank, and his Goober Growlers 119
Schnee, Bill 399
Schoenberg, Arnold 157
Schmucker, Red, and His Mountain Boys 119
Schutt, Roger "Captain Midnight" 210, 212, 216
Schuyler, Thom 301
Schwarzenegger, Arnold 286
Scruggs, Earl 6n8, 107–17, 119n6, 158
Scruggs, George Elam 109
Scruggs, Horace 110
Scruggs, Junie 114
Shaeffer, Armand 79
Seckler, Curly 113
Seeger, Mike 39n9, 43, 157
Seger, Bob 302
Sharp, Cecil 8–15, 17, 71n9
Shaver, Billy Joe 210
Shedd, Harold 301–2
Shell, Larry 319–20
Shelton, Blake 357, 360
Sherwood, Don 197

Shilkret, Nat 82–3
Shindig (television series) 193
Sholes, Steve 141–5, 148, 166
Shriver, Evelyn 277
Shumate, Jim 112
Sides, Alan 299
Siebel, Paul 271
Silverstein, Shel 208, 210, 220
Siman, Si 144
Simmons, Gene 342
Simpson, Nicole Brown 336
Simpson, O.J. 336
Sims, Frances 72n11
Sinatra, Frank 75, 122
Sirius XM 349
Sizemore, Asher 43–4
Sizemore, Little Jimmy 43–4
The Skillet Lickers 4
Skaggs, Ricky 262, 342, 345
Slocum, Tom 269
Smith, Carl 120, 122, 195
Smith, Connie 190
Smith, Hazel 208, 210, 211, 216–8, 221
Smith, Michael W. 303
Smothers Brothers 184, 188, 190, 191, 248
The Smothers Brothers Comedy Hour (television
    series)
    See Smothers Brothers
The Summer Smothers Brothers Show (television
    series)
    See Smothers Brothers
Snodgrass, Jon 308, 309 312
Snow, Hank 31, 120, 127, 132, 134, 143, 144, 211,
    213
Snyder, Jimmy 186
Sobule, Jill 340–4
Society of European State Authors & Composers
    (SESAC) 165n3, 323
Son Volt 328
Sonny and Cher 193
Sons of the Pioneers 91
SoundScan 280, 282
Southern Melody Boys 92
Springsteen, Bruce 261, 268, 342
Spotify 353
Spurlock, C.R. 245
St. John, Chuck 296–7
The Stanley Brothers 114, 158
Stanley, Ralph 63, 111, 114, 116, 265
Stapp, Jack 124, 141
Star Trek (television series) 189
Starr, Linden K. 4
Steagall, Red 188
Steinbeck, John 96, 97

Steppenwolf 334
Stewart, Jimmy 79
Stewart, Rod 300
Stokes, Leonard 61
Stone, Cliffie 153–5, 184–5, 187, 197
Stone, Oscar 122
Stoneman, Ernest 28–9
Strait, George 319, 321, 322, 324
Strange, Billy 154
Stravinsky, Igor 157
Stroud, James 299, 301–2
Stuckey, Nat 186
The Sundowners 313
Swift, Taylor 345–52, 365
Sykes, Roosevelt 102

Tanner, Gid 4, 159
Tashian, Barry 263
Taylor, Harty 71n7
Taylor, James 301
Teetot
    See Payne, Rufus
Tennes See Ramblers 62
Tennyson, Lord Alfred 17
Terhune, Max 67
Thall, Bill 67
The Thin Man (film) 364
Thomas, Keith 302
Thomas, Rufus 128
Thompson, Beazley 106
Thompson, Fred 343
Thompson, Hank 186, 195
Thompson, "Uncle Jimmy" 121
Tickner, Ed 272
Tillis, Mel 240n10, 247
Timms, Sally 306, 308
Tippin, Aaron 293–4
TMZ 349
To Kill A Mockingbird (book) 350
Town Hall Party (television series) 153–5
Tractor King Howdy Boys 312
Trailer Bride 311
Travis, Merle 147, 155
Travis, Randy 275–9, 297, 334
Travolta, John 230
Treat, Ron 301
Trinajstick, Blanche "Trina" 169–78
Tubb, Ernest 31, 100, 122, 134, 166, 173, 212, 213,
    215, 227, 228, 276, 334, 355
Tubb, Justin 132, 133, 161n5
Tucker, Tanya 345, 362
Tumble Weed 67
Tunetwisters 67
Turner, Scott 187

Twain, Shania 295, 307, 308, 317, 320, 327, 333, 349
Twitter 364
Twitty, Conway 197, 296, 321
Tyler, T. Texas 197
Tyler, Toby, and the Night Lifers 183

U2 288
Uncle Tupelo 305, 306, 309, 311n8, 312, 328
Underwood, Carrie 357, 359, 360, 365
Urban Cowboy (film) 229–43, 278

Van Halen 342
van Shelton, Ricky 275
van Zandt, Townes 253
Vaughn, Jim 200
Verdi, Giuseppe 118
Village People 342
The Voice (television series) 360

The Waco Brothers 313
Wagnon, Bill 154, 155
Wagoner, Porter 143–4, 185
Walker, Billy 175
Walker, Jeff 291
Walker, Jerry Jeff 271
Walker-Meador, Jo 166, 168
Wallace, Jerry 188
Walton, Stanley 122
Wanda Lee and Her Wanderers 183
Ward, Jerry 186
Wardell, Zeke 6
Ware, John 259
Warshaw, Nan 307–8, 312, 313
Was, Don 300
Wayne, John 289
Webb, Jimmy 181, 190, 192, 193, 204
Weir, Rusty 362
Welburn, Debbie 238
Welling, Frank 72n11
Wells, Kitty (Muriel Deason) 137–40, 173,, 185,
    260, 358n2, 360
Wells, Ruby 139
West, Kanye 342
West, Speedy 154
Wexler, Jerry 355
Whisnant, Johnny 114
Whiskey & Co. 309–10
White, Clarence 180
Whitley, Ray 72n12
Wilburn, Sally 128
Wilco 328
Wilkes, Colonel JD 310
will.i.am 342
Williams, Charlie 188

Williams, Hank 117, 122, 124, 135, 148, 166, 197,
    204, 212, 227, 228, 254, 276, 302, 304, 307,
    308, 316, 319, 327
Williams, Jr., Hank 291, 316, 327
Williams III, Hank 327
Williams, Mason 191
Williams, Mike 271
Williams, Vanessa 302
Willis, Kelly 300
Wills, Bob 90, 91, 97–8, 102, 196
Wilson, Ann
    See Heart
Wilson, Brian 193
Wilson, Gretchen 325–9, 342, 358
Wilson, "Hawk" Shaw 317
Wilson, Lonnie 334
Wilson, Nancy
    See Heart
Wilson, Parker 91
Winger, Debra 230
Winnie, Lou, and Sally 67, 68
Winterhalter, Hugo 144
Wise, Chubby 114
Wiseman, Lulu Belle 70
    See also Lulu Belle & Scotty
Wiseman, Scotty 66–7
    See Lulu Belle & Scotty
Womack, Lee Ann 321, 322
Wonder, Stevie 342
Woods, Bill 198
Wooley, Sheb 182
Worley, Paul 334, 335, 336
Wren, Bob 92
Wright, Bobby 139
Wright, Johnnie
    See Johnnie and Jack
Wright, Johnnie, Jr.
    See Bobby Wright
Wright, Louise 139
WSM Disc Jockey Convention 142, 169
WWVA Jamboree (radio broadcast) 159, 177
Wynette, Tammy 186, 211, 281

The Yas-Yas Girl 102
Yearwood, Trisha 297, 334
Yoakam, Dwight 275
Young, Chip 187
Young, Kyle 321
Young, Red 220
Young, Reggie 302
YouTube 353

Ziegler, Bonnie Kay 292
ZZ Top 334

Song Index

"Achy Breaky Heart" 290
"Act Naturally" 180
"The Akron Disaster" 72n11
"All Because of Lovin' You" 93
"All Jacked Up" 328
"American Soldier" 308
"Anything's Better Than Feeling the Blues" 337
"Are You Sure Hank Done It This Way" 319
"At My Mother's Grave" 23

"Baby Are You Gettin' Tired of Me" 317
"Bad News" 257
"Baggage Claim" 360
"The Ballad of Jed Clampett" 309
"Barbara Allen" 257
"Barnacle Bill, The Sailor" 53
"Barroom Women" 312
"Before He Cheats" 360
"Belshazzar" 127
"Better in the Long Run" 360
"Bettie, Bettie" 316
"Beyond the Blue" 332
"Big River" 128
"Bile That Cabbage Down" 120
"Billie Broke My Heart at Walgreen's and I Cried
    All the Way to Sears" 185
"Billy in the Low Ground" 5, 121
"The Birmingham Jail" 158
"Birth of the Blues" 120
"Blessed" 338, 339
"Blue" 335
"Blue Echo" 148
"Blue Suede Shoes" 128
"Blue Yodel" 34
"Blue Yodel No. 2" 34 "Blue Yodel No. 3" 34
"Bonzo Goes to Bitburg" 342
"Boot Scootin' Boogie" 291
"A Broken Wing" 331, 337
"Burning a Hole in My Pocket" 190
"Bury Me Under the Weeping Willow" 42
"By The Time I Get to Pheonix" 190
"Bye, Bye Love" 149, 151

"Cacklin' Hen" 5
"California Girls" 328
"Candy Kisses" 120
"Carry Me Back to the Old Prairie" 52
"Carroll County Accident" 185
"[The] Cattle Call" 93, 144

"C'est la Vie" 272
"The Change" 282
"Chattahoochee" 323
"Cheap Whiskey" 335
"Cheating Heart"
    See "Your Cheatin' Heart"
"Cherokee Boogie" 316
"Chewing Gum" 113
"The Christian Life" 272
"City of New Orleans" 127
"Clementine" 122
"Come to Jesus" 192
"Company's Comin'" 144
"Courtesy of The Red, White, And Blue (The
    Angry American)" 308, 340
"Crash of the Akron" 72n11
"Crazy" 334
"Crazy Arms" 316
"Crazy Ex-Girlfriend" 361
"Crazy Feeling" 246
"Cripple Creek" ["Goin' Up Cripple Creek"] 29,
    93, 112
"Cross-Eyed Cowboy from Abilene" 93
"Cry" 122
"Cry, Cry, Cry" 127
"Cry on the Shoulder of the Road" 337
"Cumberland Gap" 112, 193

"Dear Old Dixie" 112
"The Death of Floyd Collins" 23, 72n13
"Death On the Highway" 120
"Delta Dawn" 210
"Desperadoes Waiting for a Train" 210
"Devil in the Wheat Patch" 5
"D-I-V-O-R-C-E" 186
"Does the Chewing Gum Lose Its Flavor on the
    Bedpost (Overnight)" 185
"Don't Give Me No Plastic Saddle (I Want to Feel
    that Leather When I Ride)" 186
"Don't Go Near The Indians" 161
"Don't Rock the Jukebox" 327
"Don't Say Fuck around the K-I-D-S" 186
"Down at the Twist and Shout" 294
"Down on the Corner of Love" 199
"Downtown" 204
"Drivin' Wheel" 267

"Electric Slide" 290
"Even Cowgirls Get the Blues" 262

"Even If It's Wrong" 316
"Ezekiel Saw the Wheel" 104

"Faded Love and Winter Roses" 195
"Fifteen" 348, 352
"Fightin' Side of Me" 180
"Fireball Mail" 115
"Foggy Mountain Top" 109
"Forever & Always" 351
"Four Walls" 149
"Friends in Low Places" 281
"Fuck This Town" 307
"Full Time Job" 328

"Galveston" 190
"The Gambler" 247, 247n5, 249
"Gentle on My Mind" 188, 190, 192, 197, 213,
    213n7, 214
"Git Them Cold Feet Over On The Other
    Side" 120
"Goin' Up Cripple Creek"
    See "Cripple Creek"
"Going Home to Your Mother" 194
"Gone Country" 327
"Good Bye" 337
"Goodbye, Earl" 330
"Good Old Mountain Dew" ["Mountain
    Dew"] 204
"Gotta Lotta Hen House Ways" 186
"The Great Speckled Bird" 122, 184
"Greyhound Bound for Nowhere" 363
"Guitar Blues" 150
"Gunpowder and Lead" 360, 361, 366

"The Hangman Blues" 104
"Happy Girl" 332, 337
"Happy Trails" 364
"Happy Whistler" 188
"Harper Valley PTA" 161, 161n2, 186, 188
"Have You Forgotten?" 340
"Heart Like Mine" 363
"Heartaches by the Number" 228
"Heartbreak Hotel" 148
"Heart Trouble" 336
"Heavy Traffic Ahead" 115
"Hell on Heels" 364,
"Help Me Make It Through the Night" 234n7,
    339
"Here for the Party" 328
"Here We Are Again" 148
"Hey, Good Lookin'" 119
"Hey, Porter" 127
"Hick Town" 187
"Hickory Wind" 316

"High Life" 309
"Holiday" 308
"Home on the Range" 71
"Honky Tonk Heroes" 210
"Honky Tonk Song" 240n10, 316
"Honky-Tonkin'" 119
"Hop, Light, Ladies" 5
"Hot Dog" 197
"Hotel California" 324
"The House That Built Me" 363
"How Many Biscuits Kin You Eat This
    Mawnin'" 120
"How's the World Treating You" 151
"The Hunger" 210

"I Ain't Never" 316
"I Cross My Heart" 323
"I Don't Believe You've Met My Baby" 132
"I Don't Feel Like Loving You Today" 328
"I Got Candy All Over My Face" 186
"I Got the Interstate Running Through My
    Outhouse" 186
"I Kissed A Girl" 341
"I Laid My Mother Away" 124
"I Love My Lulu Belle" 28
"I Put the Blue in Her Eyes" 195
"I Ride an Old Paint" 17
"I Walk the Line" 128
"I Wanna Be Free" 360
"I Want You, I Need You, I Love You" 148
"I Was There When It Happened" 127
"I Wish I Felt This Way at Home" 195
"If I Was Jesus" 308
"If Tears Were Pennies and Heartaches Were
    Gold" 185
"The Ill Fated Akron" 72n11
"The Ill Fated Morrow Castle" 72n12
"In the Sweet Bye-and-Bye" 93
"Independence Day" 331, 332, 333, 336, 337
"Inside Your Heaven" 359
"It Is No Secret What God Can Do" 120
"It Don't Hurt Anymore" 127
"It Wasn't God Who Made Honky Tonk
    Angels" 138, 139, 185, 360
"It'll Be Her" 210

"Joe Clark" ["Old Joe Clark"] 5
"John Henry" 112
"Johnny B. Goode" 197, 199
"Just Dropped In (To See What Condition My
    Condition Is In)" 247

"Katie Hill" 5
"Keep My Skillet Good and Greasy" 113

"Keep on the Sunny Side" 38
"Kerosene" 361, 366

"Ladies Love Outlaws" 210
"Last Cheater's Waltz" 261
"Leaving Louisiana in the Broad
    Daylight" 252n5, 262
"Let Old Mother Nature Have Her Way" 120, 122
"Let's Get Drunk and Be Somebody" 186, 186n17
"Let's Invite Them On Over" 186
"Let's Live a Little" 122
"Lifetime to Prove" 317
"Like an Old-Fashioned Waltz" 268
"Little Mary Phagan" 2
"Little Old Log Cabin in the Lane" 3
"Little Ramona (Gone Hillbilly Nuts)" 316, 317
"Longneck Bottle" 281
"Look to Your Soul" 188
"Losers Lounge" 186
"Love Story" 351
"Love's The Only House" 332, 337
"Lovesick Blues" 119, 122
"Loving Her Was Easier" 216
"Lucille" 246

"MacArthur Park" 190
"Married by the Bible, Divorced by the Law" 186
"May the Bird of Paradise Fly Up Your Nose" 186
"Me 'N Opie Down by the Duck Pond" 316
"Midnight" 151
"Molly and Tenbrooks (The Race Horse
    Song)" 114
"Moon Over Naples" 204
"Moonshiner Bob" 5
"The Morrow [sic] Castle Disaster" 72n12
"Moving On" 120
"Mr. Sand Man [Sandman]" 148, 261, 265
"Mullinax" 5
"My Baby Loves Me" 335–6
"My Blue Ridge Mountain Home" 53
"My Buddy" 93
"My Cup Runneth Over with Love" 204
"My Daddy Is Only a Picture" 120
"My Daughter's Eyes" 338
"My Filipino Baby" 122
"My Life Would Make a Damn Good Country
    Song" 210

"The Newmarket Wreck" 43n13
"New San Antonio Rose" 97
"Ninety MPH Down a Dead End Street" 188
"Nobody's Child" 189
"No Letter Today" 102, 158
"Not In Front of the Kids" 195

"Okie From Muskogee" 180
"Old Cold Tater"
    See "Take an Old Cold Tater and Wait"
"Old Dan Tucker" 29, 121
"Old Folks at Home" 71
"The Old Hen Cackled and the Rooster's
    Going to Crow" 3, 158
"Old Zip Coon" 5
"On the Banks of the Sunny Tennessee"
    43n12
"On the Radio" 268
"On Top of Old Smoky" 158
"Once a Day" 339
"One Has My Name, the Other Has My
    Heart" 186
"One Long Saturday Night" 317
"One More Night Together" 185, 185n15, 187
"Only In America" 342

"Peace in the Valley" 120
"Peach-Pickin' Time in Georgia" 105
"Piano Roll Blues" 189
"The Pill" 223–5
"Pistol-Packin' Mama" 101–2
"Please Don't Help That Bear" 93
"Please Pass the Biscuits, Pappy" 105
"Politically Uncorrect" 328
"Poor People of Paris" 148
"Poor Wayfaring Stranger" 265
"The Price You Pay" 261
"Pussy, Pussy, Pussy" 93
"Put Another Log on the Fire" 220

"Rabbit in the Pea Patch" 113, 122
"Raining on Me" 328
"Raisin' McCain" 341, 343
"The Red Strokes" 289
"Redneck Woman" 326, 328
"Reuben" 110
"Reuben James" 247
"Rhythm Guitar" 258
"Riding Down the Canyon to Watch the
    Sun Go Down" 91
"Ring of Fire" 257
"Ringo" 188
"Rock All Our Babies to Sleep" 33
"Rocket 88" 125–126
"A Room Full of Roses" 236
"The Rope" 335
"Rosalita" 101
"Rose Garden" 206n5, 339
"Rubber Dolly" 93
"Ruby (Don't Take Your Love to Town)"
    247

"Run, Nigger, Run, Patteroll'll Ketch You" 6
"Safe in the Arms of Love" 337
"Sally Goodin" 112
"Satin Sheets" 339
"A Satisfied Mind" 144
"Save the Best for Last" 302
"Settin' the Woods on Fire" 144
"She Gave Me the Bird" 93
"She May Be Sour Grapes to You But She's
    Sweet Wine to Me" 186
"Shutters and Board" 187
"Six Days on the Road" 257
"Skip to Ma Lou My Darling"
    See "Skip to My Lou"
"Skip to My Lou" 29
"Skoal Ring" 328
"Smoke on the Water" 122
"Soapsuds Over the Fence" 5
"The Soldier's Sweetheart" 33
"Something's Burning" 247
"Sourwood Mountain" 29
"Stairway to Heaven" 324
"Start Today" 309
"Strangers" 336
"The Streets of Baltimore" 212, 213
"Summer Rain" 188
"Sweethearts in Heaven" 199

"The Taliban Song" 308
"Take an Old Cold Tater and Wait" 122
"Tea for Two" 185
"That Don't Impress Me Much" 308
"That Silver-Haired Daddy of Mine" 83
"That's Me" 335
"There's a Star-Spangled Banner Waving
    Somewhere" 102
"There's Evil in Ye Children" 105
"They Plowed the Old Trail Under" 82
"This One's For the Girls" 338
"Thou Shall Not Steal" 148
"Three Shif'less Skonks" 93
"The Thunder Rolls" 281, 330
"'Til I Gain Control Again" 262
"Tim McGraw" 347
"Too Old To Cut The Mustard" 120
"Tracks Run Through the City" 194
"The Train Kept a-Rollin'" 316
"Trucker's Prayer" 187
"True Blue Fool" 335
"Turn, Turn, Turn" 180

"Two More Bottles of Wine" 267, 337
"Two of a Kind" 288

"Up, Up and Away" 190
"This Uncivil War" 337

"The Wabash Cannon Ball" 122, 204
"Wabash Cannonball"
    See "The Wabash Cannon Ball"
"Walkaway Joe" 297
"Walking The Floor Over You" 122
"What Made Milwaukee Famous Has Made a
    Loser Out of Me" 186
"What's New Pussycat?" 193
"When I Stop Dreaming" 132
"When It's Round-Up Time in Texas" 93
"When It's Springtime in the Rockies" 51
"Where I Used to Have a Heart" 336
"Where Were You When the Ship Hit the
    Sand" 186
"Where Were You (When the World Stopped
    Turning)?" 340
"Where Would You Be" 333
"White Christmas" 94
"White Horse" 351
"White Liar" 363
"Who's Gonna Mow Your Grass" 199
"Who's Julie" 189
"Why Leave Something I Can't Use" 196
"Wide Open Road" 127, 129
"Wichita Lineman" 190
"Wild Hog in the Cane Brake" 5
"Wildwood Flower" 38, 257
"Will the Circle Be Unbroken?" 38
"With Lonely" 194
"Woman Walk the Line" 255
"Worried Man Blues" 38
"Wreck of the Shenandoah" 23, 72n11
"The Wreck on the Highway" 103

"You Ain't Woman Enough to Take My Man" 339
"You Are My Flower" 257–8
"You Are My Sunshine" 258
"You Decorated My Life" 247
"You May Be Wild Bill Tonight But You'll Be
    Sweet William in the Morning"
"You Win Again" 339
"You'll Never Miss Your Mother 'Till She's
    Gone" 121
"Your Cheatin' Heart" 228